Intelligence and the
National Security Strategist

Intelligence and the National Security Strategist: Enduring Issues and Challenges

Edited by Roger Z. George and Robert D. Kline

ROWMAN & LITTLEFIELD PUBLISHERS, INC.
Lanham • Boulder • New York • Toronto • Oxford

ROWMAN & LITTLEFIELD PUBLISHERS, INC.

Published in the United States of America
by Rowman & Littlefield Publishers, Inc.
A wholly owned subsidiary of The Rowman & Littlefield Publishing Group, Inc.
4501 Forbes Boulevard, Suite 200, Lanham, Maryland 20706
www.rowmanlittlefield.com

P.O. Box 317, Oxford OX2 9RU, UK

British Library Cataloguing in Publication Information Available

The National Defense University Press edition was catalogued by the
Library of Congress as follows:

Intelligence and the national security strategist : enduring issues and challenges / edited by
   Roger Z. George and Robert D. Kline ; with a foreword by Mark M. Lowenthal.
       p. cm.
    Includes bibliographical references.
    1. Military intelligence—United States. 2. National security—United States. 3. United
   States—Military policy. I. George, Roger Z., 1949– II. Kline, Robert D., 1949–
   UA251 .U51553 2003
   327.1273—dc22

                                                                            2003068852

ISBN 0-7425-4038-3 (cloth : alk. paper)
ISBN 0-7425-4039-1 (pbk. : alk. paper)

Printed in the United States of America

♾™ The paper used in this publication meets the minimum requirements of American
National Standard for Information Sciences—Permanence of Paper for Printed Library
Materials, ANSI/NISO Z39.48-1992.

Contents

Foreword xi
Mark M. Lowenthal

Preface to the Rowman & Littlefield Edition xiii

Acknowledgments xv

Introduction: Teaching Intelligence xvii
Roger Z. George and Robert D. Kline

Part I—Intelligence and the Strategist

Chapter 1
Clausewitz on Intelligence 3
Reed R. Probst

Chapter 2
Clausewitz's Contempt for Intelligence 11
Victor M. Rosello

Part II—Origins and Future of U.S. Intelligence

Chapter 3
Origins of the Central Intelligence Agency:
"Those Spooky Boys" 23
Amy B. Zegart

Chapter 4
Central Intelligence: Origin and Evolution 41
Michael Warner

Chapter 5
The Need to Reorganize the Intelligence Community 57
Larry C. Kindsvater

Part III—Intelligence and Democracy

Chapter 6
Balancing Liberty and Security..................................65
Loch K. Johnson

Chapter 7
Sharing Secrets with Lawmakers: Congress as
a User of Intelligence 85
L. Brit Snider

Chapter 8
Partisanship and the Decline of Intelligence Oversight 103
Marvin C. Ott

Chapter 9
The Role of the Federal Bureau of Investigation
in National Security 125
Harvey Rishikof

Part IV—Challenges of Technical Collection

Chapter 10
Space-Based Surveillance: Reconnaissance Satellites
Are a National Security Sine Qua Non 147
Glenn W. Goodman, Jr.

Chapter 11
Unclassified Space Eyes 153
Glenn W. Goodman, Jr.

Chapter 12
Commercial Satellite Imagery Comes of Age 159
Ann M. Florini and Yahya A. Dehqanzada

Chapter 13
"John, How Should We Explain MASINT?" 169
John D. Macartney

Chapter 14
The Time of Troubles: The U.S. National Security
Agency in the 21st Century..................................... 181
Matthew M. Aid

Part V—The Art of Clandestine Collection

Chapter 15
The In-Culture of the DO 209
Charles G. Cogan

Chapter 16
Espionage in an Age of Change: Optimizing Strategic
Intelligence Services for the Future 217
Norman B. Imler

Chapter 17
Economic Espionage 237
Randall M. Fort

Chapter 18
The Ten Commandments of Counterintelligence 251
James M. Olson

Chapter 19
A Review of the FBI's Performance in Uncovering
the Espionage Activities of Aldrich Hazen Ames 259
Michael R. Bromwich

Part VI—The Open-Source Revolution

Chapter 20
Open-Source Intelligence: New Myths, New Realities 273
Mark M. Lowenthal

Chapter 21
The Strategic Use of Open-Source Information 279
John C. Gannon

Chapter 22
Open-Source Intelligence: A Review Essay 285
Richard S. Friedman

Part VII—Challenges of Intelligence Analysis

Chapter 23
Defining the Analytic Mission: Facts, Findings,
Forecasts, and Fortunetelling 295
Jack Davis

Chapter 24

The Challenge for the Political Analyst 303
Martin Petersen

Chapter 25

Fixing the Problem of Analytical Mindsets:
Alternative Analysis 311
Roger Z. George

Chapter 26

The Intelligence Community Case Method
Program: A National Intelligence Estimate
on Yugoslavia 327
Thomas W. Shreeve

Chapter 27

Building Leverage in the Long War: Ensuring
Intelligence Community Creativity in the
Fight against Terrorism 341
James W. Harris

Part VIII—Deception, Denial, and Disclosure Problems

Chapter 28

Intelligence and Deception 359
Michael I. Handel

Chapter 29

Miscalculation, Surprise, and U.S. Intelligence 389
James J. Wirtz

Chapter 30

How Leaks of Classified Intelligence Help U.S. Adversaries:
Implications for Laws and Secrecy 399
James B. Bruce

Part IX—Perils of Policy Support

Chapter 31

What To Do When Traditional Models Fail 417
Carmen A. Medina

Chapter 32

What We Should Demand from Intelligence 425
Martin Petersen

Chapter 33
American Presidents and Their Intelligence
Communities 431
Christopher M. Andrew

Chapter 34
Inside the White House Situation Room 447
Michael B. Donley, Cornelius O'Leary, and John Montgomery

Part X—Intelligence and the Military

Chapter 35
The DCI and the Eight-Hundred-Pound Gorilla 459
Loch K. Johnson

Chapter 36
Tug of War: The CIA's Uneasy Relationship with
the Military... 479
Richard L. Russell

Chapter 37
CIA Support to *Enduring Freedom* 493
Anthony R. Williams

Chapter 38
Working with the CIA... 497
Garrett Jones

Chapter 39
U.S. Central Intelligence Agency Forces:
Covert Warriors.. 509
Andrew Koch

Appendix A
The National Security Act: Excerpts 517

Appendix B
Executive Order 12333: United States Intelligence
Activities.. 523

Appendix C
Director of Central Intelligence Directive 1/1............... 541

Appendix D
The USA PATRIOT Act: A Sketch 553

Appendix E

Executive Order Strengthened Management of the
Intelligence Community 559

Appendix F

Summary of Intelligence Reform and Terrorism
Prevention Act of 2004 567

Selected Readings 591

About the Contributors 593

Foreword

In an article I published many years ago, I noted that the years 1975–1976 represented a turning point for the scholarship of intelligence. This period saw three major investigations of the U.S. Intelligence Community, and in the years since intelligence has never been able to withdraw completely under its former cloak of secrecy. Changing as well as contending views of intelligence, a more open discussion of intelligence issues in the press, and public pressure to declassify more materials have contributed to an increased amount of available, if not always accurate, information about intelligence.

Nothing has happened in the last quarter century to affect this trend. However, as I noted then, the quality versus quantity balance was and remains a bit uneven. One still has to wade through books that are, in the end, hopelessly uninformed or breathlessly scandal-mongering. The number of good, serious books has increased, although many of these remain aimed at the intelligence professional as opposed to a wider academic or general readership.

One positive countervailing trend, however, has been the growth of intelligence as a serious academic subject. The number of colleges and universities that teach courses on various aspects of intelligence has grown. This reflects increased intellectual maturity on the part of academe, as well as a keen business sense that there was student demand that required supply. Unfortunately, it has taken a while for intelligence literature to catch up to this academic trend. Many of the best pieces remained scattered across conference proceedings and journals that were difficult to bring together into a coherent text.

This volume, edited by two faculty members at the National War College, Roger George and Robert Kline, addresses this problem and is a welcome addition to the intelligence library. The editors have ranged across the available books and, more important, articles, and brought together some of the very best, in a well-organized single volume. Anyone who has ever attempted to create an anthology will appreciate the many difficulties involved. It is a labor of love, above all else.

Aficionados of intelligence literature cannot but be impressed by the caliber of the authors represented. This volume will appeal to those who approach intelligence as a historical topic and those who approach it as a governmental activity. The organization of the volume follows the steps of the intelligence process: policymaker requirements, collection, processing and exploitation of collection, analysis, policymaker use. Of necessity, the complex issue of collection is broken down into its major component parts, various technical collections, espionage, and the often-lauded but usually neglected open source.

One unique feature of the book is a section on the important topic of deception and denial. The inclusion of contributions on intelligence and strategy, the role of intelligence in a democracy, intelligence and the military, plus documentation on the Intelligence Community round out the book.

This volume fills a gaping hole in our academic intelligence library. I believe that anyone teaching a course on intelligence will want to have this volume on his or her reading list. There is no better collection of articles on the wide range of intelligence issues. The editors have performed a commendable service for all of us who care passionately about intelligence and who seek to share this passion with others. We are fortunate to have this volume.

Mark M. Lowenthal
Assistant Director of Central Intelligence for
Analysis and Production

Preface to the Rowman & Littlefield Edition

T he topic of intelligence has been a prominent part of the public debate since 9/11 and Operation Iraqi Freedom. It is arguably a topic that is still not well understood. This book of readings on strategic intelligence was first developed to support courses the editors taught at the National War College in Washington, DC. As faculty members of the college, our goal was to enable our students—senior military officers and civilians drawn from the State Department and other national security organizations—to better understand the uses and the limits of intelligence as they prepared for leadership positions in their institutions. We were guided in part by the observation of a former CIA Director, who also served as Deputy National Security Adviser, about the fundamental problem underlying intelligence and national security:

> Presidents and their senior advisers usually are ill-informed about intelligence capabilities. Therefore, they have unrealistic expectations about what intelligence can do for them, especially when they see examples of some of the truly remarkable things we can do. And when they do learn the limitations, they are inevitably disappointed.[1]

Our original purpose was to prepare a resource exclusively for use at senior military colleges and other civilian government training programs. However, since the book's initial publication, numerous requests from both U.S. officials and private university instructors and scholars have demonstrated that there is a wider audience for the information, ideas, and insights that we have tried to provide.

The public debate about U.S. intelligence capabilities, and the organization and management of the institutions and programs that comprise the U.S. "Intelligence Community," is important. Not only should intelligence be discussed in terms of the global war on terror, but also as Americans reexamine the enduring principles and traditions, which underlie our form of democratic self-government. As the former Director of the National Security Agency and now the nation's first Deputy Director for National Intelligence reminded congressional oversight committees: "What I really need you to do is to talk to your constituents and find out where the American people want that line between security and liberty to be."[2]

One of the difficult tasks in addressing this subject is to do so in a way that explains intelligence to the public while protecting Americans' ability to perform effective operations and analysis in the service of this nation. We believe this selection of articles will help to do both. The book's chapters present the reader with a broad overview of the range of challenges faced by intelligence professionals and the consumers of what they produce. The chapters explain the purposes and distinctions between different intelligence disciplines, and they also highlight the *limits* of what technical and human intelligence can do. Additionally, the chapters trace the evolution of the U.S. Intelligence Community and raise some questions important to the ongoing debate about additional changes that may be needed in the future. Some of the chapters illustrate the enduring tensions between balancing the need for intelligence and fundamental liberty and due process issues central to our concept of government. Importantly, some chapters lay out the ways intelligence analysts attempt to provide insightful analysis to demanding policymakers, but also emphasize the limits to our knowledge and "sense-making" abilities. Finally, the chapters explain the dangers from deception and the need to protect sources and methods when the country is faced with an existent threat like global terrorism.

The continuing public discourse over the future of the U.S. Intelligence Community ensures that more books like ours will be needed to help explain the strengths and weaknesses in our intelligence system. At the end of the day, America will need an Intelligence Community that is consistent with its values and political system and one that is ultimately accountable to the public. Our hope is that our volume will make a modest contribution to informing the public as this national dialogue continues.

Roger Z. George
Robert D. Kline
March 2005

Notes

[1] Robert M. Gates, *From the Shadows* (New York: Simon & Schuster, 1996), p. 567.

[2] Lt. General Michael E. Hayden, Testimony before the open session of the Joint Inquiry of the Senate Select Committee on Intelligence and the House Permanent Select Committee on Intelligence, October 17, 2002.

Acknowledgments

To paraphrase a former First Lady, it takes a community to make a book of readings. Indeed, this volume reflects the ideas of many experts and the efforts of many institutions. We could not have completed this project without the support of three institutions and key people associated with them.

The experience of teaching at National War College was the inspiration for this collection. We treasure the opportunity to work with an outstanding faculty and a superb military-civilian leadership that helped to shape this book. Several colleagues—Harvey Rishikof, Norman B. Imler, and Marvin C. Ott—contributed to this effort. As importantly, Major General Reginal G. Clemmons, USA, the commandant of the National War College, encouraged us to expand and integrate intelligence studies into the core curriculum. The creation of the Sherman Kent Center for Intelligence Studies at the college in 1997 began what has become a close working relationship between the intelligence faculty and other members at the college.

The previous edition of this book would not have been possible without support from across the National Defense University (NDU). We found the university and its senior leaders enthusiastic about publishing a volume on intelligence that would interest students attending professional military education institutions. In particular, we want to thank Stephen J. Flanagan, director of the Institute for National Security Studies, for sponsoring this effort. The support of NDU Press— George C. Maerz, Jeffrey D. Smotherman, and Lisa M. Yambrick, under Robert A. Silano, director of publications—was marvelous. They made us feel that this was an effortless process, which we are certain is not the case in the event.

Finally, this book is being made available to military as well as other U.S. Government education institutions as a result of the far-sightedness of the Community Management Staff (CMS) at the Central Intelligence Agency. Thanks to the support of Larry Kindsvater, executive director of CMS, and Mark M. Lowenthal, associate director of Central Intelligence for Analysis and Production, the funds were made available to produce this collection on the complexities and challenges facing the Intelligence Community at the beginning of the 21st century.

Recent events attest to the continuing importance of intelligence to U.S. national security, and to the need for helping current and future leaders to understand the processes by which that intelligence is produced, along with its strengths and limitations. We hope this book makes a contribution to that end.

Roger Z. George
Robert D. Kline

Introduction: Teaching Intelligence

Roger Z. George and Robert D. Kline

Mature, thoughtful, keen, pleased to be there and anxious to make the most of it, they were a joy to teach. One learned from them as one taught.

—George F. Kennan on war college students

Teaching intelligence at a war college is an awesome responsibility because of the remarkable qualities, experiences, and commitment that senior military and civilian students bring to their studies. These officers, diplomats, and other civil servants are not average students one finds at a graduate institution. They have had direct experiences, both good and bad, with intelligence. Many have not only some prejudices but also high expectations of what U.S. intelligence should be able to do for commanders, military planners, and national security strategists. Others bring accounts of excellent and poor cooperation in dealing with intelligence officers overseas or in the interagency process. Thus, teaching intelligence to such a demanding and experienced group of students requires great skill as well as a frank dialogue about the Intelligence Community strengths and weaknesses.

Explaining the Intelligence Community and its arcane processes to future military and civilian leaders is also a major responsibility. Some students will become tomorrow's combatant commanders, Chairmen of the Joint Chiefs, assistant secretaries of state and defense, or senior directors of the National Security Council; however, virtually all will go on to greater responsibilities where their reliance on intelligence will be considerable and their information needs will impact the shape and performance of the Intelligence Community of tomorrow. Hence, making all of these future strategists better consumers of intelligence is the principal goal of any intelligence course at a senior service college. Giving them an accurate picture of what the community can and cannot do, explaining how it works and how its various cultures shape operations, and debating where it needs to change are all part of educating the next generation of senior foreign policymakers. It is notable that the Intelligence Community spends a great deal of time trying to educate its analysts, collectors, and all managers about how the policymaking process works in order to help intelligence agencies support more effectively the policy world. However, the opportunities for policymakers to get inside the intelligence world are far more limited. Thus, offering these future leaders the chance to learn about intelligence is a unique opportunity for the community to help itself be better understood and exploited more effectively.

The job of introducing the Intelligence Community to students at the military service schools has gotten easier in one respect. Ten years ago at a symposium on teaching intelligence, historian Ernest May noted, "A generation ago, the literature on intelligence was at or below the level of literature on business before the arrival of modern business history and education."

Today, however, libraries are full of literature on all aspects of intelligence. The challenge is to select among the best available sources to use in any course. Naturally, even the best books or articles contain biases on intelligence. Selecting articles for this collection, then, runs the risk of introducing both known and unknown biases into any study of intelligence. We expect that some articles will be more or less controversial but hope that all will stimulate discussion and debate among students. Unlike some training courses, educating students on intelligence matters involves raising more questions than providing answers.

A student should expect to struggle with several central questions about intelligence. First, how does intelligence function as a set of tools for statecraft? At the national level, intelligence can serve as an enabler or force multiplier for other tools of statecraft; a protective shield, with counterintelligence capabilities interfering with an opponent's use of deception or masking us to misdirect an enemy's attention and activities; and, a limited policy tool, with covert actions carrying out authorized activities in conjunction with other tools of statecraft.

Second, students need to ask: How does the multifaceted intelligence cycle actually work? An examination of the intelligence cycle will highlight the critical importance of policymakers who must help establish the Intelligence Community requirements and priorities. Having clear guidance from senior customers on what matters to them is the first step to directing collection efforts and prioritizing analytical tasks. Once requirements and priorities are understood, then students will need to master how different collection disciplines—imagery, signals intelligence, human intelligence, and open sources—can all be directed to attack important analytical problems. Understanding how the various disciplines can work together—rather than in isolation—to crack a problem is in itself an important realization; working jointly and across agencies is the key to successfully meeting the new set of transnational threats the United States faces.

The analytical phase of the intelligence cycle is equally challenging for students. The wide variety of intelligence products, not to mention the growing reliance of the community on electronic media and face-to-face briefings, reflect the reality that consumers need their intelligence delivered to them in many different fashions. While some consumers value raw intelligence reporting, others want a polished brief or the bottom line. Some policymakers insist on the Intelligence Community giving them their best guess, while others demand getting the facts first and only then entertaining what the intelligence analysts believe might be happening. In any event, students need to appreciate not only the difficulties encountered in collecting intelligence but also the inherent uncertainties embedded in any finished intelligence analysis. To become an educated consumer, the student will need to understand the limits of the analytical process and what risks are entailed in relying on conventional wisdom and unspoken mindsets that are sometimes hidden in confidently delivered intelligence analysis. The existence of deception should not surprise the military student, but knowing when one is being deceived is both art and science.

Third, the student must ask: Do the makeup and structure of the Intelligence Community make sense? As of this writing, the Intelligence Community consists of 15 separate agencies spread among numerous departments of Government; they are both civilian and military institutions. They span many missions—supporting warfighters, policy planners, counterterrorist and law enforcement officials, to name a few. With the creation of a Department of Homeland Security and the new Terrorist Threat Integration Center, we are perhaps witnessing a further expansion of the Intelligence Community and its missions. Not unlike the military services themselves, each intelligence agency reflects a particular culture that has grown up with a traditional mission. Yet redesigning the community has been on the agenda ever since the 1947 National Security Act was signed, with numerous reform proposals being recycled over the past half-century and very few implemented. A high degree of dissatisfaction remains in the Congress and the Executive Branch with the level of cooperation among agencies, the efficiency and effectiveness of having multiple agencies working on similar tasks, and repeated instances of "intelligence surprises" that appear to be the result of agencies not sharing information widely enough or soon enough. How much is the result of ingrown cultures or hidebound attitudes toward an agency's enduring mission is something that each student will need to assess.

Finally, students must address the question of how the Intelligence Community should be providing the best possible support to its wide-ranging sets of customers. Support to the warfighter is not the same as policy support to the President and his Cabinet-level advisers; moreover, the kind of skills and information needed to support law enforcement agencies against the terrorist threat is also unique and poses special problems. While most of the community is focused on supporting Executive Branch agencies, students must not forget that intelligence agencies have an obligation to support the Congress, to which it is also accountable. The issue of oversight is taken seriously but presents certain dilemmas regarding how it can be supportive of both branches of Government without being caught in the middle of Congressional-Presidential struggles over the control of foreign policy.

These four objectives are a tall order to fulfill for any course on intelligence. The articles found in this collection attempt to complement both the lectures given at war colleges and the excellent textbooks now available. We believe they present useful information and perspectives on some of the central and more enduring challenges facing U.S. intelligence. We begin by focusing on the strategist's view of intelligence, the origins of U.S. intelligence, and the role of intelligence in American democracy. The second major portion of the book consists of specific articles on different intelligence collection disciplines and the strengths and weaknesses of each. The final sections of the book address the enduring problems of performing insightful analysis, overcoming analytical bias and deception, and supporting both the national strategist and the military commander.

Part I—Intelligence and the Strategist

It is only the enlightened ruler and the wise general who will use the highest intelligence of the army for purposes of spying, and thereby they achieve great results.

—Sun Tzu

Chapter 1
Clausewitz on Intelligence

Reed R. Probst

General Carl von Clausewitz, the great Prussian theorist on war, had little in a positive sense to say about intelligence in his chapter on that subject (Book 1, Chapter 6).[1] After defining *intelligence* as "every sort of information about the enemy and his country—the basis, in short of our own plans and operations," the author branded the business as "unreliable and transient," and asserted that war based on such plans and operations "is a flimsy structure that can easily collapse and bury us in its ruins."[2]

As for the rationale behind his mistrust of intelligence, Clausewitz wrote, "Many intelligence reports in war are contradictory; even more are false, and most are uncertain." To filter out fiction from fact, the author believed an officer "must possess a standard of judgment" that could only be gained from "knowledge of men and affairs and from common sense." Furthermore, an officer's judgment "should be guided by the laws of probability."

Clausewitz also made three other principal points regarding intelligence in this chapter:

- Most intelligence is false, and the effect of fear is to multiply lies and inaccuracies. As a rule most men would rather believe bad news than good, and rather tend to exaggerate the bad news.
- This difficulty of *accurate recognition* constitutes one of the most serious sources of friction in war.
- Self-reliance is the best defense against the pressures of the moment.[3]

Clausewitz's gainsaying of intelligence is no doubt the product of his experience and circumstances. He was writing about tactical intelligence, which in his day (1780–1831) could only be collected by spies and observers and then transmitted to military headquarters by cumbersome means. Without the assistance of satellites and computers, sophisticated electronics, and advanced gadgetry, the practitioners of intelligence in the first half of the 19th century had few resources at their disposal beyond those of human reporting and personal intuition.

A careful reading of Clausewitz's book, *On War*, nevertheless shows that the author had a healthy respect for intelligence—especially the strategic kind—but also that he thoroughly understood and appreciated the analytical processes through which raw information is transformed into finished intelligence. Indeed, Clausewitz,

---

Source: Reed R. Probst, "Clausewitz on Intelligence," *Studies in Intelligence* (Fall 1985), 29–35.

who has been hailed for generations as the theoretician par excellence of war, also might serve today as a theoretician of the art of intelligence. It should come as no surprise, then, that much of what he wrote directly about war is almost equally applicable to intelligence. Take, for example, the following passage:

> Theory will have fulfilled its main task when it is used to analyze the constituent elements of (intelligence), to distinguish precisely what at first sight seems fused, to explain in full the properties of the means employed, and to show their probable effects, to define clearly the nature of the ends in view, and to illuminate all phases of (intelligence) in a thorough critical inquiry.[4]

One of the key tasks of intelligence is to provide policymakers with forecasts and warning, and the comments of Clausewitz on such matters are as valid today as they were 150 years ago. Rather than discuss the business of forecasting per se, the author zeroes in on a key determinant of the future—human will—which he characterizes as a factor by which one may produce tomorrow's forecast based on today's state of mind. In writing further about human will, Clausewitz asserts that "war never breaks out wholly unexpectedly, nor can it be spread instantaneously." For this reason, he cautions that the other side should be judged largely by what it is or does, rather than by what it ought to do.[5]

On the business of estimating, Clausewitz writes, "From the enemy's character, from his institutions, the state of his affairs and his general situation, each side, using the *laws of probability*, forms an estimate of its opponent's likely course and acts accordingly."[6]

Although the author was attracted both to trends and what he termed the "laws of probability," he had even greater regard for the element of chance. Indeed, because of chance, he argues:

> In short, absolute, so-called mathematical, factors never find a firm basis in military calculations. From the very start there is an interplay of possibilities, probabilities, good luck and bad that weaves its way throughout the length and breadth of the tapestry. In the whole range of human activities, war most closely resembles a game of cards.

And again:

> War is the realm of uncertainty; three-quarters of the factors on which action in war is based are wrapped in a fog of greater or lesser uncertainty. A sensitive and discriminating judgment is called for; a skilled intelligence to scent out the truth.[7]

Finally, Clausewitz noted with precision and clarity a common shortcoming associated with the process of estimating when he wrote, "Men are always more inclined to pitch their estimate of the enemy's strength too high than too low, such is human nature."[8] This overestimating of enemy strength can, according to Clausewitz, bring military activity to a halt.

Advice for Analysts

Perhaps the greatest insights and contributions of Clausewitz to the theory and practice of intelligence result from his comments on critical analysis. Inasmuch as such analysis constitutes a key requirement for the production of intelligence, the principles espoused by Clausewitz on this subject deserve close attention. He observed, "Critical analysis being the application of theoretical truths to actual events, it not only reduces the gap between the two but also accustoms the mind to these truths through their respected application."[9]

He then pointed out that critical analysis is far more than the preparation of a plain narrative of a historical event, for the narrative only arranges facts in sequence and at most only touches on their immediate causal links. In contrast, critical analysis involves three intellectual activities:

- Historical research, or the nontheoretical process of discovery and interpretation of facts.
- Critical analysis proper, or the tracing of effects back to their causes—an essential process for theory.
- Investigation and evaluation of the means employed. This he calls criticism proper—a process that provides the theoretical framework whereby lessons can be drawn from history.[10]

Throughout his exposition on historical inquiry, the author insists on thorough and careful work: ". . . it is vital to analyze everything down to its basic elements, to incontrovertible truth. One must not stop half-way, as is so often done, at some arbitrary assumption or hypothesis."[11]

Clausewitz then offered what can be taken as words of counsel for modern-day intelligence analysts. In a passage dealing with the problem of deducing effect from cause, he warns that true causes may be entirely unknown due to intentional concealment or to lack of recorded data. For this reason, he argues, "critical narrative (akin to modern-day intelligence comment) must usually go hand in hand with historical research." He continues:

> Even so, the disparity between cause and effect may be such that the critic [read intelligence analyst] is not justified in considering the effects as inevitable results of known causes. This is bound to produce gaps—historical results that yield no useful lesson. All a theory demands is that investigation should be resolutely carried on till such a gap is reached. At that point, judgment has to be suspended. Serious trouble arises only when known facts are forcibly stretched to explain effects; for this confers on these facts a spurious importance.[12]

From the foregoing passage, the author provides eloquent warning about concealment and deception, about the need for thorough research—even if it cannot yield instant answers or bridge existing gaps in knowledge—and about the fallacy of tailoring facts to fit misleading theories.

Clausewitz did display a faith that the search for causes will at least uncover the major issues that require further study.[13] He also strongly advocates that analysts be objective, take a broad view of the issues at hand, and avoid executing judgment based on personal, limited standards.[14]

On Probability

One of the major themes in Clausewitz's writings is that of the role of what the author variously calls chance, luck, or fate. What he says about probability is directly relevant to intelligence. Particularly for those involved in the estimative process, Clausewitz argued that one must on occasion avoid exclusive reliance on probability: "But we should not habitually prefer the course that involves the least uncertainty. . . . There are times when the utmost daring is the height of wisdom."[15]

The author also had advice that is relevant to postmortems on estimates:

> We cannot deny an inner satisfaction whenever things turn out right; when they do not, we feel a certain intellectual discomfort. That is all the meaning that should be attached to a judgment of right and wrong that we deduce from success, or rather that we find in success.[16]

Clausewitz, moreover, urged steadfastness on the part of those making judgments and assessments:

> The critic, then, having analyzed everything within the range of human calculation and belief, will let the outcome speak for that part whose deep, mysterious operation is never visible. The critic must protect this unspoken result of the workings of higher laws against the stream of uninformed opinion on the one hand, and against the gross abuses to which it may be subjected on the other.[17]

On Clarity

Clausewitz's advice on clarity will give comfort to those who must review and edit intelligence products:

> Truths should always be allowed to become self-evident. . . . We will thus avoid using an arcane and obscure language, and express ourselves in plain speech, with a sequence of clear, lucid concepts. Granted that while this cannot always be completely achieved, it must remain the aim of critical analysis.[18]

The author claimed that analysts, in their writing, have three common flaws. One is to rely on "certain narrow systems" as a basis for their work. More worrisome is "the retinue of *jargon*, *technicalities*, and *metaphors* that attend these systems." The third failing is that analysts frequently try to show off their erudition and misuse historical examples. Clausewitz asserted that "a fact that is cited in passing may be used to support the most contradictory views; and three or four examples from distant times and places, dragged in and piled up from the widest range of circumstances, tend to distract and confuse one's judgment without proving anything."[19]

Military Analysis

Because of his study of the phenomenology of war, Clausewitz has left behind a veritable bible for those involved in military analysis. His observations range from the moral elements of war to surprise, from deception to friction, and from the role of fortresses to insurrections.

On numerical superiority: "Superiority of numbers admittedly is the most important factor in the outcome of an engagement, so long as it is great enough to counterbalance all other contributing circumstances."[20]

He cites three principal moral elements: the commander's skill, the experience and courage of the troops, and their patriotic spirit. Of them, he writes:

> The relative value of each cannot be universally established. It is hard enough to discuss their potential, and even more difficult to weigh them against each other. The wisest course is not to underrate any of them—a temptation to which human judgment, being fickle, often succumbs.[21]

Clausewitz asserts that the desire to take the enemy by surprise is an outgrowth of the universal desire for relative superiority in numbers. Indeed, surprise is necessary for superiority at the decisive point. The type of surprise to which he refers is not that of a surprise attack but rather the condition achieved through planning and disposition of forces. He asserts that this type of surprise is equally feasible in defense.

According to Clausewitz, secrecy and speed are the two factors producing surprise. These factors presuppose great energy on the part of government and the commander and great efficiency on the part of the army. He warns:

> But while the wish to achieve surprise is common and, indeed, indispensable, and while it is true that it will never be completely effective, it is equally true that by its very nature surprise can rarely be outstandingly successful. It would be a mistake, therefore, to regard surprise as a key element of success in war. The principle is highly attractive in theory, but in practice it is often held up by the friction of the whole machine.[22]

On war preparations:

> Preparations for war usually take months. Concentrating troops at their main assembly points generally requires the installation of supply dumps and depots, as well as considerable troop movements, whose purpose can be guessed soon enough. It is very rare therefore that one state surprises another, either by an attack or by preparations for war. It is obvious, however, that the greater the ease with which surprise is achieved, the smaller its effectiveness, and vice versa.[23]

Clausewitz is no doubt right on most of the points cited in the passage above, but one still wonders how he would explain the degree of surprise felt by the American side at the attack on Pearl Harbor, or the Israeli surprise on the occasion of the Egyptian attack during Yom Kippur. These would be the exceptions that prove the rule.

On deception:

> Plans and orders issued for appearances only, false reports designed to confuse the enemy, etc., . . . have as a rule so little strategic value that they are used only if a ready-made opportunity presents itself. They should not be considered as a significant independent field of action at the disposal of the commander.

To prepare a sham action with sufficient thoroughness to impress an enemy requires a considerable expenditure of time and effort, and the costs increase with scale of the deception. Normally, they call for more than can be spared.[24]

Despite the gainsaying by Clausewitz, much of the success of the Normandy landings in June 1944 was due to an elaborate deception scheme that had the Germans believing that the main attack would come elsewhere.

On general insurrection, Clausewitz set forth the five conditions under which a general uprising can be effective:

- The war must be fought in the interior of the country.
- It must not be decided by a single stroke.
- The theater of operations must be fairly large.
- The national character must be suited to that type of war.
- The country must be rough and inaccessible because of mountains, or forests, marshes, or the local methods of cultivation.[25]

Again one wonders whether a present-day Clausewitz would add the factor of outside agitation and support to his list of requirements for a successful insurrection.

There are many other Clausewitzian concepts that professional intelligence officers ought to understand. First is the famous principle that "war is . . . a continuation of political activity by other means." Another is the concept of friction in war. Clausewitz understood this principle long before the legendary Murphy developed his "laws," or the expression "snafu" was coined. Still another is what Clausewitz termed the "remarkable trinity" of the phenomenon of war, by which he meant that war could only be successfully prosecuted through the harmonious interaction of the people, the army and its commander(s), and the government.[26] For the United States, Vietnam was a painful reminder of this condition.

Admittedly Clausewitz, with his detailed reasoning and cumbersome prose, is not an easy writer to follow, let alone understand, but his wisdom has easily stood the test of time. Moreover, his ideas are enjoying a resurgence in interest as each of the senior military service schools has incorporated *On War* into its curriculum, and scholars such as the Army's Colonel Harry Summers have used Clausewitzian principles to analyze recent military shortcomings.[27] For the professional intelligence officer, a careful reading of Clausewitz will result in a better understanding of the nature of conflict, of the principles of effective analysis, and of the ways of dealing more effectively with those elements hostile to the interests of the United States.

Notes

[1] Throughout this [chapter], the quotations are taken from Carl von Clausewitz, *On War*, ed. and trans. Michael Howard and Peter Paret (Princeton: Princeton University Press, 1976). The quotations are referenced by page number. Clausewitz himself spelled his first name with a "C" rather than the "K," which appears in many references to him.

[2] Clausewitz, 117.

[3] Ibid., 117–118.

[4] Ibid., 141.

[5] Ibid., 78.

[6] Ibid., 80.

[7] Ibid., 101.

[8] Ibid., 85.

[9] Ibid., 156.

[10] Ibid.

[11] Ibid.

[12] Ibid., 156–157.

[13] Ibid., 159.

[14] Ibid., 165.

[15] Ibid., 167.

[16] Ibid.

[17] Ibid.

[18] Ibid., 168.

[19] Ibid., 168–169.

[20] Ibid., 194.

[21] Ibid., 186.

[22] Ibid., 198.

[23] Ibid., 198–199.

[24] Ibid., 202–203.

[25] Ibid., 480.

[26] Ibid., 89.

[27] Harry G. Summers, Jr., *On Strategy: The Vietnam War in Context* (Washington, DC: U.S. Government Printing Office, 1983).

Chapter 2

Clausewitz's Contempt for Intelligence

Victor M. Rosello

Many intelligence reports in war are contradictory; even more are false, and most are uncertain. . . . In short, most intelligence is false.[1]

—Carl von Clausewitz, *On War*

The latest intellectual revival of classical military thought (a trademark of the U.S. military in the post-Vietnam era) has brought a proverbial breath of fresh air to our military literature. No doubt the establishment as a whole is benefiting substantially from this vigorous infusion of timeless thinking. The trend has raised the intellectual horizons of our profession and will continue to set the pace for military theorizing and doctrinal development through the next century.

During this current renaissance, it is not at all unusual to find the military theories of notable writers copiously referenced: Machiavelli, Jomini, Du Picq, Mahan, Douhet, Fuller, and Liddell Hart routinely grace the pages of professional military journals. But of the many classical writers recently repopularized, the oft-quoted Carl von Clausewitz comes to mind as the most widely read and most influential. The revived popularity of his great treatise, *On War*, has generated healthy debates within the U.S. military over the utility of such Clausewitzian concepts as "centers of gravity," "culminating points," and "fog and friction."

One highly relevant—and controversial—Clausewitzian theme concerns the subject of intelligence. A reading of his views leaves the unequivocal impression that Clausewitz did not regard intelligence highly. His apparent attitude is best summarized by the statement that introduced this [chapter]: "Many intelligence reports in war are contradictory; even more are false, and most are uncertain. . . . In short, most intelligence is false." Such a deliberate and dogmatic statement by a reverenced authority, particularly a statement so at odds with the instincts of serving soldiers, simply demands investigation. This [chapter] will thus attempt to answer the question: Why does Clausewitz seem to regard intelligence with such contempt?

Source: Victor M. Rosello, "Clausewitz's Contempt for Intelligence," *Parameters* 21 (Spring 1991), 103–114.

Clausewitz on Intelligence: A Different Focus

Research into Clausewitz's notions on intelligence is certainly not a new endeavor and has been treated with some frequency in the past.[2] So why another [essay] on this subject? A significant shortcoming with previous such investigations is a general lack of balance. Some writers are prone to validate Clausewitz by overstating "historical intelligence failures" and then subscribing to the notion that "the causes of these intelligence failures are the same as Clausewitz's reasons for distrusting intelligence."[3]

If scores were kept to measure success, however, then the trite historical examples of strategic intelligence failures that are always trotted out—Pearl Harbor, the Ardennes, the Yalu, Yom Kippur, etc.—would obviously be overshadowed by all the recorded successes of intelligence. The true test of Clausewitzian logic should be the ability of intelligence systems and organizations to produce worthwhile intelligence effectively over extended periods in support of day-to-day missions at all levels, in peace and war.

Another criticism of past examinations of Clausewitz vis-à-vis intelligence is the tendency of writers to allow themselves to be led down the metaphorical path of Clausewitzian fog-shrouded battlefields which defy attempts at penetration owing to insurmountable uncertainty. Thus writers correctly acknowledge that the pervasive Clausewitzian theme of the ascendancy of the moral domain had the most influence in Clausewitz's distrust of intelligence. These moral influences are the role of chance; the imponderables of fog and friction and their effects on the reliability of information; the limitation inherent in observation; the inability to penetrate the mind of the adversary; the dominance of preconception over fact; and the limitations of intelligence analysis.[4] Writers conclude by agreeing with Clausewitz because "in the larger picture . . . [Clausewitz's] views prevail. Intelligence can indeed magnify strength and improve command, but leaders do not always have it."[5]

Clausewitz's observations are realistic if we accept without question that intelligence is not always available and that uncertainties are always present in any intelligence system or activity. The existence of limitations, however, does not invalidate the conceptual need and usefulness of intelligence. It is from this standpoint that Clausewitz may be criticized for displaying a shallow and one-sided view.

There is the final consideration that Clausewitz was after all a child of his times. His ideas were shaped by dramatic historical events that touched him personally and professionally. For Clausewitz, the transition in warfare created by the Napoleonic Wars served as the crucible in which the foundation of his concepts on military theory developed. The Napoleonic Wars have much to tell us about war, but not all.

The Sophistication of Napoleonic Intelligence

An extensive part of Clausewitz's writings in *On War* was based on personal observation and "an examination of the five wars in which he had served."[6] It is quite likely that his perceptions of the value of intelligence also evolved from actual combat experience. Unfortunately, his first exposure to Napoleonic battle, while serving as adjutant of a Prussian infantry battalion, resulted in the greatest defeat of the Prussian army at the hands of Napoleon. The battle of Auerstadt in 1806, and the subsequent pursuit and rout of Prussian forces by Napoleon's army, left a deeply etched impression on the young Clausewitz, particularly since the debacle resulted in his humiliating capture and imprisonment by the French. Contributing to the defeat was the failure of Prussian intelligence to quickly assess the situation which developed as Napoleon maneuvered seven corps against the defenders. Notwithstanding that Prussian cavalry units were assigned the mission of reconnoitering a still-undeveloped situation, the order for their departure was transmitted late. "There was no way of knowing what was happening; reports from the front were muddled and contradictory."[7] These intelligence failures, coupled with such other adverse factors as indecision and problems of command within the Prussian organization, were branded indelibly on the mind and memory of the future theorist.

The sad state of Prussian readiness, however, was only one side of the problem. An important factor which served to reinforce the notions of chance and uncertainty in the mind of Clausewitz was the nature of the enemy opposing him: the great Napoleon Bonaparte. Of the many accolades bestowed on Napoleon, one has particular relevance for us here—his mastery of deception and operations security:[8]

> Napoleon's strategic deployments were carefully planned to set the stage for the great and decisive battle. Even before hostilities had begun, the Emperor's intentions were carefully shrouded from the enemy. Newspapers were censored, borders closed, travelers detained. Then, when the Grand Army moved, its advance was preceded by swarms of light cavalry, screening its line of advance, protecting its communications, and gathering intelligence about the location of the enemy.[9]

At the same time, according to David Chandler, "Elaborate deception schemes and secondary offensives would be devised and implemented to confuse the foe and place him off balance. All those common characteristics of twentieth-century military security were employed by Napoleon at the beginning of the nineteenth."[10]

Efforts by the opposing side to penetrate the fog of war proved inadequate. The deception plans and the priority given to operations security by Napoleon quite simply overwhelmed the existing and limited intelligence resources of his opponents:

> In the interests of security and deception, Napoleon was in the habit of continually altering the composition of his major formations . . . adding a division here, taking away a brigade there. . . . Even if . . . intelligence [of Napoleon's dispositions] was eventually discovered and digested by the enemy it was soon completely out of date. . . . Thus at no time could the foe rely on "accurate" information concerning the strength of their opponents or the placing of their units.[11]

The last line of this quotation is important because it characterizes in Clausewitz's eyes the plight of Napoleon's foes who attempted to gather information on his movements, strength, and intentions. For one facing an opponent of the caliber of Napoleon, the rudimentary level of information gathering in practice could not effectively lower the veil of brilliantly designed deception plans inherent in Napoleon's operations. Not only were Napoleon's counterintelligence means effective, but his intelligence service has often been regarded as one of the most efficient of the era, with the Emperor devoting considerable attention to the acquisition of intelligence:

Indeed, if we accept Clausewitz's definition of "intelligence"—"every sort of information about the enemy, and his country" that serves as the basis "of our own plans and operations"—then it is difficult to avoid the conclusion that Napoleon was well served by his ambassadors, his roving general aides, his chief of intelligence and the infamous Black Cabinet. In asserting that "most intelligence is false," Clausewitz reveals only that he was ignorant of this dimension of Napoleon's generalship.[12]

Napoleon's relative sophistication in intelligence matters is particularly impressive since formal intelligence organizations did not exist during his era.[13] The general staff of the Prussian army, well known to Clausewitz, was exceptionally small—limited to approximately two dozen officers.[14] With staff officers at a premium, the formal identification of intelligence officers was nonexistent.[15] In most cases it was the supreme commander who acted as the overall intelligence analyst for the field army, choosing and discarding information as he saw fit. This rudimentary method was not limited to the Prussians, but appears also to have been a characteristic of most Napoleonic-era armies.

Owing to regular changes in Napoleon's headquarters organization, many variations of the basic organization evolved. It is generally accepted, however, that from 1805 on, Imperial Headquarters was composed of three parts: the Emperor's Personal Quarters ("Maison"), a General Staff, and an Administrative Headquarters.[16] Of relevance to our discussion is the location of those sections tasked with information-gathering. This function was directed by two staff sections: the Statistical Bureau, forming part of the "Maison," and the General Staff. An intelligence function of the Statistical Bureau was to obtain information at the strategic level for use by tactical units. Its missions were wide-ranging, involving the collection and translation of newspapers and the placement of agents in all important cities to obtain information of political and military character.[17]

Information of a tactical nature was handled by the General Staff. Observation reports from the corps' cavalry patrols and interrogation reports obtained from enemy deserters and prisoners of war were passed to Napoleon through this section. Additionally, Napoleon supplemented information from the General Staff by incorporating special staff officers for missions he specifically assigned.[18] When compared with that of his adversaries, the Emperor's intelligence arm provided an appreciably more systematic and effective approach to exploiting the existing information resources, thus dispelling some of the fog of war.

The Weaknesses of Napoleonic Intelligence

Napoleon's intelligence system should not be overrated. By modern standards, Napoleon's organization had serious flaws. Although highly advanced for the period, it is evident that the French intelligence organization suffered from inadequate coordination and lack of a centralized analytical facility.[19] The various sections operated independently so that collection was not coordinated among them. And as to a central analytical center receiving the raw data, Napoleon chose to fulfill this role himself, thereby preventing a methodical effort fully dedicated to collecting, evaluating, interpreting, and transforming raw information into intelligence. This mode of operation ensured more timely decisions by Napoleon by eliminating intermediate staff layers, but it also increased the odds for making a poor decision based on incomplete assessments of the enemy situation.[20]

Of note, Napoleon's British rival at Waterloo, the Duke of Wellington, used a similar system during his earlier years, and, like Napoleon, was his own intelligence officer:

> All intelligence came to Wellington and . . . the appraisal of it was his and his alone. . . . It is not surprising that all reports of enemy movements, no matter what source they came from, whether from the outposts, the divisional or allied commanders, or officers on detached service and the rest, were brought to him as well. Nor do these reports appear to have been summarized, abstracted, or collected before they reached him, but were taken before him as they stood. What collating was done was almost certainly done by himself.[21]

By the latter stages of the war, however, Wellington was allowing his intelligence department, the Quartermaster General, the latitude of handling most of his intelligence functions.[22]

The strengths and weaknesses within the respective quasi-intelligence organizations of the Napoleonic era are relevant to the study of Clausewitz and intelligence. A thorough exploitation of enemy information was largely precluded owing to the lack of a coordinated intelligence effort and the preference of the individual commanders to act as arbiters of truth. Consequently, Clausewitz's evaluation of intelligence may be interpreted as criticism of what he perceived to be the existing and dismal state of organizational and technical incapability to penetrate the fog of war, rather than a denial of the usefulness or general need for intelligence.

Clausewitz's primary perceptual disadvantage, however, was that he fought on the wrong side of the war. Clausewitz may simply not have been aware of the qualitative edge that intelligence gave Napoleon.[23] If he had been, Clausewitz's notions of intelligence would doubtless have developed differently, perhaps along the lines of his contemporary, Jomini.

Jomini on Intelligence

The Swiss military writer Baron Antoine-Henri Jomini (1779–1869) firmly believed in the merits of intelligence. He served under Napoleon and thus "had a better appreciation for Napoleon's use of intelligence. He would argue that the role of intelligence 'is one of the chief causes of the great difference between theory and the practice of war.'"[24]

As he did with most of his treatment of the subject of war, Jomini attempted to reduce intelligence to a science which was prescriptive in its form and technique. In contrast to Clausewitz, Jomini attempted to abstract war from its political and social context by describing it in terms of rules and principles. To his credit, his writings have endured and are still studied and discussed today.[25]

Jomini's treatment of intelligence in his classic work, *The Art of War*, was limited to one subsection under the chapter heading of "Logistics." Unlike Clausewitz, whose cursory three-paragraph coverage of intelligence devolves to a negative handwringing account of why intelligence does not work, Jomini's discussion of intelligence presents a more positive outlook, accurately assessing the important role of intelligence and sketching in the intelligence sources available to the commander.

Jomini recognized the shortfalls as well as the advantages of intelligence. Like Clausewitz, he understood that uncertainty was always present on the battlefield ("uncertainty results . . . from ignorance of the enemy's position and plans").[26] However, Jomini was sufficiently astute to realize that despite difficulties and the almost impossible task of eliminating fog, intelligence has to be aggressively gathered so as to increase the commander's success on the battlefield by helping eliminate some of this uncertainty:

> One of the surest ways of forming good combinations in war would be to order movements only after obtaining perfect information of the enemy's proceedings. In fact, how can a man say what he should do himself, if he is ignorant of what his adversary is about? As it is unquestionably of the highest importance to gain this information, so it is a thing of the utmost difficulty, not to say impossibility.[27]

As with Clausewitz, Jomini accepts that not all reports are reliable. For this reason he stresses the need to use multidimensional information systems, in a sense making him a progenitor of modern all-source intelligence:

> A general should neglect no means of gaining information of the enemy's movements, and, for this purpose, should make use of reconnaissances, spies, bodies of light troops commanded by capable officers, signals, and questioning deserters and prisoners. . . . Perfect reliance should be placed on none of these means.[28]

Jomini also notes that intelligence collection alone does not hold the key to success. Good intelligence analysis must then occur so that the information can be used to form "hypotheses of probabilities." These are something akin to modern predictive intelligence or Intelligence Preparation of the Battlefield:

> As it is impossible to obtain exact information by the methods mentioned, a general should never move without arranging several courses of action for himself, based upon probable hypotheses that the relative situation of the armies enables him to make, and never losing sight of the principles of the art.[29]

Jomini understood that Napoleon's revolution in warfare (the organization of the Army into self-contained, mission-oriented, corps-size units and a command and control system to orchestrate it)[30] created new problems which complicated the ways in which the old intelligence systems worked:

> When armies camped in tents and in a single mass, information of the enemy's operations was certain because reconnoitering parties could be thrown forward in sight of the camps, and the spies could report accurately their movements; but with the existing organization into corps d'armee which either canton or bivouac, it is very difficult to learn anything about them.[31]

Rather than turning his back on the complications created by these changes (as Clausewitz may be accused of doing), Jomini chose to confront the problem by emphasizing the need to develop a workable intelligence apparatus to better serve the commander, thereby elevating the overall importance of intelligence.

Clausewitzian Intelligence or Information?

To move now from the historical context of our discussion, a controversial question develops over the issue of "intelligence" versus "information." Was Clausewitz's criticism in fact aimed at the poor quality of combat information as opposed to combat intelligence? To the casual observer this point may appear to be hair-splitting, but members of the Intelligence Community today are quick to recognize that this distinction is indeed important:

> Information is unevaluated material of every description including that derived from observations, communications, reports, rumors, imagery, and other sources from which intelligence is produced. Information itself may be true or false, accurate or inaccurate, confirmed or unconfirmed, pertinent or impertinent, positive or negative. "Intelligence" is the product resulting from the collection, evaluation, and interpretation of information.[32]

The stroke of a translator's pen not in tune with these nuances could be at the heart of some of the controversy regarding Clausewitzian notions of intelligence. For example, in the problematic chapter where Clausewitz addresses intelligence (Chapter 6, Book 1, titled "*Nachrichten Im Kriege*" in the German text), the term *Nachrichten* is a focal point of debate because it may be translated variously as "intelligence," "information," "reports," or even "news." Similarly, the word *Kenntnis* may be translated as either "information" or "knowledge."[33]

In the excellent and most recent (1984) edition of *On War*, the distinguished military historians Michael Howard and Peter Paret translated the German opening line from Chapter 6, Book 1, in a manner that has come to be widely accepted by most U.S. military readers: "By intelligence" [that is, *Nachrichten*] we mean every sort of information about the enemy and his country."[34]

Should this construction be considered the final word? An editors' note in the 1984 edition states:

> We have attempted to present Clausewitz's ideas as accurately as possible, while remaining as close to his style and vocabulary as modern English usage would permit. *But we have not hesitated to translate the same term in different ways if the context seemed to demand it* [emphasis added].[35]

Howard and Paret chose to interpret *Nachrichten* as "intelligence." The two previous English translations of *On War*, however, construed it simply as "information." More specifically, in both the 1909 and 1943 editions the opening line previously referenced reads: "By the word 'information' we denote all the knowledge which we have of the enemy and his country."[36]

According to Dr. Paret, during Clausewitz's times the modern distinction between intelligence and information did not exist. The decision to translate *Nachrichten* as "intelligence" was based on the determination that "it is most appropriate because it is the closest modern equivalent to what Clausewitz was referring to: information on the enemy and his country." In Dr. Paret's opinion, the previous translations were too literal, failing to capture the essence of Clausewitzian thought.[37]

Howard and Paret's decision becomes especially critical for modern readers of Clausewitz when they attempt to come to terms with his unflattering appraisal of intelligence as quoted in the epigraph of this [chapter]. To recall, the 1984 edition translation is as follows: "Many intelligence reports in war are contradictory; even more are false, and most are uncertain. . . . In short, most intelligence is false."[38]

The 1909 and 1943 versions of this same line read: "A great part of the information obtained in war is contradictory, a still greater part is false, and by far the greatest part somewhat doubtful. . . . In a few words, most reports are false."[39]

These translations convey significantly different meanings. Unfortunately, the 1984 edition (currently the most widely read) suggests that Clausewitz was critical of intelligence per se rather than of the confusing flow of information and reports from which intelligence must be distilled. To reiterate, it is essential to recognize that today intelligence professionals clearly distinguish between the two. The decision to regard intelligence as simply information on the enemy might be a purely academic argument, but in light of today's tendency to quote Clausewitz as an authority on modern military matters, the issue transcends academic boundaries. To accept the 1984 edition's translation of *Nachrichten* as "intelligence" is to imply that Napoleonic armies were knowingly producing the equivalent of what we today call intelligence. Such was just not the case.

Put in its proper historical context, then, Clausewitz's disparagement in *On War* of what Howard and Paret label as "intelligence" was actually directed at the raw flux of undigested "information" emanating from the theater of war. It can even be argued that because of the primitive approach to gathering and processing data in the Napoleonic era, Clausewitz never witnessed the production of true intelligence. With operational as well as intelligence problems to solve, it is no wonder that battlefield commanders serving as their own intelligence officers were habituated to false, incomplete, or misleading data on the enemy. From Clausewitz's perspective, contradiction, chance, and uncertainty were the hallmarks of battlefield information, and he was correct in taking a dim view of the prevailing state of affairs.

Concluding Thoughts

On War continues to be read, interpreted, and debated among the present generation of military professionals, just as it was debated by past generations. To reap maximum benefits from this great work, it is advisable to maintain an open mind and curb the tendency to make hasty judgments about those bold positions of Clausewitz that jar the modern sensibility. His treatment of intelligence is a perfect case in point.

Intelligence today is far from being a perfect science. Imperfect or not, however, it continues to fulfill a necessary function which encompasses provision of strategic indications and warning down through tactical support of the combat arms. The

Intelligence Community strives to "minimize uncertainty" concerning the enemy through the scientific processing and weighing of multiple sources of data.[40] "Minimizing uncertainty" is a respectable and practical standard to pursue—one fully recognizing that the Clausewitzian concepts of chance, friction, and the fog of war are still very much a part of modern conflict.

Of course, intelligence failures will never be eliminated. But for every intelligence failure there are scores of important counterintelligence and intelligence-based operational successes. The failures neither invalidate the conceptual usefulness of intelligence nor validate Clausewitz's skepticism concerning reportage on the enemy.

Observers point out the great strides that technology has made in the intelligence field, implying that technology alone is what readily distinguishes past from present intelligence.[41] In reality, the important advancements have been more fundamental. The establishment of intelligence as a formal discipline and the creation of intelligence staffs at major combat unit levels—staffs exclusively dedicated to the collection, collation, and analysis of information—are the two most revolutionary advances in the entire intelligence endeavor. Deficiencies in these areas were the crippling weaknesses of intelligence efforts during the Napoleonic era.

Like the nations and armies that fell before Napoleon's revolutionary warfighting methods, the quasi-intelligence organizations of his era failed to keep pace with the changing nature of war. Master deception and counterintelligence executed by ensuing great captains strained an antiquated and outmoded organization already incapable of consistently and systematically producing reliable intelligence.

In writing from his personal observations, Clausewitz attempted to capture the state of the art of intelligence. But, as we have seen, warfare was in transition. Advances were required in several functional areas, to include intelligence. Systems and methods had yet to catch up with operational advances on the battlefield. A glaring mismatch between ends, ways, and means came to develop. Clausewitz recognized the intelligence shortfalls and reported what he saw. To a point, he was correct. Advances in intelligence would later be made, but not during his lifetime.

If Clausewitz can be faulted, the reason may be simply that his statements on intelligence violated his own injunctions with regard to the best approach to a theory of war. He had desired to create a nonprescriptive way of thinking. By alleging flatly that "most intelligence is false," he lapsed into the very dogmatism he elsewhere abjured. Certainly he demonstrated a lack of vision in failing to foresee that the wildly confused and confusing combat information reportage of his time—as frustrating as it was—would one day be largely harnessed by the scientific method. Lacking such foresight in this instance, he could hardly have recognized that the wretched *Nachrichten* about which he complained so sorely would ultimately metamorphose into what we today call "intelligence," a sine qua non for success in war.

Notes

[1] Carl von Clausewitz, *On War*, ed. and trans. Michael Howard and Peter Paret (Princeton: Princeton University Press, 1984), 117.

2 David Kahn, "Clausewitz and Intelligence," in *Clausewitz and Modern Strategy*, ed. Michael I. Handel (London: Frank Cass, 1986), 117–126.

3 Ibid., 125.

4 Ibid., 118–120.

5 Ibid., 125.

6 Walter Goerlitz, *History of the German General Staff, 1657–1945* (New York: Praeger, 1967), 61.

7 Roger Parkinson, *Clausewitz: A Biography* (New York: Stein and Day, 1970), 310.

8 David G. Chandler, *The Campaigns of Napoleon* (New York: Macmillan, 1966), 146.

9 Gunther E. Rothenberg, *The Art of Warfare in the Age of Napoleon* (Bloomington: Indiana University Press, 1978), 147.

10 Chandler, 146.

11 Ibid., 147.

12 Jay Luvaas, "Napoleon's Use of Intelligence: The Jena Campaign of 1805," in *Leaders and Intelligence*, ed. Michael I. Handel (London: Frank Cass, 1989), 52.

13 Telephonic interview with Dr. Peter Paret, Institute for Advanced Study, Princeton, New Jersey, January 5, 1989.

14 Ibid.

15 Ibid.

16 Martin van Creveld, *Command in War* (Cambridge: Harvard University Press, 1985), 65.

17 Ibid., 66.

18 Ibid., 67.

19 John Elting, *Swords Around a Throne* (New York: The Free Press, 1988), 116.

20 Van Creveld, 68.

21 S.G.P. Ward, *Wellington's Headquarters: A Study of the Administrative Problems in the Peninsula, 1809–1814* (London: Oxford University Press, 1957), 119–120.

22 Ibid., 120.

23 Luvaas, 52.

24 Ibid.

25 John Shy, "Jomini," in *Makers of Modern Strategy: From Machiavelli to the Nuclear Age*, ed. Peter Paret with Gordon Craig and Felix Gilbert (Princeton: Princeton University Press, 1986), 144.

26 Henri Jomini, *The Art of War*, trans. G.H. Mendell and W.P. Craighill (Westport, CT: Greenwood Press, 1977), 197.

27 Ibid., 269.

28 Ibid., 274.

29 Ibid.

30 Van Creveld, 97.

31 Jomini, 270.

32 Direct quotation from superseded U.S. Army Field Manual 30–5, *Combat Intelligence*, Headquarters, Department of the Army, October 1973, 2–1. A point of interest is that this manual's definition of "information" closely matches Clausewitz's idea of the uncertain nature of most reports. See also U.S. Army Field Manual 34–1, *Intelligence and Electronic Warfare Operations*, July 1987, 2–8, 2–13; U.S. Army Field Manual 34–3, *Intelligence Analysis*, January 1986, 1–1; and Joint Chiefs of Staff Publication 1, *Dictionary of Military and Associated Terms*, Washington, DC, June 1, 1987, 184, 188, for definitions of a similar nature.

33 Carl von Clausewitz, *Vom Kriege*, ed. Werner Hahlweg (Bonn: Ferd. Dümmlers Verlag, 1980), 258: "Mit dem Worte Nachrichten bezeichen wir die ganze Kenntnis, welche man von dem Feinde und seinem Lande hat. . . ."

34 Clausewitz (Howard and Paret), 117.

35 Ibid., xi.

36 Carl von Clausewitz, *On War*, trans. J. J. Graham (London: Kegan Paul, Trench, Trubner, 1909), 75; Carl von Clausewitz, *On War*, trans. O.J. Matthijs Jolles (Washington, DC: Infantry Journal Press, 1950; reprinted from 1943 Random House edition), 51.

37 Telephonic interview.

38 Clausewitz (Howard and Paret), 117. The German original is as follows: "Ein grosser Teil der Nachrichten, die man im Kriege bekommt, ist widerspechend, ein noch grosserer ist falsch und bei weitem der grosste einer ziemlichen Ungewissheit unterworfen. Mit kurzen Worten: die meisten Nachrichten sind falsch" (Hahlwege, 258–259).

39 Clausewitz (Graham), 75–76; Clausewitz (Jolles), 51.

40 Field Manual 30–5, 2–1, and Field Manual 34–3, 1–1; also refer to the role of the intelligence analyst in reducing uncertainty.

41 Kahn, 123–124.

Part II—Origins and Future of U.S. Intelligence

A President has to know what is going on all around the world in order to be ready to act when action is needed. . . . The war taught us this lesson—that we had to collect intelligence in a manner that would make the information available where it was needed and when it was wanted, in an intelligent and understandable form.

—Harry S. Truman

Chapter 3

Origins of the Central Intelligence Agency: "Those Spooky Boys"

Amy B. Zegart

W hen most Americans think of the Central Intelligence Agency (CIA), they conjure up images of a rogue elephant, a supersecret organization gone out of control.[1] "Those spooky boys," as Secretary of State Dean Rusk called them,[2] designed exploding Cuban cigars to assassinate Fidel Castro, mined Nicaraguan harbors, planted Soviet moles, and sponsored coups from Guatemala to Vietnam. The ultimate Cold War agency, the CIA became best known for its covert, subversive operations abroad.

But this Central Intelligence Agency looks nothing like the one created by the 1947 National Security Act. When Harry Truman submitted that draft legislation in February 1947, he meant to create an intelligence confederation. Conforming to his military's wishes, the President sought a small central intelligence agency that would coordinate, evaluate, and disseminate intelligence, but not collect it. The original CIA was never supposed to engage in spying. It was never supposed to sponsor coups, influence foreign elections, or conduct any other kind of subversive operations. It was never supposed to be more than an analysis outfit, coordinating the information gathered by preexisting intelligence units in the Army, Navy, Federal Bureau of Investigation (FBI), and State Department.[3] To put it plainly, the CIA was supposed to be weak. Its provision in the National Security Act was among the least noticed and least debated of all.

At the outset, it is also important to bear in mind that the CIA's origins were much more complicated than those of the National Security Council (NSC) system or the Joint Chiefs of Staff (JCS). There were many more bureaucratic actors on the scene who had a stake in the creation of a central intelligence organization. Despite the popular perceptions generated by Tom Clancy novels and James Bond movies, American intelligence gathering was not a Cold War invention: it has existed since the Republic's founding. George Washington organized his own intelligence unit during the Revolutionary War, sending spies behind enemy lines and overseeing

Source: Amy B. Zegart, Chapter 6, "Origins of the Central Intelligence Agency: Those Spooky Boys," in *Flawed by Design: The Evolution of the CIA, JCS, and NSC* (Stanford: Stanford University Press, 1999), 163–184. Copyright © 1999 by the Board of Trustees of the Leland Stanford Junior University. Used with permission of Stanford University Press, www.sup.org.

counterespionage operations. In 1790, just 3 years after the Constitutional Convention, Congress acknowledged an executive prerogative to conduct intelligence operations and gave President Washington a secret unvouchered fund "for spies, if the gentleman so pleases."[4] Intelligence has been a component of American foreign policy ever since.

More important for our purposes, America's growing involvement in world affairs during the late 19th and early 20th centuries led to the establishment of several permanent intelligence organizations. In 1882, the Office of Naval Intelligence (ONI) was created and charged with collecting technical data about foreign naval ships and weapons. Three years later, the Department of War established its own intelligence unit, the Military Intelligence Division (MID). In 1908, the Federal Bureau of Investigation opened its doors. By the 1930s, the FBI had become the Nation's paramount counterespionage agency and had branched into running intelligence activities in Latin America. The State Department, meanwhile, had developed an expertise and a mission that focused on overt information collection. Finally, Japan's stunning surprise attack on Pearl Harbor sparked the creation of a new wartime central intelligence agency under the Joint Chiefs of Staff, the Office of Strategic Services (OSS), which collected information, analyzed raw intelligence, and carried out a range of covert subversive operations abroad, from propaganda to sabotage to paramilitary operations. By the end of World War II, these five bureaucratic actors were vying for their own places in the postwar intelligence arena. This was hardly the same straightforward War Department versus Navy Department environment that gave rise to the National Security Council (NSC) system or the Joint Chiefs of Staff.

In addition, although the CIA's statutory charter can be found alongside provisions that established the NSC system and the Joint Chiefs of Staff, questions of postwar intelligence were peripheral to the unification debate. Political players, particularly the President, were far more concerned with consolidating the military services than with establishing any kind of peacetime central intelligence agency. The JCS and even the NSC system figured directly in War-Navy unification discussions. But postwar intelligence issues were mostly hashed out along a separate, parallel negotiating track. Indeed, these issues appeared to be settled in January 1946, a full year before the Truman administration presented Congress with its final version of the National Security Act: in an executive directive, the President signaled his acceptance of a hard-won compromise intelligence plan. The arrangement protected all existing intelligence units by granting each exclusive control over its own sphere of activity and by creating a new, weak central coordinating body called the Central Intelligence Group (CIG). All sides expected this arrangement to be simply and automatically codified in the forthcoming National Security Act.

To everyone's surprise, however, the new Central Intelligence Group quickly took on a life of its own, pressing the administration for broader jurisdiction, more autonomy, and stronger legal foundations in the National Security Act. The timing could not have been worse. The warring military services were just now edging toward a comprehensive compromise unification bill. Reopening intelligence discussions at this point threatened to rekindle military opposition and derail the entire legislative package. Facing this specter, Truman and his aides were in no mood to compromise with CIG. Determined to get a military consolidation bill through Congress in 1947, the White House rejected all of CIG's demands and kept intelligence provisions as brief and as uncontroversial as possible. The administration's proposed National Security Act included the barest mention of a central intelligence agency. Ironically, such thin, vague provisions opened the door for subsequent CIA abuses. Truman's uncontroversial language would become the proverbial wolf in sheep's clothing.

The Players

Wild Bill Donovan and the Office of Strategic Services

Called an empire builder by some and Wild Bill by most, William J. Donovan began floating radical ideas for a powerful central intelligence organization as early as 1940.[5] During a European tour for President Franklin D. Roosevelt, Donovan became convinced that the existing intelligence system—which left War, Navy, State, FBI, and other intelligence units to their own devices—was incapable of providing the President with integrated intelligence analysis or operations. With U.S. involvement in the war imminent, Donovan began pressing Roosevelt for an agency that would not only coordinate these disparate intelligence components but combine intelligence collection, analysis, and subversive foreign operations under a single roof.[6] Events soon played into Donovan's hands. The surprise Japanese attack on Pearl Harbor gave rise to the OSS. With Donovan at its helm, the OSS was directed to "collect and analyze . . . strategic information" and to "plan and operate . . . special services."[7] The agency quickly evolved. By the end of the war, the OSS was engaged in a range of activities—from guerrilla warfare to clandestine activities to strategic analysis—and employed over 1,200 people.[8]

Still, the OSS was far from the all-encompassing, powerful central intelligence agency that Donovan envisioned. Placed under the Joint Chiefs of Staff, OSS faced stiff competition and firm resistance from both the Office of Naval Intelligence and the Army's G–2 intelligence branch. Anne Karalekas writes, "From the outset the military were reluctant to provide OSS with information for its research and analysis role and restricted its operations."[9] General Douglas MacArthur, she notes, excluded the OSS from the Pacific theater. FBI Director J. Edgar Hoover prohibited the OSS from conducting any domestic espionage activities and maintained the FBI's tight control over all intelligence activities in Latin America. In short, with no direct access to the President, with relatively limited autonomy, and with little cooperation from other intelligence components, the Office of Strategic Services contributed only modestly to the wartime intelligence effort.[10]

The OSS experience was central to Donovan's thinking about postwar intelligence organization. In the fall of 1944, Donovan once again took the initiative, proposing a new and improved OSS to meet American peacetime intelligence needs. According to Donovan's memo to Roosevelt of November 18, 1944, this proposed central intelligence agency would report directly to the President. It would have its own budget. It would be able to call on other intelligence agencies for personnel and information. And it would have explicit authority to gather its own intelligence, to conduct its own subversive activities abroad, and to coordinate the intelligence functions and policies of all other intelligence agencies. In short, the Donovan proposal called for a truly centralized system, dominated by a single agency.[11]

The Military, the FBI, and the Department of State

Donovan's strong central intelligence agency plan ran up against serious opposition. The Navy Department, the War Department, the Justice Department's FBI, and the Department of State all conducted intelligence activities of their own. Without objecting outright to the idea of a central coordinating agency, these actors sought to protect their own turf. As former CIA Deputy Director Ray Cline writes, "The one thing that Army, Navy, State, and the FBI agreed on was that they did not want a strong central agency controlling their collection programs."[12] A common enemy forged common bonds. Though the specific motivations and plans varied among these actors, their objective was the same: maintaining the maximum power and independence of their own intelligence operations. In an unusual coalition, sailors, soldiers, G-men, and diplomats came together and lobbied for a decentralized, confederal intelligence system. Nominally coordinated by a small central organization, the system would allow each department to run its own intelligence affairs.

The Department of the Navy. The Navy Department led the charge against Donovan's idea of a powerful central intelligence agency. This should not come as a surprise. A decentralized intelligence system fitted nicely with the Navy's unification proposals and philosophy. Decentralization and loose coordination served the Navy's interests on all fronts. Navy leaders knew that confederal organizations—be they the National Security Council, the Joint Chiefs of Staff, or some diluted central intelligence agency—offered the best odds of maintaining the department's unparalleled status, power, and influence. That was exactly what they wanted. In Cline's words, the Navy "sought a central [intelligence] structure strong enough to prevent any other agency from dominating everything but weak enough to present no threat to Navy's control of its own affairs."[13]

But there was more to the Navy's motives than naked self-interest. As Ferdinand Eberstadt's 1945 report suggests, the Navy, War, and State Departments had very different informational needs—needs that could not easily be combined or even understood by a central intelligence apparatus. Developing Navy strategy, tactics, weapons programs, and force structure required detailed technical information about enemy and allied naval forces. Similar considerations applied to the Army and Air Force. As for the State Department, diplomatic moves required both military information and intelligence about broader economic and political conditions abroad. "Each of these departments," Eberstadt concludes, "requires operating intelligence peculiar to itself. Intimate and detailed knowledge of the objectives and problems of each service is obviously indispensable to successful operation."[14] For all three departments, collecting the right information and interpreting it in the right way required specialized expertise. Such skills, they believed, were most efficiently developed and used by their own, inhouse intelligence components.

The Department of War. War and Navy Department interests coincided. While the two departments fought tooth and nail over almost every other provision of the National Security Act, they formed a united front against a strongly centralized intelligence system. Like the Office of Naval Intelligence, the Army's G–2 served the unique needs of its parent department. Operations, intelligence gathering, and analysis were all undertaken with an eye to improving War Department strategy and tactics. Though military consolidation promised a multitude of benefits for the War Department, intelligence consolidation did not. In this one area, War Department leaders willingly chanted the Navy's mantra: the more organizations, the better.

The Federal Bureau of Investigation. The FBI, like the Navy and War Departments, had good reasons to resist a highly centralized intelligence system. Initially established as the Justice Department's basic Federal law enforcement agency, the bureau quickly extended its activities to counterterrorism and counterintelligence. During the 1930s, J. Edgar Hoover's G-men were responsible for rooting out spies, for investigating sabotage, and for hunting down communist and fascist operatives within the United States. It was not long before the ever-ambitious Hoover began pushing for more. In 1939, the FBI assumed responsibility for collecting foreign intelligence in Latin America. With President Roosevelt's blessing, the bureau created a Special Intelligence Services whose 360 agents controlled Western Hemisphere intelligence activities throughout the war.[15] By 1945, Hoover's FBI had become the Nation's primary counterespionage agency, with near total control over domestic activities, and had begun venturing into overseas operations. As the war's end drew near, the bureau was naturally reluctant to cede either of these hard-won gains to Donovan's OSS or to any other organization.

An Uneasy Partner: The Department of State. The State Department sat more tenuously in this coalition. It appeared to be caught between two countervailing pressures.

On the one hand, Donovan's idea of a strong central intelligence agency threatened the Secretary of State and his colleagues. As State saw it, the line between analyzing intelligence and providing foreign policy advice was a thin one. Indeed, the State Department largely saw its mission in terms of intelligence; what else did Foreign Service officers do but collect information and use it to develop workable policy proposals and programs? For diplomats, information was power. Donovan's new agency, with its broad information-gathering mandate and direct access to the President, posed a direct challenge to the State Department's influence in foreign affairs.

On the other hand, the department's own cultural norms and organizational structure pulled in the opposite direction. Disdain for all things covert ran deep within the diplomatic corps. As Secretary of State Henry L. Stimson once put it, "gentlemen do not read each other's mail." Such sentiment had prompted the department to disband its code-breaking joint venture with the Army and Navy in 1929 and to resist creating an internal clandestine intelligence unit until after World War II. For these officials, intelligence was supposed to be gained openly, by trained diplomats who spent their time monitoring foreign news, socializing with foreign diplomats, and cabling their impressions back home to Washington.[16] If clandestine activities had to be performed at all, the feeling ran, it was better to let some other organization take responsibility. By this reasoning, a powerful central intelligence agency might not be a bad thing. At the very least, it kept the dirty business of spying from sullying the hands of diplomats.

The department's centrifugal organization only added fuel to the fire. Regional bureaus dominated the State Department's power structure. Rooted in this division was the idea that all activities, including overt intelligence collection, should be scattered across the various country and regional offices rather than concentrated in any kind of department-wide functional bureau. This resistance to creating an in-house, State Department intelligence outfit weakened the department's hand in the broader executive branch battle.

As we shall see, these countervailing pressures led the State Department to move in and out of its alliance with the Navy, the War Department, and the FBI. At first, fears of Donovan's all-powerful agency drove the department into their arms. Once Donovan's plan was off the table, however, Secretary of State James Byrnes tried to break away from the coalition and take control of *all* intelligence activities in the executive branch. But Byrnes soon found himself waging a two-front war—one against his coalition partners in the executive branch and the other against his own department. Byrnes eventually conceded, rejoined the War/Navy/FBI coalition, and lived to fight another day.

A Late Arrival: The Central Intelligence Group

The Central Intelligence Group was never supposed to become an actor in the intelligence conflict. When Harry Truman created CIG by executive directive on January 22, 1946, he believed the bureaucratic battle to be over: CIG's design represented a decisive victory for proponents of decentralized intelligence. Surrounded by superintending and advisory bodies, dependent on other departments for budgets and staffing, and limited to coordinating, correlating, evaluating, and disseminating the intelligence collected by others, CIG was designed to be a clearinghouse without strong central authority or power.[17]

Truman expected to codify this language eventually (and easily) in the National Security Act. The Central Intelligence Group had different ideas. Within 6 months of its creation, the agency began pushing for wide-ranging changes. Complaining about its "stepchild" status, CIG Director Hoyt S. Vandenberg mounted a campaign to win his agency greater autonomy, broader jurisdiction, and more power, and to enshrine all of these gains in a new statutory charter. Rather than ending the intelligence controversy, CIG's creation added one more voice to it.

The President

For Harry Truman, creating a strong peacetime central intelligence agency was never a high priority. Publicly, he remained relatively detached from intelligence hostilities, refusing to take a firm position or get out in front of the issue.[18] When moments of decision did arrive, however, the President sided with his military services. At every critical juncture of the intelligence debate, Truman opted for the weaker central intelligence agency proposed by the military. There were three major moments of decision.

The first came in September 1945, when Truman chose to disband the wartime Office of Strategic Services instead of maintaining it during peacetime, as Donovan wanted. Second, in January 1946, the President opted to coordinate intelligence through an emasculated Central Intelligence Group rather than through a much stronger State Department apparatus. Finally, in 1947, Truman proposed a CIG-like agency for the National Security Act instead of the more powerful agency recommended by CIG Director Vandenberg.

These choices may seem surprising at first. After all, we would expect any President, *ceteris paribus*, to prefer more information to less, and to favor centralized control over decentralized arrangements. By this reasoning, Truman should have been driven by the imperatives of office to reject the military's intelligence plans. However, Truman's position makes more sense when placed in context. For this President, no organizational issue appeared more important than consolidating the War and Navy Departments into an effective, efficient military apparatus. As he explained in his 1945 special message to Congress:

> We would be taking a grave risk with the national security if we did not move now to overcome permanently the present imperfections in our defense organization. However great was the need for coordination and unified command in World War II, it is sure to be greater if there is any future aggression against world peace. . . . Our combat forces must work together in one team as they have never been required to work together in the past.[19]

Unification of the Armed Forces was Harry Truman's crusade. For 2 years, the President marshaled all the energies and powers of his office to make this idea a reality. Eyeing the unification prize, Truman had little patience for anything that might jeopardize his campaign.

A new, powerful central intelligence agency threatened to do just that. Intelligence was one of the few issues on which the warring Navy and War Departments actually agreed. From the start, both services resisted any proposal that sought to concentrate intelligence authority in a single organization—be it the OSS, the State Department, or a Central Intelligence Agency. From the President's vantage point, opposing the military on this issue posed high risks and promised low rewards. Given the delicate nature of unification negotiations, Truman needed all the help he could get.[20]

Two Missing Pieces: Interest Groups and Congress

Just like the NSC system and the JCS, the CIA was created without much input from interest groups or Members of Congress. The absence of interest groups in this case is understandable. We already know that the foreign policy interest group scene was rather sparse. In addition, intelligence operations and organizations were, by nature, shrouded in secrecy. With no way to know what the issues were, even interested citizens naturally found it difficult to organize and try to influence the debate.

Legislators also played minor parts in the CIA's creation. Between 1944 and 1947, substantive debates about postwar intelligence organization stayed within the confines of the executive branch. Though House and Senate committees held a string of hearings during that time about military unification, questions of intelligence organization were rarely raised and hardly discussed. Tellingly, Truman succeeded in disbanding the wartime OSS and creating the Central Intelligence Group without any congressional involvement at all. Both changes were made by unilateral executive action.[21] Moreover, legislators appeared to duck the intelligence question even when they had an opportunity to tackle it. In 1947, the intelligence provisions of Truman's National Security Act sailed through the House and Senate with little controversy. Though the House Committee on Expenditures in the Executive Departments insisted on specifying the CIA's functions, they adopted the President's old CIG directive almost word for word. No one ever seriously considered what this new agency would or should be doing. The question hinged on whether the CIA's powers should be spelled out in legislation, not on what those powers should be.[22] Thus, National Security Act provisions ended up creating a CIA that closely resembled its CIG predecessor. This was precisely what the Truman administration wanted.

Congress acquiesced on CIA design for many of the same reasons it did on the NSC system and the JCS provisions of the National Security Act. First and foremost, average members had no real incentives to take charge of the issue. If anything, electoral considerations militated against challenging the executive branch on national security organization. There were no strong organized interests that could reward legislators for their votes. Conversely, broad-based public opinion could easily be turned against members who challenged military experts on American national security issues. Against the Cold War backdrop, these considerations prevented even congressional national security intellectuals—that is, leading legislators who tackled national issues for nonelectoral reasons—from taking a prominent role. With dim prospects of rallying their colleagues to action, congressional leaders sat on the sidelines.

The administration also made it difficult for Congress to join the intelligence debate. For one thing, placing intelligence provisions in the omnibus National Security Act deflected attention from the CIA and toward other more contentious issues such as the Secretary of Defense's powers or the Navy's autonomy. For another, White House aides deliberately adopted a strategy of "the less said, the better," making CIA provisions brief and vague.[23] Fearing that any more detailed language might reopen bureaucratic conflict or invite closer congressional scrutiny, administration officials kept controversial provisions to a minimum, presented them as stopgap measures, and promised Congress a second, separate intelligence bill in the future.[24] The approach worked: all but a few legislators were content to let the National Security Act's intelligence provisions stand unchallenged.

In sum, like the National Security Council system and the Joint Chiefs of Staff, the Central Intelligence Agency was forged out of conflict in the executive branch. A host of bureaucratic actors—the wartime OSS, the military, the FBI, the State Department, the Central Intelligence Group—all held substantial stakes in postwar intelligence organization. Each fought to achieve its own goals. President Truman was a reluctant arbiter. Preoccupied with military unification, the President took action only when necessary and always sided with his military departments. Legislators, for their part, had little reason to get involved. Flexing congressional muscles on this issue offered little in the way of electoral rewards and much in the way of potential public criticism.

Overview: Unification and the Central Intelligence Agency

The intelligence battle was a three-round affair. All rounds were fought within the executive branch, but they did not involve the same actors or the same options. Round 1, which lasted from late 1944 to the fall of 1945, pitted Wild Bill Donovan and his OSS against a coalition of the Navy, War, Justice, and State Departments. At issue was whether to transform the wartime Office of Strategic Services into a powerful, independent peacetime central intelligence agency. When the round ended, Donovan had lost. Not only did the President reject Donovan's vision of a central intelligence agency, but he disbanded OSS altogether, transferring its divisions to the Departments of War and State like spoils to the victors. In round 2, it was State versus the military; suddenly, without the OSS as a common enemy, the Navy/War/Justice/State coalition began to fray. While Secretary of State Byrnes pressed for a new State Department-controlled intelligence system, War and Navy officials stuck to their guns, continuing to support the old coalition plan for a Central Intelligence Group under joint State/War/Navy control. In the end, State conceded and CIG was established by executive directive. Round 3 featured two new players—the freshly minted Central Intelligence Group and the White House. Between January 1946 and February 1947, CIG pushed for more power and for stronger statutory foundations in the National Security Act, while Truman and his legislative drafting team, mindful of the military's position, desperately tried to quell their demands. With the entire unification bill hanging in the balance, CIG did not have much chance. The CIA that emerged from the National Security Act of 1947 satisfied the War and Navy Departments. It was weak by design.

Round 1: November 1944–September 1945

Wild Bill Donovan kicked off the conflict in November 1944 with a memo to Franklin Roosevelt.[25] In it, Donovan urged the President not only to keep OSS after the war but to vastly increase its autonomy, capabilities, and jurisdiction. Whereas the wartime OSS had to report to the Joint Chiefs of Staff, Donovan's postwar agency would be led by a director who reported directly to the President. Whereas the OSS had to make do with budgets from other departments and agencies, the postwar intelligence agency would have an independent budget. Whereas the OSS's mandate was limited, Donovan's new agency had wide-ranging authority to run its own spies and conduct subversive operations, as well as to analyze and disseminate intelligence gathered by State, ONI, G–2, the FBI, and any other governmental intelligence unit. With its own money, its direct access to the President, and its broad authority, Donovan's new agency would be suffused with power. It was designed not to coordinate existing intelligence agencies but to dominate them.

Naturally, the departmental intelligence services resisted Donovan's plan. As Thomas Troy notes, the OSS's "pretensions to permanence and power" generated "intense hostility" among other intelligence producers, particularly those in the Departments of War, the Navy, and Justice. "These had not wanted . . . OSS in the first place, had never become reconciled to it, and were determined it would never attain what they were sure it aspired to, namely, control over their intelligence and their intelligence departments."[26] In their view, effective intelligence gathering and analysis could be realized only by a decentralized system in which each department trained its own experts and developed its own priorities.

Politics made for strange bedfellows. Between November 1944 and September 1945, the Departments of State, War, the Navy, and Justice joined forces against the Donovan plan. They counterattacked along several fronts. The military spearheaded the effort, working within the JCS to develop constructive alternatives to the Donovan plan. They finished in a matter of weeks. Their counterproposal, which was issued as JIC 239/5 on January 1, 1945, diluted much of the central agency's power.[27] Instead of reporting directly to the President, the agency's director answered to a National Intelligence Authority (NIA) consisting of the Secretaries of State, War, the Navy, and a representative from the Joint Chiefs of Staff. This NIA was a far more powerful superintending authority than anything Donovan had envisioned, with nearly total control over the new agency's budgets, jurisdiction, and activities. The JCS plan also called for an intelligence advisory board, filled with the heads of all the major intelligence units, which would advise the new central agency's director. In essence, this scheme sought to create an intelligence system that was centralized in name only; sandwiched between the NIA and the advisory board, the proposed central intelligence agency would have minimal authority and power.[28]

Meanwhile, Hoover's FBI worked behind the scenes to sabotage the OSS effort. In February 1945, news of Donovan's plan made front-page headlines in three leading anti-Roosevelt papers—the *Chicago Tribune*, the *New York Daily News*, and the *Washington Times Herald*. The articles, written by Walter Trohan, carried classified details of the Donovan plan and denounced them all. "Donovan Proposes Super Spy System for Postwar New Deal; Would Take Over FBI, Secret Service, ONI and G–2 to Watch Home, Abroad," ran the *Times Herald* story. The *Chicago Tribune* declared, "New Deal Plans Super Spy System; Sleuths Would Snoop on U.S. and the World."[29] Calling the proposed central intelligence agency "an all-powerful intelligence service to spy on the postwar world and to pry into the lives of citizens at home,"[30] Trohan inflamed public fears of a U.S. Gestapo. Though J. Edgar Hoover never admitted responsibility, many observers, including Donovan and White House aide Clark Clifford, believed him to be the source of the leaks.[31]

As the JCS counterproposal made its way to the President's desk and as press leaks made Donovan's plan increasingly untenable, the Departments of State, Justice, War, and the Navy embarked on a diplomatic initiative to stall consideration of the entire intelligence issue. On April 5, 1945, just before his death, President Roosevelt asked Donovan to canvass the heads of all intelligence services about the establishment of a postwar central intelligence agency. Secretary of War Henry L. Stimson responded by sending a letter to Donovan. His position was firm and clear: as the primary protectors of U.S. national interests abroad and at home, the Departments of State, War, the Navy, and Justice had to retain complete control over their own intelligence operations. Stimson also made clear that the War Department was not standing alone. "State, War, Justice, and the Navy have together examined the proposed central intelligence service and are in substantial agreement that it should not be considered prior to the termination of hostilities against Germany and Japan," he wrote.[32] The meaning of this sentence could not have been lost on Donovan: the four most power-ful executive departments had already forged a coalition against him.[33] Delaying the intelligence issue was merely a polite—and effective—signal of their intentions.

Donovan and the Office of Strategic Services had no chance against such odds. Indeed, as Troy writes, the agency "was in a fundamentally weaker position than all its rivals and foes."[34] Forged in wartime, without any statutory authority, OSS was never intended to be anything more than a temporary creation. As such, the agency lacked institutional strength. It had no alumni to speak of, few congressional supporters, and no real broad public support. As the war wound down, public sentiment favored a quick return to business as usual, including the demobilization of wartime agencies.

This first round of conflict ended 5 months later, on September 20, 1945, when President Truman issued an executive order disbanding the Office of Strategic Ser-vices and transferring its divisions to the Departments of State and War. With the big four executive departments on the offensive, with public criticism on the rise, and with Donovan against the wall, the President's choice was easy. When the dust cleared, OSS was dead and Donovan's hopes for a strong postwar central intelligence agency were dashed.

Round 2: September 1945–January 1946

Round 2 began immediately. With OSS gone, the locus of conflict moved inside the Navy/War/Justice/State coalition. On September 20, the same day Truman eliminat-ed OSS, he asked Secretary of State James Byrnes to "take the lead in developing a com-prehensive and coordinated foreign intelligence program."[35] Why the President handed this responsibility to the State Department remains unclear; what is clear is that Byrnes and his acolytes seized the opportunity. They soon began lobbying for a State Depart-ment–controlled postwar intelligence system. The State Department plan, developed by Byrnes's special assistant for research and intelligence, Alfred McCormack, called for housing an overarching national intelligence authority within the State Department, under the exclusive authority and direction of the Secretary. Under the McCormack plan, State would be the sole conduit of intelligence reports to the President.[36]

McCormack's proposal touched off a new and bitter struggle between the Department of State and the military. To War Department and Navy Department officials, a State-run intelligence system was no better than Donovan's independent central intelligence organization. Both threatened departmental prerogatives. Both promised to undermine military control over military intelligence units. Both guar-anteed outside interference in Army, Navy, and Air Force intelligence activities. As Rhodri Jeffreys-Jones put it, "The services wished to keep their own intelligence arms intact. If there had to be a central system, they demanded a major say in it."[37]

War and Navy leaders quickly forged an alliance to resist this new threat. On October 13, 1945, Navy Secretary James Forrestal wrote Secretary of War Robert Pat-terson a memo that, among other things, praised the old JCS intelligence plan and suggested the two Secretaries "push it vigorously at the White House."[38] Days later, the Navy Department publicly released its lengthy study of military unification, the Eberstadt Report. In forceful prose, the report reiterated the Navy's support for a weakly centralized intelligence system. "Complete merger of the intelligence services of the State, War and Navy Departments is not considered feasible," the report declared.[39] On November 3, the War Department concluded its own internal study of intelligence issues. The department's final report differed in some details but agreed in principle to JCS and Navy proposals for a confederal intelligence system with minimal central control. As Troy concludes, "With these two reports in hand . . . the two secretaries had both a common position and a common front . . . and their alliance presented a serious challenge to the Secretary of State."[40]

State leaders also found themselves facing fierce opposition within their own department. Regional division heads feared the proposed State Department national intelligence authority would interfere with their own intelligence efforts. Jealously guarding their prerogatives, these Foreign Service officers wanted no part of McCormack's plan. As Under Secretary of State Dean Acheson recalled, the geographic divisions, led by Latin American Division chief Spruille Braden and Near Eastern Division chief Loy Henderson, "were moving into solid opposition to intelligence work not in their organizations and under their control." Braden later described it as a " knockdown, dragout fight."[41]

The combination of internal and external resistance proved devastating. With a two-front war on his hands, Secretary of State Byrnes did not last long. In mid-November, Byrnes began to move toward accommodation with the Secretaries of War and the Navy. In December, the military turned up the heat, sending the President copies of the State and JCS plans, along with a cover memo by Admiral Sidney Souers outlining why the President should adopt the military's proposal.[42] The critical moment came on January 6, 1946, when Byrnes, Forrestal, and Under Secretary of War Kenneth Royall met at the Shoreham Hotel. In their meeting, Forrestal reportedly told Byrnes, "Jimmy, we like you, but we don't like your plan. Just think what might happen if another William Jennings Bryan were to succeed you in the State Department."[43] Byrnes capitulated. Before the meeting ended, he agreed to rejoin the coalition and renew his support for a decentralized intelligence system.[44]

Three weeks later, President Truman made the deal official. His executive directive of January 22, 1946, created a central intelligence system that closely followed the military's recommendations. Under the directive, each department retained almost complete autonomy over its own intelligence services. A new Central Intelligence Group was created, but given no real autonomy or power. Instead of reporting directly to the President, as Donovan had wanted, CIG served under a National Intelligence Authority—a board that included the Secretaries of State, War, the Navy, and a Presidential appointee. Sitting above the central agency, the Secretaries of State, the Navy, and War were in an ideal position to protect the interests of their own intelligence components. That was not all. Truman's directive created an Intelligence Advisory Board consisting of all intelligence agency heads to "advise" the new CIG director. The Presidential order also guaranteed the continued existence of departmental intelligence agencies, provided no authority for CIG to collect intelligence or conduct covert operations, and explicitly prohibited the new agency from exercising any "internal security functions" that might infringe on the FBI's jurisdiction. Truman even gave the State, War, and Navy Departments control over CIG budgets and staffing. As Anne Karalekas notes, this was a recipe for feeble centralization. "Through budget, personnel, and oversight," she writes, "the Departments had assured themselves control over the Central Intelligence Group. CIG was a creature of Departments that were determined to maintain independent capabilities as well as their direct advisory relationship to the President." She concludes that "they succeeded in doing both."[45]

Round 3: January 1946–February 1947

At this point, all sides thought the intelligence battle was over. Donovan and his OSS were out of the picture, the State Department had come back into the fold, and the President had created a Central Intelligence Group that left each department to run its own intelligence affairs. As Truman and his warring military services now turned to drafting a compromise military unification bill, the intelligence consensus was clear: any legislation should include provisions codifying the President's CIG directive.[46] Doing so would freeze the existing intelligence system into law, insulating it from the whims or desires of future political players. On this much, at least, the War and Navy Departments agreed.

The Central Intelligence Group did not. Ink on the CIG directive had hardly dried before the agency began taking on a life and agenda of its own. CIG's problems were apparent from the start. During the early months of 1946, departmental intelligence services readily bypassed the central agency, sending their information and taking their case directly to the President. They provided CIG with a small budget and a meager, mediocre staff. They refused to share raw intelligence and ignored the agency's efforts to reconcile or synthesize conflicting information. As Anne Karalekas writes, the intelligence units "jealously guarded both their information and what they believed were their prerogatives in providing policy guidance to the President, making CIG's primary mission an exercise in futility."[47] The problem was simple: CIG's success hinged on the generosity of those who wanted it to fail. Truman's directive appeared to be working too well.

Frustrated by their agency's impotence, CIG officials soon began pressing for substantial changes. In their capacity as National Intelligence Authority members, the Secretaries of War, the Navy, and State granted some significant concessions.[48] But these were not enough. In July, CIG General Counsel Lawrence R. Houston sent a draft "Bill for the Establishment of a Central Intelligence Agency" to the White House that sought to transform CIG from a small planning staff to "a legally established, fairly sizable, operating agency."[49]

This move came as an alarming surprise to the White House, which was now deeply embroiled in the unification conflict. As Troy writes, "In this perspective, where the White House had the difficult problem of getting generals and admirals to agree on a fundamental reorganization of their services, the legislative problem of the CIG must have seemed . . . an unwelcome detail."[50] As the War and Navy Departments moved toward compromise, the President and his legislative drafting team hardened toward CIG. By January, when the military finally agreed to a comprehensive unification bill, the White House was in no mood to humor the Central Intelligence Group's demands that the legislation specifically outline CIA functions, make the director of central intelligence a statutory nonvoting member of the NSC, provide procurement authorities, or grant the CIA power to "coordinate" foreign intelligence activities and "operate centrally" where appropriate. Such controversial measures threatened to reignite military opposition and reopen the entire unification conflict.[51] Thus, as CIG pressed for more, the White House responded with less. On February 26, the President submitted his draft National Security Act to Congress. It included only the barest mention of the CIA—enough to transform the CIG directive into law and nothing more. In just 30 lines the CIA section established the agency, placed it under the National Security Council, gave it a director appointed from civilian or military life by the President (with the Senate's consent), and authorized it to inherit the "functions, personnel, property, and records" of the Central Intelligence Group.[52] Round 3 was over. CIG had lost.

Epilogue: Congress Considers the National Security Act

The CIA provisions of the National Security Act went relatively unnoticed and unaltered in Congress. Legislators concentrated instead on the more hotly contested aspects of merging the two military departments—such issues as the power of the new Secretary of Defense and the protection of the Navy's Marine Corps and aviation units. In the Senate, Armed Services Committee deliberations resulted in only two relatively minor changes to the proposed CIA, neither of which dealt with its functions or jurisdiction.[53] In fact, the committee's final report specifically noted that the agency would continue to perform the duties outlined in Truman's CIG directive until Congress could pass permanent legislation at a later date.[54] In the House, members of the Committee on Expenditures in the Executive Departments raised more questions and concerns about the CIA's "Gestapo" potential and about its unspecified functions. But transcripts clearly show such questions and concerns were overshadowed by other unification issues. Discussion of the CIA occupied just 29 out of 700 pages of House committee testimony.[55] The committee's probing did not go far or produce far-reaching changes to the bill. Quite the opposite: when House members finally decided to list CIA functions in greater detail, they simply cut and pasted from Truman's existing CIG directive.

The CIA that arose from the National Security Act of 1947 closely resembled its CIG predecessor. Like CIG, the CIA was supposed to "correlate," "evaluate," and "disseminate" intelligence from other services, but was given no authority to collect intelligence on its own or to engage in any covert operations. Like CIG, the CIA operated under the vigilance of other intelligence producers; where CIG reported to a National Intelligence Authority, the CIA operated under the National Security Council—a committee including the Secretaries of War, the Navy, State, and Defense and the President. Mimicking the CIG directive, the National Security Act protected existing intelligence components with explicit guarantees. In deference to the FBI, the law barred the CIA from exercising any "police, subpoena, law-enforcement powers, or internal-security functions." It also provided that "the Departments and other agencies of the Government shall continue to collect, evaluate, correlate, and disseminate departmental intelligence." Finally, the act borrowed two broad clauses from Truman's directive that were to have a profound impact on the CIA's subsequent development. The new agency was charged with conducting "such additional services of common concern as the National Security Council determines" and with performing "such other functions and duties related to intelligence affecting the national security as the National Security Council may from time to time direct."[56] Taken together, these CIA provisions created an agency that suited the War and Navy Departments to a T. If CIG were any guide, the CIA would pose no threat to departmental intelligence agencies.

Conclusions

Here, too, it appears that a major national security agency was forged without much congressional input and without much consideration of the national interest. Like the National Security Council system and the Joint Chiefs of Staff, the Central Intelligence Agency took shape almost exclusively within the executive branch, where bureaucratic players cared first and foremost about their own institutional interests.

The CIA was clearly a product of executive branch discussions and decisions. All three rounds of the postwar intelligence battle were fought among bureaucratic actors and were ultimately decided by the President. Round 1, which pitted OSS chief Donovan against the Navy/War/Justice/State Department coalition, ended with an Executive order disbanding the OSS and transferring its functions to the Departments of State and War. Round 2 featured internecine warfare between top State Department officials and the military. It, too, ended with unilateral Presidential action: an executive directive that implemented the military's recommendations for a weak Central Intelligence Group. In round 3, it was CIG against the White House. With the entire unification bill hanging in the balance and with military preferences about postwar intelligence well known, Truman and his legislative drafting team took decisive action. Rebuffing CIG's advances, they introduced a national security bill that included brief, vague CIA provisions. Their aim was to continue CIG under new, statutory authority while generating as little controversy as possible.[57]

Truman succeeded, thanks in large part to congressional indifference. Legislators in both chambers accepted the CIA provisions with little comment or debate. Though a few members raised alarms about the agency's potential police power and broad jurisdiction, these voices were whispers against the wind.[58] Average legislators had little incentive to probe deeply into the CIA's design, and national security intellectuals had bigger fish to fry in the unification bill. Tellingly, even those who pressed for a more specific CIA mandate ended up simply copying from Truman's CIG directive of 1946. It seems that even here, legislators were content to defer to the executive. The CIA that emerged bore an uncanny resemblance to the Central Intelligence Group. Truman himself writes that the National Security Act succeeded in "renaming" the Central Intelligence Group—implying that the act made no substantive changes to CIG's design or operations at all.[59]

There can also be little doubt that the Central Intelligence Agency was forged out of parochial rather than national interests. Creating any kind of postwar central intelligence apparatus inevitably benefited some bureaucratic actors and threatened others. While the OSS and CIG had much to gain by a strongly centralized system, the Departments of State, Justice, War, and the Navy all stood to lose. For these "big four" departments, promoting U.S. national security was never a paramount concern. Instead, these departments sought a central intelligence system that, above all, insulated their own intelligence services from outside interference. Paradoxically, their vision of an "effective" central intelligence agency was one without strong central control or coordination. The ideal CIA was a weak CIA.

But why did these departments succeed? Why did the President so readily accept their vision of postwar intelligence organization? The short answer is that Harry Truman needed the military services more than they needed him. Propelled by national interest, the President had placed military consolidation at the top of his political agenda. To him, no issue was more vital to American postwar security than unifying the War and Navy Departments into a single Department of Defense, and no price was too great to achieve success. In this context, Donovan's vision of a powerful statutory CIA never had a chance. From day one, War and Navy leaders strenuously opposed such a scheme. With no political capital to spare, the President went along. His executive actions and legislative recommendations all sought to create a central intelligence apparatus that protected departmental intelligence units rather than to ensure that the new central agency would function well.

Notes

[1] The term *rogue elephant* was first applied to the CIA by Senator Frank Church in his 1976 review of the agency's history and activities. See U.S. Senate, Select Committee to Study Governmental Operations with Respect to Intelligence Activities of the United States (Church Committee), *Final Report*, 94th Congress, 2d session (April 26, 1976), S. Rept. 94–755, Serial 13133–3–3.

[2] William M. Leary, ed., *The Central Intelligence Agency: History and Documents* (University: University of Alabama Press, 1984), 6.

[3] This point is hotly contested. Many experts believe that Harry Truman intentionally created a central intelligence agency with covert capabilities and insulation from congressional control. At the very least, they argue, Truman deliberately included two elastic clauses in the National Security Act that could be used to justify covert CIA operations. See, for example, Ray S. Cline, *The CIA Under Reagan, Bush, and Casey* (Washington, DC: Acropolis Books, 1981); and Clark Clifford, with Richard Holbrooke, *Counsel to the President* (New York: Random House, 1991). However, Truman's insertion of these clauses was merely a response to congressional enumeration of the CIA's authority. As the following discussion shows, Truman did not seek a CIA with wide discretionary powers.

[4] Christopher Andrew, *For the President's Eyes Only: Secret Intelligence and the American Presidency from Washington to Bush* (New York: HarperCollins, 1995), 6.

[5] Thomas F. Troy, *Donovan and the CIA: A History of the Establishment of the Central Intelligence Agency* (Frederick, MD: University Publications of America), 74.

[6] Anne Karalekas, "History of the Central Intelligence Agency," in Leary.

[7] Franklin D. Roosevelt, "Military Order of June 13, 1942: Office of Strategic Services," in Troy, 427.

[8] Daniel Yergin, *Shattered Peace: The Origins of the Cold War and the National Security State* (Boston: Houghton Mifflin, 1977), 215–216.

[9] Karalekas, 17.

[10] Mark M. Lowenthal, *U.S. Intelligence: Evolution and Anatomy*, 2d ed. (Westport, CT: Praeger, 1992).

[11] The complete text of Donovan's memo to the President of November 18, 1944, can be found in Troy, 445–47; and Leary, 123–25.

[12] Cline, 112.

[13] Ibid.

[14] Ferdinand Eberstadt, *Unification of the War and Navy Departments and Postwar Organization for National Security: Report to Hon. James Forrestal, Secretary of the Navy*. Printed for use of the U.S. Senate, Committee on Naval Affairs, 79th Congress, 1st session (October 22, 1945), 163.

[15] Jeffrey T. Richelson, *The U.S. Intelligence Community*, 2d ed. (Cambridge, MA: Ballinger, 1989), 136.

[16] Cline, 30–37.

[17] A full copy of Truman's CIG directive can be found in Troy, 464–65; Leary, 126–27; and Michael Warner, ed., *The CIA Under Harry Truman* (Washington, DC: Center for the Study of Intelligence, Central Intelligence Agency, 1994), 29–31.

[18] Truman's special message to Congress of December 19, 1945, is quite revealing on this count. In his most important address on foreign policy organization, his remarks focus almost exclusively on the need for consolidating the military services. Intelligence issues are mentioned only obliquely, almost in passing. In more than 14 pages of comments, the President refers to postwar intelligence organization only 3 times. In the first reference, Truman notes generally that "our military policy . . . should reflect our fullest knowledge of the capabilities and intentions of other powers." The second reference comes when he emphasizes the need for "other major aspects" of a total security program. Even here, Truman seems far more concerned with industrial mobilization and the development of scientific research programs than with a peacetime intelligence system. At the end of the paragraph, he adds, "The findings of our intelligence service must be applied to all of these." In the third reference, Truman notes that "the development of a coordinated, government-wide intelligence system is in progress," but gives no hint about how the system should be organized or what it might do. See Harry S. Truman, *Public Papers of the Presidents of the United States: Harry S. Truman, 1945–1953*, 8 vols. (Washington, DC: Government Printing Office, 1961–1966), 1:546–560.

[19] Ibid., 1:549.

[20] The President's personal beliefs also contributed to his position. Evidence suggests that Truman harbored "Gestapo" fears about concentrating intelligence authority in one organization. Presidential aide George M. Elsey recalled that Truman "wanted to be certain that *no single* [emphasis Elsey's] unit or agency of the Federal Government would have so much power that we would find ourselves, perhaps inadvertently, slipping in the direction of . . . a police state" (transcript, George M. Elsey oral history interview by Jerry N. Hess, July 10, 1970, qtd. in Rhodri Jeffreys-Jones, *The CIA and American Democracy* [New Haven: Yale University Press, 1989], 29). The Budget Bureau director, Harold Smith, agreed. In his diaries, Smith notes that the President repeatedly expressed concern about "building up a gestapo" (Ibid., Harold D. Smith Papers, Truman Library).

[21] The OSS was disbanded by executive order and CIG was created by an executive directive.

[22] Troy, 385; Lowenthal, 17.

[23] Troy; Clifford.

[24] Admiral Forrest Sherman, in U.S. House, Committee on Expenditures in the Executive Departments, *National Security Act of 1947: Hearings on H.R. 2319*, 80th Congress, 1st session, 174. Also, the administration did present a separate CIA bill to Congress 2 years later. The Central Intelligence Agency Act of 1949 regularized the CIA's budget and enabled the Director of Central Intelligence to spend funds on covert operations without notifying Congress. However, it did not specify the agency's functions, jurisdiction, or restrictions in any greater detail. See *U.S. Statutes at Large, Central Intelligence Act of 1949* (1950), 63:208–213.

[25] See Troy, 445–447.

[26] Troy, 278.

[27] The OSS wartime experience had been an exercise in frustration and bureaucratic competition. Karalekas notes, "Although by the end of the war OSS had expanded dramatically, the organization encountered considerable resistance to the execution of its mission. From the outset the military were reluctant to provide OSS with information for its research and analysis role and restricted its operations" (17).

[28] Troy, 151.

[29] Ibid., 255.

[30] Ibid.

[31] Arthur B. Darling, *The Central Intelligence Agency: An Instrument of Government, to 1950* (1953; repr., University Park: Pennsylvania State University Press, 1990); Troy; Clifford.

[32] Troy, 269.

[33] Darling; Troy.

[34] Troy, 277.

[35] "Letter from President Truman to Secretary Byrnes Concerning the Development of a Foreign Intelligence Program," in Troy, 463.

[36] Troy; Jeffreys-Jones; Clifford.

[37] Jeffreys-Jones, 34.

[38] Troy, 316.

[39] Eberstadt, 163.

[40] Troy, 319.

[41] Dean Acheson, *Present at the Creation: My Years in the State Department* (New York: W.W. Norton, 1969), 159–160.

[42] The complete text Of JIC 239/5 can be found in Troy, 451–454.

[43] Darling, 70.

[44] Darling; Troy.

[45] Karalekas, 21.

[46] It should be noted that Truman originally requested a review of the intelligence debate. It is unclear, however, whether the President directly asked that Souers, a Navy officer and author of the Eberstadt Report's intelligence sections, be charged with the task. Souers's memo can be found in Warner, 17–19. See also Troy, 339–40.

[47] Karalekas, 24.

[48] The documentary evidence on this point is striking. From May 1946 to January 1947, Truman and the military consistently included intelligence provisions in their unification proposals—intelligence provisions that clearly meant to grant CIG statutory authority without changing its design or operation in any way. On May 31, 1946, the Secretaries of War and the Navy drafted a letter outlining their points of agreement and outstanding differences on all aspects of military unification. Creation of a Central Intelligence Agency was listed among the eight agreed-upon points. The letter makes clear that this new CIA would differ in no way from the existing Central Intelligence Group. Like CIG, the CIA would "compile, analyze, and evaluate information gathered by various Government agencies" but would not collect information or conduct its own operations. Like CIG, the CIA would operate under a superintending authority of the Secretaries of State, War, the Navy, and others. To remove any doubt, the letter noted that "an organization along these lines, established by Executive order, already exists" (*Congressional Record* 1946, 7425–7426). President Truman used identical CIA language in the draft unification proposal he sent to Congress on June 15, 1946. On January 16, 1947, the War and Navy Departments finally agreed to an entire unification bill. Sending a letter of transmittal to the President, they again noted: "There shall be a . . . Central Intelligence Agency (which already exists) as agreed by the Secretary of War and the Secretary of the Navy in their letter to the President of May 31, 1946." See U.S. Senate, Committee on Armed Services, *National Defense Establishment (Unification of the Armed Services): Hearings on S. 758*, 80th Congress, 1st session (1947), 2–3.

[49] See George M. Elsey, Papers, Box 56, Harry S. Truman Library, qtd. in Demetrios Caraley, *The Politics of Military Unification: A Study of Conflict and the Policy Process* (New York: Columbia University Press, 1966).

[50] Troy, 371.

[51] Troy.

[52] U.S. House, National Security Act of 1947: Communication from the President of the United States, 80th Congress, 1st session (1947), H. Doc. 149, 10.

[53] First, the committee voted to make the President a statutory member of the National Security Council. Since the CIA reported to the NSC, this move theoretically gave the CIA greater access to the President than originally planned. However, it still fell far short of granting the agency a private channel to the President, especially since the President was not required to attend NSC meetings. Second, the committee made clear that civilians, as well as military officers, were eligible for appointment as director of central intelligence; the President's bill did not rule out civilian appointments but did not specifically mention them (Troy).

[54] Troy.

[55] U. S. House, Committee on Expenditures in the Executive Departments, *National Security Act of 1947: Hearings on H.R. 2319*, 80th Congress, 1st session (1947). Tabulations conducted by author. Note that the committee also went into executive session to discuss intelligence issues. But these sessions appear to have been brief and focused on press leaks of CIG operational activities. For more, see Darling and Troy.

[56] *U.S. Statutes at Large, National Security Act of 1947* (1948), 61:497–499.

[57] Truman's diary suggests the President intended to grant CIG statutory legitimacy without changing its substantive functions or operations in any way. See also U.S. Senate, Church Committee (1976), 71; Karalekas; Lowenthal.

[58] The most vocal legislators were Representatives Clarence Brown (R–OH), James Wadsworth (R–NY), Fred Busbey (R–IL), and Senator Millard E. Tydings (D–MD).

[59] Harry S. Truman, *Memoirs: Years of Trial and Hope* (Garden City, NY: Doubleday, 1956), 2:57–58.

Chapter 4

Central Intelligence: Origin and Evolution

Michael Warner

Historical Perspective

. . . what have appeared to be the most striking successes have often, if they are not rightly used, brought the most overwhelming disasters in their train, and conversely the most terrible calamities have, if bravely endured, actually turned out to benefit the sufferers.

—Polybius, *The Rise of the Roman Empire Book III, 7*

The explosions at Pearl Harbor still echoed in Washington when President Harry Truman and congressional leaders passed the National Security Act of 1947. A joint congressional investigation just a year earlier had concluded that the Pearl Harbor disaster illustrated America's need for a unified command structure and a better intelligence system.[1]

In almost the next breath, however, the National Security Act made important concessions to the traditional American distrust of large military establishments and centralized power. The Act (among other qualifications) ensured that the Joint Chiefs would not become a Prussian-style "General Staff," created an independent air force, and insisted that the new Central Intelligence Agency (CIA) would have no law enforcement powers. The Act also decreed that the intelligence divisions in the armed services and the civilian departments (what came to be called the Intelligence Community) would remain independent of the CIA.

Since 1947 Directors of Central Intelligence (DCIs) have served within the bounds of this ambiguous mandate. They have had the responsibility of coordinating national intelligence collection and production without a full measure of the authority they needed to do so. Many Presidents and Congresses—not to mention DCIs—have expressed their frustration with this ambiguity and have assumed that the solution to the dilemmas it created lay in concentrating more power in the office of the Director

Source: Michael Warner, ed., "Historical Perspective," in *Central Intelligence: Origin and Evolution,* Center for the Study of Intelligence, Central Intelligence Agency, 2001, available at: <http://www.cia.gov/csi/books/cia_origin/Origin_and_Evolution.pdf>.

of Central Intelligence. This centralizing impulse has prompted various reforms to increase the Director's ability to lead the Intelligence Community. For years these attempts were made by the National Security Council (NSC) through a series of NSC Intelligence Directives. In the wake of "the time of troubles" for the Intelligence Community in the mid-1970s—marked by investigations into questions about excesses and accountability—three Presidents issued successive Executive orders aimed at one goal: rationalizing American intelligence and increasing the DCI's power. Since the end of the Cold War, Congress itself has taken up the task, repeatedly amending the intelligence sections of the National Security Act.

The various regulations and amendments, however, have not fundamentally altered the "federalist" intelligence structure created in 1947. Strong centrifugal forces remain, particularly in the Department of Defense and its congressional allies. Indeed, the case for centralization seems to be countered by historical illustrations of the perils of excessive concentration. In actual practice, the successful end to the Cold War and the lack of any national intelligence disasters since then seem to militate in favor of keeping the existing structure until some crisis proves it to be in dire need of repair.

Reform after World War II

The agency began its statutory existence in September 1947—its creation ratifying, in a sense, a series of decisions taken soon after the end of the Second World War.[2] That conflict ended in the summer of 1945 with Washington decisionmakers in broad agreement that the United States needed to reform the intelligence establishment that had grown so rapidly and haphazardly during the national emergency. Nevertheless, when President Truman dissolved the wartime Office of Strategic Services (OSS) in September 1945 he had no clear plan for constructing the peacetime intelligence structure that he and his advisers believed they needed in an atomic age. President Truman wanted the reforms to be part and parcel of the "unification" of the armed services, but the overhaul of the military that the President wanted would take time to push through Congress.[3] In the interim, he created a Central Intelligence Group (CIG) to screen his incoming cables and supervise activities left over from the former OSS.

In early 1946, the White House authorized CIG to evaluate intelligence from all parts of the Government, and to absorb the remnants of OSS's espionage and counterintelligence operations.[4] Initially these disparate components of the new CIG shared little in common except an interest in foreign secrets and a sense that both strategic warning and clandestine activities abroad required "central" coordination. Indeed, these two missions came together in CIG almost by accident. Under the first two Directors of Central Intelligence, however, CIG and the Truman administration came to realize how strategic warning and clandestine activities complemented one another.

Meanwhile, the military "unification" issue overshadowed intelligence reform in congressional and White House deliberations. In mid-1946 President Truman called again on Congress to unify the armed services. That April, the Senate's Military Affairs committee had approved a unification bill that provided for a central intelligence agency, but the draft legislation had snagged in the hostile Naval Affairs committee.[5] Perhaps with that bill in mind, Secretary of War Robert Patterson and Secretary of the Navy James Forrestal in May agreed among themselves that a defense reorganization bill should also provide for a central intelligence agency. President Truman the following month sent Congress the result of the secretaries' accord (with modifications of his own), repeating his call for lawmakers to send him a unification bill to sign.[6]

The administration's judgment that a central intelligence agency was needed soon firmed into a consensus that the new Central Intelligence Group ought to form the basis of this new intelligence agency. Indeed, CIG continued to accrue missions and capabilities. Oversight of the CIG was performed by a committee called the National Intelligence Authority (NIA), comprising the Secretaries of State, War, and Navy, joined by the President's chief military adviser, Admiral William Leahy. National Intelligence Authority Directive 5 (NIAD–5), issued on July 8, 1946, provided the DCI with the basic implementation plan for the broad scope of powers envisioned in President Truman's charter for CIG. Indeed, it was NIAD–5 that created the real difference between OSS—an operations office with a sophisticated analytical capability—and CIG, a truly (albeit fledgling) national intelligence service authorized to perform strategic analysis and to conduct, coordinate, and control clandestine activities abroad.

NIAD–5 represented perhaps the most expansive charter ever granted to a Director of Central Intelligence. It allowed CIG to "centralize" research and analysis in "fields of national security intelligence that are not being presently performed or are not being adequately performed."[7] NIAD–5 also directed the DCI to coordinate all U.S. foreign intelligence activities "to ensure that the overall policies and objectives established by this Authority are properly implemented and executed." The National Intelligence Authority through this directive ordered the DCI to conduct "all organized Federal espionage and counter-espionage operations outside the United States and its possessions for the collection of foreign intelligence information required for the national security."

In NIAD–5, the National Intelligence Authority determined that many foreign intelligence missions could be "more efficiently accomplished centrally" and gave CIG the authority to accomplish them. This in effect elevated CIG to the status of being the primary foreign intelligence arm of the U.S. Government. This mandate did not, however, give CIG the controlling role in intelligence analysis that DCI Hoyt Vandenberg had sought. The NIA's authorization was carefully phrased to allay fears that the DCI would take control of departmental intelligence offices; the Cabinet departments were not about to subordinate their own limited analytical capabilities to an upstart organization. In addition, NIAD–5 did not force a consolidation of clandestine activities under CIG control. Indeed, the Army defended the independence of its Intelligence Division's own collection operations by arguing that NIAD–5 gave CIG control only over "organized" foreign intelligence operations.

National Security Act of 1947

Congress initially paid scant attention to the new Central Intelligence Group. Indeed, CIG had been established with no appropriations and authority of its own precisely to keep it beneath congressional scrutiny. As CIG gained new authority in 1946 and the White House gained confidence in its potential, however, a consensus emerged in Congress that postwar military reforms would not be complete without a simultaneous modernization of American intelligence capabilities.

The budding consensus even survived the death of the Truman administration's cherished unification bill in 1946. Ironically, prospects for unification only brightened when the opposition Republicans subsequently swept into control of the Congress in that year's elections, taking over the committee chairmanships and displacing powerful Democrats who had made themselves (in Harry Truman's words) "the principal stumbling blocks to unification."[8] With the President's goal of military modernization suddenly in sight, the White House firmly told DCI Vandenberg that enabling legislation for CIG would remain a small part of the defense reform bill then being redrafted by the President's aides, and that the intelligence section would be kept as brief as possible in order to ensure that none of its details hampered the prospects for unification.[9]

This tactic almost backfired. When President Truman sent his new bill forward in February 1947, the brevity of its intelligence provisions had the effect of attracting—not deflecting—congressional scrutiny. Members of Congress eventually debated almost every word of the intelligence section, and made various adjustments. Ultimately, however, Congress passed what was essentially the White House's draft with important sections transferred (and clarified in the process) from Truman's January 22, 1946, directive establishing CIG—thus ratifying the major provisions of that directive. Thus the Central Intelligence Agency would be an independent agency under the supervision of the National Security Council; it would conduct both analysis and clandestine activities, but would have no policy-making role and no law enforcement powers; its Director would be confirmed by the Senate and could be either a civilian or a military officer.

What did Congress believe the new CIA would do? Testimony and debates over the draft bill unmistakably show that the lawmakers above all wanted CIA to provide the proposed National Security Council—the new organization that would coordinate and guide American foreign and defense policies with the best possible information on developments abroad. Members of Congress described the information they expected CIA to provide as "full, accurate, and skillfully analyzed"; "coordinated, adequate"; and "sound." Senior military commanders testifying on the bill's behalf used similar adjectives, saying the CIA's information should be "authenticated and evaluated"; "correct"; and based on "complete coverage." When CIA provided such information, it was believed, the NSC would be able to assess accurately the relative strengths and weaknesses of America's overseas posture and adjust policies accordingly.[10]

Congress guaranteed CIA's independence and its access to departmental files in order to give it the best chance to produce authoritative information for the Nation's policymakers. CIA was to stand outside the policymaking departments of the Government, the better to "correlate and evaluate intelligence relating to the national security."[11] Although other departments and agencies would continue to handle intelligence of national importance, the agency was the only entity specifically charged by the Act with the duty of producing it. To assist in the performance of this duty, the DCI had the right to "inspect" all foreign intelligence held by other agencies, as well as the right to disseminate it as appropriate. If the DCI happened to be a military officer, then he was to be outside the chain of command of his home service; this would help him resist any temptation to shade his reports to please his superiors.[12] Finally, the agency was to provide for the U.S. Government such "services of common concern" that the NSC would determine could more efficiently be conducted "centrally." In practice, this meant espionage and other clandestine activities, as well as the collection of valuable information from open sources and American citizens.

Having approved the placement of these authorities and activities under one head, Congress in 1947 expected that CIA would provide the best possible intelligence and would coordinate clandestine operations abroad. Congress also implicitly assumed that the executive branch would manage CIA and the Intelligence Community with these purposes in mind.[13] After fixing this course in the statute books, Congress stepped back and left the White House and CIA to meet these expectations. This was how Congress resolved the apparent contradiction of creating "central intelligence" that was not centrally controlled. The institution of central intelligence would henceforth steer between the two poles of centralization and departmental autonomy.

Not Only National but Central

Congress passed the National Security Act on July 26, 1947, and President Truman immediately signed it into law. The Act gave America something new in the annals of intelligence history; no other nation had structured its foreign intelligence establishment in quite the same way. CIA would be an independent, central agency, but not a controlling one; it would both rival and complement the efforts of the departmental intelligence organizations.[14] This prescription of coordination without control guaranteed friction and duplication of intelligence efforts as the CIA and the departmental agencies pursued common targets, but it also fostered a potentially healthy competition of views and abilities.

The National Security Council guided the Intelligence Community by means of a series of directives dubbed NSCIDs (National Security Council Intelligence Directives). The original NSCIDs were issued in the months after the passage of the National Security Act. Foremost was NSCID 1, titled "Duties and Responsibilities," which replaced NIAD–5 and established the basic responsibilities of the DCI and the interagency workings of the Intelligence Community.[15]

NSCID 1 did not rewrite NIAD–5, but instead started afresh in the light of the debate over the National Security Act and the experience recently gained by the new CIA. Where the earlier document had authorized the DCI to coordinate "all Federal foreign intelligence activities" and sketched the initial outlines of his powers, NSCID 1 had to work within the lines already drawn by Congress and precedent. The Director who emerged from NSCID 1 was more circumscribed in his role and authority than previously. He was now to "make such surveys and inspections" as he needed in giving the NSC his "recommendations for the coordination of intelligence activities." Nonetheless, the DCI was—in keeping with Congress' implicit intent in the National Security Act—a substantial presence in the intelligence establishment. NSCID 1 gave the DCI an advisory committee comprising the heads of the departmental intelligence offices, and told him to "produce" intelligence (but to avoid duplicating departmental functions in doing so). The type of intelligence expected of him and his agency was "national intelligence," a new term for the information that the National Security Act called "intelligence relating to the national security."[16] The DCI was also to perform for the benefit of the existing agencies such "services of common concern" as the NSC deemed could best be provided centrally. The NSC left the particulars of these responsibilities to be specified in accompanying NSCIDs (which eventually numbered 2 through 15 by the end of the Truman administration in 1953).[17]

Under this regime, DCIs were faced with contradictory mandates: they could coordinate intelligence, but they must not control it. Since the prohibitions in the statute and the NSCIDs were so much clearer than the permissions, every DCI naturally tended to steer on the side of looser rather than tighter oversight of common Intelligence Community issues. Because of this tendency to emphasize coordination instead of control, CIA never quite became the integrator of U.S. intelligence that its Presidential and congressional parents had envisioned. The DCI never became the manager of the Intelligence Community, his agency never won the power to "inspect" the departments' operational plans or to extract community-wide consensus on disputed analytical issues, and CIA never had authority over all clandestine operations of the U.S. Government.

Revisions and Oversight

This federalized intelligence structure did not satisfy the White House. Indeed, Presidents from Dwight Eisenhower through Richard Nixon sought to adjust the NSCIDs to improve the functioning of the Intelligence Community, primarily by pushing successive DCIs to exert more control over common community issues and programs. President Eisenhower paid particular attention to this issue, approving in 1958 the first major revisions of NSCID 1. The September 1958 version of the revised directive added a preamble stressing the need for efficiency across the entire national intelligence effort, and began its first section by declaring "The Director of Central Intelligence shall coordinate the foreign intelligence activities of the United States. . . ."

The September 1958 version of NSCID 1 also added a section on "community responsibilities" that listed the duties of the DCI to foster an efficient Intelligence Community and to ensure the quality of the intelligence information available to the U.S. Government. It also emphasized to the existing departments and agencies their responsibilities to assist the DCI in these tasks. To this end, the new NSCID 1 created the United States Intelligence Board (USIB), a panel chaired by the DCI—with the Deputy Director of Central Intelligence (the DDCI) representing CIA—to coordinate a range of cooperative activities through a network of interagency committees. USIB soon built a sophisticated set of procedures, prompting former CIA Executive Director Lyman Kirkpatrick in 1973 to declare that "the USIB structure provides the community with probably the broadest and most comprehensive coordinating mechanism in the history of any nation's intelligence activities."[18]

In 1971 President Nixon turned to the topic of intelligence reform and issued a directive that precipitated the first major revision of NSCID 1 in over a decade. In the spirit of President Eisenhower's earlier initiatives, Nixon authorized a full-dress study of Intelligence Community cooperation, with an emphasis on cutting its costs and increasing its effectiveness. A committee headed by James Schlesinger of the Office of Management and Budget recommended major reforms, among them a greater role for the DCI in managing the Intelligence Community. President Nixon directed the adoption of many of these recommendations in a November 5, 1971, letter to the Cabinet secretaries and senior policymakers who oversaw the community's far-flung components.[19] The NSC issued a revised NSCID 1 in February 1972 to disseminate the new guidance to the community.

The new version retained much of the earlier text, while adding that the DCI had "four major responsibilities." He was to plan and review all intelligence activities and spending, submitting annually to the White House the community's overall "program/budget"; to produce national intelligence for the President and policymakers; to chair all community-wide advisory panels; and to establish intelligence requirements and priorities. In addition, the 1972 NSCID 1 established several objectives to guide the DCI in discharging these responsibilities. He was to seek the attainment of greater efficiency, better and more timely intelligence, and, perhaps most of all, "authoritative and responsible leadership for the community." The provision for DCI authority (albeit limited) over the Intelligence Community budget was new and significant; henceforth all subsequent directives governing the community would place at least one of the DCI's hands on the collective purse strings.

The years that followed the issuance of the 1972 version of NSCID 1 witnessed dramatic changes in the policy dynamic surrounding the Intelligence Community. For several reasons—many of them related to the Vietnam War and the Watergate scandal, but including agency misdeeds under earlier administrations as well—Congress began to impose itself directly on CIA and other parts of the Intelligence Community in the mid-1970s. The White House responded to the new mood in Congress by acting to protect what it defended as the exclusive prerogatives of the executive branch. Republican and Democratic Presidents had long been content to delegate the chore of overseeing the community to the National Security Council, but President Gerald Ford, concerned that Congress would rewrite the statutes undergirding the Intelligence Community, intervened with an Executive order that supplanted the earlier NSCIDs.

Executive Order (EO) 11905 (February 18, 1976) retained much of the language of the 1972 NSCID 1, but added much else as well. Most prominently, it established a lengthy list of restrictions on intelligence activities, which ran the gamut from a prohibition on the perusal of Federal tax returns to a ban on "political assassination." EO 11905 also revisited the traditional ground covered by the now-obsolete NSCID 1 series, assigning "duties and responsibilities" to the DCI and the various members of the Intelligence Community.

President Ford's Executive order did not diverge noticeably, however, from the earlier listings of the DCI's duties. These were now to be: acting as "executive head of the CIA and Intelligence Community staff," preparing the community's budget, requirements, and priorities; serving as "primary adviser on foreign intelligence," and implementing "special activities" (that is, covert action). Indeed, EO 11905 encouraged the DCI to devote more energy to "the supervision and direction of the

Intelligence Community." In this spirit, it revived an Eisenhower administration idea and urged the DCI to delegate "the day-to-day operation" of CIA to his Deputy Director for Central Intelligence.

President Jimmy Carter superseded EO 11905 with his own Executive Order 12036 barely 2 years later. The new order retained basically the same (albeit reordered) list of duties for the DCI in his dual role as manager of the Intelligence Community and head of CIA. It also revamped the old United States Intelligence Board, expanding the list of topics on which it was to advise the DCI and renaming it the National Foreign Intelligence Board (NFIB). Where EO 12036 differed from preceding directives was in tasking the DCI to oversee the Intelligence Community budget. President Ford's Executive order had created a three-member committee, chaired by the DCI, to prepare the budget and, when necessary, to reprogram funding.[20] Under the new provisions of EO 12036, however, the DCI now had "full and exclusive responsibility for approval of the National Foreign Intelligence Program budget." These combined powers were somewhat less sweeping than under EO 11905, but more concentrated in now being vested in the DCI alone. He would issue guidance to the community for program and budget development, evaluate the submissions of the various agencies, justify them before Congress, monitor implementation, and he could (after due consultation) reprogram funds.

President Ronald Reagan in his turn replaced the Carter directive with Executive Order 12333 (December 4, 1981), which remains in effect today. The new order deleted provisions for the NFIB and other boards, allowing the DCI to arrange interagency advisory panels as he needed (DCI William Casey quickly reinstated the NFIB on his own authority). This was, however, almost the only enhancement of the DCI's power in an Executive order that otherwise stepped back slightly from the centralization decreed by President Carter. Specifically, EO 12333 diluted DCI authority over the National Foreign Intelligence Program (NFIP) budget that EO 12036 had briefly strengthened. Where Carter had explicitly made the DCI the manager of the NFIP budgeting process, Reagan instead outlined a leading role for the DCI in developing the budget, reviewing requests for the reprogramming of funds, and monitoring implementation. The change was not dramatic, but it was significant.

Management of the Intelligence Community by Executive order during this period did not forestall increased congressional oversight. In the 1970s, both houses of Congress had created permanent intelligence oversight committees and passed legislation to tighten control of covert action. With the renewed polarization of foreign policy debates in the 1980s, both Republican and Democratic officials and lawmakers sought to "protect" intelligence from allegedly unprincipled forces that might somehow co-opt and abuse it to the detriment of the community and the Nation's security. Responding to these concerns, Congress further toughened the new regulatory, oversight, and accountability regime to check the powers and potential for abuses at CIA and other agencies. Congress ensured permanence for these changes by codifying them as amendments to law, particularly to the National Security Act of 1947.

By the late 1980s, Congress' increased oversight role (and its new appetite for finished intelligence) prompted then-DDCI Robert Gates to comment publicly that

CIA "now finds itself in a remarkable position, involuntarily poised nearly equidistant between the executive and legislative branches."[21] Not until the 1990s, however, did these changes significantly affect the "duties and responsibilities" of the DCI and the Intelligence Community.

Into a New Era

For the duration of the Cold War, the White House kept nudging successive Directors of Central Intelligence to do more to lead the Intelligence Community. DCIs more or less tried to comply. The statutory and institutional obstacles to centralization, however, proved daunting. Each DCI held budgetary and administrative sway only over the Central Intelligence Agency; the much larger budgets and staffs of the intelligence agencies in the Department of Defense (and their smaller cousins in other departments) remained firmly under Cabinet-level officials who saw no reason to cede power to a DCI. Faced with this reality, DCIs had tended to let their community coordination duties suffer and to concentrate on the management of the CIA. Congress had intended a different course, however, and in the 1990s the legislative branch began its own campaign to encourage greater coordination in the Intelligence Community.

The end of the Cold War saw a subtle shift in congressional attitudes toward intelligence. With the political need for a "peace dividend" acutely felt, Congress and the White House oversaw a gradual decline in real defense spending that affected the Intelligence Community as well. Declining defense budgets soon meant relatively declining intelligence budgets, which in turn put a premium on cost-cutting, consolidation, and efficiency. Similar concerns had surfaced during the debate over the creation of CIA (when demobilization, not the incipient Cold War, was still the primary consideration in defense budgeting).[22] To many Members of Congress in 1992—as in 1947—the answer seemed to lie in increased authority for the DCI, who in turn could motivate a leaner, more agile Intelligence Community.

Congress in the 1990s partially supplanted EO 12333 with a series of amendments to the National Security Act. Those amendments were occasionally proscriptive (like the prohibitions added in the 1980s), but often they mandated various acts by the DCI. The intelligence-related passages of the National Security Act—which had hardly been amended at all before 1980—grew from 22 pages of text in the 1990 edition of the House Permanent Select Committee on Intelligence's *Compilation of Intelligence Laws* to 48 pages in the 2000 version.[23]

Foremost among these amendments was the Intelligence Organization Act of 1992.[24] Inspired by the reforms of the Joint Chiefs of Staff accomplished in the 1986 Goldwater-Nichols Act, the legislation—for the first time in a statute—specified the roles (as opposed to the duties) of the Director of Central Intelligence.[25] The DCI was to serve as head of the Intelligence Community, as principal intelligence adviser to the President, and as head of the CIA. As principal intelligence adviser he was to provide the Nation's senior policymakers, commanders, and lawmakers with "national" intelligence that was "timely, objective, independent of political considerations, and based on all sources." As head of the agency he was to collect and evaluate intelligence (particularly from human sources), and to perform services of common concern and "such other functions and duties" as had been suggested since 1947. As head of the Intelligence Community he was to develop the community's budget, to advise the Secretary of Defense in the appointments of chiefs for the military's joint intelligence agencies, to set collection requirements and priorities, to eliminate unneeded duplication, and to coordinate the community's relationships with foreign intelligence services.

The Intelligence Organization Act also codified the DCI's budgetary powers as described in EO 12333, considerably strengthening their provisions. The act decreed that the budgets of the various components of the Intelligence Community could not be incorporated into the annual National Foreign Intelligence Program until approved by the DCI, and required all agencies to obtain DCI approval before reprogramming any NFIP funds. In addition, the Act gave the Director something new: a carefully limited authority to shift funds and personnel from one NFIP project to another (provided he obtained approvals from the White House, Congress, and the affected agency's head).

Events at mid-decade lent new urgency to the unfinished task of modernizing the Intelligence Community. At CIA, the arrest of Aldrich Ames and the spy scandal that ensued led to bipartisan calls for reform of the agency. The subsequent Republican takeover of Congress in the 1994 elections seemed to provide an opportunity for sweeping changes in the community as a whole. Finally, the reordering of national priorities after the end of the Cold War had meant substantial budget cuts for the U.S. military, resulting in reduced budgets and lower personnel ceilings for the Intelligence Community.[26] While military and intelligence resources had been reduced in the early 1990s, however, Washington committed American forces to several major overseas deployments in Africa, the Balkans, the Middle East, and the Caribbean.

The White House responded to the new situation by reordering intelligence priorities. The burgeoning military deployments demanded ever more tactical intelligence support, and President William Clinton issued a 1995 Presidential order (PDD–35) instructing the Intelligence Community to provide it. Explaining his directive at CIA headquarters a few months later, he emphasized that the community's first priority was to support "the intelligence needs of our military during an operation." Commanders in the field needed "prompt, thorough intelligence to fully inform their decisions and maximize the security of our troops."[27] Since the military spent most of the 1990s deployed in one peacekeeping operation after another (often with more than one taking place at a time), the result of the commitment in PDD–35 was a diversion of shrinking national, strategic intelligence resources to growing, tactical missions.

Congress took a little longer to respond. In 1995, congressional and outside critics coalesced in no fewer than six separate panels to study the U.S. intelligence effort and recommend reforms.[28] Almost all of the reports published by these groups endorsed a greater degree of centralization and enhanced authority for the Director of Central Intelligence.[29] The wide variance in the size and scope of the study groups—which ranged in stature from academic colloquia to the Presidentially appointed Brown-Aspin Commission—seemed to highlight their basic agreement on this issue. The Brown-Aspin Commission report perhaps expressed the feeling best. After considering arguments for decentralization, the report cited President Truman's disgust with the bureaucratic rivalry that "contributed to the disaster at Pearl Harbor" and concluded that "returning to a more decentralized system would be a step in the wrong direction." The report declined to suggest alterations in "the fundamental relationship between the DCI and the Secretary of Defense," but nonetheless urged a strengthening of "the DCI's ability to provide centralized management of the Intelligence Community."[30]

Congress heeded the conclusions and the recommendations of these several reports when it drafted the Intelligence Renewal and Reform Act of 1996. That act, among its other provisions, required the Secretary of Defense to win the concurrence of the DCI in appointing directors for the National Security Agency, the new National Imagery and Mapping Agency, and the National Reconnaissance Office. Under the Act, the DCI would also write (for the NSC) annual performance appraisals of these three agencies.[31] The Act also gave the DCI several new aides (nominated by the President and confirmed by the Senate) to assist in managing the Intelligence Community: a Deputy Director of Central Intelligence for Community Management, as well as Assistant Directors of Central Intelligence for Collection, Analysis, and Production, and Administration. It also enhanced the DCI's role as an adviser to the Pentagon's tactical and interservice intelligence programs, strengthened his limited ability to "reprogram" money and personnel between national intelligence programs, and created a subcommittee of the NSC to establish annual priorities for the Intelligence Community.

Congress did not, however, resist the shift of national means to tactical ends. The shift of intelligence resources toward support for military operations worried officials and observers of the Intelligence Community. Indeed, DCI Robert Gates complained as early as 1992 that cuts in the defense budget were forcing the military to trim tactical intelligence programs and pass their work on to the "national" intelligence services.[32] PDD–35 seemed to make the situation even more acute. More than one appraisal in the year after its issuance warned that "support to the warfighter" could demand a disproportionate share of intelligence efforts; a congressional study even blamed PDD–35, in part, for this development.[33] Nevertheless, these worries remained on the margins of the debate for several more years.

Contradictory Impulses

The net effect of the changes made by the White House and Congress under both Republican and Democratic majorities was to urge the DCI to exercise more control over the Intelligence Community while limiting his freedom to allocate "national" intelligence resources among competing priorities. Members of Congress collectively seemed impatient with executive branch implementation of reforms to streamline and motivate the community during a long decade of shrinking real defense budgets. At the same time, however, no Congress seriously considered forcing the various civilian and military agencies into a unitary system with a Director of Central Intelligence (or whatever the title) transformed into a true intelligence czar. The executive branch neither assisted nor resisted this congressional impulse to enhance the DCI's authority and the centralization of the Intelligence Community. In effect, however, the White House's aforementioned actions with regard to intelligence were anything but neutral.

The contradictory impulses affecting the Intelligence Community showed in the way the executive and legislative branches together crafted a 1996 law, the National Imagery and Mapping Agency (NIMA) Act, which created the Department of Defense agency of that name out of components from CIA and Defense. While this marked a diminution of the DCI's direct control over imagery analysis, the NIMA Act took pains to preserve DCI authority to prioritize assignments for "national imagery collection assets" and to resolve conflicts among competing priorities.[34] The net effect was ambiguous; the DCI and the CIA lost actual, day-to-day control over an important component of the Intelligence Community, but gained a statutory voice in the Nation's employment of that component.

In 1998, DCI George Tenet issued a reconstituted series of Director of Central Intelligence Directives (DCIDs), led by a new DCID 1/1, titled "The Authorities and Responsibilities of the Director of Central Intelligence as Head of the U.S. Intelligence Community." DCIDs had traditionally not been issued as policy statements; they had essentially been implementing documents for the policies established in the NSCIDs (and later in the Executive orders). DCID 1/1 stayed well within this tradition, but provided an important reference for the entire community by arranging and citing in one document the key passages of Executive Order 12333 and the amended National Security Act.

The preface to DCID 1/1 stated that it was only intended to be "illustrative." Indeed, readers were directed to the citations "for controlling language." This spare format perhaps conveyed a message more powerful than its authors realized. The DCI's newfound ability to cite so many passages of the United States Code to buttress his authority meant that his powers had grown substantially since its meager beginnings in January 1946. The fact that a DCI felt the need to cite all those passages for the edification of Intelligence Community colleagues, however, suggests that his authority still had far to go.

The blurring of the divide between "national" and "tactical" intelligence seemed at decade's end to provide unclear portents for the future of the DCI's authority. By 2000, the earlier warnings were widely seen to have been accurate. A high-level study commission recently has complained that declining intelligence resources, combined with increased demands for "warning and crisis management," have resulted in:

> an Intelligence Community that is more demand-driven. . . . That demand is also more driven by military consumers and, therefore, what the Intelligence Community is doing is narrower and more short-term than it was two decades ago.[35]

Another commission, reporting its findings on the National Reconnaissance Office, found in PDD–35 a lightning rod for its criticism:

> There appears to be no effective mechanism to alert policy-makers to the negative impact on strategic requirements that may result from strict adherence to the current Presidential Decision Directive (PDD–35) assigning top priority to military force protection. That Directive has not been reviewed recently to determine whether it has been properly applied and should remain in effect.[36]

The Elusive Vision of Central Intelligence

> Today, intelligence remains the only area of highly complex government activity where overall management across departmental and agency lines is seriously attempted.[37]

Ten years past the end of the Cold War and 5 since the spate of reform proposals in 1996, this observation by the Brown-Aspin Commission seems to remain valid. The Director of Central Intelligence is nominally stronger now; new laws and amendments have augmented his power to lead the Intelligence Community. Nevertheless, the community remains a confederated system, in which the DCI has leadership responsibilities greater than his responsibilities. The system seems roughly balanced between the need for central direction and the imperative to preserve departmental intelligence autonomy. If that balance perhaps appears to be less than optimal, there nevertheless is no obvious imperative to correct it in any fundamental way. Indeed, the 2001 report of the blue-ribbon "Commission on National Security/21st Century" (the Hart-Rudman Commission) recommended "no major structural changes" in the management of the Intelligence Community and noted that "current efforts to strengthen community management while maintaining the ongoing relationship between the DCI and the Secretary of Defense are bearing fruit."[38]

The Members of Congress who passed the National Security Act of 1947 had wanted the new Central Intelligence Agency to provide policymakers the best possible information and to coordinate clandestine operations. They assumed that the President's intelligence officer—the Director of Central Intelligence—would accomplish these objectives and left the executive branch to its own initiative for the next four decades. This was how Congress resolved the dilemma of having a "national" intelligence system that was not centrally controlled. Succeeding Presidents oversaw the Intelligence Community through a series of National Security Council Intelligence Directives and Executive orders, which recognized the gap between coordination and control and encouraged DCIs to do more to bridge it and to manage America's intelligence efforts. After the Cold War ended, however, Democratic and Republican Congresses grew impatient with the executive branch and urged that intelligence be done centrally. Nonetheless, no Congress grasped the nettle of sweeping reform, either to decentralize the system or to give the DCI command authority over military intelligence and the departmental intelligence offices. At the same time, the executive branch's insistence on using declining resources first and foremost to support military operations effectively blunted the congressional emphasis on centralization by limiting the wherewithal that DCIs and agency heads could devote to national and strategic objectives.

This ambiguity is likely to endure for the same reasons it arose in the first place: no one can agree on what should replace it. Reform faces the same obstacles that Harry Truman and his aides encountered in 1945. Everyone has a notion of how reform should be implemented, but everyone also has a specific list of changes they will not tolerate. The mix of preferences and objections produces a veto to almost every proposal, until the one that survives is the one policymakers and legislators dislike the least. Ambiguity is also likely to keep alive the durable idea—born from the Pearl Harbor disaster—that the axiomatic principles of unity of command and unity of intelligence can best be served through an increased centralization of U.S. intelligence efforts.

America's national security framework forces such ambiguities on policymakers and commanders for good reasons as well as bad. The great economic and military strength of America and the comparative material wealth of its Intelligence Community have provided a certain latitude for experimentation—and even duplication of effort—in the service of higher, political goals. In such a context, a decentralized Intelligence Community may be the only kind of system that can maintain public and military support for an independent, civilian foreign intelligence arm in America's non-parliamentary form of government, where it is possible for the two major political parties to split control over the executive and legislative branches of Government. Decentralization assures the Pentagon of military control over its tactical and joint intelligence programs. It also assures Members of Congress of both parties that the President's chief intelligence adviser cannot acquire a dangerous concentration of domestic political power or monopolize the foreign policy advice flowing into the White House. Thus we are likely to live with the decentralized intelligence system—and the impulse toward centralization—until a crisis realigns the political and bureaucratic players or compels them to cooperate in new ways.

Notes

[1] Joint Committee on the Investigation of the Pearl Harbor Attack, "Investigation of the Pearl Harbor Attack," 79th Congress, 2[d] Session, 1946, 252–253.

[2] Shorthand reference to *the agency* is commonly used, and is used herein, as synonymous with CIA. *Community* has long been used, and is herein, to denote the totality of U.S. executive branch organizations that produce and provide foreign intelligence to U.S. policymakers and military commanders.

[3] "Text of the President's Message to Congress Asking Unification of the Army and Navy," *The New York Times*, December 20, 1945, 14.

[4] President Harry S. Truman's January 22, 1946, directive establishing CIG is reprinted in U.S. Department of State, *Foreign Relations of the United States, 1945–1950, Emergence of the Intelligence Establishment* (Washington, DC: U.S. Government Printing Office, 1996) [hereafter cited as FRUS], 178–179. The first DCI, Sidney Souers, recalled in 1954 that he had been part of the collective effort (leading to CIG's establishment) to create "a central intelligence agency" that would ensure that national security policymakers "all would get the same intelligence—in contrast to the system that had prevailed, where the OSS would give one bit of intelligence to the President and not any to the secretaries of the military departments and the State Department, who had some responsibility to advise the President." Quoted in Ralph E. Weber, ed., *Spymasters: Ten CIA Officers in Their Own Words* (Wilmington, DE: Scholarly Resources, 1999), 3.

[5] David F. Rudgers, *Creating the Secret State: The Origins of the Central Intelligence Agency, 1943–1947* (Lawrence, KS: University of Kansas Press, 2000), 107.

[6] Anthony Leviero, "Truman Offers Congress 12-Point Program to Unify Armed Services of Nation," *The New York Times*, June 16, 1946. For the Patterson-Forrestal accord in May 1946, see Walter Millis, ed., *The Forrestal Diaries* (New York: Viking, 1951), 163.

[7] National Intelligence Authority Directive number 5, July 8, 1946, reprinted in FRUS, 391–392.

[8] Harry S. Truman, *Memoirs, Volume II: Years of Trial and Hope* (Garden City, NY: Doubleday, 1956), 46–47.

[9] Admiral Forrest Sherman, a member of the White House team that drafted the bill, later told the House Committee on Expenditures that he and his colleagues feared that a detailed CIA section would prompt Congress to seek similar levels of detail in the armed services' sections of the bill, forcing a re-opening of the drafting process and possibly encumbering the draft with controversial specifics. See Lyle Miller's declassified draft, "Legislative History of the Central Intelligence Agency–National Security Act of 1947," Central Intelligence Agency (Office of Legislative Council), July 25, 1967, 72.

[10] Quoted in Miller, "Legislative History," 40, 45, 47, 48, 50.

[11] Sec. 102(d)3. The phrase came from President Truman's January 22, 1946, directive establishing CIG; see FRUS, 178. The original pages of the intelligence section of the National Security Act of 1947 are reproduced in Michael Warner, ed., *The CIA under Harry Truman* (Washington, DC: Central Intelligence Agency, 1994), 131–135.

[12] The Act was amended in 1953 to provide for a Deputy Director of Central Intelligence (DDCI) with the stipulation (since removed) that the positions of DCI and DDCI must not "be occupied simultaneously by commissioned officers of the armed services, whether in an active or retired status."

[13] Ludwell Montague believed the term *Intelligence Community* made its earliest documented appearance in the minutes of a 1952 meeting of the Intelligence Advisory Committee. For the sake of consistency the term *Intelligence Community* is used throughout this [chapter], even though the size and composition of the community has changed and now includes several large entities that did not exist when the National Security Act was passed in 1947. For example, of [the 15] intelligence organizations in the community, the National Security Agency, the Defense Intelligence Agency, the National Reconnaissance Office, and the National Imagery and Mapping Agency are among the 8 intelligence organizations that come under the Department of Defense. The only independent agency (that is, not part of a policy department) is CIA. For the 1952 usage of the term, see Ludwell Lee Montague, *General Walter Bedell Smith as Director of Central Intelligence: October 1950–February 1953* (University Park, PA: Pennsylvania State University Press, 1992), 74.

[14] At the time the Act went into effect, the intelligence agencies of the U.S. Government comprised the Central Intelligence Agency, the Federal Bureau of Investigation, the Office of Intelligence Research (State), the Intelligence Division (Army), the Office of Naval Intelligence, the Directorate of Intelligence (Air Force), and associated military signals intelligence offices, principally the Army Security Agency and the Navy's OP–20–G.

[15] All versions of NSCID 1 have been declassified and are available at the National Archives and Records Administration, Record Group 263 (CIA), NN3–263–91–004, box 4, HS/HC–500.

[16] NSCID 3 (January 13, 1948) defined *national intelligence* as "integrated departmental intelligence that covers the broad aspects of national policy and national security, is of concern to more than one Department or Agency, and transcends the exclusive competence of a single Department or Agency or the Military Establishment." Its opposite was *departmental intelligence*, which NSCID 3 defined as intelligence needed by a department or agency "to execute its mission and discharge its lawful responsibilities"; see FRUS, 1109. Executive Order 11905 in 1976 retained "national intelligence" but changed its opposite to a phrase used in President Richard M. Nixon's 1971 letter, *tactical intelligence* (which the Executive order did not further define, apart from saying that the DCI shall not have responsibility for it). Executive Order 11905 also added the overarching term *foreign intelligence*, defining it as information "on the capabilities, intentions, and activities of foreign powers, organizations or their agents."

[17] It bears noting that the NSCIDs endorsed the NIA's 1946 assignment of the two main missions (strategic warning and the coordination of clandestine activities abroad) to the DCI and his Central Intelligence Group. In particular, NSCID 5 (December 12, 1947) reaffirmed NIAD–5 in directing that the DCI "shall conduct all organized Federal espionage operations outside the United States . . . except for certain agreed activities by other Departments and Agencies." See FRUS, 1106.

[18] Lyman B. Kirkpatrick, Jr., *The U.S. Intelligence Community: Foreign Policy and Domestic Activities* (New York: Hill and Wang, 1973), 39.

[19] Richard M. Nixon to the Secretary of State et al., "Organization and Management of the U.S. Foreign Intelligence Community," November 5, 1971.

[20] The panel had been created by Executive Order 11905, which titled it the "Committee on Foreign Intelligence"; it comprised the DCI (chairman), the Deputy Secretary of Defense for Intelligence, and the Deputy Assistant to the President for National Security Affairs.

[21] Robert M. Gates, "The CIA and American Foreign Policy," *Foreign Affairs* 66 (Winter 1987/1988), 225.

[22] Rhodri Jeffreys-Jones, "Why Was the CIA Established in 1947?" *Intelligence and National Security* 12 (January 1997), 30.

[23] Unless otherwise noted, all amendments to the National Security Act cited herein are published in the several editions (1993, 1998, or 2000) of the House Permanent Select Committee on Intelligence's *Compilation of Intelligence Laws*.

[24] The Intelligence Organization Act was passed as part of the Intelligence Authorization Act for fiscal year 1993. Much of its text came from S. 2198, introduced by Sen. David L. Boren (D–OK) and titled the "Intelligence Reorganization Act of 1992." S. 2198 proposed a "Director of National Intelligence" to head the Intelligence Community; subordinate to this new officer would be the newly styled "Director of the Central Intelligence Agency." Senate Select Committee on Intelligence, "S. 2198 and S. 421 to Reorganize the United States Intelligence Community," 102[d] Congress, 2[d] Session, 1992, 2. The companion bill in the House of Representatives was HR. 4165, which offered a milder version of the DNI proposal. See also Frank J. Smist, Jr., *Congress Oversees the United States Intelligence Community,*

1947–1994, 2ᵈ ed. (Knoxville: University of Tennessee Press, 1994), 286–287.

²⁵ The Goldwater-Nichols Act is widely credited with adding coherence to the Joint Chiefs of Staff structure—another creation of the National Security Act of 1947—which had long been viewed as fragmented and less effective than it should have been in advising the Commander-in-Chief. Among other reforms, Goldwater-Nichols strengthened the Chairman of the Joint Chiefs, naming him (as opposed to the Joint Chiefs as a body) the principal military adviser to the President, clarifying his place in the national chain of command, giving him a Vice Chairman and improving the Joint Staff. See Ronald H. Cole et al., *The Chairmanship of the Joint Chiefs of Staff* (Washington, DC: Office of the Chairman of the Joint Chiefs of Staff, Joint History Office, 1995), 25–38.

²⁶ Commission on National Security/21ˢᵗ Century, *Road Map for National Security: Imperative for Change* (Washington, DC: U.S. Government Printing Office, 2001), 82.

²⁷ William J. Clinton, address to the U.S. Intelligence Community, delivered at the Central Intelligence Agency's headquarters, July 14, 1995.

²⁸ The six panels' reports were Commission on the Roles and Missions of the United States Intelligence Community, *Preparing for the 21ˢᵗ Century: An Appraisal of U.S. Intelligence* (Washington, DC: U.S. Government Printing Office, 1996); House Permanent Select Committee on Intelligence, "IC21: Intelligence Community in the 21ˢᵗ Century," 104ᵗʰ Congress, 2ᵈ Session, 1996; Richard N. Haass, Project Director for the Independent Task Force, *Making Intelligence Smarter: The Future of U.S. Intelligence* (New York: Council on Foreign Relations, 1996); Abram Shulsky and Gary Schmitt, Working Group on Intelligence Reform, *The Future of U.S. Intelligence* (Washington, DC: Consortium for the Study of Intelligence, 1996); the Twentieth Century Fund Task Force on the Future of U.S. Intelligence, Stephen Bosworth, chairman, *In From the Cold* (New York: Twentieth Century Fund Press, 1996); and John Hollister Hedley, Georgetown University Institute for the Study of Diplomacy, *Checklist for the Future of Intelligence* (Washington, DC: Institute for the Study of Diplomacy, 1995).

²⁹ The lone dissenter was the Consortium for the Study of Intelligence's report, overseen by Georgetown political scientist Roy Godson and Harvard historian Ernest May. Its authors concluded, "the failure of centralization efforts can be seen as reflecting the reasonable needs of the various components of the national security bureaucracy. In any case, the centralized model was probably better suited to the Cold War, with its emphasis on 'national' level intelligence about the Soviet strategic nuclear threat, than to the present period when departmental, regional, and tactical intelligence requirements have exploded and gained new urgency" (xiv–xv). The Twentieth Century Fund's report did not discuss the DCI's responsibilities or the centralization issue, although a background paper by Allan E. Goodman (bound with the report) implicitly endorsed greater powers for the DCI (see 78).

³⁰ Commission on Roles and Missions, *Preparing for the 21ˢᵗ Century*, xix, 51–52

³¹ See Sections 808 and 815 of the Intelligence Authorization Act for Fiscal Year 1997; *Compilation of Intelligence Laws* (1998).

³² Testimony of Robert M. Gates on April 1, 1992, at the Joint Hearing, Senate Select Committee on Intelligence and House Permanent Select Committee on Intelligence, "S. 2198 and S. 421 to Reorganize the United States Intelligence Community," 102ᵈ Congress, 2ᵈ Session, 1992, 108.

³³ For expressions of official and outside concern, see "IC21: Intelligence Community in the 21ˢᵗ Century," 245. See also the joint comment by Morton I. Abramowitz and Richard Kerr in Richard N. Haass, *Making Intelligence Smarter: The Future of U.S. Intelligence*, 38.

³⁴ See Section 1112 of the National Imagery and Mapping Agency Act, which was passed as part of the National Defense Authorization Act for Fiscal Year 1997; *Compilation of Intelligence Laws* (2000).

³⁵ Commission on National Security, *Road Map for National Security*, 82.

³⁶ National Commission for the Review of the National Reconnaissance Office, Final Report (Washington, DC: U.S. Government Printing Office, 2000), 51.

³⁷ Commission on Roles and Missions, *Preparing for the 21ˢᵗ Century*, 47.

³⁸ Commission on National Security, *Road Map for National Security*, 83.

Chapter 5

The Need to Reorganize the Intelligence Community

Larry C. Kindsvater

The Intelligence Community (IC) should be reorganized to more concertedly, effectively, and efficiently address today's national security intelligence needs. No one (except the Director of Central Intelligence) and no organizational entity is actually responsible for bringing together in a unified manner the entire IC's collection and analytic capabilities to go against individual national security missions and threats, such as terrorism, North Korea, the proliferation of weapons of mass destruction, and China. To correct this deficiency, the IC must:

- refocus its management and organizational structure around substantive national security missions rather than collection
- create new IC-wide, mission-oriented centers
- have a leader who is truly "in charge."

Taken together, these changes would fundamentally revamp the way the IC functions.

Previous Reform Efforts

Reorganizing the IC is not a new idea. Over the past 50-plus years, more than 20 official commissions and executive branch studies have proposed organizational and administrative adjustments to improve the operation of the IC. Many of these previous efforts have espoused similar recommendations, such as enhancement of the Director of Central Intelligence's (DCI's) authority to manage programs, personnel, and resources across the community, or the creation of a new position—Director of National Intelligence (DNI)—to run the IC, leaving the DCI to manage the CIA.

As early as 1949, the first Hoover Commission called for the CIA to be the "central" organization of the national intelligence system.

In 1955, the second Hoover Commission recommended that the DCI concentrate on his community responsibilities and that an "executive officer" oversee the day-to-day operations of the CIA.

Source: Larry C. Kindsvater, "The Need to Reorganize the Intelligence Community," *Studies in Intelligence* 47, no. 1 (2003).

In 1971, the Schlesinger Report discussed creation of a DNI but did not propose establishing such a position over the DCI. Instead, the report simply recommended that the Nation needed a strong DCI who could control intelligence costs and production.

In 1976, the Senate Select Committee to Study Government Operations with Respect to Intelligence Activities (the Church Committee) issued a report that, inter alia, recommended that national intelligence funding be appropriated to the DCI, thereby giving him control over the entire IC budget. The report also recommended separating the DCI from the CIA.

In 1992, proposed legislation from Senator David Boren and Representative David K. McCurdy called for a DNI with programming and reprogramming authority over the entire IC and the ability to temporarily transfer personnel among IC agencies.

In 1996, the House Permanent Select Committee on Intelligence produced a staff study—IC21: The Intelligence Community in the 21st Century—that called for more corporateness across the community and strengthened central management of the IC by providing the DCI additional administrative and resource authorities. It also proposed consolidating all technical collection activities into one large agency; refining the "center" concept as employed by the CIA; and creating two deputy DCIs, one for Analysis and one for Community Management, including collection.

None of the recommendations that would fundamentally alter the management or organizational structure of the IC and significantly strengthen the DCI's managerial authorities over the IC have been implemented. Today, the DCI's only real authorities are related to managing the CIA, not the Intelligence Community. Moreover, previous recommendations for change failed to consider fully the fundamental problem plaguing the IC: the community is not managed or organized to directly address national security missions and threats. The community continues to have a "stovepipe" collection focus. From a management and organizational perspective, the community today is not much different than it was in 1947 when the National Security Act was passed.

A More Complex World Demands Change

In recent years, the escalation of transnational threats and demands for peace-making around the world have increased the imperative to strengthen the management and organization of U.S. intelligence writ large—the National Foreign Intelligence Program (NFIP, referred to in this article as the IC); and the Joint Military Intelligence Program and Tactical Intelligence and Related Activities (JMIP and TIARA), organic Department of Defense (DOD) intelligence activities supporting military operations. DOD already intends to reorganize intelligence activities under its direct control by creating, with congressional support, a DOD intelligence czar, the Under Secretary of Defense (Intelligence), or USD(I). This new position is needed because during the tight resource years of the 1990s, the military services reduced their organic tactical intelligence capabilities, trading them for the new weapons and operations/maintenance activities needed to preserve readiness. With the lack of intelligence investment, the military, for the most part, stopped making any distinction between national and tactical/operational intelligence capabilities. Today, the Joint Chiefs of Staff (JCS), the combatant commanders, and the services essentially presume that the DCI will provide the tactical intelligence they need to conduct military operations. This reliance on national systems threatens not only military operational capabilities but also our overall strategic national security posture.

The country's security requires that both national and tactical intelligence capabilities be managed and organized effectively. It would degrade IC ability to support overall national security if the national-level intelligence capabilities of the NFIP were transformed into purely tactical capabilities to meet military operational needs. National intelligence is intended to provide critical information to help protect against a strategic surprise, providing policymakers ample time to develop a response—whether diplomatic, military, or otherwise. Moreover, national intelligence provides shorter-term indications and warnings about possible impending problems to help policymakers forestall more immediate military and other conflicts. Tactical intelligence supporting military operations is primarily needed once a conflict has begun—of course, planning and funding for such intelligence capabilities must be accomplished before the conflict. Efforts to redirect national-level intelligence (NFIP) funding toward purely tactical intelligence capabilities would reduce DCI ability to provide the information demanded by his national customers—including the President, members of the National Security Council, other Cabinet officials, and the Congress.

The USD(I), hopefully, will concentrate on tactical/operational intelligence issues within DOD. Currently, no one in DOD is in charge of determining what tactical intelligence capabilities are needed to support military operations, and organizing and implementing a service-wide process to ensure that such capabilities are developed and funded. The USD(I) should accomplish these tasks by directly managing JMIP and TIARA and organizing TIARA into a functioning program.

The new global order, however, also calls for a fundamental rethinking of how the Intelligence Community (the NFIP) should be managed and organized to support critical strategic intelligence needs.

Focus on Missions

The managerial and organizational emphasis in the IC should be on national security missions and issues. Today's IC, however, is organized by collection "stovepipes," essentially independent agencies responsible for specific types of collection activity. Signals intelligence is handled by the National Security Agency (NSA), imagery intelligence by the National Imagery and Mapping Agency (NIMA), and human intelligence by the CIA and the Defense Intelligence Agency. As a result, the IC's emphasis presently is on the type of collection, first, and substantive missions/issues, second.

This structure creates a strange and dangerous managerial situation because no organization or person in the IC (except the DCI) is actually responsible for (or can be held accountable for) success or failure against the primary national security missions of the community, such as countering terrorism or understanding the threat from North Korea. Instead, the IC is managed and organized primarily according to analytic and collection capabilities that are needed to carry out these missions. No IC-wide operational organization exists to direct the collective activities of these stovepipe capabilities against specific national security missions.

Although the collection agencies are needed to manage how collection activities are implemented, what these agencies collect (and analyze) needs to be substantively managed in a centralized way by mission/issue. If the President, DCI, or Congress has an intelligence question, they should be able to do one-stop shopping based on the issue, not based on how intelligence was collected or analyzed.

"Centerize" the IC

To implement a new substantive mission focus, the IC needs to create community-wide substantive analytic/collection centers that would deal with major threats to our national security (that is, terrorism) and major regional/country areas (such as China). Such centers must be truly IC-wide organizations. They should be:

- responsible for substantively managing community-wide analysis and collection on their respective issue areas. This means that the centers would be in charge of the community's analysis on their issues, and receive and direct all IC collection against these issues.
- populated by substantive analytic experts and collection discipline/system experts from across the IC. These officers, while working for the director of the center, would be performing the functions of their home component/agency within an IC setting. Such an arrangement would improve collection by directly connecting the collection components/agencies to the substantive analytic efforts of the IC.
- headed by officers working for the DCI.

Members of the national-level requirements, analytic, and collection boards would become advisers, instead of members, to these boards, which include the Mission Requirements Board, the National Intelligence Analysis and Production Board, and the National Intelligence Collection Board.

Advisers providing direct input to the DCI's Community program and budget process would further ensure that funding for analytic and collection issues is appropriately prioritized within the IC budget and supports the DCI's strategic direction for the IC.

The centers, in turn, would be managed by a centralized IC corporation, supported by multiple subsidiaries. This central corporation would help the IC become a "real" entity, not the loose grouping of separately managed multiple agencies that it is today. The centralizing organization—the corporation—should be the Central Intelligence Agency, but not the CIA as it is organized today. The new CIA would be driven by the centers, not the existing directorates, and have an IC-wide focus and mission.

The CIA would be reorganized by making the IC centers the major subunits, comparable to today's directorates. The centers would not be located within an existing CIA directorate. The Directorates of Intelligence (DI), Operations (DO), and Science and Technology (DS&T) would continue, but the centers (separate from the directorates) would be the substantive analytic/collection focal points within the CIA and the entire IC. The other intelligence agencies—and the DI, DO, and DS&T—would, in effect, work for these centers and provide people to man them. These new

CIA centers would represent a radical departure from the way the CIA—and the IC—operates and is managed today.

The IC corporation, the CIA, would need a few other adjustments to enable it to manage the new centers effectively. The DCI, as head of the corporation (CIA) and all of its subsidiaries (NSA, NIMA, and so forth), must be tied directly to his community staff; therefore, the Office of the Deputy Director of Central Intelligence for Community Management (DDCI/CM) should be moved into CIA proper. The CIA would then have two Deputy Directors of Central Intelligence (DDCIs):

- One DDCI would manage the IC-wide substantive analytic/collection centers. This DDCI would also be responsible for the CIA directorates (DO, DI, DS&T) and other functions/activities performed by the CIA's operationally related components (such as the mission support offices).
- A second DDCI would manage IC-wide processes, including the requirements, analytic, and collection boards; and the IC-wide strategic planning, policy, program, and budget processes. This DDCI would also be responsible for other IC-wide functions/activities, such as those conducted in the offices of the Assistant DCI for Analysis and Production, the Assistant DCI for Collection, Congressional Affairs, the General Counsel, and the Inspector General.

Together, the two DDCIs would be accountable to the DCI to assure the complete integration of intelligence analysis and collection needs into IC-wide processes that strategically, as well as operationally, lead and manage intelligence activities and resources.

DCI in Charge

To make the IC-wide centers and the reorganized CIA a reality, the DCI must truly be the head of the entire community. This would require the DCI to receive additional authorities over IC personnel, agency directors, and budget. Without such new authorities, the centers and the revamped CIA would not be able to function, and today's reality would continue—with no one person in charge of the IC and no one person held accountable for its successes and failures. Specifically, the DCI would need the authority to:

- move any IC employee anywhere in the community at any time. The centers must be populated with qualified experts from across IC agencies. The DCI must be able to direct IC agencies to provide the officers necessary for the centers to function properly. This would not require a uniform personnel system across the IC; it would, however, require new legislation.
- hire/remove IC agency heads in consultation with the Secretary of Defense. If the DCI is to be in charge, the agency heads must work for the DCI and managerially be subordinate to the DCI. This arrangement would reverse today's situation where the Secretary of Defense selects IC agency heads in consultation with the DCI. New legislation would be needed to effect this change.
- move funding within or across IC agencies at any time with congressional approval. While the DCI already has the authority to propose the annual IC budget to the President and the Congress, he also would need the independent

ability to move funding around in the year of execution. At present, the Secretary of Defense must also approve such "reprogrammings" because most of the IC funding is appropriated to him. The DCI cannot be in charge of the IC if he must ask the Secretary of Defense to let him reprogram community money. This would not necessarily require appropriating IC funding to the DCI; it might be accomplished by delegating the Secretary of Defense's authority over IC funding to the DCI, either by Presidential direction or by legislation.

"Jointness" within the IC

With the above adjustments, this proposal would roughly create an IC version of the DOD joint military command structure, where the JCS, the regional combatant commanders, and the services function together. In the IC, the DCI's staff under the DDCI and DDCI/CM would carry out functions comparable to the JCS; the new CIA centers would be equivalent to the combatant commanders; and the CIA directorates and the other IC agencies would represent the services.

This type of jointness could also help the DCI attract topnotch officers to his IC staff and the centers, by designating some of the positions in these organizations as joint, comparable to the way the military does in the JCS and combatant commander staffs. If having served in such a joint IC position were required for higher-level positions within the IC agencies, hopefully the best and brightest would apply.

Conclusion

The changes recommended in this chapter would fundamentally alter how the IC actually functions, making substantive national security missions/issues/threats the driving managerial force across the IC, and creating organized entities with someone in charge who is responsible for community-wide efforts against specific national security missions. This arrangement would dramatically reduce the intelligence collection (stovepipe) management and organizational orientation of the IC. Moreover, it would place a DCI with expanded authorities at the top of an organization, the Central Intelligence Agency, that has an IC-wide (corporate) mission, responsibility, and authority.

Part III—
Intelligence and Democracy

Americans have always had an ambivalent attitude toward intelligence. When they feel threatened, they want a lot of it, and when they don't, they regard the whole thing as somewhat immoral.

—Vernon A. Walters

Chapter 6

Balancing Liberty and Security

Loch K. Johnson

We know that many Americans are uneasy about CIA and U.S. intelligence activities. They understand the need for information, and even, on occasion, for covert action. But they are uncomfortable with secrecy. And therein lies the value of congressional oversight: the reassurance to Americans that the laws are being obeyed and that there is accountability.

—DCI Robert M. Gates, *Hearings*, U.S. Senate Committee on Intelligence, 1991

The Sharing of Governmental Power

By constitutional design, the executive branch of Government in the United States is required to share its powers with the legislative and judicial branches. While this can lead to frustrations and inefficiencies, its virtue lies in the accountability that sharing provides. This legislative monitoring or review is usually referred to by the awkward term "oversight."

The concept of power sharing has roots that run deep in American tradition. "If angels were to govern men, neither external nor internal controls on government would be necessary," James Madison observed in 1788. Perhaps unable to recollect any angels he had met in public life, he advised the adoption of more secular safeguards against government abuse. "A dependence on the people" would be paramount, especially a cycle of elections. Though necessary, voting in itself would not be sufficient, however. "Experience has taught mankind the necessity of auxiliary precautions," Madison added. Between elections, the three branches of Government would have to keep a close watch on one another. In his most famous dictum, "Ambition must be made to counteract ambition."[1]

This concern about the dangers of concentrated power was widespread in the new republic. Jefferson scoffed at the notion that loyal citizens should exhibit an obsequious confidence in their leaders; instead, he recommended vigilance over those serving in high office. "Confidence is everywhere the parent of despotism," he warned. "In questions of power, then, let no more be heard of confidence in man, but bind him down from mischief by the chains of the Constitution."[2] The preeminent link in these chains was the Constitution's first article, which enumerated the powers of Congress

Source: Loch K. Johnson, Chapter Nine, "Balancing Liberty and Security," in *Bombs, Bugs, Drugs, and Thugs* (New York: New York University Press, 2000), 188–222. Copyright © 2000 by New York University Press. Reprinted by permission.

and made it clear that legislators would have a major role to play in the exercise of the war, treaty, and spending powers, along with an opportunity to impeach an executive or judicial official who violated the public trust. Contemporary political scientists have refashioned this idea as "separated institutions *sharing* powers" as a more accurate portrayal of the day-to-day reality of how the Constitution operates in practice.[3]

This idea of power sharing was endorsed in modern times by Supreme Court Justice Louis Brandeis, who reminded a new century of Americans that the founders had sought "not to promote efficiency but to preclude the exercise of arbitrary power. The purpose was not to avoid friction, but, by means of the inevitable friction incident to the distribution of the governmental powers among three departments, to save the people from autocracy."[4]

The governing arrangements envisioned by the founders have never worked perfectly. Institutional struggles over the war and the treaty powers have been particularly heated. Sometimes the powers of the President have expanded to alarming proportions, as when Abraham Lincoln assumed the status of an autocrat during the early phases of the Civil War, when Andrew Johnson acted capriciously during Reconstruction, when Lyndon B. Johnson escalated the war in Vietnam without a meaningful congressional debate, and when Richard M. Nixon helped cover up a White House espionage operation against the opposition party (the Watergate scandal).

On other occasions, the powers of Congress have grown too large, as when Joseph R. McCarthy (R–WI) grossly misused the Senate's investigative powers to harass the Truman and Eisenhower administrations and scores of private citizens. Sometimes the judiciary has overreached, as in 1936 when Justice George Sutherland issued sweeping dicta in favor of expanded Presidential powers in foreign affairs.[5]

For the most part, though, the government has abided by the founding principle of power sharing, though its precise form has always been dependent on the personalities and conditions of the times. Some personalities have been expansive in the interpretation of their office's inherent constitutional powers (compare Franklin D. Roosevelt with the more passive William Howard Taft). Some events have compelled a greater concentration of power in the hands of the executive, in times of emergency and for the sake of secrecy and swift action. The Depression, World War II, and the Cold War have been the major centralizing forces of the modern era that encouraged an aggrandizement of power by the executive branch.

Yet almost always (the Civil War excepted), dialogue and accommodation have mollified disputes among the departments of government. Presidents Andrew Johnson and Bill Clinton barely escaped removal from office through the impeachment procedure, and President Richard Nixon resigned rather than face almost certain removal. Usually, though, those in high office have been willing to display (however begrudgingly) a spirit of comity on which power sharing depends. Always at the heart of these governing arrangements is the principle of checks against power imbalances, that is, accountability, except for one domain of government that has always stood out as a conspicuous exception to the rule. Throughout most of their history, the Nation's intelligence agencies have enjoyed immunity from close oversight by outside supervisors.

The Exceptional Case of Intelligence

During America's early history, intelligence operations eluded serious supervision by Congress and the courts.[6] But even in the modern era with all the congressional oversight capabilities (budgets, staff, frequent hearings, strengthened subpoena, and other investigative authorities), the CIA and its companion agencies have sidestepped the government's usual checks and balances. Members of Congress have deferred to the expertise of intelligence officers and preferred anyway to avoid responsibility for controversial secret operations like the Bay of Pigs fiasco (1961).[7]

A former director of Central Intelligence, James R. Schlesinger, remembered a meeting he had in 1973 with John Stennis (D–MS), chair of the subcommittee dealing with intelligence on behalf of the Senate Armed Services Committee. "I went up to the Hill and said, 'Mr. Chairman, I want to tell you about some of our programs.' To which the Senator quickly replied: 'No, no, my boy, don't tell me. Just go ahead and do it—but I don't want to know!'"[8] With little scrutiny, the leaders of the Armed Services Committees in both chambers quietly allocated funds for the secret agencies into the Defense Department's annual appropriations bill.

Nor did the Executive Office of the President offer reliable accountability for the intelligence establishment. Key members of the National Security Council rarely—in some cases, never—even laid eyes on the intelligence budget. "I never saw a budget of the CIA, although I was a statutory member of the National Security Council," Dean Rusk once said, looking back over his long tenure as Secretary of State during the Kennedy and Johnson administrations.

> The CIA's budget apparently went to two or three specially cleared people in the Bureau of the Budget, then run briefly by the President, turned over to Senator [Richard] Russell [D–GA], and that was the end of it. He would lose the CIA budget in the Defense budget and he wouldn't let anybody question it. There were no public hearings on it. So again his judgment, his word on that, was the last word.[9]

Many of the CIA's activities (including aggressive covert action, collection, and counterintelligence operations) never received a thorough examination—or, in some cases, even approval—by the National Security Council.[10] When the council did endorse a covert action proposal, the decision process became slippery, according to Clark Clifford, an adviser to several Presidents from Truman onward.

> I believe on a number of occasions a plan for covert action has been presented to the NSC and authority is requested for the CIA to proceed from point A to point B. The authority will be given and the action will be launched. When point B is reached, the persons in charge feel it is necessary to go to point C, and they assume that the original authorization gives them such a right. From point C, they go to D and possibly E, and even further. This has led to some bizarre results, and when an investigation is started the excuse is blandly presented that authority was obtained from the NSC before the project was launched.[11]

Mindful of the need for closer supervision of the Intelligence Community, a few members of Congress attempted from time to time to devise new controls (particularly in the wake of intelligence flaps such as the Bay of Pigs and the CIA's infiltration of the National Student Association). But these initiatives were always defeated, as a majority of legislators remained content to abide by the rule of exception for intelligence activities, persuaded by the argument that the Nation's secret operations were too delicate for oversight and wary of consenting to operations that might prove embarrassing.

Nonetheless, some of the oversight proposals were modest efforts to strengthen the review of intelligence programs, and had they been adopted, they might have helped avoid later scandals. Other proposals were more extreme, including one—the Abourezk amendment—designed to abolish all covert actions, regardless of type or circumstance.[12] Whatever the merits of the various oversight initiatives, Congress proved unwilling to extend the doctrine of power sharing to the darker recesses of American government.

In December 1974, however, this attitude changed abruptly. In a series of articles, reporter Seymour M. Hersh of the *New York Times* disclosed that the CIA had spied on American citizens during the Vietnam War and had also attempted to topple the constitutionally elected president of Chile (Salvador Allende). Although Congress might have ignored the revelations about covert action in Chile as just another necessary chapter in the Cold War against Soviet interference in the developing world, spying on American citizens—their constituents—was an allegation they found difficult to dismiss. Both the executive and legislative branches immediately launched investigations, in what became known as the "Year of Intelligence" (or the "Intelligence Wars," in the embittered view of some CIA officials).[13]

During these inquiries in 1975, a parade of horrors emerged, everything from murder plots against foreign leaders to widespread espionage operations against American citizens whose only crime had been to protest the war in Vietnam or join the civil rights movement. The Ford administration revived the President's Foreign Intelligence Advisory Board and created the Intelligence Oversight Board, both part of the Executive Office of the Presidency and now expected to monitor the secret agencies on behalf of the chief executive. By executive order, President Gerald R. Ford banned assassination plots and tightened CIA and National Security Council approval procedures for the use of covert action. His successor, Jimmy Carter, further codified and strengthened the council's accountability for intelligence activities by means of another executive order and supporting directives.

The zeal for reform was most evident on Capitol Hill. Indeed, President Ford's initiatives were widely considered more an attempt to preempt congressional action than bold steps to rein in the secret agencies. On the last day of the legislative session in 1974, Congress enacted the first-ever statute to place controls on the use of covert action. The landmark Hughes-Ryan amendment made two far-reaching changes: first, before a covert action could be carried out, the President would have to authorize the operation through a special approval called a "finding," and second, the finding would have to be reported to the appropriate committees of Congress "in a timely fashion," thereby alerting legislative overseers that a covert action had been authorized by the White House.[14] With the enactment of this law, a few legislators were allowed into the small group of people told about covert actions, the "witting circle" in spytalk. Legislators stopped short of granting themselves authority to approve or disapprove covert actions, but at least they would have an opportunity to know about them and (by implication) to voice their objections or at the extreme even shut off funding for a proposal if they strongly opposed it.

By the spring of 1976, Senators had established a permanent committee on intelligence oversight, named the Senate Select Committee on Intelligence (SSCI, pronounced "sissy" by everyone except its members and staff, which they would sometimes prove to be) and given a mandate to provide a close accounting of intelligence budgets and day-to-day operations. The next year the House followed suit, establishing the House Permanent Select Committee on Intelligence (HPSCI, pronounced "hipsee") with largely comparable duties and expectations.

Since then, this congressional experiment in power sharing has evolved in fits and starts. Sometimes legislators have tightened the reins, most notably with passage of the Intelligence Oversight Act of 1980, the Boland amendments to curtail covert action in Nicaragua during the Reagan administration, the Intelligence Oversight Act of 1991, and, in the same year (both responses to the Iran-contra scandal), the creation of a CIA inspector general confirmed by and accountable to Congress. At other times, legislators have loosened the reins when they proved to be too restrictive, as in 1985 with the repeal of the legislation prohibiting covert action in Angola and the buckling under of legislators to President George Bush's insistence on greater Presidential discretion over reporting to the Congress on covert actions. On still other occasions, Congress has helped the intelligence agencies shelter their legitimate activities, as with the passage of an Intelligence Identities Protection Act in 1982 to prohibit the exposure of undercover intelligence officials through the publication of their names. While the pulling and tugging continued, one conclusion was without dispute: at last the secret agencies had become a part of America's system of shared powers.

On the Merits of Accountability

Has the new system of accountability been successful? Opinion remains divided on this question, as reflected in two recent studies of intelligence.[15] For one author, Kathryn Olmsted, the movement to introduce accountability into this secret world has largely failed, however well intended and proper the attempt. Despite the year-long investigations by three separate panels—one in the Senate led by Senator Frank Church (D–ID), another in the House led by Representative Otis Pike (D–NY), and a third in the White House led by Vice President Nelson Rockefeller (R–NY), the end result was little reform. The Congress was, she writes, "ultimately unwilling to shoulder its responsibilities for overseeing the intelligence community."

In her effort to determine why this was the case, Olmsted begins with an observation from Richard Helms, a former DCI pilloried by Senate investigators in 1975. Helms commented sarcastically: "Where is the legislation, the great piece of legislation, that was going to come out of the Church committee hearings? I haven't seen it."[16] Though for quite different reasons, Olmsted, too, is unimpressed by the will of legislators to supervise the Intelligence Community. The preference of Capitol Hill overseers is "to maintain their basic deference" to the secret agencies, she maintains, rather than hold them to high standards of accountability. In regard to accountability from outside the government, she finds the Nation's media equally feckless. While much of Olmsted's criticism of legislative oversight is compelling, she too easily discounts the improvements that have come about as a result of the investigations in 1975. She (and Helms) is wrong: it is not the number of laws or their level of detail that matters so much but, rather, the day-to-day monitoring of the secret agencies by legislators and their staff. By this measure, the creation of the two intelligence oversight committees has led to a much closer check on America's secret government than existed earlier.

Moreover, the oversight laws that have been passed should not be so easily discounted, especially their reporting requirements. The Intelligence Oversight Act of 1980 considerably enhanced accountability. It included a provision for *advanced* notice to Congress of *every* important covert operation (not just covert actions). Significant, too, are the Foreign Intelligence Surveillance Act (FISA) of 1978, which brought the judiciary into the ambit of intelligence oversight by requiring a special court review of requests for national security wiretaps, and the Intelligence Oversight Act of 1991, which insists on a prior, written Presidential finding for important covert actions, not *ex post facto* oral approval, as once given by President Reagan.[17] These initiatives are not shadows on the wall but, like the new inspector general statute, tough laws that have given genuine meaning to intelligence accountability. This is particularly evident when compared with the statutory void that existed before passage of the Hughes-Ryan Act.

The media also deserve more credit than Olmsted gives them. Clearly, a number of American reporters erred in the past when they accepted secret stipends from the CIA for intelligence work, blurring the line between independent journalism and espionage.[18] Moreover, reporting on intelligence matters has often been superficial (Olmsted's central point). Yet the reason for the thin coverage warrants some empathy. The secret agencies are enclosed by both real and figurative walls, just as daunting for journalists as for scholars and other outsiders. Expectations that the media will be able to break down these walls with any frequency is unrealistic, nor would most American citizens want the Nation's secrets so easily breached.

Furthermore, the media have occasionally behaved in a manner that has been not so much deferential as irresponsible. Columnist Jack Anderson had his moments of commendable reporting in the public interest, but his disclosure of Operation *Guppy* (U.S. wiretapping of Soviet limousines in Moscow) and the *Glomar Explorer* story (when the CIA attempted to salvage a sunken Soviet submarine) undermined two potentially valuable intelligence-collection operations.[19] Several members of the media with access to these stories prudently decided against printing them, on grounds that the best interests of the United States might be harmed. There are times—however few—when the media should restrain itself in the national interest.

In Olmsted's view, the "secret agencies clearly emerged the winners of their long battle with the investigators [in 1975]," for the inquiries resulted "only in restoring the CIA's credibility." Yet consider the whole new set of arrangements for closer intelligence supervision on Capitol Hill, including the establishment of SSCI and HPSCI by lopsided votes (the White House and the Intelligence Community lobbied vigorously against them). The two committees enjoy line-by-line budget authorization, competent staffs, subpoena powers, and a mandate to prevent further abuses. Consider, too, the exposés of assassination plots, domestic spying, covert action in Chile, and drug experimentation. The intelligence agencies were hardly winners in 1975. True, the CIA was not dismantled, as some feared (including then-DCI William Colby). The end result, though, was nonetheless a significant tightening of legislative supervision over the secret agencies.

As for restoring the CIA's credibility (which Olmsted seems to view as a dubious outcome), it was never the intention of the Church committee to undermine the intelligence agencies' ability to perform their legitimate work. Rather, Senator Frank Church hoped to improve U.S. intelligence by rooting out its rotten branches. Church's only major speech during the inquiry praised the CIA for its analytic skills and solid reporting to policymakers over the years.[20] His purpose was to extol the virtues of intelligence (he himself had served as an intelligence officer during World War II), renewing its legitimacy even as he criticized its excesses.

Olmsted ends her study with an important question about the evolution of intelligence oversight in the United States: Have the legislative committees caved in to the very agencies they were created to supervise? Once more she discerns a pattern of deference toward the secret agencies by their overseers, citing as an illustration a journalist's observation that within a decade after 1975, the House intelligence committee "was staffed largely by former CIA officers."

From time to time, the two oversight committees have disappointed outside advocates of strong accountability, but at other times they have also demonstrated firm resolve, depending on the mix of members and how seriously they have taken their oversight responsibilities. Representative Edward P. Boland (D–MA) stood up to the covert action chicanery in Nicaragua directed by the National Security Council staff during the Reagan years, as did Iran-contra congressional investigators in 1987. And throughout 1995–1996, both intelligence committees engaged in a wide-ranging constructive review of intelligence reform proposals.

"For a brief moment," Olmsted concludes, "[congressional investigators] forced the Nation to debate the perils of secrecy in a democracy." On the contrary, this has been an energetic and ongoing debate, continuing through the Carter years and heating up during the Reagan and Bush administrations with the Iran-contra affair. It was revived again during the Clinton years with the report of the Aspin-Brown commission in 1996, along with concomitant efforts by Congress and scholars in the private sector to ponder intelligence reform. How much intelligence is enough? What is the proper balance between liberty and security? When should legislators and the media be supportive or openly critical of sensitive intelligence operations? These are questions without definitive answers.

Whereas Olmsted is dismayed by the lack of robust intelligence oversight, the second study takes quite the opposite view. Steven F. Knott is aghast that the overabundance of oversight has supposedly stifled America's secret agencies. He reminds us that Washington, Jefferson, and Lincoln periodically resorted to unsavory covert practices. He derives from this history lesson a dubious conclusion, however, namely, that a reliance on executive discretion over intelligence activities served the Nation well in the past and would in the future as well if only the Congress would step out of the way. According to Knott, intelligence operations frequently are delicate and perishable and rely on secrecy, flexibility, timeliness, and efficiency, all of which are lost when Congress enters the picture.

Knott is impressed by precedents set in the Nation's early history and understandably so, for the founders' accomplishments are indeed impressive. His enthusiasm, though, goes too far. During the Watergate scandal, defenders of the Nixon administration insisted that the President had done nothing more than what earlier Presidents had done. "I do not share this view," properly responded a legislator during the impeachment proceedings against the President, "or the view of those who hold that all Presidents have lied, have broken the law, have compromised the Constitution. And if George Washington accepted bribes, it would not make bribery a virtue, nor would it be grounds for overlooking such acts by his successors."[21] Similarly, the fact that earlier Presidents engaged in intelligence operations without serious accountability should not condone the practice today.

Knott is a fervent critic of the post-Watergate rebellion against the imperial Presidency. He laments the "myth of innocence" that enveloped Frank Church and his band of reformers in Congress. Instead, he reminds Americans of how their most venerated early leaders were willing to engage in operations that today would send pantywaist legislators running into the press room crying foul. "The most important reform that should be made to the current system," Knott writes, "would be the elimination of the intelligence committees and the restoration of the system that existed from 1947 to 1974." In place of the congressional oversight committees, he would prefer a system of unfettered executive dominance. President Ford's "ludicrous" executive order prohibiting the assassination of foreign leaders should, for instance, be immediately repealed.

What disturbed legislators in 1975 was the extent to which many of the modern intelligence agencies had violated the law and their charters. Most legislators were shocked by the discovery of assassination plots; the creation of more than a million intelligence files on U.S. citizens; illegal mail openings, wiretaps, and cable interceptions; drug experiments against unsuspecting citizens; unlawful sequestering of chemical-biological materials; a White House spy plan against American citizens; an intelligence scheme to blackmail Dr. Martin Luther King, Jr., and encourage his suicide; the CIA's infiltration of this country's media, universities, and church groups; the FBI's incitement of violence among African Americans; covert harassment of Vietnam War dissenters and civil rights activists; and covert actions directed against not just autocracies but duly elected governments in democratic regimes.

Throughout most of the republic's history, secret operations remained small and peripheral. Now, however, our intelligence establishment has grown beyond the capacity of the President alone to monitor. The Congress must help. In Knott's opinion, however, this legislative supervision ("micromanagement," in the preferred slight) has only stymied the secret agencies. Yet most of the intelligence directors since 1975 take a different view. They have welcomed the opportunity to share the burden of their heavy responsibilities with Members of Congress. Moreover, no administration has sought to repeal the core set of laws and oversight procedures that currently guide intelligence activities. Legislators understand that this Nation must continue to have, when needed, a viable covert action capability and one that can move swiftly. According to Knott, the new oversight has caused the CIA to shy away from this option, but in fact, covert action was most extensively used during the Reagan and Bush years, well after the reforms were in place.[22]

Knott does Congress a further disservice by blaming it for the unauthorized disclosure of classified information. Studies on the subject of leaks consistently trace most back to the executive branch.[23] Knott also maintains that the oversight exercised by Congress from 1947 to 1974 was sufficiently vigorous. Every other credible study disagrees.[24] He then shifts from the improbable to the impossible: a defense of the relations between DCI William J. Casey of the Reagan administration and Congress. The fact is that Casey's standing on Capitol Hill reached rock bottom. He had nothing but disdain for the legislative branch and even managed to alienate the CIA's archdefenders in Congress (including the SSCI chair, Barry Goldwater [R–AZ]).

The choice is not between executive or legislative sovereignty over intelligence. The challenge is to use the best attributes of both branches in the service of the Nation's security. Members of Congress have a strong sense of what the American people will support, plus a large amount of foreign policy expertise in their own right. Congress provides a second opinion, carefully tendered in the executive (closed) sessions of the oversight committees by a small group of legislators in each chamber. On sensitive matters that can involve great cost and danger for the United States, a second opinion can be vital.

During the Iran-contra investigation, Vice Admiral John M. Poindexter (President Reagan's national security adviser) conceded that he had bypassed the intelligence committees in order to avoid "outside interference"[25]—as if Congress were an outsider. Granted, in the intelligence domain, debate must often take place behind closed doors. The new system of oversight, though, provides an opportunity for at least some degree of independent review by elected representatives of the American people, beyond just the President and Vice President. The alternative is covert operations by executive fiat. The unfortunate consequences of that approach, well documented by investigators in 1975 and again in the wake of the Iran-contra scandal, remain fresh in the memory of the attentive public.

Adapting to the New Era of Accountability

Regardless of whether or not one likes the idea of greater intelligence accountability, the fact remains that 1975 was a critical turning point in the history of American intelligence. Since then, the quality of oversight has depended on the degree of commitment displayed by individual legislators toward their supervisory responsibilities and how often (and persuasively) the media have reported incidents of intelligence impropriety. Generally, the level of oversight has remained relatively high compared with its near absence before 1975. With the passage of a series of amendments sponsored by HPSCI chair Edward Boland, legislative overseers responded quickly to block untoward covert actions in Nicaragua during the first half of the Reagan administration. Congress failed to sniff out the Iran-contra shenanigans at first, but disclosure of the operations (never reported to Congress, as required by law, but by a Middle Eastern newspaper) jolted the overseers back to their senses.

A New Partnership

Despite these fluctuations, the overall trend during the latter stages of the Cold War was unmistakable: Congress and the executive branch had entered into a new era of partnership in the conduct of intelligence activities. As a recent DCI put it, the CIA found itself equidistant between the two branches: "responsible and accountable to both, unwilling to act at presidential request without clearance from Congress."[26] Between 1986 and 1990, the number of CIA briefings to the congressional oversight committees, individual members, and staffers rose from a few hundred a year to 1,040 in 1986, 1,064 in 1987, 1,044 in 1988, 947 in 1989, 1,012 in 1990, and 1,000 in 1991.[27] The number of written reports sent to Congress, most of them classified, has also sharply increased since 1986. In 1991 alone, 7,000 intelligence reports went to Capitol Hill.[28]

The frequency of contact between the CIA and Congress has accelerated since the Cold War. In 1993, 1,512 meetings took place between Members of Congress and the CIA's legislative liaison staff, along with 154 one-on-one or small-group meetings between legislators and the DCI; 26 congressional hearings with the DCI as a witness; 128 hearings with other CIA witnesses; 317 other contacts with legislators; and 887 meetings and contacts with legislative staff, a 29 percent increase over 1992. In 1993, the agency provided 4,976 classified documents to legislators, along with 4,668 unclassified documents and 233 responses to constituency inquiries.[29] In 1998, CIA officials briefed members or staffers on Capitol Hill on 1,350 occasions (about five times each working day).[30]

Another sign of more serious effort to monitor the CIA and keep American citizens informed of at least some of its activities was the series of hearings in Congress, held from 1991 to 1994, in which witnesses from the Intelligence Community testified in public, a rarity during the Cold War. President Clinton's first DCI, R. James Woolsey, appeared in eight open hearings in 1993, whereas in previous years—even after the congressional investigations of 1975 and calls for greater openness—DCIs often never appeared in public hearings during an entire session of Congress or, if testifying, never more than once or twice a year.

The result is that the agency now has two masters: the President as well as Congress, and sometimes a third, as the courts increasingly adjucate intelligence-related litigation and regularly examine requests for electronic-surveillance warrants against national-security targets.

Backsliding

The degree of CIA openness should not be overstated, however. That Congress was still kept in the dark on key aspects of intelligence policy was underscored in 1994.

Although the HPSCI had been briefed, SSCI members learned only through a chance audit that the National Reconnaissance Office (NRO) had engaged in cost overruns amounting to $159 million for its new headquarters in the Virginia countryside. Subsequent reports in 1995–1996 revealed further that the NRO had accumulated a $4 billion slush fund of appropriations, without keeping Congress informed of its magnitude.[31] Woolsey produced a raft of documents purportedly showing that when he had been DCI, Congress had been briefed on the NRO budget nine different times. A CIA/Department of Defense inquiry subsequently indicated, however, that the NRO had presented this matter to legislators in piecemeal fashion that (to quote the report) "left unclear the total project cost."[32] However inadvertent the inadequacy of briefings may have been, the fact remained that the NRO had failed to keep Congress fully informed of its activities, as the spirit and the letter of the oversight laws intend. The "fully informed" standard means that intelligence officials must patiently reiterate their testimony to busy committee members and staff again and again, if necessary, with respect to any departure from normal practices (including cost overruns). Overseers have every right to this information.[33]

It was revealed in 1995 that another secret agency, this time the CIA, had also failed to report to Congress about dubious activities. The issue concerned the agency's ties to a controversial military colonel in Guatemala, Julio Roberto Alpirez, who had been providing intelligence to the United States from time to time. The media suspected the officer of being involved in the murder of an American citizen in Guatemala and also in the death of a local guerrilla insurgent married to an American woman. Under the oversight rules, the CIA should have reviewed with the congressional oversight panels the propriety of an ongoing relationship with the colonel. "Guatemala's most important lesson," concluded the *New York Times*, "is that the CIA cannot be trusted to police itself."[34]

Another, more recent case of an intelligence official who failed to understand the concept of accountability is the chief of counterintelligence in the Energy Department. In 1999, he criticized the SSCI and HPSCI chairs for their vigorous inquiry into the spy scandal at the Los Alamos National Laboratory, complaining that he had "to testify about this before fourteen different committees for two months."[35] The Los Alamos spy incident, however, revealed a serious counterintelligence breach. If legislative overseers wish to hear from the CI chief in charge of the Nation's labs one or one hundred times, that is an important part of his job. As an experienced former intelligence officer explained, "Dealing with the public is as much a function of intelligence these days as the recruiting of agents or the forecasting of future events."[36]

At least the Energy Department's CI chief avoided the even worse stance adopted by the Iran-contra bureaucrats. They either failed to inform Congress at all, or, the ultimate offense against accountability, they lied to legislators. Other officials in the Energy Department, though, did exhibit some of this regrettable behavior, despite the still-fresh memory of Iran-contra. In 1998, the department failed to file an annual report on the status of security at the Nation's labs, as required by Congress.[37] Moreover, two of the department's senior officials, including its acting head of intelligence, withheld information on the Los Alamos scandal from the House Armed Services Subcommittee on Military Procurement, even under oath and in executive session.[38]

For some people, the lessons of Iran-contra seem easily forgotten (if they were ever learned). "To my mind, to disclose as little as necessary to Congress, if they can get away with it, is not a bad thing," a former intelligence officer reportedly observed in 1991, referring to colleagues caught up in the Iran-contra affair. "I have trouble myself blaming any of those guys."[39] Similarly, the new NRO director concedes that the old ethic at his organization—which he vows he is determined to change—was at best a grudging acceptance of congressional accountability. "Legislators were considered pimples on the face of progress," he recalls. "The attitude was: 'We're not going to tell you and you can't make us.'"[40] Yet as a former SSCI staff member observed, the only hope for oversight to work depends ultimately on the "honesty and completeness in what the members of the intelligence community tell their congressional overseers."[41]

During the Congress's Los Alamos inquiries in 1999, even DCI George Tenet—formerly the SSCI staff director and well versed in the ethos of oversight—refused to provide information about the spy case to his former committee (evidently so ordered by the Department of Justice). The SSCI chairman, Senator Richard Shelby, was correct in asserting his committee's right to "have access to all information in unredacted form that pertains to our oversight responsibility."[42] Without full access to information about all intelligence activities, the oversight committees would be unable to provide the institutional balance envisioned by the Nation's founders as a safeguard against the abuse of power.

The evolution of reliable accountability for intelligence was dealt yet another blow at the beginning of the new century when it came to light in February 2000 that the CIA had never reported to the congressional oversight committees or the Justice Department evidence that implicated former DCI John Deutch in the improper handling of classified materials (while director, he took large amounts home to work on, thereby violating security procedures). There was "no excuse" for failing to report the impropriety, conceded Deutch's successor, George Tenet. "It should have been done promptly, certainly by the spring of 1997."[43] The Intelligence Community's degree of openness and cooperation with legislative overseers, then, has been uneven since the institution of greater accountability in 1975. How well have other overseers, inside and outside the government, fared in their efforts to keep the secret agencies accountable?

Oversight by the White House

During the Reagan years, the Intelligence Community benefited from a close relationship with the White House, mainly because DCI Casey was a personal friend of the President and had served as his national campaign manager. Casey became the first DCI accorded the largely honorific "cabinet rank." Furthermore, Reagan was supportive of Casey's enthusiasm for covertly countering the worldwide influence of the Soviet Union. But this free rein given to the Intelligence Community and the NSC staff led to the Iran-contra excesses. When former DCI George Bush became President, the CIA had the luxury of a chief executive who understood and appreciated intelligence as well as anyone who has served in the Nation's highest office. Accordingly, President Bush was sympathetic to most of the funding requests from the secret agencies, though he did reduce the CIA's involvement in covert actions.[44]

The Clinton admimstration [was] almost a polar opposite, with its relative inattentiveness to foreign policy (at least in the early years). Then, during the administration's first significant foreign policy crisis in Somalia, intelligence deficiencies—among them, a failure to understand the intentions, or even the whereabouts, of tribal leader General Mohamed Farah Aideed—raised doubts among White House officials about the effectiveness of the secret agencies.

In 1994, President Clinton turned to a proposal advanced by his former Secretary of Defense, Les Aspin, Vice President Al Gore, and his national security adviser, Anthony Lake, to establish a Presidential reform commission on intelligence, the President's first expression of interest in the direction that intelligence should take during his tenure. This was prompted not just by the events in Somalia; the CIA's failure to have forecast the fall of the Soviet Union also produced widespread criticism in Washington. Some critics further excoriated the intelligence agencies for underestimating the nuclear weapons programs in Iraq and North Korea. Others simply argued that with the end of the Cold War, America no longer needed a large intelligence establishment. In addition, its annual budget was an inviting target for budget cutters concerned about the spending deficit.[45] The final straw was the discovery in 1994 of a highly placed Russian mole inside the CIA, Aldrich H. Ames.

Although President Clinton understood that something had to be done, Senator John Warner (R–VA) had in mind something quite different. He envisioned a legislative probe whose main objective would be to reassure the American people that the CIA was an effective organization and should be preserved, not abolished or even substantially downsized. The SSCI, of which Warner was a senior member, accepted his view and pushed for a congressional panel of inquiry, rather than what might have been a more probing executive branch inquiry with Aspin at the helm.

The eventual compromise between the branches was a law passed in 1994 that created a joint Presidential-congressional commission on the roles and capabilities of the U.S. Intelligence Community. It authorized the President to select nine members, which he drew from the President's Foreign Intelligence Advisory Board (including its chair and subsequently the commission's chair, Les Aspin). Congressional leaders from both parties picked the remaining eight members, Senator Warner among them. The commission began its work in March 1995. When Aspin tragically died 3 months later, he was replaced by another former Secretary of Defense, Harold Brown (of the Carter administration).

The report issued by the commission in March 1996 largely met Warner's objective. Instead of recommending major reforms, the blue ribbon panel—the first significant official inquiry into intelligence policy in 20 years—extolled the good work of the secret agencies, kept their budgets intact, offered a few modest suggestions for improvement, and disappeared as a footnote to history.

The commission's boldest initiative was its attempt to help President Clinton's second intelligence chief, John M. Deutch, expand his powers. The panel recommended that the DCI have joint approval—along with the relevant department secretaries—over all intelligence agency directors. The commission further advocated greater DCI authority over community-wide budget decisions. The individual intelligence agencies (and especially the military ones) immediately laid siege to these proposals, however, drawing on the assistance of the Armed Services committees and other powerful allies in the Congress. The reform proposals largely collapsed.

Interest Groups

In 1975, a senior intelligence officer resigned from the CIA to establish the Association of Retired Intelligence Officers (ARIO).[46] Its purpose was to lobby legislators and the American people on behalf of the secret agencies. Other pressure groups came into existence soon thereafter, some for and some against the Intelligence Community. For example, as the Pentagon's budget began to shrink after the collapse of the Soviet Union, industrial manufacturers cast an eye toward the Government's ongoing requirements for espionage hardware—especially expensive satellites—to supplement dwindling contracts for tanks, ships, and aircraft. Members of Congress in districts with weapons plants—and jobs at risk—were solicited by the manufacturers for assistance in procuring intelligence-hardware deals, in the manner they once were used to obtain Department of Defense acquisitions and to forestall base closures. By the Cold War's end, interest-group politics had entered the once relatively insulated domain of intelligence policy.[47]

With respect to the Intelligence Community's own lobbying efforts on Capitol Hill, known in Washington euphemistically as "legislative liaison," in the wake of the investigations of 1975, intelligence managers began to understand a lesson already well learned by the FBI and the Pentagon, namely, the importance of defending (read selling) one's programs on Capitol Hill and beyond. The agency's Office of Congressional Affairs expanded from two staffers in 1974 to more than a dozen in 1994. The CIA's Office of General Counsel soared from 2 in 1974 to 65 in 1994 (although most of these individuals were employed to administer the new accountability rules, and only a few were given lobbying tasks). Forced somewhat out into the open in 1974 by the *New York Times* allegations of improprieties, the CIA and the other secret agencies began to devote additional resources to their public defense, in the manner of most other government bureaucracies.

Scholarly Inquiries

The same forces that led to the creation of an intelligence commission in 1994 stirred various nongovernmental groups to study intelligence reform, including panels at Georgetown University, the Council on Foreign Relations (CFR), and the Twentieth Century Fund. Perhaps the most controversial views expressed by the members of these outside panels came from the project director for the CFR report, who tried to turn back the clock on 20 years of bipartisan intelligence reform.[48] He recommended the restoration of assassination plots; use of the Peace Corps as a cover for CIA officers abroad (which has never been done); permission for intelligence officers to pretend they are American journalists, academics, or clergy traveling overseas; and more aggressive participation in coups d'état against regimes deemed unfriendly to the United States, all of which had been rejected by every major government panel of inquiry from Church, Pike, and Rockefeller through Aspin and Brown.

The Debate Continues

Since the end of the Cold War, intelligence officials have been more forthcoming in their public release of selected documents from the organization's early history, including analytic reports on the USSR in the 1950s, documents on the Cuban missile crisis, and some one million pages of secret records on the agency's probe of possible foreign ties to the assassination of President John F. Kennedy.[49] Moreover, the current DCI, George Tenet, stated in 1998 that "we plan to release well over one million pages of documents this year and more than two million next year. The CIA has done more in recent years to release information than ever before, and certainly far more than any other intelligence service in the world."[50]

However heartening these statistics may appear as an expression of greater openness, they do not mean that the information released by the Intelligence Community has been of high quality or that the quality is likely to improve in the future. More telling than the DCI's reassurances is the CIA's request in 1999 that the Justice Department rescind the authority of the Interagency Security Classification Appeals Panel (ISCAP) to declassify agency documents, a panel that has overruled denials of declassification by the secret agencies in over 50 percent of the cases.[51] A researcher with the National Security Archives concluded that the Clinton administration's release of documents on the CIA's involvement with the Pinochet government in Chile during the 1970s indicates that the agency "has much to offer here, and much to hide. They clearly are continuing to hide this history."[52]

The secret agencies remain a loose association of individual fortresses that seldom give up information about their clandestine activities. This continues to be true, even though every credible study on secrecy in America has concluded that most documents that are classified need not be if the criterion for release is whether the national interests of the United States would be injured. Of course, the Government must keep concealed the names of its agents overseas, its nuclear weapons secrets, and its sensitive methods of intelligence collection; but if we wish to remain a democracy, the Government must also keep the people better informed about the many activities of its intelligence agencies that can be made public, especially events that took place decades ago.

With its subpoena powers, budget review, control of the intelligence purse strings, and a capacity to focus public attention by way of open hearings, the Congress remains the strongest *potential* overseer for intelligence. This potential rests, though, on the question of whether its Members have the will to perform these duties, a mixed record so far. For the most part, intelligence accountability has rested on the shoulders of a few dedicated legislators and their staff aides. This limited scrutiny has led to gaps in legislative coverage of intelligence activities and sometimes an insufficient "critical mass" among legislators to focus the full committee's attention on problems that could benefit from more serious oversight. In 1996—3 years before the scandal over the alleged Chinese spying at Los Alamos—the two congressional intelligence committees were told about the possible theft of nuclear secrets from the lab but reportedly did nothing to strengthen counterintelligence at the site or at the other national laboratories.[53]

Even if the SSCI and HPSCI members spent more time on their oversight duties, they could never hope to monitor, or even understand, all the complexities of U.S. intelligence. Furthermore, the secret agencies will sometimes ignore the oversight guidance provided by Congress, no matter how good the counsel may be. In 1981, for instance, the General Accounting Office (GAO, an investigative arm of Congress) found lax counterintelligence procedures at the Nation's weapons laboratories that allowed foreign visitors too easy access to data on America's nuclear weapons. The GAO recommended appropriate corrective measures. Nine years later its investigators conducted a followup study, only to discover these security problems had grown much worse.[54]

Though certainly imperfect, accountability from Congress and other legitimate entities (like the Intelligence Oversight Board) remains important, if only for the selective examination of programs it provides; for the questioning of intelligence officers on enough things to keep people more honest; for its latent capacity to punish those who do violate their oath of office, if only by embarrassing them in the public light of investigative hearings; and for the guidance that overseers can give to bureaucrats about what the public expects from its intelligence agencies. As former DCI Robert Gates has observed:

> Some awfully crazy schemes might well have been approved had everyone present [in the White House] not known and expected hard questions, debate, and criticism from the Hill. And when, on a few occasions, Congress was kept in the dark, and such schemes did proceed, it was nearly always to the lasting regret of the Presidents involved.[55]

The current DCI concurs. "I dare say the CIA receives more oversight from the Congress than any other agency in the Federal Government," George Tenet stated. "This is not a complaint. In fact, this oversight is our most vital and direct link to the American people—a source of strength that separates us from all other countries of the world."[56]

The success of democracy will continue to depend on these checks, along with an equally indispensable ingredient, the attitudes of people in high office. One of the most thoughtful DCIs, the late William Colby, expressed a sense of optimism about the new era of intelligence accountability that came to pass on his watch:

> With today's supervision, and with the command structure trying to keep things straight, the people in CIA know what they should do and what they should not do—as distinct from the fifties, in which there were no particular rules. If CIA people today are told to violate their limits, or if they are tempted to violate those limits, one of the junior officers will surely raise that question and tell the command structure, and, if not satisfied there, he will tell the Congress, and, if not satisfied there, he will tell the press, and that is the way you control it.[57]

The Iran-contra scandal erupted not long after these words were recorded, reminding the Nation how important a personal commitment to law and integrity is to those who govern.

A cause for celebration in America's experiment with intelligence accountability is the fact that the overwhelming majority of those who serve in the intelligence agencies are men and women of enormous talent and integrity, among the best anywhere in public service or in the private sector. Jefferson's eternal vigilance will remain necessary, though, because inevitably in any organization, a few will lack honor. They will dismiss the rule of law, the philosophy of power sharing, and the principle of accountability.

Scholars and practitioners are likely to carry on the debate about the proper degree of supervision over the hidden side of America's Government. Proponents of meaningful accountability will cite Madison, Jefferson, and Brandeis; opponents, Jefferson again (this time his unchecked use of covert action in simpler days), the *Curtiss-Wright* case, and the Machiavellian perspectives of Admiral John Poindexter's testimony during the Iran-contra hearings. Proponents will warn of Big Brother intrusion at home and against tampering with democratic regimes abroad; opponents will point to the paralysis that accompanies legislative micromanagement, and the foolishness of turning the CIA into a nunnery.

The champions of oversight want reliable safeguards to preserve liberty; its critics seek more effective secret operations to shield the United States from enemies at home and abroad. The rub comes from this obvious conclusion: the Nation wants and deserves both civil liberties and a shield against foreign dangers. So the search continues to find the right formula for power sharing in this most difficult of government domains—knowing full well that no formula exists, only the hope that in a spirit of comity, the Congress, the executive, and the courts will carry on the quest for a modus vivendi that takes into account liberty and security.

Notes

[1] James Madison, "Federalist Paper no. 51," February 8, 1788, reprinted in *The Federalist* (New York: Modern Library, 1937), 337.

[2] Thomas Jefferson, Draft of the Kentucky Resolutions, October 1798, in *Jefferson* (New York: Library of America, 1984), 455.

[3] Richard E. Neustadt, *Presidential Power and the Modern Presidents* (New York: Free Press, 1990), 29, italics in original.

[4] *Myers v. United States*, 272 U.S. 52 293 (1926).

[5] *United States v. Curtiss-Wright Export Corporation* 299 U.S. 304 (1936).

[6] Stephen F. Knott, *Secret and Sanctioned: Covert Operations and the American Presidency* (New York: Oxford University Press, 1996).

[7] Jerrold L. Walden, "The CIA: A Study in the Arrogation of Administrative Powers," *George Washington Law Review* 39 (October 1970), 66–101.

[8] Interview with James R. Schlesinger, Washington, DC, June 16, 1994.

[9] Richard B. Russell Library, Richard B. Russell Oral History no. 86, taped by Hughes Cates, University of Georgia, Athens, February 22, 1977.

[10] U.S. Select Committee to Study Governmental Operations with Respect to Intelligence Activities, "Foreign and Military Intelligence," *Final Report*, S. Rept. 94–755, vol. 1, 94th Congress, 2d session (Washington, DC: U.S. Government Printing Office, May 1976), 157 (hereafter cited as the Church committee).

[11] Ibid., 158; Clifford's testimony to the Church committee, December 4, 1975.

[12] On the Abourezk amendment (named after its sponsor, James Abourezk [D–SD]), see *Congressional Record*, October 2, 1974, 33482.

[13] Loch K. Johnson, *Season of Inquiry* (Lexington: University Press of Kentucky, 1986); Kathryn Olmsted,

Challenging the Secret Government: The Post-Watergate Investigations of the CIA and FBI (Chapel Hill: University of North Carolina Press, 1996); Frank J. Smist, Jr., *Congress Oversees the United States Intelligence Community, 1947–1989* (Knoxville: University of Tennessee Press, 1990).

[14] Sec. 662 of the Foreign Assistance Act of 1994 (22 U.S.C. 2422).

[15] Olmsted; Knott.

[16] Olmsted, 3.

[17] See U.S. Senate Select Committee on Secret Military Assistance to Iran and the Nicaraguan Opposition and U.S. House Select Committee to Investigate Covert Arms Transactions with Iran (the Inouye-Hamilton committees), *Report on the Iran-Contra Affair*, S. Rept. 100–216 and H. Rept. 100–433 (Washington, DC: U.S. Government Printing Office, November 1987), 379.

[18] Loch K. Johnson, "The CIA and the Media," *Intelligence and National Security* 1 (May 1986), 143–169.

[19] Jack Anderson, "How the CIA Snooped inside Russia," *The Washington Post*, December 10, 1973, B17; on the *Glomar Explorer*, see the reports in *The New York Times*, March 20 and 26, 1975.

[20] Frank Church, "An Imperative for the CIA: Professionalism Free of Politics and Partisanship," *Congressional Record*, November 11, 1975, 35786–35788.

[21] Representative Jack Brooks (D–TX), *Impeachment Hearings*, U.S. House Judiciary Committee, 93d Congress, 2d session, 1974, in "Congress: We the People," *Program 20*, WETA television, Washington, DC (1983).

[22] Robert M. Gates, *From the Shadows* (New York: Simon and Schuster, 1996).

[23] See, for example, the citations in Loch K. Johnson, *America's Secret Power—The CIA in a Democratic Society* (New York: Oxford University Press, 1989), 295, n. 63. At a recent conference, former DCI William Webster observed that during his tenure "more leaks came out of the White House than the [congressional] Intelligence Committees"; U.S. Intelligence and the End of the Cold War Conference, Bush School of Government and Public Service, Texas A&M University, College Station, November 20, 1999.

[24] See Frederick M. Kaiser, "Congress and the Intelligence Community: Taking the Road Less Traveled," in *The Post-reform Congress*, ed. Roger H. Davidson (New York: St. Martin's Press, 1992), 279–300. See also in Davidson; Smist; and Walden.

[25] Testimony of Vice Admiral John M. Poindexter, the Inouye-Hamilton committees, *Hearings*, vol. 8, 100th Congress, 1st session (Washington, DC: U.S. Government Printing Office, 1987), 159.

[26] Gates, 61.

[27] Senior official, CIA, letter to [author], September 21, 1991.

[28] Ibid.

[29] Interview with the CIA's deputy director for congressional affairs, Langley, VA, April 1, 1994.

[30] Lloyd Salvetti, director, Center for the Study of Intelligence, remarks to Joint Military Intelligence College Conference, Defense Intelligence Agency, June 18, 1999.

[31] Unsigned editorial, "The Keys to the Spy Kingdom," *The New York Times*, May 19, 1996, E14.

[32] Quoted in David Wise, "The Spies Who Lost $4 Billion," *George*, October 1998, 84. This does not excuse the all-too-frequent incidence of legislative overseers asleep at the wheel from failing to follow through on reports of illegal covert actions during the early stages of the Iran-contra affair to (more recently) a willingness to look away as the Clinton administration planned a paramilitary covert action to assassinate Saddam Hussein in violation of an executive order. The plot was subsequently called off when the operation fell apart in the field. See Walter Pincus, "Saddam Hussein's Death Is a Goal," *The Washington Post*, February 15, 1998, A36.

[33] President Clinton proved unwilling to back Woolsey on the NRO issue. Along with the DCI's growing frustration over seldom seeing the President, this precipitated his resignation. Woolsey no doubt understood the cardinal rule for a DCI's success, as veteran intelligence officer Samuel Halpern defined it: "Unless the DCI is able to walk in to see the President at will, privately, except maybe for the secretary, just these persons—unless that's possible, you don't have a DCI"; interviewed by historian Ralph E. Weber, November 11, 1995, Arlington, VA, and published in Ralph E. Weber, ed., *Spymasters: Ten CIA Officers in Their Own Words* (Wilmington, DE: SR Books, 1999), 129.

[34] Unsigned editorial, "Making the C.I.A. Accountable," *The New York Times*, August 18, 1996, E–14.

[35] Quoted in James Risen, "Energy Secretary Delays Disciplining Staff over Spy Case," *The New York Times*, June 10, 1999, A6.

[36] Arthur S. Hulnick, "Openness: Being Public about Secret Intelligence," *International Journal of Intelligence and Counterintelligence* 12 (Winter 1999/2000), 480. The Commission to Assess the Organization of the Federal Government to Combat the Proliferation of Weapons of Mass Destruction (the Deutch commission, led by former DCI John M. Deutch) had a point, though, in calling on Congress to consolidate the number of legislative committees with oversight and budgetary responsibility for nonproliferation programs, in order to reduce confusion and an unnecessary surcharge on the time and energies of executive officials in their reporting to Congress; *Report* (Washington, DC: U.S. Government Printing Office, July 1999).

[37] Eric Schmitt, "Leading Senators Demand That U.S. Limit Overtures to China," *The New York Times*, March 14, 1999, A6.

[38] Associated Press report, "Energy Officials Admit to Ducking Spy Case Queries," *Athens* (GA) *Daily News*, April 16, 1999, 1B.

[39] Quoted in Stansfield Turner in an op-ed piece, "Purge the C.I.A. of K.G.B. Types," *The New York Times*, October 2, 1991, A19.

[40] Remarks to National Intelligence and Technology Symposium, CIA, Langley, VA, November 6, 1998.

[41] James T. Currie, "Iran-Contra and Congressional Oversight of the CIA," *International Journal of Intelligence and Counterintelligence* 11 (Summer 1998), 203.

[42] Quoted in Eric Schmitt, "Senate Panel and C.I.A. Fight on China Documents, *The New York Times*, June 5, 1998, A12.

[43] Quoted in James Risen, "C.I.A. Admits Slow Move in Security Slip," *The New York Times*, February 3, 2000, A18. Deutch's run-ins with the Operations Directorate [. . .] may have led him to believe its officers might be spying against him, thus causing him to seek refuge in his own home computer rather than the one on his desk at Langley (although access to a home computer would not be much of a technical challenge for DO operatives).

[44] Former President George Bush, letter to [author], January 23, 1994.

[45] See Tim Weiner, "C.I.A. Chief Defends Secrecy, in Spending and Spying, to Senate," *The New York Times*, February 23, 1996, A5.

[46] This group has been renamed the Association of Former Intelligence Officers (AFIO).

[47] See, for example, John Mintz, "Lockheed Martin Works to Save Its Older Spies in the Skies," *The Washington Post*, November 28, 1995, D1.

[48] Richard N. Haass, "Don't Hobble Intelligence Gathering," *The Washington Post*, February 15, 1996, A27. For the broader, less extreme views of the council's report, see Council on Foreign Relations, "Making Intelligence Smarter: The Future of U.S. Intelligence," *Report of an Independent Task Force* (New York: Council on Foreign Relations, 1996).

[49] See John M. Deutch, "C.I.A., Bunker Free, Is Declassifying Secrets," letter to the editor, *The New York Times*, May 3, 1996, A10; John Hollister Hedley, "The CIA's New Openness," *International Journal of Intelligence and Counterintelligence* 7 (Summer 1994), 129–142; and Tim Weiner, "A Blast at Secrecy in Kennedy Killing," *The New York Times*, September 29, 1998, A17.

[50] Letter to the editor, *The New York Times*, July 16, 1998, A18.

[51] Steve Aftergood, Federation of American Scientists, "Bulletins," *Secrecy & Government Bulletin* 79 (June 1999), 2.

[52] Quoted in Karen DeYoung and Vernon Loeb, "Documents Show U.S. Knew Pinochet Planned Crackdown in '73," *The Washington Post*, July 1, 1999, A23.

[53] Daniel Klaidman and Melinda Liu, "Open Secret," *Newsweek*, March 22, 1999, 31. The HPSCI staff director questions, though, whether his committee was "told directly or in such a way as to create a reaction" (personal correspondence with [author], November 29, 1999), the problem again of keeping the oversight panels well and clearly informed.

[54] Jeff Gerth, "Nuclear Lapses Known in '96, Aides Now Say," *The New York Times*, March 17, 1999, A12.

[55] Gates, 559.

[56] Remarks at *Does America Need the CIA?* Conference, Gerald R. Ford Library, November 19, 1997.

[57] William E. Colby, "Gesprach mit William E. Colby," *Der Spiegel*, January 23, 1978, 114 ([author's] translation).

Chapter 7

Sharing Secrets with Lawmakers: Congress as a User of Intelligence

L. Brit Snider

What Intelligence Information Is to Be Provided to the Congress, and Who Decides This?

Both sides seem largely content with current practice regarding the provision of published intelligence. The Hill has access to most finished intelligence published for general circulation but not to finished intelligence tailored to the needs of high-level policymakers or to "raw" unevaluated intelligence, unless a special need exists.

Briefings given in response to congressional requests are more problematic in that they often pose a "sourcing" question: how much information about intelligence sources and methods should be cited to explain the evidence underlying particular analytical judgments? The analysts responsible for preparing the briefings typically resolve this issue themselves, perhaps after consultation with the collection element(s) concerned.

If the information at issue is, in the view of the analysts, of marginal significance to their conclusions, it may be left out of the briefing altogether. If, on the other hand, sensitive source information is deemed so pertinent that it cannot in good conscience be left out of the briefing, the analyst may attempt to brief the information separately to the leadership of the committee concerned or, if the requester is an individual Member, tell him or her that sensitive source information is being omitted from the briefing. The other possibility is that the analyst will leave out of a briefing sensitive source information that is relevant, and no one will be the wiser.

An even more difficult situation arises when an analyst obtains significant but sensitive information that is not included in the finished intelligence that goes to the Hill and is not provided as part of any briefing specifically requested by Congress. An example of this problem was provided by a Central Intelligence Agency (CIA) analyst who several years ago had become aware of reporting that, if true, suggested that another government was attempting to develop weapons of mass destruction that could pose a threat to the United States. The analyst knew that such a report would be a significant concern for particular Members of Congress but was also aware that the report, if provided to those Members, would in all likelihood be leaked to the press.

Source: L. Brit Snider, "Problems and Pitfalls in the Relationship," Part V in *Sharing Secrets with Lawmakers: Congress as a User of Intelligence,* Intelligence Monograph CSI 97–10001 (Washington, DC: Center for the Study of Intelligence, February 1997). Accessed at <http://www.cia.gov/csi/monograph/lawmaker/toc.htm>.

While there was doubt among the analyst's colleagues that the reporting was credible, the analyst was convinced that it was.

The analyst was torn: "Do I take the report to the Congress and watch all hell break loose, or do I keep it to myself and risk being accused down the line of hiding significant information? I just hoped and prayed I wouldn't be caught in a trap." The analyst sought advice from a colleague in Congressional Affairs who could only offer: "Do what you think is right." Fortunately for this analyst, the report was soon included in a briefing requested by one of the intelligence committees, thus taking him off the hook.

But what if the briefing had not occurred? Was the analyst obliged to present such information on his own initiative to the relevant committees? Could he have been held accountable for a failure to do so? Does Congress expect to be advised in such circumstances?

One Member of Congress interviewed for this study said that Congress does expect "sensitive intelligence" to be brought to its attention, but he conceded there were no criteria for identifying "sensitive intelligence" as such. The Member suggested that:

> intelligence agencies need to put themselves in the place of Members and decide what information would constitute a serious matter. It might be something that could necessitate the use of military force or might relate to a terrorist threat. It may not always be something that Congress has to act on, though, and it may not always be bad news.

The Member went on to say that intelligence agencies also should have latitude in deciding who in Congress is told of such information, so long as notice reaches the pertinent Members. "Not everyone in Congress needs to know everything, but the Intelligence Community needs to communicate significant information in some fashion to the people that matter who can ensure it is factored into the decisions being made by the body as a whole."

In 1995, Director of Central Intelligence (DCI) John Deutch issued new guidelines for reporting information to the two intelligence committees. The guidelines were intended principally to ensure that operational information indicating potential oversight concerns reached the committees in a timely manner. Where substantive intelligence is concerned, the guidelines were no more specific than the existing statutory standard. While CIA and the other intelligence agencies that have adopted these guidelines occasionally report significant substantive information pursuant to them, the guidelines themselves do not move this particular train any further down the track.

On What Basis Are Distinctions Made as to Who in Congress Is Entitled to What Kind of Intelligence Support?

While all Members of Congress, by virtue of their elected positions, are entitled to have access to intelligence, clear distinctions have evolved regarding the intelligence support provided to congressional committees and to individual Members. What is the basis for these distinctions?

At one time distinctions evidently were made on the basis of security considerations. Until the two intelligence committees were created, there were no places on Capitol Hill that met the DCI's standards for storing intelligence. Now the Senate has a repository that serves Senate committees as well as individual Members. The House could establish a comparable facility if it chose to do so. In fact, the House Appropriations Committee, House National Security Committee (HNSC), and House International Relations Committee (HIRC) now have small facilities approved for the storage of intelligence.

Another possible basis for the distinctions in intelligence support would be the recipients' institutional "need to know." This might explain the more limited support provided to the Congress's "nonnational security" committees and to individual Members who do not have committee responsibilities in the national security area.

But "need to know" does not account for the difference in support accorded the intelligence committees and the other committees with jurisdiction over national security matters (for instance, the Senate Foreign Relations Committee, Senate Armed Services Committee [SASC], HIRC, and HNSC). The explanation most frequently offered is that the funding and oversight responsibilities of the intelligence committees necessitate a broader level of substantive intelligence support. In order to reach judgments on the funding and effectiveness of intelligence activities, some interviewees asserted, the intelligence committees must be familiar with what has been produced and how. The needs of the other national security committees for substantive intelligence, it is argued, are more limited. They do not need all of the intelligence that is produced—only that which is relevant to their ongoing activities. Moreover, they need to know only what the judgments of the Intelligence Community are, not how the intelligence underlying those judgments was gathered.

Although it is clear that the Intelligence Community has made a serious effort in the last 2 years to improve the intelligence support provided to the other national security committees, the distinctions that remain still rankle. A staffer for one of these committees, for example, said he "resented" the fact that his committee was not given the same information the intelligence committee was given. In particular, he could not understand why his committee could not be provided with information that would help it evaluate the reliability of the evidence underlying the conclusions reached by intelligence analysts: "[We] are the ones who have to act on this stuff, not the intelligence committee."

Agreeing to, Preparing for, and Handling Intelligence Briefings on the Hill

One intelligence official interviewed for this article said that, despite 20 years of experience in briefing the Congress, "everything is ad hoc . . . every situation is a new situation . . . you would think things would be thought through by now, but they haven't been."

Three aspects of the briefing process are discussed below.

1. Agreeing to Provide Briefings. If an intelligence agency is asked by a congressional committee to provide a briefing for its Members in closed session, the agency will usually accommodate the request, assuming that appropriate security measures are in place or can be put in place prior to the briefing.

But what about a request to provide an intelligence briefing under any of the following circumstances:

- in public session
- to a committee whose chairman is obviously seeking the briefing to obtain information for political purposes
- to a committee whose jurisdiction over the subject matter of the briefing is questionable
- to an individual Member who has a track record of unauthorized disclosures of classified information
- limited to either the majority or the minority Members or staff of a committee or the majority or minority Members of the Senate or House
- to an individual Member or group of Members who obviously plan to use the information to support their political agendas
- when the request originates with the incumbent administration, which wants certain committees or individual Members briefed because the intelligence analysis happens to support its position on a particular issue.

Intelligence agencies deal with such requests all the time. How do they respond? The most realistic answer is, "It depends."

For example, although no intelligence agency relishes a briefing in open session, it might agree to provide one, depending on which committee is making the request, what the committee's perceived need is, and whether the subject matter of the briefing can reasonably be discussed in public. Similarly, the idea of providing briefings requested by Members who have handled intelligence irresponsibly in the past may well grate, but most agencies if pressed will provide the briefing, albeit taking more care than usual with what they say.

Intelligence agencies normally will seek to avoid briefing in a partisan setting (that is, one limited to the Members or staff of one political party) or in a setting where it is apparent that their audience plans to make political use of the information provided. Nonetheless, most will if pressed provide the briefing, even at the risk that their information might be disclosed or their analysts drawn into one side of a public debate.

An example of what can happen when intelligence briefings are provided in such circumstances occurred during the 100th Congress, which was considering legislation to ease U.S. export control restrictions. In May 1987, CIA analysts were called upon to brief a variety of congressional committees concerning an alleged sale of "submarine-quieting" technology to the Soviet Union by a Japanese corporation, Toshiba, with the alleged complicity of a state-owned Norwegian firm, Kongsberg Vaapenfabrik, in violation of Western export controls. (The allegations had already been alluded to in public testimony by a Defense Department official and had been briefed to the intelligence committees several months earlier.) On June 30, 1987, largely in response to these intelligence briefings, the Senate passed an amendment to a trade bill prohibiting the United

States from doing business with either of the foreign firms. The same day a group of Republican Congressmen, wielding a sledge hammer, obliterated a Toshiba video cassette recorder on the steps of the Capitol.[1]

Later the same year, when the Japanese and Norwegian governments confirmed that their respective companies were guilty as charged and took punitive and preventive actions against them, the issue for Congress was whether the sanctions imposed earlier by the Senate should be retained in the House version of the bill.

In the meantime, the CIA analysts involved had found indications of additional export control violations by Toshiba. While the Defense and State Departments were unpersuaded by CIA's new information and were opposed to maintaining U.S. sanctions against the companies in the House bill, CIA was asked to give repeated briefings to a small group of Congressmen who continued to favor sanctions against the companies involved. Not surprisingly, the most damning information found its way into the press. The principal CIA briefer was profiled in several major newspapers, occasionally being referred to on a first-name basis by the Members who took political sustenance from his briefings.[2] For many observers, the impression created by the episode was something less than a politically neutral CIA.

Intelligence agencies run a similar risk when they agree to undertake congressional briefings at the request of an incumbent administration if the intelligence happens to support the administration's position. Yet here too, agencies are likely to accommodate the request if they believe a semblance of their independence and objectivity can be maintained.

One CIA analyst interviewed for this [chapter] recalled a request by an administration to brief undecided Members of Congress on a treaty whose implementation required congressional action. Not surprisingly, the intelligence happened to support the administration's position in favor of the treaty. CIA accommodated the request by agreeing to provide briefings to undecided Members. For those interested in receiving the briefing, analysts were sent to hold one-on-one meetings with each such Member.[3] CIA rationalized its action because other Members (on both sides of the aisle) were themselves encouraging their undecided colleagues to obtain the CIA briefing—it was not solely an administration idea—and because the briefers were careful to steer clear of any policy prescription. One of the briefers was nonetheless chagrined when a Member came up to congratulate him in the hallway on getting their side "two more votes" as a result of the briefing initiative.

2. Preparing for Briefings on the Hill. Preparations for congressional briefings also vary widely. Briefings to committees ordinarily receive the most attention. If the briefings involve a controversial topic, briefers are more likely to follow a written text that has been coordinated beforehand within the agency concerned and with relevant players in other agencies. Such briefings are also more apt to be previewed by managers at the agency concerned. Senior analysts are more likely to be tapped to do the briefing or be sent to accompany a more junior briefer.

If the briefing is essentially informational—presenting facts rather than judgments—and does not involve a controversial subject, analysts may brief on the basis of notes that are not coordinated with anyone or simply "wing it" without notes. There is no "dry run" in such instances.

If the briefing is to an individual Member or committee staff, few analysts will go to the trouble of preparing a script. The degree of their preparation will depend upon the controversy attached to the issue and how they perceive the sophistication of their audience with respect to it. Often they will "wing it" based on their knowledge of the issue.

Whether an analyst doing an intelligence briefing is "prepped" on the political "lay of the land" that he or she can expect to encounter will also depend on the controversy attached to the briefing as well as the analyst's own experience and savvy. One congressional staffer interviewed for this study saw such prepping as improper, perhaps leading analysts to alter their conclusions or the manner of their presentation to avoid conflict with Members. Most, however, saw this kind of preparation as essential, especially where the analyst was inexperienced in dealing with Congress. As one former CIA Congressional Affairs official noted:

> Most of [the analysts] see themselves as intellectually pure, immune from politics. Then they are sent to the Hill, many never recognizing what a hornet's nest they are walking into . . . Often they would not recognize where a Member was coming from with his questions, and they would give an answer that totally confused and complicated the process. Sometimes it would take us a month to work out of it.

Whether special attention is given to preparing an intelligence briefing on the Hill will also depend on the analyst's recognition that the briefing is likely to be controversial. Such recognition does not always occur. In 1993, for example, in connection with an intelligence briefing being given to a nonoversight committee on U.S.-Russian cooperation on the space shuttle, a former Congressional Affairs aide related:

> The analyst doing the briefing was unaware that the administration had taken a public position in favor of this cooperative venture where they [the White House] had stated that the Russians had the technology and expertise to make a useful contribution. The analyst's briefing took much the opposite view. When staff from the committee later raised this testimony with the White House, they went through the roof [with us] because they hadn't been told about it. The fact is, the analyst didn't realize he was putting himself at odds with them.

Analysts also do not always appreciate what information has and has not been provided to Congress prior to incorporating it into their briefings. Some might assume that information from "raw" intelligence reports or from specially tailored analysis has been made available to the Hill when, in fact, it has not. In some cases, such information may be at odds with the finished intelligence the Hill has received. Where the information is especially pertinent, it may put the analyst in the position of having to explain why it had not been previously provided. Whether the analyst is made aware of these potential pitfalls seems more a matter of happenstance than systematic planning.

In sum, in most agencies, preparations for briefings on the Hill are left by and large to individual analysts and their immediate superiors. Congressional Affairs staffs will try to ascertain in advance whether the briefings being planned satisfy the requirements of the Hill and whether the presentations are in a form that can be assimilated by a congressional audience. But what the analyst plans to say and how he or she plans to say it are normally left to the analytic office concerned. Whether this office fully appreciates the circumstances surrounding a particular briefing is by no means assured under the current system.

3. *How Analysts Handle Intelligence Briefings on the Hill.* Whether briefing Members of Congress or executive branch officials, intelligence analysts are trained to make factual, objective presentations. They are taught to base their judgments and conclusions on the available evidence. If those judgments and conclusions are premised on certain assumptions, the assumptions are identified. If the evidence needed to reach conclusion is not available, analysts are expected to say so.

By all accounts, the vast amount of intelligence analysis presented to Congress substantially meets these standards. But there have been occasions, in the view of some observers, when it has not.

"Too often," said one executive branch official, "there is a selective presentation of intelligence to the Hill . . . It may not even be witting. Every bit of evidence that analysts can construe as pointing to [a foreign policy calamity in the making] is pointed out, while very little evidence is pointed out leading away from such a conclusion."

As one former executive branch official noted, this often puts the policymaker in an awkward position:

> The Intelligence Community always seems to be saying "the sky is falling, the sky is falling." Whereas policymakers are usually the ones to say "not so fast, let me put this in context for you." Generally they will downplay the significance of the intelligence. This leads to suspicions on the Hill that policy agencies are trying to interpret intelligence for their own political purposes. Intelligence analysts, on the other hand, are given more credibility because they are seen as independent rather than pursuing the administration's policy line.

A former Congressional Affairs officer also noted the tendency of analysts to want to present a lucid picture on the Hill regardless of the quality of the evidence: "Analysts often do not go to the trouble of alerting [Members] to the quality of the information that supports their conclusions. This happens particularly when they have a good story to tell. There is a tendency to want to tell that story rather than present the holes or gaps in it." A congressional staffer put it this way: "Analysts are too focused on what the intelligence says and not what it doesn't say. Rarely will they point out to the committee when their evidence is thin."

"There is also a tendency among intelligence analysts," said another executive branch official, "to reach analytical judgments which are not theirs to make. But because they know that's what the Hill is interested in, they make them anyway." This official cited as an example an intelligence briefing in which an analyst reached a judgment that, if accepted as true, would effectively have prejudged a determination that the President, by law, was supposed to make.

Intelligence analysts are not, to be sure, in the policy business. They support policymakers; they do not make policy, nor do they opine about what policy is or should be. Indeed, it is precisely because they are not in the policy business that their analysis has value.

Members of Congress, however, often do not appreciate the principled position analysts occupy, and they attempt to draw them into policy discussions. This happens most often when the analysis being offered seems to indicate a particular policy choice and a Member wants the analyst to confirm it, or when the analysis offers no clear policy direction and a Member wants to know what conclusion the analyst would draw. Sometimes a Member's question arises so naturally that the analyst does not realize what he or she is being asked to do.

Even if the analyst demurs on the ground that he or she is not "a policy person," a Member will often press on with "well, just give me your personal opinion, then" or, "I know, but you're the expert. I've got 30 minutes to spend on this issue and that's it. So you've just got to help us on this." Or things may turn blatantly political ("So from what you've told us, the President's policy is a lot of baloney. Is that right?"). The analyst may feel his or her only choice at this point is to appear rude ("I can't answer that, sir") or ignorant ("I don't have an opinion, sir"). If the briefing is being held in open session, the pressure to respond to such questions is even greater.

Analysts who succumb to such pressure usually find themselves (and/or their bosses) on the receiving end of an angry telephone call from the policymaker(s) whose territory has been violated. Their relationship with the policymaker (whom they normally support) can be seriously jeopardized as a result.

Analysts may also find that Members who disagree with the policy that their analysis appears to support sometimes try to find fault with the analysis, either by pitting other analysts against them ("Does everyone else at the table agree with what Mr. Smith just said?") or by questioning the weight to be accorded the analysis ("Does this represent only your view, Ms. Jones, or only the view of your office? My understanding is the Secretary of Defense takes a different view").

How analysts handle such questions may be crucial to the success of the briefing. Yet most analysts are unprepared to cope with them. While analysts are accustomed to defending themselves in intellectual combat, most are not used to this kind of questioning. Few have experienced the rough and tumble, and at times downright nastiness, of the political arena.

To remedy this situation, some interviewees suggested that analysts who brief Congress be provided formal training, or at least receive instruction prior to a particular briefing, in the foibles of the political process. But it is not clear how many absolutes there are to imbue. One Congressional Affairs officer, for example, on the question of providing an opinion on a policy issue, said he advises analysts that, if the pressure from Members becomes excruciating enough, "go ahead and answer the man's question . . . we'll worry about it later."

Providing Advance Notice to Policymakers of Intelligence to Be Shared with the Congress

As a practical matter, so much intelligence is now shared with Congress that it is impossible for intelligence agencies to advise pertinent policymakers in the executive branch (primarily at the White House and the State and Defense Departments) of everything being provided. Nor are there any mechanisms for policy agencies to get "back-briefed" on what transpires on the Hill. Communications largely occur by word of mouth. Most policymakers are aware that the Hill has access to most finished intelligence and frequently receives intelligence briefings.

Intelligence agencies say they ordinarily make an effort to provide specific notice to affected policymakers if they anticipate that the intelligence to be shared with the Congress will cause problems for these policymakers. Obviously, unless the analyst or others involved in the process—such as the Congressional Affairs staff—spot a potential problem, notice will not be forthcoming.

At other times, notice is provided but, for a variety of practical reasons, does not "take." To begin with, notice is usually left until the last minute. Players in other agencies are not consulted or notified until the intelligence agency has itself resolved what its analysts will say to the Hill. Phone calls to policymakers are missed. Proposed testimony winds up in the legislative affairs office rather than with the relevant policymaker. Or, if it is sent to the policymaker, he or she is too busy to read it.

Even if the appropriate policymakers do read what intelligence agencies plan to brief to the Hill, they may be too busy to weigh in with comments. Or, if they are uncertain the briefing will produce a "flap," they may simply decide to hope for the best. Some are also concerned that, if they comment on the proposed analysis or attempt to delay it from reaching the Hill, they may be accused of "politicizing" the process, either by the analyst concerned or by the committee or Member who requested the analysis.

The fear of subjecting analysis to political influence also inhibits intelligence analysts from confronting policymakers. While analysts insist that, in giving policymakers advance notice, they do not seek their views or concurrence, they know that policymakers frequently do not see the matter that way. If the policymaker does respond with comments, criticism, or complaints, the analyst may be left in a quandary as to how to deal with the policymaker's views within his or her allotted time frame.

Various bureaucratic means are currently used to cope with the notice problem. The DCI meets regularly with senior White House staff and the heads of policy departments, sometimes using these occasions to alert them to controversies brewing on the Hill. The DCI and heads of intelligence agencies also receive calendars that show upcoming congressional briefings. Weekly teleconferences have been instituted between Congressional Affairs offices in which upcoming briefings are identified and discussed. The principal intelligence offices at State (the Bureau of Intelligence and Research) and Defense (the Defense Intelligence Agency [DIA]) participate in these teleconferences and thus are able to advise policymakers in their respective departments of scheduled hearings and briefings. On occasion, where congressional support for important foreign policy initiatives of the administration may be affected, the

National Security Council (NSC) staff has stepped in and has become the conduit for intelligence going to the Hill on a particular subject.

In the end, however, nothing short of personal contact between the analysts involved and the affected policymakers and/or their staffs is likely to be effective. By all accounts, making this connection remains a significant practical problem.

Perhaps no episode better illustrates the foibles of the congressional process and its potential consequences for analysts and policymakers alike than the briefings in October 1993 regarding a National Intelligence Estimate (NIE) on Haiti. Work began on this estimate in 1992, which turned out to be the last year of the Bush administration. After the U.S. Presidential election in November, the project was expedited to assist the President-elect in dealing with an anticipated exodus of "boat people" from Haiti to the United States. Intelligence personnel briefed officials in both the outgoing and incoming administrations on the draft NIE during the Presidential transition period. The NIE went through the normal staffing process within the Intelligence Community and ultimately was approved by acting DCI William Studeman and National Foreign Intelligence Board (NFIB) principals in early 1993.

By October, the political cauldron was bubbling. The United Nations had imposed an economic embargo on goods going into Haiti in an effort to force the military rulers there to accept the return of President Jean-Bertrand Aristide, who had been ousted in a military coup in 1991. An international flotilla, led by the United States, was assembled to enforce the embargo. In the meantime, the U.S. Government was weighing its options should the embargo fail to bring about Aristide's return. One of these options was the introduction of U.S. military forces into the country. Opposing this idea was the Senate Minority Leader, who introduced a resolution severely limiting the President's authority to send in U.S. military forces. The President, in turn, strongly objected to this proposed limitation on his authority, and negotiations were under way to work out a compromise.

Enter the NIE. In early October, a Republican staffer on the Senate Foreign Relations Committee asked CIA for a briefing on the estimate. The senior analyst responsible for the NIE was sent to do the briefing. No effort was made at this point to advise the NSC or the State Department. The briefing was given to about a half-dozen cleared members of the minority staff, who homed in immediately on issues dealing with Aristide. (It was clear to the analyst concerned that the staff already was aware of, at least in general terms, conclusions reached in the estimate.) At the end of the briefing, according to one participant, the staff said the estimate should be "briefed up to the Member level," but no specific request was made at the time.

A few days later, CIA received another request, this time from the House Permanent Select Committee on Intelligence, to brief on Haiti. The briefing was to include responses to specific questions about Aristide. This request prompted the senior analyst involved to prepare a carefully worded classified statement describing the judgments and the supporting evidence contained in the NIE. The NSC and State Department were not advised of the impending House briefing, however, until the morning of the late October day on which it was to occur.

Earlier that day, unbeknownst to the analysts involved, Senator Jesse Helms, Ranking Minority Member of the Senate Foreign Relations Committee, had asked the White House, in the name of the majority and minority leaders, for a CIA briefing to take place as soon as possible for all Senators on the portions of the NIE pertaining to Aristide. The White House staff agreed to the request and instructed CIA to arrange such a briefing. Because the agency's two senior Latin America analysts were already on the Hill to brief the House intelligence committee early that afternoon, the decision was to send them over to brief Senators after the House briefing had ended.

The briefing to the House committee proved an immediate sensation, provoking many, often hostile, questions. One Congressman reportedly said he intended to take the subject up with the President immediately after the hearing was over.

At the end of this grueling session, the analysts learned that they had to give a repeat performance to the Senate. It was now late afternoon, and they were exhausted, but a commitment had been made by the White House.

When the analysts arrived at the briefing room, they found that the Assistant Secretary of State with responsibility for Haiti was there, along with the Assistant Secretary for Legislative Affairs. When the briefing began, about 15 Senators, including Senator Helms, were present. The senior analyst briefed from the same script that he had used earlier before the House committee. As time wore on, additional Senators entered the room. Each time a new Senator arrived, the analyst would be asked to summarize what he had briefed earlier from the prepared script. According to one observer who was present, this happened four or five times, with the analyst using progressively more succinct "shorthand" to describe the judgments contained in the estimate. "By the end of the briefing," said this observer, "all nuance had disappeared."

The State Department officials in attendance were immediately put on the defensive by the Senators present and were unprepared to offer a convincing rebuttal. Senator Helms announced that the information was "something the American people needed to know about." Eight or nine Senators remained behind at the briefing to question the analysts. One of them put in a call to the White House to tell it that "the administration has a real problem on its hands."

In the weeks that followed, numerous briefings and hearings were held on the NIE. Some of these sessions involved lengthy, painstaking appraisals of the evidence that formed the basis for the estimate's conclusions. Although the President subsequently came forward with a defense of the administration's position concerning Aristide, the wounds left at the White House and at the State Department did not soon heal.

Responding to Complaints and Requests of Executive Branch Officials

Intelligence agencies acknowledge the need to provide a "heads-up" to policymakers with respect to intelligence going to the Hill that is likely to create a problem for them. The purpose of such notice is to ensure that policymakers are not "blindsided" and have adequate time to formulate a rejoinder.

Intelligence agencies are not looking for the policymakers' concurrence or comments on the substance of the briefing. Nevertheless, this is often what they receive, especially if policymakers see their program, policy, proposal, or initiative in danger of going down the drain as a result of the material being provided to Congress. Policymakers may question whether the evidence underlying the analysis is accurate or complete, whether the judgments reached by the analyst are sound, or why this is something Congress needs to know. They sometimes ask if briefing Congress can be delayed until an ongoing initiative with an affected foreign government can be completed or until that government can be officially advised. It is not uncommon for a policymaker to elevate these issues directly to the top of the intelligence agency concerned.

What are the obligations of the Intelligence Community to policymakers in these circumstances? How far can intelligence agencies go in terms of shaping the content and timing of analysis without subjecting themselves (and policymakers) to charges of politicizing intelligence?

Most intelligence agencies say that if a policymaker complains about the accuracy or completeness of intelligence analysis to be briefed to the Hill, the agencies will, in fact, review the preparatory work their analysts have done. As one senior intelligence official noted:

> Policymakers who complain about intelligence going to the Hill are crying wolf most of the time, but about 20 percent of the time they may have a point. Let's face it. Analysis can be shoddy and unprofessional. [Intelligence producers] have an obligation to make sure it's accurate and complete before it leaves here.

This may entail a de novo review of the evidence supporting the analyst's(s') conclusions and/or sending the analyst(s) involved to meet with the complaining policymaker in an effort to discern what the policymaker knows that apparently the analyst(s) do not. If the analysis proves to be inaccurate or incomplete, changes may be factored in. Ultimately, however, what is briefed to the Hill will remain the intelligence agency's call.

If, on the other hand, the policymaker's complaint is that he or she simply disagrees with the analysis or that it will adversely affect an ongoing initiative, intelligence producers typically will provide a polite turndown. "If you tell us it's wrong," said one intelligence official, "we'll fix it. But if you just say you don't like it, it goes."

Intelligence agencies sometimes will honor a request to delay providing intelligence to the Hill, depending on the circumstances. Why has the delay been requested—to avoid a legitimate diplomatic problem or because the policymaker simply wants to put off the inevitable conflict? How urgent are the needs of Congress? To what extent does the intelligence bear upon pending congressional action, as opposed to being sought by a particular Member for a limited political purpose? Intelligence agencies recognize that the longer they delay in responding to congressional requests, the more likely Congress is to perceive their action as politically inspired. As one intelligence official noted, "Information that undermines an administration's policies and initiatives is precisely what Congress most wants to know about. Any effort to delay it is going to [incur] a heavy political cost."

Understandably, many policymakers are not altogether happy with this state of affairs. One who was interviewed for this study said bluntly that:

> the system is broken and no one can fix it—not the DCI, not the White House, and not [the policy departments] . . . What intelligence is briefed to the Hill is decided by analysts . . . Much of what goes up there is irrelevant as far as the Hill is concerned and much of it is crap. But because everyone is worried about politicizing intelligence, nobody will stop it . . . In the end, it is the analysts who are the ones that politicize intelligence by deciding what will be provided and how.

A former policymaker expressed similar frustrations:

> Intelligence agencies work for the President like everybody else in the executive branch. But the intelligence they produce is not seen as subject to his control. Once it is created, a certain imperative attaches to it. No one can stop it, even if it creates political problems for the President and even if its assertions and conclusions are dubious. Anyone who tried to do so would pay a high price in terms of being charged with cooking the books . . . So it goes to the Hill where it's seen as "ground truth." The views of the policymaker, on the other hand, are treated as suspect, tainted by his association with the administration . . . Is this good government? You tell me.

The frustrations felt by these policymakers may well be overblown. Clearly, administration policy is often the beneficiary, rather than a casualty, of intelligence analysis. Nonetheless, policymakers' concerns about how Congress will perceive and use intelligence are not entirely groundless.

How Congress Uses the Intelligence It Receives

Most of the policymakers interviewed for this study faulted Congress for taking intelligence analysis too seriously. They noted that Congress is often unaware of, and does not take the time to understand, the context of the issue being addressed in intelligence briefings. They complain that what Congress often hears—particularly when analysts do not have firm evidence one way or the other—is the worst case scenario and that this, in turn, skews congressional perceptions of the issue being briefed. They also fault Congress for too readily accepting the judgments of intelligence analysts without probing the basis for them, leading to conclusions that the policymaker regards as unjustified by the evidence.

> Most of the Members and staff interviewed for this article acknowledged the need to obtain appropriate "context" in order to evaluate the intelligence they receive and conceded that at times this does not happen.[4] Some noted, however, that the fault often lies with policymakers who refuse to appear at intelligence briefings to provide "the policy side" of an issue. This happens especially when the committee making the request is not the "policymaker's committee"—that is, the committee that exercises principal jurisdiction over the department to which the policymaker belongs.

Some in Congress also fear that, if policy officials are invited to intelligence briefings, the end result is likely to be a "homogenized" presentation rather than a "gloves off" intelligence briefing. Indeed, many intelligence analysts concede that they prefer briefing congressional audiences without policymakers present in order to avoid uncomfortable situations.

Members and staff also acknowledge the frequent failure of Members to probe the judgments offered by intelligence analysts. As one Member put it:

> Many Members take what the Intelligence Community says as gospel when in fact they should look on it as an educated opinion . . . The real problem is, Members don't spend enough time probing what they hear from the Intelligence Community. If they spent more time analyzing what they were hearing, they would know more what needs to be fleshed out in order to make their own judgments.

Intelligence analysts usually cannot be counted upon for such help. They may be unwilling or unable to comment, even if asked, about the political context that surrounds a given issue. As a consequence, Members often do not receive a complete picture from an intelligence briefing.

This situation has implications not only for policymakers but also for Members themselves, especially when it later turns out that the intelligence analysis was wrong or should have been treated more circumspectly. Members who relied on such analysis in deciding how to cast a controversial vote or in formulating a position on a controversial issue may suffer politically as a consequence. They may, in turn, blame the Intelligence Community for producing what they see as shoddy analysis or, worse, for having deliberately misled them.

A graphic illustration of this problem occurred in connection with the Senate vote in December 1990 authorizing the President to send U.S. troops to the Persian Gulf. For weeks preceding this vote, the Senate intelligence committee received almost daily briefings from representatives of the Intelligence Community, given principally by a senior DIA analyst, with other community representatives also involved. These briefings focused on the strength of the Iraqi military forces. Staffers recall the committee being told "the Iraqi military was the most advanced in that part of the world, battle-tested by eight years of war with Iran. . . . The Iraqis would use chemical and biological weapons against the coalition forces . . . In all likelihood, the United States was in for a prolonged conflict of at least six months' duration involving many casualties."

Largely on the basis of these dire predictions, several Senators on the Senate Select Committee on Intelligence (SSCI)—including its chairman, David Boren of Oklahoma—as well as the Senate Armed Services Committee (SASC) chairman, Sam Nunn of Georgia, ultimately voted against the resolution authorizing the President to send troops to the Gulf. Later, when it turned out that coalition forces achieved immediate air superiority and the ground war ended in a matter of days with relatively few American casualties, the Senators who had voted in the negative were understandably upset. Some had lost considerable political support in their home states as a result of their votes. Senator Nunn later said the vote not only had hurt his credibility as chairman of the SASC but also had removed any thoughts he might have had about running for President, knowing that his vote would have been a "major debating point" in any election campaign.[5]

After all, they were Senators supposedly "in the know" and yet appeared to have egregiously misread the situation. Most felt "sandbagged" by the Intelligence Community.

"In the end," said a former committee staffer, "it was apparent the Intelligence Community didn't know squatola about the Iraqi military—what they had, how bad they were, or what they intended to do." A former intelligence official disputed this view and suggested that information may have been held back from the Congress for military operational reasons:

> The Intelligence Community knew how poorly trained the Iraqi forces were. Some of them had been dragged out of dancehalls in Baghdad in their Bermuda shorts. But, for some reason, this wasn't highlighted to the Congress . . . perhaps because they were concerned this information would leak out and it might suggest which Iraqi forces were the softest targets.

"But the real problem for the committee," said a former committee staffer, "was that it was never given 'blue team' information [information on U.S. military capabilities]. It was never advised, for example, that stealth aircraft were to be used. It was never provided an assessment of our forces versus theirs."

Senators could, of course, have done more to seek such information outside the Intelligence Community. As one staffer said, "A lot of relevant information was not provided . . . Not because it wasn't available but because it was not asked for . . . Much of it could have been obtained by any legislative assistant in any Senator's office. But no one asked." Senators might have sought a Pentagon "net assessment" of the military forces involved in the Gulf conflict.[6] Or they might have sought personal assurances from the Secretary of Defense or the Chairman of the Joint Chiefs of Staff. Indeed, several Senators on the SSCI did seek out additional information beyond what they were receiving from the Intelligence Community. At least one of them changed his position from opposition to support for the resolution on the basis of this additional information.

The administration itself might also have done more to get this kind of information into the committee's mix. Indeed, given the closeness of the Senate vote on the resolution authorizing the President to commit U.S. forces, in retrospect it is surprising to some of those interviewed for this study that no such effort was made. Some attribute this to a historical reluctance on the part of the executive to give Congress advance information about U.S. operational plans. But a former intelligence official involved in planning for the operation said a more likely explanation was that "[the] administration was so busy at that point; it paid very little attention to what was being briefed to the intelligence committees. Had they known the impact it was having, they might have done something about it, but this was really not on our screens at this point."

Several of those interviewed had little sympathy for the Members who found themselves in this position. As one noted, "they are big boys now and can look out for themselves." Another pointed out that "Members are never going to get all the information known to the executive on a particular issue . . . If they miss something, they miss something."

When Members are inadequately informed, however, regardless of who is to blame, the repercussions can extend beyond the Members themselves. For those

Senators whose votes against the Persian Gulf resolution were determined by the intelligence briefings they received, the high regard some of them had held for intelligence analysis was seriously shaken. Such feelings can later translate into negative votes where intelligence funding and oversight matters are at issue.

Selective Use of Intelligence for Political Purposes

It will surprise no one that Members and their staffs at times use intelligence, or information derived from intelligence, for political purposes. The same phenomenon is not unknown in the executive branch, but Members of Congress operate for the most part in an open political environment, whereas executive officials usually take things public only after having lost the battle internally.

Neither branch has done much to discourage the practice. Leakers of intelligence are rarely identified and even more rarely punished. As one Congressional staffer noted, "People here have the sense that, since no one enforces the rules, they are not to be taken all that seriously. It's like the tendency people have to speed up on a freeway if they never see a cop. Let me tell you, they aren't writing any tickets on this freeway."

Members of Congress are protected by the "speech and debate" clause of the Constitution, which immunizes them from criminal prosecution for what they say on the floor of either House. Nevertheless, because they are elected officials, they must think twice before saying anything that might jeopardize their standing for the next election or subject them to criticism by their colleagues. For most Members, these are strong inhibiting forces.

In any case, some Members, when they see a chance to score political points, will be tempted to do so, regardless of the source of their information. Members and staff concede as much. While most Members take care to protect the intelligence they are given, some will seek a way to turn it to their political advantage without (in their view) endangering national security. Few will be so bold as to publicly release classified information themselves, but there are many subtle ways to insinuate intelligence information into the political process. In the end, most Members and staff do not see a realistic means of controlling this practice. One staffer regarded it as "an artifact of the system." Another said, "the winds up here will blow where they will . . . Intelligence agencies know it and just have to factor it into their calculations."

Intelligence agencies, interestingly enough, actually give Congress high marks for protecting intelligence information. Apart from a handful of widely reported and somewhat dated examples, no intelligence agency personnel interviewed for this study could point to instances of compromise by Members or their staffs. In any event, no one saw the "leak" problem as sufficiently serious or widespread to warrant executive branch reconsideration of the amount or sensitivity of the intelligence shared with the Hill.

Widespread concern was expressed, however, over the growing number of cases in which Members or their staffs demand that information contained in intelligence briefings or reports be declassified or "sanitized"[7] so that the Member can make public use of it. According to many intelligence officials, the political motivation behind many of these requests is quite transparent. Many in Congress apparently have seized on this technique as a way of making selective use of intelligence in a legal way. Intelligence agencies have attempted to accommodate such requests, which has only encouraged more of them.

Failure of Congress to Assimilate Finished Intelligence

Another apparent problem is the failure of the national security committees of Congress (including the intelligence committees) to avail themselves in a meaningful way of the finished intelligence that is distributed to, or can be requested by, these committees.

Having access to, but not acting upon, information described in finished intelligence can become a source of embarrassment. This happened [. . .] to the SSCI [when] its chairman publicly criticized the Secretary of Defense for failing to respond to finished intelligence reports indicating a security threat to the Khobar Towers complex in Saudi Arabia, only to find that the SSCI had received the same intelligence reports and had done nothing with them prior to the bombing there in June 1996 that killed 19 U.S. airmen. Although the committee correctly noted that security for a military complex was not its responsibility, the fact that it had not previously raised the issue with those who were responsible weakened the impact of its chairman's criticism.

Both branches recognize the problem, but neither has been inclined to do much about it. While the national security committees would like to do a better job of availing themselves of finished intelligence available to them, they are too busy to spend much time worrying about it. Because they are able to request and obtain intelligence briefings whenever they need them, keeping up with developments in finished intelligence does not claim a high priority on their time.

Having computer access to intelligence (now limited to the two intelligence committees) also does not appear likely to solve the problem, at least until more terminals become available and committee staffs become more adept at using them. Intelligence committee staff now must take the time to go to a computer terminal that is located outside the staff's own workspaces (and that may already be in use) and search computer files for what may be relevant. Indeed, one congressional staffer said that computer access actually had made it more difficult for him than having "hard copy" intelligence.

Intelligence agencies, for their part, recognize that very little of the finished intelligence sent to the Hill is actually read. Nonetheless, just the fact that the material is there or can readily be made available offers the agencies some degree of protection. Committees cannot claim they did not know this or were denied access to that. If the committees choose not to avail themselves of the finished intelligence that is offered or provided, from the standpoint of intelligence producers, "It's their problem, not ours."

Notes

[1] The Toshiba episode is the subject of an excellent case study prepared by Anna M. Warrock and Howard Husock, entitled "Taking Toshiba Public" (Cambridge, MA: John F. Kennedy School of Government, Harvard University, 1988).

[2] "CIA Aide Tells of Toshiba Deliveries," *Washington Times*, March 9, 1988, 1.

[3] CIA rejected a suggestion by an administration representative that all undecided Members be bussed to the CIA for the briefing.

[4] One Member did express a preference for receiving intelligence briefings without policy officials attempting to provide "context." This Member also thought Congress needed to hear "the worst case" from intelligence analysts if it is trying to weigh the consequences of a particular course of action.

[5] "Nunn Regrets Vote on Gulf War," *The Washington Post*, December 26, 1996, A12.

[6] One former Senate staffer who did hear the briefings to the Senate Armed Services Committee by U.S. military officials recalled them as "every bit as pessimistic" as those presented to the SSCI.

[7] This is accomplished principally by removing references to intelligence sources and methods and recasting the analysis in more general terms.

Chapter 8

Partisanship and the Decline of Intelligence Oversight

Marvin C. Ott

The September 11, 2001, terrorist assault on the United States highlighted the absolute centrality of intelligence in the Nation's defense. National security specialists have been in general agreement for several years that the greatest postwar security threat would come from terrorist networks utilizing powerful conventional explosives and "weapons of mass destruction" (chemical, biological, and nuclear). General agreement has developed that the first line of defense against such threats lies in the formation of effective relationships with foreign intelligence and domestic counterintelligence agencies.

From this vantage point the airliner assaults on New York City and the Pentagon, and the subsequent postal anthrax attacks, constituted dramatic and costly failures of intelligence. Those failures are highlighted by the fact that the Central Intelligence Agency (CIA) and the broader Intelligence Community had been focused for nearly 3 years on Osama bin Laden's al Qaeda network as their prime terrorist target. As late as March 2001, the Director of Central Intelligence (DCI) George J. Tenet gave the U.S. Senate Intelligence Oversight Committee the following upbeat assessment of the counterterrorism effort:

> Here in open session, let me assure you that the Intelligence Community has designed a robust counter terrorism program that has preempted, disrupted, and defeated international terrorists and their activities. In most instances, we have kept terrorists off-balance, forcing them to worry about their own security and degrading their ability to plan and conduct operations.

With the mass casualty and biological warfare thresholds already crossed, chemical and nuclear terrorist attacks must now be seen as well within the realm of possibility. Under these circumstances, a highly effective Intelligence Community is not merely desirable, it is vital.

Strengthening U.S. intelligence capabilities will involve a panoply of initiatives and upgrades across the whole range of intelligence collection (technical and human), analysis, and operations. This much is widely understood. What is not appreciated is that congressional oversight of intelligence is a key element in the effective functioning

Source: Marvin C. Ott, "Partisanship and the Decline of Intelligence Oversight," *International Journal of Intelligence and Counter Intelligence* 16, no. 1 (Spring 2003). Copyright © 2003 by Frank Cass Publishers, London.

of the Intelligence Community (IC). When oversight has been capable and constructive, it has been a major asset to the IC. When degraded or misused, it has been an albatross around the neck of the intelligence agencies.

In May 2001, a Senate hearing room was the scene of a gala reception commemorating the 25th anniversary of the Senate Select Committee on Intelligence (SSCI). Creation of the SSCI was an event worth remembering because the American system for legislative oversight of intelligence is unique in the world. The quarter-century experience with that system has been eventful, with both impressive achievements and discouraging reversals. But at present, a once robust mechanism is in disarray; "Humpty Dumpty" is badly broken. But lessons can be learned. The obvious question is: Can the pieces be put back together? The answer is not at all obvious. Only through a thorough understanding of the regulatory mechanism can improvements be made.

Intel's Historical High Stakes

Although intelligence may or may not be the world's second oldest profession, it has long been a key instrument of national statecraft and even survival. Americans have tended to view the intelligence profession with some ambivalence—with attitudes ranging from romantic idealization to moral condemnation. For all that, intelligence has played a major role in U.S. security and foreign policy over the last half century. Currently, the United States spends in excess of $30 billion annually supporting an elaborate and far-flung intelligence capability, and that expenditure is on the rise. Throughout the Cold War, both the United States and the Soviet Union regarded intelligence as a key element in determining the outcome of that global struggle. At critical junctures, such as the Cuban Missile Crisis and support of the Afghan mujahidin against the Soviet occupation, the Intelligence Community was a key element in success. On the negative side, the roll call of Presidential administrations that have been burned, sometimes badly, by covert intelligence operations gone awry, is long. Presidents Dwight Eisenhower and the U–2; John F. Kennedy and the Bay of Pigs; and Ronald Reagan and Iran-contra are simply three examples. Every President since Harry S. Truman has faced some major controversy as a direct outgrowth of intelligence activities. In the Bill Clinton administration, the epicenter was China, with a succession of high profile brawls involving satellite sales, political campaign contributions, and alleged nuclear espionage.

In short, for good or ill, intelligence is a high stakes enterprise. This will be increasingly true in the years ahead. For the foreseeable future, the most likely threat to U.S. security will come from international terrorist networks—possibly tied to a "rogue" state like Iraq, or, as President George W. Bush has termed them, the "Axis of Evil," which includes Iran and North Korea. Those threats will, in turn, be imbedded in, and arise from, toxic social, economic, and political circumstances—particularly in parts of the Muslim world—producing a kind of free-floating rage that can be exploited and channeled by terrorist organizers. The burden of defense against such threats falls heavily upon various intelligence agencies working with the Federal Bureau of Investigation (FBI). As the threats become more diversified and sophisticated, the demands on intelligence collection, analysis, and operations grow apace.

The Needs of Democratic Governance

While the assertion that intelligence is important to national security is not novel, how the United States has attempted to reconcile the imperatives of an effective intelligence capability with the quite different and, in some respects, opposite, imperatives of democracy, is very much so. Modern authoritarian regimes from Josef Stalin's Soviet Union to General Augusto Pinochet's Chile to contemporary China and Cuba consider a robust (and generally brutal) intelligence establishment the key instrument of regime survival. The structure, processes, and values that animate a dictatorship, of whatever political coloration, are symbiotically compatible with a strong, intrusive intelligence apparatus.

For political democracies, however, the picture is very different. Democratic government rests on five working requirements: openness and participation, disaggregation of power, rule of law, privacy, and mutual trust. To consider each in turn:

- Democracy assumes an informed electorate capable of rational choices concerning a nation's leadership and broad policy direction. This, in turn, requires a free media, a high degree of transparency in government and decisionmaking, and the free flow of information and ideas. Intelligence operates according to entirely different principles: secrecy, need-to-know, and compartmentation of classified information.

- Democracies are typically suspicious of concentrated power and tend to devolve significant authority downward and outward toward provincial and municipal authorities. But intelligence agencies concentrate and centralize both authority and access to secrets. Such concentration is the natural concomitant to the overriding need to secure sensitive information and systems.

- Democracies are rooted in the rule of law, not personalities, and that law in turn is based on broadly held values in the society. The Justice Department took Microsoft to court under the anti-trust laws in response to a long-held American value judgment that the excessive concentration of corporate power is deleterious to public well being. Intelligence, by contrast, often requires special exemptions under domestic law, and regularly involves violating the law of other countries. In most countries, and at most times, intelligence has been a ruthless business that, in the end, recognizes only the law of success and survival, and one measure of merit: Will it work?

- Although not specifically enshrined in the U.S. Constitution, privacy has, over time, also assumed the status of a basic right. But when an individual becomes an employee of the CIA, he or she largely forfeits such rights vis-à-vis the Intelligence Community. A condition for employment is a "full scope" polygraph, designed to probe and lay bare the most private behavior and attitudes. An agency employee is subject to being repolygraphed at various intervals, and someone who becomes the subject of a security investigation may have his or her bank records and other normally confidential data examined. CIA employees, present and former, are obligated to "clear" writing for publication in advance with the agency to assure that no classified information is being revealed.

- Finally, democracy, at some fundamental level, requires a degree of mutual trust among citizens, and between citizens and the government. Within the intelligence world, the price of security is vigilance, and with vigilance goes an engrained suspicion concerning the motives and activities of coworkers. Had those who worked with Aldrich Ames, Robert Hanssen, or Jonathan Pollard been more distrustful, those agents of foreign powers would presumably have been detected much sooner.

This adds up to a dilemma. Can a democracy maintain an effective, capable intelligence service without doing violence to the norms, processes, and institutions of democracy itself? An affirmative answer is not guaranteed. Arguably, during much of the Cold War, no other nation, not even Great Britain, established effective, independent oversight of its intelligence services. In a parliamentary system, the fusing of legislature and executive creates a fundamental structural impediment to effective legislative oversight of executive intelligence entities. In the United States, however, with its almost unique separation of powers, legislative oversight is, at least in principle, feasible. Feasible does not mean workable. Obvious and difficult questions exist as to whether an institution dedicated to free debate and wide-open public access can ever be a reliable custodian of the Nation's most sensitive secrets. At the same time, congressional oversight is notably and particularly important in the case of intelligence, given its clandestine nature. The press and other watchdog organizations cannot provide the depth of public scrutiny of the Intelligence Community that they can of other Government departments.

The Senate and House intelligence committees, while engaged in the same generic enterprise, have brought their own distinct approaches to aspects of oversight. The focus here will be primarily, though not exclusively, on the Senate experience in the past two decades.[1]

Oversight Background
The history of U.S. intelligence oversight can be conveniently divided into four time periods: 1947–1975, 1976–1980, the 1980s, and the 1990s to the present.[2]

The Early Years: 1947–1975
The origins of congressional oversight of intelligence necessarily coincide with the enactment into law of the National Security Act of 1947. Prior to World War II, the United States had little real national intelligence capability. Instead, the State Department foreign service gathered and assessed information according to the gentlemanly rules prevailing in a world dominated by British and French diplomatic practice. But under the exigencies of World War II, the United States, in the form of a new Office of Strategic Services (OSS), plunged into the cold waters of clandestine intelligence. When it became clear that the world war would be succeeded by a global Cold War, Congress created, among other instrumentalities, the Central Intelligence Agency. This in turn generated a question: how would Congress oversee this new, secret entity?

The initial answer—and one that prevailed for nearly three decades—was to vest oversight authority in subcommittees of the Armed Services Committees of the

House and Senate. In practice, real authority was sharply restricted to the chairman and a handful of key members on each committee. For most of this period, the key figure was the powerful chairman of the Senate Armed Services Committee, Senator Richard B. Russell (D–GA). But as America geared up to prosecute the Cold War, Senator Russell and his colleagues had far bigger fish to fry than intelligence. Because they supported the CIA and trusted its leadership, actual intelligence oversight was minimal at most. Oversight usually took the form of a meeting between senior intelligence officials and Senator Russell and a few colleagues in his office. The main agenda item was the intelligence budget; agreement was typically reached with little difficulty. Often an entire year would pass without a single armed services subcommittee meeting on intelligence matters. In sum, "oversight" hardly existed, and what there was occurred outside the purview of most of the Congress and the public.

These *de minimis* arrangements were due not to any foot dragging on the part of CIA officials regarding consultation or testimony, but rather to aversion on the congressional end. A leading member of the committee, Senator Leverett Saltonstall (R–MA), commented at the time: "It is not a question of reluctance on the part of CIA officials to speak to us. It is a question of our reluctance, if you will, to seek information and knowledge on subjects which I personally, as a member of Congress and as a citizen, would rather not have."[3] It was all very cozy, clubby, informal, and unsystematic. In dominating the process, Senator Russell protected the fledgling intelligence agency from less friendly congressional intrusion. Periodic attempts by the Senate Foreign Relations Committee to assert even partial oversight over CIA activities were rebuffed, as were efforts by Senate Majority Leader Senator Mike Mansfield (D–MT) to establish a freestanding intelligence oversight committee modeled on the Joint Committee on Atomic Energy.

By the early 1970s, however, the era of minimal oversight was coming to an end. Senator Russell died in 1971. In 1973, the press published reports of apparent CIA involvement in a coup overthrowing the democratically elected government of Salvador Allende in Chile. Media coverage of the Vietnam War generated reports of controversial CIA programs in Vietnam and at home. In October 1974, the *New York Times* reported that the CIA and FBI had engaged in illegal intelligence operations against the antiwar movement in the United States. Meanwhile, the cumulative effect of the war and the simultaneous Watergate break-in scandal seriously undercut the traditional congressional deference enjoyed by the President in national security matters—including intelligence. The dikes built by Senator Russell against assertive congressional oversight of intelligence gave way in a flood. In 1974, Congress passed the Hughes-Ryan Amendment to the Foreign Assistance Act, which, for the first time, set a legal requirement that the President formally authorize any covert action. Specifically, the President had to "find" that a covert action was "important to the national security of the United States." The amendment also required that the President report "in a timely fashion, a description and scope of such operation" to the "appropriate Committees of the Congress."[4]

In 1975, Congress created two special investigatory committees, the Church Committee in the Senate and the Pike Committee in the House, with broad authority to examine intelligence activities across the board. In a five-volume public report after extensive hearings, the Church Committee documented a pattern of misconduct by intelligence agencies and called for the creation of a committee for continuing congressional oversight. The Pike Committee reached a similar conclusion, but its formal report was never officially released to the public.

In May 1976, the Senate created its Select Committee on Intelligence (SSCI), and in July of the following year, the House established the House Permanent Select Committee on Intelligence (HPSCI). The modern era of intelligence oversight was born.

Institutionalizing Oversight: 1976–1980

Among their first acts, both committees claimed exclusive jurisdiction within Congress over the Hughes-Ryan legislation. The most sensitive intelligence programs would thus be overseen only by the SSCI and HPSCI.

The concept involved in creating the oversight committees was straightforward enough. For congressional oversight to work, the number of committees and members involved would have to be carefully circumscribed. If every Member of Congress could claim the right of intelligence oversight, secrecy would be impossible. But jurisdiction, that is, "turf," is hard won on Capitol Hill. Even after establishment of the SSCI and HPSCI, six other committees (the Senate Panels on Armed Services, Appropriations, Foreign Relations, and their counterparts in the House) continued to claim varying degrees of intelligence oversight jurisdiction. Only with the passage of the Intelligence Oversight Act of 1980, after months of negotiations with the Carter administration, was the exclusive jurisdiction of the two intelligence committees codified. This legislation, which became Title V of the National Security Act of 1947, established, "consistent with the constitutional responsibilities of the President," specific reporting requirements for the heads of all the intelligence agencies.

Among these were the need to keep the two intelligence committees "fully and currently informed of the intelligence activities of the United States"; to report "significant anticipated intelligence activities" to the committees; to provide prior notice of covert actions, or notice in a "timely fashion" if prior notice was not given; and to report violations of law and "significant intelligence failures," again, in a timely fashion. Finally, the law retained the Hughes-Ryan requirement of Presidential findings for covert action programs.[5] The act also specified that these reporting requirements would be limited to just two committees, the SSCI and the HPSCI.

Equally important, the actual flow of intelligence information assessments, reports, briefings, and testimony rapidly increased in the late 1970s. By 1980, Congress had become a major consumer of intelligence. The oversight committees had established their jurisdiction.

Gradually earning the grudging respect of the Intelligence Community for their custodianship of sensitive intelligence, the committee staffs developed an expertise in a variety of program areas, including counterintelligence, reconnaissance systems, budget, geographic analysis, and covert action.

As a consequence, the Intelligence Community has found itself, rather uncomfortably, somewhere between the executive and legislative branches of the Government, with statutory obligations to both.[6] On numerous occasions CIA officials have responded to congressional demands for intelligence with information and analysis that has undercut prevailing administration policy.

Despite the 1980 act, and an executive order supporting it, the actual ground rules concerning exactly what intelligence would be provided to Congress and under what specific circumstances, evolved through negotiations between the oversight committees and the Intelligence Community. These understandings developed through agreement and practice rather than legislation and regulation. For example, the committees, in principle, claimed an unhindered right to all intelligence information, without exception. In practice, however, the committees generally refrained from seeking certain very sensitive intelligence (for example, the actual identities of recruited agents) as unnecessary to effective oversight. By 1980 these "rules of the road" were largely in place and the process of intelligence oversight had become effectively institutionalized.

The 1980s: The Golden Age

The decade of the 1980s, viewed in retrospect, may fairly be described as the apogee of intelligence oversight, as far as the Senate is concerned. In this period the flow of intelligence information to Congress continued to rise, despite the palpable hostility to the entire oversight process evinced by President Ronald Reagan's first DCI, William J. Casey. By 1988, the CIA was annually conducting some 1,000 briefings for Congress, transmitting over 4,000 documents, and hosting over 100 visits by congressional members and staff at intelligence facilities in the United States and overseas. By mid-decade, a fair degree of mutual trust and respect animated these institutional interactions. Most senior Intelligence Community officials had come to realize that the oversight committees were the best and most effective friends the community had on Capitol Hill. The combination of Senator David L. Boren (D–OK) and William S. Cohen (R–ME) as the SSCI chairman and vice chairman worked easily, mastered the often arcane substance of intelligence, and had no obvious political axes to grind. The professional staff, many of whom had come from positions in the Intelligence Community, was highly competent, often expert, and entirely apolitical.

A highlight of this period was an SSCI report to the Congress on whether the Intelligence Community could adequately verify Russian compliance with the Intermediate Nuclear Forces (INF) Treaty of 1987. The Senate's decision on ratification rested substantially on that question. A young, relatively junior staff member named George Tenet largely wrote the SSCI's highly detailed report to the Senate. Drawing upon the resources of the Intelligence Community, the report was a dispassionate distillation of the community's analytical judgment and technical capabilities.

The newly robust oversight process was severely tested by the Iran-contra affair. The initial phase of the SSCI's probe into possible U.S. support for the Nicaraguan anti-Sandinista contras was largely frustrated by witnesses who refused to appear (for example, Admiral John Poindexter and Colonel Oliver North), and those who dissembled and misled congressional investigators. Professor James Currie, a former SSCI staff member, cites one notable example:

On 28 November 1986, the SSCI sent a letter to President Reagan informing him that the committee would begin an investigation of the Iranian initiative and the diversion of funds. As part of that investigation, Alan Fiers testified under oath on 9 December ... [I]n response to a question from SSCI Minority Staff Director Eric Newsom about the financial condition of the contras, Fiers responded, "We have some general ideas of the amount of funding that they get, and no idea of where it comes from and how they process it." He went on to say that "Insofar as where that money came from, how they got it, and how they accounted for it, we don't have specific intelligence." None of these statements were true.[7]

In time, however, the story broke wide open and Fiers ended up giving lengthy and riveting public testimony in which he detailed the Intelligence Community's role in the affair.

In sum, the system of oversight that had prevailed in the 1980s, though imperfect, was by far the most ambitious and effective ever established in a democratic polity. How did it work? First, through congressional authority. The powers of the oversight committees included the following:

- Legislate on all matters relating to the Intelligence Community, from covert action reporting requirements, to the authorities and responsibilities of the DCI, to the CIA pension fund.
- Authorize the Intelligence Community budget for action by the full Senate after referral to the Senate Armed Services Committee.
- Investigate allegations of criminality, intelligence "failure," and/or waste, fraud, and abuse.
- Monitor CIA and other community operations and programs, including audits of expenditures.
- Determine what intelligence capabilities imply for major decisions and issues facing the Senate—for example, to judge administration claims that specific arms control agreements can be effectively verified or monitored for compliance.
- Confirm (Senate only) the most senior Intelligence Community officials as a precondition to assuming their appointments.[8]
- Receive prior notification of contemplated covert actions after the President has signed a finding but before operations have commenced.
- Access all sensitive Intelligence Community information and programs, including the authority to task Intelligence Community officials to supply such information through printed reports, letters, testimony, and briefings.

If oversight is to function effectively, Congress generally, and the oversight committees specifically, must assume a set of reciprocal obligations. Most basic, Congress must demonstrate that it can and will protect classified information. To this end committee staffs are vetted through a full FBI field investigation. Members of Congress are deemed, by virtue of their election, to have met all the requirements for a security clearance. Sensitive materials are handled by means, and according to standards, that meet or exceed those of the Intelligence Community. The committees work within secure facilities that meet all the technical requirements set by the Intelligence Community.

Every serious assessment during the 1980s of the problem of "leaks" of classified material into the public domain concluded that the sources were predominantly, if not overwhelmingly, in the executive branch—including the Intelligence Community itself, not the oversight committees. During the same period, there were no serious allegations that a foreign intelligence service had penetrated the committee staffs.

The Covert Action Dilemma

Covert action poses a special challenge to oversight. Covert actions involve intelligence programs that go beyond collecting and analyzing intelligence to actually affecting events. By their very nature, they carry with them a much higher political risk, as the Iran-contra relationship demonstrated, than normal intelligence activities. Consequently, the oversight committees have tended to spend a disproportionate amount of time and effort on these programs that, in budgetary terms, are often of minor significance.

The formal procedures of oversight require that covert action programs come to the committees for review after authorization by a Presidential finding. Congress has no authority to veto a covert action, but through the annual authorization bill it may deny funds for its implementation—a power that has been used. A DCI would be very ill advised to proceed with a covert action in the face of clear disapproval from the oversight committees.[9] All members of the oversight committees, plus a restricted number of "compartmented" staff, are normally authorized to attend a covert action hearing, whether on an existing or a newly authorized program. But, if the DCI judges a covert action to be extraordinarily sensitive, he may ask the chairmen of the two committees to restrict attendance to just themselves, their vice chairmen, plus the Senate Majority and Minority Leaders and the House Speaker and Minority Leader—the "Gang of Eight."

This restriction in participation, seldom invoked, has to date not been a source of significant controversy. But the timing of oversight review has. The Intelligence Oversight Act of 1980 and the executive order that preceded it call for a new Presidential finding to be submitted to the oversight committees "in a timely manner." Congress has made it clear on several occasions that it regards "timely" as within 48 hours from the President's signature on the finding. During the prolonged tug-of-war between the branches of Government over Iran-contra, the Reagan White House held fast to its position that the Constitution permitted the President to defer covert action notification to the Congress indefinitely if he felt circumstances so warranted. Congress did not concur with this assertion but was in no position to do anything about it. In the end, the executive and legislative branches agreed to disagree on the matter.

Relative Nonpartisanship

As another basic requirement of effective oversight, the committees must adopt a nonpolitical approach to their responsibilities. For important periods since its inception, the SSCI has been that great rarity—a genuinely nonpartisan Senate committee. The chairman from the majority party and the vice chairman from the minority acted, in effect, as co-chairmen. Behind the committee's sealed doors, out of sight of the press and public, members conducted their business as colleagues, not partisans.

Professional staff was typically selected with no reference to political affiliation. An invisible observer in the committee room during this period, not knowing one Senator from another, would have been unable to tell who was a Republican and who was a Democrat. This was remarkable in a partisan-crazed institution like the Senate.

Having served on the staffs of both the SSCI and the Senate Foreign Relations Committee during this period, I found the contrast between the two committees instructive. Foreign Relations continually operates in the public spotlight. A Member appearing at a committee hearing looks upon an audience that includes a large press table and a phalanx of television cameras. Virtually every word uttered in that environment is chosen for its political effect. But the same Member entering the SSCI hearing room faces no media or audience, except for committee staff and the few Intelligence Community witnesses providing testimony. With no gallery to play to, conversation among panel members assumed the tone of colleagues addressing issues that, for the most part, had few political ramifications.

Finally, the intelligence committees have always had to recruit and retain highly professional, expert, nonpartisan staff. The SSCI staff during the 1980s met these criteria. In many instances, staff members had developed more expertise in key areas (for example, counterintelligence programs) than their Intelligence Community counterparts. SSCI staff frequently had longer experience with a subject area than did the IC personnel, who were routinely subject to fairly frequent transfers to new responsibilities.

A notable example of staff influence involved the SSCI's chief budget officer, Keith Hall, who came to the committee from the Office of Management and Budget with a prior background in Army intelligence. (He later became Director of the National Reconnaissance Office.) On more than one occasion, the committee listened to a DCI formal budget presentation, backed by the assembled expertise of the Intelligence Community, regarding a choice among major, highly technical (and expensive) satellite systems. But, having considered the DCI's recommendation, the SSCI chose instead to adopt an alternative recommendation from Hall and his three- or four-member staff. This reflected nothing more than the Members' extraordinary confidence in the expertise of the committee staff. Senior IC officials did not always like those decisions, but they generally respected the staff judgment that lay behind them.

The quality of the SSCI staff in the 1980s and early 1990s is validated by the remarkable number of very senior Intelligence Community positions that these same individuals came to occupy in the 1990s. A partial list includes:

- Director of Central Intelligence
- CIA Inspector General
- CIA Director of Congressional Affairs
- CIA Deputy Executive Director
- Director, National Reconnaissance Office (NRO)
- Chief of Staff, Office of the DCI (formerly) and CIA Director, Resource Management Directorate of Operations (currently)
- Director, Intelligence Programs, National Security Council

- Deputy Assistant Secretary of Defense (Intelligence)
- Deputy Director, Center for Information Technology Operations
- Inspector General, NRO
- Deputy Staff Director, NRO Commission.

To find a comparable example of the staff of a single congressional committee ascending to so many of the most senior positions of a major executive agency would be very difficult. It certainly has no precedent in the history of the United States or any other intelligence community.

1990s to the Present: A Dark Age

The 1980s represented a signal achievement in creating an effective oversight system, but signs of trouble began to appear not long into the next decade. They were a reminder of just how difficult and tenuous intelligence oversight in a democracy really is.

The first indications that the system was vulnerable occurred in 1991 when Robert Gates was nominated by President George H.W. Bush to succeed William Webster as DCI. Gates was very well known to the SSCI, which would conduct his confirmation hearing. He had been Deputy Director for Intelligence (DDI) and Deputy Director for Central Intelligence (DDCI) under DCI Casey, and was again DDCI under Webster. The Reagan administration's original choice to succeed Casey, Gates' 1987 confirmation hearing became instead a lightning rod for growing Senate concerns and questions regarding the Iran-contra affair—a problem whose contours were then just becoming visible on Capitol Hill. Rather than prolong an increasingly difficult and potentially rancorous hearing process, Gates withdrew his name from consideration. In his place the administration nominated, and the SSCI confirmed, Webster, a former Director of the FBI. Judge Webster had no Iran-contra baggage, and enjoyed a reputation as "Mr. Clean"—a highly valued quality after what many considered the dubious adventurism of the Casey era. Placing a high value on good relations with Congress, Webster was determined to be forthcoming in response to oversight requirements. Because his nearly 4-year tenure as DCI set a new standard in comity between the branches of Government, intelligence oversight had reached its full flowering.

Gates Redux

Robert Gates had been a frequent and effective interlocutor between the Intelligence Community and Congress, appearing regularly as the senior administration witness at budget and other oversight hearings. He demonstrated an impressive mastery of detailed substantive material, allowing him to testify at length on complex programs, with little reliance on notes or support staff in the room. In addition, he conveyed to the committee members an understanding of how Congress works, and a general posture of support for the entire oversight enterprise.

When Gates' nomination was forwarded to the SSCI following Webster's retirement in 1991, there was a general expectation in both the administration and the committee that his hearing would progress fairly rapidly and successfully toward confirmation. Some unfinished business concerning Iran-contra remained but that was taken care of when Alan Fiers gave lengthy public testimony detailing CIA support for the contras. His account, while compelling and detailed, did not tarnish Gates to any significant degree. That left one other matter to be addressed—persistent but unconfirmed allegations that the CIA under Casey and Gates had distorted some key intelligence analysis to fit the prevailing views of the White House. In short, it was said (by whom was not clear) that intelligence had been "politicized."

The charge was serious because it went to the heart of the entire intelligence enterprise. The value of intelligence to senior policymakers and to the Nation rests to a critical degree on the confidence that the process is not corrupt—that intelligence collectors and analysts speak truth to power, however unpalatable it might be at any one time. During the Vietnam War, the Intelligence Community—to its great credit—continued to tell the White House bad news that President Lyndon Johnson did not want to hear.

Intelligence reporting and analysis might or might not be correct, but they must always be honest. If the integrity of the process and product is ever compromised, intelligence will become less than worthless because it will then be unreliable and misleading. Even the suspicion of distortion could be enough to gravely weaken this essential component of national security.

Nevertheless, prior to the Gates nomination, allegations of Casey-era manipulations had received scant attention, in either the oversight committees or the press. Consequently, the committee staff assigned to investigate them began with the assumption that the charges had little substance. That assumption was quickly challenged. As the investigation developed, the SSCI staff came into contact with former CIA analysts who provided detailed support for the allegations. Some of them provided dramatic testimony, first in secret and then in public, before the committee. Indications also increased that numerous veteran, currently serving, analysts shared the concern over politicization but, for understandable reasons, were reluctant to come forward on the public record. But six or seven then-current CIA analysts did come forward at considerable potential risk to their careers.[10] Many analysts recall that work in the DI ground to a near halt in one office after another as analysts gathered around television screens broadcasting the open hearings. Nothing comparable has happened before or since. Suddenly and surprisingly, the nomination appeared to be in serious jeopardy. Under heavy pressure from Gates himself, the Bush White House reacted by informing Republican members of the committee that the President would "go to the mat" for Gates, and wanted his nomination confirmed at all costs.

This was a crucial moment in the history of intelligence oversight because the SSCI's GOP members responded by rallying behind Gates as a matter of political loyalty and obligation. Some committee Democrats responded in kind. For the first time in a decade, the SSCI's proceedings were being heavily influenced by partisan politics. The tendency was strongly accentuated by the committee's decision to conduct largely public hearings on the Gates confirmation.

The proceedings did not become entirely partisan because the chairman, Senator Boren, supported Gates' confirmation. Despite public professions of neutrality,

Boren worked hard behind the scenes on Gates' behalf throughout the hearings. Ultimately, the nomination was saved, due largely to Boren's support and Gates' far-reaching pledges to take congressional views heavily into account during his tenure as DCI. Thus, more than any of his predecessors, he became a creature of the Congress. The *New York Times* noted the irony: "In an administration that has shown its disdain for what it considers Congressional meddling in national security issues, Mr. Gates will be the first director who is directly beholden to Congress. He has vowed to resign rather than jeopardize that relationship should differences emerge between the executive branch and the CIA."[11]

For Gates there was one more irony. George H.W. Bush lost the subsequent (1992) election, and Gates, despite his obvious desire to stay on, was not retained by the new Clinton administration. Gates thus served for only little more than a year in the job that he had won at such heavy cost.

Greater Conflict at Hand

The Gates hearing proved to be not an anomaly but a harbinger. President Bill Clinton tapped R. James Woolsey, a widely respected Washington-based attorney with conservative foreign policy views, as his DCI. Senator Boren's tenure as chairman of the SSCI ended with the 103d Congress in January 1993. Senator Dennis DeConcini (D–AZ) succeeded him for a 2-year term (1993–1994). DeConcini, who lacked Boren's accumulated expertise on intelligence matters, faced one overriding task: to reduce the post-Cold War intelligence budget in rough correspondence with ongoing reductions in the defense budget. From DeConcini's standpoint, the political and bureaucratic pressures on the budget were irresistible. The issue was not whether to cut, but where and by how much. He badly needed a DCI who would work closely with him to make the necessary reductions as thoughtfully as possible.

Instead, Woolsey repeatedly demanded that the Intelligence Community budget be *increased* and fought DeConcini at every turn. Relations between them deteriorated to the point where every matter of committee business became an issue or dispute. Consequently, Woolsey's brief tenure as DCI was, from an oversight perspective, a disaster. Senator DeConcini compounded the difficulties by selecting as SSCI staff director an old friend from Arizona with no background or interest in intelligence. George Tenet, Senator Boren's last staff director, had moved to the National Security Council (NSC) staff. The new staff director made it clear that he had little regard for his job, and conducted himself accordingly.

Nevertheless, some positives can be noted. After a rocky beginning, Senator DeConcini and his vice chairman, Senator John W. Warner (R–VA), developed a solid, cooperative working relationship. Relations between committee staff and the Intelligence Community remained generally positive and professional. This was largely due to the fact that the staff director essentially ceded his responsibilities to his deputy, who performed effectively.[12]

DeConcini's successor as chairman was Senator Arlen Specter (R–PA) for the 2-year term (1995–1996). Specter demonstrated far more interest in his ongoing Presidential candidacy than in trying to strengthen the fabric of intelligence oversight. As a Presidential aspirant, Specter was keenly interested in media/press coverage. Consequently, he initiated what was, by SSCI standards, a large number of public hearings, whereas past practice had been to conduct the vast majority of the committee's business *in camera*. Senator Specter did select a capable and experience staff director, who tried to do what he could but, with an inattentive, publicity-hungry chairman, his effectiveness was limited.

By the time the chairmanship of the committee passed to Senator Richard C. Shelby (R–AL) in January 1997, the committee's oversight capabilities had already been crippled. Most of the professional staff from the Boren era had left and been replaced, not by intelligence professionals, but by individuals selected for their political loyalties. Shelby, who brought to the chairmanship no demonstrated expertise in intelligence, selected a staff director with a narrow technical background and no real understanding of what made oversight work—or fail. Under his management, the replacement of expertise with partisanship on the staff, and with it the "dumbing down" of the committee, proceeded apace. Equally important, a change of climate took hold. In place of an attitude that valued cooperation across political party and institutional divisions, a new "us vs. them" mindset became dominant. For the GOP majority, the committee came to be viewed as a club to wield against the Clinton administration. This change becomes evident when comparing, for example, the SSCI's report on intelligence verification of the INF Treaty in the late 1980s with the committee's report on U.S. vulnerability to ballistic missile attack (regarding possible abrogation of the Anti-Ballistic Missile Treaty) in the late 1990s.

Even more than the congressional norm, the SSCI reflects its chairman. Unlike most other committees, no subcommittee chairmen share the load with the chairman or act as a counterweight to his views. Moreover, the SSCI's rules effectively give the chairman full power over the hiring, firing, and organization of the staff. All staff members are under the control of the staff director selected by the chairman.[13] This means, among other things, that bipartisanship can exist only as a gift from the chairman and the majority.

From the beginning, Senator Shelby treated the SSCI as no different than any other committee, that is, as an instrument of partisan politics.[14] Consequently, under his chairmanship the SSCI became a highly partisan body in its approach to oversight. And Shelby became a frequent presence on television, generally assuming the role of harsh critic of the Clinton administration. Still more important, partisanship took over the committee's internal workings, with staff now formally designated as majority and minority, and members acting in a largely partisan capacity. Comity and even communication between Republican and Democratic staff largely broke down. Whereas in past years, political distinctions within the staff were nonexistent, now they became pervasive. The effect was exacerbated by the obvious personal animus Senator Shelby felt for the current DCI, George Tenet. The origins and motivations for Shelby's attitude are unclear, but the reality is not. By contrast, Representative Porter J. Goss (R–FL) as consistently and publicly affirmed his high regard and support for Tenet. When George W. Bush assumed the Presidency in January 2001, Shelby recommended that Tenet be replaced, whereas Goss endorsed his retention.

Negative Responses to Partisanship

The cumulative effects of these changes in chairmanship were accentuated by changes in the membership of the committee. During the 1990s, the Senate leadership on both sides of the aisle began appointing Senators to the committee for political reasons rather than for reasons of their experience, judgment, or stature in the national security arena. The committee membership of the 1980s included such heavyweights as Democrats Sam Nunn (GA), John Glenn (OH), Lloyd Bentsen (TX), and Ernest F. Hollings (SC), along with Republicans Warren Rudman (NH), William Cohen, and John Warner. In the 1990s, a number of more junior, inexperienced, and often very partisan Senators (several of them having just moved over from the House) became members.

Partisanship is, of course, part of the Senate's very fabric. Nearly all committees function to a greater or lesser degree along partisan lines. Moreover, partisanship can give impetus to effective oversight, forcing the executive to confront issues it would rather avoid. A partisan edge may be required to uncover waste in the Department of Agriculture, or a disregard for congressional intent at the Department of Energy, or instances of taxpayer abuse at the Internal Revenue Service. But intelligence is qualitatively different from most executive functions. The information that is its product and lifeblood is too sensitive, and the potential consequences of failure are too horrific to be treated like data on public housing at the Department of Housing and Urban Development. In short, partisanship and intelligence oversight simply will not mix. Rigorous intellectual integrity is the coin of the intelligence realm. The only intelligence community worth having is one that calls the facts and their implications without heed to the political or related consequences. This standard, though high and hard, is a necessary one.

In addition, the relationship between oversight and the quality of intelligence product is not always simple or even direct. As oversight comes to reflect partisan pressures, specific pieces of high-profile analysis with controversial implications for policy may well become a target. Meanwhile, the vast majority of day-to-day analytical products will be unaffected. But when the process is perceived to be vulnerable to political manipulation in even one or two instances, the entire intelligence oeuvre will rapidly lose credibility. Put bluntly, the moment policymakers (or Senators) conclude that intelligence is being trimmed to fit the policy or political winds, the intelligence agencies might as well be closed down.

Furthermore, in the immediate post–Cold War years, the CIA was a wounded institution. Budget cuts, personnel reductions, a rapid succession of short-tenure DCIs (including a failed nomination), two of its own (Aldrich Ames and Harold Nicholson) revealed as Communist spies—all exacerbated a pervasive sense of disorientation as the overriding anti-Soviet mission evaporated. The agency badly needed the help of congressional oversight committees that were highly professional and at the top of their game. The last thing intelligence professionals needed was overseers levying competing political demands and using the intelligence product in games of political gamesmanship.

The intelligence agencies themselves take it as axiomatic that their budgets, programs, and analysis should not be political issues. So, when one of the oversight committees begins to approach its responsibilities in a partisan manner, demanding this and criticizing that to score political points, the agencies do not know how to respond. When they believe or know that the information they provide will be misused, the volition that oversight ultimately depends upon begins to erode. A perception that the oversight committees are irresponsible will in time inevitably engender a temptation to stonewall, evade, and deceive on the part of intelligence officials. At a minimum, the Intelligence Community stops seeing the committees as partners, but rather as entities to avoid if at all possible. This has already happened.

Implementation of Partisanship

The disquieting transformation of the Senate intelligence committee was put on public display during the 1997 confirmation hearings for Anthony Lake as DCI. Dr. Lake, President Clinton's first National Security Adviser, was nominated by the White House to succeed John Deutch as DCI. The confirmation hearing before the SSCI quickly became a political circus. The vitriolic, partisan exchanges among committee members during the public portion of the hearings were without precedent in its history. Chairman Shelby initially demanded that the raw files compiled during the FBI's background security investigation of Lake be made available to the committee (rather than the FBI-prepared summaries as in the past) and to the entire Republican membership of the Senate. No prior SSCI chairman would have even considered tossing the committee's most sensitive business (not to mention highly personal data on a nominee) into the lap of a party caucus.

The political environment has aggravated certain of the SSCI's long-standing structural liabilities. One often cited by Gates is the inattention and nonparticipation of most members. Senators have multiple committee assignments and, under the best of circumstances, have difficulty giving adequate time and attention to any one of them. In the case of the intelligence committee, the problem is compounded by two factors: the often arcane and technical quality of the subject matter; and the closed nature of the committee proceedings, which means that a Senator sees little or no political payoff for the time and effort expended on the panel. Consequently, only two or three members tend to be present at any given time, even in important hearings. This changes, of course, on those occasions such as the present when the committee holds public hearings.

Another structural problem involves membership turnover. The authors of the statute establishing the SSCI feared that its members would be "captured" by the Intelligence Community, and thereby lose their independence and objectivity. Members were therefore limited to a maximum term of 8 years. The result, as Gates and many others have noted, is that a Senator barely has time to master the substance of intelligence before his or her committee term is up. In the House, the problem is even more acute, with HPSCI members limited to 6 years of service.[15] But House Members have the compensating advantage of far fewer committee assignments. The effect of both turnover and inattention is a reinforcement of the staff's critical role and quality.

An additional development has further eroded the committee's effectiveness. The SSCI's relationship with the Senate Armed Services Committee is unique. As is well known, the authorization bill for the Intelligence Community for security purposes is imbedded within that for the Defense Department. Similarly, the intelligence authorization bill in the Congress is incorporated within the larger defense authorization. So, instead of going directly to the Appropriations Committee, the budget authorization determined by the SSCI goes to the Armed Services Committee. In the Boren era, the chairman of the Armed Services Committee was Sam Nunn. Boren and Nunn had close working and personal relationships, and under Nunn the Armed Services Committee largely kept its hands off the intelligence authorization.

A similar situation existed with the Appropriations Committee where Senator Robert C. Byrd (D–WV) held sway. Close cooperation extended from the chairman to other members of the three committees and to their staffs. For the SSCI, this was crucial because the far more powerful Armed Services and Appropriations committees can, if they choose, effectively override the SSCI and dictate outcomes. The essential cooperation and camaraderie that characterized relations among the three committees during the Boren-Cohen era continued largely intact under DeConcini, but began to break down under Specter, and largely disappeared under Shelby. The growth of partisanship diminished the SSCI's reputation and standing within the Senate as a whole. As a consequence, the intelligence agencies know they are dealing not only with a far more partisan SSCI, but a far weaker one as well.

The symptoms of the SSCI's deterioration are not hard to detect. One involves an increasing trend toward legislative micromanagement. In recent years, a number of SSCI-mandated Congressionally Directed Actions (CDAs), requiring a variety of often-detailed administrative initiatives, has grown steadily. Along with the CDAs has come a lengthening list of obligatory reports, many of them required annually, about intelligence programs. A debatable but fair generalization is that the quality of interaction between an oversight committee and an executive agency is in inverse proportion to the number of required CDAs and reports. The inevitable consequence is the dwindling respect for the committee and its staff within the Intelligence Community.

Hopeful Signs

Ironically, the extent to which oversight still works with regard to the Senate occurs because so many of the senior officials of the Intelligence Community come from the SSCI. To a person, they believe in the importance of congressional oversight, and have continued to act on that belief even as the Senate committee lost viability. DCI Tenet continues his effort to make oversight work. But this is obviously a very short-term situation. As new incumbents without a Capitol Hill background assume relevant senior posts on the panel, the current anomalous community-led oversight will certainly fade.

Any overall judgment on the current state of oversight should note that the HPSCI—which has had a history of being more partisan and considerably less effective than the SSCI—has performed very creditably in the last 5 years under the chairmanship of Congressman Goss. It is surely no coincidence that Goss is a former CIA career intelligence officer.

In June 2001, the SSCI, like the rest of the Senate, underwent a sudden power shift, passing unexpectedly from Republican to Democratic control. Senator Bob

Graham (D–FL) became the new chairman. It is too early to judge whether he will have any lasting success in arresting the committee's downward trajectory. He has not attempted the key task of replacing the political spear-carriers on the committee staff with professionals actually knowledgeable about intelligence and dedicated to expert, nonpartisan oversight. The reason is surely pragmatic—to do so would precipitate a major battle within the committee. Forcing a changeover in key staff assignments would be a pyrrhic victory, given the likely political costs and the short time remaining on his chairmanship.

Congressional Collaboration

The SSCI, working jointly with the HPSCI, has taken one important initiative with potentially enduring consequences. In February 2002, the two oversight committees announced a joint inquiry into the September 11, 2001, attacks and possible attendant intelligence failures. To carry out the inquiry, the committees established a single investigational staff, to be organized and run by a director, and supporting both oversight committees separate from their existing staffs. The director was to be selected by the leadership of the two committees, but would in turn have full authority to select the staff of the inquiry. According to the Senate Historian's Office, the creation of such a unified (vice joint) investigation serving both House and Senate is apparently unique in congressional history. The selection of a director was both critical—and difficult. Ultimately the choice was L. Britt Snider, until recently the CIA's Inspector General, and before that the SSCI's General Counsel. Snider, in turn, quickly assembled a staff of experienced professionals with impressive credentials.

In announcing the launching of the joint investigation, both Senator Graham and Representative Goss struck a note of objectivity and bipartisanship. Graham stated: "I have no interest in simply looking in the rear view mirror and playing the 'blame game' about what went wrong from an intelligence perspective. Rather, I wish to identify any systemic shortcomings in our intelligence community and fix these problems as soon as possible." Snider set a firm target date for completion of the inquiry and the release of a report of findings by the end of the calendar year 2002. That would be a Herculean undertaking, given the vast quantities of material to be reviewed, including 400,000 FBI documents alone.

The potential importance of the report can hardly be exaggerated. It could provide a critical part of the historical record of the September 11 attacks. In that sense, its only counterpart would be the inquiry following Pearl Harbor. Still more important, an understanding of intelligence failures and vulnerabilities could be critical in preventing future attacks of this or greater magnitude.

The Intelligence Community evidently took the inquiry very seriously, and viewed it with considerable trepidation. At the same time, full community cooperation was and is the sine qua non for a successful outcome. From all evidence, that cooperation was forthcoming—perhaps, in large part, because senior IC officials trusted Snider, whose reputation for professionalism and integrity was unassailable. But, suddenly, on April 26, 2002, Snider resigned without comment. Committee sources would say only that there had been an issue over a "personnel" decision involving the investigative staff. The circumstantial evidence strongly suggested that Snider and the staff were subjected to the same partisan political pressures that have so damaged Senate oversight in recent years.

Subsequently, however, James Risen of the *New York Times* reported that:

> the leaders of the joint House-Senate panel forced . . . Snider . . . to resign after they learned that he had hired a CIA officer who was the subject of a counterintelligence investigation. CIA officials had told Mr. Snider that the employee was under scrutiny because of problems that had surfaced in a polygraph examination. . . . Mr. Snider did not immediately inform the committee leadership when he learned of the inquiry, and crucial lawmakers were angered after they somehow found out on their own.[16]

Risen also reported that Snider's close association with DCI Tenet, begun when they worked together on the SSCI staff a decade ago, had raised some doubts among critics about his ability to "aggressively investigate the agency's performance in the months leading up to the attacks."[17] Senator Graham nevertheless praised Snider for assembling a professional staff and playing a very significant role in the panel's progress.[18]

Risen concluded, "Some members want a look back that assigns blame for the intelligence failure culminating on September 11. Others want to look forward and propose reforms in the government's counterterrorism operations." Senator Graham and Congressman Goss, he writes, "generally seem inclined to make the panel forward-looking. But Senator Shelby has made it clear that he believes Mr. Tenet's tenure at the CIA should be scrutinized to determine if he should be held accountable for the intelligence failure before September 11."[19]

Subsequently Senator Graham clearly viewed the inquiry and its report as the legacy of his chairmanship. It might have been even more. A credible, nonpolitical, and persuasive report could constitute a critical first step toward rebuilding effective oversight. But stripped of the credibility provided by Snider's involvement, the odds against its success lengthened markedly. A high-profile debacle was narrowly averted largely due to two developments. First, Snider personally persuaded the remaining joint inquiry staff not to resign in an act of sympathetic protest, and Senator Graham and Representative Goss found an able replacement in the person of Eleanor Hill, whose background and personality were remarkably similar to Snider's. A former Inspector General of the Department of Defense with substantial prior experience on Capitol Hill, most notably as Chief Counsel to the Senate Governmental Affairs Subcommittee on Investigations (a post once held by Robert Kennedy), she succeeded in maintaining the momentum of the ongoing staff work, and handled the pressures of the subsequent public hearings with a steady professionalism.

Another issue arising out of the September 11 investigation dramatically highlighted the problematic complexity of relations between the oversight committees and the executive branch. On June 19, 2002, the Cable News Network reported the content of highly classified testimony by the director of the National Security Agency before the two committees. This produced an angry reaction from the White House. The circumstances of the leak strongly suggested its emanation from the SSCI. A chagrined committee leadership immediately called for an FBI investigation of members and staff to affix blame. This was a critical moment in the history of oversight. Citing Constitutional separation of powers, the oversight committees had in the past effectively declared themselves off limits to FBI security investigations.[20] Staff members are vetted through routine FBI field investigations prior to hiring, but they are not subjected to a polygraph as are employees of the CIA and other executive intelligence agencies. But, given the explosive environment in this most recent case, the FBI was invited to question members and staff. Several members found this development highly unsettling—particularly since it came at a time when the committees (through the joint inquiry) were investigating the FBI's performance prior to September 11.

The FBI interviewed all 37 members of the House and Senate oversight committees and some 60 staff members. As the next step, the FBI asked 17 Senators to turn over their phone records, appointment calendars, and schedules that would reveal contact with the media.[21] Senator Graham announced that he would comply, but it remains unclear to what extent other Senators did so. FBI interviewers also asked their subjects if they would submit to a polygraph. If implemented, an FBI polygraph of congressional members and staff would represent a complete breach of a historic firewall.

Those familiar with the FBI know that the bureau dislikes investigations of leaks because they so seldom produce a conclusive outcome. This investigation was no exception. Although still nominally ongoing by late 2002, the FBI had not tried to actually conduct any polygraph examinations, and the firewall remained partly, but not wholly, breached.

Restoring an Institutional Asset

In sum, the U.S. system of intelligence oversight by Congress has proven to be a viable solution to a tricky problem. But the system requires a very special set of conditions to work. These include, on the IC side, a recognition that oversight is not only a legal requirement, but if done properly, an essential institutional asset. The Intelligence Community must be ready and willing to support, not resist, oversight. On the congressional side, the list of requirements is longer: nonpartisanship; an expert professional staff; a competent, experienced staff director; a chairman (hopefully supported by other members of the committee) who has mastered the substance of major issues and programs; and a good working relationship among the oversight, Armed Services, and Appropriations committees.

Clearly, under present circumstances, Senate-conducted intelligence oversight no longer measures up to these threshold requirements. Whether it can be restored to viability, or whether the damage is irreparable, remains open to question.

Notes

[1] The author's personal experience primarily involved the Senate where he was a professional staff member (1984–1992) and deputy (Minority) staff director. He was hired by a Republican chairman, and, for most of his tenure with the committee, was the "designee" of another Republican. However, neither Senator (nor the committee staff director) inquired concerning the author's political views or affiliation—which is as it should be in a nonpartisan environment.

[2] L. Britt Snider developed this organization of the historical record in his monograph, *Sharing Secrets with Lawmakers: Congress as a User of Intelligence* (Washington, DC: Center for the Study of Intelligence, February 1997).

[3] Ibid., 2.

[4] Section 662 of the Foreign Assistance Act (22 U.S.C. 2422).

[5] S. Res. 400, Sec 11. Text in "Legislative Oversight of Intelligence Activities: The U.S. Experience" report, prepared by the Select Committee on Intelligence, October 1994, 35.

[6] The *Intelligence Community* is a collective noun referring to the various executive branch intelligence agencies of the U.S. Government. S. Res. 400 gives the SSCI oversight and authorization jurisdiction over the following: "(A) The Central Intelligence Agency and Director of Central Intelligence. (B) The Defense Intelligence Agency. (C) The National Security Agency. (D) The intelligence activities of other agencies and subdivisions of the Department of Defense. (E) The intelligence activities of the Department of State. (F) The intelligence activities of the Federal Bureau of Investigation (G) Any department, agency, or subdivision which is the successor to any agency named in clause (A), (B), or (C)."

[7] James T. Currie, "Iran-Contra and Congressional Oversight of the CIA," *International Journal of Intelligence and Counter Intelligence* 11, no. 2 (Summer 1998), 198

[8] DCI, DDCI, General Counsel, Inspector General, Deputy Director for Community Management.

[9] If a new covert action is funded by a reserve release (as many are initially), the committees are technically "notified" of the release. While the administration typically does not use the reserve until the committees (including Appropriations) have cleared off, the law permits it to do so. A continuing covert action program, though, has to be funded in the annual authorization, and here the committees have denied funding on occasion.

[10] The SSCI in the person of Chairman Boren extracted a specific pledge from Robert Gates that as DCI he would not take adverse action against these analysts because of their testimony. During Gates' subsequent brief tenure as DCI the pledge was, to my knowledge, honored.

[11] Elaine Sciolino, "Senate Approves Gates by 64–31, to Head the C.I.A.," *The New York Times*, November 6, 1991, A23.

[12] For example, two high profile issues that had real potential for partisan exploitation—the Aldrich Ames spy case and controversial expenditures by the NRO on its new headquarters complex—were both handled in a professional and essentially nonpartisan fashion by the SSCI.

[13] The committee, virtually since its inception, has operated under an informal "designee" system whereby members of the committee can select a staff member who will serve as their particular resource on the committee. These designees can be political or professional depending on the requirements or nonrequirements established by the chairman.

[14] For a very different assessment of Senator Shelby's tenure, see Gregory C. McCarthy, "GOP Oversight of Intelligence in the Clinton Era," *International Journal of Intelligence and Counter Intelligence* 15, no. 1 (Spring 2002), 26–51.

[15] The term *limitation* has usually, but not always, been rigidly applied. Senator Specter successfully persuaded the Republican Leader, Senator Robert Dole (R–KS), to allow him leave the committee for 2 years to stop the clock on his tenure—and to enable him to rejoin the committee and assume the chairmanship for his remaining 2 years. Senator Mike DeWine (R–OH) has negotiated an analogous arrangement. Senator Graham was granted an extra 2 years by the Democratic leader, Senator Thomas Daschle (D–SD), to allow him to assume the chairmanship when Senator Charles Robb (D–VA), who had been next in line, was defeated for reelection.

[16] James Risen, "Reason Cited for Ousting of Terror Inquiry's Director: Staff Member's Security Problem Is Blamed," *The New York Times*, May 9, 2002, A34.

[17] Ibid.

[18] Ibid.

[19] Ibid.

[20] There is general agreement among legal experts that in the event of a criminal investigation, congressional claims based on the separation of powers would have to give way.

[21] Dana Priest, "Probe of Hill Leaks On 9/11 Is Intensified," *The Washington Post*, August 24, 2002, 1.

Chapter 9

The Role of the Federal Bureau of Investigation in National Security

Harvey Rishikof

The safest place in the world for a terrorist to be is inside the United States. . . . As long as [terrorists] don't do something that trips them up against our laws, they can do pretty much all they want.

—Brent Scowcroft, former National Security Adviser[1]

The question is whether the [Bush] administration is prepared to do the kind of head-banging that's needed to force everyone to work together and the jury is still out on that. So far, I'd give the changes a pretty low grade.

—David Benjamin, Former Staff, National Security Council on Terrorism[2]

We are at a crossroads on the role of law enforcement in national security. Before the events of September 11, 2001, the United States had established a legal and policy framework that clearly distinguished between criminal law enforcement and national security. This paradigm was established to keep in check the broad investigative powers of the Federal Bureau of Investigation (FBI) and the roles and missions of the Intelligence Community (IC). Since 1946, the law enforcement and intelligence agencies have enjoyed periods of cooperative and intensely competitive coordination within this policy structure.[3]

Yet the increase of transnational crimes—narcotics, terrorism, money laundering, economic espionage, and the trafficking of weapons of mass destruction—created challenges to the old paradigm that September 11 shattered.[4] The placing of Osama bin Laden on the FBI 10 Most Wanted List radically changed how the U.S. Government perceived law enforcement and terrorism. If bin Laden were apprehended, is he to be read his Miranda rights before being taken into custody, as stipulated by U.S. law?[5] Prior to this law enforcement strategy, a cruise missile had been launched in August 1998 to kill bin Laden for his participation in the bombing of the U.S. Embassies in Kenya and Tanzania. Was the United States at war with al Qaeda, or was al Qaeda a group similar to an organized crime family? Different rules applied depending on how this question was answered.

This chapter assesses the recent criticisms that have been made about the FBI in the national security arena, discusses recent organizational changes that have been made in the Intelligence Community with reference to the FBI, and evaluates continuing reform proposals. The chapter is not an exhaustive analysis of the current state of the FBI but more a discursive discussion of some of the main themes that have dominated the debate over the role of the FBI in national security.

After 1946, two critical documents shaped the FBI mission and roles in the area of national security: the Foreign Intelligence Surveillance Act (FISA) of 1978 and Executive Order 12333 (1981). In the wake of September 11, Congress enacted the Uniting and Strengthening America by Providing Appropriate Tools Required to Intercept and Obstruct Terror[6] (known as the USA PATRIOT Act), which fundamentally changed the FISA–Executive Order 12333 paradigm. In addition, a recent reinterpretation of the FISA by the FISA Appellate Court recrafted the historic separation of criminal and intelligence matters.

The classic reasons usually proffered for FBI weakness in national security are that the bureau is primarily and culturally focused on "making cases" for "criminal investigation" and would not share its information in an effort to maintain the integrity of the criminal prosecution, for "evidentiary" and "chain of custody reasons." The second major criticism has focused on the timidity and reluctance of the bureau to pursue investigations in the counterterrorism, counterintelligence, and national security arenas aggressively to avoid repeating the years of abuse chronicled by the Church and Pike Committees.[7] The third and related criticism of the FBI is the lack of a talented, effectively trained special agent cadre supported by a modern computerized recordkeeping process to analyze and disseminate information in a coherent and timely manner. In short, the FBI "does not know what it knows," and, when it knows it, does not perform effectively. The result is that the FBI remains a reactive institution that investigates crimes after the fact and does not prevent crimes or international incidents from happening.

Among the major organizational and programmatic solutions to these criticisms have been:

- the creation of the Department of Homeland Security (DHS) and the transfer of former FBI functions, such as the National Infrastructure Protections Center (computer security), to Homeland Security
- the reorganization of the FBI by Director Robert Mueller in 2002–2003 with renewed emphasis on a network of "FBI-local police" Joint Terrorism Task Forces
- the creation of joint intelligence–law enforcement task force organizations, such as the Terrorist Threat Integration Center (TTIC) at the Central Intelligence Agency (CIA)
- the new National Intelligence Plan by the Department of Justice to tie

together local and state law enforcement agencies for terrorist-related information gathering.[8]

In addition to these reorganization reforms, two more radical changes are being
hotly debated:

- the creation of a new domestic intelligence organization to pursue national
  security issues effectively along the lines of the British Security Service
- the creation of a czar, or director, for all intelligence issues for all IC members
  from domestic law enforcement to military intelligence.

The Recent Past: A Culture of Criminal Investigation

The classic view of the FBI is that of a law-enforcement agency designed to investigate crimes and gather evidence for criminal trial prosecutions.[9] Prevention has
never been a priority, nor has national security been the fast track for career advancement at the FBI. Although there have been periodic and celebrated national security
cases, this was not the rationale of the FBI organizational structure.

A series of FBI cases—including the FBI laboratory investigation; the shoot-
ings at Ruby Ridge, Idaho; the Waco, Texas, standoff; the Atlanta Centennial Olympic
Park bombing and the false accusation of Richard Jewell; the mishandled espionage
investigation of Wen Ho Lee; and the Robert Hanssen espionage conviction—have
created a negative image of the bureau as an effective counterintelligence agency. Successes such as the investigation and capture of double-agent Aldrich Ames at the CIA,
or the arrest and prosecution of Katrina Leung, an FBI source and Chinese double
agent, have not done enough to counter the general sense that the FBI is not up to
the task. The FBI has continued to be viewed as an organization where the dominant
culture is that of an elite national police force that does not share its information or
expertise easily with local law enforcement and other agencies. Agents continue to be
drawn primarily from police backgrounds, with little representation from outside intellectual disciplines. Outsiders have usually been restricted to the director's or deputy
director's staffs, and only very recently have significant numbers of assistant directors
been chosen from outside FBI ranks.

The most recent report criticizing the FBI for a general failure in its handling of
information concerning September 11 has been issued by the congressional committees charged with monitoring intelligence.[10] As part of the systematic findings section,
the report stresses the "serious gaps" for intelligence collection coverage between U.S.
foreign and domestic intelligence organizations: "Prior to September 11, the Intelligence Community was neither well organized nor equipped, and did not adequately
adapt, to meet the challenge posed by global terrorists focused on targets within the
domestic United States."[11] The familiar historic criticisms and errors are reiterated in
the report:

> no comprehensive strategies; declines in funding; outdated technology and insuf-
> ficient technical systems with no centralized databases; inexperienced, unquali-
> fied, under-trained analysts; lack of foreign language trained translators; poor

information sharing; and mixed results on reaching out to foreign intelligence and law enforcement services.[12]

Interestingly, the intelligence committees involved in the oversight also must bear part of the responsibility, since many of these problems have been long-term and well known.

The report further documents, specifically for September 11, how FBI Head-quarters (FBIHQ) and the field offices miscommunicated, mishandled information, disagreed upon legal standards, and did not use existing financial investigative author-ities to track potential terrorists. Of course, many links in the "wilderness of mirrors" of intelligence become clear in retrospect as "refracted intelligence" leads to the events one wants to explain. When one looks back after an event, a clear line of intelligence to the eventual event usually can be found. The "if only" or the "could have, would have, should have" line of argument creates a sad commentary on hardworking profession-als struggling to find the right answers. But in real time, straining the relevant data from the stream of information is like trying to get a drink from a fire hose.

The Rowley Critique

To understand these difficulties, it is instructive to analyze one agent's view of the September 11 events from a street-level perspective. Such a deconstruction high-lights the difficulties in solving the intelligence puzzle. Special Agent Coleen Rowley's letter from the Minneapolis Field Office to Director Robert Mueller in February 2003, which cataloged a series of concerns about how the FBI war on terrorism and the pending war with Iraq were affecting the bureau's credibility, encapsulated many of the popular concerns that the general public held about the FBI.[13]

In her letter, Rowley specifically raised parallels between the Waco, Texas, in-cident and her concerns over fighting al Qaeda domestically and any future war in Iraq. She raised questions over how information may be used to shape policy and take action. Rowley believed that the FBI's domestic experiences could be used to shape foreign policy integration for Director Mueller. Whether her analogy was persuasive is open to debate, but what is significant is how a line agent had begun to view the role of force and policy being merged in the domestic and international arenas:

> I believe the FBI, by drawing on the perspective gained from its recent history, can make a unique contribution to the discussion on Iraq. The misadventure in Waco took place well before your time as Director, but you will probably recall that David Koresh exerted the same kind of oppressive control over members of his Branch Davidian followers as Saddam Hussein does over the Iraqis. The parallel does not stop there.

> Law enforcement authorities were certain Koresh had accumulated a formidable arsenal of weapons and ammunition at his compound and may have been plan-ning on using them someday. The FBI also had evidence that he was sexually abusing young girls in the cult. After the first law enforcement assault failed, after losing the element of surprise, the Branch Davidian compound was contained and steadily increasing pressure was applied for weeks. But then the FBI decided

it could wait no longer and mounted the second assault—with disastrous consequences. The children we sought to liberate all died when Koresh and his followers set fires leading to their mass death and destruction.

The FBI, of course, cannot be blamed for what Koresh set in motion. Nevertheless, we learned some lessons from this unfortunate episode and quickly explored better ways to deal with such challenges. As a direct result of that exploration, many subsequent criminal/terrorist "standoffs" in which the FBI has been involved have been resolved peacefully and effectively. I would suggest that present circumstances vis-à-vis Iraq are very analogous, and that you consider sharing with senior administration officials the important lessons learned by the FBI at Waco.[14]

The body of the letter was an analysis of how the recent events in Iraq and the investigation of terrorism domestically were damaging the FBI mission. First, Rowley challenged the FBI as being the source for the public statement that there are 5,000 al Qaeda terrorists already in the United States. Was this figure based on any hard data or an estimate based largely on speculation? For Rowley, this figure would only feed the suspicion, inside the organization and out, that the number was largely the product of a desire to gain favor with the administration, to gain support for FBI initiatives, and possibly even to gain support for administration initiatives.

Second, she inquired about the FBI evidence with respect to a connection between al Qaeda and Iraq:

As far as the FBI is concerned, is the evidence of such a link "bulletproof," as Defense Secretary Rumsfeld claims, or "scant," as General Brent Scowcroft, Chairman of the President's Intelligence Advisory Board, has said? The answer to this is of key importance in determining whether war against Iraq makes any sense from the FBI's internal security point of view. If the FBI does have independent data verifying such a connection, it would seem such information should be shared, at least internally within the FBI.[15]

Third, if "the prevention of another terrorist attack remains the FBI's top priority," she asked, why is it that we have not attempted to interview Zacarias Moussaoui, the only suspect in U.S. custody charged with having a direct hand in the horror of September 11?

Although al-Qaeda has taken pains to compartmentalize its operations to avoid compromise by any one operative, information obtained from some al-Qaeda operatives has nonetheless proved invaluable. Moussaoui almost certainly would know of other al-Qaeda contacts, possibly in the U.S., and would also be able to alert us to the motive behind his and Mohammed Atta's interest in crop dusting.[16]

"Moreover," she contended, "little or no apparent effort has been made to interview convicted terrorist Richard Reid, who obviously depended upon other al-Qaeda operatives in fashioning his shoe explosive. Nor have possible links between Moussaoui and Reid been fully investigated."[17]

Fourth, she believed the FBI had not "adequately apprised" the administration

> of the potential damage to our liaison relationships with European intelligence
> agencies that is likely to flow from the growing tension over Iraq between senior
> U.S. officials and their counterparts in key West European countries. There are far
> more al-Qaeda operatives in Europe than in the U.S., and European intelligence
> services, including the French, are on the frontlines in investigating and pursuing
> them. Indeed, the Europeans have successfully uncovered and dismantled a num-
> ber of active cells in their countries.[18]

As she pointed out, "In the past, FBI liaison agents stationed in Europe benefited from
the expertise and cooperation of European law enforcement and intelligence officers.
Information was shared freely, and was of substantial help to us in our investigations
in the U.S. You will recall that prior to 9–11, it was the French who passed us word of
Moussaoui's link to terrorism."[19]

Fifth, Rowley questioned the logic behind the new color code system being established by DHS and the effect that it would have on the attempt of the FBI Joint Terrorism Task Forces to pursue all leads engendered by "panicky citizens," drawing resources
away from more important, well-predicated, and already established investigations.

Sixth, Rowley raised concerns about the over 1,000 persons "detained" in the
wake of September 11 who might not turn out to be terrorists but mostly illegal aliens.
Recognizing the right to deport those identified as illegal aliens during the course of
any investigation, she focused on the emphasis on field offices "to report daily the
number of detentions in order to supply grist for statements on our progress in fighting terrorism." Rowley was nervous that:

> the balance between individuals, civil liberties, and the need for effective inves-
> tigation is hard to maintain even during so-called normal times, let alone times
> of increased terrorist threat or war. It is, admittedly, a difficult balancing act. But
> from what I have observed, particular vigilance may be required to head off undue
> pressure (including subtle encouragement) to detain or "round up" suspects—
> particularly those of Arabic origin.[20]

Seventh, Rowley noted that the administration's new policy of "preemptive
strikes" abroad is not consistent with the Department of Justice (DOJ) "deadly force
policy" for law enforcement officers. She feared that the foreign policy approach would
seep into the domestic view of the appropriate use of deadly force. As she reasoned:

> DOJ policy restricts federal agents to using deadly force only when presented
> with an imminent threat of death or serious injury (essentially in self-defense or
> defense of an innocent third party). I believe it would be prudent to be on guard
> against the possibility that the looser "preemptive strike" rationale being applied
> to situations abroad could migrate back home, fostering a more permissive atti-
> tude towards shootings by law enforcement officers in this country.[21]

These points raised by Agent Rowley demonstrate the logic behind the use of
analogy between domestic and international politics and how intelligence and force
are employed. Naturally, there is a critical difference between the international and

domestic contexts—since only the domestic government controls the legitimate use of force internal to its borders. The question of how the FBI goes about its role in gathering and analyzing domestic information has become the center of attention.

The Field Office View

On this point, Agent Rowley is better known for her first letter of May 21, 2002. In this letter, she raised concerns over the FBIHQ response to evidence of terrorist activity in the United States prior to September 11, the previous investigation of the potential "20th hijacker," Zacarias Moussaoui, and his flight training as presented by the Minneapolis field office.

According to Rowley, within days of Moussaoui's arrest for his overstay of his visa when the French intelligence service confirmed his affiliations with radical fundamentalist Islamic groups and activities connected to Osama bin Laden, the agents became desperate to search the computer laptop that had been taken from Moussaoui, as well as to conduct a more thorough search of his personal effects. The initial goal of the Minneapolis agents was to obtain a criminal search warrant; however, to do so, they needed to get FBIHQ approval to ask for DOJ Office of Intelligence Policy Review's approval to contact the U.S. Attorney's Office in Minnesota. Prior to and even after receipt of information provided by the French, FBIHQ personnel argued with the Minneapolis agents about the existence of probable cause to believe that a criminal violation was in progress or had already occurred. As such, FBIHQ personnel refused to contact the Office of Intelligence Policy Review to attempt to secure the authority.[22]

In her letter, Rowley detailed the view that key FBIHQ personnel, whose job it was to assist and coordinate with field division agents on terrorism investigations and the obtaining and use of FISA searches (and who, theoretically, were privy to many more sources of intelligence information than field division agents), continued to throw up roadblocks inexplicably and undermine Minneapolis' by-now desperate efforts to obtain a FISA search warrant. This behavior continued long after the French intelligence service provided its information and probable cause became clear. In Rowley's mind, FBIHQ personnel brought up "almost ridiculous questions" in their apparent efforts to undermine the probable cause. In all of their conversations and correspondence, FBIHQ personnel never disclosed to the Minneapolis agents that the Phoenix Division had, only approximately 3 weeks earlier, warned of al Qaeda operatives in flight schools seeking flight training for potential terrorist purposes.

As a tactical choice, Rowley thought it would be better to pursue the "other route" (the FISA search warrant) first. She stated that her reason for such a choice was that there was a common perception that if the FBI could not do something through "straight-up criminal methods," it would then resort to using less-demanding intelligence methods. She stated, "Of course this isn't true, but I think the perception still exists." So, by this line of reasoning, she was afraid that if she first attempted to "go criminal" and failed to convince an Assistant U.S. Attorney, the FBI would not pass the "smell test" in subsequently seeking a FISA warrant.

Accordingly, Rowley thought the best chances therefore lay in first seeking the warrant. As she acknowledged, both of the factors that influenced her thinking are areas arguably in need of improvement: requiring an excessively high standard of probable cause in terrorism cases and getting rid of the smell test perception. She reasoned that it could even be argued that FBI agents—especially in terrorism cases, where time is of the essence—should be allowed to go directly to Federal judges to have their probable cause reviewed for arrests or searches without having to gain the prosecutorial approval.

Eventually on August 28, 2001, after a series of emails between Minneapolis and FBIHQ, Rowley wondered whether the FBIHQ agents were deliberately undercutting the FISA effort by not adding the promised intelligence information that supported Moussaoui's foreign power connection and by making several changes in the wording of the information that had been provided by the Minneapolis agent. That is, the Minneapolis agents were notified that the National Security Law Unit Chief did not think there was sufficient evidence of Moussaoui's connection to a foreign power. In essence, for Rowley, FBIHQ had failed in its role of assisting the field in making the best case for a FISA warrant.

Finally, Rowley questioned the Director's view that the way to fix the problem was to create "Super National Security Squads":

> Your plans for an FBI Headquarters' "Super Squad" simply fly in the face of an honest appraisal of the FBI's pre-September 11th failures. The Phoenix, Minneapolis, and Paris Legal Attaché Offices reacted remarkably well, exhibiting keen perception and prioritization skills regarding the terrorist threats they uncovered or were made aware of pre-September 11th. The same cannot be said for the FBI-Headquarters' bureaucracy and you want to expand that?[23]

Rowley's question was whether structural changes would be the answer:

> You are also apparently disregarding the fact that the Joint Terrorism Task Forces (JTTFs), operating out of field divisions for years (the first and chief one being New York City's JTTF), have successfully handled numerous terrorism investigations and, in some instances, successfully prevented acts of terrorism. There's no denying the need for more and better intelligence and intelligence management, but you should think carefully about how much gate keeping power should be entrusted with any HQ entity. If we are indeed in a "war," shouldn't the Generals be on the battlefield instead of sitting in a spot removed from the action while still attempting to call the shots?[24]

Taking Rowley's two memos together, the old issues that had plagued the FBI were put on display with a question as to whether the proposed structural changes would fix the internal problems.

The Present: How Does One Change an Organizational Culture?

FBI Director Mueller recognized the issues requiring reorganization, and Attorney General John Ashcroft predicted that the overhaul would occur "by shifting the FBI's structure, culture and mission to one of preventing terrorism" and issuing new Attorney General Guidelines.[25] Director Mueller wanted to focus on hiring those with expertise in computers, foreign languages, and the sciences. Better recruiting, managing, and workforce training; collaborating with other agencies; and improving the collection, analysis, and sharing of information were the keys to the new FBI.

The FBI overhaul plan included:

- restructuring FBI headquarters in Washington, DC, specifically the redefinition of the relationship between headquarters and the field
- coordinating between domestic and international operations
- upgrading the outdated FBI computer system
- increasing analytical proficiency through personnel and technology
- better recruiting, training, and managing of the workforce; hiring 900 more agents, mostly for counterterrorism, by September 2003; and reassigning 60 agents to counterterrorism.

In 1983, Ronald Reagan's Attorney General, William French Smith, had issued guidelines that modified those issued in 1976 by Gerald Ford's Attorney General, Edward Levi. The Levi Guidelines were criticized as being too restrictive and cumbersome. Indeed, many of Ashcroft's criticisms of the guidelines were similar to those lodged against the Levi Guidelines, which the Smith modifications were intended to rectify. The PATRIOT Act increased and updated a number of investigative techniques where technology had outstripped aspects of the warrant process—such as roving surveillance, pen registers, trap and trace authorities—and amended some grand jury procedures concerning the transfer of information.[26] Even with these grand jury amendments (procedures previously existed by special motion), the passage of information still requires a prosecutor to recognize the significance of the information.

Will changing Attorney General guidelines and structures solve the perceived problem?[27] Was the FBI truly hamstrung in its efforts to combat domestic terrorism prior to September 11? It is the conventional wisdom both inside and outside the FBI that prior to September 11, there were restrictions on the FBI doing its job. One former FBI official was quoted as saying, "you have to wait until you have blood on the street before the Bureau can act." Steven Emerson, a former investigative journalist turned terrorist expert, has asserted that the FBI is severely restricted in infiltrating known extremist groups, that it has no terrorism database like that of the CIA, and that it is powerless to stop extremist groups from masquerading as religious groups. Yet how much was culture or the law, and how much was self-imposed restraint?

Arguably the most significant change that has taken place is in the FISA arena, where the historic wall of separation between criminal and intelligence matters has been eroded. Prior to the change in the law by the PATRIOT Act, the DOJ had only used FISA warrants and wire taps for the primary purpose of gathering foreign intelligence. Under FISA, the Government must have a reasonable suspicion to show probable cause that the target of the surveillance is an agent of a foreign power, unlike in the Fourth Amendment context where there must be a showing of probable cause of a violation. The PATRIOT Act, by changing the language to "a significant purpose," expanded the situations in which it is appropriate to pursue an application under FISA, as interpreted by the FISA Appellate Court. In addition, the Appellate Court, by allowing for greater prosecutor involvement, similarly expanded law enforcement use of intelligence tools.

In the words of one of the drafters of the PATRIOT Act, Senator Orrin Hatch (R–UT), the act addressed the issue of the previous FISA in two significant ways: first, Congress, with Section 218 of the act, modified the primary purpose requirement for FISA surveillance and searches to allow FISA to be used where a significant (but not necessarily primary) purpose is to gather foreign intelligence information. Second, Section 504 of the PATRIOT Act specifically authorized intelligence officers who are using FISA to consult with Federal law enforcement officers to "coordinate efforts to investigate or protect against" foreign threats to national security, including international terrorism. Based on these two provisions, Hatch contended it was clear that Congress intended to allow greater use of FISA for criminal purposes and to increase the sharing of intelligence information and coordination of investigations between intelligence and law enforcement officers.[28]

The Smith and subsequent Attorney General Guidelines, however, had made it absolutely clear that the FBI did not have to wait for blood in the streets before it could investigate a terrorist group. The guidelines expressly stated, "In its efforts to *anticipate or prevent crimes*, the FBI must at times initiate investigations in advance of criminal conduct." The threshold for opening a full investigation was low: a domestic security/terrorism investigation may be opened whenever "facts or circumstances reasonably indicate that two or more persons are engaged in an enterprise for the purpose of furthering political or social goals wholly or in part through activities that involve force or violence and a violation of the criminal laws of the United States."[29] Indeed, the FBI was also authorized to open a preliminary inquiry on an even lower threshold: The bureau can begin investigating when it receives any information or allegation "whose responsible handling requires some further scrutiny." Preliminary inquiries could be conducted without headquarters approval for 90 days, during which time the FBI could conduct interviews, contact confidential sources and previously established informants, and carry out physical surveillance. Preliminary inquiries could be extended with headquarters' approval.

One of the main purposes of the Smith Guidelines was to make clear that the FBI could open an investigation based on advocacy of violence. While urging respect for the First Amendment, the guidelines stated, "When, however, statements advocate criminal activity or indicate an apparent intent to engage in crime, particularly crimes of violence, an investigation under these guidelines may be warranted."[30]

As has been further pointed out by the Center for National Security Studies (CNSS), in any given year prior to September 11, the FBI engaged in approximately two dozen full domestic terrorism investigations. Over the years since the Smith Guidelines were adopted, nearly two-thirds of these full investigations were opened before a crime had been committed. The FBI has investigated right-wing, antigovernment, antitax, paramilitary, and militia groups under this authority. The FBI characterization of White American Resistance (WAR), for instance, is typical: After opening a domestic terrorism investigation of WAR, the FBI stated, "No known acts of violence have as yet been attributed to WAR; however, leaders of the group have been encouraging members to arm themselves."[31]

The FBI had been successful in preventing terrorist crimes before they occurred. In 1993, for example, the FBI arrested several skinheads in Los Angeles after a lengthy investigation determined that they had been discussing and planning attacks on black churches, Jewish targets, and other religious targets. Calling something a church or a religious organization did not immunize it from investigation. In fact, a number of the white supremacist groups investigated by the FBI had assumed a religious mantle under the "Christian Identity" philosophy. The FBI had investigated under the pre-September 11 terrorism guidelines the Yahweh Church, a militant black group in Miami, and other religious groups.[32]

From the point of view of CNSS and other commentators, nothing in law or logic prohibited the FBI from opening investigations based on public source material or reports from private civil rights groups such as the Southern Poverty Law Center.[33] The FBI opened investigations based on any credible source, including news reports. For example, the FBI opened a civil rights investigation into the Rodney King case as soon as officials saw the broadcast of the videotape. Also, DOJ has met with abortion rights activists to solicit information about groups that may be planning attacks on abortion clinics.

As for gathering information:

> the FBI for a number of years has had an on-line computer database known as the Terrorist Information System (TIS) containing information on suspected terrorist groups and individuals. The system has over 200,000 individuals and over 3,000 organizations or enterprises. The individuals indexed include not only subjects of investigations but also known or suspected members of terrorist groups, associates, contacts, victims, and witnesses. The organizations or enterprises include not only terrorist groups but also affiliated organizations or enterprises. TIS was designed to allow the FBI to rapidly retrieve information and to make links between persons, groups or events.[34]

But as has been pointed out by numerous reports, the overall ability to access, retrieve, and analyze data was severely hampered by the lack of technology.[35]

Yet the announcement by the Department of Defense (DOD) of the creation of the Terrorism Information Awareness (TIA) Program (initially announced as the Total Information Awareness Program), to be headed by Admiral John Poindexter, U.S. Navy (Ret.), raised a hue and cry concerning the erosion of privacy even from such noted conservative columnists as William Safire. Safire lamented the creation of the "supersnoop's dream" that would combine credit card bills, magazine subscriptions, medical prescriptions, all emails, bank deposits, academic grades, travel itineraries, passport applications, driving records, bridge toll records, judicial records, hidden camera surveillance, and all other private commercial source information (for example, video store interests) to create a "virtual centralized grand database."[36] But for others, the exploitation of the integrative power of computer technology of legally available information is a necessity in the war against terrorism, and limiting its use against only non-U.S. persons for military operations outside of the country misses the nature of the terrorist threat.[37]

In short, there is increasingly more access to more information. Historically, the Federal institution that organized and controlled information involving potential crime had been the FBI. Yet as has been recognized by numerous commentators, the relation of crime, terrorism, and intelligence has many overlapping points. The question therefore remains: Does it make sense for the FBI to continue to be the agency to coordinate domestic efforts, or is some other framework required?

"Connecting the Dots": Is the Solution a New FBI or a New Organization?

As of summer 2003, countless commissions and studies already have been cataloguing the errors and failures of the FBI in the intelligence and counterterrorism fields. As the U.S. Government struggles to find the correct organizational framework, it is clear that the Federal bureaucracies, including the FBI, have not yet found the optimal resolution. The FBI, composed of 11,500 agents and approximately 40 legal attaches abroad, has only a limited set of resources as it balances all of its jurisdictions and investigations. The FBI is actively involved in training police around the world, administering the International Law Enforcement Academy in Budapest, Hungary, and increasing the bureau's overseas presence. In response to the stinging joint congressional report of July 2003, Director Mueller stated, "While the report provides a snapshot of the FBI at September 11, 2001, the picture of the FBI today shows a changed organization,"[38] having already implemented 10 of the 19 recommendations of the report, including improved terrorist analysis and better trained agents.[39]

Under the Clinton administration, the Office of the National Counterintelligence Executive for the 21st Century (NCIX) was created to act as a fusion center for terrorism and counterintelligence information. NCIX was to be a body of analytical thinkers with representation from all IC members tasked with coordinating the counterintelligence agenda with ties to relevant terrorist information. This group, as already envisioned by a Presidential Decision Directive, answered to the Director of the CIA, Attorney General, Director of the FBI, and Secretary of Defense. The existing NCIX was to be responsible for coordinating and dealing with the relevant information from each component agency. Although the concept was sound, it faltered in its execution for a variety of reasons, including competition for leadership, bureaucratic resistance, lack of resources, and an unclear mandate.

The most recent organization that resembles NCIX in approach is the new Terrorist Threat Integration Center (TTIC) at the CIA. The center is planned to have between 200 and 300 analysts with representation from the FBI, DHS, CIA, and other intelligence community members. TTIC is responsible for sifting through terrorism intelligence and ensuring that it is acted upon by providing a bridge between law enforcement and the national intelligence agencies.

But DHS also has a Directorate for Information Analysis and Infrastructure Protection. The department, as is to be expected of a fledging Federal institution defining itself in the more robust and institutionalized Intelligence Community, has had a slow start due to senior-level resignations, lack of analysts, and insufficient resources. The decision to keep the FBI and CIA as separate institutions, with DHS as a "client" for information, guaranteed that the new organization would have to struggle to establish an intelligence role. As DHS battles for identity and function, there will be continuing bureaucratic tussles over whether the department's primary focus is on acting as a "B" team that reexamines all the intelligence assembled by the FBI and CIA, as a point agency for tightening security in the local community, or as primary liaison to the private sector in the critical infrastructure sectors outlined by the Marsh Commission on security.[40]

In Britain, the Directorate of Military Intelligence, Section 5 (MI5), acts as a domestic analytical and spy agency. Being debated as an alternative solution is an American MI5, or an agency dedicated to protect the United States from terrorism and espionage.[41] This would entail restructuring the FBI, DHS, and Department of Treasury and keeping the national security, counterterrorism, and counterintelligence functions to combine all of the relevant analysts into one agency, as is currently the practice in Great Britain. MI5 is under the Office of the Home Secretary, and its agents have no arrest authority. The service is empowered with expansive investigative powers for domestic surveillance, intercepting all communications, eavesdropping, and using informants and moles.[42] Under this scenario, the FBI would function more like Scotland Yard and concentrate on traditional national crimes and organized crime violations. Presumably the new entity would also work closely with DOD assets to act as a clearinghouse for all of the relevant information from the 14 major intelligence-gathering agencies.[43] Needless to say, the resistance to the creation of MI5 comes not only from a philosophical resistance to the notion of a domestic spy agency with expanded powers but also from all the existing intelligence bureaucracies, which oppose the concept of losing such assets. The creation of DHS without significant intelligence powers reflects this dual resistance to an American MI5. Even with such an agency, the issues of sharing and analyzing information and having constitutional and Congressional accountability still remain.

Given these constraints, a group of experienced former government officials has suggested an interim MI5 approach that might be more bureaucratically acceptable to the Intelligence Community.[44] Arguing for more information domestically on terrorist cells and the need for the integration of counterintelligence with counterterrorism that goes beyond a "case-file mentality," the group calls for the creation of a new and accountable agency within the FBI. Using the National Security Agency and the National Reconnaissance Office as models, it is envisioned that the new agency embedded within the FBI would:

- have as its director a Presidential appointee who was not from law enforcement
- be responsible to the Director of the CIA
- be governed by Attorney General guidelines
- have its own independent personnel system for hiring
- have direct oversight by the FISA court and Congress.

As one can readily deduce from these proposed solutions, one of the continuing questions is: Who is in charge of integrating domestic law enforcement intelligence from the approximately 650,000 police officers, domestic Federal agencies, and foreign national intelligence sources? Although the Director of the CIA is the titular head of the IC, he or she does not control approximately 80 to 85 percent of the intelligence budget, which is under the authority of the Secretary of Defense, and as a matter of law, the CIA Director cannot operate domestically without severe legal constraints.

Terrorist organizations cut across domestic and foreign jurisdictions and have created both legal and institutional problems. To resolve this dilemma, some have proposed the creation of a czar or director for all intelligence issues, including IC members from domestic law enforcement to military intelligence.[45] The currently dual-hatted CIA Director, who is both director of the agency and head of the whole Intelligence Community, has been constrained by his day-to-day role at the agency. Even with one leader, the compartmentalization of the community may continue to hamstring effectiveness. Subordinating the FBI intelligence functions to this czar, however, may allow it to function more efficiently and concentrate on the central intelligence mission. Historically, the United States has not had success with the functioning of the energy or drug czars since there is too much opportunity to stonewall the central authority unless the requisite component parts cooperate. Integration and analysis remain the key issues.

Concluding Thoughts: Something Less Than *Minority Report*

What all the proposals for reform agree upon is that there is a problem with the FBI and, for that matter, with the Intelligence Community, in that the current institutional configuration was not established to counter the threat posed by domestic terrorism. Terrorism requires the gathering of both domestic and international intelligence to prevent attacks and provide national security. The elaborate and enviable legal and bureaucratic structures that were created to protect and guarantee privacy have become impediments to prosecuting and preventing terrorist acts. The debate has focused on how to reengineer this framework while sufficiently protecting our domestic liberties.

The Supreme Court has made critical distinctions between citizens and noncitizens, domestic and international arenas. Historically, the FISA established these distinctions and the FBI organized its investigative bureaus around them, as did the CIA and DOD. The same restraint that characterized the FBI in domestic investigations and was viewed as an appropriate curtailment on its power is now being described as an institutional weakness. Fighting organized crime and domestic terrorists, such as the abortion militants, requires some of the same skill sets, but other abilities are necessary.

The FBI has had a long tradition in counterintelligence and counterterrorism dating from the Palmer raids[46] against suspected communists in the 1920s to fighting saboteurs in World War II to anticommunist activities in the Cold War. At times, this history has not been a model of restraint and professionalism, but the bureau has been effective.[47] During the 1990s, the FBI doubled the number of personnel working on counterterrorism and more than tripled the budget in that area. Schemes to inflict harm were thwarted, such as the 1993 plot to attack New York City landmarks; a 1995 plot to bomb U.S. commercial aircraft; a 1997 plot to place pipe bombs in New York subways; and a 1999 plot to bomb the Los Angeles airport.[48] Meeting the new challenge will require refocusing on prevention.

Yet there have been a number of attempts to create fusion centers for coordination, consultative approaches, and refocus for the evolving domestic law enforcement and international intelligence missions:

- Counterterrorist Center in 1986
- National Drug Intelligence Center in 1992
- Intelligence-Law Enforcement Policy Board and Joint Intelligence-Law Enforcement Working Group in 1994
- National Counterintelligence Policy Board and National Counterintelligence Center of 1994
- Antiterrorism and Effective Death Penalty Act of 1996 (P.L. 104–132), allowing for the use of "classified material" in deportation hearings
- Presidential Decision Directives 62 (Protection Against Unconventional Threats) and 63 (Critical Infrastructure Protection), which created the National Infrastructure Protection Center at the FBI (transferred to DHS) in 1998.[49]

In 1998 and 1999, specific programs were initiated to improve the FBI focus on terrorism, with renewed emphasis on Joint Terrorism Task Forces including local police and CIA membership. Reorganizations of FBIHQ divisions with a separate division for counterterrorism were also made to overcome resistance and create responsiveness. Yet, despite all these valiant efforts to fuse these investigative and intelligence worlds, disjunction remains.[50]

The road to cultural change is through organizational structures and incentives. Director Mueller's proposed organizational changes have begun the painful process of structural change, but they do not include many areas where culture is defined and reinforced. A series of steps should take place to further this process. First, regardless of which organizational format is finally decided upon, the Director should appoint an advisory committee of seasoned experts from the private sector and the academic, legal, and intelligence communities. This would include experienced senior managers who have transformed their industries, such as computer companies, complex financial institutions, data mining firms, and foreign experts in domestic intelligence from among our allies.

Currently, positions in the upper echelons of FBI management, the senior executive service, require at least 1 year of law enforcement experience; most non-law enforcement experts have been discouraged from joining the FBI. Lower pay than that of other Government executive services is another serious disincentive. Although the goal behind the restriction was to depoliticize the agency, the unintended consequence has been the elimination of outside expertise and alternative views. The Director requires outside assistance to evaluate both plans for change and new personnel. Relying solely on inside insight and FBI recommendations makes a new director too captive.

Second, the Director should create an Inspector General (IG) for the FBI, who reports to the Director, the Attorney General, and the congressional oversight committees for national security and intelligence. The IG would have broad powers to ensure that investigations followed constitutional limits and privacy restrictions. The recent turnaround of the FBI Laboratory and the role an independent IG played in the process is proof of how effectively it can work. But the office of the Inspector General must be large enough to ensure its success. With new FBI powers there must be clear and transparent accountability. The current Office of Professional Responsibility, although staffed with agents of integrity and energy, is too small, with powers that are too limited. In the recent report of the Department of Justice IG cataloguing alleged abuses of the DOJ and FBI in the fight against terrorism,[51] a number of cases demonstrated that this is the type of transparency that builds legitimacy in the long run. Distinguishing between constitutionally protected dissent and threats to the Nation requires more than one authority making the determination.

Third, the Director should revamp the training division at Quantico, Virginia. Not only should the new agents be hired from graduate programs, policy institutes, accounting firms, and computer companies, but a new curriculum with an emphasis on terrorism analysis must be created. Here the advisory committee would be of invaluable assistance. Analysis is the key to fighting terrorism. Analysis is the key to understanding what the new crown jewels of the modern state are. Our problem is not gathering information; our problem is gathering the right information, analyzing it, and making sure the decisionmakers have it in a timely fashion. Moreover, all agencies have a shortage of Arabic, Spanish, and Mandarin Chinese speakers. In the Cold War, when there was a shortage of Russian speakers, the Government sponsored language scholarships to create a critical mass of translators. Within 4 years of the introduction of such a program, the Government hired thousands of speakers with the appropriate security clearances. The program would benefit both student and Government needs.

But we should not believe that even if all of these suggestions were taken, we would have no more acts of terrorism in the United States. Israel, a much smaller country with infinitely more experience in fighting terrorism and without our evolved sense of private liberties, still has not been able to stop suicide bombers on the West Bank and in Gaza. Moreover, our vulnerabilities to cyberattacks, suicide lone gunmen, and anthrax attacks such as the 2001 incident have demonstrated that we cannot be 100 percent successful. The amount of vulnerable structure controlled by the private sector makes Government-private sector cooperation vital but almost impossible. Many industries such as the financial sector have a structural disincentive to make known their computer vulnerabilities for fear of financial penalty. Our ports are so open that even the prepositioning of agents in the foreign ports of origin will not secure the commercial traffic.

The International Institute for Strategic Studies, a London policy think tank, estimates that approximately 20,000 jihadic soldiers graduated from the al Qaeda training camps in Afghanistan and that the U.S. operations have killed or captured around 2,000 of these militants.[52] But the more recently released joint congressional report contends that bin Laden trained between 70,000 to 120,000 terrorist recruits and was creating a "support structure" in the United States for multiple attacks.[53] These are the "alleged known" versus the number of youths who will be socialized into violence in the future. Predictions of future violence are hard to determine.

In the film *Minority Report*:

> a top detective in an experimental "pre-crime" unit wires the brains of genetically altered "precogs" (short for *precognition*) to computers that display their glimpses of the future. The super sleuth stands before the display as if he were conducting a symphony and directs the images so that he can find the perpetrators before they kill. There is no way to know if everyone who is arrested under this program would in fact have become a murderer, but in the film since the program has been in place, there has not been a single murder in the city.[54]

Unlike in the film, we probably will never have a set of precogs at the FBI or CIA who can predict when an act of violence will take place, days before it happens, so that corrective measures can be taken by the Government to stymie the event. In reality, we will have to infiltrate terror cells at home and abroad, use spy satellites to track movements, trace deposits with money-laundering specialists, increase eavesdropping, deploy code breakers, and then piece it all together,[55] overcoming turf battles, bureaucratic intransigence, incompetence, and limited budgets along the way.

In the end, terrorism is a political act. Although there may be a minority of actors who suffer from a self-destructive nihilism and for whom violence is in itself the goal, our efforts to reorganize the state are being made with political terrorism as the target. If, in the desire to fight terrorism, we create an intrusive state that erodes the right of privacy, without effective checks and accountability on government officials to avoid abuses, we will have delegitimized the very institutions created to protect ourselves—an ironic, unintended consequence in the fight against terrorism.

As we expand the FBI detention and questioning functions; as local police use profiling; as we increase Immigration and Naturalization Service magistrate powers without review; as we employ military tribunals rather than Federal courts; as we increase the use of the death penalty; as we monitor library borrowing and encourage the general public to monitor neighbors; as we use more special forces, assassination, and covert operations; as we institutionalize preemption doctrines; and as we continue to blur the line between domestic and international and citizen and noncitizen, it becomes even more imperative that we increase institutional accountability. For in the war of ideas, the war that is the terrorist's final terrain, we will have defeated ourselves if accountability is not maintained.[56]

Notes

[1] House Permanent Select Committee on Intelligence and Senate Select Committee on Intelligence, unclassified report of the joint inquiry into the terrorist attacks of September 11, 2001, July 24, 2003, S. Rept. No. 107–351, H. Rept. No. 107–792, 107th Congress, 2d Session.

[2] Quoted in Eric Lichtblau, "On Terror, Doubts Anew," *The New York Times*, July 25, 2003, 14.

[3] Mark Riebling, *Wedge: From Pearl Harbor to 9/11—How the Secret War between the FBI and CIA Has Endangered National Security* (New York: Touchstone, 2002).

[4] Richard A. Best, Jr., "Intelligence and Law Enforcement: Countering Transnational Threats to the U.S.,"

Congressional Research Service report for Congress, order code RL30252, updated December 3, 2001.

[5] Under Miranda the following rights are read to the perpetrator: "You have the right to remain silent. Anything you say can and will be used against you in a court of law. You have the right to be speak to an attorney, and to have an attorney present during any questioning. If you cannot afford a lawyer, one will be provided for you at government expense."

[6] Uniting and Strengthening America by Providing Appropriate Tools Required to Intercept and Obstruct Terror, H.R. 3162, 107th Congress (2001), October 26, 2001, Pub. L. No. 107–56.

[7] As has been noted by many, there is an inherent tension between a constitutional system that strives to protect civil liberties and one that must also work clandestinely to protect its citizens. In 1974, the *New York Times* reported how the CIA violated its own charter by spying on antiwar protesters and others on the left during the Johnson and Nixon administrations. Similar revelations about the domestic counterintelligence programs (COINTELPRO) operation at the FBI under J. Edgar Hoover led to even more widespread mistrust of the intelligence agencies. President Gerald Ford appointed a commission headed by Vice President Nelson Rockefeller to look into the allegations. That was soon followed by two congressional committees, one headed by Senator Frank Church (D–ID) and the other by Representative Otis Pike (D–NY). In the months that followed, the Pike and Church Committees shined the spotlight on an intelligence operation run amok with nobody to keep it in check. Pike and Church's investigations led to a series of reforms and legislative checks on those agencies, including the creation of the House and Senate intelligence committees. See Anthony York, "Why Can't Uncle Sam Spy? The problem is red tape, turf battles, and no spies on the ground, experts say," accessed at <http://archive.salon.com/news/feature/2001/09/18/spooks/index.html>.

[8] "Is Homeland Security Keeping America Safe," *CQ Weekly*, June 14, 2003, 1486–1487.

[9] Harvey Rishikof, editorial, *Providence Journal Online*, July 27, 2002, accessed at <http://www.projo.com/opinion/contributors/content/projo_20020727_ctrish27.721d2.htm>.

[10] House Permanent Select Committee on Intelligence and the Senate Select Committee on Intelligence, unclassified report of the joint inquiry into the terrorist attacks of September 11, 2001.

[11] Ibid., xv.

[12] Ibid., xv–xix.

[13] A copy of the February 26, 2003, letter can be found at <http://www.startribune.com/stories/484/3738192.html>.

[14] Ibid.

[15] Ibid.

[16] Ibid.

[17] Ibid.

[18] Ibid.

[19] Ibid.

[20] Ibid.

[21] Ibid.

[22] The two possible criminal violations initially identified by Minneapolis agents were violations of Title 18 United States Code Section 2332b (Acts of terrorism transcending national boundaries, which, notably, includes "creating a substantial risk of serious bodily injury to any other person by destroying or damaging any structure, conveyance, or other real or personal property within the United States or by attempting or conspiring to destroy or damage any structure, conveyance, or other real or personal property within the United States") and Section 32 (Destruction of aircraft or aircraft facilities).

[23] See "The Bombshell Memo," *Time*, May 21, 2002, accessed at <http://www.time.com/time/covers/1101020603/memo.html>.

[24] Ibid.

[25] "FBI Chief Unveils Overhaul Plan," Newsnet5 Web site, May 29, 2002, accessed at <http://www.newsnet5.com/news/1485358/detail.html>. The number of reassigned agents has been quoted to be now 1,200. See also Lichtblau.

[26] Elizabeth Bazan, "The Foreign Intelligence Surveillance Act," Congressional Research Service report RL30465, September 18, 2001. Pen registers and trap and trace are techniques used to acquire telephone numbers and now Web addresses. A *roving surveillance* "allows the authorities to tap the individual under surveillance and not one phone."

[27] The FBI Domestic Counterterrorism Program, Attorney General Guidelines, and the FBI pre-9/11 investigations, Center for National Security Studies, April 26, 1995, accessed at <http://nsi.org/Library/Terrorism/terpolcy.html>.

[28] Orrin Hatch, Statement, U.S. Senate Committee on the Judiciary, "The USA PATRIOT Act In Practice: Shedding Light on the FISA Process," September 10, 2002.

[29] Attorney General's Guidelines on General Crimes, Racketeering Enterprise, and Domestic Security/Terrorism Investigations, March 21, 1989, accessed at <http://www.usdoj.gov/ag/readingroom/generalcrimea.htm>.

[30] Ibid.

[31] Center for National Security Studies analysis, accessed at <http://nsi.org/Library/Terrorism/terpolcy.html>.

[32] Ibid.

[33] "Guide to the FBI Guidelines," Center for Democracy and Technology, accessed at <http://www.cdt.org/wiretap/020626guidelines.shtml>.

[34] Center For National Security Studies, accessed at <http://nsi.org/Library/Terrorism/terpolcy.html>.

[35] House Permanent Select Committee on Intelligence and the Senate Select Committee on Intelligence, unclassified report of the joint inquiry into the terrorist attacks of September 11, 2001.

[36] Robert H. Bork, "Civil Liberties after 9/11," *Commentary* 116, no. 1 (July/August 2003).

[37] Ibid.

[38] Quoted in David Johnston, "Report of 9/11 Panel Cites Lapses by CIA and FBI," *The New York Times*, July 25, 2003, A13.

[39] Lichtblau.

[40] John Mints, "At Homeland Security, Doubts Arise Over Intelligence," *The Washington Post*, July 22, 2003, A12; President's Commission on Critical Infrastructure Protection (General Marsh Commission), 1997; Presidential Decision Directive 63, accessed at <http://www.fas.org/irp/offdocs/pdd/pdd-63.htm>.

[41] See recommendations of the Advisory Panel to Assess Domestic Response Capabilities for Terrorism Involving Weapons of Mass Destruction (James Gilmore, chairman), Fourth Annual Report to the President and Congress of the Gilmore Commission; accessed at <http://www.rand.org/nsrd/terrpanel/terr4.pdf>.

[42] See British Security Service Web site, accessed at <www.mi5.gov.uk>; Don van Natta, Jr., "Intelligence Critics Urge U.S. to Look to British Spy Agency," *The New York Times*, July 26, 2003.

[43] John Edwards, Homeland Security Address, The Brookings Institution, Washington, DC, December 18, 2002.

[44] "America Needs More Spies," *The Economist*, July 12–18, 2003, 30–31. The group of former officials includes Robert Bryant and Howard Shapiro from the FBI; John Hamre from DOD; John Lawn from DEA; and John MacGaffin and Jeffrey Smith from CIA.

[45] William E. Odom, *Fixing Intelligence: For a More Secure America* (New Haven: Yale University Press, 2003).

[46] The Palmer Raids, named after Alexander Mitchell Palmer, U.S. Attorney General under Woodrow Wilson, were a number of quasi-legal attacks on Socialists and Communists in the United States from 1918 to 1921. With strong support from Congress and the public, Palmer clamped down on political dissent in 1919. After bombs were detonated in eight American cities—including one in Washington, DC, that damaged Palmer's home—on June 2, 1919, Palmer and his assistant J. Edgar Hoover orchestrated a series of well-publicized raids against apparent radicals and leftists under the Espionage Act of 1917 and the Sedition Act of 1918. Without warrants, Palmer's men smashed union offices and the headquarters of Communist and Socialist organizations and arrested over 10,000 people. After the Communist revolution that Palmer had predicted for May 1, 1920, failed to occur, he suffered criticism for his disregard for civil rights and was accused of orchestrating the Red Scare to secure the Presidential nomination of the Democratic Party. Information accessed at <http://www.wikipedia.org/w/wiki.phtml?title=Palmer_raids>.

[47] Ronald Kessler, *The Bureau: The Secret History of the FBI* (New York: St. Martin's Press, 2002); Ronald Kessler, *The FBI : Inside the World's Most Powerful Law Enforcement Agency* (New York: Pocket Books, 1994).

[48] House Permanent Select Committee on Intelligence and the Senate Select Committee on Intelligence, unclassified report of the joint inquiry into the terrorist attacks of September 11, 2001.

[49] Best, Jr.

[50] House Permanent Select Committee on Intelligence and the Senate Select Committee on Intelligence, unclassified report of the joint inquiry into the terrorist attacks of September 11, 2001.

[51] Office of the Inspector General, "A Review of the Federal Bureau of Investigation's Counterterrorism Program: Threat Assessment, Strategic Planning, and Resource Management." Report no. 02-38, September 2002. Accessed at <http://www.fas.org/agency/doj/oig/fbi02sum.html>.

[52] Daniel Bergner, "Where the Enemy Is Everywhere and Nowhere," *The New York Times Magazine*, July 20, 2003, 39–41.

[53] Susan Schmidt and David von Drehle, "Congressional Inquiry Faults FBI Monitoring of Hijackers," *The Washington Post*, July 25, 2003, A1, A15.

[54] Plot summary from Movie Mom's Reviews, accessed at <http://movies.yahoo.com/shop?d=hv&cf=parentsguide&id=1807592183>.

[55] Eric Lichtblau, "Connecting the Dots," *The New York Review of Books*, March 16, 2003, 15.

[56] R.D. Howard and R.L. Sawyer, *Terrorism and Counterterrorism* (New York: McGraw Hill, 2003); Harvey Rishikof, "Is it Time for a Federal Terrorist Court? Terrorists and Prosecutions: Problems, Paradigms, and Paradoxes," *Suffolk Journal of Trial and Appellate Advocacy* 8 (2003), 1.

Part IV—Challenges of Technical Collection

Now that we have technical systems ranging from satellites traveling in space over the entire globe, to aircraft flying in free airspace, to miniature sensors surreptitiously positioned close to difficult targets, we are approaching a time when we will be able to survey almost any point on the earth's surface with some sensor, and probably with more than one.

—Stansfield Turner

Chapter 10

Space-Based Surveillance: Reconnaissance Satellites Are a National Security Sine Qua Non

Glenn W. Goodman, Jr.

America's first "spy" satellite, the KH–1 Corona, conducted its first reconnaissance mission in August 1960. The satellite used photographic film to record high-resolution images of the Soviet Union from space. It released canisters of exposed film in a recovery vehicle, which fell to Earth with a parachute and were retrieved so the film could be developed.

The same method was used by subsequent U.S. photo-reconnaissance satellite types KH–2 through KH–9. The KH–1 through KH–9 (Keyhole) programs encompassed nearly 150 satellite launches between 1960 and 1972.

The heavily classified National Reconnaissance Office (NRO) was established in 1960 to design, build, and operate all U.S. reconnaissance satellites. (The U.S. Government did not publicly acknowledge the NRO's existence until 1992. Today, it falls under the Air Force.)

Imagery satellites or *overhead systems*—known as "national technical means of verification," shortened to "national technical means"—typically operate in low Earth orbits to be closer to the areas they are reconnoitering. The strong suit of U.S. imaging reconnaissance satellites to date has primarily been the monitoring of fixed facilities over periods of days and months to detect changes in activity or military readiness.

Imagery and Signals Intelligence Satellites

Space-based reconnaissance has come a long way since the KH–1 Corona. Beginning with the KH–11 Kennan/Crystal series, first launched in December 1976, U.S. electro-optical (E–O) imaging satellites have transmitted their black-and-white [television] picture-like imagery to a ground station in virtually real time using a relay satellite.

The inability of photo-reconnaissance and subsequent E–O imaging satellites to "see" through clouds has been their biggest shortcoming. As a result, development of an all-weather, space-based imaging radar, which could use radar pulses to see through clouds, fog, haze, and darkness and generate images of the ground, was initiated in late 1976. Following a successful test of the Indigo prototype satellite in early 1982, development of the Lacrosse/Vega radar imaging satellite began in 1983. The 16-ton spacecraft built by Lockheed Martin (Denver) was first launched by the space shuttle *Atlantis* in December 1988. The NRO put several more of them in orbit through 1999 using booster rockets. In August 2000, the latest Lacrosse Onyx satellite was successfully orbited.

The Lacrosse design includes a large dish radar antenna and a very long solar panel array to provide substantial electric power for the radar transmitter and produce images with high resolution—not as high as U.S. E–O imaging satellites but less than a meter in the latest versions of the satellite and in all weather.

Imagery satellites were joined in space early on by others with signals intelligence (SIGINT) payloads, operated by the NRO to support National Security Agency (NSA) collection and exploitation of intercepted message traffic and other electronic eavesdropping. In fact, the first SIGINT satellite, a device that looked like a large silver soccer ball and was called GRAB [Galactic Radiation and Background], went into low Earth orbit in May 1960 before the KH–1 Corona. It collected signals emitted by hundreds of Soviet air defense radars and retransmitted them down to ground stations for recording on magnetic tape and subsequent analysis by NSA.

SIGINT antennas and receivers can intercept radio, radar, cellular telephone, and missile test telemetry signals emitted by military forces on the ground, and [they] can detect, identify, and locate enemy emitters or pick up signs of vehicle movements or other hostile activities.

As microwave repeater towers replaced buried land lines in the Soviet Union for carrying telephone calls and data transmissions over long distances, NRO and NSA discovered that the best place to put a SIGINT satellite was in geostationary (geosynchronous) orbit (22,300 miles up, rotating at the exact same speed as the Earth). This is because microwave transmissions can be picked up in deep space as very clear signals, while satellites in low Earth orbit travel too fast through the microwave beams.

The first of a new generation of SIGINT satellites, called Rhyolite and built by TRW, was launched in 1970. It was put in geosynchronous orbit above the equator near Indonesia, which was a good position from which to collect signals emitted in the Soviet Union and China. The satellite retransmitted the signals without encryption directly to the Pine Gap ground station in Alice Springs, Australia, where they were encrypted and relayed by satellite, or the data tapes airlifted, to the NSA. The Rhyolite satellites were supplemented by Jumpseat SIGINT satellites launched into elliptical orbits from 1971 to 1985 to cover the Soviet Union's extreme northern regions.

Ground stations were added in Germany, England, and Japan, and larger, more capable SIGINT satellites targeting different types of emissions were launched over the years, with names such as Chalet/Vortex, Mercury (Advanced Vortex), Magnum/Orion, and Intruder. The billion-dollar Trumpet SIGINT satellite, with an antenna reportedly 100 meters across, was launched in 1994, 1995, and 1997, and Trumpet Mentor (Advanced Orion) in 1998.

The latest Advanced KH–11 improved Crystal E–O/infrared (IR) reconnaissance satellite (some call it the KH–12), built by TRW, was first launched into low

Earth orbit in November 1992. At least two more were launched, in December 1995 and December 1996. Akin to the bullet-shaped Hubble Space Telescope, with a large rocket engine attached on the end for maneuvering and wing-like solar panel arrays perpendicular instead of parallel to the spacecraft's main body, the Advanced KH–11 reportedly weighs 18 tons, including 7 to 8 tons of fuel. It features a rotating mirror on its top end that reflects images onto a primary optical telescope mirror measuring up to 150 inches in diameter. The Advanced KH–11's E–O and IR sensors can produce sharp digital images with a resolution approaching 0.1 meters for objects on Earth hundreds of miles away. The Advanced KH–11 also carries SIGINT receivers.

The U.S. inventory of spy satellites was reported last September to include three Advanced KH–11, two Lacrosse, and five SIGINT satellites.

Next-generation U.S. space reconnaissance capabilities are centered around NRO's Future Imagery Architecture (FIA), a planned constellation of new E–O/IR imaging and probably radar satellites that is expected to provide huge gains in imagery intelligence for tactical warfighters. Boeing Satellite Systems, Seal Beach, California, is developing the system.

In April 2002, Air Force Undersecretary Peter Teets, who is dual-hatted as director of the NRO, discounted news reports that the FIA program was in trouble, stating that he had reviewed Boeing's progress and that it was "on cost and on schedule." Boeing's FIA team, which won the $4.5 billion development contract in 1999, includes Hughes Electronics Corporation, Raytheon, Eastman Kodak, and Harris Corporation.

The Air Force plans to kick-start development of (an unclassified) space-based radar in fiscal year (FY) 2003, seeking $91 million in its research and development request. The system would offer ground moving target indicator and synthetic aperture radar capabilities from space akin to those provided today by the Air Force's 707 aircraft-mounted E–8 Joint Surveillance Target Attack Radar System (JSTARS). Space-based radar sensors could dwell for sufficient time over target areas to track moving vehicles around the clock.

Manned surveillance aircraft like the E–8 are costly to man and operate year in and year out; Air Force leaders believe that space-based radar sensors, once the up-front investment to develop and deploy the satellites has been made, could provide JSTARS–like capabilities at far lower operating costs and without risking personnel.

In 2000, Congress killed the earlier Discoverer II space-based radar program, which sought to launch a two-satellite experimental constellation in 2003. This time, the Air Force wants to use program funding to build an operational system, rather than conduct an experimental technology program like Discoverer II. The hope is that the first satellites can be launched by 2010.

Reconnaissance satellites are important strategic capabilities also sought by other advanced nations around the globe, such as Israel, France, and Germany.

Israeli Spy Satellites

Israel launched a new reconnaissance satellite into low Earth orbit on May 28, 2002. It was the OFEQ–5, built by Israel Aircraft Industries (IAI). Its predecessor, OFEQ–3, burned up the previous year on reentering the Earth's atmosphere after it ran out of life. OFEQ–5 is designed to operate in low Earth orbit at altitudes between 370 and 600 kilometers.

What is unique about OFEQ–5 is that it is a small, lightweight satellite, yet it carries high-resolution sensors. Its launch weight is only about 650 pounds (300 kilograms). It has a height of 2.3 meters and a 1.2-meter diameter. An IAI statement notes, "OFEQ–5's light weight allows for maximum agility over target to yield rapid image acquisition. It acquires images in swaths ahead of the satellite trajectory, beneath it, and lateral to it." OFEQ–5's projected life is about 4 years. Israel launched OFEQ–1, its first spy satellite, in 1988.

European Reconnaissance Satellites

France is developing a new Helios II satellite to upgrade its strategic reconnaissance capabilities. Belgium and Spain are participants in the Helios II program and Italy also may join; their own ground stations will receive optical imagery from the satellite. The first Helios II satellite is scheduled to be launched in 2004 and the second in 2008.

France's two earlier-generation Helios IA and IB satellites were launched in 1995 and 1999, respectively, and had a 4-year design life. Italy and Spain have been Helios I system participants.

Astrium, the European space company formed by EADS and BAE Systems, is the prime contractor for the Helios I and II satellites, and Alcatel Space has supplied their optical sensors.

The 5,500-pound Helios I helped locate targets for U.S. air strikes during Operation *Enduring Freedom* in Afghanistan. A French Ministry of Defense official noted that, while the resolution of Helios I images (one meter) is not as good as those from U.S. reconnaissance satellites, it was sufficient to identify major targets, such as airfields.

Germany is set to acquire its first reconnaissance satellite, SAR–Lupe. It will carry an Alcatel synthetic aperture radar (SAR), which will provide high-resolution images day or night and in all weather conditions. A constellation of five satellites will be launched between 2004 and 2007. The relatively small satellite, to be built by Orbital High Technology Bremen, will weigh about 1,700 pounds (770 kilograms) and will measure 4 by 3 by 2 meters. It will operate at an altitude of about 500 kilometers and will have a 10-year life.

France and Germany recently planned to sign a memorandum of understanding to exchange imagery from Helios II and SAR–Lupe, which would provide both countries access to both optical and radar imagery in the future.

U.S. Early-Warning Satellites

Imaging reconnaissance satellites are one key type of U.S. space-based surveillance systems; the other is missile warning satellites. Orbiting Air Force Defense Support Program (DSP) satellites have performed the attack warning function since 1970, detecting the launch of ballistic missiles worldwide from the infrared heat of their rocket plumes. The Space-based Infrared System (SBIRS, pronounced *sibbers*) is intended to be the next-generation U.S. global missile warning and tracking system.

The Air Force is developing two separate SBIRS satellite components and a single ground segment. SBIRS High will replace the DSP satellites. It will consist of four dedicated satellites in high geostationary Earth orbit and sensor payloads on two other classified host satellites in highly elliptical orbits. SBIRS High will detect and report missile launches faster and more accurately than the DSP satellites and also will detect and track shorter-range missiles with greater accuracy.

SBIRS Low will encompass more than 20 missile-tracking satellites in low Earth orbit. As a key element of the DOD planned National Missile Defense system, SBIRS Low satellites will perform precise midcourse tracking of ballistic missiles after they separate from their rocket boosters and will discriminate between missile reentry vehicles (warheads) and decoys.

The Air Force began full-scale development of SBIRS High in 1996. Lockheed Martin Space Systems Company (Sunnyvale, California) is the prime contractor and systems integrator. Northrop Grumman is developing the critical infrared sensors for SBIRS High. SBIRS High will use a combination of scanning and staring IR sensors. The scanning IR sensor will sweep wide swaths of the Earth to detect missile launches; once a launch is detected, the highly sensitive staring IR sensor will independently focus, or stare, at the launch location to pick up detailed information on the characteristics of the missile being launched.

Substantial cost overruns on the SBIRS High program put it at risk of cancellation this past spring under the provisions of the Nunn-McCurdy law. DOD programs whose unit costs increase by 25 percent or more must be reviewed and certified to Congress for continuation or be terminated. In early May, Pentagon acquisition chief Pete Aldridge certified the program for continued funding. Rather than restructuring the program, Aldridge directed that it be revised to meet realistic cost and performance profiles.

The first launch of a SBIRS High geosynchronous satellite is now expected to slip from November 2004 by 18 to 24 months. SBIRS Low got started in August 1999, when the Air Force awarded competing industry teams, led by TRW and Spectrum Astro, $275-million, 38-month Program Definition and Risk Reduction contracts. TRW's team included Raytheon, Northrop Grumman (formerly Aerojet), Motorola, Honeywell, and Ball Aerospace; Spectrum Astro's team included Northrop Grumman, Lockheed Martin, and Boeing. The Air Force planned to pick a single team to conduct the next development phase by December of this year.

A February 2001 General Accounting Office report concluded that the SBIRS Low program was "at high risk of not delivering the system on time or at cost or with the expected performance." Concerned by the program's cost growth, Congress subsequently slashed funding for SBIRS Low in FY02 defense appropriations request. As a result, the program was restructured by DOD, with congressional concurrence, to reduce its technical risks, corral its growing costs, and get it back on schedule.

On April 18, 2002, TRW was named the prime contractor of a single combined team. Spectrum Astro will play a significant role developing the spacecraft, while Raytheon and Northrop Grumman will develop the critical sensor elements of the satellite payload under competitive subcontracts to TRW.

In July 2002, TRW will submit a proposal to the DOD Missile Defense Agency for the "Cycle 1" portion of the restructured program, essentially those activities leading up to the first satellite launch in FY06 and the second in FY07. The combined industry SBIRS Low team will focus on the early development and deployment of initial missile-tracking satellites and evolve the system's capability incrementally as technology advances.

Pat Caruana, TRW Space and Electronics' vice president for missile defense and its SBIRS Low program manager from 1999 to 2001, told [*ISR Journal*]:

> One of the [Government's] desired outcomes behind the restructure of the program was to have a strong prime and then to look at the capabilities that each of the team members could bring to the table, respectively. And then determine, of those, which is the "best of the best." It really allows us a lot more collaboration on a broader industrial base for all the players that were previously in a competitive mode.

Caruana [also] noted, "The fact that the Government is retaining competition for the payload is a clear recognition that development of the payload—including the [scanning] acquisition sensor and the track sensor, the IR focal plane array development, the cryocooling—is where much of our challenge still resides."

Asked if the payload sensors will be multispectral, he responded:

> The key to SBIRS Low's success is the shortwave IR, the midwave IR, and the longwave IR—all three of them—for various elements of the sensing both in the [threat missile's] boost and post-boost phases. Principally the longwave IR for the colder bodies that SBIRS Low will look at once they deploy from the post-boost vehicle, but all three [wavebands] are involved to the degree that we can provide the best capability for [characterizing] those objects once they deploy.

Space-based surveillance sensors, although extremely costly to design, build, and launch into orbit, remain a sine qua non for major nations with international security concerns. And fortunately for those countries that can afford reconnaissance satellites, their performance capabilities from space keep improving as technology advances.

Chapter 11

Unclassified Space Eyes

Glenn W. Goodman, Jr.

The fledgling U.S. commercial satellite imagery industry received a major boost from a June 7 memorandum from George Tenet, Director of Central Intelligence, to the Director of the National Imagery and Mapping Agency (NIMA), Lt. Gen. James Clapper (USAF, Ret.). Tenet's memo stated unequivocally:

> It is the policy of the Intelligence Community to use U.S. commercial space imagery to the greatest extent possible. Therefore, I . . . [d]irect that U.S. commercial satellite imagery be the primary source of data used for government mapping [while] national technical means [classified U.S. reconnaissance satellites] will only be tasked under exceptional circumstances.

Tenet added, "My goal in establishing this policy is to stimulate, as quickly as possible, and maintain, for the foreseeable future, a robust U.S. commercial space imagery industry. . . . You should take all possible steps to remove any remaining institutional obstacles to its use in meeting government needs."

The timing of Tenet's memo was due, in large part, to pressure from congressional committees for the U.S. Government to take greater advantage of available commercial imagery. For example, the Senate Armed Services Committee's report on the fiscal year 2003 defense authorization bill had stated:

> The strategy that NIMA seemed to have adopted last year that was designed to assure the commercial remote-sensing industry of the long-term commitment and reliability of the U.S. Government as a customer appears to have been abandoned in favor of a return to a "day-to-day," as-needed approach to commercial imagery purchases. Such indecision is not in the best interests of the U.S. commercial remote-sensing industry or in the national security interests of the U.S. Government.

But Tenet's memo also reflected the maturity of the small U.S. commercial satellite imagery industry in terms of the rapidly improving availability and resolution of images of areas on the Earth's surface it now offers. Increasing numbers of commercial high-resolution imagery satellites, operated by both U.S. and foreign firms, are circling the globe, and more launches are planned. As one firm's representative [stated], "Our industry and the number and types of imagery satellites we now have in orbit have reached a sort of 'critical mass' where they can no longer be ignored."

NIMA, despite recognizing earlier the potential cost savings and benefits for military users of more substantial purchases of commercial satellite imagery, was hamstrung by low funding levels. However, in line with Tenet's memo, the Bush administration is now poised to substantially increase funding for the agency's purchases of commercial imagery and derivative products.

Tenet's memo is expected to bring about a dramatic change in the use of commercial satellite imagery by the Defense Department and the Intelligence Community that will ultimately benefit U.S. military warfighters in operations around the world.

A Little Background

Modern commercial remote-sensing satellites acquire images using digital camera systems. The systems typically consist of a telescope with mirrors that focus the captured Earth imagery onto digital imaging sensor arrays. These arrays are made up of thousands of tiny detectors that measure the energy reflecting from the Earth's surface and objects on it in different wavelengths of the electromagnetic spectrum.

Electro-optical (E–O) cameras are the most common type of satellite imaging sensor in orbit and provide the highest resolution images. However, E–O sensors can capture images only during daylight and cannot see through clouds or fog. Some satellites carry synthetic aperture radar (SAR) sensors that do not have these limitations; they can capture images of the Earth through clouds, fog, haze, and darkness. However, the resolution of the radar images is not as good as that of E–O images.

Commercial remote-sensing satellites typically circle the globe in near-polar, low Earth orbits in a little over an hour and a half. They travel in a slightly northeast-to-southwest direction on descending orbits that take them back over the exact same spot on Earth once every several days. The number of days elapsing between passes over the same spot at nadir (with the sensor looking straight down) is called the satellite's revisit rate.

A satellite with an adjustable viewing angle can acquire imagery of the same spot more often by pointing its sensor off-nadir up to hundreds of kilometers out of its normal ground track or footprint (although the imagery will be at somewhat lower resolution). This facilitates more frequent monitoring of areas hit by floods, fire, or other natural disasters.

An E–O satellite acquires imagery only on its descending orbits because the orbits are timed so the satellite is always descending on the daylight side of the Earth and ascending on the dark side. (SAR satellites acquire images during both phases of their orbits.) Most E–O satellites are sun-synchronous—that is, they move with the sun so they can make repeat passes over a particular area at the same time of day. This ensures that the sun angle and shadowing will be similar in multiple images of the same area acquired on different orbits. Image data are compressed and transmitted to a ground station on Earth.

The E–O cameras on imagery satellites are normally equipped with two types of detector arrays: panchromatic (black and white) and multispectral (color). Panchromatic imagery is acquired in the visible light band of the electromagnetic spectrum, while multispectral imagery is acquired in three or four visible light/infrared bands (red, green, blue, and near-infrared).

Multispectral imagery has lower resolution, but it reveals information that cannot be seen with the naked eye, such as the health of vegetation, the mineral content of rocks, the moisture of soil, and other invisible characteristics. Thus, multispectral imagery is highly useful for agricultural and land management–related applications.

Resolution refers to the size of the smallest object or ground feature that can be recognized in an image. The higher the resolution (spatial as opposed to spectral), the more detail is revealed in the image. And, generally, the more detailed a commercial satellite image is, the more expensive it is per unit area (dollars per square kilometer) to purchase, since it requires greater computer processing and storage space. A satellite image with high resolution, such as one meter, normally captures a smaller coverage area ("swath width") on the Earth's surface than one of lower resolution.

Emergence of an Industry

France's SPOT Image launched the first commercial remote-sensing satellite, SPOT 1 (Systeme Pour l'Observation de la Terre), in 1986. SPOT 2, 3, and 4 followed in 1990, 1993, and 1998. Those satellites have provided what today is called medium-resolution imagery—that is, 10-meter panchromatic and 20-meter multispectral imagery across a 60-kilometer (km) swath width (with 60 km x 60 km image sizes)—to predominantly government customers. (SPOT 3 is no longer in orbit.)

SPOT Image was virtually the lone player in the global national security market for commercial satellite imagery for many years and has sold images over time to DOD and the U.S. Government through its U.S. subsidiary, SPOT Image Corporation in Chantilly, Virginia. The U.S. Air Force has used SPOT imagery since the Gulf War. Following Operation *Desert Storm*, the service purchased its own Eagle Vision mobile ground stations to receive and process downlinked SPOT commercial satellite imagery and to use it for air crew mission planning and visualization. (Eagle Vision was built by EADS' Matra Systemes and Information with a Datron antenna and a data integration van from ERIM.) The three Air Force ground stations have been deployed around the world, played a valuable role in the Kosovo air war, and today receive imagery from a number of other commercial satellites besides SPOT. The U.S. Army also operates an Eagle Vision ground station.

In the early 1990s, U.S. policymakers loosened controls over the generation and dissemination of high-resolution satellite imagery, essentially to try to shape the future of the expanding global remote-sensing marketplace by encouraging American firms to take a dominant position. The Land Remote Sensing Act, passed by Congress in 1992, established a licensing regime for commercial imagery satellites. Together with President Clinton's 1994 Presidential Decision Directive (PDD)–23, it opened the door for the emergence of a U.S. commercial satellite imagery industry. Current U.S. law allows American firms to sell commercial satellite imagery with a spatial resolution of 0.5 meters on the open market, although sales to countries on the State Department's list of terrorism-supporting states are prohibited.

A U.S. firm formed in 1994 by Lockheed Martin and Raytheon, Space Imaging of Thornton, Colorado, launched the first high-resolution commercial remote-sensing satellite, IKONOS, in September 1999. The 1,600-pound satellite, built by Lockeed Martin Missiles and Space in Sunnyvale, California, provides 1-meter-resolution panchromatic and 4-meter-resolution multispectral images using a single E–O camera specially designed for IKONOS by Eastman Kodak.

This was quite a leap from existing SPOT 10-meter/20-meter images. IKONOS brought the commercial world a lot closer to the capabilities of very large U.S. national reconnaissance satellites—said to provide resolutions down to 6 inches or less—for the first time. In doing so, IKONOS generated greater awareness within DOD about what was available from commercial providers.

In December 2000, Cyprus-based ImageSat International, a global company with strong Israeli ties, got into the game when it launched its Earth Remote Observation System (EROS) A1 satellite, the first non-U.S. commercial high-resolution imagery satellite. Its panchromatic camera provides 1.8-meter resolution across a 12.5-km swath width. This resolution can be improved to one meter using a technique called oversampling, reportedly involving taking multiple overlapping images of an area or slowing the rate at which the sensor scans an area. (This reduces the swath width to 6 km, decreasing the area covered during an orbital pass.) The agile satellite, which provides global coverage, weighs only 550 pounds and can be maneuvered to point its camera up to 500 km off nadir.

ImageSat plans to offer even higher resolution (0.67 meters across a 9.5-km swath width) soon using a new technique called hypersampling, which it says involves a combination of satellite maneuvering and software enhancements to the imagery processing. The company also expects to launch its second high-resolution satellite, EROS B1, in early 2004. The larger satellite's new E–O camera will offer 0.87-meter standard panchromatic resolution as well as 3.5-meter multispectral resolution.

ImageSat's major shareholder is Israel Aircraft Industries (IAI), which built the EROS A1 satellite. Two other core investors are Israel's Elbit, whose El–Op division supplied the satellite's camera, and the U.S. company Core Software Technology, which has provided online imagery distribution.

Compared with its larger U.S. competitors in the high-resolution imagery market, ImageSat says it offers faster turnaround times for standard orders (for example, 2 weeks instead of 2 months or more) and cheaper prices. One of the unique purchase options it offers government national security customers is a satellite operating partnership, in which the customer purchases long-term use of EROS satellites over a specific area of the world and has its own ground station. The customer has exclusive control of the satellite during the time it passes over that area, telling the spacecraft's camera what spots to look at and downloading the imagery in real time to its ground station, all without ImageSat's knowledge. Israel is one such customer and has purchased exclusive use of EROS A1 imagery of the Middle East on a continuing basis.

Digital Globe (formerly EarthWatch) of Longmont, Colorado, upped the resolution ante when it launched its QuickBird satellite in October 2001. QuickBird provides the highest resolution commercial satellite imagery currently available:

0.61-meter (2-foot) panchromatic and 2.4-meter multispectral (4 bands) at nadir across a 16.5-km x 16.5-km area. The satellite was built for Digital Globe by Ball Aerospace and Technologies Corporation and is equipped with a Ball E–O camera. To achieve an adjustable viewing angle for its camera, the entire QuickBird satellite tips and tilts to change its orientation and point its sensors rather than just moving the camera itself.

On May 3, 2002, SPOT Image gained back some ground from its industry competitors when it successfully launched its new SPOT 5 satellite. It produces 2.5-meter and 5-meter panchromatic and 10-meter and 20-meter multispectral resolution imagery over a wide area (60 km x 60 km up to 60 km x 120 km). The SPOT 5 satellite was developed by the French national space agency CNES (Centre National d'Etudes Spatiales) in cooperation with Belgium and Sweden with Astrium as the prime contractor.

SPOT 5 also carries a unique high-resolution stereoscopic sensor made up of two telescopes that capture overlapping imagery of the same area on the ground from two different viewing angles during the same pass. Stereo imagery is needed to create the digital elevation models (DEMs) used in 3–D visualization-based applications, such as flight simulation, mission planning, and mission rehearsal. The consistent-quality imagery produced by SPOT 5's stereo sensor allows the company to use it directly in an automatic process at its receiving stations on the ground to produce DEMs, which will have a horizontal accuracy of 10 meters and a vertical (height) accuracy of 15 meters. Typically, remote-sensing satellites have had to capture overlapping single images from different orbital paths and manually create DEMs through laborious and expensive image processing.

Planning to join the high-resolution club soon is ORBIMAGE (Orbital Imaging Corporation), based in Dulles, Virginia, which hopes to launch its OrbView-3 satellite before the end of the year. It will carry a 1-meter panchromatic sensor and a 4-meter multispectral sensor, covering a swath width of 8 km.

With these higher-resolution imagery satellites, the commercial remote-sensing firms hope to increase their share of the civilian market, which includes supporting agriculture, urban planning by state and local governments, oil and gas exploration, utilities, and telecommunications. (Aerial photography is still a major competitor in that market, particularly for small coverage areas.) However, national governments remain the major source of demand for commercial satellite imagery.

Supplementing Classified Satellites

NIMA used IKONOS satellite imagery acquired from Space Imaging extensively during the early phases of the war in Afghanistan. (The only existing maps of that country available to U.S. forces at the outset of the conflict were Russian or 14-year-old NIMA maps.) In fact, during a 2-month period last fall, NIMA purchased exclusive use of all the commercial imagery collected by IKONOS over Afghanistan and Pakistan (470,000 square km) to keep it out of the hands of adversaries. Most of that imagery is now available for commercial purchase.

Lt. Gen. James R. Clapper, Jr., NIMA's director, has been a strong proponent of greater use of commercial satellite imagery by his agency to meet the increasing geospatial product needs of U.S. military forces. He wrote [. . .] at the time of the Tenet memo, that the National Reconnaissance Office (NRO) and NIMA recently

> completed a business plan that lays out a realistic plan of action over the next five years, based upon our budget profile for this essential imagery source. The expected outcome of this plan underscores our appreciation of the maturity of the industry and its ability to improve our readiness and responsiveness posture for military and intelligence customers. Broadly, NRO and NIMA will continue to operate, task, and exploit the government's high-end [classified national] sensors, products, and services. But it also is apparent that we can off-load some of the medium-to-low resolution imagery requirements from national collectors to commercial vendors....To do that to the maximum level possible, we will review our ordering techniques, optimize collection strategies, and drive to reduce the unit cost.

A major advantage for the U.S. Government's use of commercial satellite imagery as much as possible is that the imagery is unclassified and can thus be readily shared with U.S. allies, coalition partners, and international organizations. The great expense and infrastructure involved in protecting classified imagery from unauthorized disclosure are avoided.

One expert estimated that 70 to 80 percent of the image collection traditionally done by U.S. classified satellites is mapping-related activity rather than real intelligence-gathering and could be done cheaper and more efficiently by commercial satellites. National intelligence satellites certainly are not needed to map Afghanistan or other large potential conflict areas. In fact, U.S. regional [combatant commanders] have many unfunded mapping needs that can be met by the commercial sector.

There also are a significant number commercial firms that have developed geographical information system (GIS) software that will help exploit commercial satellite imagery to produce value-added geospatial information products for defense users. NIMA plans to outsource a substantial amount of work to such firms.

The emerging expansion of the commercial remote-sensing market is not just the result of higher-resolution commercial imagery becoming available. As an industry executive said:

> Imagery alone has value, but it has even more worth to government and industry customers when combined with faster computers to process the imagery, new GIS software that can run on a desktop computer, cheaper costs of data storage, and the ability to move imagery over the Internet to high-value customers.

It is an exciting new era for the global commercial satellite imagery industry, as the competition heats up around the world in both national security and civilian markets. The U.S. intelligence community and NIMA have lifted the barriers to a greater use of commercial imagery by U.S. Government agencies. The only issue now is how NIMA can move faster in establishing the procedures and infrastructure to integrate commercial imagery into its functions in a big way.

Chapter 12

Commercial Satellite Imagery Comes of Age

Ann M. Florini and Yahya A. Dehqanzada

The quality and detail of commercial images are taking a leap forward; governments will have to learn to live with it.

Since satellites started photographing Earth from space nearly four decades ago, their images have inspired excitement, introspection, and, often, fear. Like all information, satellite imagery is in itself neutral. But satellite imagery is a particularly powerful sort of information, revealing both comprehensive vistas and surprising details. Its benefits can be immense, but so can its costs.

The number of people able to use that imagery is exploding. By the turn of the century, new commercial satellites will have imaging capabilities approaching those of military spy satellites. But the commercial satellites possess one key difference: Their operators will sell the images to anyone.

A joint venture between two U.S. companies—Aerial Images, Inc., and Central Trading Systems, Inc.—and a Russian firm, *Sovinformsputnik*, is already selling panchromatic (black-and-white) imagery with ground resolution as small as one and a half meters across. (Ground or spatial resolution refers to the size of the objects on the ground that a satellite sensor can distinguish.) Another U.S. company, Space Imaging, has a much more sophisticated satellite that was launched in late September 1999. It can take 1-meter panchromatic and 3- to 5-meter multispectral (color) images of Earth. Over the next 5 years, nearly 20 U.S. and foreign organizations are expected to launch civilian and commercial high-resolution observation satellites in an attempt to capture a share of the growing market for remote-sensing imagery.

The Uses of Satellite Images

These new commercial satellites will make it possible for the buyers of satellite imagery to, among other things, distinguish between trucks and tanks, expose movements of large groups such as troops or refugees, and identify the probable location of natural resources. Whether this will be good or bad depends on who chooses to use the imagery and how.

Source: Ann M. Florini and Yahya A. Dehqanzada, "Commercial Satellite Imagery Comes of Age," *Issues in Science and Technology*, Fall 1999, 45–52. Reprinted with permission from *Issues in Science and Technology*. Copyright © 1999 by the University of Texas at Dallas, Richardson, Texas.

Governments, international organizations, and humanitarian groups may find it easier to respond quickly to sudden refugee movements, to document and publicize large-scale atrocities, to monitor environmental degradation, or to manage international disputes before they escalate to full-scale wars. The United Nations, for example, is studying whether satellite imagery could help to significantly curtail drug trafficking and narcotics production over the next 10 years. The International Atomic Energy Agency is evaluating commercial imagery for monitoring compliance with international arms control agreements.

But there is no way to guarantee benevolent use of satellite images. Governments, corporations, and even small groups of individuals could use commercial imagery to collect intelligence, conduct industrial espionage, plan terrorist attacks, or mount military operations. And even when intentions are good, it can be remarkably difficult to derive accurate, useful information, from the heaps of transmitted data. The media have already made major mistakes, misinterpreting images and misidentifying objects, including the number of reactors on fire during the Chernobyl nuclear accident in 1986 and the location of the Indian nuclear test sites just last year.

The Trend Toward Transparency

Bloopers notwithstanding, the advent of these satellites is important in itself and also as a case study for a trend sweeping the world: the movement toward transparency. It is more and more difficult to hide information, not only because of improvements in technology but also because of changing concepts about who is entitled to have access to what information. Across issues and around the world, the idea that governments, corporations, and other concentrations of political and economic power are obliged to provide information about themselves is gaining ground.

In politics, several countries are enacting or strengthening freedom-of-information laws that give citizens the right to examine government records. In environmental issues, the current hot topic is regulation by revelation, in which polluters are required not to stop polluting but to reveal publicly just how much they are polluting. Such requirements have had dramatic effects, shaming many companies into drastically reducing noxious emissions. In arms control, mutual inspections of sensitive military facilities have become so commonplace that it is easy to forget how revolutionary the idea was a decade or two ago. As democratic norms spread, as civil society grows stronger and more effective in its demands for information, as globalization gives people an ever-greater stake in knowing what is going on in other parts of the world, and as technology makes such knowledge easier to attain, increased transparency is the wave of the future.

The legitimacy of remote-sensing satellites themselves is part of this trend toward transparency. Images from high-resolution satellites are becoming available now not only because technology has advanced to the point of making them a potential source of substantial profits, but [also] because government policies permit and even encourage them to operate. Yet governments are concerned about just how far this new source of transparency should be allowed to go. The result is inconsistent policies produced by the conflicting desires of states to both promote and control the free flow of satellite imagery. Although fears about the impact of the new satellites are most often expressed in terms of potential military vulnerabilities, in fact their impact is likely to be far more sweeping. They shift power from the former holders of secrets to the newly informed. That has implications for national sovereignty, for the ability of corporations to keep proprietary information secret, and for the balance of power between government and those outside it.

The new satellite systems challenge sovereignty directly. If satellite operators are permitted to photograph any site anywhere and sell the images to anyone, governments lose significant control over information about their turf. Both spy and civilian satellites have been doing this for years, but operators of the spy satellites have been remarkably reticent about the information they have collected, making it relatively easy for countries to ignore them. Pakistan and India may not have liked being observed by the United States and Russia, but as long as satellite operators were not showing information about Pakistan to India and vice versa, no one got too upset. Although the civilian satellites that operated before the 1990s did provide imagery to the public, they had low resolution, generally not showing objects smaller than 10 meters across. This provides only limited military information, nothing like what will be available from the new 1-meter systems.

Under international law, countries have no grounds for objecting to being imaged from space. The existing standards, the result largely of longstanding U.S. efforts to render legitimate both military reconnaissance and civilian imaging from space, are codified in two United Nations (UN) documents. The 1967 Outer Space Treaty declared that outer space cannot be claimed as national territory, thus legitimizing satellite travel over any point on Earth. And despite years of lobbying by the former Soviet bloc and developing countries, who wanted a right of prior consent to review and possibly withhold data about their territories, the UN General Assembly in 1986 adopted legal principles regarding civilian remote sensing that made no mention of prior consent. Instead, the principles merely required that "as soon as the primary data and the processed data concerning the territory under its jurisdiction are produced, the sensed state shall have access to them on a nondiscriminatory basis and on reasonable cost terms." In other words, if a country knows it is being imaged, it is entitled to buy copies at the going rate. Even then, countries would not know who is asking for specific images and for what purposes. If an order is placed for imagery of a country's military bases, is that [a] nongovernmental organization (NGO) trying to monitor that country's compliance with some international accord or an adversary preparing for a preemptive strike?

There is a major economic concern as well. Corporations with access to satellite imagery may know more about a country's natural resources than does the country's own government, putting officials at a disadvantage when negotiating agreements such as drilling rights or mining contracts. And as we have all seen recently, highly visible refugee flows and humanitarian atrocities can attract intense attention from the international community. The growing ability of NGOs and the media to track refugee flows or environmental catastrophes may encourage more interventions, even in the face of resistance from the governments concerned. Will the lackadaisical protection of sovereignty in the 1986 legal principles continue to be acceptable to governments whose territory is being inspected?

Corporations may also feel a new sense of vulnerability if they are observed by competitors trying to keep tabs on the construction of new production facilities or to estimate the size of production runs by analyzing emissions. This is not corporate espionage as usually defined because satellite imaging is thoroughly legal. But it could make it difficult for corporations to keep their plans and practices secret.

Not only its competitors will want to keep an eye on a particular corporation. Environmentalists, for example, may find the new satellites useful for monitoring what it is doing to the environment. This use will develop more slowly than will military applications because 1-meter spatial resolution is not significantly better than existing systems for environmental monitoring. Political scientist Karen Litfin has pointed out that environmental organizations already make extensive use of existing publicly available satellite images to monitor enforcement of the U.S. Endangered Species Act, to document destruction of coral reefs, and to generate plans for ecosystem management. Environmental applications will become far more significant when hyperspectral systems are available because they will be able to make fine distinctions among colors and thus provide detailed information about chemical composition. That day is not far off; the Orbview 4 satellite, due to be launched in 2000, will carry a hyperspectral sensor.

Environmental groups are not the only organizations likely to take advantage of this new source of information. Some groups that work on security and arms control, such as the Verification Technology and Information Centre (www.fhit.org/vertic) in London and the Federation of American Scientists (www.fas.org) in Washington have already used, and publicized, satellite imagery. As publicly available imagery improves from 5-meter to 1-meter resolution, humanitarian groups may find it increasingly useful in dealing with complex emergencies and tracking refugee flows. They will be able to gather and analyze information independent of governments—an important new source of power for civil society.

In short, the new remote-sensing satellites will change who can and will know what, and thus they raise many questions. Who is regulating the remote-sensing industry, who should, and how? Does the new transparency portend an age of peace and stability, or does it create new vulnerabilities that will make the world more rather than less unstable and violent? When should satellite imagery be treated as a public good to be provided (or controlled) by governments, and when should it be treated as a private good to be created by profit seekers and sold to the highest bidder? Who gets to decide? Is it possible to reconcile the public value of the free flow of information for pressing purposes such as humanitarian relief, environmental protection, and crisis management with the needs of the satellite industry to make a profit by selling that information? Is it even possible to control and regulate the flow of images from the new satellites? Or must governments, and people, simply learn to live with relentless eyes in the sky?

Present U.S. policies fail to address some of these questions and give the wrong answers to others. By and large, U.S. policies on commercial and civilian satellites lack the long-term perspective that can help remote sensing fulfill its promise. And there are distressing signs that other countries may be following the United States down the wrong path.

The Trials of Landsat

U.S. policy on remote sensing has gyrated wildly among divergent goals. First, there has long been a dispute over the purpose of the U.S. remote-sensing program. Should it be to ensure that the world benefits from unique forms of information, or should it be to create a robust private industry in which U.S. firms would be dominant? Second, the question of which agency within the U.S. Government should take operational responsibility for the civilian remote-sensing program has never been resolved. Several different agencies use the data, but none has needed it enough to fight for the continued survival of the program. These two factors have slowed development of a private observation satellite industry and at times have nearly crippled the U.S. civilian program.

The story begins with the launch of Landsat 1 by the National Aeronautics and Space Administration (NASA) in 1972. However, Landsat 1's resolution (80 meters multispectral) was too coarse for most commercial purposes; scientists, educators, and government agencies were its principal patrons. In an effort to expand the user base and set the stage for commercialization, the Carter administration transferred the program from NASA to the National Oceanic and Atmospheric Administration (NOAA). Ronald Reagan, a strong believer in privatization, decided to pick up the pace despite several studies showing that the market for Landsat data was not nearly strong enough to sustain an independent commercial remote-sensing industry. To jump-start private initiatives, NOAA selected Earth Observation Satellite Company (EOSAT), a joint venture of RCA Corporation and Hughes Aircraft Company, to operate the Landsat satellites and market the resulting data.

The experiment failed disastrously because the market for Landsat imagery was just as poor as the studies had foretold and because the Government failed to honor its financial commitments. Prices were raised dramatically, leading to a sharp drop in demand. For several years Landsat hung by a thread.

During this low point, France launched Landsat's first competitors, which had higher resolutions and shorter revisit times; their images were outselling Landsat's by 1989. The fate of Landsat's privatization was sealed when the United States discovered its national security utility during the Gulf War. The U.S. Department of Defense spent an estimated $5 million to $6 million on Landsat imagery during Operations *Desert Shield* and *Desert Storm*. In 1992, Congress transferred control back to the Government.

But Landsat's troubles were not yet over. In 1993, Landsat 6, the only notable product of the Government's contract with EOSAT, failed to reach orbit, and the $256.5 million spacecraft plunged into the Pacific. Fortunately, Landsat 7 was launched successfully in April 1999, and it is hoped that it will return the United States to the forefront of civilian remote sensing.

Commercial Remote Sensing Emerges

Congress established the legal framework for licensing and regulating a private satellite industry in 1984, but no industry emerged until 1993, when WorldView, Inc., became the first U.S. company licensed to operate a commercial land observation satellite. Since then, 12 more U.S. companies have been licensed, and U.S. investors have put an estimated $1.2 billion into commercial remote sensing.

This explosion of capitalist interest reflects political and technological changes. First, the collapse of the Soviet Union removed barriers that stifled private initiatives. Throughout the Cold War, U.S. commercial interests were constantly subordinated to containment of the Soviet threat. Investors were deterred from developing technologies that might be subjected to Government scrutiny and regulation.

Second, a newfound faith that the market for remote-sensing data will grow exponentially has spurred expansion of the U.S. private satellite industry. Despite enormous discrepancies among various estimates of the future volume of the remote-sensing market, which range from $2 billion to $20 billion by 2000, most investors believe that if they build the systems, users will come. Potential consumers of remote-sensing data include farmers, city planners, map makers, environmentalists, emergency response teams, news organizations, surveyors, geologists, mining and oil companies, timber harvesters, and domestic as well as foreign military planners and intelligence organizations. Many of these groups already use imagery from French, Russian, and Indian satellites in addition to Landsat, but none of these match the capabilities of the new U.S. commercial systems.

Third, advances in panchromatic, multispectral, and even hyperspectral data acquisition, storage, and processing, along with the ability to quickly and efficiently transfer the data, have further supported industry growth. In the 1980s, information technology could not yet provide a robust infrastructure for data. Now, powerful personal computers capable of handling large data files, geographic information system software designed to manipulate spatial data, and new data distribution mechanisms such as CD–ROMs and the Internet have all facilitated the marketing and sale of satellite imagery.

Fourth, after Landsat commercialization failed, the U.S. Government took steps to promote an independent commercial satellite industry. Concerned that foreign competitors such as France, Russia, and India might dominate the market, President Clinton in 1994 loosened restrictions on the sale of high-resolution imagery to foreigners. The Government has also tried to promote the industry through direct subsidies to companies and guaranteed data purchases. Earth Watch, Space Imaging, and OrbImage, for example, have been awarded up to $4 million to upgrade ground systems that will facilitate transfer of data from their satellites to the National Imagery and Mapping Agency (NIMA). In addition, the Air Force has agreed to give OrbImage up to $30 million to develop and deploy the WarFighter sensor, which is capable of acquiring 8-meter hyperspectral images of Earth. Although access to most of WarFighter's imagery will be restricted to Government agencies, OrbImage will be permitted to sell 24-meter hyperspectral images to nongovernment sources. The Office of Naval Research has agreed to give Space Technology Development

Corporation approximately $60 million to develop and deploy the NEMO satellite, with 30-meter hyperspectral and 5-meter panchromatic sensors. The U.S. Intelligence Community has also agreed to purchase high-resolution satellite imagery. Since fiscal year 1998, for example, NIMA has reportedly spent about $5 million annually on commercial imagery, and Secretary of Defense William Cohen says he expects this figure to increase almost 800 percent over the next 5 years.

Shutter Control

To legitimize satellite remote sensing, the United States pushed hard, and successfully, for international legal principles allowing unimpeded passage of satellites over national territory and for unimpeded distribution of the imagery flowing from civilian satellites. To regain U.S. commercial dominance in the technology, the United States is permitting U.S.-based companies to launch commercial satellites with capabilities substantially better than those available elsewhere. But the United States, like other governments, hesitates to allow the full flowering of transparency. Now that the public provision of high-resolution satellite imagery is becoming a global phenomenon, policy contradictions are becoming glaringly apparent. What are the options?

One possibility is to take unilateral measures, such as the present policy of export control with a twist. Unlike other types of forbidden exports, where the point is to keep some technology within U.S. boundaries, imagery from U.S.-controlled satellites does not originate within the country. Satellites collect the data in outer space, then transmit them to ground stations, many of which are located in other countries. To maintain some degree of export control in this unusual situation, the United States has come up with a policy called "shutter control." The licenses NOAA has issued for commercial remote-sensing satellites contain this provision:

> During periods when national security or international obligations and/or foreign policies may be compromised, as defined by the secretary of defense or the secretary of state, respectively, the secretary of commerce may, after consultation with the appropriate agency(ies), require the licensee to limit data collection and/or distribution by the system to the extent necessitated by the given situation.

But shutter control raises some major problems. For one thing, satellite imagery is a classic example of how difficult it is to regulate goods with civilian as well as military applications. Economic interests want to maintain a major U.S. presence in what could be a large and highly profitable industry that the United States pioneered. National security interests want to prevent potential adversaries from using the imagery against the United States or its allies, and foreign policy interests prefer no publicity in certain situations.

Yet denying imagery to potential enemies undercuts the market for U.S. companies, and may only relinquish the field to other countries. Potential customers who know that their access to imagery may be cut off at any time by the vagaries of U.S. foreign policy may prefer to build commercial relationships with other, more reliable providers. These difficulties are further complicated by the fact that the U.S. military relies increasingly on these systems and therefore has a stake in their commercial success. Not only does imagery provide information for U.S. military operations, but unlike imagery from U.S. spy satellites, that information can also be shared with allies—a considerable advantage in operations such as those in Bosnia or Kosovo.

An extreme form of shutter control is to prohibit imaging of a particular area. Although it runs counter to longstanding U.S. efforts to legitimize remote sensing, the Government has already instituted one such ban. U.S. companies are forbidden to collect or sell imagery of Israel "unless such imagery is no more detailed or precise than satellite imagery . . . that is routinely available from [other] commercial sources." Furthermore, the President can extend the blackout to any other region. Israel already operates its own spy satellite (OFEQ–3) and plans to enter the commercial remote-sensing market with its 1-meter-resolution EROS–A satellite in December 1999. Thus, allegations persist that Israel is at least as interested in protecting its commercial prospects by hamstringing U.S. competitors as it is in protecting its own security.

Shutter control also faces a legal challenge. It may be unconstitutional. The media have already used satellite imagery extensively, and some news producers are eagerly anticipating the new high-resolution systems. The Radio-Television News Directors Association argues vehemently that the existing standard violates the First Amendment by allowing the Government to impose prior restraint on the flow of information, with no need to prove clear and present danger or imminent national harm. If shutter control is exercised in any but the most compelling circumstances, a court challenge is inevitable.

Even if it survives such a challenge, shutter control will do little to protect U.S. interests. Although the U.S. satellites will be more advanced than any of the systems currently in orbit other than spy satellites, they hardly have the field to themselves. Russia, France, Canada, and India are already providing high-resolution optical and radar imagery to customers throughout the world, and Israel, China, Brazil, South Korea, and Pakistan are all preparing to enter the commercial market. Potential customers will have many alternative sources of imagery.

Persuasion and Voluntary Cooperation

An alternative is to persuade other operators of high-resolution satellites to voluntarily restrict their collection and dissemination of sensitive imagery. However, the U.S. decision to limit commercial imagery of Israel was based on 50 years of close cooperation between the two countries. Would the United States be able to elicit similar concessions from other states that operate high-resolution remote-sensing satellites but do not value U.S. interests to the extent that the United States values Israel's interests? There is little reason to believe that the Russians, Chinese, or Indians would respect U.S. wishes about what imagery should be disseminated or to whom.

The prospect for controlling imagery through international agreements becomes even more precarious as remote-sensing technology proliferates, coming within the grasp of other countries. Canada, for example, plans to launch RADARSAT 2, with 3-meter resolution. Initially, NASA was to launch the satellite but expressed reservations once it became clear just how good RADARSAT's resolution would be. Whether the two countries can agree on how the imagery's distribution should be restricted remains to be seen, but Canada's recent announcement of its own shutter-control policy may help to alleviate some U.S. concerns.

If, as certainly seems possible, it proves unworkable to control the flow of information from satellites, two options remain: taking direct action to prevent satellites from seeing what they would otherwise see or learning to live with the new transparency. Direct action requires states to either hide what is on the ground or disable satellites in the sky. Satellites generally travel in fixed orbits, making it easy to predict when one will be overhead. Hiding assets from satellite observation is an old Cold War tactic. The Soviets used to deploy large numbers of fake tanks and even ships to trick the eyes in the sky. Objects can be covered with conductive material such as chicken wire to create a reflective glare that obscures whatever is underneath. One security concern for the United States is whether countries that currently do not try to conceal their activities from U.S. spy satellites will do so once they realize that commercial operators can sell imagery of them to regional adversaries. Officials fear that commercial imagery may deprive the United States of information it currently acquires from its spy satellites.

Although concealment is often possible, it will become harder as satellites proliferate. High-resolution radar capable of detecting objects as small as one meter across—day or night, in any weather, even through clouds or smoke—will reduce opportunities for carrying out sensitive activities unobserved. Moreover, many new systems can look from side to side as well as straight down, so knowing when you are being observed is not so easy.

If hiding does not work, what about countermeasures against the satellite itself? There are many ways to put satellites out of commission other than shooting them down, especially in the case of unprotected civilian systems that are of necessity in low orbits. Electronic and electro-optical countermeasures can jam or deceive satellites. Satellites can also be spoofed: interfered with electronically so that they shut down or change orbit. The operator may never know whether the malfunction is merely a technical glitch or the result of a hostile action. (And the spoofer may never know whether the target satellite was actually affected.) Such countermeasures could prove useful during crises or war to prevent access to pictures of a specific temporary activity without the legal bother of shutter control or the political hassle of negotiated restraints. But during peacetime, they would become obvious if carried out routinely to prevent imaging of a particular site.

The more dramatic approach would be to either shoot a satellite down or destroy its data-receiving stations on the ground. Short of imminent or actual war, however, it is difficult to imagine that the United States would bring international opprobrium on itself by destroying civilian satellites or committing acts of aggression against a sovereign state. If the United States could live with Soviet spy satellites during some of the most perilous moments of the Cold War, it is unthinkable that it would violate international law in order to avoid being observed by far less threatening adversaries. Moreover, the U.S. economy and national security apparatus are far more dependent on space systems than is the case in any other country. It would be self-defeating for the United States to violate the long-held international norm of noninterference with satellite operations.

Get Used to It

The instinctive reaction of governments confronted by new information technologies is to try to control them, especially when the technologies are related to power and politics. In the case of high-resolution remote-sensing satellites, however, the only practical choice is to embrace emerging transparency, take advantage of its positive effects, and learn to manage its negative consequences. No one is fully prepared for commercial high-resolution satellite imagery. The U.S. Government is trying to maintain a kind of export control over a technology that has long since proliferated beyond U.S. borders. The international community agreed more than a decade ago to permit the unimpeded flow of information from satellite imagery, but that agreement may come under considerable strain as new and far more capable satellites begin to distribute their imagery publicly and widely. Humanitarian, environmental, and arms control organizations can put the imagery to good use. Governments, however, are likely to be uncomfortable with the resulting shift in power to those outside government, especially if they include terrorists. And many, many people will make mistakes, especially in the early days. Satellite imagery is hard to interpret. Junior analysts are wrong far more often than they are right. Despite these potential problems, on balance the new transparency is likely to do more good than harm. It will allow countries to alleviate fear and suspicion by providing credible evidence that they are not mobilizing for attack. It will help governments and others cope with growing global problems by creating comprehensive sources of information that no single government has an incentive to provide. Like any information, satellite imagery is subject to misuse and misinterpretation. But the eyes in the sky have rendered sustained secrecy impractical. And in situations short of major crisis or war, secrecy rarely works to the public benefit.

Chapter 13

"John, How Should We Explain MASINT?"

John D. Macartney

Whereas SIGINT is akin to hearing, and IMINT to sight, MASINT is akin to touch, taste, and smell.[1]

In 1988, I was an Air Force colonel on detail from the Defense Intelligence Agency (DIA) to the faculty of the National War College in Washington to teach about intelligence. My Central Intelligence Agency (CIA) colleague and I offered a graduate, codeword-level course. I recall meeting in our office spaces prior to class one day, and Joel, my colleague, asked me how I thought we should explain MASINT. We both knew what the acronym stood for—measurement and signature intelligence—but, alas, that's all we knew. So, we put our heads together and decided that we would explain it to our students as a "catch-all" category of miscellaneous technical collection tools. MASINT, we told our students that afternoon, was simply technical intelligence that was neither signals intelligence (SIGINT) nor imagery intelligence (IMINT). Examples, we said, were air and water sampling, nuclear intelligence using radiation detectors and telemetry intelligence. And that was that—the term MASINT did not come up again during the remainder of the semester. The explanation we arrived at in our ignorance was actually not so far removed from the official definition.

Measurement and signature intelligence (MASINT) is technically derived intelligence (excluding traditional imagery and signal intelligence), which, when collected, processed, and analyzed, results in intelligence that detects, tracks, identifies, or describes the signatures (distinctive characteristics) of fixed or dynamic target sources.[2]

Signatures. As the definition implies, the key word in measurement and signature intelligence is *signature*. MASINT sensors come in a wide variety. What they all seem to have in common is the ability to detect and differentiate specific "signatures" that reveal the presence of particular materials or phenomenon—like underground facilities, marijuana or opium patches, industrial pollutants, anthrax, nerve gas, explosives or enemy war machines. By detecting these "signatures," MASINT can make unique contributions to intelligence in terms of specific weapons identification, chemical compositions, material content, and so on.

Source: John Macartney, "John, How Should We Explain MASINT?" in *Intelligencer: Journal of U.S. Intelligence Studies* 12, no. 1 (Summer 2001), 28–34. Copyright © 2001 by Association of Former Intelligence Officers, McLean, Virginia. Reprinted by permission.

History. MASINT has been around for years, although we used to call it by other names. Air and water sampling, radioactivity sensors, seismometers, acoustic devices, and the monitoring of missile test telemetry are old and familiar examples of MASINT. Twenty-four years ago, for example, the 1977 Camp David Accords treaty between Israel and Egypt carried in it explicit language about MASINT-type sensors that the United States was to place and maintain in the Sinai to support that treaty:

> 1) A strain-sensitive cable sensor (SSCS), which, buried in the soil, senses movement crossing it and thus acts as an invisible fence; 2) A miniature seismic intrusion detector (MINISID 111), that senses vibration caused by people from 50 meters and by vehicles from 500 meters; 3) An acoustic add-on unit (AAU), which is a communications device that transmits sounds picked up within the sensor field back to the watch station; and 4) A directional infrared intrusion detector (DIRID), which is an optical device that senses the temperature difference between the normal background and an intruder.[3]

The term *MASINT* was coined in the 1970s, and in 1986, the U.S. Intelligence Community officially recognized MASINT. In 1992 it was cast as one of four main "INTs," alongside and theoretically on par with human intelligence (HUMINT), SIGINT, and IMINT, and a Central MASINT Office (CMO) was established within DIA to be the Community-wide coordinator and advocate for MASINT programs, which are carried out across the Intelligence Community. The Air Force has taken a leading role in the high-tech MASINT business, and some 84 percent of MASINT's General Defense Intelligence Program funding and 93 percent of its manpower were Air Force provided in 1996.[4] The National Air Intelligence Center (NAIC) at Wright-Patterson Air Force Base in Ohio has been designated as the Department of Defense (DOD) and Intelligence Community prime actor for the exploitation of MASINT data.

Increased Clout. In 1999, and as a result of congressional urging, the Central MASINT Office in DIA was upgraded to an organization, with the same initials and made a major Directorate of the DIA. The Director of the CMO, now Barbara Sanderson, reports to the DCI through the Director of DIA. Since the 1999 upgrade, the Director of CMO has much increased bureaucratic and political strength and is a member of the Military Intelligence Board, the Senior Military Officers Intelligence Council, and the Intelligence Program Review Group. Further, CMO now provides guidance on MASINT content for all national and tactical intelligence programs. Also, the CMO provides independent evaluation of National Foreign Intelligence Program and Tactical Intelligence and Related Activities programs to the Director of Central Intelligence and the Deputy Secretary of Defense. Nevertheless, the CMO, whose growing organization still consists of only about 100 professionals, is far smaller and with less clout than the huge flagship organizations that run the other three INTs—CIA (HUMINT), the National Security Agency (SIGINT), or the National Imagery and Mapping Agency (NIMA) and National Reconnaissance Organization (IMINT).

Why is so little known about MASINT? Partly, it seems, because MASINT is relatively new—much of it is still on drawing boards, in laboratories, or on experimental reconnaissance vehicles. Also, the technologies involved are so exotic and complex that most of us do not have enough scientific background to understand much about MASINT. Most journalists also lack the technical background to understand MASINT, and even if they do understand it, the complexity of MASINT does not lend itself to sound bytes or newspaper articles. As a result, MASINT does not get the kind of press coverage that IMINT, SIGINT, and HUMINT routinely receive. Finally, MASINT is heavily classified. As exotic new sensors are fielded, the Intelligence Community prefers to keep them and our newest capabilities in the shadows. Which is as it should be. Nevertheless, enough information is in the public domain for us to get a general, if incomplete, picture.

I attend most of the many Association of Former Intelligence Officers and National Military Intelligence Association luncheons and symposia in the Washington, DC, area, and throughout 1998 and 1999, senior U.S. intelligence officials were telling these public forums that MASINT was gaining in importance and would soon be *the* most valuable of all the collection disciplines. More important, that is, than HUMINT, SIGINT, or IMINT. It is already indispensable, they said, for detecting weapons of mass destruction—nuclear, chemical, and biological. Quite a statement![5]

By that time, 1999, I was long retired from the Air Force and no longer held any security clearances, but I was still teaching a graduate course on intelligence—at American University's School of International Service in Washington, DC. If MASINT is that important, I thought, I should cover it in my course. As I was unable to find any useful readings on the subject for my students that year, I wrote a two-page handout based on what I could glean from the Internet and publications like *Aviation Week*. That handout was the forerunner of this [chapter].

MASINT Education. Because MASINT is so little understood even within the national security establishment, a major focus of the CMO is "missionary work," or advertising—getting the word out, explaining to Intelligence Community leaders as well as consumers what MASINT is and what it can do for them. MASINT liaison officers, or MASLOS, have been placed on the staff of each [combatant commander], while training packages have been sent out to military schools and colleges. Even civilian universities are being tied into MASINT through research projects and internship opportunities.

Computers and Database Libraries. Advances in computer technology have been critical to the rise of MASINT. Just a decade or so ago, MASINT data (acoustic signatures, multispectral imagery, etc.) was sent to laboratories where it would be painstakingly analyzed by scientists in order to tease additional information out of the data. DNA matching by the law enforcement community still follows this paradigm. But increasingly MASINT sensors are designed to operate in real time. Today, it is more likely that the sensor will be preloaded with a computerized database containing thousands of "signatures." Rather than send the data to a lab, the sensor itself will sort through the known signatures in its database to find one that matches what has just been detected and, often, the result (Mark VII tank, Firecan radar, semplex explosives, nerve gas, or whatever) will be instantly displayed to the operator, who need not be a scientist (or an intelligence officer for that matter), on an LCD screen.

One of the biggest tasks for the U.S. MASINT community today is the collection and construction of libraries of these necessary signature databases. For the sensor to make rapid and accurate identification on, for example, a battlefield, those libraries are crucial.

Trade Association. MASINT is one of the hottest areas of research and development (R&D) and defense contracting, and not surprising, there is a trade association to promote business in this area. MAST, the Measurement and Signature Technologies Association, with its headquarters in Washington, DC, was formed about 2 years ago. Made up of defense and Intelligence Community contractors, it seeks to promote the new discipline, encourage research, and provide for the exchange of information and establish a networking arena. The association's Web site is perhaps the best place for us to start zeroing in on "how to explain MASINT": http://www.mastassociation.org.

> Measurement and Signature Intelligence (MASINT) provides technically derived intelligence to detect, locate, track, identify, and describe the specific characteristics of fixed and dynamic target objects and sources. Numerous scientific disciplines and advanced technologies are applied in dedicated MASINT systems. There are also advanced MASINT processing and exploitation techniques, which broaden the usefulness of data collected by IMINT and SIGINT systems. MASINT collection systems include, but are not limited to, radar, spectroradio-metric, electro-optical, acoustic, radio frequency, nuclear detection, and seismic sensors, as well as techniques for gathering chemical, biological, nuclear, and other material samples. The MASINT discipline encompasses the full range of intelligence functions: requirements management, collection, processing, exploitation, dissemination, reporting, and archiving data. It requires the translation of technical data into recognizable and useful target features and performance characteristics. Computer, communication, data fusion, and display processing technologies now provide actionable MASINT for military operations and other near-real-time applications, as well as for threat characterization and in-depth technical analysis.

This explanation gets us a bit closer, I think, to what MASINT is all about than the official definition. On their Web site, the association goes on with a tutorial—listing and explaining six MASINT subdisciplines: Materials Intelligence, Radar Intelligence, Radio Frequency Intelligence, Geophysical Intelligence, Electro-Optical Intelligence, and Nuclear Intelligence.

■ *Materials Intelligence* is the collection, processing, and scientific analysis of gas, liquid, or solid samples. Materials intelligence is critical to collection against nuclear, chemical, and biological warfare threats. It is also important in analyzing military and civil manufacturing activities, public health concerns, and environmental problems. Samples are collected by both automatic equipment, such as air samplers, and directly by humans with access to areas of interest. Samples, once collected, may be rapidly characterized or undergo extensive forensic laboratory analysis to determine the identity and characteristics of the sources of the samples.

- *Radar Intelligence* (RADINT) is the active or passive collection of energy reflected from a target or object by line-of-sight, bi-static, or over-the-horizon radar systems. RADINT collection provides information on radar cross-sections, tracking, precise spatial measurements of components, motion and radar reflectance, and absorption characteristics for dynamic targets and objectives.
  - *Synthetic Aperture Radar* (SAR) creates a larger apparent antenna than is actually used by consistently adding together (coherently integrating) the radar returns as the host platform moves along a track with respect to the target. A SAR system coupled with advanced MASINT processing techniques provides a high-resolution, day/night collection capability. Such a capability can produce a variety of products such as change detection, terrain mapping, underwater obstacle detection, dynamic sensing of targets in clutter, and radar cross-section signature measurements.
- *Radio Frequency Intelligence* is the collection, processing, and exploitation of electromagnetic emissions from a radio frequency weapon (RFW) precursor, or an RFW simulator; collateral signals from other weapons, weapon precursors, or weapon simulators (for example, electromagnetic pulse signals associated with nuclear bursts); and spurious or unintentional signals.
  - *Electromagnetic Pulses* are measurable bursts of energy. A rapid change in a material or medium, resulting in an explosive force, produces radio frequency emissions. The RF pulse emissions associated with nuclear testing, advanced technology devices, power and propulsion systems, or other impulsive events can be used to detect, locate, identify, characterize, and target threats.
  - *Unintentional Radiation Intelligence* (RINT) involves the integration and specialized application of MASINT collection, processing, and exploitation techniques against unintentional radiation sources that are incidental to the RF propagation and operating characteristics of military and civil engines, power sources, weapons systems, electronic systems, machinery, equipment, or instruments. These techniques may be valuable in detecting, tracking, and monitoring a variety of activities of interest.
- *Geophysical Intelligence* is the collection, processing, and exploitation of phenomena transmitted through the earth (ground, water, atmosphere) and manmade structures including emitted or reflected sounds, pressure waves, vibrations, and magnetic field or ionospheric disturbances.
  - *Seismic Intelligence* is the passive collection and measurement of seismic waves or vibrations in the earth surface (for example, seismic and hydroacoustic systems detect, identify, and locate nuclear explosions on the Earth's surface, underground, and in the ocean).
  - *Acoustic Intelligence* is the collection of passive or active emitted or reflected sounds, pressure waves or vibrations in the atmosphere (ACOUSTINT) or in the water (ACINT) (for example, acoustic systems detect, identify, and track ships and submarines operating on and under the ocean).

- *Magnetic Intelligence* is the collection of detectable magnetic field anomalies in the Earth's magnetic field (land and sea) (for example, magnetometers may detect tanks or other vehicles in the area of interest).

■ *Nuclear Intelligence* (NUCINT) is information derived from nuclear radiation and other physical phenomena associated with nuclear weapons, reactors, processes, materials, devices, and facilities. Nuclear monitoring can be done remotely or during on-site inspections of nuclear facilities. Data exploitation results in characterization of nuclear weapons, reactors, and materials. A number of systems detect and monitor the world for nuclear explosions, as well as nuclear materials production.

■ *Electro-Optical Intelligence* (E–O) is the collection, processing, exploitation, and analysis of emitted or reflected energy across the optical portion (ultraviolet, visible, and infrared) of the electromagnetic spectrum. MASINT E–O provides detailed information on the radiant intensities, dynamic motion, spectral and spatial characteristics, and the materials composition of a target. E–O data collection has broad application to a variety of military, civil, economic, and environmental targets. E–O sensor devices include radiometers, spectrometers, nonliteral imaging systems, lasers, or laser radar (LADAR).

  - *Infrared Intelligence* (IRINT) is a subcategory of electro-optical that includes data collection across the infrared portion of the electromagnetic spectrum. Spectral and thermal properties are measured laser systems—strategic and tactical weapons, range finders, and illuminators.

  - *LASER Intelligence* (LASINT) is integration and specialized application of MASINT E–O, and other collection to gather data on laser systems. The focus of the collection is on laser detection, laser threat warning, and precise measurement of the frequencies, power levels, wave propagation, determination of power source, and other technical and operating characteristics associated with laser systems-strategic and tactical weapons, range finders, and illuminators.

  - *Spectroradiometric Products* include E–O spectral (frequency) and radiometric (energy) measurements. A spectral plot represents radiant intensity versus wavelength at an instant in time. The number of spectral bands in a sensor system determines the amount of detail that can be obtained about the source of the object being viewed. Sensor systems range from multispectral (2–100 bands) to hyperspectral (100–1,000 bands) to ultraspectral (1,000+ bands). More bands provide more discrete information, or greater resolution. The characteristic emission and absorption spectra serve to fingerprint or define the makeup of the feature that was observed. A radiometric plot represents the radiant intensity versus time. An example is the radiant intensity plot of a missile exhaust plume as the missile is in flight. The intensity or brightness of the object is a function of several conditions, including its temperature, surface properties or material, and how fast it is moving. For each point along a time-intensity radiometric plot, a spectral plot can be generated based on the number of spectral bands in the collector.

This spectroradiometric tool is one of the most useful for intelligence purposes and is certainly one of the more difficult for laymen to comprehend. Recall 1997, when we all watched at home on our television sets in real time as the Pathfinder wheeled robotic vehicle moved about the surface of Mars and reported 119 million miles back to Earth the chemical and mineral composition of the Red Planet's surface. That was a demonstration of a "material composition," E–O imaging sensor in action. How does that work? Well, as I understand the science here, any object with a temperature above absolute zero emits electromagnetic energy. The higher the temperature, the shorter the mean wavelength of the radiation. This basic principle is what enables multi or hyperspectral E–O/infrared sensors to remotely determine material composition. Basically, hyperspectral imagery allows the chemical analysis of material remotely— from a hand held spectrometer or from an aircraft or space platform.

Hyperspectral imaging can differentiate one crop from another (a marijuana patch in the midst of corn fields, for example) or one type of soil or mineral sample from another, from space. It can also locate beetle infestation in forests, water and soil pollutants, differentiate real foliage from camouflage, find people or vehicles under trees, and so on. By measuring the strength of growing crops, it can be used to predict future harvests and therefore future food availability, and, of course, future commodity prices. It may also be possible to detect submarines or the wakes of submarines from space, and perhaps locate nuclear, chemical, or biological weapons by reference to their remote "signatures."

The possibilities are almost limitless, and hyperspectral imaging is still in its infancy. Theoretically (and I am making this up), it would be possible to tune a hyperspectral imaging sensor to the paint used on a hostile country's military vehicles—the chemical properties of those paints. That way, a sensor could distinguish between, for example, American tanks, British tanks, and Iraqi tanks based on the chemical composition of the paint. (Of course, my example probably wouldn't work because tanks on the battlefield are likely to be covered with mud, dust, grease, or snow.)

But for purposes of discussion, let us continue with the vehicle paint example. Once you isolate the paint signatures used by various armies, one could not only put that data into intelligence sensors but also into missile guidance sensors. Thus, a missile with an on-board MASINT sensor could distinguish between enemy paint and friendly paint. This example illustrates another problem. It will be necessary to keep classified the particular signature chosen for sensors and/or guidance mechanisms. That becomes extremely sensitive information because, in our hypothetical example, if the enemy found out what signature you were using, they could rather easily change paints, or maybe just splash their paint liberally around the countryside to confuse your sensor (and your missile guidance system)—making them useless.

Of course, MASINT sensors are not limited to the chemical properties of paint. Back to tanks—perhaps a better signature would be a radar silhouette, or maybe thermal emissions, or perhaps acoustic soundings—or maybe a composite signature established by a suite of sensors. Once a reliable database of signatures for tanks is established, then sensors can be programmed to distinguish rocks or trucks from tanks as well as friendlies from enemies, and so on.

MASINT Now? Are there multi or hyperspectral sensors on today's secret U.S. spy satellites? Probably not. The current imaging system, believed to be an "Advanced KH–11," is thought to have infrared imaging capability but not a true multispectral sensor.[6] On the other hand, there are multispectral sensors on commercial satellites and their "take" is regularly used by the U.S. Intelligence Community.

Also, this country's U–2s and other reconnaissance aircraft are being fitted out with MASINT sensors.[7] And there are CMO-sponsored test satellites. One of those, COBRA BRASS, has had a multispectral imaging satellite in orbit for a year or two.[8] Another experimental program sponsored by the Air Force Research Laboratory is "MightySat II," a series of two to five small satellites (all with the same basic configuration) built by Spectrum Astro, Inc. The first MightySat II will have hyperspectral imaging capabilities while a second vehicle is expected to carry an ultraspectral imaging system.[9] Also, NIMA routinely purchases unclassified commercial imagery for intelligence purposes—much of that, it seems likely, is multi or hyperspectral with the take going to the MASINT community. So, the Intelligence Community is using hyperspectral imagery today, even if it is not yet part of our Government "spy satellite" constellation.

Commercial MASINT. What is known in the unclassified world is that Landsat, the first U.S. commercial imaging satellite, has had multispectral capabilities for many years and TRW has a commercial lightsat, LEWIS, which features hyperspectral imaging capabilities.[10] Likewise, IKONOS, launched by Space Imaging, Inc., in September 1999, has 1-meter monochromatic resolution and 4-meter multispectral pixels. Moreover, Space Imaging has developed a technique of overlaying their high-resolution images with information from the multispectral—providing high-resolution, 1-meter imagery with MASINT information tied in. In 1997, the U.S. Air Force awarded Orbital Sciences Corporation a contract to include a hyperspectral imaging capability on one of its OrbView satellites.[11] Also, *Aviation Week and Space Technology* (or any other defense oriented magazine) reveals numerous advertisements for multi and hyperspectral sensors. Lots of companies are selling, so presumably some Government agencies must be interested in buying.

MASINT Support for Military Operations (SMO). During the Cold War, MASINT was generally geared to national-level intelligence—detecting underground nuclear tests with seismometers, for example. But there has apparently been a switch in focus in recent years as new technologies have allowed for instantaneous database matching. Now there is a shift to *tactical* applications—something the "shooter" can use on the battlefield. That development is largely the result of newer sensors equipped with on-board computerized databases discussed earlier that can instantly identify a detected signature. So the emphasis is shifting from strategic systems to battlefield systems—many with a sensor-to-shooter capability that effectively cuts the intelligence officer out of the picture. As these technologies mature, more and more precision-guided munitions will have on-board MASINT sensors that can seek out enemy aircraft (tanks, ships, whatever) while sparing friendlies.

Finally, Some Examples

From what little we can glean from open sources, it is apparent that MASINT involves a good deal of "Buck Rogers"–like high-tech gadgetry. Much of that, perhaps most, seems to be in the research and development worlds. Some of these sensors are probably already operational—good for us. So, I will end this [chapter] with a sampling of some the more exotic MASINT endeavors I have come across in the open source literature and on the Internet.

- *Spectral Analysis of Jet or Rocket Exhaust.* Electro-optical or infrared sensors can detect jet or rocket engine exhausts at great distances (for example, from space), they can in some cases perform spectral analyses of the exhaust plume that identifies the type of fuel and the specific type of vehicle (MiG–29 or whatever), and even the throttle setting.[12]

- *F–15 Fire Control Radar.* Although not an intelligence sensor, the radar in the F–15 can get a count of the number of compressor blades on an approaching aircraft, well beyond visual range. And the number of blades constitutes a "signature"—thus identifying the engine itself and, therefore, the type of aircraft.

- *Acoustic Identification of Ships.* The U.S. Navy's acoustic sensors are able to differentiate types of ships and even specific ships by their acoustic "signatures."[13] Even more surprising, [sound surveillance system] arrays planted on the ocean bottom have demonstrated the capability to track and identify aircraft flying over the water.[14]

- *Laser Remote Sensing.* Since weapons of mass destruction (WMD)—chemical, biological, and nuclear—each give off distinctive signatures (or their manufacture or storage involves signatures) and since WMD proliferation is one the top priorities for the Intelligence Community, much of the MASINT effort has been pointed toward WMD detection. One project is CALIOPE. "Chemical Analysis by Laser Interrogation of Proliferation Effluents" is pointed mostly toward detection of nuclear mischief. Laser remote sensing is currently used in a number of climatology and pollution control applications, such as measuring water vapor in the atmosphere and emissions from a chemical plant. The CALIOPE program is attempting to use similar technology against suspect facilities from extreme distances, for example, space.[15]

- *Multispectral Imaging.* The Multispectral Thermal Imager (MTI) satellite is another test program of the Department of Energy's Office of Nonproliferation. The idea is that small amounts of effluent processing dust will accumulate over time and settle on the ground around a suspect manufacturing facility. The MTI satellite can be tuned to detect and identify those effluents and thus determine what is going on inside the suspect facility.[16]

- *Biosensors can identify specific pathogens.* There are already vehicle-mounted sensors in the U.S. Army that can drive into an area suspected of contamination and identify specific pathogens—anthrax, smallpox, etc. Coming out of laboratories and soon to be fielded are much smaller, hand-held units that can do the same and with the tiniest sample of pathogen.[17] This type of sensor detects individual molecules of the target material, and these "sniffers" are also being developed to search for drugs, explosives, and other contraband. These small units can be parachuted into a suspect area ahead of troops to check for contamination. Using spectral analysis principles, there are also sensors under development that are expected to detect and identify chemical agents (nerve gas) and perhaps pathogens remotely—from several miles standoff distance.[18]

■ *Airport sensors can detect minute quantities of contraband.* This falls in the airport security/law enforcement department but tells us a great deal of what is becoming possible. Biosensors, like those described above, have been developed for airports. Early versions are metal wands or metal-detector like doorframes with sensors that "sniff" for explosives or drugs. Newer versions are more sensitive and less obtrusive. If a passenger has handled explosives or drugs in the past few days, trace amounts are left behind on his or her hands—even after repeated washings—and will rub off on tickets or boarding passes. The extremely sensitive sensors scan documents—usually boarding passes, or customs declaration forms after they have been turned in—looking for telltale traces of contraband.[19]

■ *Imaging through Brick or Concrete Walls?* This advertisement from the DOD *Commerce Business Daily* of January 20, 1999 doesn't use the term MASINT but it certainly does sound MASINT-like.

The U.S. Army Intelligence Center, Fort Huachuca, Directorate of Contracting, Thunder Mountain Evaluation Center is seeking information from companies, educational institutions, or other Federal agencies that currently (or plan to) provide R&D services to the Federal Government in support of the Technical Support Working Group. The following is a set of requirements that has been developed to meet needs of various participating agencies in the Technical Support Working Group (TSWG): Systems should have capability to *image through walls* [my emphasis] of varying construction, including: (a) Interior Walls–Standard sheet rock; plaster over lath; plaster over screening materials, wood, ceramic tile, brick, cinder block, stone (marble or granite). These materials are typically installed over interior framing that is either wood or metal; and (b) Exterior Walls–Wood, brick, cinder block, stucco, vinyl or aluminum siding, concrete, and10 reinforced concrete. URL: <http://web.fie.com/htdoc/fed/dod/amy/any/proc/mti/01209907.htm>.

■ *Synthetic Aperture Radar.* SAR and Advanced SAR units allow imagery day or night and in all types of weather. Fine resolution SARs are so sensitive that they can detect, from an aircraft or UAV, small surface penetrations like footprints in soft earth.[20]

Notes

[1] "IC21: Intelligence Community in the 21ˢᵗ Century," Staff Study of the Permanent Select Committee on Intelligence, U.S. House of Representatives, 104ᵗʰ Congress (Washington, DC: Government Printing Office, April 9, 1996), 150.

[2] Department of Defense Instruction 5105.58, "Management of Measurement and Signature Intelligence (MASINT)."

[3] Barry Cherniavsky, *Early Warning Systems and the American Peacekeeping Mission*, Incidental Paper O-81-6, Harvard Program on Information Resources Policy, Cambridge, MA, July 1981, 21–22.

[4] "IC21," 166.

[5] I had related that "most important" statement to my students, and in the spring of 1999 when the late John Millis, then Staff Director of the HPSCI, was our guest lecturer, the very first question he got was about MASINT, which John had not mentioned. "The CMO must have put you up to that question!" John retorted. "Who are you?" The young man replied that Prof Mac (me) had told them MASINT was being billed as the most important of all the INTs (even if I couldn't explain it very well). A discussion followed in which Millis, a former CIA case officer himself, allowed that MASINT was useful and important, but, he went on, certainly not, in his opinion, the most important. Incidentally, the statements about the importance of MASINT were absent from briefings I attended this year and last. When asked about that, two senior intelligence officers said something to the effect that "perhaps MASINT had been oversold in previous statements."

[6] Jeffrey T. Richelson, "High Flying Spies: The Targets May be Getting More Sophisticated, but so are U.S. Intelligence Collection Systems," *Bulletin of Atomic Scientists* 52, no. 5 (September/October 1996).

[7] Part of the "Senior Year" upgrade to the U–2. See Zachary Lum, 1988, 43.

[8] Ibid.

[9] Air Force Research Laboratory, MightySat II Satellites Fact Sheet, July 1999, accessed at <http://www.vs.afrl.af.mil/Factsheets/msat2.html>.

[10] See TRW Web [site] for descriptions of Lewis and its sensor capabilities: <http://www.trw.com/seg/space_guide/space_guide.cgi?27>.

[11] Marco Antonio Caceres, "Satcoms Prosper," in Aviation Week, *1998 Aerospace Source Book*, accessed at <http://www.aviationweek.com/aviation/sourcebook/sb_space.htm>.

[12] Jeffrey T. Richelson, "MASINT: New Kid in Town," *International Journal of Intelligence and Counterintelligence* 14, no. 2 (Summer 2001), 234.

[13] *U.S. News and World Report*, April 6, 1998, 28.

[14] Jeffrey T. Richelson, *The U.S. Intelligence Community*, 4th ed. (Boulder, CO: Westview, 1999), 234.

[15] See the FAS Web [site] at <http://www.fas.org/spp/military/program/masint/caliope.htm>.

[16] See spectacular satellite test images revealing plants with suspect effluents posted at <http://www.fas.org/spp/military/program/masint/mti.htm>.

[17] David Prescovitz, "BIOAGENT CHIP: A Sensor to Detect a Biological Warfare Attack in Seconds," *Scientific American*, March 2000.

[18] ABCNews.com, November 8, 2000.

[19] Jim Krane, "Fliers May Face Secret Searches," ABPnews.com, May 29, 2000.

[20] *Design News*, October 18, 1999, 29.

Chapter 14

The Time of Troubles:
The U.S. National Security
Agency in the 21ˢᵗ Century

Matthew M. Aid

This [chapter] seeks to ask whether the U.S. National Security Agency (NSA) is doing its job or stumbling through a midlife crisis. It reviews what has occurred at NSA during the last decade. It argues that some statements that have appeared in the American press that NSA was solely responsible for some of the U.S. Intelligence Community's recent intelligence failures are factually incorrect. Furthermore, NSA's signals intelligence (SIGINT) collection capabilities have actually improved considerably during the last decade, and evidence suggests that the technological obstacles that have been often cited in press reports as contributing to NSA's current problems have not yet begun to be widely used outside of the developed countries in Western Europe and East Asia.

NSA's most pressing problem is, instead, an area that unfortunately has received little public attention in recent months, specifically the deterioration of the agency's SIGINT processing, analysis, and reporting capabilities. It is clear that NSA must recruit substantial numbers of analysts and information technology specialists in the near future, and invest money in acquiring new processing technologies in order to begin to address this problem. The agency must also take immediate steps to shore up its strained relations with its customers inside the U.S. Government and the Armed Forces. Given the transient and oftentimes fickle nature of politics, NSA must realize that it cannot depend solely on a few allies in the U.S. Congress for its continued survival.

Equally important, but more difficult, will be NSA's internal management problems, such as how to trim the agency's large bureaucracy, eliminate duplication of effort, and how to put NSA's financial accounts in order. Finally, it is time that NSA adopts a policy of greater openness about what it does and how it does it. One obvious way to do this is to declassify documents that detail the agency's significant accomplishments since the end of World War II.

Source: Matthew M. Aid, "The Time of Troubles: The U.S. National Security Agency in the Twenty-First Century," *Intelligence and National Security* 15, no. 3 (Autumn 2000), 1–32. Copyright © 2000 by Frank Cass Publishers, London. Reprinted by permission.

Anything we see is a State secret. Also if it's an illusion it's a State secret. Even if it doesn't work and never will, it's a State secret. And if it is a lie from top to bottom, then it is the hottest State secret of the lot.

—John Le Carre, *The Russia House* (1989)

On December 6, 1999, *The New Yorker* magazine carried a lengthy article by prize-winning investigative reporter Seymour M. Hersh, which revealed that America's largest intelligence organization, the National Security Agency (NSA), is currently suffering from a multitude of serious problems that are impairing its ability to generate the kind of quality information that it had produced throughout the Cold War.[1] The Hersh article prompted other news reports, almost all of which painted a bleak picture of the agency's current health and a poor prognosis for NSA's future.

The question then becomes, as one newspaper article put it, "Is the National Security Agency doing its job—or stumbling through a midlife crisis?"[2] This [chapter] seeks to determine if NSA is, in fact, in a state of crisis by reviewing what has occurred at NSA during the last decade, the agency's current SIGINT collection, processing, and reporting capabilities, the impact of technology on NSA's capacity to perform its mission, and the agency's future prospects.

The Importance of SIGINT Today

Given the intense secrecy surrounding even the most mundane aspects of the NSA's activities, it is extremely difficult for an outsider to accurately evaluate the current importance of this agency to the U.S. foreign intelligence effort. No agency of the U.S. intelligence community has been able to better insulate itself from public scrutiny, and because of the complexity of the technology involved in its work, American journalists and academics have generally tended to shy away from examining NSA's inner workings.[3]

Despite these obstacles, it is possible to sketch some of NSA's work from recently declassified documents, newspaper reports, and interviews with former and current NSA officials.

An examination of the public record revealed a curious contradiction. The somber portrait that has been painted in recent months in the American press about NSA's current state of health runs contrary to a larger body of documentation that shows that the agency remains one of the most productive members of the U.S. Intelligence Community.

It should be noted that NSA is not a single stand-alone entity. Rather, NSA sits atop an empire called the United States SIGINT System (USSS), which consists of several American intelligence organizations that conduct the U.S. Government's national SIGINT mission. The USSS is comprised of the National Security Agency, which has operational control over the three so-called Service Cryptologic Elements (SCEs), consisting of the cryptologic elements of the U.S. Army Intelligence and Security Command

(INSCOM), the Naval Security Group Command (NAVSECGRU), and the Air Intelligence Agency (AIA), as well as the thousands of SIGINT personnel assigned to the U.S. military's various unified and specified commands. NSA also exercises operational control over the joint Central Intelligence Agency (CIA)–NSA SIGINT organization called the Special Collection Service (SCS), which currently operates covert listening posts located in several dozen American diplomatic establishments around the world.[4]

The power of NSA extends well beyond the confines of the USSS. NSA works closely with the CIA's SIGINT organization, the Office of Technical Collection (OTC), which was formed in August 1993 from the merger of the old Office of SIGINT Operations (OSO) with the CIA's Office of Special Projects (OSP). A small unit comprised of only a few hundred personnel, OTC not only manages the CIA's SIGINT collection operations, both overt and covert, but also managed and conducted clandestine operations overseas that obtained foreign cryptographic systems by surreptitious means, such as embassy break-ins and subborning code clerks.[5] Since September 1997, the head of OTC has been James Runyan, a 30-year NSA veteran seconded to the CIA.[6] NSA is also deeply involved in the operations of the National Reconnaissance Office (NRO), the U.S. intelligence agency that develops, builds, and operates America's reconnaissance satellites. According to declassified documents, over 13 percent of NRO's workforce (or 300 men and women) are NSA employees, most of whom work within the NRO's SIGINT Directorate, which operates the fleet of SIGINT satellites in orbit over the Earth.[7]

Despite its huge workforce and budget, some analysts believe that NSA produces today on a dollar-for-dollar basis more "bang for the buck" than any other intelligence source, with perhaps the exception of NRO's spy satellites.[8] In 1995, NSA Director Vice Admiral John McConnell said that "There is not a single event that the U.S. worries about in a foreign policy or foreign military context that NSA does not make a very direct contribution to."[9] In 1998, John Millis, the late staff director of the House intelligence committee, characterized SIGINT as "the INT of choice of the policy maker and the military commander."[10] According to one estimate contained in a June 1, 1998, article in *U.S. News and World Report*, 80 percent of all "useful intelligence" being collected by the U.S. Intelligence Community was coming from SIGINT, although this figure is impossible to verify and seems excessively high.[11]

On the battlefields of the 1990s, SIGINT probably was clearly one of the most important sources of intelligence information available to American combat commanders.[12] NSA played a vital role during Operations *Desert Shield/Storm* in 1990–1991, collecting much of the intelligence information that allowed Allied warplanes to destroy the Iraqi national command and control infrastructure and air defense network early in the war. SIGINT also played an important role in enabling Allied forces to win the Battle of Khafji in January 1991.[13] Since the end of Operation *Desert Storm*, a wide variety of American SIGINT collection systems, including Air Force RC–135 Rivet Joint and Navy EP–3E Aries SIGINT aircraft, have continued to closely monitor Saddam Hussein's regime in Iraq as part of Operation *Southern Watch*, the ongoing military operation that enforces compliance with the United Nations' mandated no-fly zones over southern Iraq.[14]

SIGINT successfully monitored Haitian and Cuban military activities during Operation *Uphold Democracy*, the 1994 operation that ousted the military junta ruling Haiti.[15] NSA was an important source of intelligence information during the war in Bosnia from 1991 to 1996.[16] And by all accounts, NSA performed well during the 1999 conflict in Kosovo.[17]

SIGINT provided White House, Pentagon, and State Department officials and intelligence analysts with important information about foreign political, economic, and military developments, as well as details of the intelligence operations, scientific and technical developments, weapons systems capabilities, and nuclear and chemical weapons development activities of foreign countries.[18]

In 1990, SIGINT detected Pakistani military forces moving to a higher state of alert as tensions with neighboring India over the province of Kashmir escalated.[19] On February 24, 1996, NSA intercepted the communications of two Cuban MiG–29 fighters as they shot down two unarmed Cessna aircraft flown by Cuban-Americans over international waters off Cuba, killing four of the crew members.[20]

SIGINT helped the U.S. Government block attempts by foreign countries to violate United Nations (UN)-imposed sanctions on Iraq.[21] Between 1996 and 1998, NSA and the CIA operated a covert SIGINT system inside Iraq to help UN weapons inspectors locate and destroy weapons of mass destruction that the Iraqi government was trying to hide.[22]

SIGINT helped the U.S. Government thwart planned deliveries of equipment by Russia and China to Iran, Pakistan, and North Korea that could have been used to manufacture nuclear and chemical weapons. For example, in February 1998, NSA intercepts reportedly revealed that Russia's foreign intelligence service, the SVR [*Sluzhba Vneshnei Razvedki*], had facilitated the sale of Russian missile technology to Iran.[23] SIGINT and other intelligence sources revealed that beginning in November 1992, Pakistan had received from China 30 nuclear-capable CSS–6 ballistic missiles.[24] SIGINT also proved to be an important means for tracing the flow of ballistic missile technology from China to North Korea during the 1990s.[25]

And SIGINT provided State Department officials with unusually detailed insights into war crimes committed in Bosnia during the mid-1990s.[26] In January 1999, NSA radio intercepts revealed that high-ranking Yugoslavian government officials had ordered an attack on the village of Racak in Kosovo, which resulted in the massacre of 45 unarmed ethnic Albanian civilians.[27]

By all appearances, NSA's consumers seemed to be happy with the product that they were receiving during the 1990s. In a speech to NSA staff members at Fort Meade, Maryland, on May 1, 1991, President George Bush stated that "[S]ignals intelligence is a prime factor in the decisionmaking process by which we chart the course of this Nation's foreign affairs."[28] In May 1994, Defense Secretary William Perry said in a speech that "I don't make a significant decision without taking into account the products from this agency. . . . NSA's work will be a critical factor in our ability to deal with this particularly complex and particularly uncertain world."[29] In 1996, a Presidential review panel stated in its final report that "NSA's contributions continue to be cited by national policymakers and deployed military forces alike for being of immense value."[30] In March 1997,

NSA received the Joint Meritorious Unit Award from Secretary of Defense William S. Cohen for its work during the period June 1, 1991, to June 1, 1995. The award citation stated, in part, that "During this period, the Agency's constant vigilance and outstanding intelligence support in response to international conflicts, crises, and countless time-sensitive situations requiring decision-maker attention was unparalleled."[31]

All of this raises the question: Is what is described above in any way consistent with an intelligence organization that today is reportedly in a state of crisis? Even one of the loudest critics of NSA, the House Intelligence Committee, reported only 4 years ago that "NSA is an extremely successful organization," adding that "The SIGINT system performs well."[32]

What has happened in the last 4 years to change so many minds? The only way to reconcile the 2 sides of the story and discover the truth is to examine what has happened to NSA in the last 10 years.

NSA and the Peace Dividend

In the fall of 1989, the East German regime collapsed and the Berlin Wall came crashing down. On November 9, 1989, the East German government allowed its people for the first time to freely leave the country, and by June 1, 1990, the Berlin Wall had ceased to exist and all crossing points between East and West Berlin had been opened. In the next 2 years, the Warsaw Pact was dissolved, East and West Germany were united into a single country on October 1, 1990, and the Soviet Union disintegrated into 16 separate countries. The Cold War was over, and NSA's main target for almost 45 years had vanished almost overnight, forcing the agency to adapt in order to survive in the post-Cold War era.

As far as many inside the U.S. Government and Congress were concerned, the end of the Cold War meant that there was no longer a need for "all those spies." Congress demanded a "peace dividend," so the Washington budget-cutters began to trim the size of the U.S. Intelligence Community. Between 1991 and 1996, the Intelligence Community's budget was reduced by 19 percent, from approximately $34.5 billion to slightly more than $27 billion, according to press accounts.[33] NSA's budget took a harder hit than the rest of the Intelligence Community, in part because the White House, the CIA, and Congress emphasized cuts in the U.S. Intelligence Community's expensive technical collection assets.[34] Between 1990 and 1995, NSA's budget was cut by 35 percent, falling from about $5.2 billion in 1990 to $3.47 billion in fiscal year 1995. A report issued by a Presidential commission in March 1996 indicated that NSA's fiscal year 1996 budget had risen slightly to about $3.7 billion, which accounted for roughly 15 percent of the entire U.S. intelligence budget.[35]

Accompanying these deep budget cuts were substantial reductions in the number of men and women spying for America. In 1991, Congress ordered that the number of personnel employed by the U.S. Intelligence Community be cut by 17.5 percent by the end of 1999. The CIA and Defense Department later agreed to expand these personnel reductions to 22.5 percent. As a result, between 1991 and 1998, the U.S. Intelligence Community's manpower was cut by more than 20 percent, meaning that 20,559 men and women were either given early retirement or laid off.[36]

NSA's staff cuts during this period were also more severe than the other agencies comprising the Intelligence Community. The expectation in 1992 was that the size of NSA's workforce would be reduced by 17.5 percent between 1992 and 1997, which was in line with the above-mentioned congressional plan.[37] But by 1996, the U.S. SIGINT system had lost one-third of its personnel, falling from 75,000 military and civilian personnel in 1990 to slightly more than 50,000 military and civilian personnel by 1996.[38] NSA, which was the largest component of the USSS, lost about one-third of its personnel, with its manpower levels falling from about 56,000 personnel in 1990 (26,000 civilians and 30,000 military personnel) to approximately 38,000 by 1996 (20,000 civilians and 18,000 military personnel).[39]

NSA was able to slash its budget and manpower in large part by making deep cuts in the size of its SIGINT collection network. Between 1990 and 1998, NSA closed 20 of its 40 listening posts, most of which were large HF intercept stations situated around the periphery of the Soviet Union, and the size of its military SIGINT intercept force was slashed by one-third from 21,000 to 14,000 personnel.[40] NSA also trimmed the size of its civilian staff, most of whom worked at NSA headquarters at Fort Meade, by almost 7,000 men and women between 1990 and 1998.[41]

A Poor State of Affairs: The Internal Management of NSA

Carefully hidden from public view were a host of internal problems that continue to bedevil NSA today.

The first problem was that classified financial audits and internal reviews of the agency conducted in the early 1990s found that NSA possessed one of the largest, multi-layered bureaucracies in the entire U.S. Intelligence Community, which was impeding the effective management of the agency.[42] Upon becoming the director of NSA in 1992, Vice Admiral McConnell found widespread duplication of effort, inefficiency, and a huge number of personnel carried on NSA's payroll who had "little involvement in actually accomplishing the Agency's mission."[43]

The bureaucratic inefficiency of NSA manifested itself in various ways. For example, an internal study in the early 1990s found that NSA's logistics office needed 10 days to get a box of paperclips to someone inside the agency from the time it was ordered; NSA's telecommunications and computer services office took 4 months to install a desktop computer from the time an employee requested the system; and the agency's contracting office required over 6 months to award a contract after it had received all proposals and tendered offers from contractors. In one NSA directorate, on average it took 13 days to send a letter, measured from the time the letter was drafted to the time it was actually mailed, due to all of the reviews, endorsements and approvals that the letter had to go through before it could be sent.[44]

This situation had developed because historically there has been very little internal or external oversight of the agency's operations, especially during the so-called "Go-Go 1980s." A 1991 audit by the Defense Department's Inspector General revealed that "NSA did not have sufficient oversight mechanisms to ensure the Agency efficiently accomplished its mission."[45] A 1991 House intelligence committee report found "very limited internal oversight of Agency [NSA] programs," as well as no supervision of the agency by either the Department of Defense Inspector General's office or the congressional watchdog agency, the General Accounting Office (GAO).[46] In December 1995, former CIA Director John M. Deutch reportedly intervened with key Members of Congress to prevent the GAO from auditing a particularly troubled NSA project.[47] A 1996 Department of Defense Inspector General report on NSA also found that the agency still was lacking adequate internal management oversight or controls.[48]

Then there were questionable decisions made in the mid-1990s about how to spend NSA's shrinking budget. For example, despite the fact that the agency's budget and personnel were cut by one-third between 1990 and 1996, somehow the cost of paying for NSA's civilian personnel rose by a whopping 26 percent during the same years. According to a 1996 report, 40 percent of NSA's $3.7 billion fiscal year 1996 budget went to pay the salaries and benefits of the agency's civilian workforce.[49] Part of the increased personnel costs were attributable to a reported 29 percent pay increase in 1993 for NSA's senior managers, which occurred at the same time that the agency was letting thousands of its employees go.[50]

This naturally left a limited amount of money for the actual conduct of NSA's operations. During the mid-1990s, a furious battle raged between NSA's SIGINT and Information Security (INFOSEC) directorates over who got the lion's share of what remained of NSA's budget. The apparent loser in this battle was NSA's 4,000-person Technology and Systems Directorate, which ran the agency's information technology infrastructure and managed its research and development program. Faced with a financial pinch, NSA chose to cut spending on infrastructure and research and development in order to keep the core SIGINT and INFOSEC missions up and running.[51]

It should therefore come as no surprise that NSA has had a less than stellar record managing its finances over the last decade. In 1994, an investigation by the Defense Department found that NSA had wasted almost $7 million dollars on two communications security programs called "Blacker" and "Cane Ware."[52] In 1994, NSA asked Congress for $250 million to fund the purchase of a new supercomputer system to be used against advanced foreign encryption systems. When pressed to justify the need for the new computer system, NSA reportedly refused to provide Congress with information about how many computers it had, how they were being used, and took months to finally develop a plan for the use of the requested computer system.[53]

In the late 1990s, NSA spent millions of dollars on a project called "Light Core," which was an upgrade of the agency's data network. Civilian contractors working for the agency told NSA officials that the upgrade would not work, but the agency went ahead with the project anyway. According to press reports, "Today the system requires frequent technological band-aids" to keep it up and running, all of which is costing NSA millions of dollars.[54]

A 1996 audit of NSA by the DOD Inspector General (IG) found glaring management and accounting deficiencies. For instance, the IG report revealed that in 1991 and 1992 alone, NSA lost $82 million worth of equipment, which it wrote off on its financial statements rather than determine what had become of the material.[55]

Two years later, a still-classified August 1998 DOD Inspector General report, entitled *Fiscal Year 1997 Financial Statements for the National Security Agency*, found that NSA still could not track what it paid for, suffered from "material" weaknesses in its accounting system, and that the agency had not corrected the financial problems identified in the above mentioned 1996 IG audit which it had told the Pentagon had been fixed.[56] In 1998, the House intelligence committee discovered that NSA had not spent any money on programs for attacking new communications technologies that Congress had previously approved. Moreover, NSA officials were not able to provide the committee with an accurate accounting of how the funds had been spent.[57]

Where Have All the People Gone?

The second significant problem that escaped public attention until years later was that during the 1990s NSA lost many of its best employees. As noted above, NSA lost almost 7,000 of its civilian employees between 1990 and 1998.[58] But many of those employees taking early retirements in the early 1990s were some of the agency's most experienced senior managers, analysts, and technical personnel, most of whom had served with the agency for more than 20 years. Lost with these men and women was much of the agency's institutional knowledge. Then many of the agency's middle-level managers left NSA in the late 1990s for better paying jobs in the private sector.[59]

As if this was not bad enough, NSA also lost many of its best technical personnel during the 1990s, especially in the engineering, computer science, and information technology fields, most of whom left for better paying jobs in the private sector.[60] NSA also lost a large number of skilled personnel who worked in the non-technical fields, such as hundreds of highly trained linguists.[61] Former NSA officials point out that despite repeated requests, Congress did not make more money available for pay raises or retention incentives in order to help NSA keep its skilled personnel.[62]

To make matters worse, throughout the 1990s NSA experienced considerable difficulty in recruiting new personnel with the right skill sets to replace the losses. This was because of a Government-wide hiring and wage freeze in effect for most of the 1990s, and a lack of financial incentives needed to attract young potential recruits possessing the requisite technical skills that NSA needed, particularly in the computer science and information technology fields.[63]

The result was that by 1996, NSA was experiencing a particularly severe problem with the size, age, skills, and make-up of its workforce.[64] NSA's current director, Air Force Lieutenant General Michael V. Hayden, has recently admitted that NSA's staff today is largely comprised of two groups: the first consists of a large group of older senior managers who are fast nearing retirement age, and a very young group of less experienced employees who are increasingly comprised of military personnel on rotational duty with the agency. Apparently there is little in between these two groups because of high personnel attrition rates during the late 1990s.[65] NSA's consumers began to complain that the younger NSA civilian analysts and managers whom they had to deal with were inexperienced and knew less about their customers' needs than their predecessors who were let go or resigned in the early 1990s.[66]

In recent years NSA has resorted to desperate measures to try to keep as many of its remaining managers and technicians "in the fold." Between 1996 and 1998, 500 NSA personnel were "retired," and were moved immediately onto the payrolls of some of the agency's largest civilian contractors, where they continued to do the same job as when they worked at NSA. Not eligible to participate in this "Soft Landing" program are agency computer scientists, linguists, mathematicians, and engineers, whom NSA obviously wanted to keep. This meant that the only NSA personnel eligible to participate in the program were support personnel. NSA claimed that "Soft Landing" saved the Government about $25 million. Yet given how NSA has managed its finances in the past, this would seem to be a dubious claim.[67]

The Quest for Global Access: NSA's SIGINT Collection Effort

Ironically, the one area that has recently been highlighted as NSA's biggest current trouble spot—its SIGINT collection capabilities—is probably the one area where NSA is not really experiencing any significant problems at present.

It is true that NSA's SIGINT collection environment has changed dramatically in the last decade. As of 1989, the year that the Berlin Wall fell, more than 50 percent of NSA's SIGINT collection and processing assets were still dedicated to intelligence coverage of the Soviet Union. By early 1999, it is believed that SIGINT coverage of the countries that formerly comprised the Soviet Union had dropped to less than 20 percent of NSA's intercept and processing resources.[68]

Today, the agency's target list is much larger and more complicated. Since the breakup of the Soviet Union in the early 1990s, NSA's attention has been shifted to other targets. One of the most important of its priorities is expanded SIGINT coverage of international economic matters, including international trade negotiations and economic summits, bribery attempts by foreign governments and companies competing with American companies for international business, and money transfers by international banks.

NSA has moved in a significant way into the war against drugs, with the agency expanding its cooperation with the CIA and the Drug Enforcement Agency (DEA) in ongoing intelligence gathering operations aimed at rooting out and destroying international drug rings, particularly in Latin America.

And NSA's intelligence coverage of international terrorism and the sources of their financing has been expanded and refined, especially since the 1993 bombing of the World Trade Center in New York City.[69]

Then there are substantive problems that the agency has had to face because of the still ongoing technological revolution in the telecommunications field. Congressional documents and recent press reports about NSA's travails have made much of these obstacles, in some cases making it sound as if NSA has suffered the technological equivalent of the attack on Pearl Harbor. For example, the late staff director of the House intelligence committee stated that "technology has become the enemy of NSA."[70] Even NSA's Director, General Hayden, told an interviewer in 1999 that "Technology has now become a two-edged sword. . . . On the dark days, it has become the enemy."[71]

From a technological perspective, things were much simpler for NSA 50 year ago. When the agency was created in 1952, there were only 5,000 computers in the entire world, and no fax machines or cellular telephones. By the late 1990s, there were more than 180 million personal computers, 14 million fax machines, and 40 million cellular telephones in use around the world.[72] Other new telecommunications technologies that have become more widely used in the last decade include the Internet, digital signals technology, fiber-optic cables, high speed modems, and powerful commercially produced encryption systems.[73] Complicating NSA's task even further is the migration of many communications systems in the developed world to wireless networks, such as local area networks (LANs) and wide area networks (WANs).[74]

The technological revolution is also changing the face of communications on the world's battlefields. NSA has found in the last decade that some foreign military forces, particularly in Europe, have begun using new telecommunications technologies, such as spread spectrum links, laser point-to-point communications, fast frequency-hopping technology, tactical satellite communications, increased usage of millimeter-wave communications systems, data compression techniques, burst transmitters, imbedded decoy signals, increased signal directionality, encryption at all levels, and greater use of low-probability of intercept communications systems, such as walkie-talkies and even cellular telephones. All of these relatively new technologies are making NSA's SIGINT collection mission in support of U.S. military operations overseas more difficult than they were 10 years ago.[75]

Then there is the problem of how to deal with the vastly increased volume of communications traffic now coursing through the airwaves. The new telecommunications systems on the market today, such as personal computers and related communications software, cellular telephones, and fax machines, are faster, more flexible, and most importantly, cheaper to buy. Costs have fallen to the point that it is now cheaper to send an email message than to send a letter. This has led to exponential growth in the volume of digital information being transmitted around the world in the last decade. From NSA's perspective, this has meant that as the volume of communications traffic has increased, it has become increasingly difficult to find the few nuggets of intelligence gold amid all the material it is picking up every day.[76]

A small but increasing amount of international communications traffic has been moved in the last decade from the airwaves to landlines, such as fiber-optic cables, which NSA theoretically cannot intercept. It should come as no surprise that NSA and its allies have invested hundreds of millions of dollars since the late 1980s trying to come up with technical means to get at traffic passing through fiber-optic cables. As of the mid-1990s, the American and British scientists and engineers had not reportedly made any headway with this problem other than to physically tap the cables.[77]

But the most significant technological threat that NSA now faces is how to deal with the rapidly proliferating number of powerful commercially produced encryption systems available on the open market, many of which are difficult (but not impossible) for NSA to solve through conventional cryptanalytic means. For example, in recent years a new generation of 128-bit encryption systems have been developed by private companies in the United States and elsewhere that offer a degree of encryption protection for commercial users that is several tens of thousands of times greater than the previously available 40-bit and 56-bit encryption systems.

By the early 1990s, these cryptographic systems were small enough to be placed on computer chips, which meant that even laptop computers could carry the most sophisticated communications protection available.

Some have suggested that these new systems are resistant to NSA's "brute force" method of attacking foreign cipher systems with the agency's huge inventory of supercomputers, although this is hotly disputed by cryptographers in the private sector. Regardless of the merits of each side's argument, these cryptographic systems are now widely available, easy to use, and relatively inexpensive, with the price for these systems coming down as the technology improves. Efforts by NSA during the 1990s to curb the development and export of strong commercial encryption technologies have met with fierce resistance from Members of Congress, privacy advocates, and most of the American computer software industry.[78]

But in recent interviews, former NSA officials stated that the recent pessimistic commentary has distorted NSA's current SIGINT collection predicament.[79] Most of these former officials agree with an assessment contained in a 1996 House intelligence committee report, which stated that the technical challenges facing NSA are "daunting." But the officials added that many of the obstacles described above can or already have been overcome.[80] Moreover, internal NSA documents make clear that NSA and its allies are currently enjoying, from a collection perspective, a "golden age" because of the recent movement of previously unobtainable communications traffic to the airwaves where the agency's intercept operators can now get it.[81]

U.S. intelligence sources point out that the new telecommunications technologies, such as the Internet and digital communications, are almost exclusively being used in the United States and other developed countries since they are the only nations who can afford them. For example, as of 1992 there were 18 million cellular phone users worldwide, of whom 10 million were in the United States, 5 million in Europe, and 1.5 million in Japan. This meant that there were only 1.5 million cellular telephone users outside of the developed world.[82] One former NSA official stated that "Things are much more low-tech once you get outside of Western Europe and Japan."[83]

This also means that most of the usage of high-grade encryption technology has also been limited to the United States, and to a much lesser degree in Europe and Japan, because this is where the vast majority of the world's Internet and cellular phone users are located.[84]

Finally, American intelligence officials point out that the worldwide use of buried fiber-optic cable is actually quite small outside of submarine cables (most of which touch land in the United States or Great Britain) and within developed countries.[85]

More importantly, the vast majority of international communications traffic continues to flow through communications satellites, which NSA and its allies can intercept. The communications satellites operated by the International Telecommunications Satellite Organization (Intelsat) carry two-thirds of all the world's international telephone calls, almost all international television broadcasts, as well as most of the world's international telex, digital computer data, video teleconferencing, email, and fax traffic.[86]

To deal with the dramatic shifts in national intelligence requirements and the growth of new telecommunications technologies, NSA drastically reengineered its SIGINT collection network beginning in the early 1990s.[87] By the late 1990s, NSA's SIGINT collection system had become smaller but more capable and flexible than the old Cold War architecture. NSA's new SIGINT collection system consists of a mixture of SIGINT satellites, large listening posts, a growing number of covert listening posts in American embassies, as well as a sizeable number of mobile airborne, surface ship, and submarine reconnaissance platforms dedicated for SIGINT collection.[88]

A new generation of SIGINT satellites were put into orbit by NSA and the NRO during the 1990s that were significantly more capable than their predecessors. Between 1994 and 1998, four new communications intelligence (COMINT) satellites were put into geosynchronous orbit over the Earth to replace the older "Vortex/Mercury" satellites that had been in orbit since the late 1970s and early 1980s.[89] These huge satellites were far more capable than their predecessors. They could intercept not only VHF radio signals and UHF microwave telephone circuits, but also huge volumes of digital and analog computer data, facsimile traffic, computer-to-computer modem transmissions, and cellular telephone calls.[90] In addition, between 1994 and 1997 three new SIGINT satellites, called "Trumpet," were launched into elliptical Molniya orbits around the Earth. These satellites were designed to monitor radio traffic and electronic emissions coming from military targets.[91] And finally, four constellations of the new "Advanced Parcae" ocean surveillance satellite were placed into orbit on June 8, 1990, November 7, 1991, May 12, 1996, and May 22, 1999.[92]

The ground-based command, control, and communications infrastructure for these SIGINT satellites has become impressively large over the last 30 years. NSA and the CIA operate four large mission ground stations to control the SIGINT satellites, located at Menwith Hill Station in England, Bad Aibling Station in Germany, Buckley Air National Guard Base in Colorado, and Pine Gap in Australia.[93] Day-to-day management of the various SIGINT satellite systems is handled by an NSA unit called the Overhead Collection Management Center (OCMC), which is responsible for tasking the satellites currently in orbit from its operations center at Fort Meade.[94]

The U.S. Navy operates three "Classic Wizard" stations on Diego Garcia in the Indian Ocean, Guam, and Winter Harbor, Maine, to process information received from its constellations of "Advanced Parcae" ocean surveillance satellites.[95] Operational control of the Parcae ocean surveillance satellites is handled by a joint NSA–Naval Security Group Command unit called that Program Operations Coordination Group (POCG), which is also located at NSA headquarters at Fort Meade.[96]

In 1998 the NRO announced that it was developing a new and larger SIGINT satellite system that will combine the functions of all three existing SIGINT satellites now in orbit. The new satellite, which is expected to be launched in 2002–2003, would "improve SIGINT performance and avoid costs by consolidating systems, utilizing new satellite and data processing technologies." NSA will also be able to reduce the number of mission ground stations needed to process information from this satellite as part of what NSA refers to as the Integrated Overhead SIGINT Architecture.[97]

Three multi-service Regional SIGINT Operations Centers (RSOCs) were activated in the mid-1990s at the Medina Annex outside San Antonio, Texas; Fort Gordon, Georgia; and Kunia, Hawaii, each consisting of over 1,000 military and civilian personnel. The Medina RSOC performs SIGINT collection in Latin America, the Caribbean, and along the Atlantic littoral of Africa for the U.S. Southern Command (SOUTHCOM) and the U.S. Central Command (CENTCOM). The Fort Gordon RSOC provides SIGINT support to the U.S. European Command (EUCOM) and U.S. Central Command in Europe, North Africa, the Middle East, the Near East, and the Persian Gulf. The Kunia RSOC is responsible for SIGINT coverage throughout Asia on behalf of the U.S. Pacific Command (PACOM). The RSOCs replaced many of NSA's overseas listening posts that had been closed since 1990. Each RSOC receives their intercepts from national and tactical SIGINT collection assets in their overseas regions of responsibility, such as ground-based Remote Operating Facilities, SIGINT-equipped U–2 aircraft, and ships equipped with remote-controlled intercept receivers. The intercepts are relayed in real-time via satellite communications links to the RSOCs, where they are processed, analyzed, and reported.[98]

In the late 1980s, NSA began expanding the size and capabilities of its network of six satellite communications (Satcom) intercept stations around the world in order to handle the increased volume of telecommunications traffic passing through the new generation of satellites operated by Intelsat. The six NSA Satcom intercept stations are located at Sugar Grove, West Virginia; Yakima, Washington; Sabana Seca, Puerto Rico; Menwith Hill Station in England; Bad Aibling Station in Germany; and Misawa Air Base in Japan. These stations work in tandem with four Satcom intercept stations operated by NSA's UKUSA [United Kingdom–United States of America] partners, located at Morwenstow, England; Leitrim, Canada; Kojarena, Australia; and Waihopai, New Zealand.[99]

The capabilities of this network of Satcom intercept stations are impressive. As of 1998, these stations reportedly intercepted approximately 100 million messages a month that were being relayed through the 19 Intelsat satellites and four Inmarsat maritime communications satellites then in orbit over the Earth, such as regular telephone calls, digital cellular telephone traffic, fax transmissions, email messages, bank wire transfers, computer transmissions, teleconferencing and video conferencing signals. The NSA Satcom intercept stations are also now capable of intercepting data, voice and video signals passing through so-called Very Small Aperture Terminals (VSAT), which are small commercial satellite systems that use small 30-foot satellite dishes.[100]

The joint NSA–CIA Special Collection Service (SCS), which operates covert listening posts inside American diplomatic establishments abroad, has continued to grow in size and importance during the 1990s. Today the SCS controls approximately 45 covert listening posts in overseas American diplomatic establishments, which intercept military, political, police, and economic radio traffic.[101] NSA has its own covert SIGINT collection unit, the Office of Unconventional Programs, which engages in unconventional SIGINT collection operations against foreign targets that cannot be accessed by more traditional means.[102]

Then there is the multitude of mobile SIGINT collection platforms operating around the world on behalf of NSA. Today, the 3 military services fly 81 dedicated SIGINT collection aircraft, and there are an additional 38 aircraft that are configured or can be converted for SIGINT collection on short notice.[103] The U.S. Navy currently operates 61 ships that are equipped with SIGINT collection suites.[104] Finally, U.S. Navy submarine reconnaissance missions, including SIGINT collection, are now being conducted by 51 *Los Angeles*–class nuclear attack submarines and a few remaining *Sturgeon*–class attack submarines.

All of these SIGINT systems together give NSA comprehensive coverage of the full range of radio signals and electronic emitters operating today. These SIGINT collection assets are capable of not only intercepting traditional HF, VHF, and UHF radio signals, but also the new high-tech telecommunications systems, such as digital, satellite, cellular telephone and data communications traffic, and even low probability of intercept (LPI) radio emissions, that is, walkie-talkie radio traffic.[105]

NSA's SIGINT efforts are greatly assisted by the CIA and the FBI, which intensified their efforts during the 1990s to surreptitiously obtain foreign cryptographic materials. A 1996 report by the House intelligence committee stated: "Arguably, a clandestine service's greatest contribution to intelligence is the compromising of codes. The proliferation of sophisticated cryptographic systems ensures the growing importance of this role of the [CIA] Clandestine Service."[106] A 1997 congressional report stated that "adding enormously to the value of clandestine HUMINT is its contribution to clandestine technical operations and in compromising foreign cryptographic materials."[107]

Clearly getting to communications traffic is not one of the major problems currently facing NSA. If anything, the agency's access to global communications has been significantly expanded and improved during the 1990s. Moreover, the dramatic increase worldwide of communications traffic means that there is more for NSA to get, if it can find the means to process and exploit these new veins of information.[108]

This is not to say that there are not problems in the NSA SIGINT collection program. Because of the worldwide explosion in communications traffic volumes, NSA must now intercept significantly more in order to continue to produce the same amount of intelligence as it did 10 years ago. This means that NSA must maintain a much broader array of intercept capabilities than it did at the height of the Cold War, which of course means a higher pricetag in order to maintain this capability.[109]

Many of NSA's "vacuum cleaner" collection systems are, however, extremely expensive and not particularly productive. In December 1992, former NSA director Admiral William O. Studeman described a collection system which on average produced only one reportable intelligence item from one million intercept inputs.[110] And because of NSA's problems processing the intercepts that it is getting now, which is described in greater detail below, many high-ranking NSA officials believe that the addition of more collection systems would only exacerbate NSA's current problems.[111]

Finally, one longstanding problem is that there is a great deal of duplication of effort within the NSA collection effort, in large part because the agency does not have the internal management controls or oversight systems in place to make sure that the same targets were being copied by multiple sensors.[112]

Boys versus Toys: The State of the SIGINT Infrastructure

As one can see, NSA's biggest problem is not its ability to collect intelligence. In reality, the agency's biggest problem is the continuing decline of its SIGINT processing, analysis, and reporting infrastructure.

As it has done since the early 1970s, NSA spent the majority of its SIGINT budget during the 1990s on building new and very expensive SIGINT collection systems.[113] The capabilities of these new SIGINT collection systems that came online in the 1990s were impressive. As of 1995, NSA was capable of intercepting the equivalent of the entire collection of the U.S. Library of Congress (1 quadrillion bits of information) every 3 hours.[114] The problem was that NSA spent comparatively little on the equipment and personnel needed to take these intercepts and turn them into finished intelligence. An one NSA insider put it, NSA was "buying all these new toys, but they don't have the people to use them."[115] Agency insiders have pointed out in recent interviews that Congress bears much of the blame for this situation. Until 1997, both of the congressional intelligence committees pushed NSA to spend more money on new collection systems and technologies, but they did not provide the agency with the money needed for requested infrastructure improvements.[116]

What happened next was inevitable. The new high-tech collection systems produced such a massive volume of intercepts that NSA's analysts and their computers at Fort Meade were quickly swamped. As time went by, an increasing number of the intercepts went unread, and NSA's SIGINT production fell dramatically.[117] By one estimate, by the mid-1990s NSA was only processing approximately 1 percent of the intercepts that were reaching Fort Meade, down from a reported 20 percent in the late 1980s.[118] NSA's current director, Lieutenant General Michael Hayden, has admitted that NSA is collecting far more data than it processes and that the agency processes more data than it actually reports to its consumers in Washington and elsewhere.[119] In 1998, Congressman Porter J. Goss, chairman of the House intelligence committee, chastised NSA and the other members of the Intelligence Community for allowing this to happen, stating that "Expending resources to collect intelligence that is not being analyzed is simply a waste of money."[120]

The consequences of NSA's resource allocation decisions made a decade ago go even deeper. As senior American intelligence officials have recently pointed out, NSA is today producing less intelligence than it was a decade ago.[121] A former White House official was quoted as saying of NSA that "They're spending more money and working harder and getting less and less information out of sources."[122] One recent press report even indicated that the amount of SIGINT information appearing in the daily intelligence summary sent to the President of the United States, the President's Daily Brief (PDB), has declined by almost 20 percent since 1989.[123]

Solutions to this massive conundrum have not been easy to come by. NSA has sought to deal with the problem by attempting to further automate the SIGINT processing task, with a bevy of new computers being added to try to help NSA's analysts cope with the growing volume of intercepts. According to publicly available information, NSA today owns at least 26 supercomputers with a combined computing power of 5,516.83 gigaflops, making the agency the largest supercomputer operator in the world.[124] In 1993, a powerful new computer system called "Normalizer" was purchased for the specific purpose of processing, storing, and distributing time-sensitive intelligence information.[125]

But this effort has been extremely expensive and fraught with problems. For 4 days during the week of January 23, 2000, the main SIGINT processing computer at NSA failed, reportedly because of a "software anomaly." The result was an intelligence blackout, with no intelligence reports coming out of Fort Meade for more than 72 hours.[126]

Another facet of the SIGINT processing problem is that although NSA owns and operates the largest computer and telecommunications system in the Federal Government, these resources have not been particularly well managed. NSA has in its inventory today dozens of computer and communications systems that are not interoperable with other systems operated by the agency.[127]

Furthermore, NSA has not yet fielded a telecommunications network that can adequately handle the vast amount of data that moves every day between NSA headquarters, its intercept units, and its consumers. During the 1999 military operations in Kosovo, NSA had to reduce to a minimum the transmission of all routine communications traffic on its communications system in order to make room for the SIGINT information being sent from Fort Meade to U.S. and Allied forces operating in Kosovo.[128]

NSA is also experiencing increased difficulty reporting SIGINT information in a timely manner. Today, NSA's intelligence consumers are demanding that NSA get its information to them in near-real-time. This means that NSA has had to speed up the processing of information in order to meet this requirement. However, this has severely strained NSA's already tightly stretched SIGINT processing capabilities, and forced NSA to cut back on the amount of material that it processes and analyzes in order to meet its customers' short-term needs.[129]

Most informed observers of NSA have concluded that more technology is not the panacea for what ails NSA. Several past and present NSA officials have stated that what the agency desperately needs is more personnel to read what the computers process.[130] But NSA's senior management has been curiously reluctant to ask Congress for money to hire more analysts because, according to former NSA officials, personnel is not a "sexy" budget line item on Capitol Hill.[131] James Bamford, author of *The Puzzle Palace*, has written that "It has always been far easier for the NSA to persuade Congress to provide more money for a sexy new piece of technology, like a satellite with the ability to vacuum 50 percent more phone calls from the ether, than for 200 more analysts to sift through the mountains of information."[132]

NSA's director, General Hayden, has recently confirmed this assessment, telling an interviewer that "Technology alone is not the solution to the data processing problem. . . . The agency needs to add more analysts and linguists to its staff." But General Hayden has noted that hiring these highly qualified men and women in the midst of a booming economy is an extremely difficult proposition given that NSA is competing for the same people that private industry wants.[133] If NSA fails to recruit a new corps of young and talented information technology specialists, one could suggest that all else is for naught. As former NSA director General Kenneth A. Minihan put it, "If we don't win the talent war, it doesn't matter if we invest in the infrastructure."[134]

The Unhappy Customers

Not surprisingly, the people who are the unhappiest with the turn in events at NSA are its clients inside the U.S. Government. An October 1999 NSA management study found that NSA's cavalier attitude toward its customers had "created a perception among customers that NSA places higher value on its tradecraft than it does on outcomes for the nation." One NSA customer was quoted in the report as saying, "I sometimes think you give us the party line rather than the real scoop on how you spend your money. And you don't want guidance from the community."[135]

Another study conducted in the spring of 1995 revealed that there was widespread consensus among NSA's SIGINT consumers that recurring turf battles among military and civilian factions within NSA's Operations Directorate had unnecessarily created bureaucratic obstacles to the free flow of intelligence information to the agency's consumers.[136] Many of NSA's customers in the Government complained that the National SIGINT Requirements Systems (NSRS), the system by which consumers around the world tasked NSA, was obsolete and unresponsive to NSA's customer needs.[137]

There is also evidence that NSA's relationship with the Defense Department has also deteriorated somewhat in recent years. For example, in 1997 Pentagon officials complained that NSA still was reluctant to give the military the intelligence information that it needed to do its job because of concerns about compromising the security of the agency's sources. This led one Pentagon official to charge that "long-entrenched civilian NSA employees are still fighting the Cold War and are more worried about maintaining security than improving tactical warfighting capabilities."[138]

Interviews with current and former officials of the U.S. Army and Air Force cryptologic organizations confirm that there exists considerable unhappiness within the military services about their diminished role in the national SIGINT effort. One former high-ranking Army intelligence official stated that in recent years, the U.S. Army Intelligence and Security Command (INSCOM) has lost many of its strategic SIGINT missions to NSA and that there exists a widespread feeling within the military that NSA is ignoring its needs.[139] A former Navy cryptologist has publicly stated that the role of the U.S. Navy's cryptologic organization, the Naval Security Group Command, has been "reduced by NSA to a backwater effort."[140]

The Push for Modernization at NSA

On November 15, 1999, General Hayden launched a major reform program at NSA that he called the "100 Days of Change." The program was prompted by a scathing report that he received in October 1999, which described "an agency mired in bureaucratic conflict, suffering from poor leadership and losing touch with the government clients it serves." The report's principal recommendation called for scrapping NSA's entire senior leadership team so as to better deal with the multitude of other problems that NSA faces.[141] General Hayden's commitment to the reform program appears to be sincere. In December 1999, he told reporters from *Newsweek* that "the agency has got to make some changes because by standing still, we are going to fall behind very quickly."[142]

General Hayden's reform plan appears to have been partly crafted by his predecessor, Lieutenant General Minihan. In March 1997, General Minihan told his staff that NSA had to "accelerate the effort to decrease our internal bureaucracies, flatten our organization, and establish a flexible, responsive, decentralized structure suited for an environment that will be highly unpredictable and will demand continuous innovation."[143] To effect these changes, General Minihan believed that the agency's internal culture would have to be radically changed. The only problem, Minihan wrote, was that "Deep cultural changes require crisis felt by all levels of the organization."[144] The only problem was that there was no crisis around which General Minihan could mobilize support within NSA for change, and his plan was derailed by NSA's senior civilian officials.[145]

Apparently General Hayden has learned from the mistakes made by his predecessors. Not only has he adopted almost all of General Minihan's reform plan, but he has also apparently created an environment conducive to getting the money that he needs to implement his plan. Suddenly, recent congressional and press reports about NSA have almost uniformly used words that are synonymous with "crisis" to describe NSA's current condition. For example, in October 1998 the late staff director of the House intelligence committee, John Millis, said that "Signals intelligence is in a crisis."[146] The House intelligence committee, in its February 1999 annual report to Congress, concluded that "NSA is in serious trouble."[147] An October 1999 study of the agency's management stated that "NSA has been in a leadership crisis for the better part of a decade."[148] Given this sort of strong language, it is hard to see how the Clinton administration or Congress could deny any "reasonable" funding request from NSA.

The real challenge that General Hayden and his supporters face is that every one of his predecessors who tried to effect major change at NSA had to fight a continuous, uphill battle against the agency's powerful and deeply entrenched bureaucracy.[149] NSA's former senior civilian, Barbara A. McNamara, the agency's deputy director from October 1997 to July 2000, came under intense fire from reformers within NSA and outside observers, with one reporter describing her as "among the most caustic defenders of the Agency's old ways."[150]

But unlike his predecessors, Hayden has some important allies on Capitol Hill who firmly support his plan for drastic changes at NSA. In May 1998, the House intelligence committee issued a report that stated that "very large changes in the National Security Agency's culture and method of operations need to take place." The committee's report concluded that "NSA will not meet its Unified Cryptologic Architecture (UCA) goals without tackling head-on some very fundamental internal obstacles," specifically "the stultifying effect that the bureaucracy of such a large organization can have."[151]

In February 1999, the Senate intelligence committee reported that NSA's SIGINT mission "must be dramatically rejuvenated." The committee found that declining budgets and obsolete equipment were impeding NSA's ability to maintain a technical edge over its opponents, and recommended a massive modernization of NSA's SIGINT effort, greater emphasis on and more money for advanced research and development, the revitalization and NSA's recruiting and hiring program, and a complete revamping of NSA's organizational structure, including a recommendation that NSA outsource many of its administrative and support functions.[152]

Beginning in November 1999, General Hayden began enacting some of the changes that he wanted. In the first 50 days of the "100 Days of Change" program,

General Hayden junked the three management committees that heretofore had run NSA—the Senior Agency Leadership Team (SALT), the Critical Issues Group (CIG), and the Corporate Management Review Group (CMRG)—and replaced them with a single committee called the Executive Leadership Team (ELT). The membership on the ELT was to consist solely of the director, the agency's deputy director, and the heads of the operations, technology and systems, and information systems security directorates. He brought in a new chief financial officer, Beverly L. Wright, formerly the chief financial officer of the investment banking firm of Legg Mason Wood Walker, Inc., to reform NSA's financial and accounting practices. He also appointed Air Force Major General Tiiu Kera as the new deputy chief of the long-dormant Central Security Service, with a mandate to improve NSA's relationship with the Pentagon and the military services.[153]

In a further development, NSA's deputy director, Barbara McNamara, stepped down from her position in July 2000 to become NSA's liaison officer in London. Ms. McNamara's departure from her post, NSA insiders believe, will go a long way toward allowing General Hayden to implement his reform and modernization plans.[154]

But as usual, NSA officials have made it clear that their reform and modernization programs cannot be accomplished without a massive infusion of money, and Congress seems inclined to give NSA what it wants. Not coincidentally, congressional concern about NSA began at about the same time that NSA began to quietly push on Capitol Hill for more money to fund modernization of the agency. In the fall of 1998 Congress quietly approved a whopping 10 percent increase in the size of NSA's fiscal year 1999 budget. This brought NSA's annual budget over the $4 billion mark for the first time since the end of the Cold War.[155] In late 1999, Congress also approved a reported $200 million increase in NSA's fiscal year 2000 budget.[156] This year (fiscal year 2001), NSA is expected once again to ask for a substantial increase in the size of its budget so that it can triple the size of its recruiting effort and double the size of its research and development program. It remains to be seen whether NSA can recruit the people it wants in the midst of a robust economy.[157]

Conclusions

Some of the reports concerning NSA's purported problems would appear to have missed their mark. No one disputes that the SIGINT product coming out of Fort Meade remains one of the most important intelligence sources available to the Intelligence Community. But statements that have appeared in the American press that NSA was solely responsible for some of the Intelligence Community's recent intelligence failures, such as failing to detect India and Pakistan's 1998 nuclear tests, are factually incorrect.

Furthermore, NSA's SIGINT collection capabilities have actually improved considerably during the last decade, and evidence suggests that the technological obstacles that have been often cited in press reports as contributing to NSA's current problems (that is, strong encryption and fiber-optic cables) have not yet begun to be widely used outside of the developed countries in Western Europe and East Asia.

NSA's most pressing problem is an area that unfortunately has received little public attention in recent months, specifically the deterioration of the agency's SIGINT processing, analysis, and reporting capabilities. As detailed above, NSA currently does not have the computer power or the personnel to process, translate, or read even a fraction of the ever-increasing volume of communications traffic that it intercepts. It is clear that NSA must recruit substantial numbers of analysts and information technology specialists in the near future, and invest money in acquiring new processing technologies in order to begin to address this problem. And until this happens, it would seem prudent to recommend that NSA cut back its spending on new collection systems and instead use this money to restore the agency's SIGINT processing and analytic infrastructure to a semblance of health.

The agency must also take immediate steps to shore up its strained relations with its customers inside the U.S. Government and the Armed Forces in order to restore confidence in NSA's intelligence product. Moreover, given the transient and oftentimes fickle nature of politics, NSA must realize that it cannot depend solely on a few allies in Congress for its continued survival.

Equally important, but more difficult to empirically quantify, is how to effectively deal with NSA's internal management problems, such as how to trim the agency's large bureaucracy, eliminate duplication of effort and waste, put NSA's financial accounts in order, and break down the agency's cultural opposition to outside oversight of its operations. Given that NSA has not passed a single outside financial audit, it would seem unreasonable for Congress to increase the size of NSA's budget without ensuring that NSA takes steps to bring about a greater level of transparency as to how it spends its money.

And finally, it is time that NSA adopt a policy of greater openness about what it does and how it does it. One obvious way to do this is to declassify documents that detail the agency's significant accomplishments since the end of World War II. Former NSA director Vice Admiral McConnell put it best when he told the agency in 1994, "In these changing times we, as an Agency, must take advantage of appropriate opportunities to give today's customer base (which includes the general public) a clear understanding of why we are relevant."[158] Many outside observers agree with these sentiments, believing that this would go a long way toward reestablishing a semblance of confidence and trust in NSA amongst an increasingly skeptical NSA customer base and the general public.

Notes

[1] Seymour M. Hersh, "The Intelligence Gap: How the Digital Age Left Our Spies Out in the Cold," *The New Yorker*, December 6, 1999, 58ff.

[2] Neal Thompson, "Putting NSA Under Scrutiny," *Baltimore Sun*, October 18, 1998, 1C.

[3] A more detailed discussion of these matters is contained in Matthew M. Aid, "Not So Anonymous: Parting the Veil of Secrecy About the National Security Agency," in *A Culture of Secrecy: The Government Versus the People's Right to Know*, ed. Athan G. Theoharis (Lawrence: University Press of Kansas, 1998), 65–67.

[4] USSID 1, *SIGINT Operating Policy,* June 29, 1987, 1, NSA FOIA; USSID4, *SIGINT Support to Military Commanders,* July 1, 1974, 1–2, NSA FOIA; USSID 18, *Limitations and Procedures in Signals Intelligence Operations of the USSS,* October 20, 1968, 7; NSA Memo for the Special Assistant, Office of the Secretary of Defense, *NSA Transition Briefing Book,* December 9, 1980, 1; NSGTP 69304–B, *Naval Cryptology in National Security,* 1985, 59; COMNAVSECGRU FOIA; "NSA/CSS Future Day—The Services Perspective," *National Security Agency Newsletter*, October 1996, 2; Tom Bowman and Scott Shane, "Espionage from the Frontlines," *Baltimore Sun*, December 8, 1995, 1A, 20A.

[5] Central Intelligence Agency, OPAI 93–00092, *A Consumer's Guide to Intelligence*, September 1993, 12; National Performance Review, *Accompanying Report of the National Performance Review—The Intelligence Community*, September 1993, 36.

[6] CIA biographical data sheet, James L. Runyan, via Dr. Jeffrey T. Richelson; *NSAN*, November 1997, 6.

[7] Jeffrey T. Richelson, "Out of the Black: The Disclosure and Declassification of the National Reconnaissance Office," *International Journal of Intelligence and Counterintelligence*, Spring 1998, 12; organization chart, National Reconnaissance Office, October 2, 1996. The author is grateful to Jeffrey T. Richelson for making a copy of this document available.

[8] David A. Fulghum, "SIGINT Aircraft May Face Obsolescence in Five Years," *Aviation Week and Space Technology*, October 21, 1996, 54.

[9] Norman Polmar and Thomas B. Allen, *Spy Book* (New York: Random House, 1997), 402.

[10] Address at the CIRA Luncheon, October 5, 1998; John Millis' speech, *CIRA Newsletter* (Winter 1998/1999), 6.

[11] Bruce B. Auster, "What's Really Gone Wrong With the CIA!" *U.S. News and World Report*, June 1, 1998. See also Walter Pincus, "CIA Chief Cited Loss of Agency's Capabilities," *The Washington Post*, May 25, 1998, A4.

[12] Alfred Monteiro, Jr., "Mustering the Force: Cryptologic Support to Military Operations," *Defense Intelligence Journal* 4, no. 2 (Fall 1995), 70; Paul Ackerley, "Team AIA," *Spokesman*, January 1995, 4.

[13] Vice Admiral Michael McConnell, letter to Senator Sam Nunn, April 28, 1992, 6, via Jeffrey T. Richelson; Mark Urban, *UK Eyes Alpha* (London: Faber, 1996), 159, 169–170; Robert H. Scales, USA, *Certain Victory: The U.S. Army in the Gulf War* (Washington, DC: Brassey's, 1994), 189–190; Michael R. Gordon and Bernard E. Trainor, *The Generals' War* (Boston: Little, Brown, 1995), 285–287.

[14] For RC–135 missions and other USAF SIGINT operations against Iraq, see Air Intelligence Agency, *History of the Air Intelligence Agency: 1 January–31 December 1994*, vol. I, appendix C, AIA FOIA; *World Air Power Journal* 21 (Summer 1995), 13; "AFIC Crew Takes Gen. Jerome F. O'Malley Award," *Spokesman*, August 1993, 9; 1st Lt. John Henry, "Duty in the Desert," *Spokesman*, March 1995, 18; "RC–135 Takes to the Sky," *Spokesman*, April 1995, 7. For Navy airborne SIGINT missions against Iraq, see *Command History Fleet Air Reconnaissance Squadron One for CY 1992*, Enclosure 1, 3; *Command History Fleet Air Reconnaissance Squadron One for CY 1993*, Enclosure 1, 4; *Command History Fleet Air Reconnaissance Squadron Six for CY 1994*, Enclosure 1,4; *Command History Fleet Air Reconnaissance Squadron Six for CY 1995*, Enclosure 1, 3–4; *Command History Fleet Air Reconnaissance Squadron Six for CY 1996*, Enclosure 1, 3–4, all Naval Aviation History Branch, Naval Historical Center, Washington, DC.

[15] Air Intelligence Agency, *History of the Air Intelligence Agency: 1 January–31 December 1994*, vol. 1, 30–31, AIA FOIA; "Interest in ARL Grows After Aircraft's Uphold Democracy Performance," *Inside the Army*, March 13, 1995, 9; Wayne P. Gagner, "Army Electronic Warfare Gears for Contingency Operations," *Signal*, October 1996, 35; David A. Fulghum, "Communications Intercepts Pace EP–3s," *Aviation Week and Space Technology*, May 5, 1997, 53–54. David A. Fulghum, "Navy Spying Masked by Patrol Aircraft," *Aviation Week and Space Technology*, March 8, 1999, 32–33.

[16] Urban, 217; Rick Atkinson, "GIs Signal Bosnians: Yes, We're Listening," *The Washington Post*, March 18, 1996, A14; Walter Pincus, "U.S. Sought Other Bosnia Arms Sources," *The Washington Post*, April 26, 1996, A15; Charles Lane and Thom Shanker, "Bosnia: What the CIA Didn't Tell Us," *The New York Review of Books*, May 9, 1996, 11.

[17] Robert K. Ackerman, "Security Agency Transitions from Backer to Participant," *Signal*, October 1999, 23; Eric Schmitt, "Hundreds of Yugoslav Troops Said to Desert," *The New York Times*, May 20, 1999, A15; Kevin Gulick, "26th Intelligence Group: An Integral Part of European Operations," *Spokesman*, August 1999, accessed at <http://www.aia.af.mil/commopages/pa/cyberspokesman/august/cover.htm>.

[18] Kenneth W. Dam and Herbert S. Lin, eds., *Cryptography's Role in Securing the Information Society* (Washington, DC: National Academy Press, 1996), 97.

[19] Seymour M. Hersh, "On the Nuclear Edge," *The New Yorker*, March 29, 1993, 65.

[20] John M. Goshko, "Transcripts Show Joking Cuban Pilots," *The Washington Post*, February 28, 1996, 1A–A15; Barbara Crossette, "U.S. Says Cubans Knew They Fired on Civilian Planes," *The New York Times*, February 28, 1996, 1.

[21] "Sanction Busting," *Newsweek*, December 31, 1990, 4. See also Director of Central Intelligence, *Annual Report on Intelligence Community Activities*, August 22, 1997, accessed at <http://www.fas.org>.

[22] Colum Lynch, "U.S. Used UN to Spy on Iraq, Aides Say," *Boston Globe*, January 6, 1999, A1; Barton Gellman, "Annan Suspicious of UNSCOM Probe," *The Washington Post*, January 6, 1999, A1, A22; Bruce W. Nelan, "Bugging Saddam," *Time*, January 18, 1999; Seymour M. Hersh, "Saddam's Best Friend," *The New Yorker*, April 5, 1999, 32, 35; David Wise, "Fall Guy," *The Washingtonian*, July 1999, 42–43.

[23] Bill Gertz, *Betrayal* (Washington, DC: Regnery, 1999), 184–186.

[24] R. Jeffrey Smith and David B. Ottaway, "Spy Photos Suggest China Missile Trade; Pressure Builds for Sanctions Builds Over Evidence Pakistan Has M–11s," *The Washington Post*, July 3, 1995, A1; Gertz, *Betrayal*, 268.

[25] Bill Gertz, "China Breaks Vow, Sends N. Korea Missile Materials," *The Washington Times*, January 6, 2000, A16.

[26] Confidential interviews with State Department officials; regarding war crimes in Bosnia, see Roy Gutman,

"Federal Army Tied to Bosnia War Crimes/Serb Leaders 'Death Camp' Link," *Newsday*, November 1, 1995, A4; Charles Lane and Thom Shanker, "Bosnia: What the CIA Didn't Tell Us," 12–13.

[27] R. Jeffrey Smith, "Serbs Tried to Cover Up Massacre," *The Washington Post*, January 28, 1999, A1, A24; Jeffrey Fleishman, "Yugoslav Official Tied to Bid to Hide Massacre," *Philadelphia Inquirer*, January 28, 1999, 1.

[28] Remarks at a presentation ceremony for the National Security Agency Worldwide Awards in Fort Meade, MD, May 1, 1991, accessed at <http://csdl.tamu.edu/bushlibrary/papers/1991/91050101.html>.

[29] "Honoring the Best of the Best," *NSA Newsletter*, July 1994, 3.

[30] Commission on the Roles and Capabilities of the United States Intelligence Community, *Preparing for the 21st Century: An Appraisal of U.S. Intelligence* (Washington, DC: Government Printing Office, March 1, 1996), 125.

[31] "NSA Earns JMUA," *NSA Newsletter*, July 1997, 6.

[32] U.S. House of Representatives, Permanent Select Committee on Intelligence, *IC21: Intelligence Community in the 21st Century*, 104th Congress (Washington, DC: U.S. Government Printing Office, 1996), 37, 120.

[33] For 19 percent cut in the intelligence budget, see U.S. Senate, Permanent Select Committee on Intelligence, Report 104–258, *Report Authorizing Appropriations for Fiscal Year 1997 for the Intelligence Activities of the United States Government*, 104th Congress, 2d Session, April 30, 1996, 3; U.S. House of Representatives, Permanent Select Committee on Intelligence, Report 104–578, *Intelligence Authorization Act for Fiscal Year 1997*, 104th Congress, 2d Session, May 15, 1996, 8. For $34.5 billion figure, see "Spying Cost U.S. $26 Billion in Fiscal '97," *The Washington Times*, October 16, 1997.

[34] Admiral William O. Studeman, memorandum to all NSA employees, *Farewell*, April 8, 1992, NSA FOIA.

[35] The $5 billion 1990 NSA budget is from Michael Wines, "Washington Is Tired of Supporting All Those Spies," *The New York Times*, November 4, 1990, E5; and Neil Munro, "The Puzzle Palace in Post-Cold War Pieces," *Washington Technology*, August 11, 1994, 14. For the 35 percent cut in the NSA's budget, see Warren P. Strobel, "The Sound of Silence?" *U.S. News and World Report*, February 14, 2000. For fiscal year 1995 budget, see Tony Capaccio and Eric Rosenberg, "Deutsch Approves $27 Billion for Pentagon Spy Budgets," *Defense Week*, August 29, 1994, 1–13. For fiscal year 1996 budget, see R. Jeffrey Smith, "Making Connections With Dots To Decipher U.S. Spy Spending," *The Washington Post*, March 12, 1996, A11.

[36] U.S. Senate, Permanent Select Committee on Intelligence, Report 104–258; U.S. House of Representatives, Report 104–578; Charles Allen, "Intelligence Community Overview for Japanese Visitors from the Public Security Investigation Agency," June 22, 1998, accessed at <http://cryptome.org/cia-ico.htm>.

[37] Memorandum for the NSA/CSS Representative Defense, *NSA Transition Book for the Department of Defense*, December 9, 1992.

[38] For the 75,000 NSA personnel figure in 1989–1990, see Declaration of Richard W. Gronet, Director of Policy, National Security Agency, June 14, 1989, 5, in CIV. no. HM87–1564, *Ray Lindsey v. National Security Agency/Central Security Service*, U.S. District Court for the District of Maryland, Baltimore, MD. The 50,000 figure was calculated as follows: as of 1995 the total number of military cryptologic personnel stood at 27,366 officers and enlisted men (Army: 11,022; Navy: 6,697; Air Force: 8,533; Marine Corps: 1,114; total: 27,366), for which see November 16, 1994, National Military Intelligence Association (NMIA) Briefing. The author is grateful to Jeffrey T. Richelson for this information. If one adds these personnel to the 20,000+ NSA civilians, plus the NRO, SCS, CIA, and civilian contractor personnel performing SIGINT missions, one comes up with a total manpower figure of slightly more than 50,000 men and women working in the USSS.

[39] Author's estimates based on confidential interviews. For 38,000 strength figure, see Commission on the Roles and Capabilities of the United States Intelligence Community, *Preparing for the 21st Century: An Appraisal of U.S. Intelligence*, 96, 132; Smith, "Making Connections With Dots To Decipher U.S. Spy Spending."

[40] Jeffrey T. Richelson, "Cold War's Wake Transforms Signals Intelligence," *Defense Week*, July 24, 1995, 6–7; Hersh, 60; Remarks by Adm. William Studeman, Acting Director of Central Intelligence, at Marquette University, April 20, 1995, accessed at <www.fas.org/inp/cia/pro duct dci_speech_42095.html>.

[41] Strobel.

[42] Memorandum for the NSA/CSS Representative Defense, 13; NSA FOIA; Department of Defense, Office of the Inspector General, Report No. 96–03. *Final Report on the Verification Inspection of the National Security Agency*, February 13, 1996, 2, DOD FOIA; Studeman Memo; "NSA Plans for the Future," *NSAN*, January 1993, 4.

[43] Ibid.

[44] Robert L. Prestel, "TQM at NSA," *American Intelligence Journal* (Spring/Summer 1994), 44.

[45] Department of Defense, *Final Report on the Verification Inspection of the National Security Agency*.

[46] U.S. House of Representatives, Permanent Select Committee on Intelligence, Report No. 101–1008, *Report by the Permanent Select Committee on Intelligence*, 101st Congress, 2d Session, January 2, 1991, 9.

[47] Tom Bowman and Scott Shane, "Congress Has Tough Time Performing Watchdog Role," *Baltimore Sun*, December 15, 1995, 23A.

[48] Department of Defense, *Final Report on the Verification Inspection of the National Security Agency*.

[49] This works out to all average cost of $75,000 for each of NSA's approximately 20,000 civilian employees, which, if correct, suggests that NSA's staff must rank as the best paid in the entire Federal Government! Commission on the Roles and Capabilities of the United States Intelligence Community, *Preparing for the 21st Century: An Appraisal of U.S. Intelligence*, 125.

[50] "Let Them Eat Cake!" *NSA Newsletter*, June 1993, 1–5.

[51] U.S. House of Representatives, Permanent Select Committee on Intelligence, *IC21: Intelligence Community in the 21st Century*, 120–121. For the size of the Technology and Systems Directorate, see Rodney B. Sorkin Biographical Data Sheet, NSA FOIA. For cuts in infrastructure and research spending, see Commission on the Roles and Capabilities of the United States Intelligence Community, 125.

[52] Bowman and Shane.

[53] Walter Pincus, "Military Espionage Cuts Eyed," *The Washington Post*, March 17, 1995, A6.

[54] Strobel.

[55] Department of Defense, *Final Report on the Verification Inspection of the National Security Agency*, 3ff.

[56] Colin Clark, "Audit Finds NSA Finances in Jumble," *Defense Week*, August 10, 1998, 2.

[57] Walter Pincus, "Panel Ties NSA Funds to Changes at Agency," *The Washington Post*, May 7, 1998, A21.

[58] Department of Defense, *Final Report on the Verification Inspection of the National Security Agency*, 6; Scott Wilson, "NSA's Quest for Diversity Called Threat", *Baltimore Sun*, July 6, 1997; Strobel.

[59] Wilson, 1A, 19A; Richard Lardner, "The Secret's Out," *Government Executive*, August 1998.

[60] Wilson; Lardner; Hersh, *The Intelligence Gap*, 64, 73.

[61] Confidential interview.

[62] Confidential interview.

[63] Wilson; Lardner.

[64] U.S. House of Representatives, Permanent Select Committee on Intelligence, Report 104–578, *Intelligence Authorization Act for Fiscal Year 1997*, 104th Congress, 2d Session, May 15, 1996, 8.

[65] Robert K. Ackerman, "Security Agency Transitions From Backer to Participant," *Signal*, October 1990, 23.

[66] Monteiro, 75–76; General Accounting Office, NSIAD–96–6, *Personnel Practices at CIA, NSA, and DIA Compared With Those of Other Agencies*, March 1996, 5.

[67] Richard Lardner, "Soft Landing Effort Praised, Criticized: NSA, Industry Partnership Gives Agency Room to Move Under Personnel Ceilings," *Defense Information and Electronics Report*, August 21, 1998, 2; Vernon Loeb, "Finding the Secret to Downsizing? NSA Moves Workers to Private Sector," *The Washington Post*, September 29, 1998, A15.

[68] H.D.S. Greenway and Paul Quinn-Judge, "CIA Chief Voices Final Hopes and Fears," *Boston Globe*, January 15, 1993, B17; confidential interviews.

[69] Gary O'Shaughnessy, USAF, "Command Enters New Era," *Spokesman*, September 1990, 1; William M. Carley, "As Cold War Fades, Some Nations' Spies Seek Industrial Secrets," *Wall Street Journal*, June 17, 1991, A1, A5; David E. Sanger and Tim Weiner, "Emerging Role For the CIA: Economic Spy," *The New York Times*, October 15, 1995, 1, 12; Paul Blustein and Mary Jordan, "U.S. Eavesdropped on Talks, Sources Say," *The Washington Post*, October 17, 1995, B1; Shane and Bowman, "America's Fortress of Spies," 12A; Tom Bowman and Scott Shane, "Battling High-Tech Warriors," *Baltimore Sun*, December 15, 1995, 22A.

[70] Address at the CIRA Luncheon, October 5, 1998; John Millis' Speech, *CIRA Newsletter*, Winter 1998/1999, 6.

[71] Bob Brewin, Daniel Verton, and William Matthews, "NSA Playing IT Catch-Up," *Federal Computer Week*, December 6, 1999.

[72] Kenneth A. Minihan, "Math and National Security—A Perfect Match for the 21st Century," address to the Joint Meetings of the American Mathematical Society and the Mathematical Association of America, January 9, 1998, Baltimore, MD; Dana Roscoe, "NSA Hosts Special Partnership Breakfast," *NSAN*, January 2000, 4.

[73] Central Intelligence Agency, *Selected Foreign Trends in Telecommunications Technology*, 1993, in Bruce Schneier and David Banisar, *The Electronic Privacy Papers: Documents on the Battle for Privacy in the Age of Surveillance* (New York: Wiley, 1997), 596–607; U.S. Army, *The United States Army Modernization Plan*, January 1993, vol. II, annex I, Intelligence/Electronic Warfare, 1–7; Whitfield Diffie and Susan Landau, *Privacy on the Line: The Politics of Wiretapping and Encryption* (Cambridge: MIT Press, 1999), 97–99; Gregory Vistica and Evan Thomas, "Hard of Hearing," *Newsweek*, December 13, 1999.

[74] Schneier and Banisar, 602; Ackerman, 23.

[75] *U.S. Army Modernization Plan*; Department of Defense, *FY96 Electronic Warfare Plan*, April 1995, 2–2, DOD FOIA; Mark Hewish and Joris Janssen Lok, "The Intelligent War: Signals Intelligence Demands Adaptable Systems," *Jane's International Defense Review*, December 1997, 28.

[76] Ackerman, 23; Gregory Vistica and Evan Thomas, "Hard of Hearing," *Newsweek*, December 13, 1999; Jeffrey T. Richelson, "Desperately Seeking Signals," *Bulletin of Atomic Scientists*, March/April 2000, 47–51.

[77] U.S. Senate, Committee on Armed Services, *Department of Defense Authorization for Appropriations Fiscal*

Year 1994 and The Future Years Defense Program, 103ᵈ Congress, 1ˢᵗ Session (Washington, DC: Government Printing Office, 1993), 449; Urban, 245–249.

⁷⁸ An excellent compilation of documents relating to this issue can be found in Schneier and Banisar. See also U.S. House of Representatives, Committee on the Judiciary, Written Statement to the House Committee on the Judiciary, Subcommittee on Courts and Intellectual Property: Hearing on H.695 "SAFE Act," by William P. Crowell, Deputy Director, National Security Agency, March 20, 1997, 9–11; Kenneth W. Dam and Herbert S. Lin, *Cryptography's Role in Securing the Information Society* (Washington, DC: National Academy Press, 1996), 101–102; Diffie and Landau, 99–101; John Markoff, "U.S. Export Ban Hurting Makers of New Devices to Code Messages," *The New York Times*, November 19, 1990, A1, D6; Neil Munro, "The Puzzle Palace in Post-Cold War Pieces," *Washington Technology*, August 11, 1994, 14; Marcia Smith, *Encryption Technology: Congressional Issues* (Washington, DC: Congressional Research Service, February 18, 1997), 1–3.

⁷⁹ Confidential interviews.

⁸⁰ U.S. House of Representatives, 121.

⁸¹ Confidential interviews. See also Diffie and Landau, 94.

⁸² Central Intelligence Agency, *Selected Foreign Trends in Telecommunications Technology*, 1993, in Schneier and Banisar, 596.

⁸³ Confidential interview.

⁸⁴ Confidential interviews; there is an unconfirmed report that terrorist leader Osama bin Laden has used encrypted cellular telephones made in Europe, for which see Vistica and Thomas, "Hard of Hearing."

⁸⁵ Confidential interviews.

⁸⁶ Brochure, International Telecommunications Satellite Organization, *INTELSAT: The Global Telecommunications Cooperative*, 1985.

⁸⁷ Memo for the NSA/CSS Representative Defense, *NSA Transition Book for the Department of Defense*, December 9, 1992, top secret edition, 19, NSA FOIA.

⁸⁸ Claudia J. Kennedy, "Staying Ahead of the Threat and the Technology Curve," *Army*, October 1999, 152; Robert K. Ackerman, "Security Agency Transitions From Backer to Participant," *Signal*, October 1999, 23.

⁸⁹ The new geosynchronous SIGINT satellites were launched on August 25, 1994, May 14, 1995, April 24, 1996, and May 8, 1998. Jeffrey T. Richelson, *The U.S. Intelligence Community*, 4ᵗʰ ed. (Boulder, CO: Westview Press, 1999), 189; Jonathan McDowell, "U.S. Reconnaissance Satellite Programs, Part 2: Beyond Imaging," *Quest* 4, no. 4, 43; Richelson (note 1), 1; "New Blueprint for U.S. SIGINT," *Intelligence Newsletter*, October 26, 1995, 1; Richelson, "Despite Management/Budget Woes, NRO Launches Continue," 16.

⁹⁰ Confidential interview.

⁹¹ The launch dates of the "Trumpet" SIGINT satellites were May 3, 1994, July 10, 1995, and November 7, 1997. Richelson, *U.S. Intelligence Community*, 189; Richelson, "Cold War's Wake Transforms Signals Intelligence," 1. Bowman and Shane, "Battling High-Tech Warriors," 22A; McDowell; Richelson, "Despite Management/Budget Woes, NRO Launches Continue."

⁹² Richelson, *U.S. Intelligence Community*, 187; Dwayne A. Day, "A Review of Recent American Military Space Operations," *Journal of the British Interplanetary Society*, December 1993, 462–463; Pincus, "Military Espionage Cuts Eyed," A6; Craig Covault, "Titan Succeeds In NRO Flight," *Aviation Week and Space Technology*, May 31, 1999, 34–35; Bruce A. Smith, "In Orbit," July 5, 1999, 5.

⁹³ Richelson, *U.S. Intelligence Community*, 190.

⁹⁴ Confidential interviews.

⁹⁵ CINCPACFLT Instruction S3251.1 D, *Classic Wizard Reporting System*, September 23, 1991, CINCPACFLT FOIA; Richelson, *U.S. Intelligence Community*, 14.

⁹⁶ *Headquarters Naval Security Group Command 1987 Command History*, 7, COMNAVSECGRU FOIA; HQNS-GINST C5450.2D, *Naval Security Group Command Headquarters Organizational Manual*, September 17, 1980, G50–8–650–9, COMNAVSECGRU FOIA.

⁹⁷ Richelson, *U.S. Intelligence Community*, 189; R. Jeffrey Smith, "As Woolsey Struggles, CIA Suffers," *The Washington Post*, May 10, 1994, A7; "New Blueprint for U.S. SIGINT," *Intelligence Newsletter*, October 26, 1995, 1; confidential interviews.

⁹⁸ Air Intelligence Agency, *History of the Air Intelligence Agency: 1 January–31 December 1994*, vol. I, 14, 37, AIA FOIA; Draft, FM 34–37, *Regional Signal Intelligence Operations Brigade*, accessed at <http://fas.org/irp/doddir/army/fm34-37_97/7-chap.htm>; Defense Airborne Reconnaissance Office (DARO), *Unmanned Aerial Vehicles (UAV) Program Plan*, April 1994, 11–16; Richelson, *U.S. Intelligence Community*, 197–198; Ira C. Owens, "Army Intelligence in Transition," *American Intelligence Journal* (Autumn/Winter 1993/1994), 18; "Commander's Column," *Spokesman*, September 1993, 1; 1ˢᵗ Lt Tamara Cinnamo, "Medina RSOC Stands Up," *Spokesman*, October 1993, 5; Gabriel Marshall, "Road to Information Dominance," *Spokesman*, December 1995, 7.

[99] Richelson, *U.S. Intelligence Community*, 200; Duncan Campbell, "They've Got It Taped," *New Statesman*, August 12, 1998; European Parliament, Scientific and Technological Options Assessment (STOA), *Development of Surveillance Technology and Risk of Abuse of Economic Information*, April 1999, 10–11; Richelson, "Desperately Seeking Signals," 47–51.

[100] Nicky Hager, *Secret Power* (Nelson, NZ: Craig Potton, 1996), 29; Claudio Gatti, "License to Spy," *Milan Il Mondo*, March 20, 1998, 10–16, in FBIS–WEU–98–076; Elmar Gusseinov, "Scandalous Echelon," *Izvestia*, September 25, 1998, accessed at <http://www.jya.com>.

[101] Air Intelligence Agency, 39, AIA FOIA; Richelson, *U.S. Intelligence Community*, 201; Bowman and Shane, "Espionage from the Frontlines," 20A.

[102] Department of Defense, Office of Public Affairs, *Release No. 520–99: DOD Distinguished Civilian Service Awards Presented*, November 4, 1999.

[103] The U.S. Air Force's 55th Strategic Reconnaissance Wing at Offutt Air Force Base, NE, flies 16 RC–135V/W "Rivet Joint" SIGINT aircraft, 2 RC–135U "Combat Sent" ELINT collection aircraft, and 3 RC–135S "Cobra Ball" missile monitoring aircraft. The 9th Strategic Reconnaissance Wing at Beale AFB, CA, flies 32 U–2R/S high-altitude reconnaissance aircraft that can be configured with a wide range of SIGINT sensors depending on mission requirements. The U.S. Navy possesses 12 EP–3 "Aries" SIGINT aircraft, while the U.S. Army flies 48 "Guardrail" SIGINT aircraft and 6 Airborne Reconnaissance Low (ARL) aircraft that collect both imagery and SIGINT.

[104] The Navy has 13 destroyers equipped with the "Classic Outboard" SIGINT suite; and 27 *Ticonderoga*-class cruisers, 11 *Arleigh Burke*–class destroyers, 5 helicopter carriers, and 6 *Wasp*-class amphibious command ships which carry the "Combat DF" SIGINT collection system. *Cryptologic Systems Group*, accessed at <http://css.rgesvc.com.LHD-7/volume2/35.htm>; PMW 163 Programs, *Combat DF*, accessed at <http://jmios.spawar.navy.mil/programs/programdetail.cfm>; *Cryptologic Technician Training Series, Module 8—Fleet Operations—Electronic Warfare*, 1987, 3–33, 3–35; Robert Holzer and Neil Munro, "Navy Eyes Eavesdropping System," *Defense News*, November 25, 1991, 12; Norman Friedman, *The Naval Institute Guide to World Naval Weapons Systems, 1991/1992* (Annapolis, MD: Naval Institute Press, 1991), 532; and "Duty Stations," accessed at <http://www. bupers.navy.mil/codes/pers2/N132D8/ctr.>.

[105] *Signals Intelligence (SIGINT) Umbrella Study*, appendix B, "Hierarchy of SIGINT Functions, Processes, and Tasks," undated.

[106] U.S. House of Representatives, 189.

[107] U.S. House of Representatives, Permanent Select Committee on Intelligence, Report 104–578, *Intelligence Authorization Act for Fiscal Year 1998*, 105th Congress, 1st Session, June 18, 1997, 18.

[108] Kenneth A. Minihan, *NSA/CSS Position Report*, November 9, 1998, 6, NSA FOIA.

[109] Confidential interviews.

[110] Remarks by Admiral William O. Studeman, Deputy Director of Central Intelligence, at the Symposium on "National Security and National Competitiveness: Open Source Solutions," December 1, 1992, McLean, VA.

[111] Ackerman, 23.

[112] Department of Defense, 19–20; Pincus, "Panel Ties NSA Funds to Changes at Agency," A21.

[113] Thompson, "Putting NSA Under Scrutiny," 1C; Pincus, "NSA System Crash Raises Hill Worries," A19.

[114] Shane and Bowman, "America's Fortress of Spies," 12A.

[115] Thompson, "Putting NSA Under Scrutiny," 1C; Pincus, "NSA System Crash Raises Hill Worries," A19.

[116] Confidential interviews. See also U.S. House of Representatives, 121.

[117] James Bamford, "Our Best Spies Are In Space," *The New York Times*, August 20, 1998, A23; Brewin, Verton, and Matthews, "NSA Playing IT Catch-Up"; Hersh, 64; David Ignatius, "Where We Can't Snoop," A21.

[118] Loch K. Johnson, *Secret Agencies: U.S. Intelligence in a Hostile World* (New Haven, CT: Yale University Press, 1996), 21; Robert D. Steele, *Improving National Intelligence Support to Marine Corps Operational Forces: Forty Specific Recommendations*, September 3, 1991, 5, accessed at <http://www.oss.net/Papers/reform>.

[119] Ackerman, 23.

[120] Walter Pincus, "Intelligence Community Faulted by House Panel," *The Washington Post*, June 19, 1997, A19.

[121] Walter Pincus, "CIA Chief Cited Loss of Agency's Capabilities," *The Washington Post*, May 25, 1998, A4.

[122] Brewin, Verton, and Matthews.

[123] Hersh, 60.

[124] Gunter Ahrendt, *List of the World's Most Powerful Computing Sites*, January 2, 1999.

[125] *Government Executive*, December 1994, 24.

[126] John McWethy, "Major Failure: NSA Confirms Serious Computer Problem," ABCNews.com, January 29, 2000, accessed at <http://abcnews.go.com/sections/us/DailyNews/nsa000129.html>; Walter Pincus, "NSA System Inoperative for Four Days," *The Washington Post*, January 30, 2000, A2; Walter Pincus, "NSA System Crash Raises Hill Worries," *The Washington Post*, February 2, 2000, A19; Laura Sullivan, "Computer Failure at NSA Irks Intelligence Panels," *Baltimore Sun*, February 2, 2000, 9A.

[127] It was not until 1997 that NSA created the position of chief information officer (CIO), who is responsible for planning and integrating the agency's vast computer and telecommunications resources. See "The Agency's CIO," *NSA Newsletter*, July 1998, 2.

[128] For NSA owning the largest communications system in the Federal Government, see "Prestigious Roger W. Jones Award Presented," *NSA Newsletter*, December 1994, 3. For network problems, see Ackerman.

[129] Ibid.

[130] Confidential interviews.

[131] Confidential interview.

[132] Bamford.

[133] Ackerman.

[134] Ackerman, 24.

[135] Brewin, Verton, and Matthews.

[136] Monteiro, 75.

[137] Memo, COMNAVSECGRU Assistant Chief of Staff for Strategic Plans, Policy, and Readiness to Command Historian, *1996 History Report for N3/N5*, January 31, 1997, 4, COMNAVSECGRU FOIA; Monteiro, 74.

[138] David A. Fulghum, "Computer Combat Rules Frustrate the Pentagon," *Aviation Week and Space Technology*, September 15, 1997, 68.

[139] Confidential interviews.

[140] Michael S. Loescher, "Navy Cryptology is Broken," *Proceedings*, February 2000, 112.

[141] Brewin, Verton, and Matthews.

[142] Vistica and Thomas, "Hard of Hearing."

[143] "DIRNSA's Desk," *NSA Newsletter*, March 1997, 3.

[144] "Ask DIRNSA," *NSA Newsletter*, April 1998, 11.

[145] Confidential interview.

[146] Address at the CIRA Luncheon, October 5, 1998, 6.

[147] U.S. House of Representatives, Permanent Select Committee on Intelligence, Report 106–130, Part 1, *Intelligence Authorization Act for Fiscal Year 2000*, 106th Congress, 1st Session, May 7, 1999, 12.

[148] Brewin, Verton, and Matthews.

[149] James Risen, "A Top-Secret Agency Comes Under Scrutiny and May Have to Adjust," *The New York Times*, December 5, 1999; Hersh, 62; Strobel.

[150] Hersh; Richard Lardner, "NSA Deputy Director Under Fire as Hayden Pushes Reforms at Agency," *Inside the Air Force*, December 10, 1999; Strobel.

[151] U.S. House of Representatives, Permanent Select Committee on Intelligence, Report 105–508, *Intelligence Authorization Act for Fiscal Year 1999*, 105th Congress, 2d Session, May 5, 1998, 9–11; Pincus, "Panel Ties NSA Funds to Changes at Agency," A21.

[152] U.S. Senate, Select Committee on Intelligence, Report 106–3, *Special Report: Committee Activities*, 106th Congress, 1st Session, February 3, 1999, 33–34.

[153] Brewin, Verton, and Matthews; Hersh, 76; Richard Lardner, "NSA Director Aims for Control of SIGINT Agency's Budgeting Process," *Inside the Air Force*, December 10, 1999; Lardner, "NSA Deputy Director Under Fire as Hayden Pushes Reforms at Agency"; "DIRNSA's Desk," *NSA Newsletter*, January 2000, 3.

[154] "NSA Deputy Chief to Quit," *Intelligence Newsletter*, no. 375, February 3, 2000.

[155] Richard Lardner, "New National Security Agency Chief Sure to Face Major Challenges," *Inside the Pentagon*, November 5, 1998; Tabassum Zakaria, "Top Secret U.S. Spy Agency Shapes Up for a New World," *Baltimore Sun*, December 14, 1999.

[156] Hersh, 76.

[157] Zakaria.

[158] "A Message from the Director," *Communicator* 2, no. 41, October 24, 1994, 1.

Part V—The Art of Clandestine Collection

When you are not catching spies, you have bad counterintelligence, and when you are catching spies, you have bad counterintelligence, and you cannot have it both ways.

—Judge William Webster

Chapter 15

The In-Culture of the DO

Charles G. Cogan

It was strictly a coincidence. There I was, sitting in my apartment at Harvard Square, reading the *New York Times* on December 6, 1990. There was a photo of Judge William H. Webster, loose-leaf briefing book tucked under his arm like a football, on his way to Capitol Hill to uphold the truth. He was to testify before the House Armed Services Committee. It reminded me again of the Biblical citation engraved in the stone of the original CIA Headquarters Building at Langley: "and ye shall know the truth and the truth shall make you free."

Judge Webster's testimony followed that of Secretary of Defense Richard Cheney, who had spoken 2 days earlier to the Senate Armed Services Committee. Cheney, according to the *New York Times*, stated that a prolonged embargo might only give Iraq's military time to harden its defensive positions in Kuwait and southern Iraq.

As the Director of Central Intelligence (DCI), Judge Webster testified that the sanctions were having some effect on Iraq's military at the margins: the ground and air forces could probably maintain their then-current levels of combat readiness for another 9 months, and the air-sortie level could be maintained for another 3 to 6 months.

On an inside page was another photo of the DCI standing in the committee's hearing room. With him was his bearded backup briefer, Winston Wiley, from the Directorate of Intelligence (DI)—what my colleague at the Kennedy School, Dick Neustadt, refers to as the "National University."

Norb Garrett, then-director of the agency's Office of Congressional Affairs and a former officer in the Directorate of Operations (DO), also was in the photo. I thought that perhaps the wary look on Norb's face bore the trace of what I like to call "the pre-r.v. [rendezvous] option: be ready for anything to go wrong." It reflected the state of mind of an operations officer preparing for an agent meeting.

I showed the picture to some members of the staff of the National Security Program at the Kennedy School. "This," I said, "is a classic tableau of the DI and DO cultures." They did not know quite what I meant because there is a general unawareness of such figurative isoglosses even among those who have many connections to the Washington establishment. I tried to explain what I had in mind, falling back on the observation that no DO officer would be seen wearing a beard—an exaggeration to prove the point.

Source: Charles G. Cogan, "The In-Culture of the DO," *Studies in Intelligence* (Summer 1991).

Coincidentally, the next day I met with the new director of CIA's Center for the Study of Intelligence, who was making his first visit to the CIA-sponsored Intelligence and Policy Seminar at the Kennedy School. He asked me if I would write an article that would present a profile of the DO officer as a cultural type distinct from the personality model of other directorates. He noted that a profile on the DI officer had already been published.[1] Such an article might contribute to the goal of making DO officers more skillful managers. I thanked him for his perhaps misplaced confidence and said I would give it a try. (The first reflex of a DO officer is never to refuse anything outright; there might be something of value behind it, or as an extension of it.)

Hard to Define

In making my assay of the DO culture, I experienced some butterflies. I recalled a famous, infelicitous use of the word "culture," when then Deputy Director of Central Intelligence Henry Knoche, before a packed house in the CIA Auditorium, said that incoming DCI Stansfield Turner was from a different "culture."

"Culture" is a loaded word, a social science word. It lacks the precision sought by the nuts-and-bolts operations officer intensely interested in hard facts—"hard intel," as the DO expression goes.

In the mystique of the DO culture, the key word is "operational." It has that indefinable, *je ne sais quoi* quality, which one either possesses or one does not. It is the exclusionary byword for the DO officer, just as "policy" is for the diplomat and "analysis" is for the analyst—domains denied to others.

I read the article on the DI culture and found it daunting and profound. Mine, alas, would be different. I probably would use more of a narrative style. This might reflect the DO officer's syndrome of "total reporting at the time," possibly engendered by the ingrained habit of the contact report, which is written as soon as possible after a meeting with an agent or contact.

A Digression

Here, I interrupt to mention two citations. The first is by a well-known phrase-maker, who, because of his past and present positions, should probably remain anonymous: "The DI looks upon the DO the way the State Department looks upon the Agency." This is unfair and overdrawn, but the exaggeration proves the point and describes the playing field.

The second citation, which is attributable, had a deep effect on me as a new DO officer in October 1954, when the Cold War was at its height and when the "no holds barred" Doolittle Report was issued.[2] It goes right to the heart of the DO culture. It was delivered by Hugh Cunningham, then-director of training, to a group of us striplings in Alcott Hall: "We must have the greatest immorality—and we must have the greatest morality." This meant that we had to be ready to deliver blows to our Cold War enemy, while maintaining the highest standards of personal integrity.

I mentioned this aphorism many years later before a career trainee (CT) audience at CIA's Special Training Center. At the time, I was a DO division chief, and I hoped that my remarks would inspire some CTs to join our division. A member of the staff called me aside afterwards and said he did not believe that I should use such a phrase; it would have a bad effect on the CTs. Perhaps he was right, although I had not meant to suggest that one should do anything outside the regulations.

This issue is still with us, but in less stark terms than in 1954. Shortly after taking over as DCI, Judge Webster, in a talk with a Third World leader, was confronted with an observation along the lines of the following: "I don't understand it, Mr. Director. You are a judge, a man committed to upholding the law; and yet you have been placed at the head of an essentially lawless organization."

After a moment's reflection, the DCI replied to the effect that: In the United States, we obey the laws of the United States. Abroad we uphold the national security interests of the United States.

And that is the dilemma, in a nutshell.

Manipulation and Drudgery

Some CTs decide not to join the DO or drop out after they do join because of what I would call the manipulation imperative. They dislike the need to manipulate people. It is not an easy problem for a manager to handle. Nor is it easy to live with the syndrome. A lifetime of manipulation can be corrosive. There also is a boomerang effect. You end up asking yourself, "Who are my real friends?" or "Do I have any?"

And yet it is such an ambivalence, such a dialectic. We like the people we exploit, even as we exploit them. This is our "dance of intelligence." The process is a reflex: we continue to "spring to the game" when the operational opportunity arises, even when we are past the "tiger age" of a case officer.

For the DO officer, recruitment is the means, intelligence is the end. In fact, it is the product more than the process that can corrode over the long run. But we feel great satisfaction when a particular intelligence report we originate—perhaps 1 in 20—seems to have had a clear and important impact on the Washington foreign policy community.

The danger of becoming a technician, as a DO officer, is ever present. The job can become drudgery, causing a loss of imagination. One can only have reflection as an antidote. And yet: During an important meeting with an agent or foreign official, one is liable to pinch oneself and muse, "And to think I get paid for doing this."

Going Public

As a DO officer moves up the management ladder, his transformation from a private to a public personality is a difficult process. On the one hand, we are blessed with, and we work on, our manipulation skills, our people skills, and our attention to the needs and aspirations of others. To look at things from other points of view, we try to put ourselves inside the skins of others, including our foreign interlocutors. Later, however, from the reference point of public policy managers we are hidebound as a result of long years of secrecy, privacy, and compartmentation. In an anonymous business, you do not call attention to yourself.

Just as the DI officer is locked into the rigidity of his own intellectual integrity, the DO officer comes to relish as a compensation for the private personality he has constructed, the notion that knowledge is power and that anterior knowledge is the sweetest power. In the process, however, he tends to become isolated from the real world. Some elements of the DO suffer from this isolation more than others. An officer in the Soviet and Eastern Europe Division conspiring in a near-total anonymity is often quite different from what came to be known, at least until recently, as the "nation-building" or "proconsular" Third World case officer.

Other Problems

As the DO attains more maturity, we find that our inherent habits of compartmentation always need to be reexamined because they can be barriers to sound, humanistic management. Too many times a young case officer at a field station has said, "I arrived here and nobody told me what to do." Partly for reasons of need to know, the young officer often is expected largely to absorb the lore by trial and error. It becomes hands-off management, much different from the way things are done in the military or in corporate America.

In the DO management style, harmony becomes more important than authority. The desire to avoid confrontation and to acquire the supple skills needed in "dancing with wolves" in the world of operations is not always conducive to developing sound management practices. In this atmosphere, performance appraisal reports tend to become inflated.

The DO officer is primarily an overseas American. He works in his language of choice. He works with foreigners. Sometimes, he can "pass" in other cultures or, failing that, often can develop the sophistication and worldliness to be accepted in those cultures. The new case officer arriving at a station gradually comes to his own conclusion: You have to like it, and, if you cannot, you have to go home. And sometimes his wife and he disagree on this matter, but that is a whole other story.

In this overseas business we are often encountering people at their weak points, and this can lead to a great deal of unreliability, hence of disappointment. It becomes a peculiar up-and-down job, demanding protracted patience. One is forced to cultivate a sublime indifference. The environment is foreign, the traps are there ("the talking as though bugged"), and one must always wear the mask of politeness. Equability is paramount when one is in a strange land trying to persuade people to do something that is often against their nature.

Two new commandments are added to the lexicon: "thou shalt not be alarmed; thou shalt not be surprised." It is a life of expecting the unexpected, recognizing that, as a colleague of mine is fond of repeating, "bad things happen." One becomes accustomed to living with precariousness, where life becomes a series of changes of plans. Everything has to be infinitely adaptable and slippable.

Playing a Double Role

There are basically two modes in which a DO officer operates, the acting mode and the straight mode. As I used to say, "a meeting is a matter of theater." Cryptonyms may be uppermost in one's thoughts in the straight mode, while in the acting mode something quite different is coming out. But just as the DO officer is taught not to volunteer information unnecessarily, so he learns that it is vital for his own psyche not to lie unnecessarily. Deception is a tool one exercises only in pursuit of one's trade. Again, the dialectic: because we are so devious, we are the straightest people on earth.

An Insular Society

The DO officer is a unique cultural phenomenon. He does not fit anywhere. He does not fit with the military—the National Security Act of 1947 saw to that in forbidding that there be two military men at the top of the agency at the same time. And he does not fit with the State Department, even though he spends his career in symbiosis with his State colleagues.

Where the DO officer does fit is with other DO officers. The DO is an elite, if narrow, confraternity. It is a form of "ethnocentrism": a party of DO officers ceases to be a social situation and instead becomes a pleasurable encounter. Although there is some backbiting among DO officers, there is something *chevaleresque* about being a member of the DO society. Foreign intelligence interlocutors, except the British, who are so much like ourselves, have at times wistfully remarked on this esprit de corps, wishing that they could escape their own blackguard of lies. Indeed, a capital offense among DO officers is to be seen "gaming one's own," instead of reserving such tactics for actual operations.

The DO is an extremely hierarchical organization. This condition derives largely from the DO's quasimilitary origins in World War II, from its global dispersal, and from its insemination by the British, to whom intelligence is *metier de seigneur* (and, after all, it is the *seigneurs* who run the world).

I can remember when a deputy director for operations loomed at me from his desk like Jupiter. Such awe vanishes as we move up this ladder of well-defined rungs. By tradition of secrecy, we all call each other by our first names—a tradition that is fading. But the hierarchy, though understated, is not transgressed.

While the DO officer is accustomed to dealing in foreign cultures, he sometimes loses the feel of how to deal with his own. I imagine many eyebrows were raised when Robert Gates, in his speech at Princeton University a few years ago,[3] described the agency as poised somewhere between the executive and the legislative branches. He was only reflecting our devotion to Montesquieu: no one branch of the government can become so powerful as to effect a tyranny. Experience has shown that the American people want congressional oversight of the CIA. And oversight, in its ultimate sense, means that Congress can refuse to fund our activities.

What does one do, then, with this pragmatic, flexible, streamlined, punctual operative who is mainly interested in getting a job done and who consequently sometimes becomes accused of not being "political" enough? At times the DO officer's very pragmatism develops into clientitis. A program works so well on the ground, the human material is so good, and yet the people "back there" in Washington do not seem to understand. Meantime, "back there," outside the progam focus, in the DI, in State, and elsewhere, the DO officer is sometimes seen as losing his objectivity.

Detribalization

At the moment the DO officer returns to headquarters, he is a "hot property." He has been hovering between crazy actions all the time. He has spent the better part of a career in often confining overseas environments and has become too close to things. He needs detribalization. He needs fresh experiences in periodic, careful, well-thought-of dosages: senior training; specialized training in subjects such as economics, nuclear science, and computers; tours in other directorates; tours in other agencies, even domestic ones. All of these are becoming more common and less unthinkable; they are a way to impel the DO officer to remove his fixity of focus as he steps into a management role in the strange world of Washington. It requires wiping out the vestiges of an anti-intellectualism in the DO, which used to manifest itself, at least until a decade or so ago, in a disdain for senior training. It requires developing a more long-range view than is possible from a string of intense assignments that change every 2 to 3 years.

The Two Cultures

One may accept the notion that former DCI Bill Colby has advanced ("finally . . . we're achieving the basic concept of central intelligence, that it's the analyst who's at the center of things"[4]), and personnel shifts at the agency in recent years have certainly gone in step with this trend. But to pretend that all the information is out there in the marketplace, *glasnost*-like, needing only to be sifted and analyzed, is to smack of what the French call *angelisme*, roughly translated as "other-worldliness." It is the kind of intellectual know-nothingism expressed in an omniscient-sounding letter to the editor that appeared recently in *The New Republic*:

> secret information is worthless information . . . the truth emerges only from the unceasing exchange of information in the marketplace—with input from scholars, diplomats, business people and others—and not from the use of classified stamps on isolated bits of information.[5]

Thus, though the DO officer is constantly, perhaps increasingly, in a struggle with irrelevance, he knows it is not for want of a challenge. The Grail is out there: important foreign leaders, some of them tyrants, want to protect what they know.

Despite all the "bonding" and cross-fertilization that has taken place between the DI and the DO over the past several years, with symbolic and real successes, the fact remains that the two cultures are very different. Many DI officers are pained (from their point of view, one can see why) that they are associated with what the public mindlessly calls the "spooks." But both the DI and the DO know that they must continue to live as *vases communicants*, and that each is the other's strength.

Notes

[1] "The DI's Organizational Culture," *Studies in Intelligence* (Fall 1990), 21–25.

[2] *Report on the Covert Activities of the Central Intelligence Agency*, September 30, 1954: "It is now clear that we are facing an implacable enemy whose avowed objective is world domination by whatever means and by whatever cost. There are no rules in such a game. . . . If the U.S. is to survive, long-standing American concepts of 'fair play' must be

reconsidered. We . . . must learn to subvert, sabotage, and destroy our enemies by more clever, more sophisticated, and more effective methods than those used against us."

[3] Robert M. Gates, "CIA and the Making of American Foreign Policy," September 29, 1987.

[4] *The New York Times*, July 14, 1991, 12.

[5] *The New Republic*, May 13, 1991, 6.

Chapter 16

Espionage in an Age of Change: Optimizing Strategic Intelligence Services for the Future

Norman B. Imler

There have been times here in America when our intelligence services were held in suspicion, and even contempt. Now, when we face this new war, we know how much we need them.

—President George W. Bush[1]

A well-tested truism in strategic planning circles, attributed variously to Chinese theoretician Sun Tzu and Prussian General Helmuth von Moltke, holds that no plan survives first contact with the adversary. This dictum, from which flows the imperative for constant adjustment to meet the demands of a changing strategic situation, holds true across the broader realm of statecraft as well. The intelligence corollary—that first contact has the potential to yield new insights about the adversary—is suggestive of the challenges that confront all technical and human intelligence disciplines that support statecraft in the dynamic environment that the United States, and its friends and allies, face today.

An effective and integrated strategic intelligence system, practicing the intelligence equivalent of military jointness that we can refer to as *complementarity*, should be positioned to detect changes in the world security environment and warn of developments that may threaten U.S. interests. It also should serve as a resource to shape that environment to support diplomacy and policy when called upon to do so, assist the warfighter if intervention becomes necessary, and monitor the results (or absence thereof) of intervention.

The human component of intelligence (HUMINT), traditionally known as espionage, is an essential component of a comprehensive strategic intelligence system. The advantages offered by effective HUMINT remain a constant through all phases of engagement, from normal relations, through pre-conflict diplomacy and maneuvering, military action, and into post-conflict operations to restore stability. It is not unusual for human agents to acquire, under extraordinarily difficult operating conditions, critical information or insights unobtainable by other means, often at grave personal risk. Assessing this strategic service, and identifying areas for strengthening and transformation, will be the primary focus of this survey.

Within the U.S. strategic intelligence system, espionage is a principal responsibility of the Central Intelligence Agency (CIA) Directorate of Operations, also known as the Clandestine Service (CS). The CIA is charged with providing clandestine and covert strategic services to the Nation. To do so, it covers the strategic environment with well-placed collection and action resources—key among them human agents (assets)—conducting espionage, reporting, and undertaking other specialized tasks as an integral and coordinated part of a larger strategic intelligence plan. An optimized clandestine HUMINT element has human agent "boots on the ground" before, during, and after the other instruments of national power have been brought to bear.

This broad responsibility holds regardless of whether the CS is operating in a support to military operations, support to law enforcement, or support to diplomatic/policy operations context. Information derived from these assets, together with data from other functional intelligence resources such as signals intelligence (SIGINT), imagery intelligence (IMINT), measurement and signature intelligence (MASINT), and open source intelligence, in turn enables a deeper, more textured and detailed understanding of the enemy, opening new opportunities for commanders and policymakers to seek a decisive advantage and achieve strategic goals and objectives.

It is thus important that we understand the elements of HUMINT in general, and the Clandestine Service and espionage discipline in particular, as fundamental parts of a larger national intelligence whole. The Clandestine Service is a unique and versatile instrument of national power. Where it is properly structured, managed, and integrated with other intelligence functions and instruments of national power, this strategic service plays an important role in giving decisionmakers both a direct, clandestine source of information about adversaries and a hidden way of influencing those adversaries.

The challenges and opportunities facing HUMINT in this age of change are qualitatively different from those faced during the bipolar Cold War with the Soviet Union, or even the "phony peace" that held prior to September 11. In the words of former Director of Central Intelligence (DCI) R. James Woolsey, "It is as if we were struggling with a large dragon for 45 years, killed it, and then found ourselves in a jungle full of poisonous snakes—and the snakes are much harder to keep track of than the dragon ever was."[2] The fall of the Berlin Wall in 1989, the dissolution of the Soviet Union 2 years later, and a rise in the number of adversarial nonstate or loosely state-affiliated actors signaled a paradigm shift. It challenged U.S. strategic intelligence to reorient its focus to cover multiple new targets, including rogue state and nonstate group threats, the proliferation of weapons of mass destruction, international crime and narcotics, and terrorism.

At the same time, "megatrends" in the areas of technology-driven transportation and communication improvements, economic and social globalization, and relaxation of restrictions on the movements of peoples made open societies more vulnerable. In spite of initial efforts to curb it, terrorism by extremists—"fanaticism armed with power,"[3] in the words of British intelligence historian Christopher Andrew—has steadily emerged as the more prevalent and pressing of the post-Cold War security threats.

To help us consider the appropriate role for clandestine HUMINT and covert action today, this chapter seeks to identify and explore, against the national security backdrop described above, the key factors that will be among the determinants of CS mission success in this transformational era. Continued CS resilience and effectiveness depend largely on the extent to which it recognizes and adapts itself to evolving intelligence mega trends in the areas of depth of personnel expertise, continuity on targets and tasks, and integration of efforts. We begin by looking at the "origin of the species."

U.S. Clandestine Service: A Grand Strategic Intelligence Experiment

The acquisition of secret or protected information of intelligence value through human means often is referred to as "the world's second oldest profession" because of tales of espionage dating to Biblical times. Sun Tzu, the classical Chinese strategist, regarded espionage as the means to foreknowledge: ". . . what enables an intelligent government and wise military leadership to overcome others and achieve extraordinary accomplishment. . . . Foreknowledge cannot be gotten from ghosts and spirits, cannot be had by analogy, cannot be found out by calculation. It must be obtained from people, people who know the conditions of the enemy."[4]

In the United States, HUMINT programs are the overall responsibility of the CIA, which was established as a strategic, independent (that is, nondepartmental), centralized national intelligence organization after World War II, over considerable political opposition from the military services, Department of State, and Department of Justice. The political calculation of a need for autonomy was underscored recently by former CIA Inspector General Jeffrey Smith, who reminds us that "President Truman and Congress recognized that it was imperative to have an agency to collect and analyze intelligence for the President that would be independent of the departments of State and Defense."[5] The purpose behind such a design still resonates.

The CIA, America's grand experiment with national intelligence in a democracy, remains the Federal Government's only independent, nondepartmental intelligence organization. Nominally responsible for the whole of the Intelligence Community (IC), the CIA Director of Central Intelligence in reality controls less than 10 percent of the IC budget and billets. The Directorate of Operations (Clandestine Service) of the CIA is the lead IC element for the human intelligence and covert action functions, complemented by the activities of other departments and agencies, particularly in wartime. While the CS will be the primary focus of this analysis, the reader also will come to appreciate that espionage is but one aspect of strategic intelligence, all the facets of which must be integrated and coordinated at a national level to support policy effectively.

HUMINT Explored

HUMINT is not always a cloak-and-dagger pursuit. Presidents, cabinet secretaries, national security advisers, and military commanders often seek intelligence— "knowledge vital for national survival," in the words of former National War College professor Sherman Kent—through direct emissaries, as an element of their practice of grand strategy. Emissaries are used to acquire information in a low-key manner to assist in anticipating foreign developments with implications for American security and interests, and to support policymaking, issue management, and risk mitigation. These emissaries often provide information of key, time-sensitive value to their principals, and a confidential channel through which views and messages can be exchanged.

Occasionally, such representatives travel in a semiclandestine mode. They avoid publicity and sometimes even use false identities to screen their activities from outside observation. Air Force General Robert E. Huyser, for example, traveled quietly to Iran in 1979, at the request of President Jimmy Carter, to assess for the White House the prospects of the Shah's regime. The information derived from such direct observation often is extremely sensitive, and given only limited circulation within the government, for both practical and political reasons.

At another level, the U.S. Government—like most governments—dispatches and maintains a variety of official representatives worldwide as its overt eyes and ears abroad. Ambassadors, defense/military (Defense Intelligence Agency [DIA]) attaches, trade representatives (Department of Commerce), cultural (Department of State) and legal attaches (Federal Bureau of Investigation [FBI]), and political and/or economic officers (also part of the State Department), among others, represent American interests to host governments or international organizations. At the same time, it is within the scope of their responsibility to observe and report information. Such information is routinely acquired or elicited from overt, official, formal and informal sources, and other contacts. As State Department spokesman Richard Boucher observed, "We're a government. We do collect information. We talk to a lot of people. We want to know things." [6]

Still other HUMINT information is produced by the FBI, DIA Defense HUMINT Service, and by military special operators and scouts, debriefings of official travelers and émigrés, and attendance at international symposia and trade, technology, and arms shows. Unlike the products of higher-level emissaries and political confidants, most reporting from official government representatives is disseminated to policymakers, analysts, and other consumers within government, using restrictions on readership deemed appropriate by the responsible department or agency.

Espionage Explained

Finally, there is espionage, a tool that is more art than science, used for thousands of years by statesmen and commanders to obtain information from as close to the centers of gravity of an adversary, or potential adversary, as possible. Sun Tzu, a Chinese military strategist dating to about 500 BC whose treatise, *The Art of War*, is regarded as containing insights of enduring strategic relevance, observed, "It is only the enlightened ruler and the wise general who will use the highest intelligence of the army for the purposes of spying, and thereby achieve great results." [7] The duality of espionage and political action was apparent even in Sun Tzu's era, when agents sometimes had both the means to acquire needed information and control of trusted confidants who could influence events at court.

In a world acutely sensitized to the collection threats posed by reconnaissance satellites tracking overhead and eavesdroppers listening in to communications, the age-old practice of espionage endures. It is one of the few remaining ways for a leader to obtain direct information about an adversary's exact location, plans, capabilities, and intentions, without the target becoming aware that it has lost such critical information. The quiet, steady, behind-the-scenes work that led to the arrest of al Qaeda chief of operations Khalid Shaikh Mohammed on March 1, 2003, is suggestive of the potential of integrated all-source intelligence, espionage operations, and direct action in support of both policy and law enforcement.

In terms of its relationship to other intelligence functions, espionage "is often essential to providing an indication, a tip, a direction for targeting and using technical intelligence assets, such as reconnaissance or signals intelligence."[8] Likewise, human agents often are vectored to targets by information acquired through technical collection.

Clandestine Operations and Covert Action

We now turn to the primary focus of our attention, the arena of the Clandestine Service. Clandestine HUMINT is part of a group of activities—referred to during World War II as *strategic services*—conducted today by the CIA Directorate of Operations under the authority of the National Security Act of 1947 and associated public laws and executive orders. This American form of strategic service combines human intelligence and covert action functions into one component, independent of Federal political and functional departments. While these activities have been commingled in the U.S. intelligence system and do on occasion overlap or support and feed each other, we need to distinguish the clandestine from the covert:

- *Clandestine* regards activities crafted, conducted, and intended to remain secret. Clandestine HUMINT activities use special means (*tradecraft* in CIA parlance) to accomplish a collection task against a target, to produce information unobtainable by other means. This is espionage, more often referred to as spying. It is subdivided into *foreign* or *positive intelligence, operational intelligence,* and *counterintelligence,* which initially was referred to as *negative intelligence.*
- *Covert* regards activities crafted and conducted to keep the sponsor's hand hidden, or *plausibly deniable.* Covert action uses special political, economic, informational, and paramilitary means to influence a foreign situation in support of a U.S. policy goal or objective. Covert activities emphasize concealing the identity of the sponsor to avoid present and future harm to bilateral relationships. In the modern era, the timeframe for such concealment has continued to shrink.

The origins and imperatives for America's grand experiment in centralized strategic intelligence can be traced to many points in our history, with World War II perhaps being the single most relevant period for today's national security strategist. In 1939, almost 3 years before America's formal entry into the war, President Roosevelt urged the Navy Office of Naval Intelligence, the Army Military Intelligence Division, and the FBI to coordinate their intelligence activities because of his increasing concerns about the threat to U.S. interests posed by developments in Europe and Asia. In doing so, Roosevelt was striving to obtain a clearer strategic picture about an increasingly turbulent and threatening world. Instead, he found "the three intelligence services were focusing on subversion, sabotage and espionage while jealously guarding their functional missions and territorial divisions."[9]

Frustrated in his efforts to effect closer cooperation between the Navy, Army, and FBI, in the summer of 1941 President Roosevelt tapped prominent Republican lawyer and decorated World War I army veteran William Donovan to become his strategic Coordinator of Information (COI). Donovan, who as a private emissary for FDR had spent considerable time in besieged London in 1940 and early 1941 learning about strategic intelligence from the British, was an advocate of centralized intelligence collection and analysis, a concept "bitterly opposed by Navy, War and the Justice Department (especially the FBI's J. Edgar Hoover), all of whom saw the possibility that such an organization would encroach on their powers and responsibilities."[10]

COI became the Office of Strategic Services (OSS) with America's entry into World War II. Because of continuing bureaucratic opposition, the OSS was subordinated to the War Department for the duration of the war, precluded from operating in the Western hemisphere by the FBI, and restricted from operations in most of the Pacific theater by the Navy and General Douglas MacArthur. In spite of such limitations, the innovative and driven General Donovan infused the OSS with a "spirit of risk, daring, and purpose"[11] and carved out a role for his new organization wherever opportunities arose. For the new OSS, these chances to contribute to the war effort came principally in occupied Europe, the Balkans, North Africa, the Middle East, and the Indo-China theater.

As a spearhead service, the OSS developed an aggressive approach to wartime espionage, counterintelligence, special operations, and analysis. It was disbanded at war's end, the victim of continuing bureaucratic intrigue and concerns regarding the need for a Federal intelligence service in a democracy, in a time of anticipated peace. CIA historian Michael Warner comments on this intrigue by noting that "The problem for the Truman administration that fall of 1945 was that no one, including the President, knew just what he wanted, while each department and intelligence service knew fully what sorts of results it wanted to avoid."[12]

In spite of such obstacles, General Donovan's activist style, together with post-war organizational remnants and skilled operators and analysts of the OSS, became the spirit and substance—the very foundation—of the clandestine collection and covert political action elements found in today's CIA. U.S. Special Forces and the Special Operations Command (USSOCOM) also trace their heritage to the "tip of the spear" special operations elements of the OSS, which helps to explain the relative ease with which USSOCOM and CIA cooperate in the field today in the war on terrorism. In the words of current Director of Central Intelligence George J. Tenet, "OSS casts a very long shadow . . . Our present organization, standards, customs, and spiritual legacy began with the OSS, and today's Agency officers are, in essence, descendants of those who served with such commitment and distinction more than a half century ago."[13] One might anticipate that, as the frequency of large-scale military operations decreases, the importance of the role of smaller, specialized forces integrated with intelligence and supporting military arms will increase.

The CIA Directorate of Operations developed, in the roughly four decades following the National Security Act of 1947 and leading up to the brink of the dissolution of the Soviet Union, structures and processes (modus operandi) to provide the range and variety of strategic espionage and action services deemed necessary within the context of the times. These encompassed a creative and flexible workforce, a unique set of capabilities, and an unusual scope of roles and responsibilities, marked by a near-worldwide physical presence (infrastructure); a network of formal and informal relationships with foreign intelligence and security partners (liaison); sophisticated operational and security processes (tradecraft and compartmentation); and advanced technical capabilities and near-real-time worldwide secure communications (support).

In spite of these strengths, clandestine strategic service remains more art than science. Highly publicized missteps, such as the inability to oust Fidel Castro during the John F. Kennedy administration, involvement in assassination plotting during the Kennedy and Lyndon Johnson years, the arms for hostages and Nicaraguan harbor mining affairs of the Ronald Reagan years, and the abortive early efforts to support a coup against Saddam Hussein, all involved the covert action element of the CS, which operates only at the direction of the President. The successes and setbacks the CS experienced in intelligence gathering are harder to identify because of the shroud of secrecy that protects such activities but also makes thorough scrutiny difficult.

The circumstances surrounding the establishment of the COI and OSS at the outset of World War II, together with the experiences of the Cold War, are important to understand because the bureaucratic forces that resisted their creation continue to reverberate today. While 62 years have passed, these rivalries and tensions continue to impact the effectiveness of intelligence at the national level today. In an age of bureaucracy, the Clandestine Service has remained agile and responsive. Reflecting Donovan's founding spirit and drive, it has thrived as an organization, despite facing considerable challenges and suffering occasional setbacks and missteps. It is unlikely that another department could duplicate this set of strengths and experience.

The essence of clandestine HUMINT in the field is the spotting, recruiting, and handling of useful agents (foreign national sources). This is accomplished by case officers, intelligence operations officers who typically are U.S. citizens working abroad under cover. Where the Clandestine Service undertakes such operations on its own—referred to as *unilateral activities*—these are often high-risk operations, in terms of the threat to U.S. foreign relations and to human lives. The risk of such operations, in theory, is managed by selectivity, undertaking only those unilateral activities that are required to accomplish a task that cannot be accomplished by more secure and less risk-laden means. Risk also can be mitigated through the involvement of partners, sister services within the IC, military services, law enforcement, and foreign counterparts. In contrast to the assertion made that the Clandestine Service has grown risk-averse, difficult operations are undertaken when there is a calculable return for the investment and means to minimize the associated risks.

Another essential dimension of clandestine HUMINT in the modern era is *liaison*. This term describes work done in partnership with counterpart foreign intelligence and security services, on activities of mutual interest. Liaison, when it is properly conducted with due regard for the complexities, risks, and gains in play, is a specialized functional skill area in and of itself. When properly handled, it is as challenging in its own right as other elements of espionage. Liaison goes well beyond the simplistic "by giving them stuff . . . that gives us stuff"[14] description offered by a former intelligence officer in describing assistance the United States receives from friendly services in the war on terrorism. Particularly in the global wars on terrorism, international crime, and narco-trafficking, where target networks move across multiple jurisdictional lines, liaison can be a tremendous force and reach multiplier.

What Kind of Tradecraft?

The Clandestine Service evolved two distinct and competitive subcultures, each with markedly different perspectives and approaches, to meet its intelligence collection requirements.

The Quantity Subculture. When targets were accessible in what were regarded as benign or less-threatening operational environments, the natural instinct for one group of officers, broad-gauged in background who preferred to work essentially alone, was to recruit in depth. This quantity-focus subculture created a host of agents to perform a multitude of tasks. Such an approach turned out to be problematic. In many instances, individual officers could not allocate sufficient time to manage each case appropriately. Adversaries, among them the Cubans, East Germans, Chinese, and North Vietnamese, were successful in turning this aggressive recruitment approach against us. These hostile services achieved a number of counterintelligence successes, controlling or identifying and turning agents, sometimes from early on in the relationship.

The Quality Subculture. For those responsible for *internal operations*—collection activities conducted against the more difficult, hard-target environments—a different approach evolved. When foreign volunteers (walk-ins) surfaced to offer their services and risk their lives, the best of these were carefully scrutinized and tested (vetted). If they passed muster, these agents were run in place inside the target government. Such quality-focused operations took time to mature and were extraordinarily rare and fragile. They were handled by team and technology-oriented methods to ensure security and productivity over time. The primary threat to such operations came from penetrations (moles) within our own services, such as Aldrich Ames (CIA), Robert Hanssen (FBI), and Ana Montes (DIA).

During the Cold War, the strategy behind operations officer development was shaped, to a large extent, by the prevailing CS leadership view that collection challenges were met best by broad-gauged generalist case officers. Practical experience gained by overseas service was stressed. Training was deemphasized. When training was provided, it was focused primarily on language and functional familiarization, rather than on advanced, skills-oriented education.

These generalist officers could be deployed virtually anywhere overseas on a moment's notice. They were judged to be versatile enough to handle espionage and action challenges in Europe and Asia and then, as required, be shifted to deal with problems arising in Africa or Latin America. Spending the bulk of one's career overseas in multiple assignments along a single operational track became the key to advancement. Because flexibility and frequent turnovers were the established keys to promotion, a majority of officers developed careers that featured rapid changes in jobs and responsibilities, sometimes as often as once a year.

Exceptions—specialist officers in functional, regional, or country-specific disciplines—were prominent in the early days of the Clandestine Service but declined steadily in number, status, and influence throughout the Cold War as generalists grew to dominate the service. During the roughly 16-year period between the "Year of the Spy" in 1985 and the identification of such penetrations as Ames (CIA), Hanssen (FBI), and Montes (DIA), for example, Clandestine Service case officers actively were discouraged from specializing in counterintelligence. This management strategy backfired, creating the HUMINT equivalent of the hollow Army of post-war Vietnam. Deficiencies in this critical offensive and defensive intelligence discipline remain.

Naturally, with such turbulence comes a decline in core subject matter expertise, a key area of concern for the prospects of reform efforts. One cannot help but conclude that frequent assignment turnover led to a tendency to work the periphery of issues, particularly against closed authoritarian or totalitarian systems. Lengthier, more complex undertakings are, by definition, less attractive and thus less frequently pursued. Operations at the margins, in contrast, are the most likely to come to fruition during the course of one's foreshortened tour of duty. As a consequence of this pattern, the likelihood of penetration of the hardest targets—for example, those presenting the greatest strategic threat to U.S. interests such as Iraqi, North Korean, and Indian weapons of mass destruction (WMD) developments—decreases. The operational focus shifts to dependence on the surfacing of chance volunteers and defectors with key insights.

This sacrifice of depth and continuity for breadth and speed was a conscious strategic choice. However, it departed from Donovan's strategy—a blend of experts and generalists—that made the OSS effective during World War II. While it may have served the CS well during the bipolar Cold War era, its relevance in this age of change, against more complex intelligence challenges where our strategic margin for error is significantly smaller, is less certain. As Colonel David Hackworth observed regarding the Army's parallel experience in Vietnam, "constantly rotating company, battalion, and brigade commanders through Vietnam was not leading to an Army with great depth in experienced battlefield leadership, but instead the loss of more blood and lives . . . a criminal lack of continuity on the ground."[15]

Continuity is no less important for the performance of strategic intelligence tasks, especially developing and running effective clandestine human agent operations against the most difficult, hardest targets.

As the Nation turns to meet the national security challenges of the 21st century, we need to consider whether the generalist officer alone will be sufficient for the complex, multidisciplinary tasks ahead. The lessons learned by the business community with respect to knowledge acquisition, knowledge management, and continual learning might be instructive in this context. Royal Dutch Shell strategist Arie P. DeGeus observed, as far back as 1988, that "the ability to learn faster than the competition may be the only sustainable competitive advantage."[16] Endorsing and investing in a lessons-learned program, and incorporating this hard-won wisdom into mandatory, all-hands educational opportunities, may be a way to accelerate and deepen the learning of officers at all ranks.

Today's Clandestine Service exists within a national security bureaucratic structure that continues to be marked by insularity and rigidity. While the shortcomings in information sharing and fusion, coordination, and cooperation are less now than those experienced by President Roosevelt in 1939, competitive and parochial tendencies continue to limit the effective, comprehensive integration of strategic intelligence efforts. To enable us to judge this further, we will need to examine some of the key intelligence roles and responsibilities that reach beyond the foreign intelligence collection arena.

Counterstrategies: The Challenges Ahead

Over the past decade, there has been a growing reliance on specialized intelligence disciplines to *counter* the numerous security threats facing the United States. These counterstrategies often combine the aspects of clandestine information collection and action directed by the President to shape the environment.

Counterintelligence (CI). CI encompasses activities conducted, and information exploited, to protect the United States from espionage, sabotage, assassination, political influence, and other activities of our adversaries. Identifying, monitoring, neutralizing, and manipulating foreign intelligence threats are integral components of a comprehensive CI program.

Challenge: The openness of American government and society makes us vulnerable to concerted efforts of adversaries to penetrate the Nation. All of our institutions are at risk. At the same time, the CI function must be conducted in keeping with American values and in a way that supports, rather than erodes, systemic effectiveness. CI remains in disarray because of lack of consensus on how it should be organized, resourced, led, and managed at a national level, and integrated at the organizational and operational levels.

Counterterrorism (CT). CT seeks to neutralize the threat posed by foreign terror groups by interweaving collection with analytic and offensive actions to preempt, disrupt, and/or defeat terrorist threats. The CT function is heavily dependent on information sharing, information fusion, and cooperation within the IC and U.S. Government and with foreign partners.

Challenge: The scope, nature, and tenacity of such groups as al Qaeda suggest that the global war on terrorism will have to be managed, but may never be won, in spite of the destruction of the Taliban and Saddam Hussein regimes in Afghanistan and Iraq respectively. The effectiveness of CT depends on unity of purpose and action within the U.S. Government, operational (CIA and FBI) development of HUMINT-enabled access to terror groups and individual targets, and our ability to leverage what are now essential foreign relationships. The efficacy of the new Terrorist Threat

Integration Center will depend on the extent to which it comes to be viewed as the lead security element in this arena, fusing and providing human threat information at higher levels of specificity and timeliness.

Covert Action (CA). CA is employed where the United States seeks to influence events abroad, in ways that are plausibly deniable. CA includes political, economic, informational, and paramilitary activities. Like Carl von Clausewitz's description of war, CA is the extension of politics by other means. It supplements, rather than supplants, other instruments of power.

Challenge: A worldwide CA infrastructure relies heavily on human and physical assets for direct action political missions. Here again, foreign states, driven by their own national interests, often are key partners. The paramilitary aspects of CA appeal to the Pentagon, particularly given the prominent role CA, together with light and agile ground forces, played in the ousting of the Taliban regime in Afghanistan. This has injected tension into the system between those who prefer interservice cooperation as a modus operandi, and those who prefer to acquire and control this aspect of CA.

Counterproliferation (CP). CP includes programs and activities designed to identify, monitor, and thwart efforts by foreign countries and groups that seek to possess weapons capable of causing mass casualties—radiological, chemical, biological, and nuclear arms often referred to as weapons of mass destruction (WMD).

Challenge: WMD are, in many cases, accessible to foreign states and groups for little investment but require networks of individuals to weaponize a capability. CP is a relatively new, promising discipline that mirrors, on the strategic intelligence side, the overt aspects of regulatory regimes. CP is increasingly action-oriented, anticipating the shift to emphasis on preemption, and heavily dependent on science and technology and HUMINT-enabled access for success, particularly in the growing MASINT arena. A coordinated national-level CP program has yet to gel.

Counternarcotics (CN) and Countercrime. CN leverages U.S. human and technical intelligence capabilities to combat organized crime and narcotics trafficking. Crime syndicates and drug smuggling organizations, increasingly well financed, operate on an international scale and, in some instances, provide assistance to terrorist groups.

Challenge: When measured in terms of their direct impact on U.S. lives and economic productivity, international crime and narco-trafficking present significant risks to national security. However, CN remains underresourced, with roles and responsibilities at the strategic level fractured and spread among too many different departments, agencies, and organization elements, again reflecting lack of national consensus regarding a strategy.

Counter Denial and Deception (D&D). Counter D&D programs target adversary efforts to minimize the loss of protected information (denial) and inject into the collection stream, where possible, an alternative view of reality (deception) and seek to convey that to a preselected audience. Strong counter D&D programs, to foil the opponent's strategy, are critical in an age of near-transparent intelligence collection and analytic capabilities.

Challenge: Efforts to manipulate the United States at a strategic level are of constant concern, as the current investigation into forged documents on Iraqi attempts to acquire uranium from an African country suggests. D&D requires HUMINT to ask tough questions regarding the motives and sources of information of even the best of agents. However, traditional resistance within the U.S. intelligence system to incorporating a robust counter D&D capability hampers development of this critical counterstrategy.

The Sum of All Challenges

The six intelligence counterstrategies sketched out above are all critical areas of expertise for a modern intelligence service to possess. While not all are new, they are all, nevertheless, necessary to assist U.S. policymakers in understanding, managing, and, if necessary, defeating complex threats posed to national security by an extraordinarily wide and varying range of foreign adversaries. In terms of the implications for the Clandestine Service, each of these counterstrategies is heavily dependent on depth and continuity in human espionage and action capabilities, and integration with other intelligence collection means, to maximize the prospects for comprehensive and sustainable success.

These counterstrategies are also important for the CIA as an institution. Former DCI Allen Dulles commented, "Presidents always want a hidden way of doing things. That's how the CIA gets its clout with the White House."[17] In each instance, the targets of these counterstrategies are closed systems, themselves skilled in offensive and defensive intelligence and security practices and increasingly aware of the intelligence methods and techniques being used against them.

To be successful, counterstrategies require significant new levels of organization endorsement and commitment. These range from the systematic development of significant new depth of expertise, to extended continuity on targets and tasks, to broader and deeper coordination within and among intelligence components. To provide the appropriate incentives in the U.S. system, HUMINT personnel responsible for these intelligence counterstrategy disciplines and functions will require as-yet unrealized recognition and status within their organizations equivalent to other, more traditional, human intelligence disciplines; equal access to the best officers available to enable the development of a "critical mass" of skilled officers; and long-term resource support.

Such measures hold out the promise of an enduring solution to the dilemma of effective intelligence counterstrategies. On the other hand, a modern strategic service that is not prepared to throw its energies behind a comprehensive and integrated program will create seams that U.S. adversaries can continue to exploit.

Espionage and Technology: Synergies Beyond "Q"

Technology, as it is applied to clandestine intelligence collection and covert action, is another area of evolution in strategic service that benefits from greater depth, continuity, and integration. Former DCI R. James Woolsey observed, "Some today try to put the effective use of technology and classic espionage at odds with one another. Nonsense! . . . There is no hint of any such false separation between the role of science and the role of human beings undertaking the dangerous, lonely, and heroic job of espionage 'in the cause of freedom.'"[18]

During World War II, for example, General Donovan enlisted the assistance of U.S. and Allied scientific, technical, and industrial talent to develop systems and techniques to bolster OSS espionage capabilities. One such system, a small, short-range, portable two-way radio, enabled OSS agents in the field to communicate with an aircraft orbiting above, demonstrated how technology could be applied in innovative ways to facilitate, enhance, and make more secure, HUMINT collection operations at their most vulnerable point—the transfer of acquired information along a line of communication to a reception point. Technology is no less important for espionage today.

Technological approaches to target, penetrate, and monitor adversary states and groups often are heavily dependent on human agents, for insight, access and sustainment. As business strategist Michael E. Porter observed, when discussing the importance of taking a systems approach to complex challenges, "The productivity frontier—the sum of all existing best practices—is constantly shifting outward as new technologies and management approaches are developed and as new inputs become available."[19]

When it is injected into clandestine affairs, technology presents a three-dimensional challenge that grows in complexity in direct relationship to the role involved. For advanced HUMINT systems, technology, when properly recognized and incorporated, is an enabler. In this situation, technology can be leveraged to make clandestine activities more productive and secure. In foreign hands, technology is a target, against which the United States seeks to leverage its scientific and industrial advantages, to make the foreign environment more transparent. Finally, technology is a powerful weapon for opponents, to sustain their grip on power, and to project power within a region (for example, Iraq) and globally (for example, al Qaeda), which must be better understood.

America's scientific, technological, and organizational prowess, combined with its emphasis on breakthrough innovations and creative applications of technologies, gives it the potential—second to none—to leverage technology to continue to strengthen HUMINT collection capabilities. At a macro-level, the U.S. HUMINT system indeed has benefited from advances in computing power, telecommunications, miniaturization, information management, information security, and precision guidance.

Curiously, though, while the IC has invested billions of dollars to harness technology to enhance collection, HUMINT elements have been comparatively slower to integrate technology into mainstream clandestine collection culture. Rather than make technology a part of the whole, it has been kept as a separate and distinct external element, utilized as an exceptional, rather than regular, tool. Further, development of technologies to support the exploitation and analysis of HUMINT collection has been limited as well. There may be other explanations, but the net effect stands in stark contrast to Porter's conclusion that "Overall advantage or disadvantage results from all of a company's activities, not only a few."[20]

As a result, in terms of its integration into modern clandestine HUMINT, technology has tended to be segregated and used at the margins. This narrow approach has robbed the U.S. HUMINT system of the critical value technology has to offer. A strengthened partnership in this area would provide another tool with which to respond to the increasingly sophisticated efforts of adversaries to screen their developments, capabilities, and activities from scrutiny.

Espionage in a Democracy: Moral and Ethical Dimensions

No review of the HUMINT function of the U.S. intelligence system is complete without acknowledging and addressing the profound moral and ethical concerns that attend the espionage function. Lieutenant General Vernon Walters, an accomplished military officer, diplomat (and private emissary), and intelligence officer, captured this uniquely American sensitivity when he remarked, "Americans have always had an ambivalent attitude toward intelligence. When they feel threatened, they want a lot of it, and when they don't, they regard the whole thing as somewhat immoral."[21]

Taking another angle, Thomas Powers, a student of the world of intelligence and author of a book about former Clandestine Service officer and later Director of Central Intelligence Richard Helms, observed that "intelligence is the most political of professions."[22] If true, then clandestine HUMINT is among the most political of the intelligence disciplines. It carries that burden in a democracy precisely because intelligence officers engaged in espionage—involving human beings under conditions of high pressure, vulnerability, and risk, and in situations occasionally requiring quick, on-the-spot decisions—sometimes take actions that are found not to stand the light of day. These instances are rare, but they receive extraordinary scrutiny nonetheless.

Much like their business executive counterparts, HUMINT officers operate today in what ethicists David Messick and Max Bazerman termed a "moral minefield" in their examination of psychology, decisionmaking, and ethical leadership.[23] Espionage, as an organizational function, is fraught with sometimes intense external and internal competition. Social psychologists have found that hyper-competition tends, over time, to reduce the barriers to unethical behavior. When it occurs, we tend to focus on the individual—the Ames, the Hanssen, the Montes—as the aberrations of an otherwise intact and correctly functioning system. What we fail to see is that "different systems may produce different levels of unethical conduct . . . the system itself can be a cause of the problems. . . . It is an old adage that evil prevails when good people fail to act, but we rarely hold the 'good' people responsible for the evil."[24]

Clandestine HUMINT officers are sometimes regarded as "magicians" for their ability to accomplish difficult collection tasks, and other specialized actions, in the face of extraordinary obstacles. However, espionage, as with other high-risk professions, comes with its own built-in traps. As Messick and Bazerman conclude, "The tendencies to feel superior, to generate self-serving, on-the-spot moral rules, and to be overconfident about beliefs create the potential for moral shallowness and callowness."[25] They single out "over confidence" as a risk specific to several high-pressure professions, including that of intelligence officer, a factor identified earlier by CIA internal research.[26]

The potential security risks posed by a singleton officer acting outside the bounds of supervision can be seen, most recently, in what was alleged to have happened following an FBI officer's apparent loss of control in the handling of a Chinese double agent. While the full story of this case has yet to be made public, preliminary news reports are reminiscent of the classical espionage and counterintelligence dilemma characterized as a "wilderness of mirrors." Because things in this gray world are sometimes not what they appear to be, firm conclusions may prove difficult to reach. Cases with similar features in the past have been found to have impacts across larger strategic intelligence and security programs and policies. Such cases require careful study, review, and analysis, referred to as damage assessments, which continue sometimes for many years after the first discovery of a problem.

Every HUMINT organization is vulnerable to the inherent flaws of an agent-handling system where the handler works essentially alone. Modern services, to address these risks, must organize themselves accordingly. A Reaganesque "trust but verify" internal management approach is critically important and is reflected as well in Sun Tzu's underlying theme of balance, carefully apportioning rewards, and avoiding arbitrary punishments. Strategic services must be proactive, protecting themselves, and their operations, programs, and governments, by regular, clear, and frequent communication between officers and their field and headquarters components. They also must develop and provide support—such as teaming, vetting, and monitoring contacts using all-source means—to reduce the likelihood of manipulation. Structurally, these services also must support meaningful counterintelligence and counterespionage elements, and robust internal inspectorates, ombudsmen, personnel security components, and offices of professional responsibility. These units must be well resourced, with open access to information and appropriately trained personnel, to perform this difficult but necessary function thoroughly and fairly.

The higher the risk posed by, or to, an individual, the more likely such activities are to raise policy, ethical, and moral questions regarding what kinds of activities the United States needs to conduct, and how these activities should be conducted. In situations requiring face-to-face handling, the United States can and does protect itself by engaging teams of officers, rather than officers acting essentially alone, to manage potentially troublesome contacts. The lessons learned from such cases might have broader application.

At the national level, secret intelligence traditionally has been perceived as a difficult fit in a democracy, which relies on transparency of government activities to limit abuses of power. Concerns are always heightened about the dark art of "spying" in comparison to other "cleaner" bits of intelligence gathered from space or by the indirect intercept of signals "out of the ether." While citizens of democracies, who vote or otherwise participate in government, perceive this tension more acutely than do citizens of other types of states, it is important to recognize that the U.S. intelligence system incorporates multiple layers of oversight—ranging from internal checks to executive, legislative, judicial controls, and the balance of an open press—to guard against abuses.

Where it is necessary for officers in the HUMINT system to contact and deal with less than desirable individuals, such as those associated with terrorism, criminal enterprise, or narcotics trafficking, one might consider the dilemma posed by the well-grounded evaluation that such an individual possesses, or may come to possess, critical information about acts that might save dozens, hundreds, or even thousands of lives, and prevent significant, perhaps even catastrophic, damage. In those circumstances, is it reasonable to preclude contact? Doubtful. Instead, one must identify reasonable and prudent approaches to, and limitations on, forming a temporary and appropriately guarded and controlled relationship with such an individual. In doing so, however, one is left with a caveat. The likelihood that any intelligence service, however sophisticated, will be able to assert and sustain control over an individual with whom it has only limited contact, measured in some instances in only minutes or hours a month, is remote.

Americans, finally, also might take some comfort in the knowledge that the vast majority of persons who come to be clandestine or covert agents for the United States do so voluntarily, drawn symbolically by America's example, in President Reagan's description, as a "shining beacon of hope." The use of pressures such as blackmail and threats are crude techniques practiced by and best left to authoritarian states.

The Future of Strategic Services: Searching for Equilibrium

The CIA Clandestine Service, which combines clandestine HUMINT collection and covert action into one unified strategic services mission, served its purpose during the Cold War. As successes in the continuing global war on terrorism have indicated, this strategic intelligence service retains important strengths and capabilities to support policy, diplomacy, the military, and law enforcement, despite its relatively modest size and limited budget. These are intelligence strengths unique to the U.S. Government.

However, while the Clandestine Service retains a highly motivated and committed workforce, established worldwide infrastructure, effective network of liaison relationships, and operational processes perfected over the course of the last 60 years, its approach reflects the perceived imperatives of an era that now has passed. The Clandestine Service, to better meet the heightened demands and expectations of the President and national security decisionmakers, must seek and achieve a new point of equilibrium within the intelligence system. In the words of Congressman Mac Thornberry (R–TX), "Transformation is about creating an adaptive national security apparatus that can deal with changing circumstances and emerging threats."[27]

To optimize the Clandestine Service for this age of change will require a renaissance in the organization's approach to collection and action, reshaping and strengthening the three critical dimensions of personnel depth, operational continuity, and strategic integration. As President Abraham Lincoln observed during a period of transformation not unlike what we face today, "The dogmas of the quiet past are inadequate to the stormy present. The occasion is piled high with difficulty, and we must rise to the occasion. As our case is new, so we must think anew, and act anew."[28]

The complexities of modern espionage and counterstrategies require different kinds of tradeoffs than in the past. Future management of these missions will require a rebalanced generalist-specialist mix, with a far higher degree of employee functional[29] specialization (professionalization), a greater commitment of employee time on task (continuity), the elimination of incentives for employee "flow through" (assignment velocity), and a renewed commitment to employee growth (career development), to enable a thorough transformation and redirection.

This new model officer will be better equipped to surmount the challenges of tough targets through the use of what might be termed "systems HUMINT." This entails the development and execution of intelligence collection and exploitation work plans that are comprehensive and interdisciplinary in nature. For an Intelligence Community that is awash in unprocessed information, these operations will be coupled with dedicated resources linked in an end-to-end (systems) approach to intelligence production.

To face the future with confidence also will require the creation of a Clandestine Service equivalent to business resilience. At a personal level, officers must be allowed to take chances, voice alternative views, and survive failure. At the organizational level, this will be defined as the ability to sustain balance across a full spectrum of operations, protecting existing activities and programs, recovering from losses, and avoiding needless redundancies, while maintaining an ability to identify new opportunities and meet new challenges.

A more highly trained and engaged cadre will be essential to success in this area. In fact, continual learning will come to be regarded as the best investment a clandestine strategic service can make to sustain itself as a vital, viable enterprise. This conclusion echoes the findings of the British Tavistock Institute, whose research suggested that "A better way to boost productivity (is) to concentrate on the 'human side' of running an enterprise, encouraging workers to feel a valued part of the enterprise."

The demands of technology—as a target, an enabler and a weapon—suggest that the espionage-technology partnership must be strengthened fundamentally. This will permit the United States to leverage its technological superiority in a more systematic and comprehensive manner to improve intelligence gain, mitigate the loss of intelligence from other means, and maintain collection against critical targets, in spite of an adversary's efforts to camouflage or conceal activities from observation or otherwise to manipulate perceptions. This human-technical partnership is of increasing value to the U.S. HUMINT community.

Finally, human and technical intelligence systems should be engaged in developing new ways to achieve *complementarity*, the intelligence counterpart to military jointness: to understand, share, and fuse all-source information, multitask, and support and play off each other's activities, without jeopardizing critical and hard-to-replace sources and methods. Cooperation will increase familiarity, decrease suspicion and rivalry, and minimize risks associated with unilateral actions. The strategic intelligence disciplines of HUMINT, SIGINT, MASINT, and IMINT all will benefit from a revitalized dialogue that moves us beyond the old "zero sum" bureaucratic world of interservice rivalries, control-based relationships, and territorialism. If systemic resistance to cooperation continues, an intelligence equivalent to the 1986 Goldwater-Nichols Act, which induced greater military jointness through legislative action, may become necessary.

The Clandestine Service remains an important player in a grand experiment with intelligence in a democracy that is larger than the sum of its parts. Recognizing at the strategic planning level the importance of depth, continuity, and integration will help a stronger, more dynamic service to evolve that can thrive amidst these new challenges, while retaining the essence of General Donovan's founding spirit. These changes will define strategic resilience and move us confidently into the future.

As the reader continues this course of national security study, one hopes it will become apparent that policy and operational work at the national level requires an understanding of, and ability to leverage and integrate, the full range of instruments of statecraft available to support policy, strategic intelligence among them. Likewise, modern national security managers must recognize the critical need for a healthy and resilient Clandestine Service element to underpin U.S. security at home and abroad.

Finally, the author hopes this survey contributes to the continuing dialogue among national security strategists, military and civilian leaders, legislators, intelligence managers, and officers regarding how current and emerging intelligence challenges might be addressed. It is this dialogue that will ensure the Clandestine Service remains a viable and vital tool that U.S. strategists, policymakers, diplomats, and commanders can employ with confidence in the discharge of their pressing national security responsibilities.

Notes

[1] George W. Bush, speech at The Citadel, December 11, 2001; accessed at <www.whitehouse.gov/news/releases/2001/12/20011211-6.htm>.

[2] R. James Woolsey, testimony to U.S. House of Representatives, Committee on National Security, February 12, 1998.

[3] Christopher Andrew, "Strategic Intelligence and National Security," Sherman Kent Lecture, National War College, Washington, DC, December 19, 2000.

[4] Sun Tzu, *The Art of War*, trans. Thomas Cleary (Boston: Shambhala, 1988), 172.

[5] Jeffrey H. Smith, "Integrity, Intelligence and Iraq," *The Washington Post*, June 1, 2003, B7.

[6] Richard Boucher, interview with *al Jazeera*, February 12, 2003.

[7] Sun Tzu, 168.

[8] R. James Woolsey, "Honoring Two World War II Heroes," *Studies in Intelligence* 38, no. 5 (1995), 31.

[9] Dennis De Brandt, "Structuring Intelligence for War," *Studies in Intelligence*, 60th Anniversary Special Edition (June 2002), 43.

[10] Ibid.

[11] George J. Tenet, remarks on commemoration of OSS 60th anniversary, June 7, 2002.

[12] Michael Warner, "The Creation of the Central Intelligence Group," *Studies in Intelligence*, 60th Anniversary Special Edition (June 2002), 169.

[13] George J. Tenet, letter marking special edition of *Studies in Intelligence*, March 14, 2002.

[14] David E. Kaplan, "Playing Offense: The Inside Story of how U.S. Terrorist Hunters Are Going after al Qaeda," *U.S. News and World Report*, June 2, 2003, 27.

[15] David H. Hackworth, *About Face: The Odyssey of an American Warrior* (New York: Simon and Schuster, 1989), 602.

[16] Arie P. DeGeus, "Planning as Learning," *Harvard Business Review* (March/April 1988), 71.

[17] Robert Woodward, *VEIL: The Secret Wars of the CIA 1981–1987* (New York: Simon and Schuster, 1987).

[18] Woolsey, "Honoring Two World War II Heroes," 31.

[19] Michael E. Porter, "What is Strategy," *Harvard Business Review* (November/December 1996), 62.

[20] Ibid.

[21] Vernon A. Walters, *Silent Missions* (New York: Doubleday, 1978).

[22] Thomas Powers, *The Man Who Kept the Secrets: Richard Helms and the CIA* (New York: Alfred A. Knopf, 1979).

[23] David M. Messick and Max H. Bazerman, "Ethical Leadership and the Psychology of Decision Making," *Sloan Management Review* (Winter 1996), 9.

[24] Ibid., 15.

[25] Ibid.

[26] R.M. Cambridge and R.C. Shreckengost, "Are You Sure? The Subjective Probability Assessment Test," CIA Office of Training, Langley, Virginia, unpublished manuscript, 1980.

[27] Mac Thornberry, "Fostering a Culture of Innovation," *Proceedings*, April 2003, 44.

[28] Abraham Lincoln, Second Annual Message to Congress, December 1, 1862.

[29] Elliott Jacques, Tavistock Institute Study, *The Economist*, March 11, 1995, 71.

Chapter 17

Economic Espionage

Randall M. Fort

Since the demise of the Soviet Union, the headlines on the issue of economic espionage have been tantalizing: "Security Agency Debates New Role: Economic Spying"; "Should the CIA Start Spying for Corporate America?"; "Some Urge CIA to Go Further in Gathering Economic Intelligence"; and "Next for the CIA: Business Spying?"[1] These headlines reflect the considerable debate that has occurred on the issue of whether the U.S. Intelligence Community should provide direct intelligence support to the U.S. private sector.

The genesis for much of this debate has been concern over the alleged decline in U.S. economic competitiveness and the need to prevent it. Ostensibly, conducting economic espionage against foreign trade and business competitors to support the U.S. private sector would "help" U.S. competitiveness. In addition, with the end of the Cold War, U.S. intelligence must refocus its efforts and resources, and it has been suggested that supporting economic competitiveness could be defined as a new intelligence requirement. Although it may sound like a good idea, it is wrong, for reasons of practicality, utility, legality, and morality. Asking the U.S. Intelligence Community to conduct economic espionage on behalf of U.S. companies would most decidedly be a bad idea.

There is considerable misunderstanding about the issue, much of which stems from a confusion over terminology. *Economic espionage, industrial espionage, commercial spying*, and other such terms may or may not refer to the same thing, but are frequently used interchangeably. In this chapter the term *economic espionage* will be used, defined as the clandestine acquisition of economic, financial, trade, and/or proprietary information by an official intelligence service using intelligence sources and methods. Further, the key issue under consideration is not whether such intelligence should be collected, but rather whether it should be provided by the U.S. Intelligence Community to the private sector.

What Is Economic Intelligence?

An additional point of confusion arises from a misunderstanding of the appropriate role of economic intelligence compared with that of other intelligence functions. As a first principle: There is a historic and legitimate role for economic intelligence in support of government policymaking. Although economic policy has

Source: Randall M. Fort, Chapter 13, "Economic Espionage," in Roy Godson, Ernest May, and Gary Schmitt, eds., *US Intelligence at a Crossroads* (Dulles, Virginia: Brassey's, 1995), 181–197. Copyright © 1995 by the National Strategy Information Center. Reprinted by permission.

become a more visible, priority issue recently, it has been an important area of intelligence collection and analysis for many years.

The Intelligence Community (IC) has traditionally been active in three key areas: First, the IC has provided support to government officials as they make economic policy. This support has included analysis of bilateral and multilateral economic negotiations; identification of economic trends and understanding the intentions of economic competitors; integration of vast amounts of disparate data to present a complete picture of the economic and political factors affecting international stability; and helping policymakers understand the "rules of the economic game" as it is played by others (for example, to monitor foreign subsidies, lobbying, bribes, and import restraints). The Treasury Department, U.S. Trade Representative, State Department, National Security Council, and Commerce Department have all benefited considerably over the years from such support.

Second, the IC has monitored trends overseas in technology that could affect U.S. national security. The U.S. Government must be aware of foreign developments in computers, semiconductors, telecommunications, and the like, which might affect U.S. military capabilities or national security interests.

The third area of IC responsibility is economic counterintelligence, that is, the identification and neutralization of foreign intelligence services spying on U.S. citizens or companies and stealing information and/or technology for use within their own countries. With recent revelations of spying by the French and Israeli intelligence services against U.S. companies, the issue of foreign intelligence collection against U.S. economic interests has seized attention. It is not, however, a new issue.

Remember the KGB?

Throughout the Cold War, economic information was a major target for the Soviet KGB and the Warsaw Pact. In fact, the KGB dedicated significant resources to the collection of economic information—Line X from the old KGB organization chart was responsible for acquiring scientific and technical information. Additionally, the massive Soviet signals intelligence (SIGINT) site at Lourdes, Cuba, gave them unique and in-depth access to a wide spectrum of U.S. commercial communications. Although the Soviets were interested principally in technology or information relevant to building or countering weapons systems, this was not always the case. For example, in the early 1970s, the Soviets used communications intercepts to negotiate very favorable terms with U.S. companies on large wheat purchases.

Because economic information was one of the things the Cold War adversaries of the United States were trying to steal, it was also one of the things that U.S. counterintelligence (CI) services were organized to try to protect. For example, for 20 years the Federal Bureau of Investigation has operated a program called Developing Espionage and Counterintelligence Awareness (DECA), which provides briefings and information to U.S. companies, particularly defense contractors, about hostile intelligence threats and activities. In the post-Cold War world, defending against foreign intelligence threats, whether against U.S. military secrets or proprietary economic data, remains a legitimate national security interest.

Current Intelligence Support to the Private Sector

Support for U.S. business has been and remains an important policy priority for the U.S. Government. In December 1991, then Deputy Secretary of State Lawrence Eagleburger stated, "U.S. competitiveness in the global economy must become one of the pillars of U.S. foreign policy and of our projection of strength and influence."[2] More recently, Secretary of State Warren Christopher declared in a speech in March 1993 that one of the first pillars of foreign policy is that it serve the economic needs of the United States.[3] As the Government makes policy in support of U.S. competitiveness, it will be supported in part with information and analysis provided by the Intelligence Community. U.S. businesses are the indirect beneficiaries of that intelligence support because the policies are being made on the private sector's behalf.

The Intelligence Community is not, therefore, new to the issue of economic intelligence, either the collection of such information for official Government requirements or the prevention of such collection by foreign intelligence services. Further, economic issues are and will remain a foreign policy priority and therefore will be the focus of considerable activity by the Intelligence Community in order to provide support to U.S. Government officials.

A New Threat?

What is new is the suggestion by some that intelligence resources should be used in an entirely different way, to provide direct support to the U.S. private sector. This idea is sometimes justified by an attempt to define the various economic challenges as new "national security threats" worthy of treatment by traditional national security tools, such as intelligence support. One of the leading proponents of this view has been former Director of Central Intelligence (DCI) Stansfield Turner. Admiral Turner stated:

> The preeminent threat to U.S. national security now lies in the economic sphere. . . . We must, then, redefine "national security" by assigning economic strength, greater prominence. . . . If economic strength should now be recognized as a vital component of national security, parallel with military power, why should America be concerned about stealing and employing economic secrets?[4]

"America should be concerned" because such an effort directly on behalf of the private sector would do little to improve U.S. economic competitiveness and would quite likely cause great harm to other important equities. Before looking at the costs and benefits of such a program, however, it is important to address the notion that economic competitiveness should be redefined as a national security threat.

The U.S. economy has suffered from a number of economic problems and dislocations in recent years. Many of them, however, are of our own making. The immense and all but uncontrollable budget deficit, with its impact on interest rates, availability of investment capital, and so forth is 100 percent "Made in the USA." Low savings rates, onerous regulations, and tax burdens are contributing "nonforeign" factors. Some of the U.S. economic problems are the result of pressures from and actions by foreign countries, but those factors vary widely, from unfair trading practices to simply building better, cheaper products.

Regardless of the provenance of these problems, it is pernicious to define them as "threats," especially "national security threats." They are more correctly labeled economic "challenges"—obstacles that can be overcome if we follow sound economic, financial, trading, diplomatic, and business policies and practices. A "threat" is appropriately defined as something that can cause demonstrable physical harm; a national security threat is, therefore, something that can cause tangible, physical harm or destruction to the United States. For example, the existence of tens of thousands of Soviet nuclear weapons posed a considerable "threat" to U.S. national security. Thought of in another way, carrying out a "threat" implies a zero-sum game at best—one side winning means the other side would have to lose. In the worst-case national security threat scenario—a nuclear war—no participant could expect to win much.

Economics Is Not War

Economic competition, however, is not a zero-sum game. There are winners and losers, certainly, but the gains and losses transcend national boundaries. If Honda of Japan makes an excellent car and sells a large number of them in the United States, then Honda is a winner and the U.S. car companies that lost those sales are losers. But the interactions are more complicated. For one thing, American consumers who buy those excellent cars of a type and quality not produced in the United States are clear winners. American auto parts companies that sell to Honda are winners, and American companies that produce and broadcast Honda advertisements are also winners. Further, increased market share for Honda, among other reasons, led to their building production plants in the United States, which is clearly to the economic advantage of the American workers employed in those plants, not to mention the increased tax revenues available to the local jurisdictions hosting such plants. Americans who have invested in Honda have been winners, and even American car companies are better off ultimately because they have had to become more efficient and productive to meet the foreign car challenge posed by Honda and other foreign car makers.

The list of winners and losers from even the limited example of imports of Honda automobiles goes on and on, but suffice it to say that in economics, competition is not a black-and-white, zero-sum game. "America" does not "lose" when faced with foreign economic competition. That competition poses challenges to various sectors of the U.S. economy, challenges that must be overcome certainly, but these are not threats to national existence.

Undertaking a program of providing direct intelligence support to the U.S. private sector would be both a significant departure from past practice and a major operational challenge. Therefore, it should be incumbent upon those who advocate such an effort to describe how it would be accomplished. Rather than making their case, however, proponents usually sidestep or ignore this critical point. Indeed, Admiral Turner blithely stated, "There are problems galore, but these are for the Commerce Department to handle on a case-by-case basis."[5] There are certainly "problems galore," but they are beyond the ability of the Commerce Department or any other Government agency to resolve.

Practical Concerns

The first significant problem is the matter of practicality. Attempting to define a workable program to share intelligence with the private sector immediately raises a host of practical problems, both in how to implement a program as well as the consequences of doing so. One of the first questions to address is how a program would be set up and operated. There is, for example, the issue of defining the beneficiary. What sectors of the economy and what companies would be targeted for assistance, because the IC could not help them all? Who would make those choices? Would all companies within a particular sector receive assistance, or just some? Again, who would choose and on what basis—size, profitability, or market share? The U.S. Government, which wasted billions of taxpayers' dollars trying to support the development of synthetic fuels in the 1970s, would need to create a mechanism to decide which sectors and companies would be supported.

The fairness and wisdom of the selection process notwithstanding, intelligence support would ultimately come to be recognized as just another subsidy and, as such, would be subject to the same vagaries of politics as any other subsidy. Anyone who is confident that the Government could make wise and farsighted determinations about which sectors or companies to assist should look no further than the April 6, 1993, issue of the *Washington Post*. An article entitled "Hair That Defies Cutting" describes the continued existence, after 39 years, of a $180-million-per-year program to subsidize the growth of mohair wool. Strategic necessity, economic efficiency, and other such logical measures are clearly not relevant in Government (political) decisionmaking about who or what is to receive Government support and assistance. There is no reason to be confident that decisions about which companies to provide with intelligence support would be made with any more wisdom than has been shown in the mohair support program. Companies with the biggest political clout—not the greatest strategic need—would likely demand and receive the greatest support.

Who Is "Us"?

Before devising a support process, however, there is an even more fundamental question: Exactly what defines a U.S. company? The Commerce Department defines a U.S. company as any enterprise with a majority of stockholders and assets in the United States. But, in the present era of multinational corporations and voluminous international trade and investment flows, the question of nationality is becoming ever more blurred. Would overseas subsidiaries of U.S. companies be assisted? What about U.S. subsidiaries of foreign companies? Should an "American" company be provided intelligence if it would use that information to win a contract to make a product in an overseas factory, if it were in competition with a "foreign" company that, should it win the contract, would make their product in a factory located in the United States? What about "American" companies working in cooperation, via joint venture, technology sharing, or other arrangements, with foreign firms? How are those interests separated in order to share intelligence with only the American entity? These questions are not mere abstractions; they are very real issues that must be sorted out and addressed in any intelligence support program. The following concrete example is illustrative:

In February 1993, six major companies—AT&T; Motorola, Inc.; Apple, Inc.; Sony Corporation; Matsushita Industrial Electric Company; and Philips NV—announced an alliance to develop new portable communication devices. The first three are U.S.-based corporations; the last three are foreign-based. How could only the U.S. companies be helped without at least indirectly helping the foreign companies? And wouldn't helping those foreign companies hurt other U.S. companies that will surely enter the market for such devices?

These questions about what is "American" and what is "foreign" are growing more complicated and are a consequence of an increasingly economically integrated world. Secretary of Labor Robert Reich studied these issues of national corporate identity and national economic interests closely during his tenure as a professor in the Kennedy School of Government at Harvard University. Reich published two compelling articles in the *Harvard Business Review* that describe the complex and fragmented nature of today's global economic environment. In the first, he noted that:

> Today, the competitiveness of American-owned corporations is no longer the same as American competitiveness. Indeed, American ownership of the corporation is profoundly less relevant to America's economic future than the skills, training, and knowledge commanded by American workers—*workers who are increasingly employed within the United States by foreign-owned corporations*. So who is us? The answer is, the American work force, the American people, but not particularly the American corporation.[6]

The issues of corporate identity promise to become more, not less, complicated as the world economy continues with its rapid pace of integration. Those changes will affect a host of Government policies (such as corporate taxation) besides making a new initiative like economic espionage problematic. While determining the identity and national allegiance of corporations will become more difficult, Reich [as noted above] offers a straightforward answer to the question: Who is us (and therefore who or what is worthy of Government support)? It is "the American work force, the American people." Under those circumstances, it would be inappropriate for the U.S. Government to provide support to entities with uncertain identities if doing so would cause injury to other, clearly identifiable American interests (for example, the American citizens who work for foreign companies).

What Kinds of Intelligence?

Assuming one could resolve the issue of "who[m]" to support, other vexing practical problems would remain. What kinds of information should be shared with the private sector? Should companies be given tactical data about specific projects or contracts for which they are competing, or broad, strategic estimates about economic prospects in particular countries or regions? Considerations of what kinds of intelligence data should be shared strike at the heart of one of the canons of the Intelligence Community—protection of intelligence sources and methods.

Maintaining the security of sources and methods, while preparing the intelligence for purposes for which the entire collection and analysis system was not designed, would be a daunting task. The information of greatest use, especially for specific contracts or projects, might well be among the most sensitive and highly classified. Any "scrubbing" process to remove those aspects that might reveal the source could also remove or obscure the details that made the report useful in the first place. The IC would face a continuing conundrum: if the intelligence to be shared were too vague, it would be useless; but if it were too specific, then it would threaten the security of sensitive sources and methods.

The sources and methods issue may strike some nonintelligence professionals as abstract bureaucratic pettiness, but to the professional, the issue is seminal, in some cases literally a matter of life and death. As the professional intelligence officer knows well, the technical collection systems that produce much of this Nation's intelligence have cost tens of billions of taxpayer dollars and tens of millions of man-hours to design, build, operate, and maintain; a single unauthorized disclosure of information derived from one of those sources can diminish, if not destroy, its effectiveness. In the area of human intelligence collection, the stakes are even higher. If information supplied by a human agent is compromised, his or her safety and security are jeopardized. In many cases, the agents risk losing their lives.

Besides security, intelligence professionals must also be concerned about the productivity of their sources of information. Would current and future sources of information want to provide secrets to the U.S. Government if those sources thought the information was only going to advance an American company's bottom line? Clandestine collection of information would not be the only affected area. Department of State diplomatic reporting and Defense attaché reporting could also suffer if a perception were to grow overseas that anything told to the U.S. Government was to be used by U.S. companies. To the degree intelligence sources are harmed or dry up because of this, Government intelligence consumers will have less intelligence available to draw upon.

These are the realities of the intelligence business, and they cannot be ignored if intelligence products are to be shared and used outside of established security controls. Once again, real-world situations would raise complications for a support program. How would the security of shared intelligence be enforced and maintained? For example, what if an American corporate officer were the recipient of intelligence information about a foreign contract, and then left the U.S. company to work for a foreign competitor? Would he or she be bound by whatever secrecy agreement had been signed, or by their fiduciary responsibility to their new employer? In this era of corporate shake-ups and massive personnel turnover, concerns about protecting the intelligence that would be shared are very real.

Costs and Drawbacks

Just as there are practical problems of implementation, there would also be practical consequences to an economic espionage program, and many of them would affect the U.S. Government. First, the Intelligence Community is not currently organized to produce and disseminate classified information to the private sector. Undertaking such an effort would, therefore, require a new commitment of personnel and resources. In a period of declining intelligence budgets, the resources for a private

sector program would most likely be allocated at the expense of Government policymakers, who are the only economic intelligence consumers at present. Therefore,
policymakers need to ask themselves if the gain to U.S. companies would be worth the
possible loss of their own intelligence support.

A second issue for the Government to consider is the occasions, sometimes frequent, when the intelligence available on a particular issue is uncertain. Policymakers do
the best they can in such instances, but complications could easily arise if that same uncertain information were to be shared with the private sector. The private sector consumers might decide that the intelligence contradicted policy decisions, or at least cast doubt
on the viability of the policy. For example, the Government might be trying to encourage
private U.S. investment in a country or region, but if intelligence analysis shared with
the private sector indicated that the economic prospects for that area were poor, then
the U.S. companies might well choose not to invest. Government officials would end up
arguing about the accuracy of intelligence reporting and estimates not just among themselves, but also with the private sector groups they were trying to influence.

A final concern for the Government about an economic espionage program
would be its serious and deleterious impacts on U.S. foreign policy. Although the
United States is the only remaining superpower, its influence is increasingly dependent on its ability to create and maintain coalitions of different countries to support
a particular policy or achieve desired objectives. The core of many of those coalitions
is the group of countries that constituted the old Western alliance. Those are also the
countries that the United States most frequently competes against economically. To
make those countries and their companies the target of economic espionage activity
on behalf of the U.S. private sector would undermine the trust and confidence that
have served as the historic basis for the existing political alliance, and it would cripple
diplomatic efforts to build the coalitions necessary to achieve important foreign policy goals. Granted, the world is changing and the old alliance structure is not as vital as
it once was. But the consequences should be thoroughly considered before the United
States undertakes actions that could rend the existing relationships and complicate
the handling of a host of issues, such as coordinating aid by the G–7 to Russia and
confronting Serbian aggression in Bosnia.

Is It Useful?

After practicality, a second major category of problems relates to the issue of
utility. The usefulness of intelligence to the private sector has been assumed, but
that assumption has not been proven or effectively tested. Certainly the IC produces
prodigious volumes of economic and financial information, but that intelligence is
produced in response to the needs and requirements articulated by Government
consumers, not the private sector. There is no doubt that some incidental data now
being collected would be of use to a business consumer. But it would take a significant
retooling of the intelligence requirements on economic issues and the processing of
that intelligence to ensure the routine, timely delivery of relevant information.

Throughout the debate on this issue, has anyone listened to what the private
sector has to say? Or asked them if they want or need such information? Interestingly,

there has been mostly silence—not one chief executive officer or other senior official of an American corporation has gone on record advocating or supporting such a program. In fact, what little reporting there is suggests that businesses are at best dubious about the idea. In a March 1993 *Washington Post* article, local executives worried that intelligence sharing "could give an unfair advantage to big companies," and "would run the risk of 'spoiling relationships with other countries who would become suspicious of how level the information playing field is.'"[7] *Time* notes that "many U.S. executives fear that suspected CIA involvement in their business could scare off customers and suppliers overseas. They're also afraid that American companies themselves may eventually fall under the spy agency's watchful eye."[8]

Do business executives think that the IC has anything useful to offer? Apparently not. As one senior executive from a major U.S. corporation said, "If a company needs the CIA to tell them what's going on in their area of business, then they're already in Chapter 11 [bankruptcy]."[9] If sharing intelligence with the private sector is such a great idea, then why is there no demand for such support from the intended recipients? Certainly the private sector is not shy about asking for Government assistance in any number of other areas, such as import restraints, foreign market access, or tax breaks. If intelligence support for business had any utility at all, the private sector would have spoken up by now.

Legality

Would a program to provide intelligence support to the private sector be legal? As with most legal questions, the answer is, "It depends." A significant number of hurdles can be identified that would have to be surmounted if an economic espionage program were to be legal. First, are the existing legal authorities sufficient to justify and allow collecting and disseminating intelligence to a nongovernment consumer? Various enabling statutes and executive orders would need to be reviewed and possibly modified to permit a private sector support effort. Second, intelligence collected under such a program would likely include trade secrets, and the Trade Secrets Act might need changing to allow such information to be disseminated without criminal liability. Third, wire fraud statutes might also need amending if it is decided that collection of intelligence through fraud or deceit (tactics used frequently in clandestine collection) for passing to the private sector violated that statute. Fourth, the Communication Act and the Foreign Intelligence Surveillance Act might require amendments to allow dissemination of certain kinds of intelligence. Fifth, there would be a substantial risk of extensive civil litigation against the U.S. Government in both U.S. and foreign courts: management and shareholders of companies not selected to receive intelligence could sue; individuals injured by products resulting from the intelligence could sue; and companies or individuals whose trade secrets or intellectual property were taken without compensation could sue.

In addition, legal protection now afforded intelligence sources and methods would be weakened, as would the Government's ability to defeat legal discovery and Freedom of Information requests if those requests related to information that was disseminated under a support program. Additionally, treaties of trade, commerce, friendship, and navigation currently in force might be breached, and intellectual property rights treaties and agreements might be affected. Clearly such a program would be inconsistent with the longstanding U.S. policy of "national treatment" for foreign investment; that is, foreign investment should be treated the same as domestic investment—if the IC is not spying on domestic companies, then it should not spy on foreign companies.

These legal concerns are largely speculative because there has been no litigation involving economic espionage that would offer a record for more certain legal analysis. Traditionally the courts have shown great deference to the requirements of national security. But it remains to be seen if the courts would view intelligence support to the private sector as a bona fide national security issue worthy of special legal forbearance. Threats to corporate profits are not the same as threats to the Nation's existence, and the traditional balancing of secrecy (among other intelligence equities) against other legal rights might well experience a shift in the legal fulcrum to the disadvantage of intelligence interests.

The list of legal problems, while not exhaustive, is indicative of the many pitfalls inherent in any effort to assist the private sector. Given all of the obvious legal impediments (and likely many more not so obvious problems), it is hard to understand how anyone would seriously advocate such an idea. In the recent past, Congress launched a major investigation of a fantasy called the "October Surprise" from the 1980 Presidential election campaign, where there was no serious evidence of a real violation of the law. Who would be so bold (or obtuse) to launch an effort that would almost certainly violate constitutional amendments, statutes, executive orders, international treaties, and open exposure to civil liabilities? Intelligence officers asked to manage such a program should heed this warning: Today's good idea is grist for tomorrow's congressional inquisition.

Morality

Do the ends justify the means? This philosophical question should be applied to the subject of economic espionage. If economic competitiveness is really a national security priority, then national security tools could reasonably be applied to effect a desired outcome. The legitimate requirements of national security have traditionally allowed for extraordinary measures to be undertaken. For example, the United States conducts espionage abroad, activity that invariably violates the laws of the countries where it occurs. Moreover, when espionage is conducted by foreign powers in the United States, it is considered a crime. But the United States justifies its own espionage activities because they serve the defense of the Nation's security.

This [chapter] has presented the argument that economic competitiveness is not a true national security issue, and so is not worthy of application of extraordinary national security measures such as intelligence support. Those who argue that competitiveness is a national security issue, however, must explain what other steps should be taken besides providing direct intelligence support to the private sector. Given all the difficulties in structuring an economic espionage program (as previously described), are there not some ideas that would be more timely and effective? For example, why not change the law that prohibits bribery of foreign officials to enable U.S. companies to win overseas contracts? Or why not change the antitrust laws to allow combinations of more powerful U.S. companies that could better compete with foreign companies? If this is indeed a genuine national security threat, then the United States should be willing to consider other such extraordinary steps. Such sentiment is not now in evidence, however, either in Congress or among the general public.

Much attention has been given to the actions of other countries using their intelligence services to spy on U.S. companies for the benefit of their domestic business. The French, according to numerous press reports, have aggressively used the resources of their intelligence services to spy on and steal information from foreign businessmen. (Pierre Marion, former head of the French external intelligence service, DGSE [Directorate General de Securite Exteriere], bragged in his memoirs about French efforts to spy on foreign companies during his tenure.) IBM and Texas Instruments were among the U.S. companies victimized. Peter Schweizer's recent book, *Friendly Spies*, describes economic intelligence collection activities by the Israelis, Germans, Japanese, and South Koreans, as well as by the French. American proponents of economic espionage make frequent reference to these incidents in an attempt to justify a U.S. program to do the same thing. These examples are noteworthy, however, not because they are admirable but because they are reprehensible. It is instructive to remember the old saying, "Two wrongs do not make a right." There are many examples of behavior by foreign countries that Americans find objectionable. The appropriate course of action, however, is to convince the country through diplomatic or other pressures to change or modify its behavior, not to emulate it. The actions of other countries do not justify the United States doing the same thing.

In any event, countries inclined to conduct economic espionage on behalf of local businesses will face growing complications. The "blurring" of companies' national identities is happening not just in the United States, but in the rest of the world as well. The economic integration occurring in Europe as a result of the EC–92 initiatives, for example, makes intelligence support by European countries for domestic companies increasingly problematic. Even France may find itself confused about who the customer for its intelligence support should be. The new conservative government has mentioned selling many of the state-run companies (which have received much of the intelligence support) to the private sector. As those companies inevitably become more "European" and less "French," the French government will find it more difficult to target the intelligence to support specific French interests.

"What Is Sauce for the Goose Is Sauce for the Gander"

The remarkable fact is not that some governments have engaged in economic espionage, but rather that there has been relatively little of it reported and acknowledged. Given the number of intelligence services around the world, and the importance of economic issues, one would expect to have seen a great deal more of such activity. Although there may be no formal treaties, the traditional Western allies (with the exception of the French) are reluctant to conduct espionage against one another. A U.S. economic espionage program, however, would drastically change that equation. If foreign governments thought that the United States was spying on competitors and aggressively supporting U.S. companies, it would release whatever restraints that now exist and permit them to do the same. Thus, American businessmen abroad would potentially become subject to a wide range of pressures and harassments, including entrapment, robbery, and blackmail. Because the United States would be engaging in similar activity, the United States would have no moral standing to protest the treatment of its citizens. In addition, it is quite possible that many countries would be better at economic espionage than the United States (if only because the U.S. legal protection for the individual would preclude the more heavy-handed pressures), negating the value of the U.S. program. There is relatively little such activity now. Should the United States be the one to start an "intelligence war" supporting domestic businesses?

Who Will Spy?

It is not certain that intelligence professionals want to be engaged in an economic espionage program. Former DCI Robert Gates stated, "Some years ago, one of our clandestine service officers overseas said to me: 'You know, I'm prepared to give my life for my country, but not for a company.' That case officer was absolutely right."[10] Intelligence officers sign up to serve their country and defend its security. Can they be convinced that (in some cases) risking their lives—or at the very least their career success—for a company is the same as for their country? It remains an open question whether the intelligence services would extend their best efforts to support such a program, but is it worth the gamble? There is also the risk of corruption, less by individual intelligence officers participating in a program than by the intelligence agencies participating in a program. Those institutions would likely become targets of the intense business lobbying that occurs whenever the economic stakes are high, and there could be temptations to make biased decisions about allocation of resources and effort.

"Fraught with Difficulties"

Then-DCI R. James Woolsey raised eyebrows and expectations during his Senate confirmation hearing when he described economic espionage as "the hottest current topic in intelligence policy." Subsequent news stories indicate that he has reached some unenthusiastic conclusions about such an effort. One year later, he was quoted as stating that such a program would be "fraught with legal and foreign policy difficulties."[11] Woolsey's disapproving tone is not surprising. Anyone who gets past the rhetoric about economic competitiveness and closely examines the nuts and bolts of how an economic espionage program is supposed to work cannot fail to reach the same negative conclusions.

Sound management practice (and common sense) dictates that major new initiatives should be preceded by some form of cost/benefit analysis. In the case of conducting economic espionage in support of the U.S. private sector, the costs—practical, legal, and moral—as outlined previously are very high. There would undoubtedly be additional costs that would surface only upon implementation of such a plan. On the other hand, the benefits of such a program are at best uncertain and quite likely nonexistent. There are many policies and programs the U.S. Government can pursue that will improve the competitiveness of U.S. companies; conducting economic espionage to provide direct support to U.S. businesses should not be one of them.

Notes

[1] *The New York Times*, June 18, 1990; *Business Week*, October 14, 1991; *The Wall Street Journal*, August 4, 1992; *Time*, February 22, 1993.

[2] "Memorandum for all Assistant Secretaries and Bureau Directors from the Deputy Secretary of State," December 12, 1991.

[3] "Christopher Makes Case for New Aid," *The Washington Post*, March 23, 1993.

[4] Stansfield Turner, "Intelligence for a New World Order," *Foreign Affairs* 70, no. 4 (Fall 1991), 151–152.

[5] Ibid., 152.

[6] Robert Reich, "Who Is Us?" *Harvard Business Review* (January/February 1990), 54 (emphasis added). See also Robert Reich, "Who Is Them?" *Harvard Business Review* (March/April 1991).

[7] "The Idea of a CIA Linkup Spooks Some Area Executives," *The Washington Post*, March 9, 1993.

[8] *Time*.

[9] Private communication with the author.

[10] Speech by Robert M. Gates to the Economic Club of Detroit, MI, April 13, 1992.

[11] *The New York Times*, April 5, 1993.

Chapter 18

The Ten Commandments of Counterintelligence

James M. Olson

O that thou hadst hearkened to my commandments! Then had thy peace been as a river, and thy righteousness as the waves of the sea.

—Isaiah 48:18

The need for counterintelligence (CI) has not gone away, nor is it likely to. The end of the Cold War has not even meant an end to the CI threat from the former Soviet Union. The foreign intelligence service of the new democratic Russia, the *Sluzhba Vneshney Razvedki Rossii* (SVRR), has remained active against us. It was the SVRR that took over the handling of Aldrich Ames from its predecessor, the KGB [*Komitet Gosudarstvennoy Bezopasnosti*], in 1991. It was the SVRR that ran Central Intelligence Agency (CIA) officer Harold James Nicholson against us from 1994 to 1996. It was the SVRR that was handling Federal Bureau of Investigation (FBI) special agent Earl Pitts when he was arrested for espionage in 1996. It was the SVRR that planted a listening device in a conference room of the State Department in Washington in the summer of 1999. And it was the SVRR that was handling FBI special agent Robert Hanssen when he was arrested on charges of espionage in February 2001.

The Russians are not alone. There have been serious, well-publicized concerns about Chinese espionage in the United States. The Department of Energy significantly increased security at its National Laboratories last year in response to allegations that China had stolen U.S. nuclear weapons secrets.

Paul Redmond, the former Associate Deputy Director of Operations for Counterintelligence at the CIA, told the House Permanent Select Committee on Intelligence in early 2000 that a total of at least 41 countries are trying to spy on the United States. Besides mentioning Russia, China, and Cuba, he also cited several *friends*, including France, Greece, Indonesia, Israel, the Philippines, South Korea, and Taiwan. He warned of a pervasive CI threat to the United States.

Source: James M. Olson, "The Ten Commandments of Counter-Intelligence," *Studies in Intelligence* no. 11 (Fall/Winter 2001).

The United States, as the world's only remaining superpower, will be the constant target of jealousies, resentments, rivalries, and challenges to its economic well-being, security, and leadership in the world. This inevitably means that the United States will be the target of large-scale foreign espionage.

A Choice Assignment

When I joined the CIA, one of my first interim assignments was with the old CI staff. I found it fascinating. I was assigned to write a history of the *Rote Kapelle*, the Soviet espionage network in Nazi-occupied Western Europe during World War II.

With its expanded computer power, the National Security Agency was breaking out the actual messages sent between the NKVD center in Moscow and the clandestine radios of the various cells in Western Europe. Incredibly, these messages came to me.

There I was, a brand new junior officer, literally the first person in the CIA to see the day-to-day traffic from these life-and-death operations. I was deeply affected by the fear, heroism, and drama in these messages. Above all, I felt privileged to have been given such an opportunity.

Building on an earlier study of the *Rote Kapelle* by the CI staff, I completed a draft several months later that incorporated the new material. To my great surprise, this study was well received by my immediate superiors, and I was told that I was to be rewarded with a personal interview and congratulations from James Jesus Angleton, the legendary head of the CI staff from 1954 to 1974.

Angleton's office was on the second floor of the original Headquarters Building. I was first ushered into an outer office, where Angleton's aides briefed me on how to conduct myself. And then I went alone into the inner sanctum.

The room was dark, the curtains were drawn, and there was just one small lamp on Angleton's desk. I later heard that Angleton had eye trouble and that the light hurt his eyes, but I was convinced the real reason for the semidarkness was to add to his mystique. It certainly worked on me!

I nervously briefed Angleton on my study, and he listened without interrupting, just nodding from time to time. When I finished, he methodically attacked every one of my conclusions. Didn't I know the traffic was a deception? Hadn't it occurred to me that Leopold Trepper, the leader of the *Rote Kapelle*, was a German double? He went on and on, getting farther and farther out.

Even I, as a brand new officer, could tell that this great mind, this CI genius, had lost it. I thought he was around the bend. It was one of the most bizarre experiences of my career.

When the meeting was over, I was glad to get out of there, and I vowed to myself that I would never go anywhere near CI again. I did not keep that vow. In my overseas assignments with the agency, I found myself drawn toward Soviet CI operations. Nothing seemed to quicken my pulse more, and I was delighted when I was called back to headquarters in 1989 to join the new Counterintelligence Center (CIC) as Ted Price's deputy. When Ted moved upstairs in early 1991 to become the Associate Deputy Director for Operations, I was named chief of the center.

Today, many years after that initial disagreeable encounter with CI, I find it hard to believe that it is actually my picture on the wall of the CIC conference room at CIA Headquarters, where the photos of all former CIA counterintelligence chiefs are displayed. There I am, number seven in a row that begins with Angleton.

So, after a career that ended up being far more CI-oriented than I could ever have imagined, I would like to offer some personal observations in the form of The Ten Commandments of Counterintelligence. I have chosen the form of commandments because I believe the basic rules of CI are immutable and should be scrupulously followed. In my view, it makes little difference whether the adversary is the Russians, the Cubans, the East Germans, the Chinese, or someone else. It likewise makes little difference whether we are talking about good CI practices in 1985 or in 2005. Unfortunately, as I watch U.S. CI today, I am increasingly concerned that the principles I consider fundamental to effective CI are not being followed as carefully and consistently as they should be.

These commandments were not handed down to me from a mountaintop, and I make no claim that they are inspired or even definitive. They are simply the culmination, for what they are worth, of my experience. They are intended primarily for my fellow practitioners in CI today, but also for any younger officers in the Intelligence Community (IC) who might someday want to join us.

The First Commandment: Be Offensive

CI that is passive and defensive will fail. We cannot hunker down in a defensive mode and wait for things to happen. I believe we are spending far too much money on fences, safes, alarms, and other purely defensive measures to protect our secrets. That is not how we have been hurt in recent years. Spies have hurt us. Our CI mindset should be relentlessly offensive. We need to go after our CI adversaries.

Aggressive double agent (DA) operations are essential to any CI program, but not the predictable, hackneyed kind we have so often pursued. We need to push our bright and imaginative people to produce clever new scenarios for controlled operations, and we need more of them. The opposition services should be kept constantly off guard so that they never suspect that we have actually controlled the operations they believe they initiated from the beginning. When the requirements, modus operandi, and personality objectives of the DA operation have been achieved, we should in a greater number of cases pitch the opposition case officer. If only 1 out of 10 or 20 of these recruitments takes, it is worth it. And CI professionals, of course, should not rely exclusively on their own efforts. They should constantly prod their human intelligence colleagues to identify, target, and recruit officers from the opposition intelligence services. The key to CI success is penetration. For every American spy, there are several members of the opposition service who know who he or she is. No matter what it takes, we have to have penetrations.

We should operate aggressively against the nontraditional as well as the traditional adversaries. How many examples do we need of operations against Americans by so-called friendly countries to convince us that the old intelligence adage is correct: there are friendly nations, but no friendly intelligence services. If we suspect for whatever reason that the operatives of a foreign intelligence service, friend or foe, are operating against us, we should test them. We should dress up an enticing morsel, made to order for that specific target, and send it by them. If they take it, we have learned something we needed to know, and we have an operation. If they reject it, as true friends should, we have learned something, too. In either event, because we are testing a *friend*, plausible deniability has to be strictly preserved. Every foreign service is a potential nontraditional adversary; no service should get a lifetime pass from U.S. offensive CI operations.

The Second Commandment: Honor Your Professionals

It has been true for years, to varying degrees throughout the IC, that CI professionals have not been favored, to the extent they deserved, with promotions, assignments, awards, praise, esteem, or other recognition. The truth is that CI officers are not popular. They are not always welcome when they walk in. They usually bring bad news. And they are easy marks to criticize when things go wrong. Their successes are their failures. If they catch a spy, they are roasted for having taken so long. If they are not catching anyone, why not? What have they done with all that money they spent on CI? It is no-win.

For much of my career, many of our best people avoided becoming CI specialists. CI was not prestigious. It had a bad reputation. It was not fast track. It did not lead to promotions or good assignments. Angleton left a distasteful legacy that for years discredited the CI profession. Ted Price did more than anyone else in the agency to reverse that trend and to rehabilitate CI as a respected professional discipline.

Nevertheless, that battle is still not completely won. We have to do more to get our CI people promoted, recognized, and respected so that our best young officers will be attracted to follow us into what we know is a noble profession and where the need is so great.

The Third Commandment: Own the Street

This is so fundamental to CI, but it is probably the least followed of the commandments. Any CI program worthy of the name has to be able to engage the opposition on the street, the field of play for espionage. And when we do go to the street, we have to be the best service there. If we are beaten on the street, it is worse than not having been there at all.

For years, we virtually conceded the streets of the world's capitals, including the major espionage centers, to the KGB, the GRU [*Glavnoye Razvedyvatelnoye Upravleniye*], and the East European services because we either did not know how to do it or we were not willing to pay the price for a thoroughly professional, reliable, full-time, local surveillance capability.

Opposition intelligence officers have to be watched, known meeting areas have to be observed, and, when an operation goes down, often on short notice, undetectable surveillance has to cover it, identify the participants, and obtain evidence.

This capability is expensive—selection, training, vehicles, photo gear, video, radios, safe apartments, observation posts, and on and on—but, if we do not have it, we will be a second-rate CI service and will not break the major cases.

The Fourth Commandment: Know Your History

I am very discouraged when I talk to young CI officers today to find how little they know about the history of American CI. CI is a difficult and dangerous discipline. Many good, well-meaning CI people have gone wrong and made horrendous mistakes. Their failures in most cases are well documented, but the lessons are lost if our officers do not read the CI literature.

I find it inconceivable that any CI practitioner today could ply his or her trade without an in-depth knowledge of the Angleton era. Have our officers read Mangold? Have they read *Legend* and *Wilderness of Mirrors*? Do they know the Loginov case, HONETOL, MHCHAOS, Nosenko, Pollard, and Shadrin? Are they familiar with Aspillaga and the Cuban DA debacle? Have they examined our mistakes in the Ames and Howard cases? Are they staying current with recent releases like *The Mitrokhin Archive* and *The Haunted Wood*?

I believe it is an indispensable part of the formation of any American CI officer and certainly a professional obligation to study the CI failures of the past, to reflect on them, and to make sure they are not repeated.

The many CI courses being offered now are a positive step, but there will never be a substitute for a personal commitment on the part of our CI professionals to read their history, usually on their own time at home.

The Fifth Commandment: Do Not Ignore Analysis

Analysis has too often been the stepchild of CI. Throughout the CI community, we have fairly consistently understaffed it. We have sometimes tried to make it up as we go along. We have tried to do it on the cheap.

Generally speaking, operators make bad analysts. We are different kinds of people. Operators are actors, doers, movers and shakers; we are quick, maybe a little impulsive, maybe a little *cowboy*. Our best times are away from our desks. We love the street. Research and analysis are really not our thing, and when we have tried to do it, we have not been good at it.

True analysts are different. They love it. They are more cerebral, patient, and sedentary. They find things we could not. They write better.

A lot of CI programs in the past have tried to make operators double as their own analysts. As a result, in the United States, CI analysis historically has been the weakest part of the business. Professional CI analysts have been undervalued and underappreciated.

A good CI program will recruit and train true analysts in sizable numbers. I do not think it would be excessive as a rule of thumb in a top-notch CI service to be evenly divided between operators and analysts. Very few of our U.S. CI agencies come anywhere close to that ratio.

Wonderful things happen when good analysts in sufficient numbers pore over our DA reports, presence lists, signals intelligence, audio and teltap transcripts, maps, travel data, and surveillance reports. They find the clues, make the connections, and focus our efforts in the areas that will be most productive.

Many parts of the U.S. CI community have gotten the message and have incorporated trained analysts into their operations, but others have not. Across the board, we still have serious shortfalls in good, solid CI analysis.

The Sixth Commandment: Do Not Be Parochial

More harm probably has been done to U.S. CI over the years by interagency sniping and obstruction than by our enemies. I remember when the CIA and the FBI did not even talk to each other and both had disdain for the military services. It is no wonder that CI was a shambles and that some incredibly damaging spies went uncovered for so long.

Occasionally in my career, I encountered instances of sarcasm or outright bad-mouthing of other U.S. Government agencies by my officers. That kind of attitude and cynicism infected our junior officers and got in the way of cooperation. These comments often were intended to flaunt our supposed "superiority" by demeaning the capabilities of the other organizations. I dealt with these situations by telling the officers to "knock it off," and I would encourage other CI supervisors around the community to do the same.

CI is so difficult, even in the best of circumstances, that the only way to do it is together. We should not let personalities, or jealousies, or turf battles get in the way of our common mission. Our colleagues in our sister services are as dedicated, professional, hardworking, and patriotic as we are, and they deserve our respect and cooperation. The best people I have known in my career have been CI people, regardless of their organizational affiliation. So let's be collegial.

The Seventh Commandment: Train Your People

CI is a distinct discipline and an acquired skill. It is not automatically infused in us when we get our wings as case officers. It is not just a matter of applying logic and common sense to operations, but is instead a highly specialized way of seeing things and analyzing them. CI has to be learned.

I do not know how many times in my career I have heard, "No, we do not really need a separate CI section. We are all CI officers; we'll do our own CI." That is a recipe for compromise and failure.

There are no substitutes for professional CI officers, and only extensive, regular, and specialized CI training can produce them. Such training is expensive, so whenever possible we should do it on a community basis to avoid duplication and to ensure quality.

CI is a conglomerate of several disciplines and skills. A typical operation, for example, might include analysts, surveillance specialists, case officers, technical experts, and DA specialists. Each area requires its own specialized training curriculum. It takes a long time to develop CI specialists, and that means a sustained investment in CI training. We are getting better, but we are not there yet.

The Eighth Commandment: Do Not Be Shoved Aside

There are people in the intelligence business and other groups in the U.S. Government who do not particularly like CI officers. CI officers have a mixed reputation. We see problems everywhere. We can be overzealous. We get in the way of operations. We cause headaches. We are the original *black hatters*.

Case officers want their operations to be bona fide. Senior operations managers do not want to believe that their operations are controlled or penetrated by the opposition. There is a natural human tendency on the part of both case officers and senior operations managers to resist outside CI scrutiny. They believe that they are practicing good CI themselves and do not welcome being second-guessed or told how to run their operations by so-called CI specialists who are not directly involved in the operations. I have seen far more examples of this in my CI career than I care to remember.

By the same token, defense and intelligence contractors and bureaucrats running sensitive U.S. Government programs have too often tended to minimize CI threats and to resist professional CI intervention. CI officers, in their view, stir up problems and overreact to them. Their "successes" in preventing CI problems are invisible and impossible to measure, but their whistleblowing when problems are uncovered generates tremendous heat. It is not surprising that they are often viewed as a net nuisance.

When necessary, a CI service has to impose itself on the organizations and groups it is assigned to protect. A CI professional who is locked out or invited in only when it is convenient to the host cannot do his job.

My advice to my CI colleagues has always been this: "If you are blocked by some senior, obtuse, anti-CI officer, go around him or through him by going to higher management. And document all instances of denied access, lack of cooperation, or other obstruction to carrying out your CI mission. If not, when something goes wrong, as it likely will in that kind of situation, you [and] CI will take the blame."

The Ninth Commandment: Do Not Stay Too Long

CI is a hazardous profession. There should be warning signs on the walls: "A steady diet of CI can be dangerous to your health."

I do not believe anyone should make an entire, uninterrupted career of CI. We all who work in CI have seen it: the old CI hand who has gotten a bit spooky. It is hard to immerse oneself daily in the arcane and twisted world of CI without falling prey eventually to creeping paranoia, distortion, warping, and overzealousness in one's thinking. It is precisely these traits that led to some of the worst CI disasters in our history. Angleton and his coterie sadly succumbed, with devastating results. Others in the CIA and elsewhere have as well. The danger is always there.

My wife, who was working at the CIA when I met her, was well acquainted with this reputation of CI and the stories about its practitioners. When I was serving overseas and received the cable offering me the position as Ted Price's deputy in the new Counterintelligence Center, I discussed it with her that evening at home. Her response, I thought, was right on the mark: "Okay, but do not stay too long."

Sensible and productive CI needs lots of ventilation and fresh thinking. There should be constant flowthrough. Non-CI officers should be brought in regularly on rotational tours. I also believe it is imperative that a good CI service build in rotational assignments outside CI for its CI specialists. They should go spend 2 or 3 years with the operators or with the other groups they are charged to protect. They will come back refreshed, smarter, and less likely to fall into the nether world of professional CI: the school of doublethink, the us-against-them mindset, the nothing-is-what-it-seems syndrome, the wilderness of mirrors.

The Tenth Commandment: Never Give Up

The tenth and last commandment is the most important. What if the Ames mole hunters had quit after 8 years instead of going into the ninth? What if, in my own experience, we had discontinued a certain surveillance operation after 5 months instead of continuing into the sixth? CI history is full of such examples.

The FBI is making cases against Americans today that involved espionage committed in the 1960s and 1970s. The Army's Foreign Counterintelligence Activity is doing the same. The name of the game in CI is persistence. CI officers who are not patient need not apply. There is no statute of limitations for espionage, and we should not create one by our own inaction. Traitors should know that they will never be safe and will never have a peaceful night's sleep. I applauded my CI colleagues in the FBI when I read not long ago of their arrest in Florida of a former U.S. Army Reserve colonel for alleged espionage against the United States many years earlier. They obviously never gave up.

If we keep a CI investigation alive and stay on it, the next defector, the next penetration, the next tip, the next surveillance, or the next clue will break it for us.

If there were ever to be a mascot for U.S. counterintelligence, it should be the pit bull.

In Conclusion

These are my Ten Commandments of CI. Other CI professionals will have their own priorities and exhortations and will disagree with mine. That is as it should be, because as a country and as an Intelligence Community we need a vigorous debate on the future direction of U.S. CI. Not everyone will agree with the specifics, or even the priorities. What we should agree on, however, is that strong CI has to be a national priority. Recent news reports from Los Alamos, Washington, and elsewhere have again underscored the continuing need for CI vigilance.

Chapter 19

A Review of the FBI's Performance in Uncovering the Espionage Activities of Aldrich Hazen Ames

Michael R. Bromwich

Explanatory Note

On April 15, 1997, we delivered our report entitled *A Review of the FBI's Performance in Uncovering the Espionage Activities of Aldrich Hazen Ames* to the House Permanent Select Committee on Intelligence, the Senate Select Committee on Intelligence, the Attorney General, and the Director of the Federal Bureau of Investigation (FBI). We also delivered a copy to the Director of the Central Intelligence Agency (CIA). The report itself is nearly 400 pages long and constitutes a careful and comprehensive review of the FBI's performance in uncovering the espionage activities of Aldrich Ames. The report is the culmination of a lengthy effort by a dedicated group of people from the Office of the Inspector General (OIG) and the FBI.

The report contains extraordinarily sensitive classified information, thus making it impossible for us to distribute the report itself to a wider audience. We have therefore developed this unclassified executive summary to provide the outline of our findings. We thought it important to report on the scope of our investigation, our findings, and our recommendations. We believe this unclassified executive summary accomplishes that objective.

We wish to acknowledge the very substantial cooperation we received from Frederick P. Hitz, the Inspector General of the CIA, and his staff during the course of our review. We also wish to acknowledge the full cooperation of the FBI in enabling the investigative team to obtain pertinent documents and interview witnesses with knowledge of the relevant facts.

Most of all, I want to pay tribute to the members of the team whose efforts are well-reflected in the full report but can only be glimpsed in this necessarily abbreviated unclassified executive summary. They made many personal and professional sacrifices over the course of this review, and I am greatly in their debt for the

Source: Michael R. Bromwich, Office of the Inspector General, U.S. Department of Justice, "A Review of the FBI's Performance in Uncovering the Espionage Activities of Aldrich Hazen Ames (April 1997)," unclassified Executive Summary accessed at <http://www.fas.org/irp/agency/doj/oig/amesxsm1.htm>.

outstanding work they did during this investigation and in the drafting of our report. The Special Investigative Counsel and the OIG members of the team are listed on the signature page of this unclassified executive summary. We did not list the members of the team from the FBI at their request. Nevertheless, I deeply appreciate their efforts in this shared enterprise.

I. Introduction

In this report, the Office of the Inspector General of the Department of Justice (DOJ) examines the performance of the FBI in uncovering the espionage activities of former CIA Directorate of Operations officer Aldrich Hazen Ames. Because Presidential Executive Order 12333 gives the FBI primary responsibility for combatting espionage conducted within United States borders, Ames' espionage on behalf of the Soviet Union, and later Russia, fell within the FBI's jurisdiction.

Ames served as a CIA officer for nearly 30 years, spending a significant portion of his career in the CIA's Soviet/East European Division. On February 21, 1994, Ames was arrested by FBI agents and charged with conspiracy to commit espionage. Ames pleaded guilty, and on April 28, 1994, he was sentenced to life imprisonment.

After his arrest, Ames disclosed that he had engaged in espionage for 9 years— from the spring of 1985 until his arrest in February 1994. During that time, Ames provided a wealth of classified information to his handlers. In particular, Ames provided information to the KGB [*Komitet Gosudarstvennoy Bezopasnosti*] that led to the compromise and execution of at least 10 CIA and FBI intelligence sources. Assessments following Ames' arrest have indicated that Ames' betrayal will continue to have a negative effect on this Nation's intelligence efforts for years to come.

After Ames' arrest, the Senate Select Committee on Intelligence (SSCI) recommended that the CIA Inspector General investigate the CIA's performance in connection with Ames. In September 1994, the CIA Inspector General issued a report detailing deficiencies in the CIA's counterintelligence effort and management of personnel. After reviewing various issues relating to the Ames matter, the House Permanent Select Committee on Intelligence (HPSCI) issued a report recommending an examination of the FBI's performance in connection with Ames. We initiated our review in response to that recommendation.

II. Summary of the DOJ Inspector General Investigation

The Inspector General assembled a team of 11 agents and analysts to pursue this review. The team was led by an Assistant U.S. Attorney on detail to the OIG. Ultimately, the team reviewed more than 26,000 pages of material from the FBI, CIA, SSCI, and HPSCI. These documents concerned the full 9-year scope of Ames' espionage activities, as well as the debriefings and damage assessments that followed his arrest. While our review was largely driven by questions and issues raised in the reports issued by HPSCI and SSCI, our own investigation disclosed additional areas for inquiry.

The team conducted more than 100 interviews during the course of the review. We sought to interview all FBI and CIA personnel who had significant involvement with what became the Ames investigation during the period of 1985 to 1994. We interviewed much of the operational hierarchy of the FBI's Intelligence/National Security Division during this same period, as well as the leaders of the CIA's Soviet/East European Division and the Counterintelligence Center. We also interviewed Ames at the U.S. Penitentiary in Allenwood, Pennsylvania.

Our final report is nearly 400 pages in length. Because of the extremely sensitive information it contains, it is classified at the top secret level. Copies of our final report were provided to a very limited audience including the Attorney General, the director of the FBI, the director of the CIA, and the chairman, vice chairman, and staff directors of both the HPSCI and SSCI. We prepared this unclassified executive summary as a means of disseminating the results of our review more widely.

III. The FBI's Performance in Uncovering Ames

The story of the Ames case begins with a catastrophic and unprecedented loss of Soviet intelligence sources suffered by the CIA and FBI in 1985 and 1986. Both agencies initially mounted efforts aimed at determining the cause of these losses (which stemmed from Ames' collaboration with the KGB) but as time passed, the level of attention devoted to this issue by the FBI and CIA sharply declined. In our report, we examine in detail the flow of information between the CIA and FBI concerning the 1985–1986 losses, and the FBI's actions in response to the information it received. We also focus on what information the FBI received from the CIA concerning Ames (who fell under suspicion at the CIA in late 1989) and evaluate whether the FBI's actions related to this information were reasonable under the circumstances. We did not examine in detail the FBI's performance after it opened an investigation of Ames. That investigation, once it was initiated, was handled by the FBI with professionalism and thoroughness.

In conducting our review, we found it useful to divide the period from 1985 to 1994 into three phases. The first phase concerns the time span between the first reported loss of CIA and FBI Soviet intelligence sources in 1985, and the completion, in September 1987, of a report by an FBI task force created to determine what caused valuable FBI Soviet sources to be compromised. In its report, the FBI reached no firm conclusions concerning the cause of its intelligence losses and did not analyze those losses and their relationship to losses suffered by the CIA.

The second phase described in our report reviews relevant events occurring between September 1987, when the FBI task force issued its report, and mid-1991, when the CIA and the FBI embarked on a joint review of the 1985–1986 losses. During this period, the FBI investigated other unrelated espionage cases and made attempts to obtain intelligence information about the 1985–1986 compromises. However, the FBI did not pursue any analytical or investigative effort focused specifically on determining the cause of both the FBI's and the CIA's 1985–1986 losses. Potentially incriminating information concerning Ames was developed at the CIA in November 1989, but was not provided to the FBI.

The third phase of the chronology developed during our investigation concerns the time span between mid-1991 and Ames' arrest in February 1994, and focuses on the work of a joint FBI/CIA team that was formed in mid-1991 to determine the cause of the 1985–1986 losses. By August 1992, this team had collected compelling circumstantial evidence implicating Ames, but the team did not suggest to anyone at FBI Headquarters or at the FBI's Washington Field Office that the FBI should open an investigation of Ames. Although certain supervisors at FBI Headquarters and at the FBI's Washington Field Office were aware that Ames was a top mole suspect, none of these managers requested a written report detailing any of the information concerning Ames. The FBI waited until after the joint team's final report was issued in March 1993 before opening an investigation of Ames. That investigation ultimately led to Ames' arrest in February 1994.

Our review revealed that throughout nearly the entire 9-year period of Ames' espionage, FBI management devoted inadequate attention to determining the cause of the sudden, unprecedented, and catastrophic losses suffered by both the FBI and CIA in their Soviet intelligence programs. Indeed, FBI's senior management was almost entirely unaware of the scope and significance of the mid-1980s losses and of the FBI's limited efforts to determine their cause. FBI senior management's lack of knowledge concerning the intelligence losses contributed to the FBI's failure to devote priority attention to this matter, particularly after 1987. Moreover, the FBI never showed any sustained interest, prior to mid-1991, in investigating the enormous intelligence losses suffered by the CIA. Even when a joint effort was initiated in mid-1991, that effort suffered from inadequate management attention as well as insufficient resources.

The inadequate briefing of senior FBI managers also led to the FBI's failure to fulfill its statutory obligation under Section 502 of the National Security Act of 1947 (50 United States Code, Section 413 [a]) to notify the congressional intelligence committees of "any significant intelligence failure[s]." Clearly, the entire scope of the losses sustained by the FBI and CIA in 1985 and 1986 falls within the meaning of the statute's notice provision. The FBI's senior managers never understood the scope and significance of these losses, however, and therefore were in no position even to consider briefing Congress on this matter.

A. Findings Concerning the FBI's Performance During the 1985 to September 1987 Period

In 1986, the FBI learned that two of its most important Soviet assets had been compromised. The FBI quickly formed a task force of six agents, code-named ANLACE, to determine how these critical assets had been compromised.

The ANLACE Task Force soon encountered serious obstacles in attempting to determine how the FBI's assets were compromised. When agents attempted to construct an access list showing the FBI personnel who had knowledge of the assets, they determined that as many as 250 FBI employees at the FBI's Washington Field Office alone likely had knowledge of these cases. Given this fact, the ANLACE team made no effort to determine whether any FBI employee with knowledge of the cases had any special vulnerabilities, such as unreported contacts with Soviets, alcohol or drug dependency, or a sudden and unexplained increase in wealth. Instead, once the task force had completed its examination of the operational details of the compromised cases, the investigation of their compromise turned largely to potential explanations outside the FBI, and primarily at the CIA, about which the ANLACE team knew very little.

Ultimately, the ANLACE Task Force issued a final report in September 1987 that failed to resolve the cause or causes of the FBI's recent losses. While the report stated that the ANLACE team had found no evidence of a current penetration of the FBI, the report did not reveal that the team had essentially conducted no investigation of FBI personnel with access to the compromised cases. In addition, the ANLACE report failed to disclose that the CIA, which had had access to information concerning the FBI's compromised cases, was simultaneously suffering unprecedented asset losses in its Soviet program.

As a result of the information that Ames delivered to the Soviets in June 1985, the CIA had suffered major losses in its Soviet asset pool. Those losses were reported to ANLACE team members and to their FBI Headquarters supervisors at a series of joint FBI/CIA conferences between December 1986 and December 1988. By early 1987, CIA personnel attending these joint conferences had reported to the FBI that the CIA's Soviet program had rapidly suffered unprecedented losses of its most significant assets at the same time the FBI was experiencing its asset losses. The ANLACE team did not disclose this fact in the ANLACE report, however, and our investigation revealed that senior FBI managers at that time, including the FBI director and the assistant director-in-charge of the Intelligence Division, never gained a true understanding of the scope and significance of the CIA's asset losses in 1985 and 1986.

In sum, between 1986 and September 1987, the FBI was a passive recipient of information concerning the serious losses suffered by the CIA in its Soviet program. Senior FBI managers were unaware of the CIA's losses, while mid-level FBI supervisors and FBI line personnel appear to have believed that receipt of this information imposed no responsibility on the FBI. Although the events of 1985 and 1986 strongly suggested that the CIA and FBI asset losses were related, the FBI made little effort to convince the CIA to embark on a joint investigation of this problem. Numerous FBI and CIA personnel whom we interviewed agreed that the FBI and the CIA should have pursued a joint investigation of the 1985–1986 compromises once the scope of the losses became clear. The FBI's failure to press for a joint investigation with the CIA stemmed primarily from the inadequate briefing of the FBI's most senior management and from the FBI's understanding, at this time, that the CIA would resist sharing sensitive intelligence information.

If the FBI and CIA had initiated a joint investigation of these losses in 1987 or 1988, there is reason to believe that Ames would have emerged as a mole suspect. Access lists developed after mid-1991, but which could have been prepared earlier, showed that Ames was one of only about 40 CIA employees with across-the-board access to the assets compromised in 1985 and 1986. If certain investigative steps were undertaken with respect to these individuals, such as determining whether any had had unreported contacts with Soviets, or had suddenly evidenced unexplained wealth, Ames would have come under suspicion. Indeed, the most compelling circumstantial evidence against Ames—the correlation between several meetings he had in 1985 and 1986 with a Soviet diplomat and large cash deposits that he had made to his bank accounts the next business day following those meetings—was available in record form in 1987 and 1988. However, because there was no joint investigation at this time and because the necessary investigative steps were not taken, this information was not requested by either CIA or FBI investigators until the summer of 1992.

B. Findings Concerning the FBI's Performance During the September 1987 to mid-1991 Period

During the September 1987 to mid-1991 period, the FBI investigated other unrelated espionage cases and made some attempts to obtain information about the 1985–1986 compromises. However, the FBI did not initiate any analytical or investigative effort specifically dedicated to resolving the cause of both the FBI's and CIA's 1985–1986 asset losses. Moreover, the FBI showed no interest in pursuing a joint investigation with the CIA regarding these losses even after learning at the joint FBI/CIA conferences in 1988 that the number of compromises in the 1985–1986 period was vastly higher than any previous 2-year time period.

In addition to revealing the CIA's unprecedented Soviet asset losses at these joint meetings, CIA personnel also conveyed their realization that potential non-mole explanations for the losses were fading. During the 1986–1987 period, the CIA had struggled to determine former CIA employee (and later defector to the Soviet Union) Edward Lee Howard's access to the compromised cases, investigated whether U.S. Marine guard Clayton Lonetree had permitted Soviets to enter the American Embassy in Moscow, and tested CIA communications systems in the United States and Moscow. At the FBI/CIA joint meetings in 1988, FBI personnel were told that no evidence had been found that Lonetree had permitted the KGB to enter the Moscow Embassy and that tests of CIA communications systems had found no penetration. The FBI also learned that Howard could not have betrayed some of the compromised cases, particularly those that had been initiated after his 1983 resignation from the CIA.

By 1988, the FBI's own counterintelligence experts were convinced that the 1985–1986 asset losses had been caused by human penetration. The quick, decisive arrest and execution of FBI and CIA sources indicated that the Soviets had obtained reliable, detailed information from a mole who likely had across-the-board access to sensitive Soviet operations. And a 1988 FBI analytical study detailing the continuing, serious disruption and unexplained compromises that were taking place in the FBI's Soviet program indicated that a mole could still be at work. FBI personnel were also beginning to recognize at this time the obvious relationship between the CIA and FBI Soviet asset losses. Indeed, the FBI's 1988 analytical study concerning the FBI's Soviet program explicitly suggested that a relatively well-placed penetration of the CIA could have compromised the lost FBI operations.

None of this information or analysis, however, led the FBI to intensify its own efforts to resolve the cause of the 1985–1986 losses, or to consider joint action with the CIA. After the ANLACE Task Force issued its report in September 1987, the team disbanded, leaving the FBI without any analytical or investigative effort aimed at resolving the cause of the FBI's and the CIA's 1985–1986 losses. In addition, the FBI's limited efforts at cooperation with the CIA on the penetration issue during this period ended with the last joint FBI/CIA conference in December 1988. The personnel at each agency who had focused on the lost assets issue went on to other duties and largely ceased communications on this subject.

The failure of the CIA and the FBI to pursue a joint investigation of the lost assets issue prior to 1991 significantly delayed the detection of Ames' espionage. Neither internal CIA and FBI records concerning Ames' 1985–1986 unreported meetings with a Soviet diplomat, nor bank records showing Ames' subsequent large cash deposits, were examined. Moreover, potentially incriminating information concerning Ames that became available at the CIA at this time was not properly referred to the FBI for investigation.

By late 1989, CIA personnel began to receive highly disturbing information concerning Ames' finances. A CIA colleague of Ames reported to CIA counterintelligence personnel that Ames, who had been experiencing financial difficulties prior to 1986, experienced a sudden, unexplained improvement in his finances. This CIA employee reported that Ames had purchased a $540,000 house in 1989 and engaged in lavish spending, all on a Government salary of $40,000 to $50,000 a year. The CIA employee's tip also specifically linked Ames' sudden wealth to his knowledge of the cases compromised in 1985 and 1986.

The CIA's investigation of this lead regarding Ames quickly revealed more disturbing information, including the fact that Ames had purchased his $540,000 home in 1989 for cash, that is, with no mortgage, and that he had engaged in three substantial cash transactions, totalling more than $50,000, between 1985 and 1989. Despite these facts and the existence of a 1988 FBI/CIA Memorandum of Understanding stating that the CIA would provide timely notice to the FBI of any conduct by CIA officers that raised counterintelligence concerns, no information concerning Ames was provided to the FBI prior to mid-1991.

If a joint FBI/CIA team had existed during the 1987 to 1990 period, it is reasonable to assume that the CIA employee's tip in November 1989 and the other financial information discovered by the CIA concerning Ames would have come to that team's attention, as it did to the joint team that was established in 1991 (the Special Investigations Unit [SIU]). And once the joint FBI/CIA team learned of the potentially incriminating information concerning Ames' sudden increase in wealth and his access to the compromised cases, the FBI would have had sufficient information to justify an investigation of Ames.

Early FBI involvement in the investigation of Ames also would have had the potential to accelerate significantly his eventual identification as the source of the asset losses. Instead, the financial investigation of Ames from November 1989 to March 1993 was pursued exclusively by a CIA officer who had limited training and experience in conducting financial investigations. And because this CIA officer had numerous other responsibilities, several years passed without any sustained effort to resolve questions concerning the source of Ames' sudden wealth.

Because the CIA possessed information that cast suspicion on Ames, and chose not to share this information with the FBI prior to 1991, the CIA must bear primary responsibility for the failure of investigators to focus on Ames during the September 1987 to mid-1991 period. The FBI's subsidiary responsibility stems primarily from its continuing failure during this same time period to seek a joint investigation with the CIA of the catastrophic losses sustained in 1985 and 1986.

The FBI's failure to focus on this matter resulted from management inattention and inadequate briefing of senior management. Our investigation revealed that during the 1987 to 1991 period, the FBI's most senior management, particularly the director and the assistant director-in-charge of the Intelligence Division, had little awareness of the 1985–1986 asset losses, the FBI's continuing operational difficulties in its Soviet program, or FBI projects related to these issues.

This lack of management attention to and involvement with the lost assets issue led the FBI to devote inadequate resources to resolving the cause of this problem during the 1987 to 1991 period. By 1988, it was clear that American intelligence had suffered catastrophic damage in its most important program. Espionage was the most likely cause of the damage. Yet the FBI's stance was passive concerning the lost assets issue throughout the 1987 to 1991 period, both with respect to the CIA's losses and with respect to the FBI's own disrupted operations. Given the significance of the losses suffered in 1985 and 1986, and the continued disruption in the FBI's Soviet operations, the FBI should have initiated an intensive effort aimed at determining the cause or causes of these setbacks. Unfortunately, no such effort was undertaken.

While management inattention and the inadequate briefing of senior management were important elements in the FBI's failure to take action, our review also revealed some confusion at the FBI with respect to the FBI's responsibility to address extraordinary intelligence losses, particularly at the CIA. We conclude that once espionage has emerged as a leading candidate for explaining such losses, the FBI, as the lead counterintelligence agency in this country, must aggressively investigate those losses. Here, the FBI ignored the obvious disaster at the CIA, even when the FBI's own operations had suffered—and were continuing to suffer—disruptions and compromises.

C. Findings Concerning the FBI's Performance During the Period from mid-1991 to Ames' Arrest in February 1994

In mid-1991, CIA officials independently decided to undertake a new effort to resolve the cause of the 1985–1986 losses. When FBI personnel learned of this effort, they expressed an interest in participating, and the concept of a joint FBI/CIA investigation of the 1985–1986 losses was born. This joint effort, referred to as the Special Investigations Unit (SIU), was based at the CIA; its staff consisted of two CIA counterintelligence officers, an FBI special agent, and an FBI analyst.

While reaching agreement on the personnel who would be assigned to this joint effort, the FBI and the CIA had little discussion concerning the new team's mission, the time period in which it would complete its work, and the product the new team would produce. It was never clear to team members whether the SIU was supposed to conduct an analytical study of the 1985–1986 losses or to pursue an investigation of certain leading mole suspects. As a result, part of the SIU pursued each strategy, resulting in the dilution of personnel resources that were already inadequate.

Once assigned to the SIU, the two FBI representatives had little substantive contact with their supervisor at FBI Headquarters. While the supervisor had told his FBI superiors that the FBI members of the SIU would be required to submit reports on a monthly basis and that the CIA and FBI would meet monthly concerning the SIU, our review revealed that the two FBI members of the SIU submitted written reports to their supervisor on only three occasions during the 2-year life of the SIU, and that only two joint meetings concerning the unit took place between CIA and FBI supervisory personnel.

The two FBI members of the SIU also had little substantive contact with a special investigative squad formed at the FBI's Washington Field Office to investigate mole suspects identified by the SIU. Agents on this special squad were told by FBI supervisors that the SIU team would produce a list of suspects for investigation by the spring of 1992. However, the SIU did not issue its final report until March 1993, by which time the special investigative squad had largely disbanded.

After arriving at the CIA, the FBI members of the SIU quickly became aware of the information developed by CIA personnel concerning Ames. This evidence included Ames' broad access to the cases compromised in 1985 and 1986; the sudden increase in wealth he enjoyed in the mid- to late 1980s; the absence of a mortgage on his $540,000 home purchased in 1989; and his large and unexplained cash transactions in 1985, 1986, and 1989. The FBI members of the SIU also interviewed the CIA employee who had provided the original tip concerning Ames' finances. This individual outlined the improvement in Ames' financial circumstances and further explained that Ames' in-laws could not account for this change.

While the FBI members of the SIU were given full access to the information that had been developed concerning Ames, and were kept apprised of additional information as it was obtained, they had almost no involvement in the investigation of Ames. One of the CIA members of the SIU collected information for a chronology concerning Ames' access and duties at the CIA, while another CIA officer pursued a financial investigation of Ames in the same intermittent fashion that had characterized the 1989 to 1991 period. The other members of the SIU, including the FBI participants, undertook a traditional analytical approach to resolving the cause of the 1985–1986 losses. This approach involved a comprehensive analysis of numerous files concerning the compromised CIA and FBI Soviet cases in an effort to discover patterns and similarities.

In the spring of 1992, the CIA officer pursuing the financial investigation of Ames was directed by his CIA superiors to complete an in-depth analysis of Ames' finances. In June 1992, the CIA officer sent letters to Ames' banks and credit card providers requesting financial information. The resulting credit card statements showed that Ames was charging expenditures of as much as $30,000 per month, while the monthly statements for Ames' bank accounts showed that hundreds of thousands of dollars had flowed through those accounts over the previous 5 years.

At this same time, the CIA member of the SIU who had developed the Ames chronology was analyzing information obtained from CIA and FBI files concerning Ames' contacts with Soviets in 1985 and 1986. In August 1992, this CIA employee discovered a strong correlation between several of Ames' meetings with a Soviet diplomat in 1985 and 1986 and Ames' large cash deposits into his bank accounts. These deposits were usually made on the next business day after Ames met with the Soviet. In addition to this financial information, the SIU's analytical study of the compromised cases had revealed that Ames had had access to nearly all of the operations that were compromised in 1985 and 1986.

All of this information was shared with the full SIU team, including the FBI members, and with certain CIA supervisors. Despite the compelling circumstantial evidence of Ames' involvement in espionage, however, no member of the SIU and no one in CIA's management suggested to anyone at FBI Headquarters or at the FBI's Washington Field Office that an investigation of Ames should be opened. Although certain supervisors at FBI Headquarters and the Washington Field Office were aware that Ames was a top mole suspect, none of these managers requested a written report detailing any of the information concerning Ames. Both CIA and FBI personnel decided to wait for the SIU's final report before taking any action.

The SIU issued its final report in March 1993, approximately a year later than expected. After concluding that there was a penetration of the CIA, the report presented a series of access lists showing which CIA employees had had broad access to the compromised cases. By the time the report was issued, however, the squad formed at the FBI's Washington Field Office to investigate mole suspects identified by the SIU had almost entirely disbanded. Having never received a list of prime suspects from the SIU, the squad members had returned to their home offices. After the report was issued, the FBI assembled another investigative team at its Washington Field Office. This team opened an intensive investigation focusing on Ames which resulted in his arrest in February 1994.

We found that the SIU effort and the FBI's contribution to that effort were undermined by a number of factors. The failure of FBI and CIA managers to reach an understanding as to the mission, duration, and objectives of the SIU led to confusion on these subjects both within the SIU and at the FBI. Given the unusual nature of the SIU effort and its important objective, the FBI's supervision of FBI personnel assigned to the SIU was inappropriately lax. Coordination between the SIU and FBI investigative squad was poor, as evidenced by the squad's dissolution before the SIU had even issued its final report. And the decision that the FBI members of the SIU would report to FBI Headquarters rather than to supervisors at the FBI's Washington Field Office isolated the FBI members of the SIU from the investigators who were charged with pursuing the mole suspects that the SIU identified. In addition, because of continuing communications and reporting failures, top FBI management had virtually no knowledge of the pursuit of an active and extremely damaging mole at CIA Headquarters.

IV. Summary of Recommendations

We found that the lack of knowledge and experience in counterintelligence work among certain FBI senior managers seriously hampered the FBI's effort in uncovering Ames' espionage. We recommend that the FBI promulgate a policy mandating that the assistant director-in-charge of the National Security Division, and his/her deputy assistant director-in-charge for Operations, possess a strong background in counter-intelligence work.

Former FBI directors told us that they had not been informed of important facts concerning the 1985–1986 asset losses and the Ames case. The FBI should establish policies designed to ensure that the director is informed of significant counterintelligence successes and failures. Records reflecting such briefings should be maintained by the director's office. The FBI should also promulgate policies designed to ensure that officials responsible for briefing Congress on intelligence matters are familiar with the FBI's statutory briefing obligations under Section 502 of the National Security Act of 1947.

We also recommend that the Director of Central Intelligence (DCI) work together with the FBI, CIA, and other members of the Intelligence Community (IC), as appropriate, to draft policies ensuring that the CIA, FBI, and other IC members cooperate to resolve significant intelligence losses involving operations about which they collectively have information. The DCI should also work with the CIA, FBI, and other IC members to formulate guidelines designed to ensure that the FBI, CIA, and other IC managers reach agreement concerning the mission, strategy, resources, objectives, duration, and reporting structure for any joint efforts. In addition, written FBI policies should require that FBI managers closely supervise their personnel during such joint operations.

While all FBI personnel interviewed agreed that in the Ames investigation the correlation between Ames' meetings with a Soviet diplomat and his cash deposits provided sufficient information to open an investigation of Ames, these facts were not communicated in writing to an FBI supervisor until after initiation of the Ames investigation. The FBI should review its policies and procedures to ensure that when FBI personnel learn of specific facts that might justify an investigation, they inform their supervisors in writing of this information.

Throughout our review, we encountered analytical reports prepared by FBI personnel that had not been evaluated or effectively used by FBI supervisors. We recommend that the FBI adopt a policy mandating an evaluation of such reports to determine whether the conclusions are valid and whether any further action is warranted.

Finally, the FBI was unable to provide our review team with a definitive answer concerning the distribution of various top secret documents. Given the sensitive nature of such documents, the FBI should develop and maintain a better record-keeping system for tracking their dissemination.

V. Conclusion

Our review found that the FBI allocated enormous resources to the investigation of Ames once it was initiated and that the Ames investigation was efficiently and professionally pursued. Based in part on incriminating documents recovered from Ames' residential trash, the FBI built an overwhelming case against him that led him to plead guilty to espionage charges following his February 1994 arrest.

The ultimate success of the Ames investigation, however, highlights the damage caused by the failure of the CIA and FBI to cooperate fully earlier in investigating the

1985–1986 asset losses. The success of the investigation also indicates that proper attention by FBI's senior management to the serious intelligence losses sustained in 1985 and 1986, and better communication concerning these matters within the FBI, would have likely led to an earlier discovery of Ames, thus cutting short his career of espionage.

Part VI—The Open-Source Revolution

I would say that something upward of 95 percent of what we need to know could be very well obtained by the careful and competent study of perfectly legitimate sources of information open and available to us in the rich library and archival holdings of this country.

—George F. Kennan

Chapter 20

Open-Source Intelligence: New Myths, New Realities

Mark M. Lowenthal

Introduction

For the most of the past year I have been in the business of providing open-source information and open-source intelligence—there *is* a difference—to Government agencies, primarily within the Intelligence Community (IC). As with all new ventures, our record is mixed—some real successes and some difficulties, both expected and unexpected. But we have had enough experience to date, I believe, to give greater shape to how the IC should be thinking about creating a stronger and more productive open-source presence in its all-source analysis and collection.

Let us, briefly, define our terms. By *open-source information*, we mean any and all information that can be derived from overt collection: all types of media, government reports and other documents, scientific research and reports, commercial vendors of information, the Internet, and so on. The main qualifiers to open-source information are that it does not require any type of clandestine collection techniques to obtain it and that it must be obtained through means that entirely meet the copyright and commercial requirements of vendors where applicable. *Open-source intelligence* (OSINT), in sharp contrast to its raw foundation, applies the proven methods of the Intelligence Community to open-source information, and transforms volumes of information into an unclassified intelligence product that represents judicious source discovery and validation, multisource integration, and subject-matter expertise. Finally, one can go a step further and distinguish between OSINT as produced in the private sector, and validated OSINT approved for dissemination by an all-source intelligence producer with full access to traditional classified sources of intelligence, which are used to validate the OSINT. For our general purposes, we will talk about OSINT as encompassing both open-source information and validated OSINT unique to the IC.

The Intelligence Community and OSINT

The idea of the Intelligence Community using OSINT is not new. It has always been recognized that open sources provided a useful stream of information for all-source collection and analysis. A current IC senior official has estimated that even during the height of the Cold War, some 20 percent of the information collected on the Soviet Union came from open sources. Indeed, one of the most venerable offices of the Intelligence Community, the Foreign Broadcast Information Service (FBIS), has been dedicated to collecting and *publishing* openly mass media from around the world, and selling the product to any and all buyers.

In the late 1980s, the IC recognized that the nature of the information world had begun to change. Not only was information technology beginning to improve by geometric bounds, but the amount of information actually available through open sources was growing as well. COSPO, the Community Open-Source Program Office, was the IC attempt to arrive at a more coherent approach to the open-source issues, both technology and content.

The view here, and one that is admittedly not shared by all, is that COSPO was unable to fulfill its mission. At least three factors were to blame. First, despite all of the lip service given to the importance of OSINT, there remains an ingrained IC prejudice—sometimes no more than a subliminal one, but a prejudice nonetheless—against open sources. There will always be IC officials, and some of their policy customers, who believe that the greater the difficulty involved in collecting the intelligence, the better the intelligence has to be. It remains difficult but imperative to convey the message that I tried to convey to a deputy director for operations during my tenure as staff director of the House intelligence committee: "We don't give you brownie points for collecting intelligence by the hardest means available." The IC remains unable to appreciate the view expressed by former Deputy DCI Richard Kerr: "The IC has to learn that it no longer controls most of its own sources." Nor, for that matter, has the IC been willing to act upon the findings of the Aspin-Brown Commission on Intelligence, which held that IC access to open sources is "severely deficient" and that this should be a "top priority" for funding.

The second reason that COSPO failed to achieve its mission was a very American failing. COSPO became seduced by the occasionally chimerical lure of technology. Too much of its emphasis went to finding an ever elusive technology that would solve the open-source problem of multiple and diverse sources. As good as information technology has become, it has not provided the types of answers that COSPO sought. Moreover, in chasing the chimera of technology, COSPO tended to lose sight of its real goal: *content*. If the technology does not produce intelligence that analysts can use, it is pointless. Technology for the sake of technology is a waste.

Finally, COSPO hit a wall—the firewall of security. COSPO presumed that it could select several important open sources, bring them inside the firewall, and satisfy the majority of IC needs. Nothing could be more dangerous, for at one stroke it guides the all-source analysts to a single, very limited "safe" site for some open sources, while failing to establish organizational, security, procurement, and training protocols for assuring IC access to the full range of open sources and services, most of which change so frequently as to make a neat "importation" solution both impossible to achieve or to fund.

COSPO became little more than a venue for the various open-source managers in each of the intelligence agencies to meet. But that very role underscores the futility of IC open-source policy. For no other collection discipline do we have separate programs in separate agencies. Indeed, it would be ludicrous to suggest CIA, DIA [Defense Intelligence Agency], and INR [the Department of State's Bureau of Intelligence and Research] each have their own imagery or signals programs. For OSINT, however, this sort of duplicative frittering of resources was deemed acceptable. Moreover, with each agency left to its own open-source devices, there has been little accountability for failing to collect, process, and exploit open sources.

New Myths, New Realities

The one-and-a-half-year production of open-source intelligence for a variety of clients has led us to face a series of new myths and new realities.

Myth 1: OSINT as a Threat and a Savior. One of the prejudices of the IC toward OSINT is their view that some OSINT advocates believe that open sources can provide most of what the IC needs. Anyone foolish enough to believe this would clearly have no knowledge of the realities of intelligence. As long as there is vital information that needs to be obtained and is being denied us, there will always be a significant role for clandestine collection of all sorts. Moreover, we are not talking just about information on rogue states, major threats, and so on. Sometimes our allies and partners are also our problems, in such areas as trade, international pollution, and so forth.

At the same time, some OSINT advocates, like all true believers, see and tout promises they cannot fulfill. Some of these advocates are the people described above, who have little understanding or appreciation of the IC. Others, interestingly, are IC veterans who find themselves turned off by any number of problems: the large gap between collection and processing/exploitation, that leaves so much collection unused; the continuing problem of overclassification—much of it imposed by the Directorate of Operations—that impedes useful and necessary sharing of information; or their own sense of the proper balance between open and clandestine sources.

There is a middle ground that few seem willing to occupy: OSINT as a significant collection discipline in its own right, properly balanced with the other collection sources in a true all-source plan. The reality, however, is that the conceit of the IC and the frustration of open-source advocates makes this middle ground untenable as yet.

Myth 2: The Technology Silver Bullet. The COSPO experience notwithstanding, the IC continues to hunt for that technology silver bullet. As noted above, this is a typical American response to a host of problems. Moreover, the IC has thrived on pushing the technology envelope farther and farther. Right now, for example, the IC is spending money to find some search engine that will make Internet searches easier, while spending even more money to make the Internet available to each analyst. Although the IC has come to appreciate that the private sector in information technology is now outpacing the IC, there seems to be some lingering nostalgia for the "good old days" when the IC was the leading edge.

Our private sector open-source experience has taught us that there is no silver bullet out there. There are many technologies available: faster computers and better search engines. But what is lost in these technology hunts is the fact that technology is no more than a means to an end; it is not the end in itself. Moreover, technology only facilitates collection at some very raw level. It cannot replace skilled analysts who make difficult choices about what to collect and what to analyze. As with all other intelligence, OSINT collection is only the beginning. Even OSINT needs to be processed and exploited.

Even with the best technology in the world, open-source collection remains a grinding job, sifting through dozens or even hundreds of possible items of interest, depending on the topic at hand. Assuming that the collector is also not the analyst—a point to which I shall return—a second sifting process takes place, as the collected material is then resifted and shaped into an analytical product. All of this requires humans—not machines—who are familiar with the stated requirements, the customer's needs, the issue itself—to make intelligence choices.

(A humorous aside here: one lesson we have learned is that the rift between collectors and analysts is generic, not systemic to the DO [Directorate of Operations] and the DI [Directorate of Information]. Even open-source collectors believe they have found a trove of sparkling gems in their searches. Open-source analysts see many worthless pieces of glass and wonder why these items were selected. The collectors wonder why the analysts do not appreciate what they have received, and also become very frustrated when the analysts fail to pass on 7 out of 10 of their variations on each theme each day. As an analyst, I can assure you that the analysts are correct and the collectors are wrong!)

We understand the basic outlines of information technology. We understand the basic paths that computers will take and now only wonder as to their increased speed and decreased cost. But only the most confirmed (and misguided) technology enthusiast would trust the actual content of his product to a machine versus humans.

Myth 3: OSINT Can Be Treated Differently. For a variety of reasons, the IC has treated OSINT very differently from the other collection disciplines. We would not expect the designer of a technical collection system to be either a cryptographer or a photo interpreter for the material that his system collected. But the IC has been perfectly willing to allow analysts to serve as their own OSINT collectors. Even within OSINT, these are two very different functions.

One of the reasons OSINT has not made the contribution that it might is that it has not had a dedicated, end-to-end process as have imagery, signals, espionage, and so forth. OSINT has been treated as something that gets absorbed as part of one's professional development or something that is obtained during one's free time by reading a newspaper or browsing the Internet. Unless and until OSINT has dedicated collectors, processors, and exploiters—either in-house or out—it will remain an adjunct rather than a contributor. For all of the flaws of the Intelligence Community, the *model* (emphasis stressed) of collectors, processors and exploiters, and analysts works. This model works so well that it would boost OSINT tremendously if this model were applied to it. Indeed, there is nothing about OSINT that argues strongly in favor of not using this model except for the continuing prejudice of the IC.

There is, in fact, a more serious reason for treating OSINT with the same depth of commitment as with the other disciplines: OSINT is vastly overrated with respect to both ease of accessibility and reliability of coverage. OSINT is not easy. Even the most sophisticated commercial online services have huge gaps in coverage, delay times before most of their content is posted, and severely constrained search and retrieval engines. Moreover, 50 to 80 percent of what one needs from the OSINT world is *not* available online or in English.

Myth 4: OSINT = the Internet. One of the greatest myths now surrounding OSINT is the view that OSINT means surfing the Internet. The Internet is the world's largest bulletin board; anyone and everyone is free to tack up whatever information they want. This is not to suggest that the Internet is not a useful OSINT source. It is. But the relationship of the Internet to open source is somewhat akin to the relationship of human intelligence to all-source: it is a sliver, some of whose reliability is often in doubt.

One of the worst aspects of the Internet is the amount of time required to run a useful search. The Internet may be one of the great black holes of time management. That is why the notion of allowing analysts to do their own Internet surfing is so alarming. Analysts will find themselves half-intrigued and half-frustrated as they guess at search strategies. The amount of time they spend will hardly justify the results of their search.

As with all other collection disciplines, one needs skilled collectors to search the Internet. But more importantly, one needs senior open-source collection managers who can develop successful search plans across all potential OSINT sources, not just the Internet.

Myth 5: OSINT = Text. A less damaging but still pervasive myth is the one that views OSINT as nothing more than clippings, reports, and so on—text. Certainly this is a mainstay of OSINT, but we have to think broader. Commercial imagery is at a point now where it can contribute more to OSINT and should be at a point in the next several years where that contribution should grow dramatically. Other visual inputs—maps, charts, tables—are easily done now. Some OSINT pioneers are also thinking about applying standard signals intelligence techniques, such as traffic and pattern analysis, to OSINT. So we need to think of OSINT as much more than text and as a potential contributor not only to the all-source process as a whole but to each of the other collection disciplines.

Moreover, one can take a step further back in the process and think of OSINT as a collection management tool. If the required information is available via OSINT, knowing that frees up scarce clandestine collection resources for those issues where OSINT cannot help. Indeed, if OSINT had a greater perceived value within the IC, it would be the collection discipline of *first* resort largely to serve that vital collection management function, while also providing a rich context for both targeting collection and evaluating what is collected.

Thus, if we only think of OSINT as a text provider, we are once again undervaluing its potential contribution.

Myth 6: The IC Has an OSINT Policy. Knowing that it has used and still uses OSINT hardly qualifies as an IC OSINT policy. Certainly we have no policy on the use and the future of OSINT that would bear any resemblance to the other collection disciplines. Instead, we have had a division of rather small funding pots, across too many agencies, to allow each of them to buy the technology or information or the vendor services they believe that they need for OSINT. The various DCI directives on COSPO and OSINT have not achieved the coordination and coherence of which they speak. Instead of an OSINT policy, the IC has a bunch of disparate OSINT operations that are likely to be somewhat duplicative and are unlikely to achieve the bang for the buck of a coherent OSINT approach: IC wide, looking at both technology and content, but remembering that content is the ultimate goal.

At the same time, the consumers of intelligence receive huge quantities of un-solicited OSINT and find that they can achieve information sharing goals themselves, using OSINT, without IC support. The creation of the Virtual Information Center in the Pacific Command, by the J–5, rather than the J–2, stands as a case in point. If the IC does not develop a policy and a concept of operations for dealing with OSINT, it will find its consumers turning more and more to homegrown OSINT solutions that are not solutions at all, but rather makeshift alternatives to the IC.

Conclusion—Some Final Observations

Despite the attention that has been given to OSINT, especially in the joint revolutions of the personal computer and the fall of the Soviet empire, it remains an underappreciated and underutilized source. The commercial OSINT world itself has its own problems in terms of efficiency, economies of scale, and consistently user-friendly products. But there is no silver bullet out there that will automatically solve those problems and create a human-free OSINT chain that has much value.

The myths currently surrounding OSINT warp some of the realities. Address-ing those realities and debunking those myths would go a long way toward helping OSINT be the INT it should be and the INT that could be of much greater assistance to the all-source intelligence process.

Chapter 21

The Strategic Use of Open-Source Information

John C. Gannon

The Intelligence Community (IC) is well known as an espionage service. Much less well known is the fact that it is one of the world's biggest information-based businesses, collecting and analyzing open-source information. Open source has long been a high IC priority. Today open-source information has become a major challenge to the IC. The IC response to the challenge is very much a dynamic work in progress.

Open-source information is not what it used to be. Ten years ago, "open source" generally meant information from foreign newspapers and the electronic media, which was collected mostly by the Foreign Broadcast Information Service (FBIS). Open source was "frosting on the cake" of intelligence material dominated by signals, imagery, and human-source clandestine collection.

Today, open source has expanded well beyond frosting and comprises a large part of the cake itself. It has become indispensable to the production of authoritative analysis. It increasingly contains the best information to answer some of the most important questions posed to the community. Media reports now are just a small piece of the open-source pie, which comprises a vast array of documents and reports publicly retrievable but often difficult to find in today's high-volume, high-speed information flow. Open sources provide vital information for the policymakers, whom the IC serves. Accessing, collecting, and analyzing open-source information, in short, is a multifaceted challenge that can only be met with a multifront response or strategy.

This [chapter] examines three aspects of the open-source challenge/response dynamic: its critical importance; how the IC is using technology to help the analyst cope with the information glut; and the need for interaction with the private sector.

Critical Importance of Open Source

The world for the IC analyst has changed dramatically since the end of the Cold War. A decade ago *global coverage* largely meant a comprehensive strategy to collect against and analyze the Soviet Union—the IC's single strategic threat. Today, global coverage entails the responsibility to assess diverse, complex, and dispersed

Source: John C. Gannon, "The Strategic Use of Open-Source Information," *Studies in Intelligence* 45, no. 3 (2001), 67–71.

threats around the world. In additional to traditional intelligence concerns—such as the future of Russia and China, political turmoil in Indonesia, and civil conflicts in Africa—the new environment features many nontraditional missions. The IC now provides intelligence about peacekeeping operations, humanitarian assistance, sanctions monitoring, information warfare, and combating international organized crime, as well as placing greater emphasis on such transnational issues as counter-terrorism, counternarcotics, and counterproliferation. Many of these missions are operationally focused, requiring growing proportions of the analytic and collection work force to function in an ad hoc crisis mode.

Open-source information now dominates the universe of the intelligence analyst, a fact that is unlikely to change for the foreseeable future. The revolution in information technology and telecommunications has fundamentally transformed the globe that the IC covers, the services that it provides to consumers, and the workplace in which its people function.

- Information abounds. A growing volume of open-source material is relevant to intelligence needs. Closed societies in the former Soviet Union and Eastern Europe have opened up, and reliable information now is widely available. Fifteen years ago, information on the Balkans was scarce, foreign newspapers took weeks to arrive at an analyst's desk, and policymakers were willing to wait days or even weeks for a paper on the issues.

- Today everything moves faster, and people are better informed. The revolution in information technology has vastly increased the volume and speed of the information flow across the globe and across computer screens. Technology makes analysts more efficient, but it also increases the demand from consumers. Intelligence requirements tend to be sharper and more time-sensitive. Analysts often receive newspaper and media reports before the people in the countries where the reports are generated, and intelligence consumers will not tolerate waiting days for a response.

- Governments have less and less capacity to control information flows. International organized crime groups, terrorists, narcotraffickers, and weapons proliferators are taking advantage of the new technologies, bypassing governments or seeking to undermine them when governments try to block their illegal activities. Chances are these criminal networks will be using laptop computers, establishing their own Web sites, and using sophisticated encryption. In the years ahead, these enhanced capabilities will raise the profile of transnational issues that are already putting heavy demands on intelligence collection and analysis.

Dealing with the Information Glut

The enhanced *speed* of communication is a distinct advantage in today's world where intelligence analysts are as comfortable in cyberspace as in the office space of top consumers. The Washington-based analyst can send a message and get a response from a post in a remote country faster than it used to take to exchange notes by pneumatic tube with counterparts in the same building.

The expanding *volume* of open-source information, however, presents a greater challenge. During the Cold War, the job of the IC was to piece together bits of secret information. Each piece of raw intelligence was a carefully acquired golden nugget. Today, the IC is still mining for information but facing an avalanche from both open-source and classified collection systems.

Technology is a major part of the answer to the magnitude of the open-source challenge, but it is no substitute for the other essential component: skilled people. The IC must invest more in technology to provide the analytic tools needed to assess and exploit the vast amount of information available, and it must invest more in people, whose expertise is crucial for prioritizing, interpreting, and analyzing this information. The greater the volume of information to assess, the stronger must be the expertise to evaluate it.

The number of sources and the overall amount of data to which an analyst has access make the process of finding precise information or hidden clues extremely difficult. How can the analyst know where to start looking? What data might be relevant and what should be ignored? When intelligence analysts query databases, they need to know how to ask the questions in a way that will get useful answers, and they need analytic tools to help them extract the right data. Automated analysis tools—data mining and retrieval techniques—provide significant opportunities to help solve the information overload problem.

Cognitive analytic tools are under development in both the private sector and the government to facilitate management of the information glut, enhancing the IC's ability to filter, search, and prioritize potentially overwhelming volumes of information.

- *Clustering* lets analysts exploit the most useful data sets first, helping the IC perform its warning function. Clustering is particularly helpful when the volume of information, as with open source, makes it difficult to recognize meaningful patterns and relationships.
- *Link analysis* helps to establish relationships between a known problem and unknown actors and detect patterns of activities that warrant particular attention.
- *Time-series analysis* can enable analysts to track actions over time so that unusual patterns of activity can be identified.
- *Visualization* allows analysts to see complex data—including link and time-series analysis—laid out in new and varied formats that promote analytic insight.
- *Automated database population* is designed to free analysts from the tedious and time-consuming function of manually inputting information into databases, reducing the potential for errors and inconsistencies.

One of the strongest and most consistent needs of IC analysts is to search and exploit both classified and unclassified information from a single workstation. The community is working on this and on ways to standardize information and tag it using metadata—or reference information—to make it easier to search, structure, and enter information into databases.

FBIS is developing a single, open-source "portal" that will organize and cross-reference FBIS products, information that FBIS has collected via the Internet as well as other multimedia material.

- The portal, to be accessible from desktops and expected to be fully operational by 2002, will provide analysts with a one-stop shop for all open-source intelligence, whether collected by FBIS or not.
- Material on the portal will be indexed, archived, and accessible via a powerful, easy-to-use search engine.

Enhancing IC Cooperation

Collaborative tools offer a critical opportunity for enhanced cooperation among the IC's 13 agencies, DCI centers, the National Intelligence Council, and literally hundreds of collection and analysis offices. The problem of sharing data among such a large number of organizations is immense, in particular because different agencies have different security standards. Each organization has private intelligence holdings that are extraordinarily sensitive. The IC has to resolve the issue of multilevel security and need-to-know concerns by developing robust and flexible communities of interest using collaborative tools.

New tools are needed to enhance cooperation in two areas:

- Collaboration in the production process to increase speed and accuracy.
- Expertise-based collaboration—to enable a team of analysts to work on a project for several weeks or months.

Several collaborative tools currently available or soon to be deployed include the capability to share both textual and graphic information in real time. These new tools will allow analysts to discuss contentious analytic issues; share information like maps, imagery, and database information; and coordinate draft assessments. This would all be done on line, from their own workspaces, resulting in substantial savings of time and effort over current practices. Future requirements emphasize broad deployment of collaborative tools, relying on mature commercial off-the-shelf platforms performing to standards that allow interoperability across the IC.

Another important aspect of enhanced collaboration is distributed knowledge. The IC will never have a database that contains all information available to all organizations, due to the individual missions of each organization. The ability to share major holdings of multiple agencies and to present an integrated view to the analyst's desktop, however, is critical and possible—but no easy task!

Finally, the IC has some challenges that few private sector organizations face. It deals, for example, extensively in foreign languages—lots of them. FBIS translates and disseminates information in many languages. Automated translation tools are getting better but still do not function adequately. The IC remains heavily dependent on trained linguists.

Working with the Private Sector

The information technology (IT) relationship between the U.S. Government and industry has undergone a dramatic transformation in recent years. By itself, the IC simply cannot stay ahead of the technological curve and it knows it. Today, government no longer dominates research and development (R&D) and the information marketplace—the private sector does. The IT industry's R&D is focused primarily on commercial applications; the IC's requirements increasingly will have to be satisfied by products developed for commercial use. The IC needs to develop close and enduring partnerships in the commercial world to benefit from both the private sector's continuing pursuit of new technology and its best practices in dealing with the open-source challenge.

In 50 years, the IC has gone from large, stationary mainframes with a handful of dumb workstations to portable multiservice devices that will communicate, compute, and run offices. This represents a dramatic leveling of information costs and affects the way the IC does its work. In many ways, however, the community still thinks and organizes itself with immobile information systems. It is continuing to invest great amounts in stationary hardware systems, while many of its targets—terrorists, narcotraffickers, and organized crime syndicates—are becoming increasingly mobile in their operations. Perhaps private industry will come up with ways to liberate analysts from their cubicles, while at the same time ensuring the security of their work.

The CIA has developed two organizations to build and sustain outside partnerships: the Office of Advanced Intelligence Tools (AIT) and In-Q-Tel.

- In 1997, CIA's Directorate of Science and Technology and its Directorate of Intelligence collaborated in the formation of AIT. The office works inside CIA with analysts to determine their needs and outside CIA with vendors to identify state-of-the-art cognitive and collaborative tools.
- CIA launched In-Q-Tel in 1999 as a nonprofit corporation designed to bring together the best of the academic, business, and private research worlds to exploit new and emerging information technologies.[1] Its mission is twofold: first, to accept strategic problems and develop a "portfolio" of innovative IT solutions, ranging from exploration to demonstration; and, second, to fuel private research, development, and application of information technologies of strategic national interest for the benefit of all partners.

In-Q-Tel is not designed to conduct research itself; rather, it will orchestrate the work of numerous partner organizations working in teams. In-Q-Tel's initial projects focus on four interrelated intelligence challenges:

- *Agency use of the Internet*, particularly Internet search and privacy issues.
- *Information security*, a crosscutting issue that permeates all organizational functions. In-Q-Tel will engage information security from the perspectives of hardening and intrusion detection; monitoring and profiling of information use and misuse; and network and data protection.
- *Analytic data processing capabilities*, including geospatial and multimedia data fusion/integration, all-source analysis, and computer data forensics.

- *Distributed information technology infrastructure,* to facilitate data dispersal to multiple organizations/agencies anywhere in the world.

The IC leadership recognizes that partnerships with outside technical and academic experts, as well as vendors, are essential to enabling us to stay on top of the information technology curve. Among analysts, the attitude and behavior toward the outside world is slowly changing, but the IC needs to provide more incentives for analysts to get out from behind their desks to engage with substantive experts and other outside sources of useful—and increasingly critical—information that cannot be captured by clandestine collectors or traditional open-source collectors such as FBIS. This is an imperative, not an option. It has been said that "Opportunities are like sunrises. If you wait too long, you miss them." The IC cannot afford to miss today's opportunities because it is too inwardly focused. It does not intend to do so.

Conclusion

For most of its history, the Intelligence Community has operated as an industrial enterprise, with compartmentation as a key operating metaphor. In the process, a set of impressive organizations has been created; however, they are now being overtaken by events. In the post-industrial world pervaded by information technology, networks defeat hierarchies, and agility becomes a prerequisite for organizational success. Even with the impressive gains of the past few years, dealing with the open-source challenge will necessarily be a work in progress for some time to come. Open source is not a traditional collection challenge, and there is no single solution. Meeting the challenge requires a multifront strategy, and it will take time for the IC to get this right.

The IC recognizes that it can succeed only if it exploits the changes taking place in the information revolution and in information industries. The community always will have security concerns but cannot allow them to deter it from taking advantage of the opportunities inherent in the emerging environment.

The leadership has committed the IC to a corporate strategy that will leverage the best practices and resources of the whole government and the private sector to provide the President and U.S. policymakers the information advantage they need.

Note

[1] The new corporation was first launched in February 1999 as In-Q-It, but changed its name to In-Q-Tel in December 1999 to prevent confusion with the financial software giant Intuit. "In-Tel" is self-explanatory, while the "Q" stands for technical innovation—derived from the James Bond character who developed Bond's spy gear.

Chapter 22

Open-Source Intelligence:
A Review Essay

Richard S. Friedman

Ninety percent of intelligence comes from open sources. The other ten percent, the clandestine work, is just the more dramatic. The real intelligence hero is Sherlock Holmes, not James Bond.[1]

—Lieutenant General Samuel V. Wilson, USA (Ret.), former director,
Defense Intelligence Agency

Former Ambassador to Algeria L. Craig Johnstone . . . recently told a Washington conference that during his assignment in Algeria, he bought and installed a satellite dish enabling him to watch CNN [the Cable News Network] so he could have access to global news. He recalled:

> The first week I had it running was the week of the Arab League summit in Algiers and, for whatever reason, the Department was interested in finding out whether Yasser Arafat would attend the summit. No one knew, and the day of the summit Washington was getting more frantic. We in the Embassy were banned from the summit site so there was no way we could find out whether or not Yasser Arafat would show. Finally, at about noon I was home for lunch and watching CNN when the office of the Secretary of State called. The staffer on the other end asked if there was anything at all he could tell the Secretary about Arafat's participation. And just then, on CNN I saw a live picture of Yasser Arafat arriving at the conference. "He is definitely at the conference," I reported. The staffer was ecstatic and went off to tell the Secretary. The next day I received a congratulatory phone call from the NEA bureau for pulling the rabbit out of the hat. How did you find out, they asked? The secret was mine. But I knew then and there that the business of diplomacy had changed, and that the role of embassies, how we do business in the world, also had to change.[2]

Ambassador Johnstone's story provides an example of the value of information from open sources. Allen W. Dulles, when he was Director of Central Intelligence, acknowledged to a congressional committee, "More than 80 percent of intelligence

Source: Richard S. Friedman, "Open Source Intelligence: A Review Essay," *Parameters* 28, no. 2 (Summer 1998), 159–165.

is obtained from open sources." Whether the amount of intelligence coming from open sources is 90 percent, 80 percent, or some other figure, experienced intelligence professionals agree that most *information* processed into finished *intelligence* may be available from open sources. This [chapter] explores the significance of a trend toward increased recognition of the role of open-source information and discusses what this may mean for intelligence consumers at every level.

The use of information from open sources (OSINT) for intelligence production is not a new phenomenon. Intelligence services in most nations have always made use of OSINT obtained by working with scholars in academia, debriefing business travelers and tourists, and examining foreign press and broadcast media. Intelligence prepared from sources available to the general public draws from books, periodicals, and other print publications such as catalogues, brochures, pamphlets, and advertisements. Also included are radio and television broadcasts and a more recent technological innovation, the Internet. Collectively, these are frequently referred to as open media resources. Intelligence—information and analysis that is *not* available to the public—is prepared for use by policymakers and military leaders inside the government. Intelligence is categorized customarily according to the source from which it is obtained. Today, five sources are recognized:

- Reports from human [intelligence] (HUMINT)
- Photo imagery, including satellite
- Measurements and signature intelligence: physical attributes of intelligence targets
- Open-source intelligence
- Interception of communications and other signals.

While most discussions of open-source intelligence seem to concentrate on intelligence collection, it is important to view intelligence trends in conjunction with developments in its traditional components. These components are:

- *Costs.* With decreasing national security budgets, government leaders are having to examine their infrastructure. As military forces become more dependent on off-the-shelf commercial technology, intelligence organizations appear headed toward greater reliance on open-source intelligence.
- *Sources.* Cost-driven decisions dictate that a significant quantity of intelligence requirements can be filled by a properly designed comprehensive monitoring of open sources, either by the intelligence establishment itself or by private organizations. A particular advantage of open-source intelligence is that the product can be maintained at a low level of classification required for these sources and methods. This outcome allows relatively wide dissemination and distribution when compared with material from other sources. This characteristic of open-source intelligence is particularly important in coalition operations.
- *Methods.* It has been demonstrated many times that good intelligence production relies on all-source assessment. Traditional intelligence structures and methods have been optimized for designated core or central missions, and today many of these remain structured to meet Cold War requirements and

scenarios. Current and likely future contingencies seem less likely to involve major hard military net assessments and diplomatic intelligence than was the case between 1945 and 1991. Current and future contingencies probably will continue a trend toward soft analyses of complex socioeconomic, technological, and political problems, and of issues that will include such items as international organized crime, information warfare, peacekeeping operations, and activities associated with special operations and low-intensity conflict.[3]

- *Targets.* Intelligence targets of greatest concern to U.S. leaders have changed since the collapse of the Soviet Union, the accompanying geopolitical upheavals (such as political deterioration in the Balkans), and changes in Western perceptions of global security interests (for example, the significance of the Middle East). Intelligence agencies must now focus their activities on a far broader range of targets and potential targets than was common in the Cold War era. Today, intelligence professionals have to be concerned with terrorism, major international crime, and arms proliferation, including programs in some areas to produce weapons of mass destruction. They have to be prepared for possible military intervention on short notice in overseas conflicts or for humanitarian relief. Some of these targets require constant scrutiny in substantial depth; for others, broad general surveillance will suffice—provided a reserve or surge capability is maintained.[4]

Although many aspects of intelligence work are changing, for the near term the preponderance of them will probably remain familiar. Today's emerging main problem is how to deal with new and indistinct boundaries among and between intelligence organizations and functions, and increasing ambiguity in roles and missions. Any intelligence officer who has ever worked at a senior level knows that senior policymakers and government officials abhor ambiguity; they want timely, accurate intelligence. As Peter Schwartz, a recognized futurist, founding member of the Global Business Network, and author of *The Art of the Long View*, told his audience at the Colloquium on the 21st Century, "We will see not only changing rules of the game, but new games. There is an emerging competitive information marketplace in which nonstate intelligence will be cheap, fast, and out of control."[5]

Enthusiastic proponents of open-source intelligence argue that the information revolution is transforming the bulk of any nation's intelligence requirements and reducing the need to rely upon traditional human and technical means and methods. But Robin W. Winks, distinguished Yale University historian who served in the Office of Strategic Services during World War II and in its successor, the Central Intelligence Agency, concluded, "Research and analysis are at the core of intelligence.... [Most] 'facts' are without meaning; someone must analyze even the most easily obtained data."[6]

The emerging debate between investing in technology and developing competent analysts concerns itself basically with the value and role of open-source intelligence. To understand some of the forces that are shaping the debate, we need to weigh the relative benefits of primary and secondary sources, two discrete subsidiary classes of open-source material. *Primary* sources, generally taken to include print and electronic media, have always provided information of value to the Intelligence Community in current intelligence, indications and warning, as well as background information used by analysts in their work. What the so-called information revolution has done is to increase the ability of users to gain access and to manipulate the information, and although most intelligence managers do not believe that the number of primary sources has expanded greatly, the number of *secondary* sources has increased exponentially. To compound the analyst's problem, the objectivity and reliability of many secondary sources are often questionable. We will need more experience before we can accept expansion of secondary sources as a benefit to the management of national security.

The largest general open-source collection in the world is the Library of Congress. To replace the original library, which was destroyed during the War of 1812, Congress in 1815 purchased the private library of former President Thomas Jefferson, greatly increasing the collection's size and scope. The Library of Congress now includes works in more than 450 languages and comprises more than 28 million books, periodicals, and pamphlets as well as manuscripts, maps, newspapers, music scores, microfilms, motion pictures, photographs, recordings, prints, and drawings. The library's services also include research and reference facilities, which coordinate with or amplify local and regional library resources.

There are also several thousand databases available from commercial organizations; LEXIS/NEXIS, Dialog, Reuters, and the *New York Times* come to mind.[7] Any discussion of contemporary open sources must now include the Internet and the World Wide Web (WWW). The World Wide Web (developed in 1989) is a collection of files, called Web sites or Web pages, identified by uniform resource locators (URLs). Computer programs called browsers retrieve these files.

The term *Internet* describes the interconnection of computer networks, particularly the global interconnection of government, education, and business computer networks, available to the public. In early 1996, the Internet connected more than 25 million computers in more than 180 countries.[8] The Internet provides an immense quantity and variety of open-source information and must be increasingly looked upon as a source for intelligence purposes.[9]

The Internet and the World Wide Web exemplify technology that is not yet mature. One hallmark of immature technology is an underlying anarchy and a potential for disinformation. In October 1938, when radio broadcasting was emerging as a reliable source of information, producer-director Orson Welles, in his weekly radio show Mercury Theater, presented a dramatization of an 1898 H.G. Wells story, *War of the Worlds*. The broadcast, which purported to be an account of an invasion of Earth from outer space, created a panic in which thousands of individuals took to the streets, convinced that Martians had really invaded Earth. Orson Welles later admitted that he had never expected the radio audience to take the story so literally, and that he had learned a lesson in the effectiveness and reach of the new medium in which content was struggling to catch up to technology.

Recent examples with the Internet and its spin-offs suggest that email abuses, careless gossip reported as fact, and the repeated information anarchy of cyberspace have become progressively chaotic. This does not mean that the Internet and the Web cannot be considered seriously for intelligence work, but it does mean that intelligence officers must exercise a vigilant and disciplined approach to any data or information they acquire from on-line sources.

In December 1997, senior officials from Germany, Canada, France, Italy, Japan, Britain, Russia, and the United States (the Group of Eight industrialized nations) gathered in Washington to explore the transnational nature of computerized crime, with specific attention to opportunities for criminals to exploit the Internet's legal vacuum. Among the facts presented to the officials were these:

- Almost 82 million computers worldwide are now connected, according to a Dataquest Market Research Report.
- By 2001 the number of linked computers is expected to reach 268 million.
- The FBI estimated that by 1997, the value of computer crime in the United States had reached $10 billion per year.
- Government agencies are fertile ground for hackers; in 1995 the Pentagon was attacked by hackers 250,000 times, with a 64 percent success rate. The Department of Justice and the Central Intelligence Agency have also been hacked. And the tension over access to Iraqi weapon sites in late 1997 and early 1998 produced a surge of attempts to penetrate U.S. Department of Defense databases.
- The San Francisco-based Computer Security Institute surveyed 536 companies or government agencies, 75 percent of which reported substantial financial losses at the hands of computer criminals.

The principal significance of these facts for the intelligence officer is that Internet sources are subject to manipulation and deception. Consequently, counterintelligence and security processing will henceforth have to include *cyberspace* during analysis.

Perhaps the greatest value to military organizations in this array of adjustments following the end of the Cold War and the proliferation of technologies is freedom from confinement to a fixed geographic site for ready access to basic unclassified references. Modern communications will free deployed military from the need to transport large quantities of reference material (classified and unclassified) during operations. Military forces in the field can now tap into an immense quantity of information resources in near-real-time. Four relevant types are:

- Basic intelligence, such as infrastructure, geography, and order of battle
- Cultural intelligence concerning the society in which the force may be required to operate
- Information of a contextual nature which relates to operational or intelligence message traffic
- Current intelligence reporting concerning the situation in the operational area.

Since the quantities of information available are great and much of the information is often irrelevant, staffs of deployed units may find it difficult to use the information productively. Deployed organizations may well have to establish forward and rear intelligence activities. The threat of information warfare will have to be taken into account in planning and executing split-echelon operations.

Providing unclassified information to the general public as well as to officials is the objective of democratic governments in their declarations of open and immediate reporting. Even the tabloid press has never advocated a freedom that would deliberately compromise national security or put the lives of service members at risk, yet there can be unintended consequences from such expanded openness. The British government learned this during the 1982 Falklands campaign when a BBC [British Broadcasting Corporation] reporter inadvertently revealed operational plans for what proved to be a costly assault at Goose Green by the Parachute Regiment: the enemy was listening. During Operation *Desert Storm*, the U.S. Government and its coalition partners would encounter other problems. While CNN was reporting directly from the theater of operations, government control of mass communications was in effect in Israel, Jordan, and Saudi Arabia, as it was in Iraq. The sites of Scud attacks on Israel were quickly cordoned off by the authorities; media representatives were granted access only after a response had been determined by the Israeli government. The state-owned Iraqi media not only repeatedly told its citizens they were winning the struggle, but it also manipulated reporting of the use of the Patriot missile against the Scud, ensuring that CNN and others reported only what the Iraqi government wished. Coalition anti-Scud measures soon were placed under direct control of Washington.

Intelligence consumers, government officials, and policymakers have not been complaining about a shortage of information; they are suffering from a saturation. The flood of mass-produced data now available and the ensuing overload means that collection is no longer the principal problem. The greater challenge facing intelligence organizations is analysis, consolidation, and timely dispatch of data and results to the individuals who need it. Effectiveness in this process will depend upon allocation of human resources among those responsible for analysis and others responsible for its transmission. An information management executive will consider any increase in volume as proof that information is being managed better, even more efficiently. But the information manager is not in the business of analysis, so he or she is not interested in how well or poorly the information is interpreted, or even if it contains misinformation or inaccuracy. One cannot equate increased throughput to improved situation awareness within a theater of operations.

Nevertheless, the quantitative arguments of information managers recently have become more effective than those of the Intelligence Community with respect to open-source policy. The last time a similar contention occurred, the proponents of technical intelligence argued that they had the key to ultimate wisdom. As the late Ray Cline, one-time Deputy Director of Intelligence at CIA and later Director of the Department of State's Intelligence and Research Bureau observed:

> The technical miracle has greatly reduced the burden on the secret agent. Lives need not now be risked in gathering facts that can easily be seen by the eye of the camera. . . . Instead the agent concentrates on gathering ideas, plans, and intentions, all carried in the minds of men and to be discovered only from their talk or

their written records. Nobody has yet taken a photograph of what goes on inside people's heads. *Espionage is now the guided search for the missing links of information that other sources do not reveal* [emphasis added]. It is still an indispensable element in an increasingly complicated business.[10]

Claims of open-source enthusiasts need to be examined in context. Those making extravagant claims sometimes have little vested interest in the role and value of open-source materials, or even the knowledge or experience to make reliable judgments about the broader issue of multidisciplined all-source analysis by skilled intelligence analysts. The communications revolution is presenting intelligence organizations with a new challenge far beyond that of mass production. Like other enterprises, intelligence now faces competition from directions believed to have been impossible only a few years ago.

As has been true with commerce and industry, intelligence will have to remodel its organization, form new associations, tailor or customize its products, and question its fundamental missions. So long as there are nations led by aggressive totalitarian rulers inclined toward terrorism, or there are fanatics equipped with lethal weapons, democracies will continue to need effective secret services.

Notes

[1] David Reed, "Aspiring to Spying," *The Washington Times*, November 14, 1997, 1.

[2] Remarks at opening session of the Conference Series on International Affairs in the 21st Century, U.S. State Department, Washington, DC, November 18, 1997.

[3] U.S. military operations in Somalia, Haiti, and Bosnia are examples of requirements of a different nature.

[4] It is important to keep in mind an old intelligence maxim: "You can't surge HUMINT!"

[5] Peter Schwartz, address at the Colloquium on the 21st Century, Washington, DC, October 21, 1997.

[6] Robin W. Winks, *Cloak and Gown: Scholars in the Secret War, 1939–1961*, 2d ed. (New Haven: Yale University Press, 1996), 62.

[7] One source estimates the current total to be more than 8,000 such databases.

[8] The Internet was initially developed in 1973 and linked computer networks at universities and laboratories in the United States. This was done for the Defense Advanced Research Projects Agency (DARPA). The project was designed to allow various researchers to communicate directly in connection with their work. It was also developed with the idea in mind that it could provide a nuclear-survivable communications system.

[9] Current estimates suggest that around 30 million individuals and more than 40,000 networks are connected, numbers which appear to be increasing rapidly. The quantity of data on the Internet is huge. One estimate is total content between two and three terabytes. (A terabyte is one million megabytes.) A typical public library of some 300,000 books has about three terabytes of data. Rajiv Chandrasekaran, "In California, Creating a Web of the Past," *The Washington Post*, September 22, 1996, H1. An essay by James Kievit and Steven Metz, "The Internet Strategist: An Assessment of On-line Resources," *Parameters* 26 (Summer 1996), 130–145, available on the Internet, is an excellent introduction and guide.

[10] Ray Cline, "Introduction," in *The Intelligence War*, ed. William V. Kennedy (London: Salamander Press, 1984), 8.

Part VII—Challenges of Intelligence Analysis

We need new ways of thinking so we can solve the problems created by the old ways of thinking.

—Albert Einstein

Chapter 23

Defining the Analytic Mission: Facts, Findings, Forecasts, and Fortunetelling

Jack Davis

In the post-Cold War era of declining resources for intelligence and increasing criticism of analytic performance, definition of the professional mission of the Central Intelligence Agency's (CIA's) Directorate of Intelligence (DI) has become an important task for leaders and wellwishers alike. An agreed and realistic definition would boost morale and productivity by helping to determine how to select, train, deploy, and reward analysts and their managers. Clarification of mission would also provide guidance on what to do more of and less of; in effect, on how analysts and their managers should invest the nth hour of a busy day.

Mission definition, to cite a former Deputy Director for Intelligence (DDI), is by its nature a "difficult and somewhat metaphysical" task.[1] I write in part to encourage readers to join in the quest for a satisfactory characterization of the role of intelligence analysis.

The mission statement I offer, warts and all, is intended to meet three overlapping standards: [to] provide key policy officials with distinctive professional support they will choose to rely on; promote the national interest by contributing to sound policymaking; [and] ensure appropriate funding from Congress. *Intelligence analysis is the process of providing objective and effective support to help U.S. policymakers, by means of information on and assessments on events overseas, to carry out their mission of formulating and implementing national security policy.*

Under the requirements of this definition, a DI analyst's work has to provide values that are taken seriously by policymakers as well as exhibit rigorous treatment of evidence, inference, and judgment. The national interest is not well served by an unimpeachably objective assessment that key officials judge to add little value to their policymaking processes.

The needs of policymakers—especially what hands-on officials seek in support of their daily management of issues—have to be a central concern of intelligence makers. This is no trivial point. Former policy officials are quick to say on the record

Source: Jack Davis, "Defining the Analytic Mission: Facts, Findings, Forecasts, and Fortunetelling," *Studies in Intelligence*, Special November 2002 Issue, 25–30.

that they did not read some of the products the agency sent to help them because they saw no loss in not knowing what was in them.[2]

At the same time, the national interest is not well served by an assessment much admired by policy officials that does not meet the standards of sound analytic tradecraft. Carefully weighed evidence and rigorously structured argumentation must form the core of the analysts' papers and briefings, not their opinions or those of policy officials. This point too is made by former policy officials, both on and off the record.[3]

Analysts and managers who participated in the dozen runnings of the "Workshop on Reaching Policymakers" conducted during 1993–1994 raised two thoughtful challenges to this definition of the DI mission as elaborated in their reading books and in-class exercises:[4]

- First, that the emphasis on close support of policy officials encourages politicization of analysis.
- Second, that constraints on analysts' opinions also debase the intelligence mission.

Politicization

Effective analysis requires the analyst to intrude into the policymaking process—to organize the available information and assumptions on contentious issues and to assist in implementing goals, including long-shot policy objectives. Analysts have to treat the most important policymakers working their accounts as "clients" in need of such professional services. Or, to use the former DDI's sports analogy, as *football coaches* in need of the specialized assistance that only *scouts* working on their behalf can provide.[5]

Why? Because policymaking is the only national security game in town. Intelligence analysts have to work through policymakers to contribute to the national interest (and, on a more pedestrian level, to earn their pay).

That said, can intelligence professionals provide close analytic support on difficult and debatable policy issues (Cuba, Caucasus, China) without opening themselves up to charges of politicization?

I know of no generally accepted definition of politicization, although it is usually meant to imply the breach of professionalism on the part of intelligence analysts and managers. Politicization cannot reasonably be defined to mean providing support to the policymaking process because that is why intelligence analysis exists in the first place. At least, under my definition of mission, it cannot mean *effective* support—that is, sought-after and useful information and insight that gets at the policymakers' operational concerns about avoiding dangers and seizing opportunities.

Also, a meaningful definition of politicization should take account of the reality that the mixing of policymaking with personal, bureaucratic, and partisan politics is as American as apple pie. More than one former policymaker has observed that senior officials spend at least as much time trying to leverage their U.S. counterparts in Washington as they do working directly against their problems overseas.

If effective relations between intelligence and policy professionals require the former to provide close support to the daily business of the latter, any mission statement that seals off intelligence analysis from politics seals it off from a significant (that is, fundable) role in the policymaking process.

That said and accepted, politicization as a debasement of professionalism cannot refer to intelligence assessments that seek to structure the substantive debates of competing policy officials by addressing contentious factors that could influence the outcome of their policy deliberations. Nor can it mean providing professional analytic support to the politically tinged action agendas that can emerge from the process. If the President wants to defy what the analysts see as the ground truth in country X, analysts are professionally obligated both to point out the long odds and to provide judgments and insights to shorten those odds.

Politicization, then, should be defined as something much different from close professional support to policymakers and policymaking. I define it as the distortion of analysis by setting aside or otherwise failing to meet the standards of objectivity in setting forth information and judgments—in order to support a world view or policy preference.

Debasement of professional norms has happened in the past when analysts and their managers have given in to bullying from a policy official or have deliberately distorted the analytic process at their own initiative. Politicization also takes place when analysts and managers, with or without awareness, let their own policy biases skew the marshaling of evidence and judgments.

The analytic profession needs to erect strong institutional guards against politicization; whatever its roots, it erodes confidence in the integrity of analysis, at times on the part of colleague analysts, at times on the part of policy officials. I contend that *objectivity* as I have defined it—a professional ethic that celebrates tough-mindedness and clarity in applying rules of evidence, inference, and judgment—is the only realistic safeguard.

Here, *realistic* means a practice that works without turning off the policymaker as client and thus, over time, congressional funding as well. Trying to guard integrity by distancing the analyst from policymaking will not do.

Two additional observations on taking an experience-based measure of the danger of politicization: First, policymakers want to succeed. And most have learned that faulty premises, while they can at times turn policy debates, undercut the prospects for policy success. As one former ranking official explained his own strong commitment to objectivity: "Policymakers are like surgeons. They don't last long if they ignore what they see when they cut an issue open."[6]

Finally, close professional ties between analysts and policymakers usually promote frankness, mutual respect, and even mutual dependence. In my experience, these in turn promote analysis to help understand and deal with tough problems, not analysis to please.

The Analytic Food Chain

A question asked these days by DI analysts, in hallways as well as classrooms, is whether intelligence professionals are still entitled to an opinion. Based on the proposed mission definition, the answer has to be *no*. The authority to interpret today's events and predict tomorrow's developments in DI papers and briefings has to be earned, first by hard work in amassing and arraying the available evidence, and then by constructing and clarifying the argument, behind all judgments. Sound tradecraft works equally well as protection against politicization and as the basis for more reliable analysis generally.

I endorse the efforts by DI leaders to place greater emphasis in papers and briefings on careful consideration of evidence and on judgments anchored in research expertise and sound reasoning. Survival of the DI as an independent cadre of analysts depends in good measure on its commitment to use rigorous analytic tradecraft to distinguish its work on behalf of policymakers from that of journalists, policy advocates, and other wordsmiths working the national security field.[7]

This in turn requires pushing DI assessments down what I call the *analytic food chain*: From fortunetelling to forecasts, and ultimately to facts and findings. Here, I use the following definitions:

- *Facts*: verified information related to an intelligence issue (for example, events, measured characteristics)
- *Findings*: expert knowledge based on organized information that indicates, for example, what is increasing, decreasing, changing, taking on a pattern
- *Forecasts*: judgments (interpretations, predictions) based on facts and findings and defended by sound and clear argumentation
- *Fortunetelling*: inadequately explained and defended judgments.

The DI effort represents in part an adjustment to internal and external criticism of the quality of analysis. The managers professionally responsible for all issuances from the directorate and the constituent offices want analysts to be more explicit about what they know and how they know it, as well as what they do not know that could affect the issue being addressed. One goal is to reduce avoidable error by relying more on evidence and logic and less on rhetoric and authority. As the former DDI put his bid for adding greater rigor, and thus greater modesty, to analysts' judgments, "We are not in the prophecy business."

More significantly, the DI's increased emphasis on facts and findings is a response to signals from hands-on policymakers that the analysts' in-depth knowledge helps them get through daily rounds of making decisions and taking actions. As a rule, they find that insights from what is known provide more *added value* than predictions about what is unknown, even unknowable. Why? Departmental assistant secretaries, NSC [National Security Council] staff directors, and like policy officials see themselves as the *analysts of last resort*—the assessors who make the judgments for the President and other bosses on what is going on in country X and what lies ahead on issue Y. What these hands-on policy officials want most from intelligence professionals is solid information and sound argumentation for reaching *their own* bottom-line conclusions.[8]

In this sense, the role of intelligence analysis is to *reduce uncertainty for policy officials*. On many issues—what next for the Russian economy, for Cuban politics, for South Africa's military, for Iranian science and technology—neither intelligence nor policy professionals can eliminate uncertainty. The latter, though, would prefer to be as well informed as possible before trying to seize opportunities and ward off dangers.

How best does the intelligence analyst reduce uncertainty for key policymakers? To use the scout-coach analogy, not by predicting the score before the game is played, but by providing specialized information and insights that help the policy official in making the best game plan. And, during the game or implementation phase of policy, the analyst sits in the stands with a powerful pair of binoculars and a book full of findings on the opponent's strengths and weaknesses to provide help in calling individual plays.

Policy officials are explicit and nearly unanimous here. The reason they prefer customized assessments (for example, timely and actionable memorandums) to broadcast publications (for example, feature articles in the National Intelligence Daily [NID; since 1998 called the Senior Executive Intelligence Brief]) is that they want to be helped up their individual learning curves. A former official attested that at one time he had been spending 60-plus hours a week on an important negotiation. He was insulted when the agency sent him a NID feature telling the "story" of the week's events: "I am the story. Please tell me what you know that I don't know."[9]

Similarly, the main reason many policy officials prefer oral briefings to written products is because they welcome the opportunity to "cross-examine" the analyst, probing for what he or she knows that could be helpful in making decisions amidst inevitable uncertainty.

Facts

Based on the casual sample of DI papers I have read over the last year or so, I see a decided increase in evidence-based analysis targeted for small numbers of hands-on policy officials. But analysts, and some managers, still complain that presenting factual materials is some kind of subanalytic pursuit—and a disruption of their "real work."

I would argue that weighing evidence to determine what is known about a complex affair is a central *analytic* responsibility. An analyst can never be too well versed in the rules of evidence. What standard of proof is needed to determine what a foreign leader said? What he meant? What he fears and hopes? What he plans to do next?

Again, knowing and applying rules of evidence is no trivial matter, if analysts expect policy officials to rely on intelligence reports in making decisions on whether, when, and how to take action. Some veteran analysts, myself included, are willing to admit that at times they placed credence in highly classified information that turned out to be either third-hand speculation or an attempt at deception.

Findings

I believe that research findings or organized information on subjects of importance to policymakers will over time become the analysts' most important and appreciated contribution to the policymaking process.

Communication technology is eroding the analyst's advantage in being first to know what happened yesterday. The policymakers' preference to make their own bottom-line call on the important issues on their agenda is eroding the analyst's advantage in being the first to predict what will happen tomorrow. These trends increase the relative importance of having organized information at the ready to inform both the analysts' interpretations and predictions and those of policy officials.

The challenge to the DI here is to provide the same resources and recognition to research that leads to a powerful database—say, for analyzing the political strength of contending forces in important countries—that once were given to published research papers. By powerful I mean solidly grounded, up to date, ready to go to the support of a memo or briefing, and set up to be used by the next tenant of the substantive account. With accelerating changes in policy agenda and analyst assignments and increased reliance on "analytic teams," corporate and not individual findings will count most.

Anchoring Judgments

By definition, analytic judgments are inherently subject to error. Analysts interpret, explain, and predict on matters they do not or cannot know with full confidence. There is, then, no such thing as safe estimating. The peril of unintended consequences can be reduced, however, by anchoring estimative judgments via tradecraft that takes account of findings and warrants sound argumentation and precise communication of conclusion, reasoning, risk, and alternatives. Under my classification of analysis, these processes define a *forecast*.

The distinction between forecasting and fortunetelling is not that the first always provides a correct and the second an incorrect answer. The difference is that policy readers can see that forecasts are secured by findings and rigorous and transparent argumentation. Fortunetelling comes across to the reader as unanchored judgments. Perhaps the analyst possesses ample data and has reasoned carefully. But the reader cannot know that this is the case or that the analyst has not relied instead on incomplete evidence, speculation, and bias. One veteran policy official refers to inadequately explained judgments as "the tablets handed down by the intelligence priesthood."[10]

Linchpin analysis is one way of showing managers and policy officials alike that all the bases have been touched. *Linchpin analysis*, a colorful term for structured forecasting, is an anchoring tool that seeks to reduce the hazard of self-inflicted error as well as policymaker misinterpretation. At a minimum, linchpin tradecraft induces rigor through a series of *predrafting checkpoints*, outlined below. Analysts can also use it to organize and evaluate their texts when addressing issues of high uncertainty. Reviewing managers can use linchpin standards to assure that the argument in such assessments is sound and clear:

- First, analysts identify the main uncertain factors or key variables they judge likely to drive the outcome of the issue. This forces systematic attention to the range of and relationships among factors at play.
- Second, analysts determine the *linchpin premises* or working assumptions about the drivers. This encourages testing of the key subordinate judgments that hold the estimative conclusion together.
- Third, because the premises that warrant the bottom-line conclusion are subject to debate as well as error, analysts marshal findings and reasoning in defense of the linchpins.
- Finally, because of the U.S. stake in the outcome, analysts address the circumstances under which unexpected developments could occur. What *indicators* or

patterns of development could emerge to signal that the linchpins were unreliable? And *what triggers* or dramatic internal and external events could reverse the expected momentum?

Linchpin tradecraft, again, is a tool to incorporate rigor into analysis of matters of considerable uncertainty. It is not an end in itself. Every analytic assignment represents distinct challenges regarding subject and audience and thus distinct challenges regarding how to explicate the judgments. Experienced analysts can achieve the same analytical insurance provided by linchpin tradecraft via a variety of anchoring practices.

That said, the institutional standard should be fixed: When a DI paper or briefing makes estimative judgments on issues of importance to U.S. national security interests, policy readers are provided with precise and powerful backup argumentation.

But what if—as has happened—a policymaker at a briefing session wants the analyst to *hold the analysis and just make a call*? Policy officials vary at least as much as analysts, and at times, some will ask for a bottom line laid bare.

Even here, I recommend the analyst substitute an *if, then projection* for a prediction. Explain what is driving the situation and the related linchpin premises. Make clear the call is based on these staying on track. Cause-and-effect analysis will take an extra minute. But the requester will know he or she is dealing with a DI analyst.

The NID may be the toughest nut to crack because most articles do not lend adequate space for argumentation. At least to me, this makes the case that analyst commentary should avoid prediction and rely instead on findings (especially what is seen as new and different in the reported events). Here, too, when a need to address future developments is deemed unavoidable, projections should be substituted for predictions.

There is a difference, for example, between predicting the success or failure of a military offensive, a political scheme, or an economic initiative and pointing to the precedents and patterns that will influence the outcome. Anchoring judgments to findings can often be executed economically, in terms of the space required to meet the standard of sound and distinctive analytic tradecraft.

Notes

[1] Douglas J. MacEachin, *The Tradecraft of Analysis: Challenge and Change in the CIA* (Washington, DC: Central Intelligence Agency, 1994), 3.

[2] See, for example, Jack Davis, "A Policymaker's Perspective on Intelligence," *Studies in Intelligence* (Summer 1994), which cites Ambassador Robert Blackwill, former NSC Staff Senior Director.

[3] Interview with Paul D. Wolfowitz, former Under Secretary of Defense for Policy, December 13, 1994.

[4] The "Workshops on Reaching Policymakers through Opportunity Analysis" were taught jointly with L. Keith Gardiner.

[5] Douglas J. MacEachin at the Meeting of the Working Group on Intelligence Reform, Consortium for the Study of Intelligence, February 7, 1994.

[6] A former policy official at the meeting cited above.

[7] MacEachin, *Tradecraft of Analysis*.

[8] Interview with Herman J. Cohen, former Assistant Secretary of State for Africa, August 20, 1994.

[9] A former policy official at a meeting sponsored jointly by CIA's Center for the Study of Intelligence and the Institute for the Study of Diplomacy, Georgetown University, March 1993.

[10] Wolfowitz interview.

Chapter 24

The Challenge for the Political Analyst

Martin Petersen

Over 30 years as a political analyst and manager of analysts has convinced me that it is harder for political, leadership, and country analysts to be taken seriously by the policymaking audience than economic or scientific analysts, to name but two. There are good reasons why this is the case, and they have nothing to do with the expertise of political analysts, their integrity, or the complexity of the issues involved. Rather, it is the nature of the beast—politics—that makes policymakers more skeptical of what political analysis can offer and adds to the credibility burden that all analysts share.

Establishing credibility is different than establishing access. The Central Intelligence Agency (CIA) label is often enough to open a door, but the CIA label does not necessarily translate into credibility. Getting an intelligence product read does not mean it has credibility either. This is a political town, and it is smart politics to know what the CIA is saying, especially if the analysis is likely to influence policy on a contentious issue.

Credibility exists when the product is seen as relevant, timely, expert, objective, and informed. With credibility comes impact. There can be no impact without credibility. The goal of intelligence analysis is not to determine the outcome of the policy process, but rather to put the policymaker in the best position possible to make the best-informed decision possible. Impact occurs when, in the words of Sherman Kent, we "raise the level of the debate," and, in the words of Director Richard Helms, "level the playing field."

Establishing credibility and having impact start with understanding the nature of our audience—not the *who*, in this case, but the *what*. Policymakers are political animals. Four generalizations can be made about them—and it is these generalizations that make the credibility hurdle higher for political, leadership, and country analysts.

Four Facts of Life

My experience has convinced me of the essential validity of four broad characterizations of the policy audience. I think of them as "the facts of life" for all analysts. There is an element of hyperbole here, perhaps, but at the center is a core of hard truth.

Source: Martin Petersen, "The Challenge for the Political Analyst," *Studies in Intelligence* 47, no. 1 (2003), 51–56.

First, all policymakers, regardless of their training, area of expertise, or track record, believe themselves to be excellent political analysts. What money is to New York and celebrity is to Los Angeles, politics and the knowledge of politics is to Washington. Policymakers know they are politically savvy—that is why they are in the positions they are in—and they have tremendous and justified confidence in their own political judgment. Moreover, they consume vast amounts of raw intelligence—the same stuff intelligence analysts are reading—and they often have friends with powerful connections who share information with them but not with the Intelligence Community. Policymakers may or may not question the physics that underpins the missile report or the numbers that support the economic outlook item, but they will argue politics.

Second, policymakers are overwhelmingly "people" people. They think in terms of people, not history or trends. They see politics as people making deals, people maneuvering for advantage, people acting. Historical precedents and larger political, military, economic, or social forces register less than individuals. From a policymaker's perspective, France, China, Russia, and so on do not act; their counterparts in these countries act. History is made by powerful people like themselves.

Third, policymakers have met the people intelligence analysts write about. In many cases, they have known them for years, both in and out of power. As a result, senior officials believe that they know these people in a way that the analyst does not and cannot. It is hard to dispute this. Policymakers are therefore inclined to believe that the analyst has little to offer beyond a few facts.

Fourth, policymakers believe they read all people equally well. One reason they are where they are is because they have excellent people skills. Policymakers will acknowledge the importance of culture, but they are convinced that they can see through the culture to the person. And, given some time, they believe that they can read intentions and influence the other person, especially if they have met the individual more than once.

Tough audience. Senior officials are smart, talented, confident, comfortable in their judgment, and almost always better plugged in than analysts. If the Intelligence Community is to help policymakers make the best-informed decisions possible, then analysts must bring something to the party—in short, they need to be seen as credible sources of needed expertise. The key is not our objectivity. Senior officials more often than not know the answer they want and are looking for the intelligence to support it. The key is our ability to put the political behavior that policymakers see into a larger cultural and historical context—that they do not see—with enough sophistication to demonstrate that the context matters.

The Foundation of Credibility

"Matters" is the key word in that last sentence. Achieving a degree of insight that recognizes the importance of context rests on an analyst mastering six broad types of knowledge. Political, leadership, and country analysts must continually work to deepen their command of these subjects. Following the daily traffic can make you current; absent expertise in these areas, you cannot be credible.

First, know your own history and culture. It is the key to being aware of the innate biases that shape our perceptions of others. Specifically, it is important to know well the history that the United States has with the country you are working on. More generally, it is important to be conscious of U.S. values and the preferred American style, and how well those mesh with the values and style of the country in question. In *Special Providence: American Foreign Policy and How It Changed the World*, Walter Russell Mead argues that there are basically four different American views of the world and that the four are always competing with one another for control of U.S. foreign policy.[1] Mead may be right or wrong, but every administration has a certain bias or predisposition—a Bush administration is different than a Clinton administration. Analysts must understand that and factor it into their thinking—not because they need to tailor their product to fit the bias, but because that bias preconditions how other nations interact with us.

Equally important is the ability to recognize when American cultural biases and values are likely to lead to miscommunication or produce tension in a foreign relationship. In *The Art of War*, Sun Tzu advises that it is as important to know yourself as it is to know your enemy. The American emphasis on law and legal forms is an example. In the United States, strangers meet, come to agreement, draft a legal document, abide by it, and on occasion go to court to settle differences. What is important is the law, and the law and the procedures and trappings that surround it are held in high regard.

In China, the personal relationship is paramount. There is no agreement or understanding absent the personal relationship, which is more binding than a legal document. Indeed, law, as we understand it, is at odds with the great Confucian tradition, which stresses moral men and holds law itself in low regard. Among China's many proverbs are: "Let householders avoid litigation, for once you go to the law there is nothing but trouble"; "Though you are very angry, do not go to the law; though you are very hungry, do not be a thief"; and "No punishment on the Bench and no law below it." There are many reasons why agreements with China have been difficult to reach and harder to sustain, but one factor is probably the very different value each side attaches to written agreements. In some Asian cultures, appearance is more important than reality, which is also at odds with the U.S. emphasis on explicit, transparent, precise, and binding agreements.

Second, learn their history, but learn it as they teach it. If you are a Japanese high school student, you probably have the impression that Japan was forced into World War II, that the war was a noble effort to rid East Asia of Western colonialism, and that the two great victims in the war were the Jews, who endured the Holocaust, and the Japanese, who were victims of the atomic bomb. Japanese aggression, the "rape of Nanking," comfort women, and the systematic abuse of prisoners are not taught. And the Japanese are not unique. There is the history of the Balkans . . . and then there is the history of the Balkans according to the Serbs, according to the Croats, according to the Albanians, and so forth. Robert Kaplan, the noted author of *Balkan Ghosts* and *Eastward to Tartary*, was once asked what he liked to read. He replied: the classics of Western philosophy, ancient histories by Greeks and Romans, and travel books from the 19th and early 20th centuries, because clues to the present are in understanding the past. I would only add that the key to understanding people today is to understand their past as they understand it.

In all lives, there are key moments. These are the events that shape a person's worldview and act as filters through which subsequent events are perceived. Political, leadership, and country analysts should be able to identify the two or three seminal events in a generation's lifespan. These are the hard lessons of history that seep into a nation's bones. For my father's generation, it was the Great Depression, World War II, and the Cold War. For mine, it was Vietnam, the Cold War, and the prosperity and disillusionment of the 1960s. The events of September 11 will be one of the seminal moments for my daughter's generation. For China's aged leaders, it is the Western dominance of China, the Japanese invasion, and the Cultural Revolution. Although these events recede, the lessons that they taught—consciously or unconsciously—do not fade. Psychologists tell us that as we grow older, we become less open to new ideas and more inclined to look back when trying to see ahead.

Third, it is important that analysts study the philosophy, literature, and key thinkers of whatever country they work on. This is especially true if an analyst is working on a non-Western country or one whose philosophical outlook does not flow from the Enlightenment. The works of leading intellectuals will tell you what a people believes about itself, especially what it believes to be best about itself. It is these beliefs that shape the views of the political elite.

Philosophy and art speak volumes about what a culture believes about the nature of man, the role of government, and the temporal world. Confucian philosophy identifies five basic relationships: emperor to subject, father to son, husband to wife, elder brother to younger brother, and friend to friend. Note that only one is considered to be between equals, and friend-to-friend relationships are rare. Thus, friendship means something different in China than it does in the United States—when Beijing calls someone an "old friend of China," it is an attempt to confer a sense of obligation on the honoree—and the notion that the normal order of things is superior-inferior helps to explain why China often acts as it does. The Japanese take this to another level: Not only is relative power a defining principle of social organization, but also obligations generally flow up and not down. Classic Indian and Buddhist philosophy is more focused on the spiritual world than the temporal one, which has implications for how these societies historically have looked at progress and material achievement—the antithesis of the Protestant ethic.

An understanding of creation myths and religion (which are not always the same thing) is also very important. You cannot comprehend Western culture without knowing about Catholicism, the Reformation, and Protestantism. The Japanese creation myth explains the importance of the emperor in Japanese society, the Japanese feeling of being unique, and the relative worth of anyone who is not Japanese. Buddhism, Christianity, and most other major religions have a form of the Golden Rule; Shinto does not.

Fourth, analysts must understand the three key elements of power, which are culture bound: how power is acquired, the preferred means of wielding power, and the acceptable and unacceptable uses of power. These are the real rules of the game and they supersede constitutions. China and Japan both have long histories of real power being wielded by people who are not in the top position. Deng Xiaoping's only title at one point was Chairman of the Chinese Contract Bridge Association, and he was honorary chairman at that.

As important, a thorough understanding of how power works is the key to putting individual events in perspective and even recognizing when the game—and not just the players—is changing. In China, the military historically has been held in low regard. A proverb says: "You do not make nails out of good iron or soldiers out of good men." Some of the civil-military tension in China today is a reflection of this ancient attitude. Mao's tactics in launching the Cultural Revolution went beyond accepted political norms, and much of what has happened in China since then reflects a conscious effort on the part of the leadership to see that the system does not and cannot produce another Mao. Because scholarship is so revered, students in Asia have a moral authority that students in the West lack. Asian students see themselves as a moral beacon for society. They have weight and their actions have a political significance that often exceeds their raw numbers, which helps to explain the Chinese government's reaction to the students in Tienanmen Square, and the historic sensitivity to student demonstrations in South Korea, Indonesia, and Thailand.

Fifth, study the popular culture. How people play, what they read, and which entertainments they prefer say a great deal about how individuals relate to one another. Popular culture determines what is considered fair and proper and defines obligations between people and groups, characteristics that shape the attitudes, prejudices, and expectations of other nations. Wellington's assessment that Waterloo was won on the playing fields of Eton may or may not be correct, but the fact that the notion has become part of what it means to be British—as well as notions of fair play and what's cricket—speaks to expected and accepted behavior. The bold, unexpected stroke from the sword of a samurai that defeats an adversary in a single blow is much admired in Japanese culture; in the United States, it is considered cowardly behavior when its expression is Pearl Harbor. Two of the most entertaining and enlightening books on Japanese popular culture are Ian Buruma's *Behind the Mask* and Robert Whiting's *You Gotta Have Wa*. The first is about Japanese movies and comic books and the second examines baseball in Japan and what happens to Americans when they play there.

And this works both ways. Foreign impressions of—and, more importantly, expectations about—the United States are shaped by American films and television. For better or worse, violent westerns, *Baywatch,* and *Jerry Springer* are synonymous with the United States for many in Europe and Asia. Conclusions about American strength and resolve drawn from an erroneous reading of American popular culture and materialism misled Japanese military leaders in the 1930s and Saddam Hussein in the 1990s. They will probably not be the last leaders to make this miscalculation.

Sixth, there is no substitute for the ability to speak or read the language of the country. Beyond the practical benefits of being able to travel easily, read widely, and converse with ordinary people, language can provide insights into what other cultures value and how they see the world. When written together, the Chinese symbols for "woman" and "male child" make the word "good." The symbol for "roof" written above the symbol for "woman" means "peace." The words for "danger" and "opportunity" when combined together become the word "crisis." The analyst with language can get out of the capital, ride the local transportation, and gain the feel of a place that is not possible otherwise. The ability to start a sentence with "when I was in" adds greatly to an analyst's credibility when the place is not the capital city. Everyone gets to the capital.

It is important for analysts to recognize that language is the test of choice for the non-expert. It is an easy measure; either you have it or you do not. And if you do not have command of the language, you are less credible in the eyes of many whom you are trying to serve. Pointing to the lack of language skills is the easiest way for critics to cast doubt on an individual's expertise and call into question the quality of the analysis.

From Credibility to Impact

The six broad areas of knowledge help to build credibility, but DI tradecraft holds the key to impact. Nothing kills credibility quicker than the unsupported assertion. In briefings and reports, every use of such words as "suggests," "could," and "likely" should send up a flare in the analyst's mind. Unless these troublesome words are bolstered by facts or demonstrated expertise, we are just another opinion in a town full of opinion—and, for a sizeable portion of our audience on any issue, we have the wrong opinion. The fact that the analyst is an expert in his or her own right carries very little weight for all the reasons that constitute the "four facts of life" discussed earlier.

The problem is not the use of "suggests" or similar verbs, or even the judgment itself. The problem is that too often what is behind the judgment is invisible to the audience. When no hard evidence is available and analysts are forced to rely on their expertise and experience in making a call, the tradecraft solution is to allow the expertise behind the judgment to show through by using an example from one of the six broad areas of knowledge to illustrate or amplify the point. A historical precedent, the parsing of a foreign word or phrase, or a reference to cultural practice has all been used to good effect in the past to buttress a judgment or establish credibility before offering the judgment.

If there is no evidence or precedent or cultural factoid to support the judgment—if we are in effect listing possible outcomes—then we should not make the judgment at all because it tends to undercut not only the credibility of the current work but also the credibility of future work. Tossing out possibilities does not raise the level of the debate or help the policymaker make better decisions. Unsupported assertions only add to the clutter. The exception to this rule is when we are specifically asked to list or rank possibilities; even in this circumstance, however, we owe the policy audience our rationale for settling on a particular set of possible developments.[2]

Analysts can do three things to help themselves when the evidence is thin and the situation is moving quickly:

- Articulate and examine their assumptions about the country they work on and the problem at hand. If an analyst cannot articulate what he or she assumes to be true, then the analyst has only the faintest idea of where he or she can go wrong. Assumptions more often than not are the underpinnings of unsupported assertions and frequently are the product of an analyst's command (or lack of command) of the six broad areas of knowledge. Because analysts are so close to the issue, managers and reviewers bear a special responsibility to probe for assumptions and question their validity.

■ Solicit the views of other experts. When analysts can cite other experts, whether private sector or foreign liaison, they add to their own credibility—experts talk to other experts—as well as buttress their argument.

■ Use hindsight in fast-moving situations. A colleague of mine made it a practice to reread older reporting during a crisis. From clandestine reports in particular, he gained insights into the present. Things that he had missed previously, that had not made sense, or that he had not fully appreciated jumped off the page and suddenly had a powerful ability to explain and predict.

Final Observations

The bar is higher for political, leadership, and country analysts than it is for others, but all analysts, regardless of discipline, have a credibility challenge. Economic analysts writing for economists and military analysts writing for the military audience must pass the same tests with their policymakers as political analysts face with all policymakers. Achieving a passing grade lies in mastering the six areas of expertise. The military analyst who speaks the language and has walked the ground has greater credibility than one who does not and has not. The economic analyst who understands a country's culture and knows how values may influence choice has an edge, especially when the issue is less the consequences of a policy than which policy a leader may opt for. When analysts switch accounts, they take on an obligation to study the history, culture, and language, as well as the current developments of their new country. To do less is to do our job less well. To do less is to be less than fully proficient on matters of critical importance to our national security.

Lastly, our credibility is on the line every time we write or brief. We can strengthen credibility gradually over time, or we can lose it in a heartbeat. In either case, we start all over again every 4 years when the policymaking community changes. It is a fact of life.

Notes

[1] According to Mead, the four schools are the Hamiltonian, which favors international commerce and institutions; the Jeffersonian, which frowns on international entanglements; the Jacksonian, which does not shy away from using military force; and the Wilsonian, which is internationalist but based on moral principles. See Walter Russell Mead, *Special Providence: American Foreign Policy and How It Changed the World* (New York: Alfred Knopf, 2001).

[2] For an example of how the agency handled one such tasking exceptionally well, see Bob Woodward, *Bush at War* (New York: Simon and Schuster, 2002), 132–133.

Chapter 25

Fixing the Problem of Analytical Mindsets: Alternative Analysis

Roger Z. George

The main difference between professional scholars or intelligence officers on the one hand, and all other people on the other hand, is that the former are supposed to have had more training in the techniques of guarding against their own intellectual frailties.

—Sherman Kent, 1949[1]

The surprise to me is not that there have been and will continue to be surprises, but that we are surprised that there are surprises. . . . As von Clausewitz wrote, "The unexpected is the prince of the battlefield."

—Donald Rumsfeld, 1998

I am conscious every day of how important it is for our analysts to challenge the conventional wisdom, to separate what we really know from what we merely think, to consider alternative outcomes—in short, not to fall victim to mindset, overconfidence, or anyone's pet paradigm.

—John McLaughlin, 2001

Ever since Pearl Harbor, the U.S. Intelligence Community, senior civilian policymakers, and military strategists have been fixated on improving their understanding of America's adversaries and on averting major surprises that would threaten the Nation's security. The controversy over the October 2002 National Intelligence Estimate (NIE) on Iraqi weapons of mass destruction (WMD) is merely the latest example of how reality can deviate from our best attempts to characterize it. In many, if not most, cases, the paternity of surprise is usually traced to an intelligence failure, which can take many forms. Failure can stem from failures of access, such as the inability to penetrate a terrorist cell; from the missed collection of an event or activity, such as the 1998 Indian nuclear test; and from ineffective dissemination of intelligence information, as was the case prior to the events of September 11.

Failure can also be the product of flawed work by intelligence analysts or of flaws in how intelligence information is understood and used by policymakers and military commanders. This chapter focuses on the tradecraft of analysis and the ways in which analysts work to test the integrity of the data they receive, as well as the integrity of the inferences and conclusions they draw from it. The chapter also seeks to show that efforts to improve that tradecraft have been a continuing concern, and it focuses specifically on the problem of *mindset*—the cognitive bias brought to each situation by analysts and by the policymakers and military leaders who depend on their work. Combating the problem of mindsets, both in preparing and in using intelligence products, is a key challenge for both analyst and user. There are techniques that have proven helpful in dealing with the problem of mindsets, and this chapter explores how the Central Intelligence Agency (CIA) came to see the value of these techniques as well as the challenges they present.

The "Second Oldest Profession" and a Contemporary Concern

Lamenting the state of intelligence during the Napoleonic War, Carl von Clausewitz noted, "Many intelligence reports are contradictory; even more are false, and most are uncertain."[2] Clausewitz aptly captures the frustration and disappointment that so many generals and statesmen express with the quality of the intelligence on which they must base critical decisions. Good intelligence analysis can aid America's strategists in understanding enemy intentions and capabilities, in considering the broader context of events and how other actors might behave, and in forecasting the short- and long-term risks and opportunities that different courses of action present. Ultimately, however, strategists, no less than intelligence analysts, must develop a sharp appreciation for what intelligence can and cannot be expected to provide, and they must rely on their own intellectual abilities and expertise when reaching momentous decisions of war and peace. The success of their policies often depends on how well strategists—not just intelligence analysts—accurately assess, understand, and exploit the international environment in which they are operating.

Mindsets can pose a fatal trap in that process: history is full of examples in which commanders have gotten it wrong because they held to an inaccurate picture of what others valued, or what their goals, intentions, or capabilities were. A simple definition of a *mindset* might be a set of expectations through which a human being sees the world. Over time, the strategist and intelligence analyst will develop these expectations based on how past events have occurred; each will draw general conclusions about the relationships among important international phenomena, about how states typically behave (for example, maximizing power vis-à-vis others), or about the motivations of foreign leaders. As new events occur, data consistent with earlier patterns of beliefs are more likely to be accepted as valid, while data that conflict with an analyst's expectations are discounted or set aside. It is human nature, according to many psychological studies, for individuals to "perceive what they expect to perceive," and holding such mindsets is virtually unavoidable.[3] The more expert one becomes, the firmer becomes one's set of expectations about the world. While these mindsets can be helpful in sorting through incoming data, they become an Achilles' heel to professional strategists or intelligence analysts when they become out of touch with new international dynamics. Knowing when a mindset is becoming obsolete and in need of revision can test the mettle of the best expert.

There are no perfect or permanent solutions to this challenge. However, over the past 10 years, recognition has grown that the application of rigorous analytic techniques can help significantly in averting the likelihood of surprise by uncovering analytical mindsets and sensitizing policymakers to the inherent uncertainty surrounding the major international developments they confront. America's strategists would do well to understand these advances in analytical tradecraft in order to encourage the Intelligence Community to exploit them better and to guard against susceptibility to distorted or inaccurate views of the world.

The study of intelligence analysis is a relatively new field. While spying is an old art, and the exploitation and analysis of the spy's information have always been part of the business, few practitioners concentrated on how best to organize analysis for the best possible results. In the United States, multidisciplinary intelligence analysis—as a central and discrete function—began only as recently as the 1940s, when a small group of historians was assembled as the Research and Analysis (RA) branch within what soon became the Office of Strategic Services. RA was the precursor to today's CIA Directorate of Intelligence (DI). From the beginning, the problem of mindsets was recognized as one of the key impediments to effective intelligence analysis.

Sherman Kent—a Yale historian, wartime member of the Office of Strategic Services, and faculty member at the National War College in 1947—was one of the earliest intelligence officers to identify the problem of mindsets as a barrier to proper interpretation of international developments. Kent became known as the father of modern American intelligence analysis for his efforts to codify the elements of good intelligence analysis and to argue that intelligence analysis is another social science discipline with its own set of methodological problems. As a member of CIA Board of National Estimates, established in 1949, Kent spent most of his career trying to instill academic rigor into the new profession of intelligence analysis. In a groundbreaking book, *Strategic Intelligence for American World Policy*, he emphasized the importance of marshalling the best minds with access to the most complete information in order to give U.S. policymakers the foresight necessary to make good decisions. If expertise and information were available, applying the scientific method would ensure the development of the right conclusions. Assembling facts, developing hypotheses, and critically weighing evidence was the mission of the intelligence analyst. Moreover, the measure of good analysis was the ability to establish one or more hypotheses that best approximate a situation's ground truth.

Yet Kent also warned that the intelligence profession had its own unique methodological problems. First, "in our business we are as likely to be faced by the problem of a plethora of raw intelligence as by one of its paucity. In many of our tasks we have so large a volume of data that no single person can read, evaluate, and mentally file it all."[4] How, then, can intelligence analysts guard against the difficulties inherent in analyzing a mountain of data, much of which may be incomplete, inaccurate, or false, without running the risk of improperly interpreting it? Second, Kent acknowledged that analysts come to their profession possessing different temperaments and abilities in conceiving alternative hypotheses about the world: "Some minds are fertile in the generation of new hypotheses and roam freely and widely among them," while "other minds not merely are sterile in this respect but actively resist the new idea."[5] Producing the best strategic intelligence requires people who are not only imaginative in their hypotheses but also able to identify and adjust for their own analytical preconceptions and prejudices. Despite all the technological advances made in U.S. intelligence capabilities, the battle against mindsets, or what Kent described as "intellectual frailties," remains unfinished business.

An Enduring Analytical Problem: Mindsets

One of the most challenging tasks for the analyst is identifying the proper analytical framework for interpreting incomplete information. For example, in hindsight, we know that information existed on and before December 7, 1941, that might have warned us of a surprise attack against the U.S. Fleet in Honolulu; instead, partly because of Japan's war in China and occupation of Indochina in 1941, we anticipated an attack in East Asia and were unprepared to think about an attack on what we might now call the Homeland. A comment attributed to Secretary of the Interior Harold Ickes reveals a mindset that also contributed to the disaster: "It seems to be pretty well understood . . . that the Japanese are pretty poor airmen." In 1950, we had reports of increasing Chinese military movements but dismissed the possibility of China entering the Korean War. In September 1962, the U.S. Intelligence Community reported increasing Soviet shipments of military equipment to Cuba but discounted as too provocative the possibility of the Soviets introducing offensive missiles to be a rational decision. In defending his own incorrect estimate, Sherman Kent wrote in 1964, "No estimating process can be expected to divine exactly when the enemy is about to make a dramatically wrong decision. We were not brought up to *under*estimate our enemies." Whether this was *mirror-imaging* (imposing an American definition of rationality on an adversary) or simply a lack of understanding how a foreign leadership assesses risks and opportunities, the results were disastrous for the Intelligence Community generally and Kent personally.[6]

The misinterpretation of Soviet intentions in 1962 was not to be the last time the CIA and other American intelligence analysts fell into the mindset trap. Nor have we been alone in suffering from this symptom. In October 1973, for example, the Yom Kippur War broke out, despite repeated U.S. intelligence assessments that the probability of war was low. In the face of mounting evidence that Egypt and Syria were mobilizing, both U.S. and Israeli intelligence analysts continued to insist that this data could be read as *defensive* rather than *offensive* movement. The dominant analytical mindset was that the Arab state militaries were inferior to Israeli military might and could not possibly harbor realistic expectations of victory against the Israel Defense Forces.[7] U.S. and Israeli analysts were ultimately proven correct; the combined Syrian and Egyptian armies were not able to defeat Israel. Nonetheless, Arab political leaders were able to achieve far more important political objectives—namely, inflicting a costly tactical surprise on Israel, puncturing its sense of invulnerability, and forcing the United States and Soviet Union to reinvigorate a stalled negotiating process. As Henry Kissinger recounts, Egyptian President Anwar Sadat told us what he was doing, and we refused to believe him.[8] Again and again, whether it was the Soviet invasion of Afghanistan or Saddam Hussein's

1990 attack on Kuwait, analysts have had to admit that their set of assumptions about foreign actors' intentions have been frequently wide of the mark.

Writing more recently about analytical tradecraft, Richards Heuer has identified a lack of imagination rather than a lack of information as the culprit. Analysts naturally favor information that fits their well-formed mental models and often dismiss other information that might support an alternative hypothesis. Or they minimize the importance of intelligence gaps and foreign deception and denial efforts, believing U.S. intelligence systems are spoof-proof or American analysts are too clever to be outwitted by third-class intelligence services. Even more invidious, the more expert one becomes, the more likely one is to discount the possibility of surprise. "The disadvantage of a mindset," notes Heuer, "is that it can color and control our perception to the extent that an experienced specialist may be among the last to see what is really happening when events take a new and unexpected turn."[9]

Ironically, despite its impressive record of developing sophisticated analytical methodologies to understand closed societies and complex international trends, the CIA has not been able to overcome the fundamental challenge of eliminating these human cognitive blinders to unexpected events. Despite the efforts of Kent and others, as the Cold War drew to a close, senior intelligence managers became more aware of their discipline's weak intellectual underpinnings.[10]

Tradecraft 2000: Building Blocks for Alternative Analysis

With the collapse of the Soviet Union and outbreak of the first Gulf War, senior intelligence managers began to take stock of their analytical profession and its deficiencies. In 1993–1994, a major reappraisal of DI tradecraft found that what really mattered to policymakers was not the opinion of DI analysts, but instead "what we know and how we know it." A clear distinction was needed between what were known facts and what were analysts' findings. Moreover, these findings were no longer considered unassailable, particularly if policymakers were not able to understand readily the analytic assumptions and logic that supported those conclusions. As the somewhat critical Paul Wolfowitz put it, "I frequently think I am as capable of coming up with an informed opinion about a matter as any number of the people within the Intelligence Community who feel that they have been uniquely anointed with this responsibility."[11]

Out of this review came the most noticeable change in CIA analytical tradecraft since the establishment of the Directorate of Intelligence. In simple terms, new DI guidelines were crafted to make CIA analysis transparent to the policymaker, which paralleled similar guidance that General Colin Powell gave to his intelligence staff:

- What do we know? How do we know it?
- What do we *not* know?
- And, only lastly, what do we think?[12]

To inculcate these basic principles of good analysis, the DI conducted 2-week-long workshops for all intelligence analysts and many managers. Termed *Tradecraft 2000*, these workshops became virtually mandatory for junior analysts to strengthen their craft. Many first-line managers of analysts had also internalized these principles by serving as instructors for the Tradecraft 2000 courses.

A new art form called *linchpin analysis* was created. Intelligence assessments were to be constructed by using the following steps:

- identify the main uncertain factors or key variables (drivers) that will determine an outcome
- identify working assumptions (linchpin premises) about how the key drivers will operate
- advance convincing evidence and reasoning to support the linchpin premises
- address any indicators or signposts that would render linchpin premises unreliable
- ask what dramatic events or triggers could reverse the expected outcomes.[13]

Behind this seemingly simple recipe for good analysis stood a radical admission. Namely, CIA had to regain credibility with its policymakers by establishing more rigor and transparency in its analysis. Moreover, CIA was convinced that to remain relevant to the policy process, it would have to provide more customized support to policymakers. Instead of marketing general assessments to the broadest possible set of consumers—from Assistant Secretaries down to the junior desk officer—the DI would aim to support senior-level policymakers and tailor its analysis to their specific intelligence needs. What flowed from this new vision was a redesign of many intelligence products, in which the DI would target a very small number of customers who already knew their issues extremely well; moreover, in some cases it also meant providing sensitive information regarding sources and methods in order to give senior policymakers a firmer basis for placing confidence in CIA assessments. Simultaneously, the DI began deploying increasing numbers of senior officers to key policymaking agencies (such as the National Security Council and Departments of State and Defense) and providing cabinet and subcabinet level customers with daily personal briefers who could provide them with the latest information tailored to their agendas and give them a direct channel to CIA expertise.

The Jeremiah and Rumsfeld Commissions: Push for Greater Change and Alternative Analysis

By the mid 1990s, in the midst of what would prove to be nearly a decade of shrinking intelligence budgets, there was growing recognition that a customer-focused approach to intelligence analysis served to prioritize limited analytical resources. By 1995, the CIA analytic ranks had shrunk by 17 percent from 1990 levels. By the end of the 1990s, the DI had declined by 22 percent.[14] In the post-Cold War order, fewer analysts meant satisfying only senior civilian and military leaders' intelligence needs, focusing analytical attention to their specific agenda items and accepting a lower level of global coverage against second- and third-order intelligence topics.

Then, in May 1998, India exploded five nuclear devices at an underground test facility without any CIA warning to policymakers. Soon after, the Pakistanis did the expected and conducted tests of their own. Congressional oversight committees demanded to know how such an intelligence surprise could occur. Responding to this pressure, as well as Clinton administration officials' grumbling about the lack of advance warning, Director of Central Intelligence (DCI) George Tenet asked retired Admiral David Jeremiah to review the record to see what had led to this failure to warn the administration. While the report remains classified, Admiral Jeremiah noted at his June 1998 press conference that his "bottom line is that both the intelligence *and* the policy communities had an underlying mindset going into these tests that the BJP [Bharatiya Janata Party—the newly governing Indian party] would behave as we behave." As in the 1962 Cuban Special National Intelligence Estimate, CIA analysts were accused of harboring a mindset that hampered their ability to see the world as a foreign government might. Going further, Admiral Jeremiah proposed that CIA analysts be more aggressive in thinking through how the other side might behave: "you could argue that you need to have a contrarian view that might be part of our warning process, ought to include some divergent thinkers who look at the same evidence and come to a different conclusion and then you test that different set of conclusions against other evidence to see if it could be valid."[15]

Almost simultaneously, the 1998 Commission to Assess the Ballistic Missile Threat to the United States issued a similar assessment. It found "analysts unwilling to make estimates that extended beyond the hard evidence they had in hand, which effectively precluded developing and testing *alternative* hypotheses about actual foreign programs taking place."[16] Congress asked the commission, which was headed by Donald Rumsfeld, to review the Intelligence Community analysis of the global ballistic missile forecast because there was significant concern that the National Intelligence Estimate had played down the long-term threat at a time when the Clinton administration was deliberating on the deployment of a national missile defense system. The commission provided its views to the congressional oversight committees in July 1998. Its general conclusions were that "the threat to the U.S. posed by these emerging capabilities is broader, more mature and evolving more rapidly than has been reported in estimates and reports by the Intelligence Community."[17] The commission found that if analysts had considered not only what they knew but also what they did *not* know, they might have been able to "employ alternative hypotheses" and thereby develop better indicators and collection priorities that could have narrowed information gaps and thus led to better assessments. More importantly, commissioners believed that the result would be "earlier warning than if analysts wait for proof of a capability in the form of hard evidence of a test or a deployment."[18]

These two commissions' recommendations, along with a separate in-house Inspector General Report on alternative analysis, renewed interest in and attention to the state of DI analytical tradecraft.[19] Among other works, Richards Heuer's own book on mindsets became required reading among senior intelligence officers. Published in 1999, his *Psychology of Intelligence Analysis* became the intellectual foundation for a major revamping of DI analytical training. As Heuer saw it, the Directorate's analytical objectives should be to:

- encourage products that clearly delineate their assumptions and chains of inference and specify the degree and source of uncertainty involved in the conclusions
- support analyses that periodically reexamine key problems from the ground up in order to avoid the pitfalls of the incremental approach
- emphasize procedures that expose and elaborate alternative points of view
- educate consumers about the limitations as well as the capabilities of intelligence analysis; define a set of realistic expectations as a standard against which to judge analytical performance.[20]

Collectively, these developments led to a new push for improvements in analytic practice, specifically the adoption of techniques to deal with the recurring problem of mindsets that shaped analytic judgments.

What Is Alternative Analysis?

Alternative analysis (AA) seeks to impose an explicit self-review by using specific techniques to reveal unconscious analytical assumptions or to challenge weak evidence or logic and to consider alternative hypotheses or outcomes even in the absence of convincing evidence. Simply put, intelligence analysts are now obliged to question explicitly and rigorously the assumptions that underlie their conclusions and guard against conventional wisdom masking a fundamental change in the dynamics of an issue. In many ways, AA merely builds upon the earlier Tradecraft 2000 emphasis that encouraged analysts to identify linchpin assumptions, key drivers, indicators, and triggers to future events. Unlike Tradecraft 2000, however, AA seeks to display this analytical self-review to the policymaker and not merely to use it as an in-house critique. The most powerful techniques include:

- Key Assumptions Checks
- Devil's Advocacy
- Team A/Team B
- Red Cell exercises
- Contingency "What If" Analysis
- High-Impact/Low-Probability Analysis
- Scenario Development.

There are similarities and overlap in some of these techniques, and most are designed to highlight uncertainty and identify intelligence collection gaps. What follows is a short description of the techniques and how they can be exploited.

Key Assumptions Checks. When drafting important analysis that contains far-reaching conclusions, analysts must identify key linchpin assumptions as well as key drivers or factors that shape these assumptions. By explicitly citing the assumptions and drivers, analysts can test the validity of the relationships between the two. Take, for example, analysis that concludes a foreign government is likely to introduce painful economic reforms without creating major instability. In this case, the analyst might need to identify as a key assumption that "security forces will remain loyal and willing to use lethal force to maintain order." If that assumption does not hold, or if there should be signs of dissatisfaction within the security services, then perhaps the analyst's judgment that the leadership will impose reforms is less well founded. By making a list of critical assumptions and drivers transparent to the policymaker, analysts allow the reader to see the argumentation behind the key conclusion, consider whether the assumptions are valid, and understand what evidence might then lead analysts to alter their judgments.

Devil's Advocacy. This technique is most valuable for challenging a deeply ingrained view of an issue. When confidence in an important, perhaps war-or-peace, judgment is high, the use of such contrarian analysis can be more than justified. To be sure, making such a case sometimes involves a contrived argument that selectively uses information to challenge conventional wisdom. The art of devil's advocacy is to turn accepted linchpin assumptions and key drivers on their heads. For example, the conventional assumption about India's Bharatiya Janata Party in 1998 was that it would not test a nuclear device because it was a leading a fragile coalition. A devil's advocate might have argued, on the contrary, that the key to stabilizing a weak coalition would be a dramatic symbolic act to mobilize Indian nationalism behind the newly elected government. In May 1998, that view would have been contrarian and not supported by official Indian statements given to the U.S. Government; however, in hindsight, a contrary analysis might have sensitized U.S. policymakers to uncertainty about how a newly elected and unproven government might perceive its own national interests. Similarly, a devil's advocate might have been assigned the task of arguing that Saddam Hussein intended to invade Kuwait in 1990 in order to challenge the conventional view that Iraq was using a high-stakes bluff to extract concessions from other Arab states.

Ever since 1973, Israeli military intelligence has performed devil's advocacy selectively to convince itself that its neighbors' military maneuvers are not disguised preparations for war. The Defense Intelligence Agency has employed this technique periodically to challenge conventional views of strategic military issues. One need not believe in the position to argue a contrary case—indeed, the reality is that most devil's advocacy proves to be unpersuasive. Still, the exercise has value in raising confidence levels in and perhaps refining the prevailing analytic judgment. However, its chief drawback is that contrived advocacy can be too easily dismissed if senior intelligence officials and policymakers do not put much credence in the technique.

Team A/Team B. This technique has been used periodically when major strategic issues have been judged too important to let conventional wisdom drive policy. For example, in 1976, then-DCI George Bush invited a Team B of outside experts to examine National Intelligence Estimates of Soviet strategic force developments and to propose its own conclusions.[21] Similarly, the 1998 Rumsfeld Commission was, in essence, a Team B exercise that challenged the underlying assumptions of CIA analysis of foreign ballistic missile developments. The technique, however, need not be used only when national policy issues are at stake. Whenever there are strongly held opposing views of an issue, there is utility in laying out each side's linchpin assumptions and key drivers, and then explicitly describing how the data support their conclusions. In presenting both sides of an argument, advocates on either team are exposed to an alternative way of thinking about an issue. Thus, it opens a dialogue over analytical assumptions and logic rather than simply focusing on the key conclusions of either side's analysis. Unlike devil's advocacy, this approach is not contrived analysis. In the real world, there are usually analysts on both sides of an issue. Thus, the Team A/Team B method can take advantage of analytical disagreements and put both sides of important issues before the policymaker.

Red Cell Exercises. As the Jeremiah Commission noted, the Intelligence Community should make more frequent use of a red cell approach to analyzing foreign government behavior and avoid the tendency to mirror-image our adversaries. A *red cell* is a group of analysts assembled to roleplay senior leaders of a foreign government or entity and to propose courses of actions that would complicate American foreign and security policy objectives. Through this technique, analysts attempt to step out of an American strategic logic and instead reflect the mode of thinking by an adversary. To be effective, the red cell draws from country experts who understand the culture as well as the political system; to the extent possible, these analysts try to look at the situation from the enemy's vantage point and produce recommendations that would approximate the cultural norms, decisionmaking style, and nationalist rhetoric used within actual foreign governing circles. As a written art form, then, a red cell might have produced a briefing book for Saddam Hussein or Slobodan Milosevic on how to counter American diplomatic and military pressures.

These red cell products are aimed at provoking thinking among policymakers and strategists and are not designed to be consensus-driven assessments. They are seldom formally coordinated with mainline analytical units. Various agencies have used red cell analysis to model how foreign leaders might develop diplomatic strategies, conduct negotiations, or wage asymmetric warfare against the United States. Most recently, in response to the terrorist attacks on September 11, the DCI has established his own red cell to "think unconventionally about the full range of analytic issues." This work is shared, but not coordinated, with other offices in the Directorate of Intelligence. It is explicitly identified as "intended to provoke thought rather than provide authoritative assessment." The subject matter can range widely, from thinking like al Qaeda cells to understanding what kinds of information campaigns would be most effective in countering terrorist recruitment propaganda. One difficulty with this kind of outside-the-box analysis is that it can blur the line between intelligence analysis and policy advocacy. For example, it is a short step from postulating what a credible terrorist recruitment strategy might be to identifying vulnerabilities of such a strategy and proposing measures that could undermine it. Red cell analysts are sometimes encouraged to think up creative courses of action that might undermine adversaries, without any expectation that they would reflect the analysts' policy preferences. Properly done and with the explicit caveats about its intended purposes, such red cell work has found an eager policymaking audience and contributed to more creative strategic planning.

Contingency "What If" Analysis. While most conventional intelligence analysis focuses on what analysts believe is the most likely outcome, contingency "what if" analysis focuses on what the causes and consequences of an unlikely event might be. For example, what if India decided to conduct nuclear tests and sought to deceive the

United States? The analysts would then be forced to consider what motives might be behind such a decision; they also would ask what the signposts or indicators might be that we would expect to see, or, alternately, how the Indians might try to hide preparations from us, and what the indications would be of such deception. Moreover, how might the Indians justify conducting a test despite expected American displeasure? Thinking through these sorts of questions forces analysts and policymakers to appreciate what they do not know as much as what they do know. Could the Indians be actively misleading us? Do U.S. diplomats have access to the small circle of decisionmakers who would actually make such a decision? Would a foreign government official lie to U.S. diplomats? How might a newly elected government judge the results to be more positive than we would? The virtue of such "what if" thinking is that it forces analysts to get out of the most obvious American ways of thinking. Unlike devil's advocacy, the thinking is not contrived to argue a specific outcome regardless of the merits of the case; instead, it asks the awkward question that might lead to further questions regarding the quality of U.S. intelligence information, the presence of deception, or a possibly faulty linchpin assumption that underlies current intelligence judgments. It might have permitted policymakers to see that the Indians could easily tolerate U.S. criticism and sanctions if it caused more trouble for the Pakistanis—who shortly thereafter tested in response—and led to wider popular support for a newly elected Indian government.

High-Impact/Low-Probability Analysis (HI/LP). Like "what if" analysis, this technique focuses on the examination of unlikely events, but ones that would have huge consequences for the United States. Analysts accept that an event such as an Indian nuclear test has significant implications and thus focus on the possible ways by which the Indian government might decide to conduct a test. In this case, analysts look for plausible combinations of domestic and international factors that could precipitate an unlikely event to occur. What changes in key assumptions, or different sets of key drivers, would have to be present to overturn the current analytical line that India would not test a nuclear device? Laying out such argumentation is probably most useful as a longer analysis for a policymaker who is already expert on the issues and likely shares the conventional wisdom. The high-impact/low-probability analysis is more valuable to such specialists as a check on their own thinking and less valuable to the policymaker who is a generalist and does not have a well-formed opinion on the issue.

Scenario Development. When analysts face more mysteries (unknowable) than secrets (discoverable), it can be very useful to address intelligence questions by using the technique of multiple scenario development. This powerful approach explores a range of possible outcomes when there are many unknowns and no certainty about a single outcome. Typically, a group of experts will use structured brainstorming to identify key factors and forces that will shape an issue. First, experts will agree that a focal issue (for example, the testing of nuclear weapons in South Asia) is sufficiently important to justify exploring a range of futures. Next, experts describe what they believe is the conventional wisdom and general assumptions about the issue (such as a belief that neither India nor Pakistan would test because of international condemnation and possible sanctions). In the course of their brainstorming, analysts list areas of relative certainty (relative economic/political dependence on the United States, technological capabilities to test, government control over nuclear materials, decisionmaking processes, and so forth) and identify critical uncertainties (stability of governing coalitions, role of public opinion, and perception of threat). Among those areas of uncertainty, analysts then select two or more key uncertainties (defined as *drivers*) and develop a matrix of possible alternative scenarios.

One possible scenario matrix, for example, might display the relative stability of the Indian government coalition (from highly stable to highly unstable) as one axis and array a range of Indian threat perceptions (from highly benign to highly threatening) as the other axis. This will produce at least four different conditions—a highly stable or unstable coalition within a highly threatening or very benign environment. Analysts can then openly speculate as to the likely actions taken by a government under these different conditions. They can also select the scenarios that are most divergent from the conventional wisdom and most threatening to U.S. interests for further examination. Typically, analysts will look for key developments or indicators that are associated with a specific scenario; these signposts will indicate the emergence of a scenario that will challenge U.S. policy objectives. The virtue of scenario analysis is that it allows the decisionmaker to imagine what might happen under a range of plausible outcomes and what actions might be needed to reduce the damage or take advantage of the opportunities posed. While the conventional wisdom ("India will not test") can be described as one plausible scenario, analysts are able to expose policymakers to alternative futures that challenge them to think through what they might face if current analysis is operating under faulty assumptions or with less than complete information.

Institutionalizing Change

As a first sign of senior CIA support to improve analytical tradecraft, the Sherman Kent School for Intelligence Analysis was opened in May 2000. Created with the primary mission of developing a more professional analytical cadre, the school now offers a wide variety of courses, including a 4-month, entry-level career analyst course as well as discipline-specific training on military, scientific, economic, leadership, and political analysis techniques. The Kent School's new analyst training includes AA techniques,[22] specifically aimed at more explicit testing of prevailing analytical judgments. This course emphasizes the use of contrarian analysis, making prevailing linchpin assumptions explicit in DI writing and identifying best practices in alternative analysis that could be adopted throughout the DI. Since 1999, AA workshops have instructed more than one-third of the Directorate's analysts—as well as other Intelligence Community analysts—in the proper use of these techniques. As an outgrowth of the AA workshops, the Directorate of Intelligence also produced a short primer that described the purposes and applications of different AA techniques that could be used by individual analysts or teams to challenge their own thinking and to stimulate intelligence analysis that would sensitize policymakers to the uncertainties surrounding some key intelligence judgments.[23]

Limitations of Alternative Analysis

The second pitfall in using AA techniques is that some of the methodologies are arcane. A key assumptions check assumes that the reader has a fairly sophisticated grasp of an issue. The decision to use this or other techniques will always rest on knowing the customers, their level of knowledge, and their interest in having CIA challenge their thinking on a vital issue. Naturally, there always will be senior policymakers who are not experts in their own right and who will wonder why the CIA is questioning its own analysis of a critical issue. Moreover, unless policymakers have actually been through a scenario development exercise, they probably will not understand the process by which scenarios were developed. Very few have the luxury of participating in lengthy workshops that scenario exercises often require.

In truth, some of these techniques turn out to be of most benefit to those who use them. Experience has shown that analysts as well as policymakers who have participated in scenario development workshops value the brainstorming exercise but find the written product less helpful. Inevitably, the scenarios cannot capture all the interesting insights shared among experts and policymakers during the 1- or 2-day workshops.[24] Similarly, the value of devil's advocacy is primarily its challenging the weaker assumptions or evidentiary base of a current intelligence judgment. Since most of this contrarian analysis will be proven wrong and reaffirm the conventional wisdom rather than replace it, there is little value in publishing it. Only when devil's advocacy is judged useful to provoke a dialogue between policymakers and intelligence analysts would it serve the DI interest to disseminate such analysis. In the end, the process of using unconventional analytical techniques is where the most learning occurs. The reported findings are not always judged as insightful as the critical thinking that went into the process.

Third, using alternative analysis will create friction within analytical ranks if there is a well-accepted view of important intelligence issues. Trying to argue against the current analytical line can be seen as undermining teamwork or even a sign of personal self-promotion. Hence, unless there is higher-level receptivity to AA, the analyst eager to try out devil's advocacy or other contrarian techniques against an analytical unit's conventional wisdom could face considerable resistance, if not open hostility. Senior intelligence leaders must encourage the use of these techniques as an important tradecraft tool that all analysts should practice. Even so, when strong views are held within an analytical office, trying to set up a Team A/Team B exercise or conduct devil's advocacy against the prevailing wisdom can set analysts on edge. The use of public investigative commissions, like the ones chaired by Admiral Jeremiah and Donald Rumsfeld, tend to accentuate the adversarial nature of these reviews. Many analysts will react defensively to the notion of using a Team A/Team B approach, if it is perceived to be a blatant condemnation of their analysis and tradecraft. Some analysts can become so personally invested in being proven right that their obstinacy derails any hope of understanding the assumptions and logic behind analytical judgments or of learning how to improve analysis.

Fourth, alternative analysis can be resource-intensive. Many managers believe it must be used sparingly and only on the most important topics. Few intelligence analysts, much less their managers, will wish to invest the time and effort into conducting

AA on a third-order issue that does not confront policymakers with major difficulties. To focus on a highly unlikely event that will not make a difference to anyone in Washington would be just as foolish as not conducting it against critical issues where the risks of being wrong might be catastrophic. Clearly, where there are major equities at stake and where DI invests substantial resources—such as on Iraq, Iran, North Korea, China, and counterterrorism—then the case can be made to employ these techniques periodically to test judgments and highlight where confidence in conventional wisdom might be unjustified.

It is unrealistic, and a poor use of scarce analytical resources, to proselytize the use of AA everywhere and every day. As a rule, intelligence managers will have to be convinced that the issue is sufficiently important to justify using these techniques; the consequences of being wrong would be a major surprise to the U.S. intelligence and policy communities; and the use of the techniques will raise policymaker understanding of the issue and the uncertainties surrounding it. Similarly, good judgment is required in deciding when to present alternative analysis to the policymaker. Contrarian analysis can be downright irritating to the policymaking community after it has completed a major policy review and selected a course of action; had this same analysis been presented a few months earlier, however, it might have been well received and helpful in stimulating and raising the level of the policy debate.

Evolution or Revolution in Tradecraft?

Over the past 60 years, have we seen an evolution or revolution in analytical tradecraft? The jury is still out. There is no question that the analytical tradecraft has changed markedly since the end of the Cold War. The CIA is using alternative analysis more explicitly to challenge its own analysis, raise important questions to policymakers, and reduce susceptibility to surprise. The CIA is also providing a much fuller range of training opportunities for new and mid-career analysts, who will improve their skills and understanding of policymaker needs. The establishment of the Sherman Kent School in 2000 was a major step toward professionalizing the CIA analytical ranks and providing a center where best practices in analytical tradecraft can be identified and used in advanced analytical training courses. Perhaps more far-reaching will be the fostering of new analytical units that are designed to emphasize unconventional, nonlinear thinking. Already, the directorate is home to several such groups. The Office of Transnational Issues has expanded the domain of its Strategic Analysis Group, which regularly conducts alternative analysis, uses sophisticated gaming and simulation techniques, and actively solicits outside expertise to challenge and enrich its own analysis. Similarly, the Kent School's small staff in the Global Futures Partnership (GFP) has become an in-house incubator of novel ideas and counterintuitive thinking. As its name implies, the GFP is active in partnering with American and even foreign academies interested in futures work that touches on global issues of mutual concern.

However, there remains room for improvement. Has the Directorate of Intelligence employed these analytical tradecraft techniques enough? Are intelligence managers supportive enough of them? Do policymakers themselves understand the value of these techniques and encourage their use to sharpen the agency's own analytical skills? The answer to these questions is probably still no.

On the positive side, senior CIA officials have openly embraced the philosophy of challenging analysts to be more self-critical and skeptical of their own infallibility. Connecting the dots or putting the puzzle pieces together will always remain easier after the fact, but the Intelligence Community is obliged to strive creatively to assemble evidence of threats and opportunities in as many ways as is possible before the fact. As Deputy DCI John McLaughlin put it in 2001, "Our country and its interests are at their most vulnerable if its intelligence professionals are not always ready for something completely different."[25] In the wake of September 11, the practice of thinking differently is the strongest defense against the unexpected.

Notes

[1] Sherman Kent, *Strategic Intelligence for American World Policy* (Princeton: Princeton University Press, 1949).

[2] Carl von Clausewitz, *On War*, ed. and trans. Michael Howard and Peter Paret (Princeton: Princeton University Press, 1986), 117.

[3] See Richards Heuer, *The Psychology of Intelligence Analysis* (Washington, DC: Center for the Study of Intelligence, 1999). Chapter 2, "Perception: Why Can't We See What Is There To Be Seen?" lays out the psychological basis for mindsets.

[4] Sherman Kent, "A Crucial Estimate Relived," *Studies in Intelligence* 8, no. 2 (Spring 1964), 6.

[5] Ibid., 7.

[6] According to many accounts, Director of Central Intelligence John McCone, who was alone in believing the Soviets might risk placing offensive missiles in Cuba, never quite recovered confidence in the Office of National Estimates or in Kent's judgment.

[7] Both the United States and Israel conducted extensive postmortems on this intelligence surprise. In Israel, the 2-year-long Agranat Commission issued extensive findings as well as punished senior intelligence officials. One recommendation was that Israeli military intelligence create a devil's advocacy unit within its analytic directorate that would have the authority to challenge "conventional wisdom" and draft contrarian analysis to ensure that all possible hypotheses about hostile military movements were explored. A description of this unit is found in Lt. Col. Shmuel, "The Imperative of Criticism: The Role of Intelligence Review," *IDF Journal* 2, no. 3 (May 1985), 62–69.

[8] See Henry A. Kissinger, *Years of Upheaval* (Boston: Little Brown, 1972). Chapter 11, "The Middle East War," discusses at length "why we were surprised.... [Anwar] Sadat boldly all but told us what he was going to do and we did not believe him. He overwhelmed us with information and let us draw the wrong conclusion."

[9] Heuer, 5.

[10] Director of Central Intelligence Robert Gates, as a former Deputy Director of Intelligence and Deputy National Security Adviser in the first Bush administration, was an early critic of the CIA's analytical performance. As both consumer and producer of intelligence, he signaled the necessity of tradecraft reforms that were to become more formalized in the 1990s.

[11] Quoted in Roy Godson, Ernest R. May, and Gary Schmitt, eds., *U.S. Intelligence at the Crossroads: Agendas for Reform* (Washington, DC: Brassey's, 1995), 76.

[12] Colin Powell, *Doctrine for Intelligence Support to Joint Operations* (Washington, DC: DOD/JCS Joint Publication 2.0, March 2000), III–5: "Tell me what you know... tell me what you don't know... tell me what you think... always distinguish which is which."

[13] Jack Davis, "Changes in Analytic Tradecraft in CIA's Directorate of Intelligence," Product Evaluation Staff/Directorate of Intelligence, April 1995, 8.

[14] John McLaughlin, "The Changing Nature of CIA Analysis in the Post-Soviet World," remarks at the Conference on CIA's Analysis of the Soviet Union 1947–1991, March 9, 2001, 3.

[15] News conference on the Jeremiah Report, June 2, 1998, accessed at <http://www.fas.org/irp/cia/product/jeremiah.html>. The report also highlighted scarce imagery assets and improper collection priorities as well as clever Indian deception and denial as among the root causes for this surprise.

[16] Report of the Commission to Assess the Ballistic Missile Threat to the United States, March 18, 1999, unclassified

version of the Intelligence Side Letter, 6, accessed at <http://www.fas.org/irp/threat/missile/sideletter.htm>. Members of the commission included Donald H. Rumsfeld (Chairman), Paul D. Wolfowitz, and former Director of Central Intelligence R. James Woolsey.

[17] Executive Summary of the Report of the Commission to Investigate the Ballistic Missile Threat to the United States, July 15, 1998, Pursuant to Public Law 201, 104th Congress.

[18] Ibid., 7.

[19] Office of Inspector General, Alternative Analysis in the Directorate of Intelligence, Central Intelligence Agency, 1999, cited in Jack Davis, "Improving CIA Analytic Performance: Strategic Warning," Sherman Kent Center for Intelligence Analysis Occasional Papers, 4.

[20] Heuer, 16.

[21] For a detailed review of this exercise, see John Prados, *The Soviet Estimate: United States Intelligence and Soviet Strategic Forces* (Princeton: Princeton University Press, 1986), especially 245–257. The Senate Select Committee on Intelligence issued a detailed report of its findings of the Team A/Team B exercise and concluded, "There is a need for competitive and alternative analyses. Both within the estimative body and with respect to outside expertise, competing and on occasion alternative estimates should be encouraged." Quoted in Harold Ford, "Annex Three: The A–B Team Experiment in Competitive Estimating 1976," *Estimative Intelligence: The Purposes and Problems of National Intelligence Estimating* (Lanham, MD: University Press of America, 1993), 267–268.

[22] This course has since been renamed Advanced Analytical Techniques.

[23] The DI Office of Policy Support produced a 25-page alternative analysis primer that was provided to every DI analyst and made available to all alternative analysis workshops and to other interested agencies.

[24] Like simulation exercises, another technique not discussed in this chapter, scenario development, requires considerable planning and logistics. The Directorate of Intelligence Strategic Assessment Group and the Global Futures Partnership both conduct these 1- or 2-day workshops that bring together senior experts from both inside and outside the government.

[25] McLaughlin, 6.

Chapter 26

The Intelligence Community Case Method Program: A National Intelligence Estimate on Yugoslavia

Thomas W. Shreeve

- Yugoslavia will cease to function as a federal state within one year, and will probably dissolve within two. Economic reform will not stave off the breakup.
- Serbia will block Slovene and Croat attempts to form an all-Yugoslav confederation.
- There will be a protracted armed uprising by Albanians in Kosovo. A full-scale, inter-republic war is unlikely, but serious intercommunal conflict will accompany the breakup and will continue afterward. The violence will be intractable and bitter.
- There is little the United States and its European allies can do to preserve Yugoslav unity. Yugoslavs will see such efforts as contradictory to advocacy of democracy and self-determination.

These eight sentences were the first substantive text in National Intelligence Estimate (NIE) 15–90, published in October 1990 and entitled "Yugoslavia Transformed." The sentences appeared on page iii of the NIE. A map of the region was on page iv; the key judgments (see appendix to this chapter) were on page v. By all accounts, the NIE was what policymakers generally said they wanted from the Intelligence Community: it was analytically sound, prescient, and well written. It was also fundamentally inconsistent with what U.S. policymakers wanted to happen in the former Yugoslavia, and it had almost no impact on U.S. policy. The process through which it was created and its fate, however, may provide insights into the analytic process and the relationship between intelligence analysis and the formulation of U.S. foreign policy.

Yugoslavia: A Troubled History

In his 1996 bestseller entitled *The Clash of Civilizations and the Remaking of World Order*, Harvard University political scientist Samuel Huntington referred to:

Source: This case study is based on open sources cited in the text, documents held by the U.S. Intelligence Community, and interviews with officials involved in the events described. Used with the permission of Thomas W. Shreeve, Thomas W. Shreeve & Associates, LLC.

the great historical line that has existed for centuries separating Western Christian peoples from Muslim and Orthodox peoples. This line dates back to the division of the Roman Empire in the fourth century and to the creation of the Holy Roman Empire in the tenth century. It has been in roughly its current place for at least five hundred years. . . . In the Balkans, of course, this line coincides with the historical division between the Austro-Hungarian and Ottoman empires. It is the cultural border of Europe, and in the post-Cold War world it is also the political and economic border of Europe and the West.

Huntington and other scholars observed also that this dividing line between civilizations ran straight through the former Yugoslavia along the border separating Slovenia and Croatia from the other republics. Yugoslavia and other nations of the Baltic region thus had the misfortune of lying at a point where the tectonic plates of two major civilizations collided, resulting in cultural anomalies that appeared to resist resolution. Historically, the Balkans had so long been prone to chaos and instability that the term "Balkanized" had come to describe any collection of polities that were fractious and divisive to the point of being dysfunctional.

The modern nation of Yugoslavia was created in 1918 out of the post-World War I wreckage of the Austro-Hungarian and Ottoman empires. The new country was called "The Kingdom of the Serbs, Croats, and Slovenes" for the three nations from which it was formed. (The name of the country was changed to Yugoslavia—"the Land of the South Slavs"—in 1929.) For Serbia, which had been an independent nation since the Congress of Berlin in 1878, this represented an opportunity to unite Serbs scattered for centuries throughout the two collapsed empires. (The Serbian royal house of Karadjordjevic was given hereditary rule over the new monarchy in recognition of Serbia's role on the winning side in World War I and of the numerical plurality of Serbs throughout the new nation.) Croatia joined the new state mainly to be among the winners of World War I and to counter Italian ambitions along the Dalmatian coast. For Slovenia, the smallest of the three components, union provided security against territorial claims by Italy and Austria.

During World War II, Germany and Italy invaded and partitioned Yugoslavia, creating a pro-Nazi puppet state in Croatia. (Many Croats participated with willing enthusiasm in efforts by the German Army to quell local resistance, particularly from among Serbian elements of the population.) Guerrilla forces under a number of Yugoslav leaders fought stubbornly against the invaders and their local allies. An estimated one million Yugoslavs died during this period, most of them slain by fellow Yugoslavs. A charismatic former Communist Party apparatchik named Josip Broz Tito emerged as the most effective partisan commander of the war. American and British forces—appreciating Tito's ability to tie down some 10 German divisions in Yugoslavia's remote and mountainous terrain—provided him with aid and supplies.

After Germany's defeat in World War II, Tito and his partisans crushed the remaining pro-Nazi resistance—mainly in Croatia—and took power in the now-communist state. Yugoslavia under Tito consisted of six republics, including Serbia, Croatia, Slovenia, Bosnia-Herzegovina, Macedonia, and Montenegro. There were also two autonomous provinces of Serbia, including Kosovo and Vojvodina. The nation's internal boundaries roughly reflected ethnic and historical divisions, but the population was so thoroughly mixed that it proved impossible to separate the various ethnic groups clearly. This was especially true of the Serbs, who were widely dispersed in varying concentrations except in Slovenia, where there were few Serbs. The Muslims were concentrated almost entirely in Bosnia-Herzegovina, but there were also many Muslims among Kosovo's Albanian population, which had grown to comprise about 90 percent of the province's total. (The Muslims of Yugoslavia had the highest birthrate in Europe.) Nationalistic tensions had long plagued the region, but under Tito's strong and occasionally ruthless leadership, these were largely suppressed. (As a dedicated communist, Tito—who was himself part Croat and part Slovene—disparaged nationalism as inconsistent with communist ideology.)

In 1948, the United States supported Tito despite his politics when he broke with Soviet dictator Josef Stalin. Successive U.S. administrations continued to support the notion of Yugoslav independence from the Soviet Union at a time when Yugoslavia successfully asserted a growing role in Europe and even internationally in the so-called non-aligned movement. In his 1996 book entitled *Origins of a Catastrophe*, Warren Zimmerman, the last U.S. Ambassador to Yugoslavia, wrote of the hope in Washington that:

> Yugoslavia could become a model for independence as well as for an Eastern European political system that, though regrettably communist, could be more open politically and more decentralized economically than the Soviet satellites. Yugoslavia's position between hostile Eastern and Western camps made its unity a major Western concern. As long as the Cold War continued, Yugoslavia was a protected and sometimes pampered child of American and Western diplomacy.

By the mid-1960s, according to a number of historians and other observers, growing disparities in economic growth rates began to provoke dissatisfaction—particularly in Slovenia and Croatia—with Tito's rigid centralization. These two republics, the nation's most heavily industrialized, realized with increasing resentment that they were making disproportionate contributions to the federal budget while receiving little in terms of investment. A movement toward economic and cultural decentralization gathered steam, especially in Croatia, in the late 1960s and early 1970s.

In 1974, the ailing Tito bequeathed to Yugoslavia a constitution that was to come into full effect after his death, which occurred 6 years later. The effect of Tito's constitution was to bolster the power of the constituent republics of Yugoslavia at the expense of the power of the central government. "In fact," Ambassador Zimmermann wrote, "the government of Yugoslavia was constitutionally the weakest in Europe. . . . The old dictator's reasons can only be guessed at. Possibly he didn't want any more Titos, possibly he wanted to deny Serbia the opportunity to reestablish its pre-World War II dominance over Yugoslavia's political institutions." Whatever his reasons, Tito left behind a central government that was "federal" in name only. Its cumbersome, rotating eight-member presidency in Belgrade, for example, consisted of one representative from each of the six republics and two autonomous provinces. "Yugoslavia became feudalized," according to John Zametica, writing for the International Institute for Strategic Studies in 1992, "an unwieldy collection of eight small states with small economies competing against each other. The system was designed to offer decentralization as a substitute of political pluralism. In fact, it was a recipe for chaos."

Growing decentralization of Yugoslavia's constituent elements occurred at a time when the nation's economy was performing badly. Unemployment was increasing during the 1980s, and production was falling. Foreign indebtedness grew sharply, and inflation reached exceptionally high levels. Moreover, the forces of nationalism, apparently dormant under Tito, began to reemerge. For example, the ethnic Albanians of Kosovo briefly revolted in 1981. In 1987 in Serbia, former communist apparatchik Slobodan Milosovic rose to power by appealing increasingly to Serbia's historically virulent sense of nationalism.

Senior officials in the United States were aware of these trends and concerned about their implications for Yugoslavia's future. For example, Ambassador Zimmermann wrote that when he returned to Yugoslavia after a long absence, Yugoslav Foreign Minister Budimir Loncar told him: "You have to understand what's happened to Yugoslavia since you were last here. With Tito gone we have become a completely decentralized country. The federal government has very little influence, and no control, over the six republics."

Changing Times

With the collapse of the Soviet Union, the position of Yugoslavia shifted in the calculation of U.S. foreign policy, according to a number of senior officials and others. In early 1989, shortly after being confirmed as the ambassador to Yugoslavia, Warren Zimmermann sought out Lawrence Eagleburger, who had just been appointed Deputy Secretary of State in the incoming Bush administration and was widely acknowledged as among the foremost U.S. experts on the Balkans.

Mindful of the profound geopolitical shift in Eastern Europe that had accompanied the end of the Cold War, Zimmermann and Eagleburger agreed that in his introductory calls in Belgrade and in the republican capitals, Zimmermann should deliver a new message. In his 1996 book, Zimmermann recalled their conclusion:

> I would say [to Yugoslav officials] that Yugoslavia and the Balkans remained important to U.S. interests, but that Yugoslavia no longer enjoyed its former geopolitical significance as a balance between [the North Atlantic Treaty Organization] and the Warsaw Pact. It was no longer unique, since both Poland and Hungary now had more open political and economic systems. Its failures in the human rights area, which the United States had tended to downplay because of America's security interests, now loomed larger, especially in the province of Kosovo, where an authoritarian Serbian regime was systematically depriving the Albanian majority of its basic civil liberties. . . . Not least, I would reassert to the Yugoslav authorities the traditional mantra of U.S. policy toward Yugoslavia—our support for its unity, independence, and territorial integrity. But I would add that we could only support the country's

unity in the context of progress toward democracy; we would be strongly opposed to unity imposed or maintained by force.

Both Eagleburger and Zimmermann were well informed on Yugoslav matters. Both were career foreign service officers, and both had served in Yugoslavia earlier in their respective careers. Eagleburger had spent 8 years there, beginning in 1962 when he was only 32 years old. Shortly after he arrived, there was a very severe earthquake in Skopje, the capital of Macedonia. Eagleburger had taken over and skillfully directed the successful relief operation, including the construction of an Army hospital. As a result, he was regarded as a hero by many Yugoslavs and was warmly welcomed when he returned as U.S. ambassador in the late 1970s. He made no secret of his high regard for Yugoslavia. Zimmermann had served in Yugoslavia beginning in 1968. In his 1996 book, Zimmermann wrote: "They say that every diplomat has a special posting, a place that shines brightest in imagination and memory. For me Yugoslavia was such a place." Zimmermann in particular wrote glowingly and at length of Yugoslavia's historic charm, the physical beauty of its mountains and lakes, and the warmth and friendliness of its people.

As the trend toward decentralization in Yugoslavia appeared to accelerate, U.S. policymakers with a focus on Europe began to express concern regarding the country's future. For example, Ambassador Robert L. Hutchings, who was a leading specialist on Eastern Europe and Yugoslavia and National Security Council (NSC) Director at the time the NIE was published, later wrote in his book, entitled *American Diplomacy and the End of the Cold War,* that "By the time of Marshal Josip Tito's death in 1980, Yugoslavia was neither centralized enough for effective leadership in Belgrade nor decentralized enough for genuine federalism to take hold. And the galvanizing element of a Soviet threat was fast disappearing."

Some Western observers of events in Yugoslavia expressed occasional frustration with the chronic divisiveness of its people, particularly over matters of religious faith. The Serbs were Orthodox, the Croats and Slovenes shared a common Central European Catholic culture, and the Muslims—comprising about 10 percent of the total population but heavily concentrated in the republic of Bosnia-Herzegovina and in Kosovo—were the descendants of local residents who had converted to Islam during the rule by the Ottoman Empire, perhaps hoping it would help them prosper under Ottoman/Turkish domination.

This sense of frustration was particularly true of the Americans, raised as they were in a culture that placed a high value on religious tolerance. The advantages of unity in Yugoslavia over disintegration appeared obvious, a "no-brainer," as one senior U.S. official described it, if only the Yugoslavs could reconcile their differences and look to the future instead of the past. At a time when few Western European observers appeared to share the growing sense of urgency in Washington regarding the future of Yugoslavia and its implications for Europe, it was difficult, according to a number of present and former U.S. policymakers, to figure out what to do. The Intelligence Community would try to help.

Intelligence Analysis and Policy Formulation

In 1990, the process known as *intelligence analysis* was carried out in many parts of the vast apparatus collectively called the Intelligence Community. Broadly defined, this consisted of about a dozen agencies focused on national security issues and Federal law enforcement issues that had national security implications. In some cases, intelligence analysts were members of major Cabinet-level departments of the U.S. Government such as State, Defense, Justice, or Treasury. These and others had components that focused on intelligence analytic activities on behalf of their respective departments. For example, the State Department had its Bureau of Intelligence and Research (INR) and the Defense Department had the Defense Intelligence Agency (DIA) to meet their respective intelligence analytic needs. The Central Intelligence Agency (CIA), by contrast, was not a part of a larger department but instead was independent of all of them. Its analytic arm, known as the Directorate of Intelligence or DI, was also much larger than any of the other intelligence analytic components.

The job of the intelligence analysts was to sift through all the information that could be acquired, openly or clandestinely, on a wide range of topics and form judgments that could be useful in clarifying the ambiguity surrounding the many issues that were of interest to foreign policy decisionmakers. The analysts were usually assigned to a fairly narrow range of issues, either by focusing on a specific nation or region, or through focus on a specific global issue such as terrorism or weapons proliferation. Typically, analysts had advanced degrees in area studies, history, political science, and many other fields; many had studied their assigned areas, or accounts, as they were called at CIA, for years.

Getting their views across to their policymaking consumers required rigorous, systematic thinking, usually followed by creation and publication of a written document—of which there were several different types—or communication in an oral briefing. The various, carefully defined types of *finished intelligence*, as the written works were called, were collectively known as *artforms*. The shortest of these were in the Intelligence Community's two "morning newspapers," called the National Intelligence Daily (NID; since renamed the Senior Executive Intelligence Brief) and the President's Daily Brief (PDB). At the time, these two artforms were about 10 pages in length and contained short, narrowly focused pieces on a wide variety of topics of current interest. The NID went to a large number of policymakers, senior military commands, and to Members of Congress. The PDB was distributed to a very small group consisting of the President and Vice President, the Secretaries of Defense and State, the Chairman of the Joint Chiefs of Staff, and at times a handful of others; it was typically shorter and more focused on matters of interest to the most senior levels of the U.S. Government. Longer artforms included intelligence assessments, interagency intelligence memoranda, research papers, and component-specific reviews of different kinds. Most of these forms of finished intelligence, including those with a focus on current events as well as the longer-term pieces, required coordination among analysts of different components or even of different agencies. The artforms produced by junior analysts also were subject to review—often extensive—before they could be published.

The National Intelligence Council (NIC) was the Intelligence Community's center for mid-term and long-term strategic thinking and the source of all National Intelligence Estimates (NIEs) and Special National Intelligence Estimates (SNIEs). The NIEs were published in accordance with plans drawn up by a committee of intelligence and policymaking representatives and often took months to write. The SNIEs were estimates that had not been placed on the annual schedule because no one could foresee the need for a judgment on a specific question. These tended to be written in response to urgent requests by policymakers confronted by some sort of crisis. Estimates represented the voice of the Intelligence Community; they went out over the signature of the Director of Central Intelligence (DCI), and consensus was highly valued in the publication process. Despite being formally sponsored by the DCI, by convention a DCI—who is a political appointee—is not expected to meddle with the analytic conclusions reflected in NIEs and SNIEs. A DCI could and occasionally did offer judgments to the President that were at odds with those in the NIC's written products.

As a result of the extensive coordination required to write them, NIEs and SNIEs were sometimes criticized for being the "lowest common denominator" judgments available in the analytic community. Nevertheless, they were broadly considered the analytic profession's most prestigious products, and they were sometimes controversial if major disagreements among analysts did emerge or if their conclusions were at odds with an administration's policies. In some circles, an analyst could not convincingly claim the status of a proven veteran until he or she had participated in an NIE or a SNIE.

Physically located at CIA headquarters building in Langley, Virginia, the NIC was composed of veteran analysts from throughout the Intelligence Community, including the Cabinet-level departments and the CIA. The council occasionally included former diplomats, retired flag officers, and prominent academics who had demonstrated an understanding of the policy process. As in other analytic components at lower levels, the National Intelligence Officers (NIOs) who comprised the council focused on specific regions, such as the NIO for Europe, or on specific topics, such as the NIO for Warning. Assignment to the NIC was considered the mark of senior, top-gun status among analysts.

Over the many years since the establishment of the Intelligence Community, analysts and policymakers had come to an elaborate though largely implicit understanding of the relationship between intelligence analysis and policy formulation. Both sides revealed an understanding of the relationship, although its nuances in any particular case were subtle and sometimes obscure. Analysts took the dynamics of the relationship seriously, as evidenced by the occasional articles on this topic published in professional journals, including the CIA's in-house journal, *Studies in Intelligence*, to highlight controversial issues and record important milestones in the intelligence profession.

At the core of the relationship, from the analysts' perspective, was the analysts' right to speak truth to power and to say what they thought. Analysts insisted on this intellectual independence to the point of being combative about it; analytic training at CIA, for example, explicitly included a consideration of how to recognize policymakers' attempts at politicization of analysis and what to do about it. Analysts who had stood their ground in the face of political pressure sometimes achieved almost legendary status in the analytic culture.

From the policymakers' viewpoint, the mutually agreed limit to analysts' right to free speech was an absolute injunction against delivering policy advice in a finished intelligence artform. The foreign policy decisionmakers for whom the analysts were writing considered themselves the masters of policy formulation, and the analysts existed to serve them by delivering the analysts' best judgments, which the policy community was then free to consider and either accept, reject, or something in between. But whatever the outcome, it was the policymakers—appointed by the President—and not the civil service analysts who would be responsible for the decisions.

In those cases in which the policymaking intelligence consumer was a highly qualified veteran, this often meant that considerable skepticism awaited an analytic judgment at odds with the administration's views on a subject. For example, at the time of the Yugoslavia NIE in October 1990, the Special Assistant to the President for National Security Affairs was retired General Brent Scowcroft, who was abundantly qualified to serve as an analyst of Eastern European affairs and in fact had done so during his earlier assignment as the defense attaché in Belgrade many years before. Equally important, Scowcroft and then-Deputy Secretary Eagleburger were close friends and had served together under Henry Kissinger in previous administrations.

NIE 15–90: "Yugoslavia Transformed"

Veteran CIA analysts, including some who had served in the region in the early 1980s and followed Yugoslavia closely, had begun to change their views on the country's cohesion. As one senior analyst who had served as Assistant NIO for Eastern Europe in the early 1980s put it, there had been a widespread assumption among Intelligence Community analysts in the early 1980s that Yugoslavia probably would survive Tito's death. The Serbs—numerically the dominant group, although scattered among several of the republics other than Serbia—had long sought to be in a single sovereign entity. Also, the officer corps of the Yugoslav People's Army (*Jugoslavenska Narodna Armija*, or JNA) was overwhelmingly Serbian, and as one of the few truly "national" institutions in Yugoslavia was thought to be in a position to prevent the nation's collapse. Moreover, economic incentives for remaining integrated were strong, since the republics' economies by themselves were too small to be viable.

Despite these reasons for remaining unified, according to this senior analyst, throughout the 1980s there were increasing signs that the Tito-era glue that held Yugoslavia together was beginning to melt. "This was especially true of Slovenia and Croatia." As he put it, "For them at least, the economic reasons for remaining in the Yugoslav federation were evaporating." Moreover, analysts sensed that throughout the 1980s the Embassy in Belgrade was constantly under pressure to overemphasize encouraging economic indicators that portrayed the Yugoslav economy as healthier than it really was. "The Embassy didn't want to cause concern among U.S. and other Western investors," this analyst claimed.

The NIO for Europe during these events was Marten van Heuven,[1] who also was closely acquainted with Zimmermann and Eagleburger. A historian by training and a graduate of Yale Law School, van Heuven was a career foreign service officer. He retired from the State Department in 1987 and joined the NIC. Van Heuven stated that by late 1989, he shared the widespread U.S. and Western European perception that instability in Yugoslavia would invite Soviet meddling and provide an unfavorable precedent for other parts of the former Warsaw Pact, and it might threaten NATO. The prevailing U.S. vision for a post-Cold War Europe, van Heuven stated, could be characterized as "Europe whole and free," and the collapse of Yugoslavia would, he and others believed, hinder that objective.

In November 1989, van Heuven attended an experts' conference on Yugoslavia at which the country's prospects were carefully reviewed. Van Heuven left the conference with a sense that the forces for disintegration were considerably stronger than the U.S. foreign policy establishment appeared to realize. He stated later that it was at this point that he realized the need for an NIE on Yugoslavia that might jar the administration's apparently sanguine assumptions.

In May 1990, van Heuven went to Yugoslavia to conduct his own assessment of the situation. From Belgrade, he wrote a cable in which he described Yugoslavia as "in permanent, low-level crisis," with pressures building for a collapse of the federation that had held together since 1945. The ethnic problems alone, van Heuven believed, were fast becoming irresolvable. Still, he recalled later, he did not believe that disintegration was a foregone conclusion.

Soon after he returned from Belgrade, van Heuven assigned the task of drafting an NIE to the NIC staff. Van Heuven chose as the first principal drafter a retired State Department officer who was a veteran analyst and considered well informed on Yugoslavian and Eastern European affairs. In the first draft, which was completed during the summer of 1990, the author reviewed the evidence for and against the probability of Yugoslavia's disintegration and concluded that there was more reason for the republics to stay together than to split apart. "They will muddle through, because the collapse of the nation is so dark a future that the Yugoslavs, especially the JNA officer corps, won't allow it to happen" was how van Heuven characterized the analytic conclusion of the first draft of the NIE.

Van Heuven was not satisfied. His trip to Yugoslavia the previous May had convinced him, he said later, that the prospects for a unified Yugoslav federation were far less rosy than the first draft suggested. Moreover, unless Yugoslavia's unraveling could be accomplished in a controlled, graduated way—something the Yugoslavs themselves were unlikely to be able to do—the outcome was increasingly likely to be violent. Others at the NIC and elsewhere in the analytic community agreed. Van Heuven then assigned the task of drafting the NIE to other experienced observers of events in Yugoslavia, including a senior Yugoslav political analyst who in earlier assignments had served in the region and was intimately familiar with the issues involved.

This analyst believed that it was principally the Soviet threat of possible intervention that had held Yugoslavia together after Tito's death. After the Soviet Union itself began to unravel in 1989, this threat diminished to the point where it could be disregarded, especially in Slovenia and Croatia, to which he had traveled frequently. "I could see they wanted out of Yugoslavia," the analyst recalled during his visits:

The Serbs didn't care much about Slovenia, since there were no Serbs there, but they did care about Croatia, which has a large Serb minority. They knew also that if Slovenia seceded, Croatia would follow. The Serbs also were becoming increasingly nationalistic at this time, led by Milosevic, who had come up through the Communist Party but was a crafty politician and could see that communism was fading, particularly as a mechanism for keeping him in power. At the same time, the Slovenes and Croats were becoming increasingly uncomfortable with staying in the federation on what they regarded as Serbia's terms: a Yugoslavia that really amounted to a "Greater Serbia."

This political analyst described the first draft of the NIE as similar to what he himself might have written immediately after Tito's death. It presented an accurate picture of the situation then, but in the years since then, the situation had changed. The forces of nationalism had grown much stronger, especially in Serbia and Croatia, at a time when the reasons for staying together had all diminished, at least in the perception of the Yugoslavs themselves, and the Soviet threat had vanished.

"There was little internal disagreement among the major contributors [at the NIC]," according to the analysts, "and there were no footnotes [suggesting dissent] from the conclusions of the NIE."

The View from Belgrade

From Belgrade, Ambassador Warren Zimmermann had been steadily reporting on the unfolding situation. In early February 1990, he noted in a cable that unrest in Kosovo was growing, despite a "show of force" by the JNA apparently intended to cow the Albanian population into continued acceptance of Serbian dominance. In March, Zimmermann traveled to Macedonia, where he found signs of increasing nationalism along with growing support for a multiparty system. "The United States continues to support the unity of a democratic Yugoslavia" was the message Zimmermann tried to convey, according to his cables in March and April.

In April and May, Zimmermann cabled that Yugoslavia's existence probably was at stake in the coming elections in Slovenia and Croatia. If the elections brought to power those who favored a looser confederation or even independence, he wrote, many feared that the breakup could not be achieved peacefully, as the increasingly bellicose Serbs led by Milosevic asserted dominance. Zimmermann strongly urged greater U.S. support for Yugoslavia's beleaguered president, Ante Marcovic, a former business executive widely regarded as a political reformer and principled anti-communist. Later, Zimmermann reported on Milosevic's June 26, 1990, speech in Belgrade in which Milosevic raised the prospect of an independent Serbia outside the Yugoslav federation and outlined tough terms for Kosovo's Albanians: submit to Serb control or face the threat of force. In August, Zimmermann described growing unrest among the Serb population of Croatia as the Serbs there set up roadblocks and called for a referendum to claim Serbian autonomy within Croatia.

On September 27, about 2 weeks before the release of NIE 15–90, Zimmermann sent a comprehensive cable to State Department headquarters in which he outlined his personal views on Yugoslavia's future. The nation's unity had substantially decayed, he wrote, over the past 6 months, mainly as the forces of nationalism had grown to the point where political decentralization was almost inevitable:

> Kosovo may well prove to be the rock on which Yugoslavia founders. It is difficult to imagine a way in which Yugoslavia could be reconfigured to allow Serbs, Albanians, and Slovenes/Croats to want to live together voluntarily in the same country. Serbs are determined to pay any price to keep Kosovo within Serbia, in spite of the fact that the province's population is less than 10 percent Serbian. Albanians seem equally determined not to remain voluntarily in any form of union with Serbia. Slovenes and Croats, for their part, have no interest in a Yugoslavia that employs the kind of repressive measures that Serbia is using to work its will on the Kosovo Albanians.

A Balkan intelligence analyst who was returning to the United States from temporary duty in the Persian Gulf in the late summer of 1990 tells another story. He traveled by way of Belgrade, and while visiting the U.S. Embassy there, received a summons from Ambassador Zimmermann, who had just seen a copy of the second draft of NIE 15–90. This analyst recalled that Zimmermann was very upset with the draft: "He said it was too pessimistic, and would prove to be self-fulfilling."

In his later recollections, Zimmermann described the NIE as bold, clear, and objective. He had seen intelligence "shaped" to fit policy in the Vietnam experience, he said, and so he favored the intellectual independence from policy that the authors of the NIE had obviously enjoyed. "But I sat in a different seat from the authors of the NIE," Zimmermann said:

> It was my duty to carry out U.S. policy, which was to favor continued unity, mainly through trying to help Marcovic. We in Belgrade were advocates, not analysts, so the NIE caused me huge problems. Its message was that there was nothing we could do to change the outcome, a conclusion that made it much harder for the policy to work. I feared that State [Department headquarters] and the National Security Council would read the NIE as indicating that the situation was hopeless, so I urged top officials to continue with the policy. I foresaw violence if Yugoslavia fell apart, so I tried to focus on getting people not to give up on Yugoslavia, even though I knew that the chances of peaceful transition were dwindling. . . . The NIE was based on powerful evidence, but the outcome it predicted was not inevitable. I wanted to prevent the NIE from becoming a "self-fulfilling prophecy." [A peaceful transition] was still worth fighting for, even if the chances of achieving it were diminishing. I would say that even as late as September there were at least two options we could have envisioned: a gradual, balanced transition to a loose confederation of some kind, or at least what I would call "managed disaster." But we didn't get either one.

Soon after its publication, the NIE evidently was leaked to the *New York Times*. Under the headline "Yugoslavia Seen Breaking Up Soon—CIA Paper Predicts Action in 18 Months and Adds Civil War Is Likely," reporter David Binder revealed the NIE conclusions in detail. Binder also claimed that "the CIA's pessimism" was shared by some State Department officials, including Lawrence Eagleburger.

U.S. policymaker attention by this point was in large measure focused on the Middle East following the Iraqi invasion of Kuwait in early August 1990, and several analysts who participated in the NIE and its subsequent fate agreed that it was increasingly difficult to capture the attention of the policy community for an issue that had long been considered basically marginal to U.S. interests and, in any case, mainly a concern for the Western Europeans to address. Nothing much happened as a result of its publication. "No one was providing any alternatives," a senior Balkan analyst said. "Politicians like to feel that they can influence events, but in this case the message was that there was nothing they could do."

John Gannon, then-CIA Deputy Director for European Analysis (and later Deputy Director for Intelligence), had supervised agency analysis of Eastern Europe and had watched events in Yugoslavia carefully:

> The Estimate was correct, but it was issued at a time when the Administration had a different view; policymakers believed it was not in U.S. interests to develop a policy based on the breakup of Yugoslavia, which was an outcome they did not want to occur. Further, the NIE did not engage the policymakers in ways that were useful. And it is important to remember that the breakup was not in fact inevitable. Tito showed that strong leadership could hold Yugoslavia together. In retrospect, analysts may not appreciate that their certainty was not entirely justified.

Asked why the NIE had so little apparent impact, a former Assistant NIO for Eastern Europe said that there was a lack of policy concern. "The United States simply stopped caring about Yugoslavia," he said. "If Yugoslavia had fallen apart without bloodshed, we would have seen no U.S. interest at all. It is only atrocities that catch our attention."

"[The Yugoslavs] would have been better off if they had stayed together," according to General Brent Scowcroft's later recollections, "but their collapse was not central to U.S. interests as long as it could be contained. As for the NIE, I certainly read it but I don't remember if it influenced me or not. I thought it was skewed against the Serbs, and it seemed unduly pessimistic. Its conclusions suggested that there was nothing that we could do to alter the outcome. It left the reader with the sense that there were no options beyond accepting the inevitable."

David Gompert, who was a senior member of the National Security Staff when the NIE was published, recalled that there was in fact considerable NSC and other top-level concern regarding Yugoslavia's future. "What we wanted was a slow-motion collapse, if we could get it," Gompert said, "but that turned out to be impossible." Resolution of the conflict would have required armed U.S. intervention, he added, an option that was never even mentioned at the time:

> The fuse had already been lit before the NIE came out. So the NIE wasn't "news" for those of us who had been following developments there. It was not a surprise. I thought it would have greater impact than it did. The Administration was stuck with an irresolvable dilemma: we couldn't favor a breakup, and we couldn't favor

forced unity. We knew that the status quo was unacceptable to the Slovenes and the Croats, and we told them, "If you declare independence unilaterally, you will start a war." Their response, basically, was "So what?"

Secretary of State James Baker made a last-ditch effort to push the various factions into more conciliatory positions when he visited Belgrade and other capitals in June 1991. This effort failed. Slovenia declared independence immediately after Baker's visit; this was followed quickly by a similar declaration by Croatia. As predicted, the Serbs made only a token effort to suppress the Slovenes' bid for independence, since there were almost no Serbs in Slovenia. The Croatian secession drew a sharp but limited response from the JNA, by that point a Serbian and no longer a Yugoslavian army. After mounting evidence of Croatian military effectiveness, Serbian forces withdrew.

A prolonged civil conflict followed, lasting for the next several years. It was marked, as the NIE had predicted, by vicious behavior on all sides, mostly by the Serbs and particularly in Bosnia-Herzegovina and in Kosovo. An estimated 200,000 people were killed, and many more displaced. Eventually, U.S. and NATO forces intervened to put an end to the fighting. Several leaders of the former Yugoslavia, including Prime Minister Milosevic—who was overthrown by a popular uprising in Serbia—were later arrested for a variety of war crimes and other offenses.

Appendix: The Key Judgments of NIE 15–90 (October 1990)

The old Yugoslavian federation is coming to an end because the reservoir of political will holding Yugoslavia together is gone. Within a year the federal system will no longer exist; within 2 years Yugoslavia will probably have dissolved as a state.

Although elsewhere in Eastern Europe economic and political reform will be interdependent, Yugoslavia's future will be decided by political and ethnic factors. Even successful economic reforms will not hold the country together.

The strongest cohesive forces at work in Yugoslavia are those *within* Serbia, Croatia, and Slovenia. They are a mix of national pride, local economic aspirations, and historically antagonistic religious and cultural identifications. In Slovenia, and to a lesser extent Croatia, the new nationalism is [W]estward-looking, democratic, and entrepreneurial; in Serbia, it is rooted in statist economics, military tradition, and a preference for strong central government led by a dynamic personality.

Neither the Communist Party nor the JNA will be able to hold the federation together. The party is in a shambles; the army has lost prestige because of its strong Communist Party identification and because much of the country considers it a Serb-dominated institution. No all-Yugoslav political movement has emerged to fill the void left by the collapse of the Titoist vision of a Yugoslav state, and none will.

Alternatives to dissolution now being discussed in various quarters are unlikely to succeed. A loose confederation will appeal to Croatia and Slovenia, but Serbs will block this in an effort to preserve Serb influence. Moreover, a Serb-dominated attempt to muddle through, using the old federal institutions and military brinkmanship to block independence, will not be tolerated by the newly enfranchised, nationalistic electorates of the breakaway republics. Serbs know this.

It is likely that Serbian repression in Kosovo will result in an armed uprising by the majority Albanian population, supported by large Albanian minorities in Macedonia and Montenegro. This, in turn, will create strong pressure on those republics to associate themselves closely with Serbia.

A slide from sporadic and spontaneous ethnic violence into organized inter-republic civil war is also a danger, but it is unlikely during the period of this Estimate. Serbia's commitment of resources to pacification of the Albanians in Kosovo will constrain its ability to use military means to bring Serbian minorities in the western part of the country under its direct control. The Serbs, however, will attempt to foment uprisings by Serb minorities elsewhere—particularly in Croatia and Bosnia-Herzegovina—and large-scale ethnic violence is likely.

The United States will have little capacity to preserve Yugoslav unity, notwithstanding the influence it has had there in the past. But leaders from various republics will make claims on U.S. officials to advance their partisan objectives. Federal and Serb leaders will emphasize statements in support of territorial integrity. Slovenes, Croats, and Kosovars, however, will play up U.S. pressure for improved performance on human rights and self-determination. Thus, Washington will continue to be drawn into the heated arena of inter-ethnic conflict and will be expected to respond in some manner to the contrary claims of all parties.

The Soviet Union will have only an indirect influence—for example, through multinational forums—on the outcome in Yugoslavia. The Europeans have some leverage, but they are not going to use it to hold the old Yugoslavia together.

This case study is based on open sources cited in the text; documents held by the U.S. Intelligence Community; and interviews with intelligence and policy officials who were directly involved in the events described. The study was written in May 2003 by Thomas W. Shreeve. It may not be used outside the National Defense University without permission from the director of the U.S. Intelligence Community Case Method Program. The NIE was originally classified SECRET but has since been declassified and approved for release. For further information, please call Thomas W. Shreeve & Associates, LLC, at 703–848–9003.

Note

[1] Robert Hutchings had been Assistant NIO for Europe, responsible for Eastern Europe, during the first part of Van Heuven's tenure as NIO. Hutchings became NSC Director for Eastern Europe prior to the production of the Yugoslav NIE.

Chapter 27

Building Leverage in the Long War: Ensuring Intelligence Community Creativity in the Fight against Terrorism

James W. Harris

Executive Summary

Intelligence is often cited as a critical element in the war against terrorism and, indeed, it is. The U.S. Intelligence Community has a golden opportunity to develop the capabilities that will make a decisive difference in a war that may last a generation or more. The adversary will not disappear as the campaign to root al Qaeda out of Afghanistan winds down. It is essential that intelligence make the transition to the longer-term fight, and the time to begin that transition is at hand.

The adversary is what some call self-organized terrorism. It grows out of a struggle within the Islamic world between secularism and old traditions. With grass-roots origins, the adversary will morph and adapt, regroup, generate new leadership, shift geographic locus, adjust tactics, and evolve into a collection of cells and networks different from the ones we have engaged fairly successfully since September 11. The goal should be to minimize the frequency and scale of future battles against terrorism before their onset rather than merely to enable the Intelligence Community to support policy and military operations once crises are in full swing—a reactive task it already does well.

In the war ahead, the adaptable nature of the adversary will demand an equally agile U.S. intelligence effort. More resources and better human intelligence will help. But an agile Intelligence Community will require something else: that the Intelligence Community at last dispense with the internal barriers that stifle communications and collaboration. Building an agile intelligence capability will require that internal communications improve, that robust and perhaps formal alliances with external centers of expertise be constructed, and that a genuine multidisciplinary analytic effort blossom and achieve a creative flair that is not typical of bureaucratic enterprises.

Metrics will be needed for measuring progress in the effort. They should include measures of improved communication within the Intelligence Community, structures that connect the Intelligence Community to the best and the brightest outside the world of intelligence, and indicators of true analytic innovation. Intelligent risk-taking and the ability of individual initiative to overcome bureaucratic caution would be central themes in a successful effort.

Introduction

The House and Senate intelligence oversight committees are set to conduct a rare joint investigation of U.S. intelligence gaps in the September 11 terrorist attacks on New York and Washington. Rep. Porter Goss (R–FL), chairman of the House Permanent Select Committee on Intelligence, has stressed that the investigation is not meant to produce "whom shall we hang" recommendations but should instead focus on constructive remedies to intelligence shortfalls. Nevertheless, Sen. Richard Shelby (R–AL), vice chairman of the Senate intelligence committee, was sharply critical of Director of Central Intelligence George Tenet during recent public testimony, and it is fair to say that Shelby has a lot of company. What will come out of the intelligence review—new initiatives to combat terrorism or finger-pointing? Will the Intelligence Community be any better prepared to combat terrorism after the joint investigation has been completed and its recommendations made?

Getting beyond Finger-pointing

Tragedies like the terrorist attacks on the World Trade Center and the Pentagon are certain to produce three tribulations: hot-tempered and hastily written allegations of intelligence failure in the popular literature, postmortem studies of the intelligence record by groups inside and outside government, and follow-on official commissions advocating far-reaching reorganization of the U.S. intelligence apparatus. Of those three things, only one hard-hitting postmortem is certain to be useful, and several such studies are under way or on the drawing board.

The actions suggested by follow-on official commissions never seem to eliminate subsequent intelligence shortfalls. Finger-pointing has a singularly unproductive history. The mission of the Intelligence Community has been revisited since the end of the Cold War. Countless reorganizations later, the Intelligence Community has not yet been "fixed" to the Nation's collective satisfaction. If there is blame to assign, it must be shared by the Intelligence Community and those who have had a hand in "reforming" it, such as the Church and Pike Committees in the 1970s and other reform efforts since then.[1]

It would be fair to point out that U.S. intelligence counterterrorist programs have actually recorded a fair number of operational successes, as noted in a balanced assessment of what intelligence can and cannot be expected to accomplish.[2] For example, the Intelligence Community is publicly credited with thwarting planned attacks on the Lincoln and Holland Tunnels in 1993 and attacks against airports on the West Coast on the eve of the millennium.[3] But intelligence cannot achieve omniscience, and if we wait long enough we are bound to be surprised by unfolding events. Osama bin

Laden founded the structure that became al Qaeda during the Afghan war against the Soviets, and it took him two decades to achieve his present notoriety.

What Really Surprised Us about September 11?

It is not as though the Intelligence Community had never contemplated assaults on the American homeland. In his unclassified testimony of February 7, 2001, Tenet effectively described the sorry state of Afghanistan, the corruption of the Taliban, and the danger posed by the al Qaeda network:

> Terrorists are also becoming more operationally adept and more technically sophisticated in order to defeat counterterrorism measures. For example, as we have increased security around government and military facilities, terrorists are seeking out "softer" targets that provide opportunities for mass casualties.[4]

He warned plainly of the threat to U.S. citizens from bin Laden, noting that terrorist assaults appeared increasingly likely to be directed against soft targets rather than against U.S. military assets, as was the attack on the USS *Cole* in October 2000.

Before September 11, the public was probably lulled by a drop in press coverage of terrorist attacks, the statistics about relatively few casualties from terrorism, and a misunderstanding of the adversary's changing approach to risk-taking. According to "Patterns of Global Terrorism 2000," compiled by the U.S. Department of State, the number of terrorist incidents worldwide increased in 2000, but only because of a sharp uptick in assaults against pipelines in Colombia.[5] Discounting the incidents in Colombia, the number of U.S. casualties from terrorism showed no upward trend. The attack on the USS *Cole* did not resonate like an attack on the American homeland would a year later. Partly as a result, terrorism moved down on the list of problems to be dealt with by the Bush administration.[6] The September 11 attacks, ironically, interrupted the last stage of the administration's own defense review, which was to focus on the need to retool the Department of Defense to deal with longer-term threats.[7]

In such an atmosphere, providing warning is the intelligence officer's most difficult task. The devil is partly in the details: it is impossible to preempt a threat without knowledge of the specific plot or plots, and it is almost impossible to unearth all of them. Preempting a general threat, as Tenet was attempting to do in his testimony almost 7 months before the assaults on New York and Washington, is even harder. Warning is inconvenient when it calls for a change in our basic approach to a national security issue—such as mandating a real commitment to homeland security—and it is especially difficult when it comes in advance of the specific events that will convincingly demonstrate the need for a policy adjustment.

Inside government, bureaucratic politics and internal organizational struggles for resources are forces that define issues and indeed often carry the day in debates in the Intelligence Community and on policy. Thus, advance warning of details that would discredit the advocates of business as usual is often unwelcome and can go unheeded. All things considered, and acknowledging that there is no excuse, it is hard to imagine the report or intelligence briefing that would have forced the government to conduct national security business as differently before the tragedy of September 11 as it has in the aftermath.

The Intelligence Community, and especially the Central Intelligence Agency, has a workforce and information resources that agencies in the rest of the Federal Government properly envy. Whatever its record before September 11, the Intelligence Community reacted quickly and constructively to the event. Instead of finger-pointing, therefore, we need to ask in the aftermath of September 11 how intelligence can be brought to the level of efficiency needed in the long term. The likelihood is that terrorist threats against the United States will be here for a generation or more, and what is different and novel about the challenge at hand should be considered. That challenge is considerable.

The Challenge of the Long War

What we are seeing is not the more familiar state-supported terrorism, which has been in gradual decline for two decades. Rather, the terrorism we face is decentralized, self-generating, and tied to the existence of failed states and the battle for the soul of Islam. Two dimensions of the threat should disturb us and influence any initiatives taken to improve intelligence.

First, the United States is caught up in what Michael Doran of Princeton University calls "somebody else's civil war."[8] In almost every Sunni Muslim country, he points out, there are calls by conservative religious elements for the revival of very old traditions. Those elements view modern Western civilization as threatening the survival of traditional Islam as Western civilization bolsters the real enemy—secularism. The struggle is not new, but the identification of America as an ally of the enemies of Islam has gathered momentum with U.S. policy support for secular, corrupt regimes throughout the Middle East and with escalating Palestinian-Israeli tensions.

Civil wars are agony for all participants. Economic historian Brad DeLong is one of several authors who recently compared the contemporary struggles among Islamic factions with the Protestant Reformation of the 16th century. He writes:

> The parallels are striking. A dominant clergy and aristocracy that seem to have . . . succumbed to materialism; a rising literate middle class; the mass distribution of personal copies of the Holy Book so that people can read it and think for themselves; and then terror—as those who have convinced themselves that they hear the will of God take action. In Europe, it lasted for 120 years—with one-third of Germany dying in the 30 Years War.[9]

One can argue the details of those parallels, but it is reasonable to expect that the struggle between secularism and Muslim tradition will last for another generation or more, and that the numbers of casualties that will result from the struggle will shock American sensibilities.

Second, while the threat from al Qaeda is different from that from state-sponsored terrorism—because of its grassroots flavor—al Qaeda differs from many other grassroots terrorist movements, such as Hamas. Al Qaeda's objectives are on a grand scale rather than local and specialized. Hamas is concerned with the plight of the

Table 1. **Self-Organized Terrorism Compared with Conventional Military Threats**

Dimension	Conventional Military Threat	Self-Organized Terrorism
Organization	Hierarchical, formal	Flat, informal, networked
Leadership	Concentrated, institutional authority	Primarily symbolic, with role in fundraising
Loyalty	A state and a polity	A tradition
Coalition partners	Formal, perhaps shifting	Informal, but likely enduring from conflict to conflict
Command and control	Centralized, with clear power relationships	Decentralized, with no one fully in charge
Role of intelligence gathering and analysis	Powerful, primarily offensive	Weak, primarily defensive
Denial and deception	Useful, but of secondary importance	Well developed, critical to mission
Doctrinal development	Derived from formal study, historic experience, simulation, gaming	Evolutionary, trial and error
Other security obligations	Numerous, including regional security, peacekeeping, formal alliances	None
Weapons arsenal	Built through formal acquisition; takes years, even decades; resources abundant	Adaptable, evolves quickly via natural selection; resources a constant
Financing mechanism	Formal budget, funded by taxes	Contributions from nongovernmental organizations, crime, narcotics

Palestinians. In contrast, al Qaeda is quite literally the irregular force that represents one side in the "Islamic Reformation."[10] Thus, it presents an even more radical departure from the models of conventional warfare to which America has been long accustomed and with which the U.S. Intelligence Community was originally built to cope. The United States is comfortable fighting adversaries that are similar to itself and is equally comfortable collecting intelligence against such adversaries. But as table 1 makes clear, the new adversary has a completely different nature, and "mirror imaging" is thus likely to fail. This adversary is an evolving, adapting force—a network with roots that spread everywhere and for which models of deterrence fail.[11]

The protracted struggle will be daunting, and defeating a broad-based self-organized network such as al Qaeda is an unprecedented chore.[12] Vietnam gave us a glimpse of the challenge, but even there the other side featured a government and command-and-control machinery for U.S. forces to target. The al Qaeda brand of terrorism more closely resembles a virus that morphs as its environment changes. To further complicate matters, individual nodes are capable of evolving their own strategy and "gaming" their opposition, as September 11 so convincingly demonstrated. They are capable of self-healing, dispersal, reassembly, and innovation. Our challenge is to outwit and then outfight an adversary that adapts rather than plans and that remains capable of decentralized changes in strategy against our vulnerabilities.

To gain an appreciation of what may be in store for the United States, it is useful to compare the present stage of terrorism to the days of evolving communism in the 1920s and 1930s. The useful historical metaphor is not an ossified Soviet Union but the early days of largely autonomous, independently operated and financed cells. Those cells organized local labor movements, fostered radical political causes, acted with global reach, and attracted the sympathies of otherwise moderate citizens. What might a U.S. Intelligence Community—had one existed in anything like its present form—have done to improve American prospects in the future Cold War with the Soviet Union, and what might the present Intelligence Community do now to protect our interests during the Islamic Reformation?

In many respects we have been lucky that the evolution of the adversary is not more advanced. It seems unlikely, given the course of the war in Afghanistan, that the adversary had a complete prepackaged war plan that could have unfolded autonomously once the battle was under way and that would have been invulnerable to allied strikes against its command-and-control infrastructure in Afghanistan. This is likely to be one of the lessons the adaptable adversary takes from the current war: its combat operations have to be completely scripted well in advance of the first battle so that the larger war cannot be interrupted by unfriendly bombing or ground force operations. The Intelligence Community needs to ask what further adaptation of the adversary the war in Afghanistan will foster.

The White House and senior Intelligence Community management should recognize that they have been lucky that the development of a radiological bomb or nuclear device by this adversary is not further along. They have to wonder how long their luck will hold. Has the U.S. Intelligence Community yet imagined the full range of models of weapons development that the adversary may employ? Is it sensitive to the right signals of the alternative development paths as they may appear in raw intelligence reporting over the next several years? Does this analytic challenge—and others that demand similarly unconventional imagination—reside only on the drawing board of the Intelligence Community, and if so, why?

The Need for New Approaches to Intelligence

The magnitude of the threat and the fact that the new terrorist groups bear little resemblance to either conventional armies or state-sponsored terrorist organizations ensure that al Qaeda and its follow-on movements will demand innovations in U.S. intelligence. Changes in the intelligence craft must go beyond redrawing the intelligence organizational chart and redesigning its chain of command. The collection of raw intelligence will remain critical, but it will also remain insufficient against an adversary that is a dynamic, evolving force. No central authority within the network of terrorist organizations can control, or has the responsibility for designing, future operations against our interests. Thus, there is no triumph of intelligence collection that can completely remedy all of our intelligence shortfalls. The Intelligence Community will win small battles against terrorism, but it is still at risk of losing far larger ones.

In addition to gathering even more raw intelligence, we need to counter the adaptable adversary with our own adaptation.[13] A $30-billion U.S. intelligence empire, coupled with a Department of Defense (DOD) that vastly outspends even its most threatening rivals, has most of the advantages, to be sure. But hierarchies are handicapped when confronted by flexible, highly adaptable, and networked enemies. A partial list of remedies to U.S. intelligence's shortcomings is given in table 2. It is not surprising that several of these remedies are either on the drawing board or actually being implemented within the Intelligence Community. How vigorously they will be undertaken or how quickly they will mature cannot yet be known.

Breaking Down Barriers

The U.S. Intelligence Community remains handicapped by internal barriers and walls meant to protect intelligence sources and methods—at a time the outside world, by interesting contrast, apparently sees the value in making unprecedented investments in getting connected ("connectivity").

There is no clearer manifestation of stifling hierarchy than Intelligence Community "stovepipes" that have persisted for years and that prevent many of the people working against terrorist targets from effectively communicating with each other. At times, the stovepipes even prevent organizations from becoming aware of each other's existence.[14] U.S. intelligence components working against terrorist targets need the ability to share data and analyses spontaneously (as academic experts do when communicating routinely over the Internet); they should not be forced to deal with a maze of bureaucratic and security-derived obstacles. That is one of the hurdles implicitly referenced by Tenet in the September 16, 2001, admonition to the Intelligence Community to erase bureaucratic blockages to fighting the war on terrorism effectively.[15] The Intelligence Community's electronic connectivity in addressing the nonstate-sponsored terrorist threat is ironically held hostage to counterintelligence concerns that emanate from threats from state actors, who, unlike al Qaeda, have ample budgets to staff their own intelligence apparatus and target it against Washington.

It is no coincidence that most multidisciplinary intelligence analysts and collectors function in largely separate electronic compartments.[16] The "need to know" principle, of course, cannot be jettisoned entirely, but the tradeoff between protecting security and promoting collegiality certainly bears recalibration. The current stovepipe approach—which erects barriers to lateral collaboration by restricting communications and rewarding only bureaucratic loyalty within the organization—makes it possible for unrelated intelligence components in different institutions to do essentially the same work against terrorist targets—wasting resources and preventing many professionals from leveraging the efforts of counterparts who remain outside their immediate circle. Good academics invest considerable energy in finding out about the research efforts of their colleagues in other institutions; Intelligence Community

Table 2. **Self-Organized Terrorism Compared with Conventional Military Threats**

Proposal	Details
Community information technology (IT) architecture	Create seamless IT system that is shared globally; agency systems are mutually compatible and integrated, though heterogeneous and classified
Universal connectivity	All professionals working terrorism are on the same system and can reach one another easily
Full reach network	Identical email, browsing, collaboration suites for all users
Local autonomy	Local users can create a Web presence at their volition on the Intelligence Community classified Internet, enabling more effective collaboration
Spontaneous organization	Communities of interest can assemble as they deem necessary; individual judgments about the utility of organizing carry the day
External research center	Off-campus facility to promote research collaboration and host visitors from academia and the private sector
Counterterrorism "skunk works"	Institution that promotes innovative ideas and creative approaches unencumbered by traditional bureaucratic restraints
Terrorism red teams	Standing groups of experts with the task of simulating the planning of the adversary's exploitation of U.S. vulnerabilities
Counterstrategy organization	Internal think tank empowered to integrate research, red team, and game results with raw intelligence to develop clear picture of adversary strategy
Denial and deception cell	Special study group charged with countering adversary measures to deceive U.S. and allied intelligence and devising novel means of deceiving the adversary
Gaming and simulation center	On-campus facility on scale of national war colleges that is charged with gaming terrorism with participation of U.S. and allied intelligence and policy communities
Software development initiative	Program to seed development of software tools to further highly advanced analysis and data processing
Long-term input into development of collection systems	Integrated effort empowered to represent counterterrorist community in developing long-term collection platforms

professionals would reap dividends from similar efforts that at least match those of their academic counterparts.

Also, the people fighting terrorism need to break down barriers to their ability to form alliances with external centers of expertise. In recent years the Intelligence Community has improved analysts' access to all of the resources made available by the information revolution. It is safe to say that Intelligence Community data systems are unparalleled. Some elements of the analytic community have created outreach programs to get beyond the walls protecting classified data. But for those in the counterterrorism community, more needs to be done to create connections with substantive experts who do not yet have all the security clearances. No organization, not even one large and deep, can have a monopoly on expertise—especially on a subject as complex as the Islamic Reformation.

Creative alliances with think tanks, academics, and other centers of expertise should be a force multiplier. Intelligence Community business practices should promote rather than impede informal and mutually beneficial contact between the analyst and the business community. With the stakes as high as they are, some of those prospective relationships even deserve to be formal, institutionalized partnerships.

Bolstering In-House Analysis

U.S. intelligence must integrate operational intelligence (intelligence that supports operational planning and covert action), at which the community already excels, with true multidisciplinary expertise, thus capitalizing on expertise in politics, demographics, economics, and culture. The original focus of the Counterterrorism Center, created by then-Director of Central Intelligence William Casey, was almost exclusively operational, leaving all multidisciplinary analysis to the Office of Near East, South Asian, and African Analysis and similar components in the Directorate of Intelligence. As al Qaeda gathered momentum in the 1990s and the Middle East peace process eroded, the burden on operators and analysts alike to put out daily fires intensified, leaving little time for the sort of research and honest digging that was routine in the Intelligence Community during the Cold War. The press of daily tasks also reinforced the Intelligence Community's tendency to insulate.

The Intelligence Community needs and deserves an unparalleled center of excellence on the roots and substance of terrorism—one that makes the time to do its own research while routinely exchanging insights with a well-developed network of allies on the outside. At the very least, the Intelligence Community needs an analytic effort that carries great prestige rather than one subordinated to supporting operational planning and covert action.

In the course of bolstering analysis, there is considerable room for more creative approaches, and it makes sense to ask if the Intelligence Community needs its own analytic "skunk works" to foster such methods. These approaches include assembling "red teams" whose purpose is to simulate adversary strategy and doctrine, perhaps replicating, to the extent feasible, the decentralized nature of the threat. Military intelligence units do this from time to time during conflict, and DOD has become adept at using this approach to test its own vulnerabilities. The Intelligence Community should be equally practiced at exploring adversary strategy, especially that of an evolving, adapting enemy whose future stratagems are not yet on the drawing board. The analysis of adversary strategy should have an identifiable and respected bureaucratic base of operation, informed by the most creative thinking of experts in the defense community and in the private sector. Red team mechanisms should be standing requirements, rather than the one-time experiments that are routinely applied to issues such as terrorist innovation with nuclear technologies.

Table 2 summarizes a series of steps to bolster intelligence that are clearly attainable. They include measures that would enable Intelligence Community analysts to take advantage of all of the benefits of large-scale information networks that are enjoyed by the academic and research communities that use the Internet to share data and locate expertise spontaneously and the ability to organize communities of interest as soon as the benefits are evident. Other measures are targeted at institutionalizing alliances between experts in and outside the Intelligence Community and at fostering creative analytic approaches. Still other steps are meant to sharpen the collection of raw intelligence by taking advantage of deeper analytic expertise, thus better focusing human-source intelligence, signals, imagery, and other intelligence collection systems.

Modeling and Simulation

The Intelligence Community should develop new software tools to support both data processing and analysis. The Intelligence Community should be using new techniques to explore the evolution of terrorist networks and their adaptability. One new approach, agent-based modeling, focuses on bottom-up computer simulation of human interaction and generates exactly the form of decentralized, spontaneous organization of social networks that we observe in the formation of political movements and in the world of terrorism. A decade ago, an adaptable network of adversaries could have been spoken of only metaphorically. As agent-based modeling shows, with recent advances in computing power and software, synthetic adversary networks can be built in digital space and their evolution simulated harmlessly. In addition, the Intelligence Community should routinely adopt the best practices of DOD and the private sector for modeling and simulation. At the same time, the Intelligence Community should prod DOD to create new warfare models that go beyond evaluating conventional weapons systems. To be able to influence and shape DOD modeling, the Intelligence Community must become so good at modeling and simulation that it can influence the development of those arts outside its own walls.

The art of analytic gaming remains a uniquely effective tool for assessing the interplay of competing strategies, as senior military officers learn in staff colleges. A properly framed game can shed light on the calculations of both adversaries and coalition partners. It is surprising that Intelligence Community components have not more robustly and routinely exploited this technique for assessing terrorism. There is now expertise to draw from within the Intelligence Community and a greater appetite for experimentation than existed a year or two ago.

Those techniques might illuminate many examples of adversary strategy that could surprise us next time. Their strategy may depend on how much the terrorists have learned from the strikes against the United States and the war in Afghanistan. For example, attempts by al Qaeda to inspire jihad in places like Pakistan failed dismally, but the attacks on September 11 appear to have prompted an unlikely spontaneous partnership with whoever conducted the anthrax attacks in the United States in the weeks that followed. Will the terrorists design their own approach with a more creative view of spontaneous partnerships next time? How does the Intelligence Community assess their capacity for learning?

The Intelligence Community should continue to counter denial and deception efforts by terrorist networks. Denial and deception analysis is a relatively new element in the intelligence toolkit and refers to measures to counteract the efforts of U.S. adversaries to escape detection by U.S. intelligence satellites and other collection means, as well as measures to counteract adversary efforts to purposefully mislead U.S. intelligence by generating data that point in the wrong direction. Washington cannot allow the adversary to play games with the U.S. Intelligence Community by placing false leads and producing false warnings. It is uncertain whether the general alerts issued by the Office of Homeland Security during late 2001 were prompted by clever manipulation on the part of terrorist networks that, if they were paying attention, surely noticed that they had the capacity to take the American economy partially offline for days at a time by allowing their own communications to leak. It may be no coincidence that senior al Qaeda leaders in late 2001 publicly framed future assaults on America as attacks on the U.S. economy. The Intelligence Community must determine the magnitude of the threat to the economy and the strategies likely to be used in an attack aimed solely at economic destruction.

The realization, on the part of senior management of the Intelligence Community, of the need for creative new approaches is encouraging. Until shortly after September 11, the Intelligence Community was not in the traditional multidisciplinary analysis business, but the creation of the Office of Terrorism Analysis within the CIA's Counterterrorism Center changed that. This kind of initiative in analytic methodology holds promise, and efforts to reinvigorate the long-term effort to generate more creative raw intelligence collection are in the works. Moreover, in the last 3 or 4 years the Directorate of Intelligence has taken measures to create and sustain "out-of-the-box" analytic approaches to difficult intelligence issues, as well as to develop mechanisms to tap expertise outside the Intelligence Community. What is needed now is a period of growth and development of those programs and the spread of best practices into the counterterrorism community.

The Focus on What Is Secret

It is de rigueur for an analysis of intelligence priorities to cite the need to invest in human intelligence collection. Indeed, in a speech to CIA employees in May 1998, Tenet cited counterterrorism as an essential reason to strengthen the Directorate of Operations.[17]

The war on terrorism will place intense pressure on all intelligence collection systems, and it may do so for a generation or more. The Intelligence Community will be tempted to "solve" the intelligence problem by throwing resources at collection systems. Although more resources would help, even with more data the Intelligence Community is likely to be frustrated by its failure to prevent every attack on U.S. interests. The adaptable adversaries who will make up the future terrorist threat will have the incentives and the means to "game" Western intelligence collection systems. Collection needs to be sharp and focused on what counts rather than hopelessly broad. Ironically, improving the analytic component of counterterrorism may be the most promising way to ensure that collection initiatives are well focused. The issue is not exclusively tactical intelligence but also enabling the counterterrorism community to tailor long-term development of collection systems to targets.

Accordingly, we should dispense with the destructive idea that the analytic corps of the Intelligence Community should confine its attention to the dimensions of the terrorism problem that play to its "comparative advantage" of secret information. Intelligence Community analysts will either have the expertise required to get the job done or not. In the long run, it is the job of the Intelligence Community to develop both analytic expertise and classified data sources on issues of interest to the national security community. That is, the Intelligence Community must give priority to collecting the information that the policymakers most need and want.

Metrics: How Will We Know We're Headed in the Right Direction?

If a metric were invented to measure the progress of the Intelligence Community in the fight against terrorism, there would be tension between the wish to base measurements on results and the desire to base measurements on actions taken by U.S. intelligence agencies. Both metrics are important. The United States must resist the temptation to interpret certain tactical victories, especially those enabled by a convenient but perhaps unique ally like the Northern Alliance, as evidence that it has solved the problem. An adversary intent on surprising us will be comfortable with long lulls in its fight against the United States. Those lulls will not necessarily mean that the United States has won the battle, any more than they did in 1998 and 1999.

If all goes well, some Intelligence Community initiatives will succeed and others will fail. The successes will be informed by lessons from the failures, which will be short-lived and corrected. Any metric the Intelligence Community employs to gauge progress—and it must use metrics—needs to make room for intelligent risk-taking. According to economist Hal Varian, an American expert in technology and innovation at the University of California, Berkeley, the keys to any successful business community revolution are experimentation, capitalization, management, competition, and consolidation.[18] Applying that paradigm to the U.S. Intelligence Community, it makes sense to credit the mid-1980s creation of the Counterterrorism Center as the critical first innovation in the fight against terrorism. It was an improvement, but one that did not go far enough. Its mission was almost solely intended to augment the collection of human source intelligence—not to deepen expertise and produce breakthroughs in intellectual capital that might enable us to outwit the adversary. In those instances in which the terrorists made mistakes, intelligence analysis assisted some successful efforts to interdict terrorist plots against U.S. interests. But intelligence analysis and human-source collection left us vulnerable to terrorist plots in which the terrorists used better tradecraft.

The Intelligence Community thus needs a more risk-taking and failure-tolerant management approach. This national security issue is not one on which to save pennies or to let the possibility of failure suppress innovative approaches. In the medium term, three broad metrics should suggest progress: connectivity is well established, multidisciplinary analysis is diverse and prospering, and individual initiative reigns supreme. Broader dividends will follow if high scores are achieved on those metrics.

Progress Improving Connectivity

Other improvements are essential as we complete the innovation phase. For one, the successful intelligence enterprise, like its adversary, will be networked and agile. One indicator is the development of strong ties between Intelligence Community entities working on counterterrorism issues. That will require creation of collaborative mechanisms that do not yet exist. In particular, professionals in the counterterrorist community who work in different buildings, different cities, and different agencies and on different local computer networks will have the ability to create their own collaborative ties rather than wait for senior managers to authorize them and make the required hardware available. The need to form such ties and use them in countering terrorism will be the final compelling reason to reform the management of Intelligence Community information systems.

A connected community will be one that knows immediately where to find the specialized bit of expertise or the arcane fact that makes the difference in a piece of analysis or in a clandestine collection program.

One critical step is integrating the Office of Homeland Security into the Intelligence Community's information networks and its client base for its most sophisticated and elaborate products. The Office of Homeland Security is a new organization with the teething problems invariably associated with a new bureaucracy, but the Intelligence Community should take on the mission of integrating the office into its operations and analysis.

Strengthening Multidisciplinary Analysis

Multidisciplinary analytic approaches to counterterrorism are new, and they will take time to establish and capitalize intellectually. If all goes well, managers of counterterrorism analysis will make room for research and teamwork under the press of daily deadlines, especially when the current war in Afghanistan wanes and demands for current intelligence support are less pressing. Perhaps the most telling measure of the health of the intelligence analysis function will be how the transition from the current war to the longer-term fight is handled and whether analysts are given the chance to take the time to dig deep and think creatively.

If developments are moving along the right track, the more creative approaches to analysis will be well staffed, reasonably funded, and institutionalized within the counterterrorism community. No approach would remain untested for its applicability to the counterterrorism problem. The output would be reports and briefings based on research, workshops, conferences, games, red teams, advanced data processing, advanced analytic software, and collaboration across agencies and institutions—not to mention the improved collection of raw intelligence that all of this may help to make possible. The optimum mix of approaches will take time to determine, but it will be diverse and not focused exclusively on current analysis.

There must also be accountability. Eventually, clever approaches must produce both actionable products and new intellectual capital, which would be shared within the community at large. High standards must apply to the new counterterrorism product line.

Fostering Individual Initiative

Common wisdom is that the U.S. Intelligence Community is so vast and its organizational structure so complex that changing its leadership or altering its organizational chart is not likely to accomplish much. But lessons drawn from the hierarchical, military model can miss the point. The successful intelligence enterprise can be sufficiently agile if, like its adversary, the terrorist network, it is driven largely by individual initiative rather than commanded entirely from the top. Senior Intelligence Community leaders, while being careful in crafting their daily message to the Oval Office, need to engage in creative delegation and promote initiative and creative thinking (including so-called out-of-the-box thinking) by the workforce.

Another reason to empower individuals is the efficiency gains produced by reducing layers of supervision. The Intelligence Community is not only stovepiped, but it is also riddled with layers of management designed to provide redundancy in an effort to avoid mistakes. Analysts have traditionally been subject to multiple layers of supervisory review, as well as to additional review by editorial staffs. Although there has been an effort to streamline the review process in recent years, there remain abundant economies to be realized by placing the individual analyst closer to the decisionmakers who are the end users of the product and relying on individual accountability to ensure quality.

Emphasis on the individual would represent a sharp break with the past. Intelligence Community senior leaders are accustomed to being the authors of new initiatives rather than their enablers. Meanwhile, managers and senior analysts climbing the ranks are used to avoiding risks that would take them off the fast track. The tendency to confine risk-taking to the top and to constrain individual initiative because it might lead to a mistake is one of the things that must change if the fight against terrorism is to succeed.

Conclusion

Good intelligence will accomplish only so much. Policymakers must also be inclined to new approaches, and they need to be receptive to messages from the Intelligence Community that are inconvenient to the daily policy agenda. The Intelligence Community will be doing its duty if two things that mark all successful intelligence enterprises are mastered: forging a close connection to policy and being persistent when it has to persuade an audience of the need to do something different. The Intelligence

Community must have the will to resist the temptation to sacrifice one of those things for the sake of the other.

Two indicators will be telling. First, the "resource mix" in the Intelligence Community must be optimized without being held prisoner to debilitating bickering. One vulnerability is likely to be internal Intelligence Community struggles over resources, as competing collection systems argue the case for more people and funding at the expense of each other and at the expense of creative analysis. By focusing excessively on any one intelligence collection resource, including human-source reporting, we run the risk of producing occasional operational successes (when the Intelligence Community is fortunate enough to get access to just the right cell or terrorist communications channel) at the expense of preventing national traumas in other instances (when the terrorists are merely lucky or when they outsmart our best efforts). This is a principal legacy of September 11. Strong Intelligence Community leadership and alert congressional oversight can avert such an outcome.

Second, when all is said and done, the joint House and Senate investigations will need to focus on Intelligence Community culture and business practices, not merely on the organizational chart. That means going beyond finding scapegoats and redrawing lines of subordination and hierarchy. And the professionals who are in the business of intelligence gathering and analysis must be part of developing the solution, not merely held responsible for implementing a plan designed by an outside group. If those professionals are doing business as usual several years hence, we will have failed to get it right.

In sum, the Intelligence Community needs to become as agile and as innovative as its terrorist adversary. It can take constructive cues from counterparts outside the realm of intelligence collection or analysis: the network of experts and data sources in the Nation's best think tanks, its best universities, its best war colleges, its best consultancies. It is a matter of where to set the bar and how to unleash the Intelligence Community's talents. Improving communications, emphasizing individual initiative, reducing bureaucratic barriers, and boosting multidisciplinary analysis are keys in the months ahead.

Notes

[1] The Select Committee to Study Governmental Operations with Respect to Intelligence Activities, chaired by Sen. Frank Church (D–ID), was established on January 27, 1975, to investigate abuses by intelligence agencies. The committee focused on major reforms. Parallel investigations were conducted by another committee chaired by Rep. Otis Pike (D–NY).

[2] Richard K. Betts, "Fixing Intelligence," *Foreign Affairs* 81, no. 1 (January/February 2002).

[3] Ibid.

[4] George Tenet, testimony before the Senate Select Committee on Intelligence, February 7, 2001, accessed at <http://www.odci.gov/cia/public_affairs/speeches/2001/UNCLASWWT_02072001.html>.

[5] U.S. Department of State, <www.state.gov/s/ct/rls/pgtrpt/2000>.

[6] Barton Gellman, "A Strategy's Curious Evolution," *The Washington Post*, January 20, 2002.

[7] Portions of the defense review did concern asymmetric and other forms of fourth-generation warfare. An early introduction to these issues can be found in Martin Van Creveld, *The Transformation of War* (New York: Free Press, 1991).

[8] Michael Doran, "Somebody Else's Civil War," *Foreign Affairs* 81, no. 1 (January/February 2002).

[9] Brad DeLong, <www.j-bradford-delong.net/TotW/Islamic_Reformation.html>.

[10] Stressing the global nature of the threat, Tenet is reported to have told the Cabinet principals in the days immediately following September 11, "You've got a 60-country problem." Dan Balz, Bob Woodward, and Jeff Himmelman, "Ten Days in September," *The Washington Post,* January 27, 2002.

[11] This discussion draws from two streams of literature, one dealing with self-organization and the other with network-centric warfare as applied to terrorism. Representative of the first is Stuart Kauffman, *At Home in the Universe: The Search for the Laws of Self-Organization and Complexity* (New York: Oxford University Press, 1996). The second is represented best by David Ronfeldt and John Arquilla, "Networks, Netwars, and the Fight for the Future," on FirstMonday.org, October 2001, accessed at <www.firstmonday.org/issues/issue6_10/ronfeldt/index.html>. Ronfeldt is a senior social scientist at RAND, and Arquilla is a professor at the Naval Postgraduate School.

[12] Self-organization and the operation of networks are relatively new ideas in the conduct of warfare. Self-organization refers to the propensity of the elements of a system to establish order without central oversight, as though doing so spontaneously. The idea is especially germane to biological and political systems, in which cells begin to work synergistically—in the early development of an organism or when a political movement is quickly "born" of commonly shared but only recently formed opinions. Financial markets also exhibit self-organization when bubbles are created out of the dynamics of expectations of individual participants. Networks also exhibit emerging structure as nodes are added and connectivity multiplies disproportionately. For further information, see Kauffman, as well as Ronfeldt and Arquilla.

[12] Experts at the RAND Corporation make similar recommendations for countering adversaries on the conventional military battlefield: the U.S. military counters dispersed, decentralized foes with "swarming tactics" that are enabled by the adaptability of our own forces. See, for example, John Matsumora et al., "The Army after Next: Exploring New Concepts and Technologies for the Light Battle Force," RAND Corporation, DB-258-A, 1999, accessed at <www.rand.org/publications/electronic/force.html>, and the list of other publicly available publications on the RAND Web site.

[13] The creation of the Counterterrorism Center (CTC) in the mid-1980s was intended to achieve improved connectivity by bringing together professionals from different intelligence and law enforcement agencies. For its day, the CTC was a dramatic step in the right direction. The CTC, however, was conceived as a largely operational entity and lacked strong ties to the broad community of intelligence analysts and to other centers of multidisciplinary expertise outside the Intelligence Community.

[14] The message has been referenced frequently in the press and in other literature; see Betts.

[15] Analysts directly supporting the collection of raw intelligence are not so removed.

[16] See www.cia.gov for the text of the speech.

[17] Hal Varian, "Five Habits of Very Effective Revolutions," *Forbes ASAP*, February 21, 2000, accessed at <www.forbes.com/asap/00/0221/073.htm>.

Part VIII—Deception, Denial, and Disclosure Problems

In wartime, truth is so precious that she should always be attended by a bodyguard of lies.

—Winston Churchill

Chapter 28

Intelligence and Deception

Michael I. Handel

The ultimate goal of stratagem is to make the enemy quite certain, very decisive, and wrong.[1]

If surprise is indeed the most important "Key to Victory," then stratagem is the Key to surprise.[2]

Ming: Lay on many deceptive operations, Be seen in the west and march out of the east; lure him in the north and strike him in the south. Drive him crazy and bewilder him so that he disperses his forces in confusion.[3]

Deception can be found in any human activity which involves competition over scarce resources or any other desired benefits that are limited in supply. Whenever and wherever a situation exists—in business, economic life, politics on all levels, love—through which an advantage can be gained by cheating, there will always be individuals or groups who will resort to it. Although in civilian affairs, cheating, deception, or fraud are usually punishable by law or by informal sanctions (such as the loss of credibility or reputation in certain circles), this not the case in war nor, to a lesser extent, in international politics, which have their own norms and morality (that is, raison d'etat). Deception in international politics (not to be discussed in this chapter) and more frequently in war is rewarded by greater achievements and success. While extremely helpful in war, deception has frequently failed, or failed to achieve its intended objectives, and on occasions has even proved to be counterproductive. Despite this word of caution, deception must be seen as an accepted and integral part of any rational conduct of war. In the words of Sun Tzu, "All warfare is based on deception."[4]

Deception in war must be considered a rational and necessary type of activity because it acts as a force multiplier; that is, it magnifies the strength or power of the successful deceiver.[5] Forgoing the use of deception in war undermines one's own strength. Therefore, when all other elements of strength in war are roughly equal, deception will further amplify the available strength of a state—or allow it to use its force more economically—by achieving a quicker victory at a lower cost and with fewer casualties.

Source: Michael I. Handel, "Intelligence and Deception," in John Gooch and Amos Perlmutter, eds., *Military Deception and Strategic Surprise* (New York: Frank Cass and Co., 1982), 122–154. Copyright © 1982 by Frank Cass Publishers. Reprinted by permission.

In the case of unequal opponents, deception (and surprise) can help the weaker side compensate for its numerical or other inadequacies. For that reason, the side that is at a disadvantage often has a more powerful incentive to resort to deceptive strategy and tactics. This was recognized by Clausewitz, who cannot be said to have otherwise emphasized the importance of deception as part of war.

> The weaker the forces that are at the disposal of the supreme commander, the more appealing the use of cunning becomes. In a state of weakness and insignificance, when prudence, judgment, and ability no longer suffice, cunning may well appear the only hope. The bleaker the situation, with everything concentrating on a single desperate attempt, more readily cunning is joined to daring. Released from all future considerations, and liberated from thoughts of later retribution, boldness and cunning will be free to augment each other to the point of concentrating a faint glimmer of hope into a single beam of light which may yet kindle a flame.[6]

This implies the existence of an inverse relationship between strength and the incentive to use deception. This observation can frequently be found in military history: during World War II, the British had a more powerful incentive to use strategic deception than the Germans did; and as long as the Israelis perceived themselves as being weaker than their Arab opponents (in 1948, 1956, 1967), they often employed stratagem and deception, while the Arabs, who perceived themselves as superior, did not. In 1973, however, the reversal of these perceptions saw a concomitant change in the incentive to resort to deception: the Israelis relied more on material strength while the Arabs had to resort to deception, which they had earlier neglected.

Enjoying overwhelming material superiority in the Vietnam War or even in World War II, when deception was left primarily in the hands of the British, the United States used deception rarely with a few exceptions on the tactical level. In the early stages of the Korean War (for example, MacArthur's landing in Inchon) when the Americans were weak, they did resort to the combination mentioned by Clausewitz of readiness to take very high risks (a maximax strategy) and the use of deception and surprise. Then, as the United States increased in strength in the later stages of the Korean War, they failed to employ those elements. The landing in Inchon may, however, be related more to General MacArthur's character and style than to a real change in the U.S. high command's approach to war.

While the tendency of more powerful states to rely more on "brute force" can be understood, it certainly cannot be justified. The strong and powerful need not waste their strength or increase their own costs just because they are stronger. Strength not accompanied by stratagem and deception will become sterile and will inevitably decline. Perhaps for that very reason, the more powerful military establishments must make a conscious effort systematically to incorporate deception into their military thinking.

The rational use of deception can be achieved in a number of ways. One type of deception attempts to misdirect the enemy's attention, causing him to concentrate his forces in the wrong place. By doing this, the deceiver tries to make his adversary violate the principle of concentration of forces in space.[7]

Well-known examples of this are the Allied deception plans that diverted German attention from the beaches of Normandy to Norway and/or Pas de Calais as possible landing sites for an Allied invasion.[8] Similarly, in 1940, the Germans helped the Allies to deceive themselves by causing them to concentrate their troops in Northern France on the Belgian border rather than opposite the Ardennes.[9]

A second and related type of deception attempts to make the adversary violate the so-called principle of the economy of force.[10] The intention here is to cause the opponent to waste his resources (for example, time, ammunition, weapons, manpower, fuel) in unimportant directions or preferably on nonexistent targets. A simple example would be to make an adversary fire a large number of scarce and expensive anti-aircraft missiles at a cheap remotely piloted vehicle decoy or an artificially created radar signature instead of at real attacking aircraft; during the Battle of Britain, the British caused the Germans to attack nonexistent airfields and factories by setting up phony targets and interfering with German electronic navigation aids. Other, much more complicated strategic or technological ploys to make the enemy waste his resources can also be designed. Information can be spread through a variety of sources that a revolutionary technological breakthrough (such as the development of "death rays" or "particle beam weapons")[11] has been achieved; this will induce the enemy to invest huge amounts of money, scientific man-hours, and time in the wrong direction—whereas the deceiver knows it will lead to a dead end or be too costly to be useful in practice.

A third type of deception, which is also related to the two mentioned earlier, is designed to surprise the opponent—to create a situation that will later catch him off-guard, unprepared for action when it comes. In this case, the variety of deceptive ploys and methods most frequently employed are intended to dull his senses and create the impression that no offensive plans are entertained by the deceiver. This can be done through the maintenance—and in fact cultivation—of normal political and economic relations up to the moment of attack, as was Hitler's policy toward Russia until the eve of *Barbarossa* in June 1941.[12]

When two or more states are already at war it is much more difficult to launch a surprise attack out of the blue. On such occasions, the deceiver frequently tries to create the impression of routine activities by very gradually conditioning the adversary to a certain repetitive pattern of behavior. Just such a ruse was employed by the Germans when they jammed British radar stations in order to enable the German battle cruisers the *Scharnhorst* and the *Gneisenau* and the cruiser *Prinz Eugen* to break out of the English Channel undetected on the night of February 11, 1942. "The German radar officers, headed by General Wolfgang Martini, had subtly increased the intensity of their jamming over a period so that we could get acclimatized to it, without realizing that it was now so intense that our radar was almost useless."[13]

Another way of moving large concentrations of troops towards an attack without alerting the adversary is to disguise those preparations as military maneuvers. Secrecy is further enhanced in many such cases when not even the participating troops are informed that they are about to go into action. A favorite of the Soviet Union, this last ploy was used on the eve of the Soviet attack on Manchuria in 1945 and the invasion of Czechoslovakia in 1968. A similar deception cover was carried out by the Syrians and Egyptians before their attack on Israel in October 1973.

In the final analysis, all types of deception operations can be said to be directed at misleading, misinforming, or confusing an opponent on only two basic types of questions. The first is to deceive him concerning one's own intentions; the second is to deceive him concerning one's own capabilities.[14] A successful deception operation can be aimed primarily in one of these directions, although it frequently includes both at the same time. After all, intentions and capabilities are closely related to one another in the conduct of war.[15] Thus, convincing an opponent that one lacks certain capabilities may also convince him that because of the absence of such capabilities, the deceiving side also has no intention of carrying out a given type of operation. For example, the Egyptians on the eve of the Yom Kippur War spread rumors that their anti-aircraft missile systems had been short of certain spare parts (capabilities) since the expulsion of the Soviet advisers in June 1972, and that therefore they obviously were not yet ready to initiate war (intentions).[16]

Deception concerning intentions will always try to conceal the actual goals and plans of the deceiver. This can be achieved through secrecy (a passive mode of deception) or through a more elaborate active deception plot that diverts the opponent's attention from the real set of intentions to another. In fact, the more active type of deception must always be based on the successful concealment of one's real intentions in addition to the development of a decoy of fake intentions. Any breach of security concerning one's actual intentions will of course lead to failure and probably to self-deception, and may even become an instrument for the adversary's own deceptions, in that the enemy can pretend to be deceived while in fact he is anticipating the deceiver's move and planning to spring his own surprise or trap.

In complex deception operations, it is therefore extremely important to have a special unit that will try to ascertain whether the adversary has really swallowed the bait or is only pretending to have been deceived.[17] Penetration of the enemy's intelligence and/or his command echelons is essential. Through the use of ULTRA, the British in World War II were unusually successful in following up and monitoring complex deceptions. The detailed deciphering of German codes enabled British intelligence continuously to check and recheck the degree of success of its deception plans and then to modify them accordingly in order to make them even more effective.[18]

Returning to the question of deception intended to conceal one's real intentions, we find a number of examples. Before launching their first offensive against the Italian 10th Army in the Western Desert in December 1940, the British under Wavell had successfully convinced the Italians that their intentions were defensive. Here is how the official British history summarizes this deception operation.

> The fact is that in war, it is usually possible to produce some sort of evidence in support of almost every course of action open to the enemy; the art lies in knowing what to make of it all. In this case, the Italian Air Force (in the Western Desert) had observed and reported movements and dispositions with fair accuracy—indeed, it was often intended by the British that they should. The important point is that

these reports were consistent with what the 10th Army were convinced was happening. They themselves were very much occupied with their own preparations for renewing the advance, and were only too ready to interpret the air reports as indicating that the British were actively improving their defensive arrangements. The British attempt at strategic deception was therefore successful.[19]

The British and Americans did not and could not hide their intention to invade somewhere in Southern Europe, but led the Germans to believe that they would invade Sardinia, Southern France, and Greece instead of Sicily, which was the more obvious target. Similarly, Operation *Fortitude*, the code name for the deception preparations for Operation *Overlord* (the invasion of Normandy) did not try to hide Allied intentions to invade Europe or even more specifically to cross the Channel, but focused German attention on Pas de Calais.[20] So successful was this stratagem that the Germans, anticipating a major attack in Pas de Calais, had most of their forces in that area a few days after the invasion of Normandy was well under way. There is, by the way, very little doubt that the greatest deception efforts ever invested in a military operation were part of the preparation for the invasion of Normandy, 1944. *Overlord* was covered by numerous complementary deception operations (not all of which are probably known even to this day) which required careful and elaborate coordination and a meticulous follow-up operation in order to estimate the extent to which the Germans were indeed deceived. This tremendous and ultimately successful investment in deception plans for D-Day is not surprising. Landing operations are notoriously tricky and involve unusually high risks. The sheer number of participants in Operation *Overlord* (the largest landing operation in history) made it even more essential to use elaborate deception plans in order to conceal the preparations and areas selected for attack. The success of the Allied deception plans is amazing even today, and no doubt was achieved through meticulous preparation, good luck, and the poor quality of German intelligence. The surprise achieved in Operation *Overlord* was total—one of the few cases of a "surprise out of the blue" with no real warning time, any lead warning time, or alert.[21]

In planning their attack on Egypt in collaboration with the British and French in 1956, the Israelis deliberately created the impression that they intended to attack Jordan by concentrating their troops closer to the Jordanian border and by escalating their reprisal raids against Jordan.[22] (Secrecy was so well kept that the British ambassador was sent to protest to the Foreign Ministry against Israeli reprisals and to warn against an attack on Jordan, while the British Government knew that the real object of the forthcoming attack would be Egypt.)

In mid-May 1967, President Nasser decided to send Egyptian troops into the Sinai, thereby initiating the crisis which continued to escalate through the month. By the end of May, Israel and Egypt were fully mobilized and ready for war. By June 2, it became clear to the Israeli Government that war was unavoidable. The problem was how to launch a successful surprise attack while both sides were fully mobilized and alert. As part of a deception plan to conceal Israel's intention to go to war, Dayan told a British journalist on June 2 that it was both too early and too late for Israel to go to war. He repeated this statement during a news conference on June 3:

> It is too late for a spontaneous military reaction to Egypt's blockade of the Tiran Straits . . . and still too early to learn any conclusions of the possible outcome of diplomatic action. The Government . . . embarked on diplomacy and we must give it a chance.[23]

Furthermore, it was decided to release a number of reservists during the weekend to create the impression that preparation and alert had been reduced. It is very possible that other plans which never became known were also implemented. In this case, the deception was simple and successful, and Israel achieved total surprise on the morning of June 5, despite the crisis atmosphere and intensified intelligence alert.[24]

It is perhaps little known that the preparations for the Israeli raid on Entebbe in July 1976 also included a deception plan intended to misdirect primarily the Americans, who were apparently watching by satellite. The deception plan indicated (mainly through spreading rumors to the press) that the Israelis planned to launch a large-scale attack on PLO targets in Lebanon in order to capture hostages who could be traded for the hijacked passengers in Entebbe. As far as is known, this deception plan successfully directed attention away from the possibility of a direct raid on Entebbe itself. The attack was a total surprise for everyone.

During peacetime or before the initiation of hostilities, it is possible, as is well known from the extensive literature on surprise attack, successfully to conceal the intention to attack; once a state of war and conflict already exists, the intention to attack in one place or another is already taken for granted. Under such circumstances, deception becomes much more important because it has to give the adversary the wrong expectations concerning one's inevitable and known intention to take action. The fewer the directions of possible attack, the more important a deception cover will be. Since it was almost inevitable that the Allies would have to attack across the Channel, the probability of success had to be increased by deception.

Deception can also be employed to mislead an opponent about the deceiver's military, primarily material, capabilities. The discussion of deception in this particular context is also a convenient opportunity to demonstrate some of the potential dangers and possible damage that can result from miscalculations and the wrong application of this art. It is important to emphasize that deception is by no means always a panacea for weakness or difficult situations, nor is it always as successful as most of the enthusiastic literature about it seems to indicate.

The use of deception to mislead an opponent concerning military capabilities can be divided into two types. The first is intended to create an exaggerated evaluation of capabilities in terms of both quantity and quality; the second attempts to conceal existing capabilities. The former type of bluff is normally practiced by a weaker state trying to deter a more powerful adversary, translate an imaginative superiority in military capabilities into political gains, or gain enough time to close a dangerous capability gap. The second type of deception concerning capabilities tries to hide a state's real capabilities primarily in order to create an impression that it is incapable of executing certain offensive plans, that is, to conceal its offensive intentions. Both types of capability-oriented deceptions need not (particularly in wartime) be contradictory or mutually exclusive. A state may wish simultaneously to conceal certain capabilities and inflate others (for example, in terms of absolute quantities or relative quantities at different places, rates of production, qualitative achievements).

The attempt to deceive by pretending to have larger than existing capabilities is well known in time of both peace and war. As already mentioned above, the intention behind this type of ploy is normally to deter a stronger adversary. This was the trick played by the Germans from 1936 onward on the French in particular and less successfully on the British and other nations concerning the real strength of the nascent *Luftwaffe*. The Germans did their utmost to impress foreign visitors such as Charles Lindbergh; Italian Air Marshal, Italo Balbo; RAF Air Vice Marshal, Christopher Courtney; and later the chief of the French Air Force, General Joseph Vuillemin. The Germans staged exciting air shows, flew in most of their latest aircraft to those airfields the guests were visiting, casually reported high production rates for advanced aircraft that in fact never went beyond the experimental stage, and gave tours of aircraft factories:

> In general, perceptions in the West of the *Luftwaffe*'s strength were exaggerated precisely as Hitler and Goring intended. Aerial blackmailing of Germany's neighbors became an important ingredient in Hitler's diplomatic negotiations which led to his brilliant series of triumphs; the policy of appeasement was founded partially on the fear of the *Luftwaffe*.[25]

The exaggerated strength attributed to the *Luftwaffe* combined with the fear of British and French political leaders that "the bomber will always get through" helped the Nazis to extract considerable political concessions from the West.[26]

Perhaps the best and also most extreme instance of an attempt by a country to inflate its military capabilities was that of Fascist Italy in the 1930s. Signor Mussolini tried to impress on all foreign observers the power of the Italian armed forces—although in this case he probably deceived no one but himself:

> By another confusing piece of legerdemain, in 1938 the composition of [Italian] army divisions had been reduced from three regiments to two. This appealed to Mussolini because it enabled him to say that fascism had sixty divisions instead of barely half as many, but the change caused enormous disorganization just when the war was about to begin; and because he forgot what he had done, several years later he tragically miscalculated the true strength of his forces. It seems to have deceived few other people except himself.[27]

Like Hitler, Mussolini tried—without much success—to impress foreign observers with the superior quantitative and qualitative strength of the Italian Air Force:

> By 1935 Italy claimed most of the international records for flying, and this was a great achievement. The chief of the air staff informed parliament that they had been won with ordinary machines. It was his further boast that Italy no longer needed the help of foreign technology in this field, and indeed that Italian planes were not only

"the best in the world" but in wartime would be able to control the whole Mediterranean. Such statements were, as they were intended to be, greeted with enormous enthusiasm, and the authorities proceeded to draw the conclusion that the Italian air force was second to none, and that Italy must be impregnable.[28]

Italy did its best to exaggerate the figures on the number of Italian aircraft.

> When the Second World War broke out, figures were given to show that Italy had 8,530 planes, but the air ministry privately admitted in April 1939 that there were only 3,000 front-line aircraft, and the naval information service reduced this to under a thousand. On further investigation the figure turned out to be 454 bombers and 129 fighters, nearly all of which were inferior in speed and equipment to contemporary British planes. . . . [Mussolini] can hardly have been intending to bluff foreign observers, because they had their own means of knowing that the official figures of the air ministry were nonsense, and indeed the British were quite sure that the efficiency of the Italian air force was growing less, not greater; the intention was to bluff Italians, and unfortunately it succeeded. [29]

The Italian navy was not in much better shape. Although its battleships and battle cruisers looked elegant and impressive, they were poorly designed. They were built for high speed and therefore were thinly armored; they had no radars or any effective anti-submarine detection capability. Their submarine fleet was the largest in the world (1939) but had no firing computers. It was ill organized and its doctrine, training, and tactics were obsolete. It was good for displays but not for war.

Mussolini successfully deceived not only himself but from May 1938 onwards, Hitler also. During Hitler's visit to Italy in May 1938 Mussolini put before him a seemingly impressive military show.

> The Italian military services performed much better during Hitler's visit in May 1938. An excellent one-battalion exercise combined with a superficially competent show by the navy (which included a simultaneous submerging and surfacing by eighty-six Italian submarines) to give Hitler the impression that Mussolini had revitalized Italy's military forces.[30]

Hitler was duly impressed and deceived concerning Italian capabilities until Italy's defeats in 1940. This misperception cost Germany and Italy dearly later on. Hitler's professional military advisers on the other hand were not as impressed as he was by the Italian military public relations campaign. They reported that the Italian army was poorly equipped and badly trained, and unlike Hitler, they viewed Italy as a military burden, not an asset, which they would prefer to see neutral rather than fighting on Germany's side.[31]

Another example of an attempt to deceive an adversary by inflating one's capabilities was premier Nikita S. Khrushchev's boast (following the launching of the first Soviet sputnik satellite) about the tremendous superiority the USSR had obtained over the United States in the design, testing, and production of intercontinental ballistic missiles (ICBMs). Initially the Soviet Union exaggerated the stage of ICBM development; later it exaggerated and in fact lied about their massive production, and finally it considerably misrepresented their capabilities and accuracy. The Russians were indeed ahead of the United States in launching satellites and their space program, but there was no direct connection at all between their successful space program and the military deployment of ICBMs. Western intelligence, however, could obtain little information on Soviet military ICBM strength, and the Russians used the opportunity to deceive the world (especially the Americans) concerning the advanced deployment of their ICBMs. Statements such as the following were common throughout 1957 and 1958: "We now have all the rockets we need: long range rockets, intermediate rockets, and short range rockets" (Khrushchev). "I think it is no secret that there now exists a range of missiles with the aid of which it is possible to fulfill any assignment of operational and strategic importance" (Khrushchev). "The fact that the Soviet Union was the first to launch an artificial earth satellite, which within a month was followed by another, says a lot. If necessary, tomorrow we can launch 10–20 satellites. All that is required for this is to replace the warhead of an intercontinental ballistic rocket with the necessary instruments. There is a satellite for you" (Khrushchev).[32] In fact, there was little connection between the Soviet space program and its military ICBM program, which lagged way behind. This was not so, of course, in the minds of Western political and military leaders who had little reliable information but were at first impressed by the Soviet space program.

The Americans, who initially believed Khrushchev's statement, accepted the existence of a dangerous "missile gap" and as a result redoubled their efforts to "catch up" with the Soviet Union. By the time of the Cuban missile crisis, the United States had not only closed this fictitious missile gap but ironically had achieved a tremendous lead over the USSR in the military deployment of ICBMs. (One common explanation for the Russian planting of medium range ballistic missiles—MRBMs—in Cuba was exactly the need to close an ICBM missile gap favoring the United States.)

Successful "inflated capability" deceptions can be too much of a good thing. Exaggerated fear of German air superiority led the British (and French) to make excessive political concessions in the short run in order to gain time to catch up with the Germans—but at the same time also to increase their own investment in air power and anti-aircraft defenses (radar in particular). By the time war broke out, the British were in much better shape to meet the German challenge. Hitler may have thus defeated his own purpose in the long run.

Khrushchev's missile gap hoax created a panic in the United States and touched off such an accelerated effort to close the purported gap that within 4 years the United States gained a tremendous edge over the Soviet Union. This was translated into concrete political gains for the United States and a loss of face for the Soviet Union during the missile crisis in Cuba. Ultimately, Khrushchev paid for his hoax with his own career.[33]

The second danger of a successful "capability deception" is that in the end the deceiver may indeed believe his own bluff and at the same time ignore the corrective measures taken by his adversary. That is, the deceiver may see a bluff as reality or a temporary advantage as reflecting a permanent position of superiority which in fact does not exist. What may have been true in 1937 or 1938 was not true by 1939 or 1940 for the relative air strength of the British or Germans. What was true in 1951 was no longer true by 1962. The deceiver may, however, fall into his own trap when he decides to take action which is based on a past real or imagined balance of capabilities. This type of successful deception which culminates in self-deception may have caused Hitler to attack Great Britain (or even open the Second World War) believing as he did in the superiority of the *Luftwaffe*; it led Mussolini to his adventures in Ethiopia, Albania, and Greece, and may have convinced Khrushchev that the Soviet Union was strong enough to challenge the United States in its own backyard in Cuba (whereas the United States probably never had and will never have again such an advantage in capabilities over the Soviet Union).

Thus, successful deception operations intended to inflate capabilities can create three types of serious dangers for the deceiver himself. The first is that the deceived target state will redouble its efforts to improve its own capabilities in reaction to the imagined threat and therefore will gain the upper hand even if it did not intend to do so initially; second, the deceiver's bluff might be called and his weakness will be exposed; thirdly, there is the pitfall of self-deception, that is, accepting one's own bluff as reality and acting upon it.

The other type of capability-related deception is exactly the opposite, namely, it tries to hide and minimize the deceiver's real strength in order to surprise the opponent on the battlefield with unexpected capabilities that may lead to his defeat. While attempts to exaggerate one's own capabilities can often be identified with ambitious and aggressive leaders (for example, Hitler, Mussolini, Khrushchev, Nasser), attempts to conceal one's real strength are more frequently implemented by military leaders and military organizations whose standard operating procedures require secrecy and discretion.

Between 1956 and 1967, for example, the Israel Defense Forces (IDF) carefully concealed its real numerical strength and qualitative improvements. Success in concealing or camouflaging its strength is certainly one of the explanations for the astounding blitzkrieg-type victory that Israel achieved over its Arab neighbors in June 1967. Arab intelligence services completely failed to get an accurate picture of Israel's actual military strength, a fact which contributed to Nasser's decision to initiate the May crisis in 1967. But again, success in concealing one's real strength can also be a double-edged sword. The weakness Israel projected in 1967 was not the intended goal but rather the unplanned byproduct of secrecy. It diminished and weakened Israel's deterrence and tempted the Arabs to attack. Had Israel's real strength been known, deterrence might have succeeded and war could have been avoided. It can therefore be argued again that strategic deception can be too much of a good thing and must be used judiciously.[34]

A similar example is the secrecy maintained by the Soviet Union until 1941 concerning its military capabilities. Given the earlier external threats to the Soviet Union, the long-held tradition of conspiracy and its closed nature, the closed nature of the Soviet political system, and Stalin's own paranoia, the emphasis on total secrecy in the Soviet Union is not surprising. For that reason, the Germans had very poor intelligence concerning the real strength of the Soviet Union. On the eve of *Barbarossa*, German intelligence may have underestimated Soviet strength by as much as 120 divisions (at that time German intelligence had identified 247 Soviet divisions and soon after the war broke out as many as 360). Had the Germans known the real strength of the Soviet Union, they might have decided not to attack at all, as Hitler later told the Italian Foreign Minister, Count Ciano. Excessive Soviet secrecy had therefore led to the collapse of Soviet deterrence and to a war the Soviet Union did not want.[35] The continued closed nature of Soviet society today will have its price too. The United States may overreact to perceptions of exaggerated Soviet strength by investing huge sums in its own military machine—more than it perhaps would if more were known about current Soviet real capabilities and intentions.

Capabilities can normally be concealed best in closed and/or homogeneous societies which are difficult to penetrate (for example, Soviet Union, Japan, Israel in particular until 1967), if and when the opponent's intelligence is weak. In today's world of spy satellites, electronic intelligence, and high-altitude air photography, it is, of course, much more difficult to conceal material military capabilities (although one can assume that in the age of satellite intelligence new types of deception and camouflage have been developed).

At this point, it may be useful to make a distinction between passive deception and active deception. Passive deception is primarily based on secrecy and camouflage,[36] on hiding and concealing one's intentions and/or capabilities from the adversary. Some experts view passive deception as inferior and not likely to succeed against any competent intelligence organization. This, as we have already seen above, is not necessarily true. While measures of secrecy do not have the same aura of romance and intellectual excitement as that associated with active deception, they can frequently be as effective as any more elaborate type of deception operation. Moreover, active types of deception are dependent on the success of passive deception. What is even more important, passive deception can tremendously complicate and therefore increase the costs of intelligence work—in terms of time, money, and the like. A recent example appeared in Jack Anderson's column in the *Washington Post*. The U.S. Defense Intelligence Agency (DIA) was interested in determining the caliber of the cannon mounted on the new Soviet T–64 and T–72 tanks. It spent over $18 million on this project (including computer time, satellite photographs and their development, electronic eavesdropping) and could not find the answer. The DIA finally discovered that the British and French had obtained the same information for next to nothing.[37] Given the freedom and lack of discretion of the American press, the Soviet Union can normally acquire similar information with little effort and expense (or to be more exact, at the cost of subscribing to major U.S. publications). The number of very successful passive concealment deception operations concerning capabilities is very impressive indeed: for instance, the development of the proximity fuze by the United States (and Britain) during the Second World War, and the development of the "window" radar jamming chaff by the British for the bomber offensive over Germany.[38] These two examples illustrate not only the decisive importance of passive deception but also the critical nature of timing—when exactly to introduce a new weapon in order to obtain the best possible results.[39] This problem is related to the study of technological surprise, a subject which has received scant attention in the open literature on intelligence so far.[40] Finally, of course, there are the atypical examples of ULTRA and the development of the atomic bomb.

In contrast to passive deception, active deception normally involves a calculated policy of disclosing half-truths supported by appropriate "proof" signals or other material evidence. This information must be picked up by the intelligence network of the deceived. The deceived must "discover" the evidence himself; he must work hard for it to be more convinced of its authenticity and importance. (Frequently, information that is easily obtained appears to be less credible and of doubtful value.[41] This may have something to do with human psychology, which tends to equate a better product with higher cost.)[42]

Deception operations must be tailored in each case to the deceived's unique character and conditions. To be sure that his adversary will indeed pick up the threads of evidence himself, the deceiver must prepare the bait taking into account the quality of the deceived intelligence, his methods of work and his agents, his perceptual frame of mind, his cultural framework, and other factors.

Deception should not be taken simply as a gratifying intellectual exercise. Deception that is too sophisticated and elegant may be intellectually satisfying to those who create it, but may not be picked up by the intended victim. Israel, for instance, often found that very polished and seemingly simple deception plans were not picked up by Arab intelligence organizations because they are not good enough to identify the bait offered. There is an obvious danger that the message developed by the deception planners is understood by them in the context of the endless meetings in which alternatives were weighed and details worked out. They are so familiar with their own thinking that they risk overlooking the degree to which the message is clear to them only because *they know what to look for* (author's emphasis).[43] Similarly, Ewen Montagu in *Beyond Top Secret U* (one of the best studies of deception) repeatedly emphasizes the need to match the bait to the character and level of sophistication of the intended victim.

> It occupied a great deal of time and energy but it was fascinating work. In a way it was like a mixture of constructing a crossword puzzle and sawing a jigsaw puzzle and then waiting to see whether the recipient could and would solve the clues and place the bits together successfully, except that it was we who would get the prize if the recipient succeeded. We had no illusions about the efficiency of the German *Abwehr*, so we had to make sure that the puzzle was not too difficult for them to solve.[44]

Part of the art of deception is to learn to think like the adversary.[45] What may make sense for the deceiving side may not necessarily make sense to the intended victim. The bait must be designed on the basis of reliable intelligence on how he thinks and what information is available to him; this in turn requires a high degree of penetration into the adversary's most guarded secrets.

It is worth quoting Montagu on this aspect at some length. In his book, he discusses a proposal for a detailed deception plan intended to ease the pressure on the Russians by creating an imaginary threat for the Germans at the Bay of Biscay area. The additional advantage of such a deception operation was that it would also force the Germans to thin out their defenses in the Channel area. Montagu proposed this deception plan on the basis of information received through ULTRA (the deciphering of top-secret German codes), which indicated that the *Abwehr*, German army, and the *Luftwaffe* were particularly afraid of such a possibility (Montagu, for instance, suggested that they try to strengthen existing German fears). His plan, though, did not win the approval of the Chiefs of Staff.

> They [the Chiefs of Staff] turned it down flat on the grounds that an attack on the Biscay coast was so impossible that the deception would be incredible. With great respect, that last point usurped our function—we were the experts on deception, they were wholly ignorant about this art. If they thought, as they apparently did, that the deception would be useful, it was for us to decide whether we could put it over.
>
> Their reason was that they knew that the Biscay coast was outside the range of our fighter aircraft, so the necessary cover could not be given for a prolonged invasion, and they knew that we hadn't got enough aircraft carriers to spare to give fighter cover even for an "in and out" operation of real magnitude—all of which was of course quite correct. But they couldn't make themselves think as Germans. The Germans did not know what our Chiefs of Staff did and, on their information, they did think that we had enough forces and material for us to risk at least a major in and out operation under Russian pressure.
>
> It was SO important to deception work to be able to put oneself completely in the mind of the enemy, to think as they would think on their information and decide what they would do—ignoring what you knew yourself and what you could do. . . . We had given the Chiefs of Staff the facts about the Bay of Biscay operation and they ought to have done better. But perhaps I am being unfair to them. Service training is not the same as that of a barrister. We have to learn throughout our career to put ourselves in our opponent's place and try to anticipate what he will think and what he will do on his information.[46]

Unfortunately, deception is a creative art and not an exact science or even a craft. For that reason it is difficult to teach someone how to deceive unless he has a natural instinct for it. This explains why, despite the large number of war memoirs and detailed military histories which discuss deception, little has been written on the theory of deception or how to practice it.[47] It is normally assumed that some military or political leaders are "deception-minded" while others are not. There is probably no systematic, structured way to teach the art of deception, as it is impossible to teach someone to become an original painter. Perhaps the only way to learn the art of deception is through one's own experience.

What are some of the conditions which facilitate the development of the art of active deception? In the first place, active deception requires that an individual or an organization (preferably a small one) be able to see things from the enemy's vantage point. This will require, as mentioned above, a good knowledge of his culture, language, mode of operation, procedures, and the like. To design the bait or the deception ploy, the deceiver must be both practical and imaginative, and not allow himself the temptation to be too sophisticated or enjoy deception for its own sake. He (almost every important deception operation originates and is developed in its early stages as the brainchild of one individual) must have a flexible combinatorial mind—a mind which works by breaking down ideas, concepts, or "words" into their basic components, and then recombining them in a variety of ways. (One example of this type of thinking may be found in the game of Scrabble.) He must be able to transcend the routine type of thinking or procedures normally imposed by large organizations and bureaucracies. Barton Whaley has tried but failed to find "some general personality type with the ability to understand and use surprise and deception and to associate its reverse type with the failure to do so."[48] But perhaps one general pattern of personality emerges for the greatest past users of deception. They are highly individualistic and competitive; they would not easily fit into a large organization or into any type of routine work and tend to work by themselves. They are often convinced of the superiority of their own opinions. They do in some ways fit the supposed character of the lonely, eccentric bohemian artist, only the art they practice is different. This is apparently the only common denominator for great practitioners of deception such as Churchill, MacArthur, Hitler, Dayan, and T. E. Lawrence. Conversely, individuals who feel comfortable in larger groups, who prefer the democratic consensus type of agreements, and who can easily get involved in routine work will make poor candidates.

From an organizational point of view, the art of deception can be practiced only by organizations that are willing to delegate a considerable amount of authority to, and have confidence in, a small group of people.[49] In short, there must be tolerance for the existence of "artists" among "bureaucrats" and enough confidence and patience not to insist on immediate results. Such an organization (normally of course an intelligence organization) must be able to maintain the highest degree of secrecy. It has above all to be able to obtain the best possible information on the adversary and to penetrate his ranks by using spies, deciphering his codes, and so on, in order to know what he knows, what he wants to know, and how he obtains his own information. Conversely, the more successful an organization is in avoiding the penetration of its own ranks, the more it will be able to carry out its own deception operations. (Barton Whaley in his extensive research on deception claims that he found no case of a deception operation that has failed or has been intercepted by an adversary.[50]) Finally, for the success of any type of deception operation, it is imperative to coordinate the policies of all other organizations that might inadvertently disclose or undermine such an operation.

It is much more difficult to advise a potential victim of deception on how to avoid or discover such a ploy. In this respect, the difficulties involved in avoiding deception are very similar to the difficulties inherent in anticipating a forthcoming surprise attack. Military history shows that surprises are in fact inevitable. Whaley has therefore concluded that not only are even the most sophisticated deceivers the victims of deception (as quoted above), but that "exhortations to avoid being deceived are . . . as uselessly homiletic as those to use it."[51]

Nevertheless, some evident though not necessarily effective precautions can be taken. Intelligence services must continuously ask themselves what are the most obvious and most reasonable directions from which an adversary might attack, even if the available evidence contradicts such contingencies. This can perhaps best be done by asking how one would do the same thing oneself. Such estimates can be prepared by analysts who are not familiar with the information available and who work only by trying to think as the enemy would. Only in the second stage must such an analysis be corroborated with available intelligence information.

Another, and again not very helpful, way to avoid deception is to be wary of information which falls too neatly into a single pattern that seems to exclude other, no less reasonable possible courses of action. R.V. Jones has added the following advice:

> Both for deception and unmasking, one of the personal qualities required is being able to imagine yourself in the position of your adversary and to look at reality from his point of view; this includes not only being able to sense the world through his eyes and ears, and their modern analogues such as photographic and electronic reconnaissance, but also to absorb the background of his experience and hopes, for it is against these that he will interpret the clues collected by his intelligence system. Thus it was not too difficult to convince the Germans that the "Jay" system was going to depend on beams because they would naturally be gratified by our copying their techniques. To guard against this weakness when one is in danger of being deceived, I can only recommend Crow's Law, formulated by my late friend John Crow: "Do not think what you want to think until you know what you ought to know." And if a good guide to successful intelligence is Occam's razor—hypotheses are not to be multiplied without necessity—then an equally relevant guide to avoid being deceived is to multiply your channels of observation as far as possible.[52]

Although this last bit of advice may sound very reasonable, it can also create its own problems. Instead of bringing in better or more reliable information, more channels may only add more "noise" or additional deceptions. I suspect that R.V. Jones meant that one should obtain a variety (rather than simply quantity) of opinions which may contradict his suggestion not to multiply hypotheses. Alternatively, it can be said that what is important is reliable information—but of course that is exactly the basic and unsolvable problem of all intelligence work.

Another piece of advice not unlike that of R.V. Jones' but based on psychological tests is not to put too much confidence in conclusions drawn from a very small body of consistent data. This is because conclusions drawn from very small samples are highly unreliable. (Tests have shown that people usually tend to be overly sensitive to consistency.[53]) Heuer's final advice is very similar to that of R.V. Jones:

> As a general rule, we are more often on the side of being too wedded to our established views and thus too quick to reject information that does not fit these views, than on the side of being too quick to reverse our beliefs. Thus, most of us would do well to be more open to evidence and ideas that are at variance with our preconceptions.[54]

Alas one is tempted to say on the basis of historical evidence that "to be closed-minded is human."

Totalitarian regimes, such as those of Nazi Germany, Fascist Italy, Japan of the 1930s, or the Soviet Union under Stalin and his successors (until this very day)[55] seem to have fewer scruples about using deception and fraud as an accepted, perhaps even common, means in the conduct of their foreign policy in times of peace.[56] This may be because they view the period of peace merely as a "cease-fire" in a continuous and unending war over resources and ideology. In a permanent state of war and zero-sum game competition for survival, all means and methods can be justified. Hitler's foreign policy is in fact nothing but a history of deception and fraud. In times of peace, this seems to give the totalitarian states a considerable edge over the "naïve" Western democracies; yet this very edge may be their undoing in the long run both in peace and in war. Some of the reasons for this counterproductive impact of deception are obvious while others are more subtle.

To begin with, those who frequently deceive quickly lose credibility; so what they can do one, two, or three times in succession they cannot do indefinitely. Although they may continue to believe in the efficacy of deception, their peaceful adversaries have already learned their lesson. As a result, they may find themselves in a position in which no state will voluntarily seek any agreements with them, and they will force the deceived to be more alert, to have better intelligence, and eventually to resort to similar means.

Paradoxically the "naïve," trusting states may turn out to be much better at the game of deception. One explanation for this is very simple. Someone who is known to be "naïve" and honest will find it hard to lose his reputation and can therefore cheat and deceive much better when he wants (at least for a while). Not expecting him to play by their own rules, his adversaries may therefore be caught off guard.

This possibility can be briefly presented in the form of a "paradox": The more one has a reputation for honesty—the easier it is to lie when one wants to. Or even more briefly: Honest people/states can deceive the best.

This may be why the Germans fell so easily for British deception. They probably could not bring themselves to believe that the same nation which let itself be deceived time and again in peacetime would develop the art of deception to new heights in times of war. While this explanation holds true for the Germans, it might not describe the attitude of the Soviet Union, whose communist ideology assumes that the capitalists will always try to deceive and that therefore they should never be trusted in the first place.[57] Stalin may have deceived himself by imagining deception behind too many moves of other states. Thus when Churchill and the British warned him on the basis of knowledge acquired by ULTRA of impending German attack in 1941, he refused to believe them and viewed this information as an attempt to drag the Soviet Union into a war against Germany in order to ease the pressure in the West. Given Stalin's communist background and his paranoia, such an attitude is not altogether surprising.[58]

A second and more interesting explanation, which will require further research to substantiate it, is that those who practice deception continuously during peacetime, as did the Germans and the Russians, usually have to establish special agencies for that purpose (normally as part of their intelligence organizations). The operation of deception by professional military men or government officials will tend to routinize the planning and execution of deception, and over an extended period of time this will in turn undermine their creativity and flair for the art of deception. By the time they reach the point where they view deception as a regular rather than special operation, their level of effectiveness will already have dropped. (This phenomenon can also be detected in the routinized deception operations of the CIA in the 1960s and early 1970s before such practices were brought to a halt in the United States.[59])

On the other hand, the Western democracies, and the British in particular, benefited considerably from their late entry into this particular field of intelligence. In both the First and Second World Wars, the British and Americans started to reorganize their intelligence organizations either immediately before the war broke out or soon afterwards. Therefore, unlike the German and Soviet intelligence organizations which were based primarily on "professionals," the British and American intelligence organizations were staffed primarily with amateurs recruited from all sections of civilian (but mainly from academic) life.[60]

Amateurs frequently bring with them new enthusiasm, a creative imagination, informality, perhaps some academic openness, and a somewhat more detached and objective search for veritas—all of which are intellectual qualities highly useful for intelligence work in general and deception work in particular. This fresh start allows them to reexamine old problems from a new point of view, unlike the pre-war professional intelligence bureaucrats: they were not obliged to commit themselves to earlier, not always fully rational, traditions or old policies. The pre-war professionals certainly viewed with considerable resentment the massive penetration of their organizations by the "professional-type" amateurs.

> The Western democracies, unlike the Germans, drafted civilians as intelligence officers even of army groups (that is, military field position) with great success. First-class minds became expert on the enemy; with no worries about career, they could both be kept in a post for the duration of the war and express their opinions more forcefully.[61]

The more conservative German officer corps strongly resisted the integration of intelligence officers into the *Wehrmacht* and all other branches of the armed forces. Their conservatism, tradition, and aversion to civilian intellectuals did not allow them to tap the enormous intelligence potential of civilian amateurs. While this type of resistance to civilians was also manifested by British intelligence professionals, this was easily quashed. It was perhaps easier for the British, given the successful contribution of civilian amateurs during the First World War.

The amateurs, however, did very well indeed.

> The mobilization of British intelligence for the two World Wars provides at least a partial vindication for the now unfashionable virtues of British amateurism. To a remarkable degree the British intelligence system during the First World War was the result of the brilliant last-minute improvisation by enthusiastic volunteers. That the volunteers failed to achieve more—for example, at Jutland and Cambrai—was due chiefly to the short-sightedness of the professionals. The renaissance of the British intelligence community at the beginning of the Second World War after

two decades of considerable neglect was, once again, largely the work of brilliant amateurs, able in some cases to build on the achievements of their predecessors. And the man chiefly responsible for the coordination of the British intelligence effort for the first time in its modern history was a much criticized amateur strategist, Winston Churchill.[62]

For a field such as deception, which leaves so much to imagination and creativity, the amateurs proved to be ideal practitioners who, in the final analysis, outsmarted the professionals.

This may be one of the best explanations for the curious and dismal failures of German strategic intelligence and its almost complete neglect of deception during the Second World War. David Kahn thus reaches the conclusion that

> ... Germany lost the intelligence war. At every one of the strategic turning points of World War II, her intelligence failed. It underestimated Russia, blacked out before the North African invasion, awaited the Sicily landing in the Balkans, and fell for thinking the Normandy landing a feint.[63]

These mistakes were caused not only by the inherent structural weakness of German intelligence but also by the Allied deception operations. Among others, Kahn gives the following basic reasons for German intelligence failures:[64]

- "unjustified arrogance, which caused Germany to lose touch with reality." Early and easily attained military successes caused the Germans to feel vastly superior to their adversaries, to feel that they were immortal. This, combined with their traditional nationalism, assumed racial superiority, and ethnocentric view of the world reduced their incentive to learn about others. Such arrogance and feelings of superiority also caused the Arabs in 1948 and 1967 to wage war against Israel with almost no intelligence and knowledge about Israel. To a lesser extent, arrogance also blinded the Israelis in 1973 and the Americans vis-à-vis the Japanese on the eve of Pearl Harbor. As already mentioned, deception operations in particular require an intimate knowledge and understanding of the adversary, and perhaps even a certain degree of compassion and respect.
- "Aggression, which led to the neglect of intelligence." This is a more subtle point based on an understanding of military strategy, in particular on Clausewitz's writings. Clausewitz viewed defense as the stronger mode of warfare and also as passive and reactive in nature (neither of which is necessarily true).

> "What is the concept of defense?" asked Clausewitz. The parrying of a blow. What is its characteristic feature? Awaiting the blow. Now an army can await a blow only if it believes that a blow is planned, and such a belief can only be created by information about the enemy. Defense requires intelligence. There can be, in other words, no defense without intelligence.[65]

The offense on the other hand is "complete in itself." It can decide when, how, and where to attack. It can concentrate on a superior force at the point of its choice and can frequently dictate the early moves on the battlefield as it has planned. For that reason, the offense is less dependent on the availability of intelligence than the defense. "The information about enemy intentions, while helpful and to a certain degree always present (for the offensive), is not essential to an offensive victory. . . . In other words, while intelligence is integral to the defense, it is only contingent to the offense. As a result—and this is a crucial point—emphasizing the offensive tends toward a neglect of intelligence."[66]

This explanation is elegant but it is not necessarily true from the military point of view, although it seems to describe existing psychological attitudes. (It is not true from a strictly military point of view because a successful offensive may require as much, perhaps even more, detailed information than the defensive. Indeed, the lack of adequate German intelligence on the Soviet Union in 1941 proved to be disastrous.)

Kahn's point on the negative incentive of an offensive-minded military to invest in intelligence work may thus be true psychologically and certainly can be accepted as an important explanation of German military behavior. It may, however, be somewhat less powerful as a general explanation. In any event, Nazi Germany's offensive and military doctrine of blitzkrieg did not stress the central contribution of intelligence to warfare. By the time the Germans were on the defensive, it was too late for them to begin building the infrastructure necessary for intelligence work. The Allies, especially the British, who were strategically on the defensive when the war broke out, greatly appreciated the importance of intelligence work and invested heavily in it. By the time they went over to the offensive, they had the advantage of a superior intelligence organization.

- "The authority structure of the Nazi State, which gravely impaired its intelligence." Governments based on the "fuhrer principle," the "cult of personality," or any other dogma which makes the leader infallible create at the highest strategic decisionmaking level of the state an environment which is not conducive to "objective" and "rational" intelligence work. The leader who always knows best, who intimidates his advisers, and who cannot be criticized will render even the best intelligence work useless. Thus, Stalin refused to listen to any intelligence indicating the possibility of a German surprise attack. Hitler frequently ignored the intelligence information given to him and refused to listen to information that contradicted his views. Later on his subordinates, on their own initiative, ceased to supply him with "depressing intelligence" or with negative information about failures, possible dangers, or the superiority of the enemy. The fact that during the 1930s until the outbreak of war, and actually until the Battle of Britain and the invasion of Russia, Hitler's intuition was often more successful than the rational advice of the military professionals certainly made things worse. Dictators, leaders who know best, and heads of state who do not encourage their aides to express a larger variety of opinions are bad intelligence consumers. Eventually they receive only the information they want to hear and consequently lose touch with reality, creating the conditions which ultimately lead to self-deception and to their own defeat.[67] "Successful deception" at a time of peace by totalitarian regimes may therefore not be a reassuring guarantee of similar success in times of war.[68]

Deception is cheap. It is neither labor- nor capital-intensive. It is among the least expensive types of modern intelligence work yet yields a high return for a relatively small investment. Even if deception were more expensive than the material and other investments in the military operation it was designed to cover, it would still be worth investment if it led to a quick and decisive victory instead of a protracted war of attrition. Even the most complicated and elaborate deception normally involves only a relatively small number of men. Barton Whaley has estimated that the total number of participants in the deception operations for the Allied invasion of Europe in 1944—the largest deception operation in history—was "in all perhaps 2,000 soldiers, sailors, and airmen; but none of whom were regular first line combat troops."[69] Smaller, less intricate deception operations involve no more than a few dozen to at the most a few hundred men.

The material investment is in most cases also negligible. Making use of cheap and readily available resources, it will often require a fair amount of radio and other electronic gear to simulate or create intensified radio traffic in one direction or another, some wood and canvas, and film set experts to build dummy aircraft, tanks, or other installations. It can involve the movement back and forth into an observed area during the day of already existing military equipment. More often than not it is even cheaper than this, since deception operations above all involve "non-material" and purely verbal and intellectual activities such as spreading rumors, organizing campaigns to manipulate the publication of certain information in the press, planting agents, passing deceptive information to the enemy, and following up the planted information. The top-secret nature of deception demands a limitation of the number of participants to the bare minimum necessary.[70]

If the costs of deception are relatively small, the benefits can be considerable if not decisive. Deception will facilitate surprise, which in turn ". . . multiplies the chances for quick and decisive military success, whether measured in terms of sought goals, ground taken, or casualty ratios."[71] Effective deception will cause the adversary to waste his resources, to spread his forces thinly, to vacate or reduce the strength of his forces at the decisive point of attack, to tie considerable forces up at the wrong place at the worst time; it will divert his attention from critical to trivial areas of interest, numb his alertness and reduce his readiness, increase his confusion, and reduce his certainty. In short, reducing the cost for the deceiver implies increasing the cost for the deceived.

The possible presence of deception behind every intelligence operation, behind every piece of information obtained will cause serious problems and a degree of doubt in any important intelligence work. The ever-present possibility of deception always introduces "noise" into the collection and analytical work of intelligence and weakens the clarity of the signals received. Consequently, there is no sense in forfeiting the use of deception or ignoring its contribution to every facet and level of planning for action in war. That would be as irrational as someone who refuses to receive interest for money deposited in the bank. In war as a rational activity, there is never a reason to make life easier for the adversary or more difficult for oneself. Therefore, even if deception is not always used as part of a military plan or strategy (which would be a mistake) the adversary must always live under the impression that deception is being practiced. As a result, deception is always a present factor whether or not it is being practiced. Deception, like surprise, must therefore be seen as inevitable in conflict, as an inherent part of intelligence work and war that can never be discounted.[72]

Since no effective measures to counter or identify deception have yet been developed, the inevitable conclusion is that deception—even if it does not achieve its original goals—almost never fails and will therefore always favor the deceiver, the initiating party. "Perceptual and cognitive biases strongly favor the deceiver as long as the goal of deception is to reinforce a target's preconceptions or simply create ambiguity and doubt about the deceiver's intention."[73] Rationality dictates that a move which involves little cost and little risk of failure should always be included in one's repertoire.

Deception as a dilemma and predicament of intelligence work has been described in the following way:

> Alertness to the possibility of deception can influence the degree of one's openness to new information, but not necessarily in a desirable direction. The impetus for changing one's estimate of the situation can only come from the recognition of an incompatibility between a present estimate and some new evidence. If people can explain new evidence to their own satisfaction with little change in their existing beliefs, they will rarely feel the need for drastic revision of these beliefs. Deception provides a readily "available" explanation for discrepant evidence; if the evidence does not fit one's preconceptions, it may be dismissed as deception. Further, the more alert or suspicious one is of deception, the more readily available is this explanation. Alertness to deception presumably prompts a more careful and systematic review of the evidence. But anticipation of deception also leads the analyst to be more skeptical of all the evidence, and to the extent that evidence is deemed unreliable, the analyst's preconceptions must play a greater role in determining which evidence to believe. This leads to a paradox: The more alert we are to deception, the more likely we are to be deceived.[74]

Experience and conditioning can work two opposite ways. The first is that once victimized by deception, one finds it difficult to accept any information as reliable. The other is that once a source of information is thought to be trustworthy it is difficult to discredit it.

Excessive alertness to the possibility of deception can have its price too. After the success of the Allied deception operation covering their landing in Sicily (Operation *Mincemeat*) the Germans became overly sensitive to the possibility of being deceived. When the detailed plans of the impending landing in Normandy fell into their hands via the British Embassy in Ankara (*Cicero*) they were convinced that this was yet another clever Allied deception; consequently, they refused to accept the detailed plan as authentic. Conversely, a double agent who supplied the Germans with useless information was used by the Allies to supply the Germans with the correct date of the operation in order to discredit it. Once proven correct on such a vital piece of information the Germans continued to accept his information even if useless.

In the final analysis, whether the enemy plants a deception plan to fit our preconceptions or we perceive a deception where in fact it does not exist, it can be said that from a strictly logical and perceptual point of view, "We are never deceived, we deceive ourselves."[75]

It must be emphasized that deception is not a panacea which can replace the other military factors required for success in war. Believing that deception can correct or eliminate other sources of weakness courts military disaster. The best deception is useless if it is not backed by military power or if it cannot be properly exploited. To try to manage a war (or avoid one) through overreliance on deception is impossible and can only end in strategic failure.

Occasionally, deception operations—whether simple or complex—can fail to achieve their intended goals or even be counterproductive. This can happen as we have seen in one of three possible ways:

- The enemy simply fails to catch the bait of deception offered to him. This can happen either when the quality of his intelligence work is low or when the bait has not been carefully matched to his perceptions (that is, "shooting over his head").
- There is a contradiction between the short- and long-term impacts of deception. In other words, deception which is very successful and credible in the short run can be counterproductive in the long run. In such cases, deception can be too successful. This problem will arise when a deception plan is designed to intimidate the adversary and convince him of his relative weakness. Such feelings of insecurity and weakness will usually hasten a corrective change in the adversary's policies, eventually transforming his "weakness" into an advantage. In addition, this type of problem can often be correlated with self-deception: that is, flushed by his early successes, the deceiver will convince himself that what is actually a temporary advantage is a permanent one. As a result, he will underestimate his adversary and overestimate his own capabilities.
- The adversary has learned of the deception plan and will use it against the deceiver. This is one reason why deception plans require good intelligence and continuous feedback from the target about what the enemy knows or does not know.

Any deceiver will be in a much more vulnerable position if he assumes his deception is working, whereas in reality his opponent is manipulating it to his advantage. I know of no such double or even infinite regression types of deception, but they cannot be discounted in theory or in practice, although the likelihood of their occurrence is very small.[76]

To deceive successfully may become more difficult, certainly much more complicated, in the future. In a world of high-altitude reconnaissance aircraft, intelligence satellites with high-resolution photographic equipment and a variety of other sensors, and AWACS aircraft that can trace any movements on air, sea, or land at distances up to more than 350 miles, deception will not come easy. To these factors we can add the contribution of high-powered computers to cryptanalysis and the fact that everyone monitors his opponent's telephone, radio, and cable communications. If in the Second World War deception seemed primarily to be the game of academics from a large variety of disciplines, future deceptions will primarily require the work of electronic and computer experts. Inevitably deception will become less of an art and more of a science; this will be true chiefly in the execution of the deception plan and perhaps less so on the initiation level. Modern deception will require much greater skill in highly technical areas, as well as detailed and systematic preparations (perhaps a large number of exercises, laboratory war games, and the like). Greater efforts for the preparation of deception plans will have to be made in peacetime so that they will be available if war breaks out. Thus it appears that deception will be left less and less in the hands of amateurs and again more in the hands of professionals, intelligence bureaucrats, and "engineers." Such a trend may be unavoidable but may also limit the scope of deception operations primarily to super-sophisticated electronic warfare, neglecting the more traditional classical *ruses de guerre*. This should be avoided at all costs, so that the advance of the modern science of deception does not exclude the ancient art of deception.

Finally, to paraphrase David Dilks, it can be said that "It would exaggerate to say that successful deception by itself enables wars to be won. But it is precisely when the resources are stretched and the tasks many, when the forces are evenly matched and the issue trembles in the balance, that successful deception matters most." [77]

Notes

[1] Barton Whaley, *Stratagem: Deception and Surprise in War* (Cambridge: MIT Center for International Studies, 1969), 135.

[2] Ibid., 263.

[3] Sun Tzu, *The Art of War*, trans. Samuel B. Griffith (New York: Oxford University Press, 1973), 133.

[4] Ibid., 66.

[5] Charles Cruickshank, in *Deception in World War II* (Oxford: Oxford University Press, 1979), says, "Deception in war is the act of misleading the enemy into doing something, so that his strategic or tactical position will be weakened" (1).

[6] Carl von Clausewitz, *On War*, ed. and trans. Michael Howard and Peter Paret (Princeton: Princeton University Press, 1976), 203. Clausewitz did not view deception as an important element in war and thought that frequently it was not worth the bother:

> To prepare a sham action with efficient thoroughness to impress an enemy requires a considerable expenditure of time and effort, and the costs increase with scale of the deception. Normally they call for more than can be spared, and consequently so-called strategic feints rarely have the desired effect. It is dangerous, in fact, to use substantial forces over any length of time merely to create an illusion; there is always the risk that nothing will be gained and that the troops deployed will not be available when they are really needed (203).

This is certainly a narrow view in more than one way. This Prussian attitude may have been accepted by the Germans but certainly not by the British or ancient Chinese. In any case the only criterion with which to judge deception is not how much it costs, but how effective it is. Will it reduce costs in terms of casualties? Will it lead to a major surprise and therefore to decisive results? As far as deception is concerned, Sun Tzu is more modern and rational than Clausewitz.

[7] Ibid., 204.

[8] For this deception plan, see, for example; Ewen Montagu, *Beyond Top Secret U* (London: Corgi Books, 1979); Cruickshank, *Deception in World War II*; J. C. Masterman, *The Double-Cross System* (New Haven: Yale University Press, 1972), chap. 11, 145–163.

[9] For the German plan of attack in the West in 1940, see Hans-Adolf Jacobsen, *Dokumente zur Vorgeschichte des Westfeldzuges 1939–1940* (Berlin: Musterschmidt July, 1956); Hans-Adolf Jacobsen, *Fall Gelb: Der Kampf um Den*

Deutschen Operationplan zur Westoffensive 1940 (Wiesbaden: Franz Steiner, 1957); Ulrich Liss, *Westfront 1939–1940* (Neckargemund: Kurt Vorwinkel, 1959); Major L. F. Ellis, *The War in France and Flanders 1939–1940* (London: HMSO, 1953); Telford Taylor, *The March of Conquest: The German Victories in Western Europe—1940* (New York: Simon and Schuster, 1958).

[10] Clausewitz, 213.

[11] On the "death ray," see R. V. Jones, *Most Secret War: British Scientific Intelligence 1939–1945* (London: Hamish Hamilton, 1978), 63. Mussolini never lost his faith in the death ray! "In the last month of his life, Mussolini, search-ing for an alibi, traced the beginning of decline in his fortunes to the fact that Marconi before his death in 1937, had refused to impart the secret of a death ray which he had brought to perfection." Denis Mack Smith, *Mussolini's Roman Empire* (New York: Penguin Books, 1977).

[12] See Barton Whaley, *Codeword* Barbarossa (Cambridge: MIT Press, 1973); John Erickson, *The Road to Stalingrad: Stalin's War With Germany,* vol. I (New York: Harper and Row, 1975), chaps. 2 and 3; Gerhard L. Weinberg, *Germany and the Soviet Union 1939–1941* (Leiden: E. J. Brill, 1954); Vladimir Petrov, *"June 22, 1941": Soviet Historians and the German Invasion* (Columbia: University of South Carolina Press, 1968). Stalin told Harry Hopkins "…that the Russian army had been confronted with a surprise attack; he himself believed that Hitler would not strike." *Hitler made no demands on Russia* (my emphasis); quoted in Nathan Leites, *A Study of Bolshevism* (Glencoe, IL: Free Press, 1953), 497.

[13] See Jones, 233–235. The British kept an eye on the German warships for a long while. There were a few indica-tions of a possible German attempt to break out of Brest between February 10–15. But the continued routine watch by the British dulled their attention. Jones brings the following quote from Frances Bacon's essay *Of Delayes* in this context: "Nay, it were better, to meet some Dangers halfe way, though they come nothing neare, than to keepe too long a watch, upon their Approaches: For if a Man watch too long, it is odds he will fall asleepe" (235).

[14] R.V. Jones in his essay "Intelligence, Deception, and Surprise" presented at the 8th Annual Conference of the Fletcher School of Law and Diplomacy–Tufts University International Security Studies program, April 1979. He has summarized as follows the negative and positive objectives of all deception operations. Most of the deception goals on his list can be classified under one of the two basic deception types I have suggested: (1) deception concerning inten-tions or (2) deception concerning capabilities.

NEGATIVE OBJECTIVES	POSITIVE OBJECTIVES
Prevent the enemy from deducing at least one of the following:	Persuade the enemy to deduce:
i. Where you are.	i. You are somewhere else.
ii. What weapons and forces you have at your disposal. (cap.)	ii. Your weapons and forces are different from what they are. (cap.)
iii. What you intend to do. (int.)	iii. You intend to do something else. (int.)
iv. Where you intend to do it. (int.)	iv. You intend to do it elsewhere. (int.)
v. When you intend to do it.	v. You intend to do it at a different time. (int.)
vi. How you intend to do it. (int.)	vi. You intend to do it in a different manner. (int.)
vii. Your knowledge of the enemy's intentions and techniques. (cap.)	vii. Your knowledge of the enemy is either greater or less than it actually is. (cap.)
viii. How successful his operations are.	
viii. His operations are either more or less successful than they actually are.	
int. = intention	
cap. = capability	

This table is based on his essay which can also be found in Uri Raanan, Robert L. Pfaltzgraff, and Warren H. Milberg, *Intelligence Policy and National Security* (London: Macmillan, 1981). Similarly: "Therefore, when capable, feign incapacity; when active, in activity. When near, make it appear that you are far away; when far away, that you are near" (Sun Tzu, 66). Katherine Herbig and Donald Daniel, in their paper "Propositions On Military Deception," classify all military deceptions in two categories: one group is termed "ambiguity-increasing" deception, which seeks to compound uncertainties on the deceived side, and the second is the misleading type, which is designed to reduce ambiguity by building up the attractiveness of one wrong alternative.

[15] For a detailed analysis of this problem, see Michael I. Handel, "Perception, Deception, and Surprise: The Case of the Yom Kippur War," The Leonard Davis Institute Occasional Paper No. 19 (Jerusalem: The Hebrew University, 1976); or Michael I. Handel, "The Yom Kippur War and the Inevitability of Surprise," *International Studies Quarterly* 21, no. 3 (September 19, 1977), 461–502.

[16] Handel, "Perception, Deception, and Surprise."

[17] On the importance of intelligence feedback from the target, see Herbig and Daniel.

[18] The literature on ULTRA's contribution to British Intelligence operations and to the war effort in general is

growing very rapidly. For a sample, see Ralph Bennet, *ULTRA In the West: The Normandy Campaign of 1944–1945* (New York: Scribner's, 1980); Patrick Beesly, *Very Special Intelligence: The Story of the Admiralty's Operational Intelligence Centre 1939–1945* (Garden City, NY: Doubleday, 1978); Ronald Lewin, *ULTRA Goes to War* (New York: McGraw Hill, 1978); P. J. Calvocoressi, "The Secrets of Enigma," *The Listener* 97, 70–71, 112–114, 135–137; David Kahn, "Codebreaking in World Wars I and II: The Major Successes and Failures, Their Causes and Their Effects," *The Historical Journal* 23, no. 3 (1980), 618–639; Jurgen Rohwer, "*Der Einfluss Der Allierten Funkaufklarung Auf Den Verlauf Des Zweiten Weltkrieges*," Vierteljahrshefte fur Zeitgeschichte 23, no. 3 (July 1979), 525–570. On the Polish contribution, see Richard A. Woytak, *On the Border of War and Peace: Polish Intelligence and Diplomacy in 1937–1939 and the Origins of The ULTRA Secret* (New York: Columbia University Press, 1979). ULTRA was of course an invaluable follow-up instrument extremely useful for the elaborate British deception operations in World War II. See Montagu, *Beyond Top Secret U.*

[19] Major-General I.S.O. Playfair, *The Mediterranean and Middle East: The Early Successes Against Italy. History of the Second World War*, vol. 1 (London: HMSO, 1954), 274.

[20] For the success of *Overlord* see, among others: Anthony Cave Brown, *Bodyguard of Lies* (New York: Harper and Row, 1975); Gilles Perrault, *The Secret of D-Day* (Boston: Little Brown, 1965); Cornelius Ryan, *The Longest Day* (London: Gollancz, 1959). All are competent journalistic accounts. Hans Speidel, *We Defended Normandy* (London: Herbert Jenkins, 1951); Gordon A. Harrison, *Cross Channel Attack* (Washington, DC: Office of the Chief of Military History, Department of the Army, 1951); L.F. Ellis, *Victory in the West* (London: HMSO, 1962), vol. 1. The definitive history of *Overlord* in light of ULTRA has still to be written.

[21] Surprise is relative and only rarely complete or total. In most cases of sudden attack, the surprised side normally had enough information and warning signals to indicate the possibility of a forthcoming attack—its timing, place, direction, and the like. In many successful surprise attacks, the attacker achieves only a partial degree of surprise. Attacks out of the blue, that is, achieving total surprise without any warning, are almost nonexistent. Surprise attacks preceded by a very small number of warning signals indicating an impending attack are also rare. The Allied attack across the Channel was, from the German point of view, preceded by only very few signals indicating the existence of an immediate danger and therefore comes as close as possible to an attack out of the blue. The possible degrees of surprise that can be achieved and the relativity of surprise to warning or alert can be presented on the following continuum:

THE RELATIVITY OF SURPRISE

Zero Warning	*Some Warning*	*Partial Alert*	*Full Alert*
Attack out of the blue. No signals.	A high ratio of noise to signals, no alert.	Some mobilization. Some clear signals received.	Full mobilization. The attack is anticipated, preempted, or intercepted.
Very rare.	Most cases.	Some cases.	Very rare.

[22] See Michael I. Handel, "Strategic Surprise in Four Middle Eastern Wars," in *Strategic Military Surprise*, ed. Klaus Knorr and Patrick Morgan (New Brunswick, NJ: Transaction Books, 1983).

[23] Quoted in Whaley, 575.

[24] For a detailed analysis, see Handel, "Strategic Surprise in Four Middle Eastern Wars."

[25] Quoted from Edward L. Homze, *Arming the Luftwaffe: The Reich Air Ministry and the German Aircraft Industry 1919–1939* (Lincoln: University of Nebraska Press, 1976), 169. See also Walter Bernhardt, *Die Deutsche Aufrusturg, 1934–1939* (Frankfurt: Bernard and Aufrusturg, Grofe, 1962); Williamson Murray, "The Change in the European Balance of Power 1938–1939" (Ph.D. diss., Yale University, 1975), chap. 3, 58–90; John Edwin Wood, "The *Luftwaffe* as a Factor in British Policy 1935–1939" (Ph.D. diss., Tulane University, 1965); Michael Mihalka, *German Strategic Deception in the 1930s* (Santa Monica: The RAND Corporation, July 1980, N–1557–NA). David Dilks in his article "Appeasement and Intelligence" claims there is evidence that part of the deception campaign concerning the strength of the *Luftwaffe* and the possibility of a German "knockout" air bombardment on Britain and Holland was planted by the German anti-Hitler elements in order to force Great Britain to accelerate its reassurement and pledge itself to a continental commitment. David Dilks, ed., *Retreat From Power: Studies in Britain's Foreign Policy of the Twentieth Century*, vol. 1, 1906–1939 (London: Macmillan, 1981), 158.

[26] Exaggerated strength was attributed to the *Luftwaffe* more by British civilian leaders than by British intelligence estimates. But psychology and fear proved to be more powerful than the cold intelligence calculations. See Murray, 71–72; also H. Montgomery Hyde, *British Air Policy Between the Wars 1918–1939* (London: Heinemann, 1976); Gerhard L. Weinberg, *The Foreign Policy of Hitler's Germany: Starting World War II, 1937–1939* (Chicago: Chicago University Press, 1980), 22–23; 164–165; also Gordon Scott Smith, "RAF War Plans and British Foreign Policy 1935–1940" (Ph.D. diss., Massachusetts Institute of Technology, June 1966), in particular chapter 3, 71–99. The problem was that not only did the British exaggerate German capabilities, they also overestimated the devastation of strategic air

bombardments. The Committee of Imperial Defence estimated in 1937 that 60 days of strategic bombing in England would result in 600,000 dead and 1,200,000 injuries (Smith, 86).

> Certainly appeasement was a consequence of a serious misunderstanding of Hitler's intentions and capabilities. This misunderstanding, however, was reinforced by the fear of the "knock-out blow." Had the fear of the "knock-out blow" not been so great it might have been easier for the appeasers to see their folly in trying to meet Hitler's demands. Fear of the "knock-out blow" made the appeasers even more prepared to accept German demands than they might otherwise have been. The consequences of war were visualized as so awful that almost any cost was worth paying if war could be avoided. From the Air Ministry poured forth the facts and figures that made war seem impossible, the true opiate of the appeasers (Smith, 167–168).

[27] Quoted from Denis Mack Smith, *Mussolini's Roman Empire* (New York: Viking Press, 1976), 170, 174–175.

[28] Ibid., 174. During the Second World War itself the Italians and Japanese never developed new or advanced weapons. "Their equipment was for the most part imitative and as the war continued inferior in design." Alan S. Milward, *War, Economy, and Society 1939–1945* (Berkeley: University of California Press, 1977), 175.

[29] Mack Smith, 174, 177–178.

[30] Murray, 213.

[31] After the war, the *Luftwaffe*'s General Plochner claimed that he had warned Hitler about the low quality of the Italian armed forces. The words he used to describe his Italian allies were unkind indeed:

> I reminded him [Hitler] that a King of Naples had once said the following about them [the Italians]: "You can take as much trouble with the Italians as you want, you can give them the very best weapons, a mountain of ammunition to practice with, you can dress them in red, blue or green uniforms, but you will never succeed in transforming them into a useful military instrument. There are two principles to which they will always remain true. The first is: when the enemy comes in view, the best thing that you can do is to run the other way; and the second: better to be a coward for five minutes than dead all your life." I told Hitler the only thing that had changed in Italy was Mussolini's big mouth, which was trying to convince the Italians that they had been the real victors of Vittorio Veneto.

Quoted in Murray, 217. While the Italian philosophy of life might have seemed strange to a Prussian, there are certainly a few good things that could be said for it.

[32] For the missile gap story, Khrushchev's policy, and the American reaction, see Edgar Bottome, *The Missile Gap: A Study of the Formulation of Military and Political Policy* (Rutherford, NJ: Fairleigh Dickinson University Press, 1971); Arnold L. Horelick and Myron Rush, *Strategic Power and Soviet Foreign Policy* (Chicago: Chicago University Press, 1966), from which the quotes were taken; Lawrence Freedman, *U.S. Intelligence and the Soviet Strategic Threat* (Boulder: Westview Press, 1977), 62–80. Another, different capability-oriented deception must be mentioned in this context. Even if U.S. intelligence was aware of the fact that no real missile gap existed between the United States and the USSR or soon learned that it was a hoax, it was in the interest of the U.S. Air Force or Army to maintain this myth in order to justify a greater investment in their own capabilities. Very frequently before the Pentagon budget is decided, rumors of the real and imagined new strength of the Red Army are spread. This deception whether consciously or unconsciously can be expected of almost any military organization.

[33] For other wartime deception operations that backfired or got out of control, see R. V. Jones, "Intelligence and Deception," 8–11.

[34] The Israelis did not plan or want to go to war in 1967. The May Crisis caught them completely off-guard. The veil of secrecy concerning their real strength did involve conscious deception planning; what was not realized at the time was that too much secrecy concerning capabilities will project an image of weakness, which in turn could lead to a war no one desired. See Handel, "Strategic Surprises in Four Middle Eastern Wars."

[35] On the German underestimation of Soviet capabilities see, among others: Lyman Kirkpatrick, *Captains Without Eyes: Intelligence Failures in World War II* (London: Macmillan, 1969), 15, 51, 268; Barry A. Leach, *German Strategy Against Russia 1939–1941* (Oxford: Oxford University Press, 1973), 91–94, 270; Albert Seaton, *The Russo-German War 1941–1945* (New York: Praeger, 1972), 43–50; Seweryn Bialer, ed., *Stalin and His Generals* (New York: Pegasus, 1969); Robert Cecil, *Hitler's Decision to Invade Russia 1941* (London: Davis-Poynter, 1975); David Kahn, *Hitler's Spies: German Military Intelligence in World War II* (New York: Macmillan, 1978), 457–461. Herbert Goldhamer suggests that Soviet secrecy brought about the collapse of Soviet deterrence and led to a war the Soviet Union wanted to avoid:

> Soviet deterrence policy, even though combined with massive forces, failed in the end to deter the Nazis. Perhaps a continuation of past Soviet overt hospitality would have served the Soviet Union better than did the Nazi-Soviet pact. Perhaps, too, Soviet military secrecy—also a form of manipulation of perceptions—may have had an anti-deterrent effect since it led Nazi intelligence to estimate at only one half of its true value the number of Soviet divisions that would be available after the onset of war.

Herbert Goldhamer, *Reality and Belief in Military Affairs* (Santa Monica: The RAND Corporation, February 1979, R–2448–NA), 39, 111.

[36] For "passive deception," see Seymour Reit, *Masquerade: The Amazing Camouflage Deceptions of World War II* (New York: Hawthorn, 1978); G. Barkas, *The Camouflage Story* (London: Cassell, 1952).

[37] Jack Anderson, "Old Fashioned Spying Methods Often the Best," *The Washington Post*, November 24, 1981, D15.

[38] See R. V. Jones, *Most Secret War*; Alfred Price, *Instruments of Darkness: The History of Electronic Warfare* (New York: Scribner, 1978); Alfred Price, *Battle Over the Reich* (New York: Charles Scribner, 1973); Brian Johnson, *The Secret War* (London: Methuen, 1978).

[39] A detailed case study of this problem can be found in Ralph Baldwin, *The Deadly Fuze: Secret Weapons of World War II* (San Rafael, CA: Presidio Press, 1980). "Window" was also a classical case of the problem of timing in the introduction of new weapons.

[40] On this see Michael I. Handel, "Surprise and Change in Diplomacy," *International Security* 4, no. 4 (Spring 1980), 57–85, and Michael I. Handel, "Avoiding Political and Technological Surprise in the 1980s," in *Intelligence Requirements for the 1980s: Analysis and Estimates*, ed. Roy Godson (New Brunswick: Transaction Books, 1980), 85–111.

[41] "The perfect deception plan is like a jigsaw puzzle. Pieces of information are allowed to reach the enemy in such a way as to convince him that he has discovered them by accident. If he puts them together himself he is far more likely to believe that the intended picture is a true one" (Cruickshank, 1).

[42] A case in mind is *Cicero* while operating in the British Embassy in Ankara, who supplied the Germans with detailed information on Operation *Overlord*, which the Germans refused to believe could be true. L.C. Mayzisch, *Operation* Cicero (London: Fitzgibbon, 1950).

[43] Quoted from Richards J. Heuer, Jr., "Strategic Deception: A Psychological Perspective," a paper presented at the 21st Annual Convention of the International Studies Association, Los Angeles, California, March 1980, 17–18. An abbreviated and less exciting version of this excellent paper also appeared in *International Studies Quarterly* 25, no. 2 (June 1981), 294–327, under the title "Strategic Deception and Counter-deception."

[44] Montagu, 60.

[45] For an original discussion (if somewhat exaggerated) of the need to try to see things also from the adversary's point of view, see Ken Booth, *Strategy and Ethnocentrism* (London: Croom Heim, 1979).

[46] Montagu, 138–139.

[47] The only systematic discussion of deception work is to be found in Whaley, *Stratagem: Deception and Surprise in War*; Whaley, *Codeword* Barbarossa; Daniel and Herbig, *Strategic Military Deception: Perspectives on its Study and Use*. Of the published memoirs the best by far are those of Montagu, R. V. Jones, and Masterman.

[48] Whaley, *Stratagem: Deception and Surprise in War*, 6–12, 11.

[49] Montagu claims he had more difficulties in convincing his superiors of the utility of deception than in executing the deception plans themselves. "To deceive the German High Command was nothing like as difficult as it was to persuade their British opposite numbers that we could do that." Evan Montagu, *The Man Who Never Was* (Philadelphia: Lippincott, 1954), 37.

[50] R. V. Jones brings one example of a German deception plan to cover the number of V–2 launching sites—which actually helped Allied intelligence to deduce the correct number and rote of fire. "Intelligence and Deception," 22.

[51] Whaley, *Stratagem: Deception and Surprise in War*, 147.

[52] R. V. Jones, "Intelligence and Deception," 23.

[53] Heuer, 28. Like R. V. Jones, he suggests:

> The bias favoring a small amount of consistent information over a large body of less consistent data supports the common maxim in deception operations that the deceiver should control as many information channels as possible in order to reduce the amount of discrepant information available to the target. Deception can be effective even with a small amount of information as long as the target does not receive contradictory data. Not only should the notional picture be consistent, but the deceiver should actively discredit the real picture as well. To achieve maximum consistency, it is necessary to discredit the true as well as to build up the false (Heuer, 33–34).

[54] Heuer, 45.

[55] On recent Soviet deception and disinformation practices, see Joseph D. Douglass, Jr., "Soviet Disinformation," *Strategic Review* (Winter 1981), 16–25; "State Department Documents Soviet Disinformation and Forgeries" in *American Bar Association Standing Committee Law and National Security Intelligence Report* 3, nos. 11, 12 (November and December 1981); also Ladislav Bittman, *The Deception Game: Czechoslovak Intelligence in Soviet Political Warfare* (Syracuse: Syracuse University Research Corporation, 1972).

[56] See Goldhamer; Mihalka; and Michael I. Handel, *The Diplomacy of Surprise: Hitler, Nixon, Sadat* (Cambridge: Harvard Center for International Affairs, 1981).

[57] For a detailed analysis of Communist and Soviet attitudes to deception, see Leites, 324–340.

[58] Stalin's belief that every act of diplomacy (let alone war) involved deception is characterized by his statement that:

> When bourgeois diplomats prepare war, they begin with increased stress to talk about "Peace" and about "friendly relations." If some Minister of Foreign Affairs begins to advocate a "peace conference" you can infer that his government has already ordered new dreadnoughts and planes. With a diplomat words must diverge from acts—what kind of diplomat would he otherwise be? Words are one thing and acts something different. Good words are masks for bad deeds. A sincere diplomat would equal dry water, wooden iron. (*Sotsial Demokrat*, January 12 (25), 1913, quoted in Leites, 325.)

For a comment on the inevitability of at least some deception in diplomacy, see Thomas A. Bailey, *The Art of Diplomacy: The American Experience* (New York: Appleton-Century Crafts, 1968), 165–166. Also Paul W. Blackstock, *The Strategy of Subversion* (Chicago: Quadrangle, 1964); Paul W. Blackstock, *Agents of Deceit: Frauds, Forgeries, and Political Intrigue Among Nations* (Chicago: Quadrangle Books, 1966).

[59] For an interesting analysis of this phenomenon, see Patrick J. McGarvey, *CIA: The Myth and the Madness* (Baltimore: Penguin, 1974).

[60] See Christopher M. Andrew, *The Mobilization of British Intelligence for the World Wars* (Washington, DC: International Security Studies no. 12, The Woodrow Wilson Center, undated).

[61] Kahn, 533.

[62] Andrew, 28. The advantage of British amateurism was also evident in the war in the Western Desert, in which British desert navigation amateurs from before the war were much better than the Germans in long-range navigation raids and commando-type operations carried out behind the German lines. See Ronald Lewin, *The Life and Death of the Afrika Korps* (London: Corgi, 1979), in particular 12–13; also W. B. Kennedy Shaw, *Long Range Desert Group* (London: Collins, 1945); Virginia Cowles, *The Phantom Major* (London); Valadimir Peniakoff (Popski), *Private Army* (London: Jonathan Cape, 1950). German professionalism under Rommel clearly had its advantages too.

[63] Kahn, 523.

[64] Ibid., 524–243.

[65] Ibid., 528.

[66] Ibid.

[67] For a detailed analysis see Handel, *The Diplomacy of Surprise: Hitler, Nixon, Sadat.*

[68] David Kahn mentions two other reasons for the failure of German intelligence during the Second World War which are of less interest in this context. They are German anti-semitism, which caused the flight of knowledge and brains from Germany and simultaneously added to the Allies' pool of knowledge. The second was the poor organization and large number of competing German intelligence agencies, which caused considerable waste of resources, lack of coordination, fragmentation, and hostility between the various organizations.

[69] Whaley, 233.

[70] The exception is expensive and complicated cryptanalysis and decoding operations such as ULTRA which require a large number of participants. These of course relate to intelligence operations in general, not only to deception work. In retrospect, one of the amazing things about ULTRA was the length of time it remained an undisclosed secret.

[71] Whaley, 234.

[72] See Handel, *Perception, Deception and Surprise: The Case of the Yom Kippur War*, also in *International Studies Quarterly* 21, no. 1 (September 1977), 461–502, and Richard K. Betts, "Analysis, War and Decision: Why Intelligence Failures are Inevitable," *World Politics* 31, no. 1 (October 1978), 661–680. The inevitability of surprise (and deception) therefore make the suggestion that the very "knowledge that cover and deception is being deployed must be denied to enemy" seem to be useless. It must always be assumed in situations of war and intense conflict that the adversary will use some kind of deception in any intelligent and rational military planning. See Herbig and Daniel, 21.

[73] Heuer, 43. It is important not to confuse initiative and passivity (or non-use) in the use of deception, with the offensive and defensive uses of deception. Charles Cruikshank in his discussion of German deception in *Deception in World War II* seems to commit such an error when he suggests, "Deception may help the side holding the initiative, but is not much use to the side on the defensive" (206). It may be true that it is easier to design and implement deception on the offensive—but it is not less important on the defensive. This contradicts Cruikshank's own example of the successful deceptive measures taken during the Battle of Britain (chapter 1). The defender should by no means give up the advantages of deception (primarily technological and scientific types of deception). This can be done by causing the attacker to waste his energy on phony targets or on heavily defended targets; by pretending to have more capabilities at weaker points of defense and less capabilities of stronger points; by interfering with the enemy's navigation aids; by pretending to launch counterattacks at the enemy's rear or to outflank him—which will force him to spread his forces, and the like.

[74] Heuer, 47. I have suggested elsewhere the other following paradoxes (or inherent contradictions) of intelligence work:

- As a result of the great difficulties in differentiating between "signals" and "noise" in strategic warning, both valid and invalid information must be treated on a similar basis. In effect, all that exists is noise, not signals.

- The greater the risk, the less likely it seems, and the less risky it actually becomes. Thus, the greater the risk, the smaller it becomes.

- The sounds of silence. A quiet international environment can act as background noise which, by conditioning observers to a peaceful routine, actually covers preparations for war.

- The greater the credibility of an intelligence agency over time, the less its reports and conclusions are questioned; therefore, the greater the risk in the long run of overrelying on its findings.

- Self-negating prophecy. Information on a forthcoming enemy attack leads to counter-mobilization which, in turn, prompts the enemy to delay or cancel his plans. It is thus impossible—even in retrospect—to know whether counter-mobilization is justified or not.

- The more information is collected, the more difficult it becomes to filter, organize, and process it in time to be of relevant use.

- The more information is collected, the more noise will be added.

- The more alerts that are sounded, the less meaningful they become (alert fatigue).

Making working systems more sensitive reduces the risk of surprise but increases the number of false alarms.

[75] Johann Wolfgang von Goethe, quoted in Handel, *Perception, Deception and Surprise,* 9.

[76] This is very common in detective stories, films (such as *The Sting, Sleuth,* and so on), and drama (such as works by the Swiss playwright Friedrich Durrenmat) or "Spy versus Spy" in *Mad* magazine.

[77] Dilks, "Appeasement and Intelligence," 169.

Chapter 29

Miscalculation, Surprise, and U.S. Intelligence

James J. Wirtz

During the early fall of 1962, U.S. intelligence analysts noted that Soviet strategic inferiority created an incentive for the Kremlin to place nuclear weapons close to America's shores, but they concluded that the Soviets would not deploy missiles in Cuba because that same strategic inferiority made such a gambit too risky. As the history of the Cuban missile crisis demonstrates, however, the Intelligence Community was only partially correct in its estimate of Soviet behavior. Analysts accurately assessed the risks involved in this Soviet initiative, but they underestimated Khrushchev's willingness to up the ante after his bluff—*Sputnik* diplomacy—had been called. Indeed, the irony of the situation did not escape members of the Intelligence Community following the denouement of the crisis. One senior analyst, focusing on analysts' *ex ante* identification of the risks involved in the Soviet deployment of missiles in Cuba, noted that it was Khrushchev, not the U.S. Intelligence Community, who had erred by ignoring the dangers of such a provocative enterprise.[1]

Even though the Intelligence Community foiled the Soviet effort to deploy covertly nuclear delivery systems in Cuba, the episode represents a phenomenon common to instances of surprise. More often than not, victims of surprise have remarked before the event that the opponent would make a big mistake by launching an attack. Before Pearl Harbor, for example, Admiral Kimmel, Commander of the Pacific Fleet, predicted that an attack on Hawaii would be "national suicide" for the Japanese, a prediction that nearly came to pass by the end of World War II.[2]

Before the 1968 Tet Offensive, Americans also believed that it would be foolish for the Viet Cong to stand up to U.S. firepower by launching a sustained attack. The Communists achieved their political objectives during the Tet attacks by producing a shift in public and elite attitudes in the United States toward American involvement in the Vietnam War. As military analysts anticipated, however, the Viet Cong were virtually annihilated during the campaign.[3]

Americans are not the only ones who have noted that an adversary would make a serious mistake by attacking. On the eve of the Yom Kippur War, Israeli analysts estimated that an Egyptian attack would be foolhardy because of overwhelming Israeli

Source: James J. Wirtz, "Miscalculation, Surprise, and U.S. Intelligence," *Studies in Intelligence* (Special November 2002 Issue), 85–93.

military superiority. Even though Egypt's political position improved after the war, Israel, as anticipated by its intelligence analysts, overcame the setbacks fostered by surprise and inflicted a crushing military defeat on the Egyptians.[4]

The fact that countries sometimes fall victim to surprise attack because they fail to anticipate their opponent's mistakes has been recognized by scholars interested in failures of intelligence.[5] Indeed, the task of identifying the opponent's initiatives and miscalculations creates a problem for intelligence analysts that is difficult to overcome. Past studies have focused on the difficulties faced by intelligence analysts in anticipating their opponent's mistakes and persuading senior political and military decisionmakers that an adversary is about to undertake an irrational or unwise action. This [chapter], however, examines the influence of miscalculation on the occurrence of surprise from a different perspective.

Given the relationship between the failure to anticipate an opponent's mistakes and falling victim to surprise, the purpose of this [chapter] is to explore the consequences of this phenomenon for the U.S. Intelligence Community now that the traditional American focus on the Soviet military threat to Western Europe appears less appropriate. In the aftermath of the Cold War, the challenge to the [first] Bush administration's vision of a "new world order"—evidenced by Operation *Desert Storm*—could continue to emanate from the Third World.

This shift in the focus of U.S. foreign and defense policy toward the "periphery" reflects a change in the potential adversaries and issues that have preoccupied Americans over the last 40 years. It also raises fundamental questions about how the Intelligence Community, which was designed to meet the Soviet threat, will cope with developments in the Third World.

Surprise and Miscalculation

Military analysts have long focused on the benefits derived from launching surprise attacks. A variety of ideas have been advanced to explain why surprise has a detrimental impact on the opponent. Sun Tzu, for example, seems to suggest that surprise, and psychological warfare in general, can paralyze the opponent by destroying the enemy commander's "conception of reality," thereby wrecking well-laid plans.[6] More recently, scholars have focused on the "force-multiplier" effect produced by surprise attack. They suggest that surprise allows one side "to take the initiative by concentrating superior forces at the time and place of its choosing, thereby improving the likelihood of achieving a decisive victory."[7] In contrast, others note that surprise temporarily suspends the paradoxical nature of warfare, the strategic interaction between combatants that ultimately governs the outcome of a conflict. Once surprised, the ability of the victim to respond to the attacker's initiative is reduced drastically. Under these circumstances, warfare becomes less of a strategic situation, in which participants must tailor their initiatives to meet their opponent's likely response, and more of an exercise in administration.[8]

The effort to achieve surprise has its drawbacks. For example, nations have to cloak their intentions and capabilities in secrecy. But secrecy often impedes the military preparations needed to launch an attack: actions taken to maximize the scope and intensity of an initiative can warn an opponent of what is about to transpire.[9] Deceptive efforts can consume vast resources that could be put to better use in the main attack. Because of these drawbacks and the fact that policymakers can never be sure in advance that their operations actually will surprise their opponent, military initiatives that depend on the element of surprise are risky. But, because of the paradoxical nature of warfare, the risk in basing a military operation on surprise can be viewed in a positive light. The greater the risk inherent in an initiative, "the less likely it seems [from the opponent's perspective], and the less risky it actually becomes. Thus, the greater the risk, the smaller it becomes."[10]

Even after accounting for the paradoxical nature of warfare, the effort to achieve surprise is not without its costs. Despite this fact, policymakers contemplating military action generally view the task of gaining surprise as well worth the effort because of the force-multiplier effect surprise yields. Because of the risks involved in launching a surprise attack, however, states facing weaker opponents generally avoid military operations that depend on surprise. In a sense, nations facing weaker antagonists enjoy the luxury of launching more predictable operations to achieve their objectives.[11] Conversely, nations facing stronger opponents have to seek force multipliers whenever possible. As a result, military actions requiring surprise are more attractive to weaker states when they face stronger opponents.[12]

Three Kinds of Mistakes

The relationship between miscalculation and surprise becomes apparent when one considers it is the weaker antagonist in a conflict that is most attracted to the benefits and least deterred by the drawbacks inherent in attaining surprise. The weaker combatant, because of its inferior position, enjoys less of a margin for error than its stronger opponent. This reduced margin for error increases the possibility of significant miscalculation. The fact that the weaker participant in the conflict is drawn to operations depending on surprise aggravates this situation. Even though there are infinite ways miscalculation can occur under these circumstances, three types of mistakes are common when states try to achieve surprise over stronger opponents.

First, in launching a surprise attack, the weaker side can miscalculate the advantage (the force-multiplier effect) provided by catching its victim unaware. Even though surprise provides an advantage, it does not provide enough of an advantage to overwhelm the opponent. The German Ardennes offensive in 1944, for example, surprised the Allies and initially led to substantial German gains. Yet, in the final analysis, the Allies possessed such an overwhelming advantage that they were able to stop the German offensive. Paradoxically, this miscalculation, which ultimately doomed the German attack to failure, was largely responsible for the surprise achieved during the offensive. From the Allied perspective, it made more military "sense" for the Germans to husband their resources in a coordinated defense of their homeland rather than risk limited resources in a dangerous gamble.[13]

Second, miscalculation sometimes resembles a "preferred strategy." Surprise is incorporated into plans to secure battlefield victories, but the attainment of political objectives depends less on the success of the surprise attack and more on the victim's overall response to hostilities. Pearl Harbor is a case in point. The Japanese estimated that the United States would not be willing to pay the price to resist Japan's efforts to increase its "co-prosperity sphere," a reasonable prediction given the dire threat posed to Europe and the United States by the Nazis. But, to succeed, the Japanese attack on Pearl Harbor had to incorporate the element of surprise. By surprising the United States with a successful attack, however, the Japanese changed the political mood in the United States. Isolationist sentiments vanished as the destruction of Japan became a widely shared priority among Americans. In this case, the surprise needed to guarantee battlefield success eliminated the possibility that the Japanese would be able to attain their political objectives. By arousing the United States, a country that had to remain at least tolerant of the expansion of the co-prosperity sphere, the Japanese success at Pearl Harbor doomed Japan's war effort to failure.

Third, miscalculation can be produced when statesmen and officers from divergent cultural backgrounds, reflected in their military styles and strategies, become embroiled in a conflict. This type of miscalculation occurs in a relative sense. It usually emerges when one or both sides engage in mirror-imaging: the projection of one sides' values, strategies, or political objectives and constraints on the opponent.[14] Instead of estimating the opponent's behavior in terms of the opponent's approach to warfare, estimates are based on the approach to conflict embraced by the individuals conducting the analysis.

The North Vietnamese decision to launch the Tet Offensive, for example, illustrates how the Communists projected their own values and theories to predict the behavior of the South Vietnamese population during the offensive. Hanoi misinterpreted anti-American sentiment in South Vietnam as evidence of support for its cause, leading it to expect that the southern population would launch a revolt against the Saigon regime in support of the Tet Offensive. The North Vietnamese interpreted domestic unrest in South Vietnam through their own analytical lens of "people's war," which incorporated the idea that the "struggle against imperialism" would culminate in a general uprising. This misinterpretation of public opinion constitutes the major Communist miscalculation during the Tet Offensive. But, because U.S. intelligence analysts did not fully understand the role played by a general uprising in the Vietnamese Communists' conception of people's war, they discounted as propaganda Communist calls to the people of South Vietnam to revolt. In effect, the Communists miscalculated by projecting their concepts and values on the people of South Vietnam, and the Americans miscalculated by projecting their concepts and values in their interpretation of the Communist effort to instigate a general uprising.[15]

All told, the relationship between miscalculation and the decision of one side in a conflict to surprise a stronger antagonist provides more evidence supporting the existing analytical consensus among those interested in the study of intelligence failure. Although this consensus has been criticized, analysts have concluded that failures of intelligence are more or less inevitable. The difficulty in anticipating the "rational" actions of an opponent pales in comparison to the problems inherent in identifying the miscalculations that could be at the heart of an adversary's decisions to launch a surprise attack. Even if these mistakes are identified, it might be too much to ask of senior commanders to base their plans on the premise that the opponent is about to undertake a reckless gamble. As General Davidson, the officer in charge of U.S. military intelligence in Vietnam, noted in the aftermath of the Tet Offensive, "Even had I known exactly what was to take place, it was so preposterous that I probably would have been unable to sell it to anybody."[16] In effect, the relationship among miscalculation, the decision to launch a surprise attack, and the fact that surprise is rarely decisive in the overall context of a conflict, constitute one factor contributing to a pattern in the history of war—the inevitability of intelligence failure.

Surprise after the Cold War

From a systemic perspective, the end of the Cold War could increase the problems faced by analysts as the focus on the Soviet Union and the bipolar character of international relations begins to wane. Instead of concentrating the majority of intelligence resources against one adversary, the number of potential adversaries faced by the United States could proliferate either in a relative or an absolute sense.

It would be an exaggeration to state that the Cold War represented the "best of all worlds," but bipolarity did offer important advantages to the U.S. Intelligence Community. In the past, analysts enjoyed the luxury of focusing on the Union of Soviet Socialist Republics (USSR). The concentration of advanced collection methods, analytical resources, and even popular interest allowed the Intelligence Community to monitor events in the USSR in detail. The procurement of technical collection systems to track Soviet military developments was virtually guaranteed by bipartisan agreement on the need to verify arms control treaties. Moreover, the longevity of the Cold War and the stability produced by bipolarity over time created a degree of predictability in Soviet-American relations. As one analyst recently noted: "The later Cold War saw fewer crises largely because the rules of the game and the boundaries of the two superpowers' spheres of influence were more clearly worked out after 1962."[17]

The simplicity of a bipolar world also is reflected in the problems that did not preoccupy intelligence analysts. For example, the Intelligence Community did not have to estimate the potential danger of shifting alliances or spend much energy determining whether the Soviets would react to major changes in the strategic balance. Most important, surprise was not a predominant phenomenon in Soviet-American relations. As the military balance between the superpowers reached parity, the drawbacks, not the benefits, inherent in incorporating the element of surprise into military initiatives probably became increasingly salient to policymakers on both sides. In an age of mutual assured destruction, when neither side could be characterized as weaker than the other, the force-multiplier effect provided by surprise was insufficient to tip the military balance to either side's advantage.

In effect, by the end of the Cold War, there were few incentives for the superpowers to surprise each other with their initiatives. It also was unlikely that policymakers in Washington or Moscow would make the types of miscalculations that often form the basis for decisions to launch surprise attacks. The transparency engendered by high technology and constant vigilance, combined with decades of diplomatic interaction, helped statesmen on both sides to become familiar with each other's culture, military doctrines, and operating procedures.

New Challenges

Following the Cold War, however, the benign situation facing the U.S. Intelligence Community is likely to change in three important respects. First, the number of potential threats facing the United States could proliferate, raising organizational and theoretical problems for analysts. From an organizational perspective, the Cold War created a de facto hierarchy among intelligence requirements; now, analysts will have to base this hierarchy on their estimates alone without a Cold War framework to serve as a guide. Shifting estimates will produce changes in these hierarchies, and analysts probably also will be unable to rank-order threats in the future. Under these circumstances, intelligence officials could face pressures to curtail certain activities, needed to sustain expertise in one area, to strengthen the resources devoted to monitoring events in areas that are of current interest to policymakers.

From a theoretical perspective, the attempt to meet a larger number of intelligence requirements could reduce the intensity of the intelligence effort directed at a particular country or region. Even though the Intelligence Community monitored events in the USSR in extraordinary detail, it would appear unlikely that analysts could similarly monitor events in two countries simultaneously. If breadth of knowledge comes to replace depth of knowledge in intelligence estimates, the degree of expertise and information about certain nations could fall below a critical level, thereby increasing the likelihood of intelligence failure.

Second, the different perspectives of Soviet and American policymakers created by their divergent historical, ideological, and cultural circumstances pale in comparison to the gulf that sometimes exists between Western statesmen and Third World elites. In this type of situation, mirror-imaging becomes more likely as analysts try to overcome a lack of expertise or data produced by organizational shortcomings by substituting Western values or concepts for missing, or incomprehensible, information. Moreover, the consequences of mirror-imaging become more profound for the simple reason that Western values or concepts are unlikely to generate significant insights into the intentions of potential opponents. The existence of this cultural gulf, however, complicates the task faced by analysts in at least one other important respect. Ethnocentrism cuts both ways.

Third World policymakers probably also will engage in mirror-imaging, employing their own values and concepts to interpret U.S. intentions. Indeed, because they often lack large intelligence organizations committed to providing independent analyses, the mirror-imaging of Third World statesmen could be based on personal experience. If this occurs, policymakers in the Third World will be more likely to miscalculate, and it will be difficult for American analysts to anticipate the national mistakes produced as statesmen project their individual biases on the United States.

Third, unlike the USSR, Third World nations would be at a significant military disadvantage vis-à-vis the United States. As a result, they will have a strong incentive to include surprise in their initiatives. Third World nations are more likely to seek the force-multiplier effect produced by surprise in planning military operations against the United States or its friends in the "periphery." The proliferation of the number of potential adversaries, the increasing cultural gulf between U.S. analysts and Third World policymakers, and the probability that Third World adversaries will be attracted to the benefits provided by surprise will create a more challenging environment for the Intelligence Community.

The Persian Gulf Crisis

The scenario of Iraq's invasion of Kuwait and the subsequent international response to Saddam Hussein's initiative could be repeated in the years ahead. Saddam's campaign in the Gulf appeared to be based on a "preferred strategy" that projected an insignificant Western and Arab reaction to the seizure of Kuwait. But Saddam appeared to make two significant mistakes.

First, Saddam and his advisers miscalculated the way nations outside the Persian Gulf region would respond to the seizure of Kuwait. The origins of this mistake lie apparently in the ethnocentric view of the world embraced by Iraq's leadership and in the regional focus of its strategic deliberations. In April 1990, for example, Saddam told members of a visiting U.S. congressional delegation that "we know that an all-out campaign is being waged against us in America and in the countries of Europe" and that Iraq intended to liberate itself from "the blackmail of the Zionist lobby."[18] Admittedly, the conspiratorial overtones of Saddam's analysis are unique, but his tendency to view international initiatives unrelated to his country as directed against his nation is a common occurrence among statesmen. In the case of Iraq, however, these misperceptions are aggravated by the way policy is formulated at the pinnacle of the Iraqi government. Surrounded by sycophants with little experience outside the cutthroat competition of Iraqi politics, Saddam enjoys dictatorial powers and tolerates little, if any, policy or political dissent.

Under these circumstances, isolation and lack of debate—far more extensive than the pressure for consensus produced by the related phenomenon of groupthink—are reflected in policy deliberations and policymakers' views of the world. The Iraqi leadership's highly self-centered and regional perspective led to three significant mistakes concerning the non-Arab world's response to the invasion of Kuwait:

- failure to recognize the implications of the historic change in Soviet-U.S. relations
- failure to appreciate American domestic politics
- failure to anticipate international condemnation of the seizure of Kuwait.

If the invasion of Kuwait had come 5 years earlier or 5 years later, the United States might not have been able to respond on such a massive scale. Five years earlier, the Soviets, in support of their Iraqi client, probably would have objected to American intervention in the Gulf. It also would have been difficult for the United States to withdraw its two armored divisions from Western Europe to prosecute a land campaign in Iraq. Saddam and his advisers, however, seemed oblivious to the end of the Cold

War and the increased likelihood that the superpowers would collaborate in resisting Iraqi aggression.

The Iraqis probably hoped that the Soviets would resist U.S. intervention in the Gulf or continue to supply Iraq with weapons. The actual Soviet response to the crisis probably came as a rude shock to Saddam. Iraq was even forced to warn the USSR against divulging Iraqi military secrets to United Nations (UN) forces, a warning that the Soviets apparently ignored.[19]

If the Iraqi invasion had occurred 5 years later, the United States might have lacked the military capability to intervene massively against Saddam. In the months proceeding the invasion, Congress was debating the extent of military budget reductions. In this sense, time was on Iraq's side. America's ability to project force in the Persian Gulf would have diminished in the years ahead. Moreover, even though the debate over military budgets has been overshadowed by events in the Gulf, the existence of this debate virtually guaranteed that there would be an influential constituency within the United States for the use of force against Iraq. In other words, those proposing only moderate reductions in military capability could point to Iraq's aggression as evidence that the United States still needs to maintain significant forces.

In addition to miscalculating the superpower response to the invasion, the Iraqi leadership apparently underestimated the international condemnation that would follow the seizure of Kuwait. Baghdad then compounded the damage done by this initial miscalculation by using foreign nationals as human shields to deter air attacks against strategic facilities. By indiscriminately threatening foreigners, Saddam antagonized nations—Japan is a case in point—that might have preferred to remain aloof from the crisis. The hostage ploy actually helped turn a regional dispute into a conflict between Iraq and a global coalition organized under UN auspices. UN resolutions affirmed the legal and moral basis of U.S. intervention in the conflict, and they also eliminated the incentives for Saddam's former arms suppliers to continue their sales to Iraq. The blows of virtually universal condemnation, UN sanctions, and termination of arms shipments to Iraq must have been a rude awakening for Saddam and his advisers.

The Arab Reaction

Iraq's leadership misunderstood how its deception strategy, needed to secure the element of surprise for the invasion, would reduce the odds of Arab acquiescence to the seizure of Kuwait. Arab passivity would have reduced the likelihood of international intervention in the crisis. The Saudi decision to resist Saddam was crucial, for example, because it allowed the United States, the United Kingdom, and France to make use of Saudi Arabia's extensive network of airfields and military facilities. If all Arab leaders had followed in the footsteps of Jordan's King Hussein, who defended Iraq's actions, U.S. military intervention would have been problematic or even politically impossible.

Admittedly, it is difficult to escape the conclusion that Saddam's estimate of the Arab reaction to his initiative was at least as misguided as his miscalculation of the general international response to the invasion of Kuwait. Still, Iraq's deception campaign directly antagonized Arab states in the region. The Iraqis not only relied on diplomacy to create reasonable doubts about their intentions, but Saddam himself apparently also took advantage of the good intentions of Arab leaders, especially Egypt's President Mubarak, who had tried to broker an equitable resolution of the border dispute between Iraq and Kuwait. Even after the invasion, the Iraqi leadership maintained the deception campaign by reassuring Saudi leaders that the invasion had been a "mistake."[20]

Burned once by Iraqi trickery, Arab elites even turned a deaf ear to Iraqi promises to transform any confrontation in the Gulf into an Arab-Israeli war. Saddam had failed to realize how his strategy of deception would ultimately undermine the political basis—Arab acquiescence to his ambitions—of his overall campaign plan. Because of this miscalculation, the invasion of Kuwait began to fail just as Iraqi troops occupied the entire country.

Conclusion

Initial reports indicate that the U.S. Intelligence Community did not fail to collect information about the buildup of Iraqi forces in preparation for the invasion. But Saddam's deception strategy succeeded in at least temporarily inhibiting a vigorous U.S. and international reaction to the impending threat against Kuwait. Although a few dissenting opinions were voiced, diplomats and intelligence analysts tended to interpret the massing of Iraqi forces along the Kuwaiti border as simply a facet of Saddam's diplomatic campaign to pressure Kuwait.[21] As a result, Saddam's military moves benefited from the element of surprise. Even though Iraq did not need a force multiplier to overwhelm Kuwaiti defenses, surprise was needed to present the international community with a *fait accompli*, thereby strengthening Iraq's position in Kuwait.

In light of the situation in the Persian Gulf and the historic changes in Europe, what does the future hold for the U.S. Intelligence Community? If current trends continue, efforts to deceive the United States could increase as a proliferating number of competitors try to gain the element of surprise for their actions. It also will be harder to overcome deception strategies; it will be increasingly difficult for analysts to anticipate the mistakes made by adversaries by bridging the cultural gulf that exists between Westerners and Third World opponents.

But Iraq's recent surprise attack also demonstrates the continued relevance of many of the concepts used to explain and, to a degree, to anticipate surprise. The preferred strategy embraced by Saddam, his myopia, and his miscalculation of the force-multiplier effect produced by surprise are not without precedent. His selective use of analogies—such as the Vietnam analogy—to anticipate the U.S. response to his initiatives also is a common phenomenon. To take advantage of these continuities across time and cultures, however, analysts have to integrate deliberately into their estimates an awareness of how different historical, cultural, military, religious, and ideological backgrounds influence the strategic deliberations of their opponents. This is no small task. But effort in this direction, undertaken by both the academic and intelligence communities, could improve the ability of U.S. analysis to anticipate the types of challenges that could threaten "the new world order."

Notes

[1] Raymond L. Garthoff, *Reflections on the Cuban Missile Crisis* (Washington, DC: The Brookings Institution, 1989), 46, 157.

[2] Husband E. Kimmel, quoted in Roberta Wohistetter, *Pearl Harbor: Warning and Decision* (Stanford: Stanford University Press, 1962), 55.

[3] James J. Wirtz, "Deception and the Tet Offensive," *The Journal of Strategic Studies* (June 1990), 82–98.

[4] Eliot A. Cohen and John Gooch, *Military Misfortunes: The Anatomy of Failure in War* (New York: The Free Press, 1990), 129–131.

[5] Wirtz, 94; Garthoff, 157; Michael I. Handel, ed., *Leaders and Intelligence* (London: Frank Cass and Co., 1989), 26–27.

[6] Sun Tzu, *The Art of War*, trans. Samuel B. Griffith (Oxford: Oxford University Press, 1963), 66–69, 77.

[7] Michael I. Handel, "Intelligence and the Problem of Strategic Surprise," *The Journal of Strategic Studies* (September 1984), 230.

[8] Edward N. Luttwak, *Strategy: The Logic of War and Peace* (Cambridge: Harvard University Press, 1987), 8.

[9] The difficulty of concealing initiatives from one's opponent while still concentrating sufficient forces to have a decisive effect was long ago recognized by Clausewitz. See Carl von Clausewitz, *On War*, ed. Michael Howard and Peter Paret (Princeton: Princeton University Press, 1967), 199.

[10] Michael I. Handel, *Perception, Deception, and Surprise: The Case of the Yom Kippur War* (Jerusalem: The Leonard David Institute, 1976), 16.

[11] John J. Mearsheimer, *Conventional Deterrence* (Ithaca: Cornell University Press, 1983), 34.

[12] Handel, "Intelligence and the Problem of Strategic Surprise," 230.

[13] On the Ardennes offensive, see Hugh M. Cole, *The Ardennes: Battle of the Bulge* (Washington, DC: Office of the Chief of Military History, 1965).

[14] For a discussion of the relationship between mirror-imaging and surprise, see Richard K. Betts, *Surprise Attack: Lessons for Defense Planning* (Washington, DC: The Brookings Institution, 1982), 122.

[15] Wirtz, 93–94.

[16] Davidson, quoted in William C. Westmoreland, *A Soldier Reports* (Garden City, NY: Doubleday, 1976), 122.

[17] Stephen Van Evera, "Primed for Peace: Europe After the Cold War," *International Security* (Winter 1990/1991), 45; Handel, "Intelligence and the Problem of Strategic Surprise," 230.

[18] R. Jeffrey Smith, "U.S. Forces Seen as Only Option," *The Washington Post*, September 30, 1990, 23.

[19] Edward Cody, "Iraq Warns Soviets Against Giving U.S. Military Information," *The Washington Post*, October 13, 1990, 17.

[20] Judith Miller, "Saudis Tell of Iraq Hot-Line Drama," *The New York Times*, October 4, 1990, 15.

[21] Rowan Scarborough, "CIA, Defense Saw Different Aims in Buildup," *The Washington Times,* August 3, 1990, 11; Rowland Evans and Robert Novak, "Saddam's Dangerous Vision," *The Washington Post*, August 3, 1990, 23.

Chapter 30

How Leaks of Classified Intelligence Help U.S. Adversaries: Implications for Laws and Secrecy

James B. Bruce[1]

It is "obvious and inarguable" that no governmental interest is more compelling than the security of the Nation.

—U.S. Supreme Court in *Haig v. Agee* (1981)

To succeed, intelligence requires secrets. And secrecy is under assault. The future of U.S. intelligence effectiveness depends to a very significant degree on keeping its secrets about collection sources and methods and analytical techniques. When secrecy is breached, foreign targets of U.S. intelligence—such as adversary countries and terrorists—learn about intelligence techniques and operations, and then often develop *denial and deception* countermeasures to them. As a result, the effectiveness of intelligence declines, to the detriment of the national security policymakers and warfighters and the citizenry that it is meant to serve.

For years, the U.S. press has been an open vault of classified information on U.S. intelligence collection sources and methods. But now the problem is worse than ever before, given the scope and seriousness of leaks coupled with the power of electronic dissemination and search engines. The principal sources of intelligence information for U.S. newspapers, magazines, television, books, and the Internet are unauthorized disclosures of classified information. Press leaks reveal, individually and cumulatively, much about how secret intelligence works—and, by extension, how to defeat it.

This significant issue—the unauthorized disclosure of classified intelligence—has been extraordinarily resistant to correctives. It will never be solved without a frontal assault on many levels, and an essential one is U.S. law. This chapter addresses key legal issues in gaining better control over unauthorized disclosures that appear in

Source: This chapter is a slightly revised version of James B. Bruce, "Laws and Leaks of Classified Intelligence: The Consequences of Permissive Neglect," *Studies in Intelligence* 47, no. 1 (March 2003), 39–49.

the press. It advocates a range of legal solutions that have not been tried before, some of which are controversial. The views expressed here are my own.

Importantly, I would not hold these views had I not come to them from the vantage point of 21 years in the intelligence business, and particularly my last 8 with the Foreign Denial and Deception Committee. This committee represents an interagency effort to understand how foreign adversaries learn about, then try to defeat, our secret intelligence collection activities. I have come to appreciate that unauthorized disclosures of classified intelligence pose a serious, seemingly intractable, problem for U.S. national security. The Director of Central Intelligence (DCI), George Tenet, made the point in an interview that unauthorized disclosures "have become one of the biggest threats to the survival of U.S. Intelligence."[2] A skeptical public can rightly question whether the DCI might not be exaggerating the seriousness of the problem. Unfortunately, he is not, and no intelligence specialist who is knowledgeable about the damage caused by leaks would disagree.

This presents an important anomaly in public discourse: Nearly all of the compelling evidence supporting the argument that leaks cause serious damage is available only in the classified domain. It thus seems daunting to make a persuasive public case for legal correctives to address unauthorized disclosures when so little of the evidence for it can be discussed publicly. Proponents for better laws—it will soon become clear why I am one of these—sometimes feel that this is not a fair fight. Freedom-of-the-press advocates and professional journalists exert disproportionate influence on this debate, at least when compared to advocates of criminal penalties for the leaking and publishing of sensitive classified intelligence. But I have come to believe that First Amendment objections to criminal penalties for disclosing classified *intelligence* now demand a more critical reconsideration than we have given them to date.[3] When we can link these important constitutional issues in a balanced and dispassionate way, it will be more of a fair fight, a more reasoned debate.

The Seriousness of Unauthorized Disclosures

Any sources and methods of intelligence will remain guarded in secret. My administration will not talk about how we gather intelligence, if we gather intelligence, and what the intelligence says. That's for the protection of the American people.

> —President George W. Bush, following the September 11, 2001,
> terrorist attacks on the World Trade Center and the Pentagon[4]

It is a myth, too commonly held outside the Intelligence Community (IC), that leaks really do not do much harm. The genealogy of this erroneous view traces to the publication of the *Pentagon Papers* in 1971. After much Government carping about all the damage that those top-secret revelations in the press would do to U.S. national security, few today would claim that any damage was done at all. And I am unaware of any that was done to intelligence. The *Pentagon Papers* flap took us off the scent. The view that leaks are harmless is further nourished by other popular myths that the Government overclassifies everything—including intelligence—and classifies way too much.

This seduction has become a creed among anti-secrecy proponents without clearances. But I would argue that this, too, at least in regard to intelligence, is wrong.

A recent classified study of media leaks has convincingly shown that leaks do cause a great deal of harm to intelligence effectiveness against priority national security issues, including terrorism. This is principally because the press has become a major source for sensitive information for our adversaries about U.S. intelligence—what it knows, what it does, and how it does it. Unfortunately, serious leaks of U.S. intelligence cumulatively provide substantial information to foreign adversaries. At the Central Intelligence Agency (CIA) alone, since 1995 there have been hundreds of investigations of potential media leaks of agency information, and a significant number of these have been referred to the Department of Justice for follow-up action. Leaks that have damaged the National Security Agency (NSA) signals intelligence sources and methods also number in the hundreds in recent years; dozens of these cases have also been referred to Justice. The National Imagery and Mapping Agency (NIMA) has experienced roughly a hundred leaks just since 2000 that have damaged U.S. imagery collection effectiveness. Many dozens of leaks on the activities and programs of the National Reconnaissance Office (NRO) have also helped foreign adversaries develop countermeasures to spaceborne collection operations. The Defense Intelligence Agency (DIA) and the military services, too, have suffered collection losses as a result of media leaks.

It is impossible to measure the damage done to U.S. intelligence through these leaks, but knowledgeable specialists assess the cumulative impact as truly significant. Some losses are permanent and irreversible; others can be recovered, though sometimes only partially, and with the expenditure of substantial resources that could well be spent elsewhere.

While leaks of classified information are often intended to influence or inform U.S. audiences, foreign intelligence services and terrorists are close and voracious readers of the American press. They are keenly alert to revelations of U.S. classified information. For example, Stanislav Lunev, a former Russian military intelligence officer, wrote:

> I was amazed—and Moscow was very appreciative—at how many times I found very sensitive information in American newspapers. In my view, Americans tend to care more about scooping their competition than about national security, which made my job easier.[5]

I call this the *Lunev Axiom*: Classified intelligence disclosed in the press is the effective equivalent of intelligence gathered through foreign espionage. Several reported examples of Cold War-era intelligence losses due to press leaks concerned:

- Soviet ICBM testing, 1958. A *New York Times* story on January 31, 1958, reported that the United States was able to monitor the 8-hour countdown broadcasts for Soviet missile launches from Tyuratam (now Baykonur), Kazakhstan, which provided enough lead time to dispatch U.S. aircraft to observe the splashdowns and, thus, collect data used to estimate the accuracy of the intercontinental ballistic missiles. Following publication of the article,

Moscow cut the countdown broadcasts to 4 hours, too little time for U.S. aircraft to reach the landing area. Occurring in the midst of the missile-gap controversy, the publication of the press item left President Dwight Eisenhower livid. Reportedly, some intelligence was lost forever, and, to recoup the remainder, the U.S. Air Force had to rebuild an Alaskan airfield at a cost of millions of dollars.[6]

■ Politburo conversations, 1971. In a September 16, 1971, column in *The Washington Post*, Jack Anderson wrote that U.S. intelligence was successfully intercepting telephone conversations from limousines used by members of the Soviet Politburo in Moscow. British historian Christopher Andrew says that this U.S. collection program producing highly sensitive information ended abruptly after Anderson's revelations.[7]

■ Soviet submarines, 1975. The *Los Angeles Times* published a story on February 7, 1975, that the CIA had mounted an operation to recover a sunken Soviet submarine from the Pacific Ocean floor. The *New York Times* ran its own version the next day. After this story broke, Jack Anderson further publicized the secret operation on national television on March 18. In his memoir, former DCI William Colby wrote: "There was not a chance that we could send the *Glomar* [*Explorer*] out again on an intelligence project without risking the lives of our crew and inciting a major international incident. . . . The *Glomar* project stopped because it was exposed."[8]

Importantly, not only Russian intelligence officers understand this. Key adversaries of the United States, such as China and al Qaeda, derive a significant amount of their information on the United States and U.S. intelligence from the media, including the Internet. What we need to understand are the legal implications of this key principle.

How Leaks Hurt: Some Post-Soviet Examples

The Intelligence Community faces improved foreign countermeasures as adversaries use leaks to expand their understanding of U.S. intelligence. Some more recent examples will illustrate the point.

M–11s in Pakistan. In the mid-1990s, dozens of press articles covered the issue of whether Chinese M–11 missiles had been covertly transferred to Pakistan. If missiles had been acquired, Pakistan could be found in violation of the Missile Technology Control Regime (MTCR), to which it was a signatory. Under the National Defense Authorization Act, U.S. law mandates sanctions against proven MTCR violators.

Reports in the Washington press claimed that U.S. intelligence had indeed found missiles in Pakistan but that the information apparently was not solid enough to trigger sanctions. Based on numerous leaks, readers of both the *Washington Times* and the *Washington Post* learned that intelligence had failed to convince the Department of State of the missiles' existence. "Spy satellites," the press announced, were unable to "confirm" the presence of such missiles. The message from the press coverage was, in effect, that any nation—such as Pakistan or other signatories to the MTCR who sought to circumvent its terms—could avert U.S. sanctions if they neutralized intelligence by shielding missiles from satellite observation. These articles not only suggested to Pakistan and China that some key denial measures were succeeding but also spelled out specific countermeasures that other potential violators could take to prevent U.S. intelligence from satisfying the standards needed for sanctions under the MTCR.

Indian nuclear testing. U.S. imaging capabilities are a favorite press topic. An example is leaked intelligence about India's nuclear program in the mid-1990s. Unauthorized disclosures about issues such as this have revealed to our adversaries, directly and indirectly, unique elements that underpin our analytic tradecraft. Thoughtful manipulation by adversaries, as well as friends, of such knowledge exposed in the press impairs our ability to provide policymakers with timely intelligence before they are taken by surprise—as happened when the Intelligence Community failed to warn of the Indian nuclear tests in May 1998.[9]

Liaison relationships. Effective intelligence depends on cooperative relationships with friendly governments and individuals who trust the United States to protect their confidences. Press disclosures can—and sometimes do—undermine these relationships, making both governments and individuals reluctant to share information, thereby inhibiting intelligence support crucial to informed policymaking, counterterrorist efforts, and, when necessary, military operations.

Iraqi weapons of mass destruction. In 1998, newspaper reports provided lengthy coverage of the United Nations Special Commission charged with inspecting Iraq's weapons of mass destruction (WMD) facilities following the Gulf War. These reports were widely cited in subsequent worldwide media coverage. Although the articles contained many inaccuracies, information in them interfered with the U.S. Government's ability to aggressively pursue its policy on Iraqi weapons inspections. Other serious leaks clearly have degraded Washington's ability to obtain intelligence on Iraq. Damaging press disclosures based on imagery-derived intelligence on Iraq have included the movement of missile systems, construction of a new command and control network, and the dispersal of WMD equipment following the September 11, 2001, terrorist attacks in New York and Washington.

Al Qaeda terrorism. Terrorists feed on leaks. Through their investigations into whether the September 11 attacks resulted from intelligence failure, Congress and the special commission will learn that important intelligence collection capabilities against Osama bin Laden and al Qaeda were lost in the several years preceding September 2001. With the concurrence of NSA, the White House officially released just one example of these leaks. As press spokesman Ari Fleischer explained:

> And let me give you a specific example why, in our democracy and in our open system, it is vital that certain information remain secret. In 1998, for example, as a result of an inappropriate leak of NSA information, it was revealed about NSA being able to listen to Osama bin Laden on his satellite phone. As a result of the disclosure, he stopped using it. As a result of the public disclosure, the United States was denied the opportunity to monitor and gain information that could have been very valuable for protecting our country.[10]

What the public cannot easily know, because the overwhelming bulk of this intelligence must necessarily remain classified, is that the bin Laden example cited here is just the tip of the iceberg. In recent years, all intelligence agencies—CIA, NSA, NIMA, NRO, and DIA, to cite just the larger ones—have lost important collection capabilities, including against high-value terrorist targets. These losses have impaired human operations, signals intelligence, and imagery collection. And they have deprived U.S. analysts and policymakers of critical information, unavailable elsewhere, that they should have had.

Weak Enforcement

The seriousness of the [unauthorized disclosures] issue has outpaced the capacity of extant administrative and law enforcement mechanisms to address the problem effectively.

—Attorney General John Ashcroft[11]

Logic and facts reveal a highly inverse correlation between law enforcement and leaks: the less the enforcement, the greater the leaks of classified information—and probably the other way around as well. A statistical approach is impossible, however, because there has been only a single example of any prosecution for an intelligence leak—Navy analyst Samuel Loring Morison in 1985. The glaring absence of criminal penalties for leaking and publishing classified intelligence establishes a law enforcement climate of utter indifference—actually permissive neglect. The unofficial message seems to be: Leak all you want, and no matter how much, or how serious, nothing will happen to you.

Perversely, for perpetrators there seem to be only benefits to leaking. Anonymous Government officials seek to skew public debate in their favor by selectively leaking intelligence that supports their favored policy positions. Journalists and book publishers can gain policy influence, brandishing relevant intelligence that their opponents may not have seen, and cannot easily refute—at least not in the press, without more leaks. But also, over time, journalists and writers can gain public renown and recognition—better newspaper, magazine, and book sales—as well as bigger incomes and profits, merely by exploiting the classified materials that law-breaking Government officials provide to them. This unholy alliance works exceedingly well as long as the legal climate remains indifferent to it.

Laws on Leaks

Is leaking classified intelligence against the law? Probably—but one would not know it from the prosecution data: only Morison would know for certain, and he was pardoned as President Bill Clinton was leaving office. President Clinton also vetoed the Shelby Amendment, an anti-leaks law written into the fiscal year 2001 Intelligence Authorization Act.

It is precisely the legal ambiguity of leaking that is the heart of this problem. Certainly there are laws against it—chiefly the 1917 espionage law (Title 18 USC §§ 793 (d)–(e) and 798) and the narrower Intelligence Identities Protection Act (Title

50 USC § 421). One could devote a whole legal seminar to what is wrong with these laws—and I urge legal experts to address this. But suffice it here to offer a non-lawyer's view that a law that is almost never enforced is either unneeded or useless. I contend that effective anti-leaks laws are urgently needed—but since the present ones are not enforced and virtually unenforceable, they are useless. Worse, consistent conspicuous failure to enforce these laws actually encourages the very crimes that they proscribe.

This problem is not new. The Willard Report (after its chairman Richard K. Willard, then-Deputy Assistant Attorney General) drew an unsettling conclusion two decades ago:

> In summary, past experience with leak investigations has been largely unsuccessful and uniformly frustrating for all concerned. . . . This whole system has been so ineffectual as to perpetuate the notion that the Government can do nothing to stop the leaks.[12]

Legal correctives proposed in the Willard Report resulted in draft legislation in 1984. Although supported by the Office of Management and Budget and the Reagan administration, the Intelligence Community later withdrew the draft legislation due to a perceived lack of support.

Twelve years later, responding to a request from the Assistant to the President for National Security Affairs, the National Counterintelligence Policy Board completed another study and reported no discernible change in the Government's ability to control leaks. The 1996 report explained the continuing failure to control leaks as a result of three key factors:

- a lack of political will to deal firmly and consistently with unauthorized executive branch and congressional leakers
- the use of unauthorized disclosures as a vehicle to influence policy
- the difficulty of prosecuting cases under existing statutes. Notably, not one of the five efforts to obtain legislation on unauthorized disclosures between 1981 and 1995 succeeded.[13]

Why are press leaks so hard to investigate? In brief, the Government sources for classified information that is disclosed in the U.S. press are enormously difficult to identify. Intelligence that is disseminated to more than a few dozen officials will rarely be investigated if leaked because the list of potential offenders is already too long. Any intelligence that is disseminated electronically—as volumes are today—is largely shielded from any leaks investigations because identifying a single guilty leaker among hundreds or even thousands of innocent readers as a practical matter is extremely difficult.

Further, investigations within the intelligence agencies can rarely extend to consumers of their intelligence products—most of whom have policy equities to defend or oppose but have little discernible incentive to protect sources and methods or little understanding of the risks to them that leaking poses. And, unlike most of their intelligence-producer counterparts, intelligence consumers will probably never have to face a routine polygraph examination.

Moreover, because intelligence agencies are for the most part not law enforcement agencies, Federal press leak investigations require high-level authorization that is not routinely granted and must compete with other national security priorities, such as terrorism or espionage, for limited investigative resources. Also, long-standing enforcement policy (not law) has, to date, not sought to target journalists as a means of identifying their Government sources.

Finally, Government officials who provide classified information to the press are sometimes believed to be very senior, and thus more politically insulated from investigations, while lower-ranking officials who leak may be responding to higher-level direction, thus rationalizing a disclosure as "authorized." Even as this kind of disclosure averts the formal declassification review process, it also complicates the legal issue by adding ambiguity over whether such a disclosure is authorized or not.

Given the palpable history of failure to protect classified intelligence information from press disclosures—and given the epidemic proportions of leaks and the deleterious consequences they wreak in foreign D&D countermeasures that reduce the effectiveness of U.S. collection—it is fair to question why past failed approaches should be expected to work today. They will not.

There has never been a general criminal penalty for unauthorized disclosures of classified intelligence. Although intelligence leaks technically can be prosecuted under the espionage statutes (18 USC §§ 793 and 798), only the single case, *United States v. Morison*, ever has been. Given that literally thousands of press leaks have occurred in recent years—many serious and virtually all without legal penalty—it is clear that current laws do not provide an effective deterrent to leakers or to journalists and their media outlets that knowingly publish classified intelligence.

Federal law enforcement officers would probably agree that bad laws are hard to enforce. A penetrating critique of what passes for anti-leak laws is provided in a comprehensive note in the June 1985 *Virginia Law Review* by Eric Ballou and Kyle McSlarrow. Although written before the Morison prosecution, the chief points remain as valid today as when written. A key passage highlights the responsibility of Congress:

> The disjointed array of statutes shows that Congress does not have a comprehensive scheme to deal with the problem of leaks. The existing statutes either prohibit those disclosures with a specific intent to harm the United States or to advantage a foreign nation, or they apply only to a few narrowly defined categories of disclosures. The specific intent statutes do not apply to information leaks because of their high culpability standard. Those statutes are more appropriate to the problem of classic espionage. As a result, persons who leak [classified] information to further public debate may do so with impunity, as long as the information they disclose is not protected by one of the more narrowly directed statutes. A second infirmity of the specific intent statutes is that they only protect information relating to the national defense. These statutes do not cover diplomatic secrets, nonmilitary technology, and other nonmilitary secrets that affect the country's security. The more narrowly directed statutes, although protecting some of this information, nonetheless constitute an incomplete solution to the problem of leaks.

Congress has ignored large categories of information that should not be disclosed with impunity. In summary, Congress has not constructed a principled and consistent scheme of criminal sanctions to punish the disclosure of vital government secrets. Moreover, persons who leak government secrets are but one side of the problem; the government must also pursue remedies against those who publish secrets. Like the disclosure provisions, however, the statutes relevant to the publication of government secrets are vaguely drafted and incomplete.[14]

A Call for New Laws

Given the intractable nature of controlling leaks, we need to try remedies that have not been tried before. I defer to the drafting skills of competent attorneys to translate any promising ideas here into workable legislation. My suggestions are grouped into three categories: Write new laws. Amend old ones. And enforce them all—new or old.

Given the fact that many thousands of leaks of classified intelligence in recent years have seriously damaged intelligence effectiveness, thereby jeopardizing the Nation's security—and that existing penalties provide no effective deterrent to leaking—we urgently need a comprehensive anti-leaks statute to empower law enforcement and investigators to better protect intelligence. A new law should:

- unambiguously criminalize unauthorized disclosures of classified intelligence
- hold Government leakers accountable for providing classified intelligence to persons who do not have authorized access to that information, irrespective of intent; and hold unauthorized recipients accountable for publishing information that they know to be classified
- define *intelligence information*—including substantive content, activities, operations, sources and methods—distinctly from *defense information*, creating a discrete protected category for intelligence that does not require proof that it is related to military defense
- provide better protection to especially sensitive and highly classified intelligence information in trials and other judicial proceedings than is presently afforded through the Classified Information Procedures Act.

Congress can ensure that such legislation is drafted in a manner that is consistent with constitutional requirements.

In addition, a separate new law should be crafted to provide the same protection to technical sensors deployed on any platform (space, air, land, and sea) that is now afforded to human operations. Such a law would constitute a technical counterpart to the Intelligence Identities Protection Act (50 USC § 421).

Accountability

Should journalists have legal accountability? Absolutely, in my view. Few would dispute that the first line of enforcement must be drawn at offending Government officials who unlawfully steal and disclose classified intelligence. Like citizens everywhere, Government officers have different opinions on the propriety of holding journalists legally accountable for publishing it. Still, I believe that to be fully effective, a worthy law should also hold uncleared publicists—that is, journalists, writers, publishing companies, media networks, and Web sites that traffic in classified information—accountable for intelligence disclosures. Specifically, media representatives should be held responsible for publicizing—thus, making available to terrorists and other U.S. adversaries—intelligence information that they know to be classified.[15] Whether journalists understand it or not—and many probably do not—the public exposure of significant intelligence often damages intelligence effectiveness by compromising valuable U.S. sources and methods. Journalists should also be held responsible under present criminal statutes for unlawful possession of classified documents when they have them.

Legal accountability for journalists is necessary because declassification authority is assigned by law exclusively to Government officials, elected and appointed, through lawful procedures. Journalists who publish classified intelligence arrogate to themselves an authority legally vested in Government that they do not by right possess. In publishing classified intelligence, no journalist can convincingly claim the constitutional right to do so. Any journalist's First Amendment right to publish information does not appear to—and should not—extend to disclosing lawfully classified intelligence information. In any case, a constitutional claim of the right to publish classified intelligence remains to be established.

A close reading of Title 18 USC § 798 (sometimes referred to as the signals intelligence [SIGINT] statute) and 50 USC § 421 (the Intelligence Identities Protection Act, sometimes referred to as the human intelligence [HUMINT] statute) shows that journalists are already legally accountable for publishing leaked classified intelligence. But since no one has ever been prosecuted under these statutes, they remain unenforced and yet to be tested in the courts.

Like Government officials, journalists also exercise a public trust. But they exercise it without any apparent legal accountability for violating the public trust when they reveal the Nation's secrets. This is wrong. Legal accountability for journalists is especially needed in the absence of an enforceable code of ethics for journalist conduct. The overwhelming majority of journalists do not publish classified information, and some recognize the ethical implications of compromising sensitive intelligence sources and methods.[16] But a few egregious offenders traffic heavily in classified intelligence. In one example, Steven Aftergood, director of the Federation of the American Scientists' anti-secrecy project, wrote: "Over the past couple of years, Mr. [Bill] Gertz [of the *Washington Times*] has written more stories based on classified Government documents than you can shake a stick at, infuriating Clinton administration officials and making a mockery of official classification policy." Aftergood also repeated a statement from Gertz that ran in the conservative *Weekly Standard*: "We believe in stories that make you say 'holy shit' when you read them," the columnist boasted.[17] The complete lack of accountability of such journalists for costly compromises of information that jeopardize the Nation's security must change under the force of law.

First Amendment Issues

Constitutional experts will address First Amendment implications of any proposed laws that may be interpreted to constrain freedom of the press. Importantly, the Supreme Court has not recognized an absolute right of publication. But neither has it made clear its conception of acceptable restrictions. Still, I believe that holding publishers of classified intelligence legally accountable under carefully drawn legislation would not be proscribed by the First Amendment.

Constitutional arguments that address First Amendment issues will have to consider the following:

- The Government's exclusive authority to classify—and declassify—Government information is firmly established in law.
- The protection of sources and methods is also well established in both statutory law and judicial decisions, including a Supreme Court decision in *Central Intelligence Agency v. Sims* that recognizes the Government's "compelling interest" in protecting the confidentiality of intelligence sources.
- Congress' willingness to regulate publications disclosing intelligence where the potential for serious harm exists is already established in the Intelligence Identities Protection Act (50 USC § 421), and in the SIGINT statute (18 USC § 798) as well.[18]
- One leaker (a Government employee, not a journalist) has been convicted of providing classified information to the press, and this decision was upheld on appeal.[19]
- Publishing classified intelligence has not been established as a constitutionally protected right.
- A compelling argument can be made for extending the *harm principle* to protecting classified intelligence from press exposure when the Nation's security is jeopardized as a consequence. For example, the media's assistance (unwitting, to be sure) to the terrorists who planned and conducted the attacks in New York and Washington on September 11, 2001, provides a vivid example of harm to intelligence—and thus to the Nation—that deserved better protection than we now afford it.[20]

Of course, the inherent tension between First Amendment rights and the Government's interest in protecting national security is dynamic and may never be solved with finality. But the current balance so favors First Amendment rights that compelling constitutional interests involving national security can be superseded. Here we should entertain redressing a potential constitutional imbalance by reconsidering a time-tested democratic principle first developed by the preeminent philosopher of liberty, John Stuart Mill: "the only purpose for which power can rightfully be exercised over any member of a civilized community, against his will, is to prevent harm to others."[21]

Under the harm principle—for example, yelling "FIRE!" in a crowded theater when there is none—a variety of exceptions to free speech are well established in American law, such as obscenity, defamation, breach of peace, and "fighting words."

To this list we should add: "the compromise of U.S. intelligence required in the service of the Nation's security."

Improving Existing Laws

Referring to the conclusion of the 1996 report of the National Counterintelligence Policy Board, if we lack the political will to write a new law—and I am convinced that lack of will is our chief obstacle here—then I urge that we amend our present, defective laws to help us curtail the loss of present and future U.S. intelligence capabilities.

The statutory responsibility to "protect intelligence sources and methods from unauthorized disclosures" is explicitly assigned to the Director of Central Intelligence in the National Security Act of 1947 (Section 103), and similarly in the Central Intelligence Agency Act of 1949. The protection of sources and methods is also further authorized in Freedom of Information Act (FOIA) exemptions (in 5 USC § 552 (b) (1) and (b) (3)), and in several significant court cases including the Supreme Court decisions in *Snepp v. United States* and *Central Intelligence Agency v. Sims.* In *Snepp*, the Court established that "The government has a compelling interest in protecting both the secrecy of information important to our national security and the appearance of confidentiality so essential to the effective operation of our foreign intelligence service."[22]

Thus, perhaps the simplest approach to improving existing statutes is to amend the National Security Act of 1947 by melding Title 18 provisions criminalizing unauthorized disclosures of classified information with the well-established legal principle that intelligence sources and methods deserve special protection. Such an amendment would insert new language establishing criminal penalties for Government officials who leak classified information that damages sources and methods, as well as for uncleared writers and publishers who publicize this classified information in the media. Such language could be inserted immediately after Section 604, and the present Section 607 could be amended to specifically define "intelligence sources and methods."[23]

We could also amend the 1917 espionage statute (Title 18 USC § 793) to establish a distinct legal identity for intelligence information, activities, operations, sources, and methods—apart from national defense. Since considerable intelligence activities can be argued as unconnected with national defense, stricter definition would remove the need to satisfy an additional prosecutorial burden. We should also ease the burden of intent or "willfulness" standards, requiring only that the Government show that classified intelligence information was publicly disclosed. I would restrict any "intent" burden only to establishing a leaker's intent to knowingly *disclose* classified intelligence instead of the higher culpability bar of establishing intended *damage* to the Nation.

I believe that we should also amend the Intelligence Identities Protection Act (50 USC § 421) to remove the burden of establishing patterns of disclosures, since some singular disclosures are so serious, perhaps resulting in loss of life, that legal penalties for exposing sensitive agents who risk their lives to help the United States and its allies must be clearly established. The intent standard should also be relaxed because agent identities can be revealed to discerning readers (such as foreign intelligence services or terrorist organizations) through merely descriptive information even when actual names are withheld. And, unless we craft a new law to accomplish this, I would broaden the scope of this narrow statute that now covers only human operations to also apply to technical collection activity, including from spaceborne sensors.

Further, we should amend 18 USC § 794 to include nonstate actors such as terrorist organizations, along with "foreign governments or agents thereof" as is currently written, and soften the intent burden analogous to the amended § 793 above.

Finally, we need to amend the Classified Information Procedures Act to afford much greater protection during investigative and judicial proceedings for highly sensitive compartmented information, which, when leaked, may not even be investigated or officially reported for prosecution. This legal timidity results from an understandable Government incentive to avoid calling further attention to a particularly sensitive activity or capability. The U.S. Government has shown a debilitating reluctance to pursue legal remedies for the most serious leaks partly because subsequent courtroom publicity of sensitive information subverts its first objective of protecting such information from further disclosures.

Strengthening Enforcement

Until those who, without authority, reveal classified information are deterred by the real prospect of productive investigations and strict application of appropriate penalties, they will have no reason to stop their harmful actions.

—Attorney General John Ashcroft[24]

Better enforcement will also require real political will—surely more than we have seen since *United States v. Morison*. Where to begin? First, acknowledge the Lunev Axiom: Recognize that Government leakers and the journalists who publish the classified materials they provide do the equivalent work of spies. Even if their motives differ, the effects can be the same. Through press leaks, unauthorized disclosures can be every bit as damaging as espionage because of the focused exploitation of the U.S. press by adversaries. If leakers and journalists were caught providing the same classified information clandestinely to a foreign power, they could, and some probably would, be prosecuted for espionage. But if published in the press—where leaked sensitive information becomes available to all foreign governments and terrorists, not just one—leakers and journalists alike derive effective immunity from prosecution under a Government that lacks the will to enforce its laws.

Let me state this categorically: Adversarial foreign countries and terrorists rely heavily on the U.S. press to acquire sensitive information about intelligence in order to deploy countermeasures against it. Since such disclosures can have the same effect as espionage, we should treat Government leakers and their collaborating journalists as subject to the same laws that apply to spies whose work is more clandestine, but sometimes no more damaging. While the espionage statutes are, for the most part, seriously flawed in their applicability to leaks, for the present they are all that we have. Also, to date, neither leaker nor publisher has been taken to account under laws specifically designed to protect against damaging disclosures of sensitive signals or human intelligence. We should thus begin by trying to enforce the three pertinent laws now on the books: 18 USC § 793 against leakers; 18 USC § 798 against leakers and publishers of classified SIGINT information; and 50 USC § 421 against leakers and publishers who expose HUMINT sources.

We should also enforce 18 USC § 794 against leakers and publishers of classified intelligence whose disclosures injure the United States and advantage foreign nations just as surely as any spies' disclosures that are provided clandestinely. Further, we should empanel grand juries to determine criminal offenses for serious unauthorized disclosures, and compel journalists under *Branzburg v. Hayes* (408 US 665, 1972) to identify their law-breaking Government sources of classified intelligence. In addition, we should subpoena in the course of legal proceedings to recover stolen Government property—classified intelligence documents that we believe are in the possession of Government leakers or journalists, and thus outside the normal physical protections that the U.S. Government provides to sensitive classified intelligence information. Government officials, journalists, and publishers who are found to be in possession of documentary classified intelligence should also be prosecuted under 18 USC § 641 for possession of stolen Government property.

We need to recognize that sensitive intelligence information is classified by this Government for good reasons—precisely because its protection really is essential to the security of the Nation. But the legal protections we afford it are woefully insufficient, and not nearly as good as those we provide to other Government or Government-protected information—such as banking, agricultural, and census data, and even crop estimates and insider trading for securities—whose acquisition by foreign adversaries and terrorists would not make any difference at all.

Consequences of Not Acting

"If the law supposed that," said Mr. Bumble, "the law is an ass."

—Charles Dickens, *Oliver Twist*

The consequences of legal inaction are high—perhaps higher than we should ask the American citizen to bear. Years of inaction, indifference, and permissive neglect are taking an enormous and unacceptable toll on U.S. intelligence capabilities. And the toll is higher still since September 11, 2001. Intelligence leaks do serious and often irreversible damage to our sensitive collection capabilities. By publicly unveiling unique and often fragile collection capabilities through leaks, the media actively help our adversaries to weaken U.S. intelligence. These disclosures offer valuable insights to our enemies—at no cost to them—into possible errors in their assessments of how well or poorly U.S. intelligence works against them, as well as useful feedback on how well they succeed or fail in countering U.S. intelligence. This kind of feedback not only facilitates more effective intelligence denial activities, it also increases the risk of foreign manipulation of our intelligence for deception operations.

Unless comprehensive measures with teeth are taken to identify and hold leakers and their publishing collaborators accountable for the significant, often irreversible, damage they inflict on vital U.S. intelligence capabilities, the damage will continue unabated. Conceivably, without some legally effective corrective action, the situation could even worsen, leading to intelligence on significant national security issues that is less accurate, less complete, and less timely than it would be without foreign countermeasures made possible by unauthorized disclosures. Warning of surprise attacks against the United States by terrorists or other hostile adversaries could be further degraded. Moreover, multi-billion-dollar collection programs could become less effective—and therefore, less cost-effective—than they would otherwise be if foreign adversaries were not learning how to neutralize or manipulate such programs through unauthorized disclosures.

The alternative is better intelligence capabilities for the United States. This can result through no added costs by merely better protecting the sources and methods we now have and those that are in the pipeline. Stemming press leaks will afford significantly better protection. Better laws—and enforcement of these laws—will make this possible. If we continue to be encumbered by a failure of will, our present climate of permissive neglect will become one of pernicious neglect.

Notes

[1] This chapter is a slightly revised version of an article entitled "Laws and Leaks of Classified Intelligence: The Consequences of Permissive Neglect," in *Studies in Intelligence* 47, no. 1 (March 2003), 39–49. While this chapter has been reviewed by the Central Intelligence Agency for classified content, the views expressed here are those of the author, and not necessarily those of CIA, the National Intelligence Council, or other U.S. Government organizations.

[2] *USA Today*, October 11, 2000, 15A.

[3] The scope of my concern with classified information here extends only to *intelligence*, which encompasses intelligence *information, activities, operations, sources,* and *methods*. I exclude from my purview other kinds of classified information, such as military (for example, war plans and weapons systems) and diplomatic secrets, not because they are unimportant, but because I believe that intelligence increasingly requires a distinct legal identity.

[4] *The New York Times*, September 14, 2001, 18.

[5] Stanislav Lunev, *Through the Eyes of the Enemy* (Washington, DC: Regnery Publishing, 1998), 135.

[6] Wayne Jackson, *Allen Welsh Dulles, Director of Central Intelligence* (July 1973, declassified history, volume 4, 29–31, Record Group 263, National Archives).

[7] Christopher Andrew, *For the President's Eyes Only* (New York: Harper Perennial, 1966), 359.

[8] William Colby, *Honorable Men: My Life in the CIA* (London: Hutchinson, 1978), 413–418.

[9] In the case of India's nuclear program, damaging press leaks further disclosed sources and methods beyond the data revealed in the official demarches delivered in 1995 and 1996.

[10] White House press statement, June 20, 2002; accessed at <http://www.whitehouse.gov/news/releases/2002/06/20020620-12.html>.

[11] Letter to the Speaker of the House in compliance with Section 310 of the Intelligence Authorization Act for Fiscal Year 2002, October 15, 2002, 4.

[12] *Report of the Interdepartmental Group on Unauthorized Disclosures of Classified Information*, March 31, 1982, prepared for the President.

[13] National Counterintelligence Policy Board, *Report to the NSC on Unauthorized Media Leak Disclosures*, March 1996, C2–4.

[14] Eric E. Ballou and Kyle E. McSlarrow, "Plugging the Leak: A Case for Legislative Resolution of the Conflict between Demands of Secrecy and the Need for an Open Government," *Virginia Law Review*, June 1985, 5. See also Michael Hurt, "Leaking National Security Secrets: Effects on Security and Measures to Mitigate," *National Security Studies Quarterly* 8, no. 4 (Autumn 2001); and Harold Edgar and Benno C. Schmidt, "The Espionage Statutes and the

Publication of Defense Information," *Columbia Law Review* 73, no. 5 (May 1973), 929–1087.

[15] The concept that persons outside of government as well as inside it should face criminal penalties for knowingly disclosing classified information is discussed in Ballou and McSlarrow, section I.B.2, and has been discussed at least since 1957; see the Wright Commission's *Report of the Commission on Government Security* (Washington, DC: Government Printing Office, 1957), xxiii.

[16] See David Ignatius, "When Does Blowing Secrets Cross the Line?" *The Washington Post*, July 2, 2000; and Ed Offley, "We are Aiding Osama bin Laden," *Defense Watch*, September 24, 2001.

[17] Steven Aftergood, *Secrecy and Government Bulletin*, no. 64 (January 1997), 1.

[18] Ballou and McSlarrow.

[19] *United States v. Morison*, 844 F.2d 1057, 4th Circuit, cert denied, 488 US 908, 1988.

[20] The significant example identified by Ari Fleischer (see note 10) is far from an isolated case. Numerous others in the classified literature show damage to counterterrorist capabilities in all collection disciplines, particularly SIGINT and HUMINT.

[21] John Stuart Mill, *On Liberty*, 1859.

[22] *Snepp v. United States*, 444 US 507, 509 n.3 (1980), and *Central Intelligence Agency v. Sims*, 471 US 159, 177 (1985). In *Sims*, the Court anticipated the Lunev Axiom and implicitly identified a D&D rationale in protecting sources and methods: "Foreign intelligence services have both the capacity to gather and analyze any information that is in the public domain and the substantial expertise in deducing the identities of intelligence sources from seemingly unimportant details . . . ." Cited in Ballou and McSlarrow. Discussion here is also based on Jay Ryan, "Criminalizing the Publication of Classified Information: The Clash between National Security and the First Amendment," unpublished paper, April 24, 2003, 6–8.

[23] Ryan, 9–10.

[24] Letter to the Speaker of the House, 5.

Part IX—Perils of Policy Support

Our experience with a number of administrations was that they started with the expectation that intelligence would solve every problem, or that it could not do anything right, and then moved to the opposite view.

—Richard J. Kerr, former DDCI

Chapter 31

What To Do When Traditional Models Fail

Carmen A. Medina

The great challenge facing analysts and managers in the Directorate of Intelligence (DI) is providing real insight to smart policymakers. Meeting this challenge is hard, but intelligence officers have long believed that careful attention to the tradecraft of intelligence analysis would lead to work that added value to the information available to policymakers. During its 50-plus years, the Central Intelligence Agency (CIA), we believed, evolved a model that needed only successful execution to produce quality intelligence analysis. When we faltered, we blamed the analysts (or the collectors), but not the model.

What if the failing, however, lies not with the analysts but with the model they are asked to follow? Customer needs and preferences are changing rapidly, as is the environment in which intelligence analysis operates. Yet the DI's approach to analysis has hardly changed over the years. A DI analyst from decades ago would recognize most of what a typical analyst does today, from reading traffic to preparing finished intelligence. Stability is often comforting, but in the DI's case, change may be what is most needed.

The Current Model

On the CIA's public Internet Web site, the DI defines its mission as the provision of timely, accurate, and objective intelligence analysis on the full range of national security threats and foreign policy issues facing the United States. The Web site outlines the different types of analytic support that might be useful to a customer at any given time. DI officers provide analysis that helps officials work through their policy agendas by: addressing day-to-day events; apprising consumers of developments and providing related background information; assessing the significance of developments and warning of near-term consequences; and signaling potentially dangerous situations in the future.

A key aspect of this model is that it focuses first on developments. In fact, the analysts' work process is structured around developments. They spend the first quarter or more of their workday reading through the "overnight traffic" to determine

Source: Carmen A. Medina, "What to Do When Traditional Models Fail," *Studies in Intelligence* 46, no. 3 (2002), 35–40.

what is new. They report what is new to their colleagues and superiors and then often to the policymaking community. The "new thing" may be an event—the death of a world leader or the precipitous decline of an Asian currency. Or it may be an item of intelligence reporting on a situation of interest—from signals, imagery, human-source, open-source, or other type of collection. This basic model has guided the DI's work for decades.

More recently, DI managers have realized that the specific interests of customers must have greater weight in determining what to do on any given day. As a result, the model has acquired an additional step—understanding customer feedback to determine policymaker interests. This new step, however, merely supplements the pivot around which the analytic work turns—identification of the new development.

Critical, sometimes unstated, assumptions underpin this tradecraft model:

- Assumption 1: Policymakers need a service that tells them what is going on in the world or in their particular area of concern.
- Assumption 2: Policymakers need help in determining what an event means.
- Assumption 3: The CIA and specifically the DI have unique information about what is happening.
- Assumption 4: DI analysts are particularly insightful about what these developments may mean.

When Models Fail

Models work only as long as they suit the environment in which they operate. If reality changes, then it is a good bet that the model needs to evolve as well. The DI's tradecraft model was developed during the 1960s and 1970s and optimized against the characteristics of that period. It was an era of information scarcity—truth about the world's many closed societies was a rare commodity. Communicating across borders and with other governments was hard—government leaders rarely talked to each other on the phone and summits among world leaders were unusual events. Ideology was a key driver in international relations—it was always important to know how far left or right a government would tack. These traits do not describe today's environment.

Analysts today have to add value in an era of information abundance. The policymaker, an intelligence consumer, has many more ways of staying informed about recent developments, intelligence-related or not. The responses to a survey of customers of the Senior Executive Intelligence Bulletin (SEIB) [formerly called the National Intelligence Daily] conducted in late 2000 are illustrative. When asked to identify the unclassified information sources they relied on, 85 percent of the respondents picked all four of the following sources: foreign newspapers and weekly periodicals; U.S. newspapers and weekly periodicals; their professional networks; and official, informal communications, such as email.

Policymakers today also read raw intelligence reports on a regular basis. Twenty to 30 years ago, analysts in the DI had the fastest access to incoming intelligence information and could count on seeing particularly critical cables before policymakers. Today, thanks to information technology, policymakers often read the raw traffic at the same time as, if not before, analysts. In a 1998–1999 survey, SEIB customers were asked, "What other sources of daily intelligence do you read?" Almost one-half of the respondents volunteered that they often read raw traffic. Given that "raw traffic" was not offered as a specific choice, the real percentage was almost certainly higher than the write-in responses indicated.

Analysts today have to dig deep to surpass the analytic abilities of their customers. Modern communication technologies and evolving diplomatic practices now allow government leaders to communicate with each other freely and often. U.S. officials even talk to opposition party leaders. This makes it much easier for policymakers to be their own analysts—to gain insights into the intentions of other governments and decipher what developments may mean. The DI has probably always underestimated the extent to which policymakers serve as their own analysts. Arguably, policymakers have never needed the DI to tell them that riots undermine governments or that currency crises shake investor confidence. Today, however, they no longer even need much help deconflicting signals from other governments.

Analysts today have to reach beyond political analysis, an area in which it is particularly hard to provide value to policymakers. The ideological orientation of governments is no longer the important issue in international relations; it has been replaced by a growing list of nontraditional issues that tend to defy ideological definition. In the DI, however, political analysis is still king. We want to follow the ins and outs of political activity in any number of countries even though the audience for this type of analysis is not as broad as it once was. A recent study of articles in the SEIB, for example, revealed that 70 percent dealt mostly with analysis of political developments. In contrast, a much wider variety of issues was covered in memos written directly in response to questions from senior customers. Only about one-third of those memos—whose topics presumably matched what was most on the policymakers' minds—covered political matters, and many of those discussed the behavior and attitudes of foreign leaders, a subcategory of political analysis that remains of high interest to senior policymakers.

The move toward nontraditional issues is already under way, evidenced by the creation of specialized centers to deal with terrorism, weapons proliferation, and narcotics and crime. Nonetheless, too many of our flagship products still reflect a political analysis bias. We need to do a better job aligning our publishing strategies with emerging realities.

Analysis in some other conventional areas can still provide value-added, but, like political analysis, the challenge is greater than before. Economic analysis faces daunting competition from the open-source world and those analysts need either to serve consumers who are not economic specialists or to identify niche substantive areas where the agency can still provide unique support. Scientific and military analyses are borderline issues that defy easy solutions. A number of our senior customers, particularly in civilian agencies, cannot serve as their own experts on technical topics, so there is more room for the intelligence analyst to provide value-added. The issue for military analysis, however, is which agency should be primarily responsible. This is now a crowded field, occupied not only by the DI and the Defense Intelligence

Agency, but, increasingly more to the point, by the strong intelligence centers at the unified military commands. The DI is still in the process of defining its comparative advantage in military analysis.

Analysis that Fits the New Environment

So, how does the DI, or anyone, do intelligence analysis in an era of information abundance, well-connected policymakers, and nontraditional issues? First, we need new assumptions:

- New Assumption 1: Most of the time, policymakers have a good sense of what is going on in their areas of concern.
- New Assumption 2. Policymakers frequently understand the direct consequences of events and their immediate significance.
- New Assumption 3: The CIA—and particularly the DI—often lacks unique information about developments, especially in the political and economic spheres. Raw intelligence is ubiquitous and can get to policymakers before it reaches the analysts.
- New Assumption 4: Policymakers need the greatest help understanding nontraditional intelligence issues. There is still a market for political analysis and certainly for related leadership analysis, but to be successful in traditional areas the DI must generate unique insights into relatively well-understood problems.

A DI optimized against these assumptions would understand current developments, but only as the necessary foundation for its real contribution to policymakers. Analysts would specialize in complex analysis of the most difficult problems. They would focus on the policymakers' hardest questions. Their goals would include identifying new opportunities for policymaking and warning first of discontinuities that could spell danger.

What does this mean in practical terms? How would the practice of intelligence analysis change?

Analysts must focus on the customer. For many analysts, particularly those involved in political work, the focus would shift from tracking developments in their particular accounts to addressing the specific, hard questions of policymakers. An analyst, for example, would often start her day by reviewing feedback and tasking from customers, instead of first reading the morning traffic. We need to use technology and a network of high-caliber representatives at policy agencies to create stronger links between analysts and customers.

Analysts must concentrate on ideas, not intelligence. Because the DI has no monopoly over the dissemination of intelligence reporting, synthesizing it for others is a poor investment of its time and talent. This particularly applies to political and economic analysis; policymakers do in fact often need help deciphering technical reports on such issues as proliferation and information warfare. In many substantive fields, the DI can best serve the policymaker by tackling the hard questions and trying to develop more reliable ways of identifying and understanding emerging issues. To do this kind of work well, the DI will need keen critical thinkers open to unconventional ideas, perhaps even more than it will need regional experts. Customers are actually pretty good at letting us know what issues keep them up at night; we have to stop dismissing these questions as either too hard or not intelligence-related.

To free analysts to do this work, we will need to deemphasize products that largely describe what has just happened. This will be hard because there are customers who want such products, which are seen as convenient, free goods. But if our relatively painless experience last year with the elimination of the *Economic Intelligence Weekly*, a decades-old publication that reviewed economic developments, is any guide, policymaker demand for such products is shallow at best.

Analysts must think beyond finished intelligence. Analysts are schooled in the need to produce validated, finished intelligence—"finished" meaning that it has been carefully considered, officially reviewed, coordinated with colleagues, and sent out under official cover. The main problem is that such products often cannot keep pace with events or even with information sources. DI officers who deal frequently with customers—including those who carry the *President's Daily Brief* to the most senior officials—report that many products short of finished intelligence often satisfy the needs of policymakers. These include annotated raw intelligence, quick answers to specific questions, informal trip reports, and memoranda of conversation. Too many intelligence analysts and managers remain fixated on formal products even as policymakers move further away from them in their own work. As anyone who has done a recent tour at a U.S. Embassy knows, most of the real scoop on world events is now exchanged in informal emails and telephone calls. Our adherence to the increasingly outdated concept of finished intelligence is what makes the DI wary of such informal intelligence practices as electronic "chat rooms" and other collaborative venues.[1]

Analysts must look to the Centers as models. If you sit long enough on a DI career service panel, you will still hear some managers say that certain analysts in the Counterterrorism Center or the Crime and Narcotics Center are not doing real DI work. They are producing little in the way of finished intelligence, and they are spending a lot of time doing individual tasks that meet very specific customer needs. Instead of being perceived as outside the DI mainstream, the Centers should be recognized as early adapters of the new model. Their focus on customer requirements, collaborative work, and less formal products speaks to the future.

Now for Something Completely Heretical

As policymakers continue to raise the standards for intelligence analysis, we may need to change more than just our assumptions and work habits. The fundamental characteristics of intelligence analysis, carefully developed during the last half of the 20th century, may in fact need to be completely rewritten. The transition might look something like the following:

The Old Analysis	*21st-Century Analysis*
Cautious/Careful	Aggressive/Bold/Courageous
Fact-based	Intuitive
Concrete/Reality-based	Metaphor-rich

Linear/Trend-based	Complex
Expert-based	Humble/Inclusive/Diverse
Hierarchical	Collaborative
Precedent-based	Precedent-shattering
Worst-case/Warning-focused	Opportunistic/Optimistic
Text-based	Image-rich
Detached/Neutral	Customer-driven/Policy-relevant

The qualities of "old analysis" are familiar to any intelligence professional. We pride ourselves on carefully basing our judgments on fact, on our expertise, on our ability to warn, and on our neutrality. Some might argue that these are clearly the analytic qualities that must persist under any scenario, regardless of whether we have addressed the needs of our customers.

Perhaps not. To really help smart policymakers, we may need to adopt new practices, new habits of thinking, and new ways of communicating our analysis.

To tell a policymaker something he does not already know, we have to be prepared to take risks in our thinking, to "go to print" with new, adventurous analytic lines before anyone else. This is not always our current style. Almost everything an analyst learns teaches her to be conservative: do not jump to conclusions, consider all sources, coordinate your views with colleagues. At best, an analyst will occasionally lean forward, when in fact she must strive to be several steps ahead of the policymaker on a regular basis.

It is difficult to generate new ideas when you have to stay close to the facts. New ideas are often intuitive, based on one or two stray bits of information that coalesce into new insight. Analysts in the 21st century will not only have to develop their intuition, they—and their managers—will also have to trust it.

Analysts today spend considerable time identifying patterns in recent events and then projecting them onto the future. This is trend analysis. Unfortunately, policymakers who are smart—and most are—can easily do this for themselves. The analysts' real value increasingly will lie in identifying discontinuities that shatter precedents and trends.

Analysts are often good at identifying what is not likely to work in a given situation; however, policymakers are usually more interested in figuring out what can work. While courses in the Intelligence Community teach analysts how to warn, there are no handbooks on how to identify new opportunities for policymakers.

The most controversial contention may be that 21st-century analysts will need to become less independent and neutral in favor of greater tailoring to customer needs. Some critics have already noted that our customer focus in recent years is eroding our detachment from policymaking. The usual answer is to assert that customer focus and neutrality are compatible; but in truth they are not completely. The more we care, as we should, that we have an impact on the policymaking community, the less neutral we become, in the sense that we select our topics based on customer interests and we analyze those aspects that are most relevant to policymakers. Analysts understandably are confused by this new direction. They were taught, they say, to produce intelligence analysis that focuses on events and developments, not customers. It is not their job to worry about whether or not it has impact.

This is the most significant and difficult consequence of working in an information-rich era lacking in significant ideological conflict. Analytic detachment and neutrality are values bred of the Cold War, when foreign policy observers often compensated for lack of information with ideologically based assertions. Intelligence analysts correctly tried not to do that—they were reliably objective.

Being completely neutral and independent in the future, however, may only gain us irrelevance. We need, of course, integrity in our analysis—we must be willing to say things that are uncomfortable for the Pentagon or the State Department and that are not compatible with the goals of policymakers. But we should not pretend that integrity and neutrality are the same thing or that they are dependent on each other. Neutrality implies distance from the customer and some near-mystical ability to parse the truth completely free from bias or prejudice. Integrity, on the other hand, rests on professional standards and the willingness to provide the most complete answer to a customer's question, even if it is not the answer he wants to hear. Neutrality cannot be used to justify analytic celibacy and disengagement from the customer. If forced to choose between analytic detachment and impact on policymaking, the 21st-century analyst must choose the latter.

Note

[1] The need to escape the constraints of finished intelligence was highlighted more than 5 years ago by Carol Dumaine, a DI officer currently leading the Directorate's Global Futures Partnership, who has written extensively on new models for intelligence analysis. In 1996, for example, in a submission to an in-house electronic discussion database, she noted that the future intelligence officer would "produce unfinished intelligence—all of it on line, interactive, iterative, multidimensional, an interdisciplinary fabric of specialist contributions, and available 24 hours a day to trusted consumers."

Chapter 32

What We Should Demand from Intelligence

Martin Petersen

There are no policy failures. There are only policy successes and intelligence failures.

—A senior State Department official only half in jest

There is no political cost in attacking the CIA.

—A senior White House official

There are two certainties in the intelligence profession: the consequences of being wrong grow every day; and sooner or later you will be wrong. There is actually a third reality as well. An unhappy turn of events, especially if it is a surprise, is likely to bring forth charges of failure and prescriptions for remedy. The recent Rumsfeld and Jeremiah Commissions are but the latest groups to examine the performance of the Intelligence Community and find shortcomings, many of which the community agreed with. But evaluating the performance of intelligence is difficult and rarely clear cut. In the public reaction to the Indian and Pakistani nuclear tests, there is yet again evidence that even people with unique access to the secret world can and do disagree about the effectiveness of intelligence. Senator Richard C. Shelby, chairman of the Senate Select Committee on Intelligence, stated the event represented a "colossal" intelligence failure, while Vice Chairman Senator John F. Kerry indicated that it seemed to be as much or more a policy failure.[1] Director of Central Intelligence George J. Tenet stuck to the facts and left the value judgments to others. "We did not get it right. Period," he said.[2]

As sincere and well taken as the various criticisms and findings often are—and we are likely to see more debate in the national security community in the next 2 years as a change of administration draws closer—there is almost always something important missing in both the criticisms and the fixes: a clear statement of what we expect intelligence to do and how we see the world and the role of the United States in

Source: Martin Petersen, "The Challenge for the Political Analyst," *Studies in Intelligence* 47, no. 1 (2003), 51–56.

it. The first is really the performance standards to which the American people should hold the Intelligence Community.[3] The second is the scope of the intelligence mission and our national tolerance for risk. Without such an articulation, it is impossible to measure progress against the goal of building an Intelligence Community that meets U.S. needs in the 21st century and weighing the tradeoffs in getting there.

What Intelligence Cannot Do

There are three things intelligence cannot do and foremost among these is prophesy the future. No one's crystal ball is that clear. It was never possible, but the end of the Cold War has made prediction even more problematic. The passing of the bipolar world coupled with the process of global democratization has produced more international actors, each with more variables, which in turn means less predictability. Russia today is a more difficult intelligence problem in many ways than the former Soviet Union. Gone too are the great ideologies that gave shape and direction to much of the politics of this century. Foreign relations, which has always been iterative and reactive, is even more a game of tactical adjustment, which makes end points even harder to identify. The communications revolution means the game is also faster with stronger global linkages between events, which adds complexity and reduces predictability.

A further complication is the nature of the issues intelligence is asked to address and the nature of the information that bears on those issues. Intelligence is about discovering other people's secrets, which they go to great lengths to conceal. Moreover, the rise of nonstate actors—terrorists, narcotraffickers, international crime organizations, and so forth—increasingly poses serious security challenges to U.S. interests. In the future it may even be difficult to know when we are under attack, especially if the attack is biological or of an information warfare nature. This problem will grow as opponents become more aware of U.S. intelligence capabilities and how to defeat them. This is partly due to leaks that compromise sources and methods, but it is also a product of our success. Nations and non-state actors study the mistakes of others and develop sophisticated denial and deception techniques.

The information explosion does give the Intelligence Community more data to work with, but the noise-to-signal ratio is great. Moreover, this information remains as it has always been: fragmentary and often contradictory. Intelligence, and especially intelligence success, is about the interpretation of data more than it is about the collection of information. And here, as always, the game is akin to putting a puzzle together without all the pieces, or a box top to guide you, and with several parts of other puzzles thrown in.

Given all this, prediction is often, at best, a misuse of resources. More significantly, by focusing on the end-state, the Intelligence Community may miss present opportunities for advancing U.S. interests. The intelligence function is unique in that it focuses on reality, the way the world is. Almost everyone else in the national security structure is focused on changing that reality through policy, not on forecasting whether they will succeed.

If intelligence cannot predict the future, neither can it—nor should it—attempt to tell the policymaker which course to take. This is fundamentally a political decision, often a partisan one, and one that must reflect U.S. domestic priorities as well. The United States cannot afford an Intelligence Community that is either partisan or tempted to defend its policy preferences as it goes about collection and analysis.

Lastly, intelligence cannot remove risk. There will always be surprises, and sadly some of these will take American lives and property.

What Intelligence Can Do

If intelligence cannot tell how events will turn out or make policy or eliminate risk, what can it do? It can light the way to better, more effective policy, policy that advances U.S. interests. In a very real sense it can make our guy smarter than their guy when it counts, whether that is on the battlefield or at the negotiating table. It can help manage risk. Ideally it may reduce it, perhaps even minimize it, but certainly make it clear to U.S decisionmakers.

While it cannot predict the future, intelligence can identify current developments and trends that will shape the future and affect U.S. interests. Moreover, intelligence can isolate individual variables that influence these broader developments so policymakers can focus on what is important. Intelligence can also establish the relationship between these variables and trends and chart the changes in them, giving decisionmakers a much better understanding of the situation they face.

The North Korean case is illustrative. Intelligence cannot predict when the regime will collapse, but it can establish that this is a regime on a downward spiral that is unlikely to be reversed. Most important it can establish for policymakers which factors have the greatest impact on the rate of decline, the relationship between those factors, how they have changed over the years, a sense of the rate of decline, and the significance of all this for the United States. Through intelligence the President and his closest advisers gain their understanding of the scope and complexity of the North Korean problems and develop a feel for how urgent they are.

Intelligence can provide the other fellow's perspective. Good collection and good analysis often provide the only insight into how our allies and adversaries truly see their own situation, assess their options, and gauge our likely response. Effective U.S. policy often rests less on how things are than on how our interlocutors assess them to be. Intelligence alone is able to provide insight into what works and does not work when it is necessary to influence a Saddam Hussein's or Kim Chong-il's perception of reality. Intelligence can identify who has influence and the limits of the Iraqi or North Korean political system. Through intelligence the President and his advisers gain their understanding of what may be possible.

Intelligence can identify the risks in a situation but it can also point out the opportunities. Especially in a crisis situation, the Intelligence Community is uniquely positioned in the national security structure to "get ahead of the story," that is, to look beyond the immediate focus of policymaker attention, explore the "what ifs," watch for the rapids and the openings in them. While intelligence must take great care not to cross the line into policy advocacy, it can, however, through an understanding of the factors in a situation and the other fellow's perspective, point out to the President and his advisers vulnerabilities and points of leverage.

And intelligence can shine a light on the consequences of choice including the option of not choosing. Because there is a natural tendency for the policymaker to focus on the issue at hand, the Intelligence Community can provide the broader perspective. Intelligence analysis, in particular, can draw the attention of the President and his team to the link between the issue at hand and other U.S. equities. It can also identify the longer-term lessons allies and adversaries are likely to draw.

Standards of Perfomance

All this has a direct bearing on how Congress, policymakers, and the American public should evaluate the performance of the Intelligence Community. Because the consequences of error can be so great, the standards must be high. And performance must be gauged over time; snapshots can distort both success and failure.

Specifically, the American public must demand that its intelligence services do those things enumerated above: correctly identify the trends and developments that most directly affect U.S. interests, assess the key variables and the forces at work in those situations, provide insight into the motives and goals of the other actors, point out the risks and opportunities for the United States, and explore the longer term consequences of actions taken.

In addition, intelligence must provide clear warning of events that threaten U.S. lives and security. Born of the ashes of Pearl Harbor, the Central Intelligence Agency (CIA), in particular, bears this responsibility. In today's complex world these threats are as likely to come from non-state actors as they are from a hostile power, and exceptional judgment is required in the execution of this duty. To warn of everything is to warn of nothing.

Intelligence must deliver its product in a timely fashion and in a form that decisionmakers can use. Critical collection and insightful analysis are worthless if they arrive too late to inform policy or if the form of the product exceeds the capacity of the President and his decisionmakers to absorb it. Too much intelligence is as bad as too little.

The Intelligence Community must demonstrate flexibility, both in its ability to refocus resources as new problems emerge and older ones recede and in its ability to take on board new information and rethink old conclusions.

And the Intelligence Community must be true to its core values. Its work must be as objective as humanly possible. It must resist pressure from policymakers to "get on the team" and the temptation to develop policy views of its own. Perhaps its greatest value to the Nation is its ability to deliver unhappy news day-in and day-out to the President and Congress and have that information accepted on its merits. To this end the Intelligence Community must make a clear distinction in its work between what it knows for fact and what it concludes. The community must also indicate its level of confidence in its judgments, laying out its own uncertainties where necessary and examining assumptions.

The American public must demand two other things as well. As secret organizations in a democracy, intelligence agencies have a special obligation to reflect both the composition and the values of the larger society. A key aspect of this is a hiring program that reaches out to all segments of the U.S. population and greater, more open interaction between intelligence officers and the wider public. The public also must demand that congressional oversight remain strong and nonpartisan.

How Much Is Enough?

Performance is also a product of resources. The more we spend on intelligence, the more we have a right to demand from it. In fiscal year 1998 the United States spent a little less than $27 billion on intelligence and intelligence-related activities. A small fraction of this is the CIA budget; the military intelligence services and the large collection agencies like the National Security Agency and the National Reconnaissance Office spend the overwhelming majority. It is hard to conceive that this amount may somehow be insufficient to U.S. needs or that there are not efficiencies to be achieved.

But part of the answer to how much is enough depends on the role the United States chooses to play in the world. If the United States sees itself, as most Americans seem to believe, as a global power with global interests, and thus a requirement to act globally, it requires a robust, global intelligence service. To state the obvious, this is expensive.

And it is perhaps truer now than it has ever been that knowledge is power. The strengthening of global linkages, the interplay between various issues, and the speed with which events in one place can affect developments elsewhere are evident in the Asian financial crisis, terrorism by non-state actors, and the instability in democratizing states. The Russian financial and political crises probably pose a greater threat to U.S. interests at present than do Russian military capabilities. As never before the security of the United States depends on our ability to gather, collate, and interpret open-source and secret data on a real-time basis, and only intelligence can do this.

Since the end of the Cold War, and especially in the last 5 years, we have seen significant changes in the intelligence mission. The issues that intelligence is expected to address have grown, not decreased. Proliferation, terrorism, international crime, the environment, and narcotics consume a major share of all intelligence resources, and rightly so because these are some of the most immediate and frightening security threats we face. Ironically, the end of the Cold War has stimulated more, not less, interest in areas of the world that were viewed 10 years ago principally as arenas in the East-West conflict. Moreover, policymaker requirements for collection and analysis on these areas are more varied and the issues more complex than in the past. We have also seen a rise in the number of consumers of intelligence; not the least of these is Congress and the military commands.

So there is more work that requires greater sophistication for more people but there are fewer resources. The CIA is significantly smaller in both people and dollars than it was at the end of the second Reagan administration, and it has responded by cutting back its capabilities in some parts of the world, reducing its investment in its people and technology, and ending collection and analysis on some subjects. The Rumsfeld and Jeremiah Reports have raised concerns about some of these issues.

There is no answer to the question of how much is enough. Ultimately this is a political decision that can only be made by Congress and the administration in consultation with the American people. Intelligence and national security must compete with other priorities such as education and health care. It really comes down to our national comfort level: how much risk is the public prepared to live with. If real resources devoted to intelligence are down as much as a quarter since the end of the Cold War, as some outside observers suggest, then the corresponding question becomes, is the world that much less threatening? If the answer is yes, then the Intelligence Community is rightsized to meet the challenges the United States faces, and all that is required is continued internal adjustment. If the conclusion is that the world is not less threatening, then the resource issue needs to be revisited or the expectation of what intelligence can do needs to be adjusted downward.

Notes

[1] See CNN Interactive, May 12, 1998, for Senator Shelby's remarks. For Senator Kerry's remarks, see his exchange with Senator Moynihan on the Senate floor May 13, 1998.

[2] See the Press Statement by the Director of Central Intelligence (DCI) on the Release of the Jeremiah Report, June 2, 1998. DCI Tenet also stated that the CIA had a "professional responsibility to stand up, acknowledge that, and learn from it."

[3] The Intelligence Community includes the Central Intelligence Agency, the Bureau of Intelligence and Research at the Department of State, the Defense Intelligence Agency, the National Reconnaissance Office, the National Imagery and Mapping Agency, and the intelligence arms of the various armed services, plus elements of a number of other organizations that are not normally thought of as having an intelligence role: the Departments of Energy, Commerce, Treasury, Customs, the Federal Bureau of Investigation, the Drug Enforcement Administration, and so forth.

Chapter 33

American Presidents and Their Intelligence Communities

Christopher M. Andrew

D uring the Revolutionary War (1775–1783), thanks chiefly to General George Washington, American intelligence and covert action outclassed those of Britain. Washington's early experience in the French and Indian Wars had convinced him that "There is nothing more necessary than good Intelligence to frustrate a designing enemy, & nothing that requires greater pains to obtain." His correspondence with the officers of the Continental Army contained frequent requests for "the earliest Advises of every piece of Intelligence, which you shall judge of Importance." Washington's passion for intelligence, however, sometimes made him reluctant to delegate. He wrote absent-mindedly to one of his agents: "It runs in my head that I was to corrispond with you by a fictitious name, if so I have forgotten the name and must be reminded of it again." Two centuries later, the head of the intelligence community, William Casey, told a Senate committee, "I claim that my first predecessor as Director of Central Intelligence was . . . George Washington, who appointed himself." The next 30 Presidents, however, rarely showed much enthusiasm for intelligence operations. Not until the Cold War did any of Washington's successors rival his flair for intelligence.

Age of Innocence

During the 19th and 20th centuries, relations between Presidents and their Intelligence Communities have gone through three distinct phases. The first and longest was the *Age of Innocence,* which endured, with few interruptions, until the Second World War. Despite the experience of the Revolutionary War, the United States was the last major power to acquire a professional foreign intelligence service and a codebreaking agency. Because of its relative isolation and self-sufficiency, it had less need of foreign intelligence than the great powers of Europe. During the First World War, the United States was thus ill-equipped to compete with the intelligence agencies of the main combatants. President Woodrow Wilson seemed proud of his own ignorance. After the war, he publicly poked fun at his own prewar innocence: "Let me testify to this my fellow citizens, I not only did not know it until we got into this war, but I did not

Source: Christopher M. Andrew, "American Presidents and Their Intelligence Communities," *The Journal of Strategic Studies* 10, no. 4, 95–111. Copyright © Frank Cass Publishers. Reprinted by permission.

believe it when I was told that it was true, that Germany was not the only country that maintained a secret service." The success of British intelligence in exploiting the naïveté of Wilson during the First World War and of Franklin Roosevelt at the start of the Second laid the foundations for an unprecedented Anglo-American intelligence alliance which still remains the most special part of the Special Relationship.

During the 1914–1918 War, both German and British intelligence agencies found it much easier to operate in the United States than in wartorn Europe. Immediately after the outbreak of war in Europe, Germany took the offensive in a secret war within the United States. "The German government," writes Wilson's biographer, Arthur S. Link, ". . . mounted a massive campaign on American soil of intrigue, espionage, and sabotage unprecedented in modern times by one allegedly friendly power against another." The most spectacular exploit of the German agents was the huge explosion at the freight yard on Black Tom Island in New York harbor in July 1916, which destroyed 2 million pounds of explosives awaiting shipment to Russia. Almost every window in Jersey City is said to have been shattered by the blast. This and other covert operations proved a public relations disaster for the German cause.

The disaster was skillfully exploited by British intelligence. Profiting from American innocence and German bungling, it gradually succeeded in winning the confidence not merely of the fragmented American intelligence community but also of President Wilson himself. The youthful British station chief in the United States, Sir William Wiseman, became the confidant of Wilson's confidant and chief adviser, Colonel Edward House, and through House succeeded in gaining access to the President. Wiseman found Wilson "ready to discuss everything on the frankest terms." He was probably the only intelligence officer ever to be informed (by House) that the President of the United States found his reports "a perfect joy." Lord Northcliffe concluded during his official missions to the United States in 1917 that Wiseman was "the only person, English or American, who had access at any time to the President or Colonel House." Though Northcliffe was guilty of some exaggeration, there is no doubt that Wilson had greater confidence in Wiseman than in his own Secretary of State; he spent much of his 1918 summer vacation in Wiseman's company.

Like Wilson, Franklin Roosevelt was initially more impressed by the British intelligence services than by those of the United States. Roosevelt's experience as Wilson's Assistant Secretary of the Navy goes far to explain his later willingness as President to begin intelligence collaboration with Britain even before Pearl Harbor. During a visit to London in 1918, FDR had listened spellbound as Rear Admiral Sir Reginald "Blinker" Hall, Director of Naval Intelligence and the most powerful of Britain's First World War intelligence chiefs, explained how British spies crossed the German-Danish border each night, went by boat to the North Sea island of Sylt and thence by flying boat to Harwich. When Hall's Second World War successor, Rear Admiral John Godfrey, visited Washington in the summer of 1941, he was amazed to be regaled by FDR's recollections of these and other amazing operations of Britain's "wonderful intelligence service" in 1914–1918. Godfrey thought it prudent not to tell the President that the exploits which had so impressed him a quarter of a century earlier were in fact wholly fictitious. Hall had invented them to conceal from the young Assistant Secretary of the

Navy that his best intelligence came from the Admiralty's codebreakers rather than from spies. Had Roosevelt realized how much signals intelligence (SIGINT) the Admiralty produced, he might well have deduced—correctly—that Britain was tapping the American transatlantic cable, which for part of the winter of 1916–1917 also carried German diplomatic traffic. And had he deduced that, he might have suspected—also correctly—that the British had broken American as well as German codes. The celebrated revelation of the Zimmermann telegram, which smoothed the United States' entry into the First World War in April 1917 by disclosing an absurd German plot to lure Mexico into the war, was at one level a successful British deception. To conceal the fact that the German telegram had been intercepted on an American cable, Hall pretended that he had first obtained it by espionage in Mexico City.

At the beginning of the Second World War, British intelligence once again took advantage of Roosevelt's naïveté. In October 1940, FDR approved SIGINT collaboration with the British, unaware that the British were simultaneously breaking American ciphers. Sir William Stephenson, the wartime station chief of the British Secret Intelligence Service (SIS) and head of British Security Coordination (BSC) in New York, set out to emulate the earlier triumphs of Wiseman and Hall. Convinced that brilliantly stage-managed revelation of German intrigues in Mexico early in 1917 had played a critical role in bringing the United States into the First World War, Stephenson planned to use similar intelligence on Nazi conspiracies in Latin America to persuade Roosevelt to enter the Second. Since, however, there were no real Nazi conspiracies of sufficient importance, Stephenson decided to invent them. Among the BSC forgeries with which he deceived Roosevelt was a forged map which, he claimed, had been obtained by British agents from a German diplomatic courier in Argentina. Roosevelt made this shocking document the centerpiece of his "Navy and Total Defense Day Address" on October 27, 1941:

> I have in my possession a secret map, made in Germany by Hitler's government by planners of the New World Order... The geographical experts of Berlin have ruthlessly obliterated all the existing boundary lines; they have divided South America into five vassal states, bringing the whole continent under their domination. ...This map, my friends, makes clear the Nazi design not only against South America but against the United States as well.

Roosevelt's most outspoken attack on Nazi Germany before Hitler's declaration of war on the United States thus relied on bogus intelligence foisted on him by Sir William Stephenson.

By far the best genuine intelligence available to Roosevelt before Pearl Harbor was MAGIC (decrypted Japanese diplomatic traffic). FDR, however, failed to grasp its importance. Though he took a personal, if ill-informed, interest in spies and secret agents, and personally appointed Colonel William J. "Wild Bill" Donovan to the new post of Coordinator of Information in July 1941 (and, a year later, as head of the Office of Strategic Services, OSS), he tolerated an astonishing level of confusion in the production of SIGINT. To resolve interservice rivalry after the breaking of the Japanese "Purple" cipher in September 1940, Roosevelt approved an absurd arrangement by which Japanese intercepts on odd dates were decrypted by military cryptanalysts and on even dates by their naval rivals. Early in 1941 he sanctioned another eccentric interservice compromise which gave his naval aide the right to supply him with MAGIC during odd months and accorded the same privilege to his military aide in even months. But there was no provision for supplying the President with SIGINT either on Sundays or on weekday evenings. It is impossible to imagine Churchill tolerating such a system for a single day. The compromise began to break down in the summer after the President's military aide, General Edwin "Pa" Watson, absentmindedly filed a MAGIC folder in his wastepaper basket. The bizarre odd/even date cryptanalytic compromise continued to cause confusion until Pearl Harbor. In the early hours of Saturday, December 6, 1941, a naval listening station near Seattle picked up the first 13 parts of the now celebrated "14-part message" containing the Japanese rejection of the final American terms for settling the crisis. The intercepts were forwarded by teleprinter to the Navy Office in Washington. As December 6 was an even date, the Navy, to its dismay, had to pass the intercepts on to the Army. Since the civilian staff of the Military Signal Intelligence Service stopped work for the weekend at midday on Saturdays, the Army, to its even greater chagrin, had to enlist naval assistance on an Army day while it tried desperately to salvage military honor by arranging a civilian night shift until the next Navy day began at midnight. While the bureaucratic black comedy continued in Washington, the Japanese fleet crept up, unnoticed, on Hawaii.

After Pearl Harbor, FDR mostly left the management of wartime intelligence to his commanders and chief advisers. With little interference from the President (unlike Churchill), the American and British high commands made better use of intelligence than ever before in the history of warfare. Roosevelt's lack of understanding of intelligence meant, however, that the American Intelligence Community never approached the level of coordination achieved by its British ally. Even after the reforms which followed Pearl Harbor, for example, the American military and naval SIGINT agencies collaborated more successfully with the British than they did with each other. The gifted intelligence analysts of OSS were hamstrung by being denied access to SIGINT.

Age of Transformation

American entry into the Second World War nonetheless began a second phase in the relationship between the Presidency and the Intelligence Community: the *Age of Transformation,* which saw the emergence of the United States as an intelligence superpower during the 1940s and 1950s. The President who did the most to shape today's U.S. Intelligence Community was, ironically, the postwar President who understood the least about intelligence. During his 3 months as Roosevelt's last Vice President, Harry Truman had been kept in ignorance of intelligence as of many other affairs of state. On becoming President in April 1945, he was initially hostile to the idea of peacetime espionage. But both his briefings on ULTRA (of which he had previously known nothing) and his own experience of MAGIC during the final stages of the war against Japan persuaded him of the importance of SIGINT. Truman's biographers fail to mention that a week before he closed down OSS in September 1945, he signed a secret order authorizing the Secretaries of War and the Navy "to continue collaboration in the field of communications intelligence between the United States Army and Navy and the British, and to extend, modify or discontinue this collaboration, as determined to be in the best interests of the United States." That collaboration was to lead in June 1948 to the signing of the UKUSA SIGINT agreement by Britain, the United States, Canada, Australia, and New Zealand. Though it ranks as the first global peacetime intelligence alliance, the UKUSA agreement is still as conspicuously absent from most histories of the Cold War as ULTRA was from histories of the Second World War published before the mid-1970s.[1]

The almost total absence of SIGINT from histories of the Cold War reflects, first and foremost, the lack of source material. Not a single decrypt produced by the National Security Agency (NSA), the largest and most expensive intelligence agency in the history of Western civilization, has yet been declassified. More than 40 years after the Korean War, we know far less about American SIGINT during that conflict (though its role, according to a CIA assessment, was "critical") than we knew about ULTRA 30 years after the Second World War. When NSA files for the Cold War period finally become available some time during the 21st century, they are certain to generate thousands of doctoral dissertations and some interesting reassessments of American foreign policy. These reassessments will no doubt include George Bush's policy during the abortive Russian coup of August 1991. NSA had remarkable success in monitoring the communications of two of the coup leaders, KGB chief Vladimir Kryuchkov and Marshal Dmitri Yazov, with regional military commands. Small wonder that Bush described SIGINT as "a prime factor" in the making of his foreign policy.

The sources for Presidents' involvement with human intelligence (HUMINT) are vastly more numerous than for SIGINT. The gaps in the available archives are nonetheless considerable. Hardly any of the President's Daily Briefs, for example, have yet been declassified. Despite the problems of sources, however, it is clear that Truman took longer to come to terms with HUMINT than with SIGINT. Early in 1946 he approved the creation of the Central Intelligence Group (CIG), a small analytical agency intended to collate and process intelligence collected by the rest of the Intelligence Community. Truman celebrated the occasion with a notably eccentric White House lunch. The President solemnly presented his guests with black cloaks, black hats, and wooden daggers, then called forward his chief of staff, Fleet Admiral William D. Leahy, and stuck a large black moustache on his upper lip. As this comic ritual indicates, Truman still did not take the idea of American peacetime espionage entirely seriously. What he hoped for from the CIG was help in coping with the daily deluge of sometimes contradictory cables, dispatches, and reports on the complex problems of the outside world. He told the first Director of Central Intelligence (Director of the CIA) Rear Admiral Sidney W. Souers, whom he dubbed "Director of Centralized Snooping," that what he needed was a "digest every day, a summary of the dispatches flowing from the various departments, either from State to our ambassadors or from the Navy and War departments to their forces abroad, wherever such messages might have some influence on our foreign policy." Thus was born what later became the President's Daily Brief. According to one of its early assistant editors, R. Jack Smith (later CIA Deputy Director for Intelligence), "It seemed almost that the only CIG activity President Truman deemed important was the daily summary."

By the summer of 1946, according to his special counsel, Clark Clifford, Truman "felt he had given the CIG concept a fair test and that it had failed." He accepted, in principle, the case for the creation of the Central Intelligence Agency, but insisted that it be postponed until after the establishment of a single Department of Defense, which he regarded as a greater priority. "I never had any thought when I set up the CIA," claimed Truman in retirement, "that it would be injected into peacetime cloak and dagger operations." It is hard to imagine Truman authorizing the 1961 landing in the Bay of Pigs or the other operations to dispose of Fidel Castro approved by his successors. But it is equally difficult to take at face value his later attempts to disclaim all responsibility for covert action. In 1964, Allen Dulles (DCI from 1953 to 1961) privately reminded Truman of his own "very important part" in the origins of covert action. Dulles wrote to the Agency General Counsel, Lawrence Houston:

> I . . . reviewed with Mr. Truman the part he had had in supplementing the overt Truman Doctrine affecting Greece and Turkey with the procedures largely implemented by CIA to meet the creeping subversion of communism, which could not be met by open intervention, [or] military aid, under the Truman plan. I reviewed the various covert steps which had been taken under his authority in suppressing the Huk rebellion in the Philippines, of the problems we had faced during the Italian elections in 1948, and outlined in some detail the various points raised in the memorandum furnished me [on other covert operations]. . . . At no time did Mr Truman express other than complete agreement with the viewpoint I expressed.

Contrary to the maxim prominently displayed on Truman's desk, the buck—so far as covert action was concerned—was intended to stop well short of the Oval Office. In June 1948, Truman signed NSC (National Security Council) 10/2, formally establishing the principle of "plausible deniability." Covert operations, Truman ordered, were to be "so planned and executed that any U.S. Government responsibility for them is not evident to unauthorized persons and that if uncovered the U.S. Government can plausibly disclaim any responsibility for them." So far from being, as he later claimed, entirely opposed to "peacetime cloak and dagger operations," Truman was the first President to found a peacetime covert action agency, and to take steps to distance the President from responsibility for its actions.

General Dwight D. Eisenhower was the first President since Washington already well informed about intelligence when he took the oath of office. Ike had been convinced of its importance both by the shock of Pearl Harbor and by his own experience as a wartime supreme commander. His administration was second only to Truman's in shaping the postwar Intelligence Community. Ike learned at first hand during the Second World War the value of SIGINT. Soon after his arrival in Britain in June 1942 as commander of American military forces, he was briefed personally on ULTRA by Churchill, one of its greatest enthusiasts, after dinner at Chequers, the country home of British prime ministers. At the end of the war, Eisenhower sent his "heartfelt" congratulations to the staff of the British SIGINT agency at Bletchley; he told Churchill's intelligence chief, Major-General Sir Stewart Menzies, that ULTRA had been "of priceless value to me . . . It has simplified my task as commander enormously. It has saved thousands of British and American lives and, in no small way, contributed to the speed with which the enemy was routed and eventually forced to surrender." During Ike's two terms as President, unprecedented peacetime resources were poured into SIGINT. By 1956, NSA had almost 9,000 employees, with as many more again working under NSA direction in the service cryptologic agencies. Though Eisenhower understood little of computer science, he was determined that NSA—like Bletchley—should have the most advanced SIGINT technology. In 1957, he authorized Project Lightning, the world's largest government-supported computer research program. NSA headquarters at Fort Meade, Maryland, contained the biggest and most sophisticated computer complex in the world.

During the Second World War, Eisenhower also acquired a passion for imagery intelligence (IMINT) which lasted for the rest of his life. His curiosity for what could be observed from the air was so great that on Independence Day 1944, to the alarm of his staff, he asked the Ninth Air Force commander, 37-year-old Major-General Elwood R. "Pete" Qesada, to fly him over German-occupied France jammed in the rear seat of a Mustang P–51 single-engine fighter. The main gap in U.S. intelligence when Eisenhower became President was, he believed, IMINT from the Soviet Union. He made frequent references to the postwar findings of the U.S. Strategic Bombing Surveys, which emphasized the accuracy and importance of aerial photography in both the European and Pacific theaters. The surprise caused by the Soviet test of a thermonuclear device in 1953 added urgency to Eisenhower's demand for the IMINT gap to be rectified. So did the "bomber-gap" controversy inaugurated in 1954 by the problems of estimating the numbers of Soviet BISON bombers.

The IMINT revolution of the 1950s, begun by the U–2 spyplane and continued by the spy satellite, owed much to Eisenhower's own enthusiasm for it. From the moment the U–2 flew its first mission over the Soviet Union on July 4, 1956, Eisenhower personally reviewed and approved every flight. The main priority of U–2 missions over the Soviet Union until they were abruptly halted in May 1960 was to seek out and monitor intercontinental ballistic missile (ICBM) production and deployment sites as well as atomic energy facilities. Besides the one launch pad at the main test center at Ty-ura Tam, ICBMs were discovered at only one other site at Plesetsk. Imagery intelligence reassured Eisenhower that the United States was ahead of the Soviet Union in both weapons development and the deployment of strategic weapons. "It is no exaggeration to say," he wrote in his memoirs, "that . . . there was rarely a day when I failed to give earnest study to reports of our progress and to estimates of Soviet capabilities." The U–2, he claimed, "provided proof that the horrors of the alleged 'bomber gap' and the later 'missile gap' were nothing more than imaginative creations of irresponsibility."

Soon after Kennedy's election victory in 1960, Eisenhower sat in on a series of secret meetings during which Richard Bissell, the CIA Director of Plans [operations], and Art Lundahl, Director of the National Photographic Interpretation Center (NPIC), two of the most gifted and persuasive briefers in American history, described in detail the remarkable progress made by imagery intelligence since the mid-1950s.

Ike triumphantly told the President-elect, "The enemy has no aerial photographic systems like ours!" The sudden revelation of the extraordinary intelligence on the Soviet Union provided by overhead reconnaissance made an indelible impression on Kennedy. During the election campaign, he had attacked the Eisenhower administration for allowing "a missile gap" to develop between the United States and the Soviet Union. IMINT showed that the gap did not exist. According to one of the IMINT experts involved in these and later briefings, "Eisenhower and Kennedy shared an insatiable craving for knowledge of their Soviet adversary, and photo interpretation became a prime source of satisfying that craving." Lundahl's relationship with Kennedy became as close and confident as it had been with Eisenhower. He later became the only photographic analyst ever to be awarded, among his many honors, both the National Security Medal and an honorary British knighthood.

The IMINT which revealed the presence of Soviet missile sites on Cuba in the autumn of 1962 justified the high hopes placed in it by Kennedy. But NPIC analysts were able to interpret the U–2 photographs so successfully only because of the detailed intelligence on missile site construction provided by Colonel Oleg Penkovsky, an Anglo-American mole in Soviet military intelligence. The early warning provided by the Intelligence Community gave EXCOM (the President's crisis committee) a week in which to consider its response to the most dangerous crisis of the Cold War. "Intelligence," said the future DCI, Richard Helms, "bought [Kennedy] the time he needed."

To a much greater degree than is usually recognized, the IMINT revolution stabilized the Cold War. Had the United States remained as ignorant about the Soviet nuclear strike force as it had been up to the mid-1950s, there would have been more and worse "missile gap" controversies and missile crises. At the very least, the Cold War would have become distinctly colder. Had the Soviet missile sites in Cuba been discovered, as Soviet leader Nikita Khrushchev had intended, only when they became operational, a peaceful resolution of the crisis would have been much more difficult.

Age of Uncertainty

In less than a quarter of a century, thanks to the Second World War and the Cold War, the United States had become an intelligence superpower. Roosevelt, Truman, Eisenhower, and Kennedy were all, in different ways, personally involved in that transformation. The Age of Transformation, however, was succeeded by an *Age of Uncertainty* which still continues. Since Kennedy's assassination in 1963, Presidents have tended, more often than not, to take for granted their daily diet of all-source global intelligence. Indeed, they have frequently seemed disappointed by it. All remember international crises which took them by surprise, and most are inclined to treat the surprises as intelligence failures. "What the hell do those clowns do out there in Langley?" President Nixon demanded after the unexpected overthrow of the Cambodian leader, Prince Sihanouk, in 1970. Eight years later, Jimmy Carter asked much the same question, more politely phrased, when he was suddenly informed that the Shah was in danger of losing his throne.

The Intelligence Community has had its fair share of failures. Presidents' recurrent disappointment with the intelligence they have received since the Cuban Missile Crisis, however, has also derived from the exaggerated expectations created by the emergence of the United States as an intelligence superpower. The more sophisticated intelligence has become, the higher Presidential expectations have risen. According to Robert Gates (DCI, 1991–1993): ". . . Presidents expect that, for what they spend on intelligence, the product should be able to predict coups, upheavals, riots, intentions, military moves, and the like with accuracy." Though good intelligence diminishes surprise, however, even the best cannot always prevent it. Some intelligence analysts during the Cold War, argues Gates, showed "a confidence in their judgments they [could] not reasonably justify." Anxious to impress each incoming President with the sophistication of its product, the Intelligence Community was understandably reluctant to emphasize its own limitations. It was thus partly responsible for raising unrealistic expectations in the White House. As former Presidents and their advisers look back on the Cold War, they tend to forget the truth of Eisenhower's dictum that intelligence on "what the Soviets *did* not have" was often as important as information on what they did. If subsequent Presidents had possessed as little intelligence on the Soviet Union as Truman, the conclusion of the Strategic Arms Limitation Treaty I agreements with the Soviet Union in 1972 would have been impossible. The secret "national technical means" developed by the Intelligence Community made it possible first to limit, and then to control, the nuclear arms race.

The key to the major successes and failures of American intelligence lies as much in the Oval Office as at Langley. Among postwar Presidents, only three—Eisenhower, Kennedy (briefly), and Bush—have shown a flair for intelligence. Kennedy's assassination was a disaster for the CIA. His immediate successors, Lyndon Johnson and Richard Nixon, rank among the ablest of all American Presidents in the spheres of, respectively, domestic and foreign policy. Neither, however, was emotionally equipped to manage the Intelligence Community. Johnson absurdly suspected the Agency of having plotted to make sure he lost the Democratic nomination to Kennedy in 1960. John McCone, a remarkably able DCI, eventually resigned because of his inability to gain the President's ear. Johnson replaced him with his devoted Texan supporter, retired Vice Admiral William F. "Red" Raborn, Jr., the least successful of all DCIs. Not until the Tet Offensive of early 1968 did Johnson prove temperamentally capable of coming to terms with gloomy CIA estimates on the Vietnam War. Richard Helms, Raborn's deputy (and, later, his successor), recalled LBJ complaining at a private dinner in the White House family quarters:

> Let me tell you about these intelligence guys. When I was growing up in Texas, we had a cow named Bessie. I'd go out early and milk her. I'd get her in the stanchion, seat myself, and squeeze out a pail of fresh milk. One day I'd worked hard and gotten a full pail of milk, but I wasn't paying attention, and old Bessie swung her shit-smeared tail through that bucket of milk. Now, you know, that's what these intelligence guys do. You work hard and get a good program or policy going, and they swing a shit-smeared tail through it.[2]

There was no danger that Raborn, like McCone, would be tempted to play the role of Bessie.

Despite Richard Nixon's flair for international relations, his election as President was another blow for the CIA. At Nixon's first meeting after his election victory with his future National Security Adviser, Henry Kissinger, he denounced the CIA as a group of "Ivy League liberals who had always opposed him politically." Besides his generalized suspicions of Langley "liberals," Nixon clung—like Johnson—to the absurd conspiracy theory that the Agency had conspired to lose him the 1960 election to Kennedy. He was convinced that the CIA had secretly given information intended to undermine the Republican program to Senator Stuart Symington, whom Kennedy had made head of a special committee on the Defense Establishment during the election campaign. According to Richard Helms, "He believed Allen Dulles had fed Stuart Symington with information on the missile gap—why I never understood, but I want to tell you it lingered." Nixon, wrote the CIA deputy leader, Jack Smith, "never forgot or forgave" the CIA for his defeat by Kennedy.

Though Presidents often underestimated the value of the intelligence they received during the Cold War, they frequently overestimated the secret power which covert action put at their command. Even Truman, after at first opposing covert action, approved a series of secret operations in the Soviet bloc which were doomed to failure. Eisenhower's misjudgments in the field of covert action were on a much larger scale. Though the Second World War taught Ike the value of SIGINT and IMINT, it left him with a distorted understanding of HUMINT. He saw the role of human intelligence agencies less in terms of intelligence collection than as a means of continuing in peacetime the wartime covert operations carried out behind enemy lines by OSS, the British Special Operations Executive, partisans, and resistance movements. Covert action was a central part of Eisenhower's Cold War strategy. He changed the motto on the massive rosewood desk in the Oval Office from Truman's "The Buck Stops Here" to *Suaviter in modo, fortiter in re* (Gently in manner, strong in deed). Eisenhower was a master of what Fred Greenstein has called "hidden-hand leadership." Behind the ready smile and the relaxed manner lay iron resolution. He left the public role of the uncompromising Cold War warrior to the Secretary of State, John Foster Dulles, while he himself tried to radiate goodwill as well as firmness. It was Eisenhower, not Dulles, however, who made foreign policy. Covert action was an essential part of that policy, offering an apparently effective alternative to the unacceptable risks and costs of open military intervention. He believed there was no other way of fighting the Cold War effectively against a ruthless enemy. "I have come to the conclusion," he wrote privately, "that some of our traditional ideas of international sportsmanship are scarcely applicable in the morass in which the world now founders."

Eisenhower's DCI, Allen Dulles, said later that 1953 and 1954 were his best years in the CIA. As one Agency official put it, he had "the American flag flying at his back and the President behind him." The apparent ease with which Prime Minister Mossadeq was overthrown in Iran and Arbenz was forced from power in Guatemala reinforced Eisenhower's exaggerated expectations of what covert action could achieve. Truman's last DCI, Walter Bedell Smith (Ike's former wartime chief of staff), privately predicted on handing over to Allen Dulles that covert action in the Eisenhower Presidency would get out of hand. "In short," according to a CIA in-house history,

> Bedell Smith anticipated a fiasco like the Bay of Pigs, although that did not happen until eight years later. In December 1959, J. C. King, head of the CIA's Western Hemisphere Division, recommended to Allen Dulles that "thorough consideration be given to the elimination of Fidel Castro."

The DCI showed no immediate enthusiasm for killing Castro. The President, however, demanded "drastic" action. Eisenhower loyalists have found it difficult to accept that the President could have authorized the farcically unsuccessful plots to assassinate Castro subsequently devised by the CIA. It is, however, barely conceivable that the decision to kill Castro was made without the President's knowledge and against his wishes. Nor was Castro the only foreign leader Ike was prepared to have assassinated. Just as Eisenhower had regarded the initial proposals of the 5412 [Covert Action] Committee for dealing with Castro as too feeble, so he expressed "extremely strong feelings" on the inadequacy of its initial plans for covert action against the pro-Soviet prime minister of the former Belgian Congo, Patrice Lumumba. Thus admonished by the President, the Committee "finally agreed that planning for the Congo would not necessarily rule out 'consideration' of any particular kind of activity which might contribute to getting rid of Lumumba."

Kennedy inherited from Eisenhower a disastrously exaggerated notion of the proper limits of covert action. It seems likely that the impression made on Kennedy soon after his election victory by Bissell's dramatic exposition of the wonders of IMINT may have helped to blind him to the limitations of the covert operations being run by Bissell's directorate in Cuba. A new administration with the fresh and critical minds assembled in the Kennedy Camelot might have been expected to see through the wishful thinking behind the Cuban operation. That they did not do so was due in part to their ignorance of peacetime intelligence. But though Kennedy blamed himself after the Bay of Pigs for having been "so stupid," the fiasco did nothing to deter him from continuing covert attempts to topple Castro. The main pressure for Operation *Mongoose*, which was intended to "overthrow the Communist regime," came not from the CIA but from the White House. And though Kennedy's supporters, like Eisenhower's, find it difficult to accept, the strong probability is that the continued attempts to assassinate Castro had the blessing of the President.

Until the 1970s, the failures of covert action had few domestic consequences for the Presidency. Remarkably, Kennedy's personal popularity actually rose in the wake of the Bay of Pigs. With the Watergate scandal, however, the national mood began to change. The most powerful government ever to fall as a result of American covert action was that of the United States itself in 1974. Secret operations had an irresistible, and ultimately fatal, attraction for the conspiratorial side of Nixon's complex personality. He became the first President to set up a White House covert action unit to operate against his political enemies. The bungling of the Watergate burglars outdid even that at the Bay of Pigs. Nixon's attempted coverup cost him the Presidency. The fate of his successors in the White House during the 1970s and 1980s was also, though in different ways, powerfully affected by covert action. By pardoning Nixon, and thus appearing to condone his attempted cover-up of Watergate, Ford probably sacrificed the 1976 Presidential election. The failure of the covert operation to rescue the Tehran hostages may have cost Carter the next election in 1980. Iran-Contra, which revived both the bungling and the illegality of White House covert action in the Nixon era (albeit against very different targets), reduced Reagan's administration to its lowest ebb and for a few months put his survival as President in doubt.

"Of all the Presidents I worked for [from 1968 to 1993]," says Robert Gates, "only Bush did not have exaggerated expectations of intelligence." Bush was the first DCI to be elected President. His experience at Langley gave him a clearer grasp than perhaps any previous President of what it was reasonable to expect from an intelligence estimate. "Measuring intentions," he rightly emphasized, "... is an extraordinarily difficult task." Bush's own electoral defeat in November 1992, forecast by almost no political pundit after his triumph in the Gulf War 18 months earlier, aptly illustrated the difficulties of political prediction. Some of the columnists who failed to foresee Bush's electoral demise nonetheless castigated the CIA for failing to predict political change in the Soviet Union with far greater accuracy than they themselves had shown in forecasting the outcome of a Presidential election in the United States.

Victory in the Cold War and the disintegration of the Soviet bloc during the Bush administration served to prolong the Age of Uncertainty. To a greater extent than most other modern intelligence communities, that of the United States was a product of the Cold War. In its main intelligence ally, Britain, both the major collection agencies, the Secret Intelligence Service and Government Communication Headquarters, and the main assessment system, the Joint Intelligence Committee, were already in place during the Second World War. The United States's principal postwar intelligence adversaries, the KGB and the GRU, went back, despite changes in their names, almost to the foundation of the Soviet state. By contrast, the main American agencies, CIA, National Security Agency, National Reconnaissance Office, and the Defense Intelligence Agency, as well as the National Security Council, though drawing on some earlier precedents, were all founded during the Cold War. The end of the Cold War thus produced greater uncertainty in the United States about the function of foreign intelligence than in most other Western states. To paraphrase Dean Acheson's famous remark about post-imperial Britain, the U.S. Intelligence Community at the beginning of the Clinton administration seemed to many observers, probably including the new President, to have lost an old enemy and not yet found a new role.

Bush's view of the post-Cold War role of the American Intelligence Community was probably clearer than Clinton's. "In sum," Bush told an audience at Langley in November 1991, "intelligence remains our basic national instrument for anticipating danger, military, political, and economic." For all the talk of peace dividends and new intelligence horizons, the main future intelligence priority remains the traditional need to monitor threats to American security. In the euphoria generated by the end of the Cold War, there was a tendency to forget that the nuclear age had not also ended. Though the prospect of an Armageddon between nuclear superpowers has—at least temporarily—receded, other dangers remained.

In the spring of 1990 both the Intelligence Community and the Bush administration were gravely concerned by the apparent danger of nuclear confrontation between Pakistan and India. Though almost unnoticed by the media at the time, that episode undoubtedly foreshadows some of the international crises which will preoccupy the Presidents of the next century. It also illustrates the crucial role that intelligence will continue to play in alerting Presidents to potential Third World conflicts involving the use of weapons of mass destruction.

In May 1990, India massed 200,000 troops, including five brigades of its main attack force, in the disputed territory of Kashmir, close to the Pakistan border. In a conventional war, it was clear that Pakistan would risk a repetition of the disastrous 2-week defeat of December 1971, which had led to the loss of Bangladesh (then East Pakistan). Intelligence reports to Bush concluded that, by mid-May, Pakistan had assembled at least 6, perhaps 10, nuclear weapons, and might already have deployed them on her American-built F–16 jet fighters. Nuclear planning, analysts suspected, was in the hands not of the Pakistani Prime Minister, Benazir Bhutto, but of President Ghulam Ishaq Khan, and the Army chief of staff, General Mirza Aslam Beg. Both, the CIA believed, were capable of ordering a nuclear strike against New Delhi rather than run the risk of another humiliation at the hands of the Indian Army. India, with a larger arsenal than Pakistan, would certainly respond in kind. "The Intelligence Community," recalls Robert Gates, "was not predicting an immediate nuclear war. But they *were* predicting a series of clashes that would lead to a conventional war that they believed would then inevitably go nuclear." The Deputy DCI, Richard J. Kerr, who coordinated the intelligence assessment in May 1990, was convinced that "We were right on the edge. . . . The Intelligence Community believed that without some intervention the two parties could miscalculate—and miscalculation could lead to a nuclear exchange."

At the height of the crisis Bush ordered Gates to fly as his personal representative on an urgent mission first to President Khan and General Beg in Islamabad, and then to the Indian Prime Minister, Vishwanath Pratap Singh, in New Delhi. Gates took with him personal letters from Bush appealing for restraint from both sides. "The card that I played heavily," he recalls, "was that I was not a diplomat but an intelligence officer by training, and that the reason I was there was that the American Government, watching the two sides, had become convinced that they were blundering toward a war and that they [might] not even know it." To demonstrate the accuracy of American intelligence, Gates "told the Pakistanis and the Indians in excruciating detail what their own forces were doing—right down to the deployment of individual aircraft and units down to the company level, distances between artillery units, and numbers of tanks in various places." President Khan told Gates that he could give the Indians a secret assurance that Pakistani training camps for Kashmiri "freedom fighters" would be closed down. At a meeting with Indian leaders in New Delhi on May 21, Gates gained permission for American military attaches to visit the frontier region in Kashmir and neighboring Rajasthan. They were able to report that Indian forces were ending their exercises and that no invasion was imminent. About 2 weeks after Gates left New Delhi, intelligence reports revealed that the leading officials in the Indian and Pakistani foreign ministries had begun regular meetings and that the two governments had agreed to other confidence-building measures. For a brief period, however, the intelligence reaching Bush had suggested perhaps the most serious threat of nuclear conflict since the Cuban Missile Crisis.

Like all previous inventions in human history, chemical, biological, and nuclear weapons will—sooner or later—inevitably proliferate. DCI James Woolsey told the House Select Intelligence Committee in 1993 that by the year 2000, 20 states are likely to possess intermediate-range ballistic missiles. Without a combination of traditional human spies and advanced technical intelligence, the United States will find it impossible either to monitor or to slow down the proliferation of weapons of mass destruction.

Conclusion

The fortunes of the Intelligence Community in the 21st century will continue to be heavily influenced by the personalities, as well as the policies, of the Presidents they have served. In a high-tech world, the human factor remains crucially important. The character and experience of the President help to determine not merely how much interest, but also what sort of interest, he takes in intelligence. Franklin Roosevelt's temperament led him to take a much keener interest in spies and covert operations than in cryptanalysis—despite the fact that codebreakers provided by far the best intelligence available to him. Truman's personality, by contrast, made him initially far less suspicious of codebreakers than of spies. The attitudes to the Intelligence Community of every incoming President since Truman have been significantly, sometimes strikingly, different from those of his predecessor. Even the new President's choice of DCI—as witness, for example, Carter's nomination of former Vice Admiral Stansfield Turner and Reagan's of William J. Casey—can have a major impact on the Intelligence Community. The influence of the DCI varies—sometimes greatly—from one administration to the next. Bush's relations with Robert Gates were closer than those between any President and DCI since the days of Eisenhower and Allen Dulles. Clinton, by contrast, had only a distant relationship with Woolsey. Whereas Bush, himself a former DCI, was a committed supporter of the CIA, Clinton's dissatisfaction with the Agency's performance helped to prompt Woolsey's resignation in December 1994.

Many of the future threats to American security in the 21st century are still unpredictable at the end of the 20th. But as the world becomes increasingly compressed into a global village, these threats will surely become both more numerous and more varied than during the Cold War. Changing threats will doubtless prompt further changes in the American Intelligence Community. Bush may well have been right, however, to argue during his valedictory address to the CIA in January 1993 that "We need more intelligence, not less." The Presidents of the next century, like their Cold War predecessors, will continue to find an enormously expensive global intelligence system both fallible and indispensable.

Notes

[1] The few books which mention the UKUSA agreement usually give the date as 1947. Dr. Louis Tordella, Deputy Director of NSA from 1958 to 1974, who was present at the signing, confirms that the date was 1948. See Christopher Andrew, "The Making of the Anglo-American SIGINT Alliance," in *In the Name of Intelligence: Essays in Honor of Walter Pforzheimer*, ed. Hayden B. Peake and Samuel Halpern (Washington, DC: NIBC Press, 1994).

[2] I owe this quotation to Dr. Robert Gates.

Chapter 34

Inside the White House Situation Room

Michael B. Donley, Cornelius O'Leary, and John Montgomery

G o to the southwest gate of the White House complex, present the guard with identification, and state your business. If you are on the appointment list, an escort will be called. Walk up West Executive Avenue and turn right into the West Basement entrance; another guard will check your pass for White House access. Take the first right, down a few stairs. To the left is the White House Mess, on the right is a locked door.

Behind these layers of security is the White House Situation Room (WHSR), a conference room surrounded on three sides by two small offices, multiple workstations, computers, and communications equipment. The conference room is soundproofed and well appointed but small and slightly cramped. The technical equipment is up to date, though not necessarily "leading edge"; every square foot of space is functional. Visitors typically are impressed by the location and technology, but they are often surprised at the small size.

While it is widely known that important meetings are held here, the importance of the WHSR in the daily life of the National Security Council (NSC) and White House staff and its critical role in Washington's network of key national security operations and intelligence centers is less understood. This [chapter] is intended to fill that void. We believe there is a longstanding need within middle and senior levels of the Intelligence Community (IC) for a basic understanding of NSC and White House functions and how current intelligence information is provided to key decisionmakers, including the President.

Mission, Organization, Functions

The WHSR was established by President Kennedy after the Bay of Pigs disaster in 1961. That crisis revealed a need for rapid and secure Presidential communications and for White House coordination of the many external communications channels of national security information which led to the President.[1] Since then, the mission of the "Sit Room" has been to provide current intelligence and crisis support to the NSC staff, the National Security Adviser, and the President. The Sit Room staff is composed

Source: Michael B. Donley, Cornelius O'Leary, and John Montgomery, "Inside the White House Situation Room," *Studies in Intelligence,* Semiannual Edition No. 1 (1997).

of approximately 30 personnel, organized around 5 watch teams that provide 7-day, 24-hour monitoring of international events. A generic watch team includes three duty officers, a communications assistant, and an intelligence analyst. The number and composition of personnel varies, depending on shift requirements and workload.

Sit Room personnel are handpicked from nominations made by military and civilian intelligence agencies for approximately 2-year tours. This is a close, high-visibility work environment. Egos are checked at the door, as captured in the admonition of a former Sit Room director to incoming duty officers: "Just remember that there are many important people who work in the White House, and you're not one of them." Personal characteristics count: an even temperament, coolness under pressure, and the ability to have a coherent, professional, no-notice conversation with the President of the United States.

Sit Room functions are perhaps described best in the daily routine of activities. The day begins with the watch team's preparation of the Morning Book. Prepared for the President, Vice President, and most senior White House staff, the Morning Book contains a copy of the National Intelligence Daily [since 1998 called the Senior Executive Intelligence Brief], the State Department Morning Summary, and diplomatic cables and intelligence reports. These cables and reports are selected based on their relevance to ongoing diplomatic initiatives and/or specific subject matter on the President's schedule. The Morning Book is usually in the car when the National Security Adviser is picked up for work. The morning routine also includes the President's Daily Brief, which is prepared by CIA, hand-delivered, and briefed by a CIA officer to the President and other NSC principals.[2]

In addition, the watch teams produce morning and evening summaries of highly selective material. These summaries, targeted on current interagency issues, are transmitted electronically to the NSC staff. Such summaries, which draw on a number of finished interagency products, field reports, and newswires, may also elicit a request for the original product. The Sit Room staff does not perform intelligence analysis or render the kind of formal interagency judgments found in National Intelligence Estimates. But it is important to recognize that, especially at the White House, there is always more intelligence information available than there is time for senior decisionmakers to read, and it falls to the Sit Room to boil that information down to its essential elements.

In a typical 24-hour day, the Sit Room will provide alerts on breaking events to NSC and White House personnel. Triggered by specific events and followed with consultations among operations and intelligence centers, the alert notification process results in a rapid series of phone calls to key officials. Responsibility for informing the President belongs to the National Security Adviser. Later, a written "Sit Room Note" will be prepared summarizing the event with up-to-the-minute reports from other centers, perhaps including a photo, diagram, or map. At the direction of the National Security Adviser, such a note might be delivered by a duty officer directly to the Oval Office or the President's residential quarters. After hours, depending on their personal style or interest, the President or Vice President might call the Sit Room directly or drop by unannounced for a quick update.

The advent of 24-hour-a-day television news broadcasting as well as radio has added a new dynamic to warning and alert operations. Not only do duty officers pore over hundreds of incoming cables, but they also are constantly bombarded by on-site television broadcasts from the crisis area and newswire services pumping a steady volume of information destined for the morning front pages. The duty officer's task is to ensure that the President and National Security Adviser are not only informed of the current situation but also how the situation is being portrayed by the media. Less-than-objective images can sometimes place the duty officer in a position of having to produce "negative" intelligence to put the event into context. Occasionally, it may even prove necessary to tell the principal that the events as portrayed by the press are incorrect.

While the advancements in telecommunications have placed more pressure on the watch standers, they have also simplified the exchange of information among participating agencies. The same satellites that allow news reporting from the field also allow forward crisis support elements to extract information from remote databases, provide for timely reporting, and, in some cases, video teleconferencing.

Another typical Sit Room activity is arranging the President's phone calls and other sensitive communications with foreign heads of state. This includes coordinating the timing of such calls at each end, providing interpreters where necessary, and appropriate security and recordkeeping. In this function, the Sit Room coordinates closely with the White House Communications Agency, which supplies communications technicians to the watch teams.

The importance of the Sit Room's communications function cannot be overstated. In all situations other than nuclear war or physical threats against the President, the Sit Room is in effect the 24-hour, one-stop shop for the White House staff. The Sit Room is also the funnel through which most communications, especially classified information, will pass when the President is not in residence. It is an essential link, providing the traveling White House with access to all the information available from Washington's national security community.

Essential Relationships

There are two essential relationships that the Situation Room has to maintain if it is to be successful in providing timely information to the Oval Office. The most important relationship is with the NSC's Executive Secretary, who reports directly to the National Security Adviser and the Deputy.

As statutory head of the NSC staff, the Executive Secretary is the primary point of contact for the White House Staff Secretary and the key player in moving national security information to and from the Oval Office.[3] National-security-related memorandums from departments and agencies to the President are transmitted through the NSC's Executive Secretary for staffing to the appropriate office. When staffing is complete, finished packages for the National Security Adviser or the President are sent back up the chain through the Executive Secretary. When the President makes a decision or approves a course of action, the Executive Secretary formally communicates the decision to affected departments and agencies. Thus, virtually all national security correspondence passes through the Executive Secretary.

For this reason, the Sit Room has often been administratively assigned to the Office of the Executive Secretary. With inclusion of the Sit Room, the Executive Secretary becomes the focal point for all information going to the National Security Adviser, from the deliberative ("slow paper") policy process to fast-moving perishable intelligence and crisis information. As coordinator of the President's national security schedule, the Office of the Executive Secretary also has an enormous reservoir of policy and operational information at its fingertips. It is through this key relationship that the Sit Room will first hear of a proposed Presidential trip abroad or a potential call to a foreign head of state.

A second essential connection for the WHSR is its relationship with the National Security Adviser, formally known as the Assistant to the President for National Security Affairs. He and the Deputy are the officials most "in the know," and they are in frequent and direct contact with NSC principals and key subordinates. Because of the Sit Room's role in the alert process, as the funnel for national security information when the President is traveling, and its 24-hour capability, a close working relationship with the National Security Adviser usually develops. For the system to work at its best, a special trust has to be established among the National Security Adviser, the Executive Secretary, and the Sit Room director.

This trust is especially important in establishing the thresholds for warning and alert after hours and providing advance notice of future events. Upon the death of a foreign head of state, for example, it may not be necessary to awaken the National Security Adviser or the President in the middle of the night. If there are no threats to American citizens involved and no action for the President to take, perhaps a "wake-up" notification at 5 a.m. would suffice. Similarly, it is not unusual for the Sit Room director to be included in sensitive interagency meetings before initiation of military operations or for the National Security Adviser to instruct the Sit Room that a special "Eyes Only" message should be brought directly upstairs. Establishing such trust can be developed only through close and routine personal interactions.

Through daily interaction with the Executive Secretary and National Security Adviser (including the Deputy), and routine access to the schedules and agenda of interagency meetings, the Sit Room director is able to provide effective operational guidance to watch teams. The teams are then in a better position to assess the value or importance of incoming cables and newswires in the context of long-range policy issues under discussion at the highest levels, as well as fast-breaking crises that will demand Presidential attention. This intimate knowledge of the President's schedule makes the Sit Room unique among Washington-area operations and intelligence centers.

Support to the NSC Staff

The NSC staff is organized into regional and functional directorates located in the Old Executive Office Building (OEOB). A directorate is headed by a senior director, appointed by the President to coordinate and oversee Presidential policy in a particular area. A senior director's counterpart at State or Defense would be at the assistant secretary level. The senior director supports the National Security Adviser, in effect coordinating the interagency policy agenda in that area. The directorates are best described as a mile wide and an inch deep because they usually consist only of a senior director assisted by two to four directors. On a day-to-day basis, the Sit Room supports the NSC directorates by electronically routing nearly 1,000 messages to staff members, scanning cables, newswires, and press reports, and monitoring CNN for fast-breaking events.

It is important that the NSC's Directorate for Intelligence Programs not be confused with Sit Room operations. The Intelligence Directorate oversees interagency intelligence policies and programs such as covert action findings, counterintelligence, major procurement projects, and the interagency intelligence budget; it has no responsibility for production, dissemination, or coordination of current intelligence.[4]

Direct Sit Room contact with the NSC staff increases markedly during crises. In some cases, such as Iraq's invasion of Kuwait and the 1991 coup attempt against President Gorbachev, it is not unusual for the senior director to move into the Sit Room to be closer to the crisis and take advantage of the on-duty staff and its communications services. This approach, however, has limitations: the Sit Room watch teams may lack the specific regional expertise appropriate to the crisis; Sit Room spaces are cramped and not suited physically to accommodate longer term crisis operations; and watch teams have a continuing responsibility to monitor other global events.

Intelligence Support to Policymakers

Efforts to strengthen intelligence support to policymakers have a long history. Every administration seems to reach its own modus vivendi, squaring expectations with realities between the policy and intelligence communities. As in the creation of the Sit Room itself, postcrisis evaluations are often the catalyst for change. Many adjustments in organization, process, and personnel have been made over the years in response to the problems perceived at the time. We describe below a model that was used successfully in the late 1980s to strengthen intelligence support at the NSC senior director and Interagency Working Group level.

In the late 1980s, the connectivity of the Sit Room to the NSC staff benefited from the assignment of several regional and functional intelligence analysts to the Sit Room staff. These analysts worked for the Sit Room director but had offices in the OEOB and were assigned to the NSC's regional and functional directorates. Their job was to provide tailored current intelligence support to the staff and to provide a focal point for Sit Room support in the directorates. Though a recent casualty of personnel cutbacks, this approach was developed after several years of trial and error focused on improving internal and external intelligence support for the National Security Adviser and NSC staff.

Use of intelligence analysts to provide daily intelligence augmentation to NSC directorates was previously considered necessary to keep up with even the normal volume of relevant intelligence and cable traffic. At the same time, resulting from their close association with the policy staff, intelligence analysts also garnered an insider's perspective of interagency policy deliberations. This perspective strengthened the Sit

Room's ability to anticipate specific intelligence requirements. During crises, the senior director would have a familiar face to coordinate intelligence support in the Sit Room, and who would know where to find key information in the IC. In turn, the Sit Room watch team would be augmented by appropriate functional or regional expertise from an intelligence analyst familiar with current interagency policy deliberations. It proved on many occasions to be a useful marriage.

Use of on-scene intelligence analysts was also a valuable means for the IC to enhance its support to the White House. With insights gained by daily interaction with the NSC directors, the analysts communicated the precise current needs of the directorates to the IC's production elements. The analysts served as a sounding board for IC-initiated studies and would discuss with NSC directors the gist of draft or just-published studies, often resulting in requests for deskside briefings.

Finally, the analysts were responsible for framing the bulk of issues in the Sit Room's Weekly Emphasis List, which was often exchanged with other agencies.

Once again, it is important not to confuse the role of the Sit Room watch team or intelligence analysts with the role of other, more senior players in the interagency intelligence process. The interagency process includes National Intelligence Officers (NIOs) who are responsible for coordinating the preparation and adjudication of formal, interagency National Intelligence Estimates in support of the policy community. NIOs are often included in senior-level interagency meetings and provide feedback and tasking to the IC. Where the NIO is focused on *future* (although sometimes near-term) requirements for collection, production, and analysis, the Sit Room analyst was focused on access to *today's* information already available in the Community, and closer coordination at the working level.

This model worked for several reasons: it supported (rather than competed with) the senior policymakers' role as crisis managers; the Sit Room's role as the NSC focal point for current intelligence was reinforced; midcareer analysts were careful not to intrude on NIO responsibilities; and it worked the same way with the same people in both routine and crisis environments.

Interagency Connections

In addition to providing current intelligence support to the NSC staff in important regional and functional areas, the Sit Room has a more independent role to play as an operations and intelligence center. There is a constant need for daily coordination on current issues with other centers, especially at the Department of Defense, State, and CIA. This coordination takes place largely out of view of the NSC staff and leadership, but is nonetheless critical to the effectiveness of the interagency system. When less formal coordination has been found inadequate, formal interagency groups have been chartered by the President or National Security Adviser to strengthen connectivity among operations and intelligence centers, improve the flow of information, develop common practices and procedures where possible, and coordinate hardware and software decisions concerning interagency communications systems.

Sit Room responsibilities sometimes extend beyond intelligence and national security functions. Maintaining connectivity with the Federal Emergency Management Agency, the Departments of Justice, Transportation, Commerce and others, the Sit Room is frequently the initial point of White House notification for domestic disasters, including everything from earthquakes, fires, and floods to Haitian refugees and Federal prison riots. The periodic inclusion of Coast Guard and other Federal agency personnel as Sit Room duty officers has sometimes proved helpful in these crises, because the Sit Room can be called upon to facilitate initial coordination of crisis response within the White House until an appropriate interagency task force is formed.

Comparisons with Other Washington-area Centers

Perhaps the most distinguishing feature of the Sit Room is its proximity to the President. As in real estate, the operative principles are location, location, and location. To be sure, the President gets most important intelligence advice and inputs from the Director of Central Intelligence, NIOs, and other key officials; but they cannot be at the White House 24 hours a day. The Sit Room will often be the "first phone call" when senior White House officials are looking for the latest intelligence information, and it will always play a key role in synthesizing cables and intelligence products originated by other agencies.[5]

A second feature is that the Sit Room is both an operations and intelligence center for the White House. These activities are divided in the majority of departments and agencies. In the Department of Defense, for example, the National Military Command Center is collocated but separate from the National Military Joint Intelligence Center. Likewise, in State and CIA headquarters, operations and intelligence activities are separated. In the White House, this means that the relationship between policy development and current intelligence can be extremely close.

The close connectivity between intelligence and policy also means that the White House is not a passive consumer of intelligence. Even at the national level, information has an "operational" and sometimes "tactical" dimension. Diplomatic and intelligence cables may be closely correlated with Presidential events, perhaps allowing a glimpse of the talking points of a foreign head of state only hours or minutes before he meets with the President.

A third feature is the small size of the Sit Room staff and its many consequences. By all measures, the Sit Room is the smallest of the Washington-area operations or intelligence centers. This has come to mean a somewhat more junior staff. Senior duty officers are perhaps O–3, or GS–12 or 13 equivalents, as compared to O–6 or GS–15 equivalents elsewhere. Limitations of size and depth, however, can in part be offset by quality personnel, high standards of performance, the Sit Room's interagency character, excellent technical support, and the motivation that comes with working inside the White House.

The Sit Room does have inherent limitations in the size and depth of staff, and it lacks the many advantages of a large intelligence agency. At the same time, the Sit Room does not need such advantages to fulfill its mission, and it should not be considered a peer competitor for influence in the IC. But the implications of the Sit

Room's proximity to the President should not be underrated. Despite its limitations, the Sit Room by virtue of its location has greater access and potential impact on White House officials than any of Washington's other operations and intelligence centers.

Implications for Leadership

A better understanding of the role of the WHSR has important implications for NSC leadership and for the intelligence agencies which supply both information and personnel to the NSC staff, including the Sit Room.

There is a need within the NSC for continuing education and dialogue among staff and leadership about the role and potential of the Sit Room in support of NSC activities. An orientation to Sit Room operations should be mandatory for incoming NSC staff officers. Likewise, an orientation to the NSC and interagency process should be mandatory for incoming Sit Room duty officers.

In addition, the National Security Adviser, Executive Secretary, and Sit Room director should nurture in their personal interactions a routine concept of operations for crisis management. The enemy in crises is confusion and "ad hocracy"; responsibilities and expectations should be as clear as possible. Sit Room personnel provide some of what little continuity exists within the NSC staff, and they are often able to observe potential gaps in the complex, fast-moving crisis management process. Routine and open dialogue among key NSC officials is essential for getting the most from the Sit Room staff.

The messages for the IC are equally clear. First, departmental and agency watch teams should be better educated about who works at the Sit Room and what they do. Operations and intelligence center personnel need to know that access is sometimes more important than rank. When a Sit Room duty officer phones, even though he or she may be junior in rank or grade, take the call and get the answer. Do not view the Sit Room as an institutional threat; support the White House in any attempt to find information and accept that the deadlines imposed, however unreasonable, will be for good reason. The IC should be confident that Sit Room information requests are for legitimate purposes and will not be mishandled.

Second, send your best and treat them well when they return. Personnel nominated to serve as Sit Room duty officers should have operations/intelligence center experience. These are junior to midlevel personnel going to an outside assignment—not always regarded as a career-enhancing move. But the destination is crucial; these junior personnel may have more contact with senior officials than certain agency directors. Personal screening of nominations by the leadership of supporting agencies is called for, as well as personal debriefings. In addition, look for opportunities to augment the Sit Room staff or NSC directorates with mid- to senior-level intelligence analysts during periods of intense activity or crisis.

When Sit Room duty officers return to your agency for their next assignment, ensure that the personnel system makes the most of their experience. Promotion boards do not always recognize the signature of the National Security Adviser or his Deputy on personnel evaluation or promotion recommendation forms. Take a close look at planned career progression, and concentrate on placement that takes advantage of the White House experience and enlarges the individual's Sit Room-attained knowledge of the IC.

Conclusion

Greater knowledge about the role of the WHSR has the potential for several beneficial effects within the IC. These include strengthening current intelligence support within the NSC staff and the White House; improving the timeliness of intelligence support during crises; enhancing the quality of individual agency products in support of national leadership; and better internal use of department and agency personnel with White House experience. In current intelligence and crisis support, the Situation Room is well positioned at the working level to assist in bridging the needs of the policy and intelligence communities. IC effectiveness would be improved with better understanding of how the White House works, how the President gets information, and how decisions are made.

Notes

[1] Bromley Smith, "Organizational History of the National Security Council During the Kennedy and Johnson Administrations," unpublished monograph, courtesy of the NSC staff, 51.

[2] Further unclassified background on the President's Daily Brief can be found in "PDB, the Only News Not Fit for Anyone Else To Read," *The Washington Post*, August 27, 1994, 7.

[3] 50 U.S.C. 402, Sec. 10 1 (c).

[4] An example of the coordination and oversight performed by the NSC's Intelligence Directorate may be found in David G. Major, "Operation 'Famish': The Integration of Counterintelligence into the National Strategic Decision-making Process," *Defense Intelligence Journal* 4, no. 1 (Spring 1995).

[5] For a broader and more fulsome treatment of the White House-CIA relationship, see Robert M. Gates, "An Opportunity Unfulfilled: The Use and Perceptions of Intelligence at the White House," *Washington Quarterly* (Winter 1989), 9.

Part X—Intelligence and the Military

Far too few senior commanders understand the Intelligence Community.

—General Alfred M. Gray, USMC (Ret.)

Chapter 35

The DCI and the Eight-Hundred-Pound Gorilla

Loch K. Johnson

What has been gathered will be dispersed.

—Buddhist saying

The jack of hearts has a major liability: he has only one eye. America's Directors of Central Intelligence (DCIs) have longed for perfect vision with respect to foreign threats, yet they too have suffered from partial blindness. This malady is inescapable in one sense, because no one—not even vast and expensive espionage organizations—can know all there is to know about world events, especially when adversaries are determined to hide their activities. This vision impairment can, however, be corrected to some extent, for in part it reflects both bureaucratic rivalries and an imbalance of missions among the Nation's intelligence agencies. The inability of DCIs to give Presidents a consistently integrated perspective on global affairs creates a major disconnection between the challenges faced and the capacity of the intelligence agencies always to respond effectively.

A Season of Change

The mid-1990s were meant to be a period of change for America's intelligence organizations. An array of reform-minded commissions and study groups, inside and outside the Government, scrutinized the state of U.S. intelligence, found it wanting, and offered a variety of correctives.[1] But on even the most fundamental points of how the secret agencies should be organized and what their missions should entail, the various panels of inquiry often disagreed with one another.

This lack of consensus came as no surprise to those who had tracked the Intelligence Community's troubled history during the Cold War. A series of controversial missteps, including the domestic spy scandals uncovered in 1974–1975, had raised questions about the state of American intelligence. Worrisome, too, was the CIA's use of extreme covert actions, even the recruitment of Mafia hit men to assassinate

Cuba's Fidel Castro (revealed in 1975). Then in the 1980s came the excesses of the Iran-contra affair and the failure to anticipate the sudden collapse of the Soviet empire. In the inquiries that followed, some critics called for sweeping reforms, even the abolition of the CIA, but others seemed content to leave the secret agencies to their own devices.[2]

Further evidence that a movement for intelligence reform would not be easy could be found in the testimony and management decisions of recent DCIs. Some directors readily expressed their dismay that the Intelligence Community was so resistant to supervision by the director's office. Admiral Stansfield Turner, DCI from 1977 to 1981, claimed that running the CIA was "like operating a power plant from a control room with a wall containing many impressive levers that, on the other side of the wall, had been disconnected."[3] Turner's response was to accelerate the downsizing of the CIA's subdivision most resistant to higher management: the Directorate of Operations (DO), home of the agency's spy handlers. This reduction in personnel had begun 4 years earlier by order of DCI James R. Schlesinger (1973), who for his efforts came to be known inside headquarters as "the most unpopular director in CIA's history."[4] Similarly, Admiral Turner's tenure is viewed by insiders as a dark chapter in the agency's history. First an academic (Schlesinger) and then not long after a Navy man (Turner)—both intelligence outsiders, or "irregulars," not bound to a specific career service[5]—had dared to interfere with the agency's sacrosanct internal structure.

One of Turner's successors recalls how the CIA had intentionally obstructed the admiral's efforts to gain control of the permanent intelligence bureaucracy. "I had learned a valuable lesson working for him," writes Robert M. Gates, a career CIA officer. "I now knew that I never wanted to be DCI—anyone who wanted the job clearly didn't understand it."[6] Although Gates eventually did become director (1991–1993) despite these misgivings, his memoirs recall his frustrations as the Nation's spymaster. Even with this career "regular" at the helm, the intelligence bureaucracy—again, most notably the Operations Directorate—resisted change mandated from the management suites on the seventh floor at Langley Headquarters. Had Gates come up through the ranks in the Operations Directorate, rather than the Intelligence Directorate, he no doubt would have been more palatable to DO personnel.

Downsizing the CIA and the other secret agencies has not been the only reform pursued by DCIs. On the contrary, for the directors during the 1980s, the answer to a more effective Intelligence Community was an expansion of its programs. The new growth took place within each of the intelligence agencies, with little attention to how their work might be most effectively integrated. The result of this approach was the creation of large, fragmented systems, which are ideal climates for the pursuit of parochial interests by individual program directors. As one authority of bureaucracies has noted, "This involves seeking higher salaries, better perquisites, greater reputations, and more power; dispensing more patronage; increasing programmatic outputs; and it adds up to immense pressures to expand organizations and increase budgets."[7] The various agency directors throughout the Intelligence Community have acted accordingly, and their combined budgets ballooned from $20 billion annually at the end of the Carter administration to $30 billion annually during the Reagan and Bush administrations.[8]

Organizational Dilemmas Facing the Intelligence Community

The Intelligence Community reflects the organizational complexity of American government with its many agencies, differing cultural perspectives, and various modi operandi. The community's centrifugal forces raise a pertinent issue of governance: is it possible to integrate the secret agencies more closely in order to give U.S. policymakers a more comprehensive and cohesive understanding of global threats and opportunities? One thing is certain: the simple redrawing of boxes on an organizational diagram is unlikely to help. Writing about intelligence, a leading academic expert on bureaucracy has wisely cautioned that it is "difficult to achieve a given outcome by changing an organizational chart."[9] Before exploring possible ways of better integrating intelligence, we should first look at the extent of fragmentation within the community. A starting place is to examine the CIA's own considerable internal disaggregation.

CIA Structural Divisions

The CIA has within its walls five major organizational divisions: the Directorate of Intelligence (DI), the Directorate of Operations (DO), the Directorate of Administration (DA), the Directorate of Science and Technology (DS&T), and the Office of the Director of Central Intelligence, each with an elaborate set of subsidiaries. More significant still in trying to understand the difficulties of governing just this agency alone (the other dozen aside) is its multitude of cultural keeps. These informal cultural fissures add to the formal divisions in producing, for intelligence directors and policymakers alike, a dismaying institutional fragmentation.

Cultural Divides

The CIA's internal cultures reflect the divergent training and outlook of each of the directorates' intelligence officers. The members of each directorate usually share basic values and practices that distinguish them from those that staff the rest of the agency. Among the cultural groupings are scholarly analysts with expertise in foreign political, military, and economic systems, located in the Directorate of Intelligence; scientists, in the Directorate of Science and Technology; case officers, propagandists, paramilitary officers, and counterintelligence specialists, in the Directorate of Operations; administrators and security officers, in the Directorate of Administration; and managers, attorneys, inspectors, arms control specialists, and legislative liaison personnel, in the Office of the DCI.

The Analysts

The analysts are the CIA's scholars, usually Ph.D.s and area specialists. During the CIA's early days, the stereotypical analyst was an Ivy League professor replete with elbow-patched tweed jacket complemented by the mandatory button-down collar and regimental striped tie, but today they are generally less tweedy and come from colleges outside the Ivy League. Nonetheless, many are educated in the Nation's top private schools, and most have an academic air about them. Their job is to sift through secret information procured abroad, blend it with information in the public domain ("open source"), and prepare short, up-to-date reports ("current intelligence") or longer "estimates" ("research intelligence") on world conditions for consideration by the President and other policy officials. Analysts are meant to be—and usually are—thoughtful, unbiased, and empirical, with a sharp eye for nuance and the academician's training to consider every perspective. The milieu of the analyst is the library, increasingly the virtual one inside a word processor, aided by the ongoing development of ties with colleagues through a secure computer network across the Intelligence Community (called Intelink). The ethos—in theory at least and usually in practice—is objectivity, and the goal is to provide decisionmakers with accurate, timely, and relevant information and insight, free of policy spin or bureaucratic parochialism.

The Case Officer

Although in the same building as the Directorate of Intelligence, the Directorate of Operations is another world, largely sealed off from the rest of the CIA. (In an attempt to overcome this separation, a recent experiment in "collocation" has seated a small percentage of DO and DI personnel together, although some DO officers have already skittered away from the project, as if on the rim of a vortex.) Some of its personnel, known as case or operations officers, live abroad and are responsible for recruiting and handling native agents or "assets" who, if they are both prick-eared and well positioned, can collect useful information in their respective countries, from sources both open (Iraqi newspapers) and closed (military documents in a safe at the intelligence headquarters of the Iraqi government).

The successful case officer, typically a gregarious sort, completes a tour of duty overseas having recruited a stable of new agents. Indeed, the criterion of success for CIA case officers was once the number of assets that he or she had recruited.[10] Recruitment is still very important, but promotion boards now take other skills into account as well. Whereas analysts are trained to value "all-source" intelligence—data drawn from all of America's spy machines and espionage assets (blended with open sources)—case officers are aficionados of old-fashioned human spying or, in their terminology, HUMINT. This, in their opinion, is ground truth; their assets, with whom they frequently develop close personal relations, are (ideally) in the enemy's secret councils or at least have access to someone who is. The case officer spends most of his or her career abroad and believes that this experience provides a better sense of the target country than that held by the narrowly specialized Ph.D. analyst—Rodin's "The Thinker" stuck behind a desk at Langley and venturing overseas only occasionally.

These differing perspectives can lead to disagreements and sometimes even hostility between the two cultures. Until a truce ("partnership") was signed in 1995, DI personnel could not even enter the DO's suite of offices at headquarters, barred by special combination locks that kept out all but the elite cadre of the "real" intelligence officers, those who learned the lessons of espionage during their overseas assignments. According to a former senior CIA official, as recently as the Reagan administration DO officers refused even to tell the DCI's Intelligence Community staff "what was going on overseas."[11]

Covert Action Specialists

Within the Directorate of Operations is the Covert Action Staff (CAS), always the most controversial of the agency's subsidiaries—and the most cosseted. This unit plans and manages operations designed to influence (and sometimes to overthrow) foreign governments through the use of propaganda, political and economic manipulation, and paramilitary (PM) or warlike activities.

One wing of the CAS suite of offices resembles those of a metropolitan newspaper, with "journalists" writing articles for placement in foreign media. Another buzzes with political campaign activities, as specialists produce everything from bumper stickers and brochures to political pins and leaflets meant to benefit pro-U.S. candidates in foreign elections. In still other offices, economic experts concoct schemes to disrupt an adversary's monetary system or to mine harbors as a means for disrupting the enemy's maritime commerce. Although the art form has declined since the end of the Cold War, most of the clandestine operations during the struggle against Communism took the form of propaganda, particularly the use of articles placed in foreign newspapers and magazines to discredit the leaders of the USSR.

One of the CAS offices has the Latin phrase *Actiones Praecipuae* above the entrance, indicating the site of the Special Activities Division, home of the paramilitary cadre—macho war fighters sporting blue-tinted aviation glasses and rolled shirt sleeves and displaying a certain swagger that comes from having faced danger abroad. These intelligence officers relish the peril of unmarked air flights behind enemy lines and the command of speedboats in hostile waters. Given the choice, they would prefer (at least in the lingering and overdrawn Rambo cartoon image from the Cold War days, which CAS officers are not above nurturing) to scale enemy walls in the dead of night, knife between the teeth, rather than fret over analytic nuances in a report destined for the President.

During the Cold War, CAS officers frequented the world's hot spots, blowing up bridges in Vietnam and Laos and concocting assassination plots against pro-Soviet leaders in the developing world ("terminate with extreme prejudice," the order would read). Their involvement in these primordial pursuits earned them the monikers "knuckle-draggers" and "snake eaters," evoking the image of men crawling on their bellies through foreign jungles. (Some journalists labeled them "The Gang That Couldn't Shoot Straight," since none of the assassination plots succeeded.) "The analysts are a bunch of academics," summed up a former DCI, "while the DO types would be entirely comfortable in the Marine Corps."[12]

The Counterintelligence Corps

Farther down the hall in the DO are the CIA's counterintelligence specialists, another breed unto themselves. Counterintelligence (CI) is the art of thwarting hostile intelligence operations directed against the United States. In these suites, paranoia is paramount: a distrust of everyone, for perhaps even one's best friend might be a Russian or Chinese "mole."

Some CI officers possess the countenance of Talmudic scholars poring over faded intelligence archives in search of clues to which foreign intelligence officer may be susceptible to recruitment (the best way of discovering what operations the enemy is running against the United States is to penetrate its foreign intelligence service with a mole of one's own). Other CI officers are cut from quite different cloth: muscular security guards who check safes to ensure they are properly locked at the close of business and monitor the internal CIA computer databanks to guard against personnel surfing outside the narrow province of one's "need-to-know." They also keep an eye on CIA officers overseas, say, during happy hour at local watering holes, in order to warn them away from socializing with individuals who may be hostile intelligence officers or their "cut-outs" (intermediaries).

When James Angleton ran the CIA Counterintelligence Staff within the DO (1954–1974), it resembled Arthur Conan Doyle's *Lost World*: remote, unchartered, mysterious. Angleton personally carried out aggressive penetration operations against foreign targets, often without the knowledge of the U.S. ambassador, the DCI, or even his most immediate supervisor, the deputy director for operations (DDO). His charge was to catch foreign spies, especially those run by the Soviet intelligence services; how he did it was up to him—or so he decided.[13]

The Techies

In another domain all their own are the scientists of the S&T Directorate, the technological wizards—"techies" or "techno-weenies"—made famous for moviegoers by Major Boothroyd (aka "Q") in the James Bond films. In the early days, they helped the Air Force build airplane and satellite surveillance "platforms" (most famously, the U–2), now a task shared by the National Reconnaissance Office and the Air Force. The scientists in DS&T design and manufacture state-of-the-art espionage devices, from tools for picking locks and burglary ("black-bag" or "second-story job") to clandestine communications facilities and disguises that can utterly transform an agent's physiognomy. In the most notorious intervals of their history, DS&T scientists have crafted exotic killing instruments for assassination plots (including a highly efficient poison dart gun or "nondiscernible microbioinoculator"), conducted LSD experiments on unwitting personnel (among them one of their own scientists, who subsequently committed suicide), and provided wig disguises for Watergate conspirators (though without knowing their criminal political intentions). Just as every university campus is culturally divided between "hard" scientists and other faculty members, so is there some distance between the CIA's scientists and the rest of the organization. The CIAs techies are essentially a lab-based support service, often driven by a stronger interest in pure research than in the traditional concerns of spy agencies.

The Admin

The Directorate of Administration keeps the agency's floors mopped and its cafeterias well stocked with food and drink. Yet it, too, has its pockets of insularity, especially the dreaded "admin" inspectors and the Office of Personnel Security. These intelligence officers are the cause of periodic dyspepsia inside the CIA, because of their marmoreal demeanor and officious enforcement of security regulations: everything from correctly wearing one's identification badge to never leaving a classified document out of its safe at night. The admin also descend from time to time on the

CIA's Embassy-based offices abroad ("stations"), conducting detailed audits and white-glove inspections.

The DA also administers the agency's lie-detector or polygraph tests to prospective employees and, at least every 5 years (a rule honored more in the breach than in the commission), to career intelligence officers as a check on their loyalty. Taking a lie detector test is always stressful and can also be a demeaning experience. In some instances, the polygraph unfairly casts doubt on the test taker's integrity, without confirming evidence. The machine is far from infallible. It failed to uncover Aldrich H. Ames, Wu-Tai Chin, and other traitors inside the Intelligence Community. Now and then, though, the lie detector has proved to be a useful security device for uncovering foreign espionage agents (CIA traitor Harold Nicholson became a suspect after failing a routine polygraph test in 1995), as well as for catching thieves and even, on one occasion, a murderer who confessed to killing his wife. But whatever the polygraph's merits or demerits,[14] it nonetheless contributes to the cultural tensions between an element within the DA and the rest of the agency, as does a concern (however unfounded) among some CIA officers that financial and medical information acquired by security personnel might be misused to harm an individual's career.

The Seventh Floor

The CIA's intelligence managers, the DCI and his immediate entourage of deputy and executive directors and their retinue of aides, reside on the seventh floor. At this level, personnel are forced into a less parochial perspective, as their job descriptions require them to plan for the entire community, however resistant the individual agencies may be to central guidance.

Depending on the particular objectives of individual DCIs (some are more community oriented than others), this management group does try to improve cooperation in intelligence collection and analysis. The goal is to overcome turf battles between the agencies, focusing instead on producing the best possible analysis for the decisionmakers. To this end, the DCI tries to behave as a genuine director of central intelligence, not just the director of the Central Intelligence Agency. If most of the other units inside the CIA's building are centrifugal or fragmenting in their organizational effect, the DO and his staff represent a degree of centripetal or centralizing influence both within the CIA and throughout the wider community.

The extent of this centralization has been modest over the years, however. Even those employees on the seventh floor meant to assist the DCI in communitywide activities can yield to narrower interests. The DCI's legal counselors, legislative liaison team, arms control experts, and the inspector general, for instance, are chiefly concerned with (respectively) legalisms, the congressional perspective, arms-accord monitoring, and accountability. These professional interests may or may not help the DCI's quest for greater community integration—if, in fact, that is even the director's goal. As a result of this internal fragmentation throughout the CIA, from the labyrinth of basement corridors to the seventh floor, DCIs have found their hands full with the task of leading the CIA—let alone all the other agencies in the community.

The DCI's First Job: Running the CIA

No DCI has successfully negotiated the straits between the Scylla of the CIA and the Charybdis of the Intelligence Community. Managing the agency is obviously a less daunting challenge for a DCI than guiding the entire community (which is essentially a dozen other CIAs—indeed, some many times larger), yet none has managed to grasp even the CIA's reins tightly in hand. Admiral Turner described the leadership dilemma as he saw it during the Carter years:

> These differing outlooks [of the CIA's internal directorates] give rise to a lot of pushing and pulling on what position the agency as a whole should take on specific questions. In any other organization such disputes would be brought to the person at the top, who would have to adjudicate them. Not so at the CIA. There, the branch heads go a very long way to compromise with each other rather than let an issue reach the DCI for resolution. The last thing [the directorates] want is for the DCI to become a strong central authority. In adjudicating between them he might favor one or the other, and the others would lose some of their traditional freedom.[15]

The admiral attributed the independence of the CIA's operating directorates to a combination of three influences: their initial separateness at the beginning of the agency's history in 1947, each with distinctive and (in his view) "haphazard" evolutionary arcs; the philosophy of a need-to-know compartmentalization (or what the CIA refers to as "compartmentation") of activities that, for security reasons, fractures the sharing of information along directorate and even office lines; and their differing responsibilities (collection, analysis, and technical support). In what manner does the CIA's professional intelligence bureaucracy want the DCI to govern? In Turner's opinion, by leaving the CIA alone and concentrating on outside political battles with the White House, the Congress, and the public—a blend of public relations and Washington infighting to protect agency budgets and programs.

Admiral Turner was not willing to tolerate this degree of internal autonomy, believing that in order to combat foreign threats more effectively, information had to be shared more equitably, both inside the CIA and across the community. Moreover, excessive internal discretion in the past had led, he was convinced, to the intelligence abuses documented by White House and congressional investigators in 1975. Yet try as he might, Turner conceded that he had little success in overcoming the centrifugal forces at Langley, and his experience in attempting to discipline improper behavior by two renegade CIA officers in the Operations Directorate illustrates the point. Rather than support his efforts, the agency closed ranks against him, sharply resisting intrusion by this outside military man and his uniformed aides (quickly dubbed "the Navy mafia" by inside regulars). As Turner recalled, "Not one CIA professional concurred with my instant reaction to fire the two men."[16]

President Bill Clinton's first DCI, R. James Woolsey (another irregular), had a similar experience in 1994. When cracking down on the lax security that allowed DO officer Ames to sell secrets to the Kremlin, he found to his amazement and chagrin that the Directorate's own leaders had chosen to confer medals on the very individuals he was attempting to punish, clearly a signal from the DO regulars to back off their turf. Apparently intimidated, Woolsey ignored the recommendations of the CIA's inspector general (Frederick P. Hitz) in favor of dismissals and other tough sanctions, deciding instead merely to reprimand 11 senior DO managers. When Woolsey's successor, John Deutch (also an irregular, a former MIT chemistry professor and provost), sought to discipline DO officers for improper activities in Guatemala, he became the first director ever booed by senior intelligence officers assembled in "the Bubble," the Agency's main auditorium.[17]

The DCI's Second Challenge: Running the Community

Admiral Turner also did not have much success in leading the wider community, but none of the other DCIs that followed him has done much better. Turner's immediate successor, the controversial outsider William J. Casey (1981–1987), devoted little attention to issues of community integration (although he did take an active interest in national intelligence estimates, detailed reports based on communitywide sources). Indeed, he bypassed altogether the agency's normal procedures and the community during the centerpiece operation of his tenure, the Iran-contra affair.

Another outsider, former FBI director William H. Webster (1987–1991), followed by insider Gates, both achieved some success in integrating the Intelligence Community based on the creation of interagency intelligence "fusion" centers and task forces. Although the next DCI, Woolsey (1993–1995), built some bridges between the CIA and the Pentagon (where he had once served), his role as a community leader was modest as well.

Subsequently, DCI Deutch (1995–1996), who had also served in the Defense Department, further tightened the ties between the agency and the Pentagon and strengthened the feeble Community Management Staff in his search for better interagency coordination. In addition, both Woolsey and Deutch enriched the DCI's top board of analysts, the National Intelligence Council, by drawing in more communitywide personnel, and responding to Washington's budget-cutting pressures, they experimented with pooling a communitywide legislative liaison staff. But all these efforts represented only piecemeal attempts to integrate the secret agencies, despite Deutch's euphoric hope to "orchestrate the symphony" of the community's component parts.[18]

Fusion Centers

"The basic themes of American governmental institutions are distrust and disaggregation," notes a political scientist.[19] Nothing so exemplifies this phenomenon as the Intelligence Community. In response to the centrifugal tendencies both within the CIA and—more pronounced still—throughout the community, recent DCIs have experimented with fusion centers that concentrate on specific intelligence problems. These fusion centers include the Center for CIA Security, the Center for Support Coordination, the DCI Center for Security Evaluation, the DCI Nonproliferation Center (NPC), the DCI Counterterrorist Center (CTC), the Counterintelligence Center, the

National HUMINT Requirements Tasking Center, the DCI Crime and Narcotics Center (CNC), and the DCI Environmental Center (DEC).

These centers offer planning, research, analysis, technical support, and operations all in one place ("one-stop shopping," officials in the centers boast), bringing together community experts to focus on specific threats to the United States. They encourage the sharing of information across agencies, in contrast to the more traditional emphasis on separate agency hierarchies, competition, and the hoarding of knowledge. Seated in the same suite of offices within easy conversational reach are CIA, Federal Bureau of Investigation (FBI), and other intelligence officers with common specialties (such as counterterrorism). Currently, each center is housed in, and dominated by, the CIA, yet the number of communitywide experts participating in several of the centers is steadily increasing, and the organizations are becoming more truly all-source integrators of information, analysis, and operations.

Task Forces

In another effort to overcome internal CIA and communitywide fragmentation, recent intelligence directors have experimented with using special task forces to deal with specific problems. Some dozen in number, they have addressed such matters as covert action, information management, and future planning. Director Woolsey put together one of the most successful task forces to monitor intelligence needs for UN and NATO forces in Bosnia. Field commanders and Washington policymakers alike commended this communitywide team for its exemplary all-source ethos and reporting of timely, useful information from the Balkans. A comparable team also performed with merit during the war in Kosovo in 1999.

Centers and task forces notwithstanding, disaggregation remains the order of the day for the Intelligence Community. The community resembles nothing so much as a byzantine mosaic—or, in the apt description of one observer, "a Hobbesian state of nature."[20] This fragmentation poses a staggering leadership challenge for any DCI who hopes to piece together, on behalf of the President, all-source intelligence products from all parts of the community. Little wonder that a deputy DCI once threw up his hands in despair and declared the community nothing more than a "tribal federation."[21] The movement toward centrism has gained some momentum, albeit at a glacial pace, and this description remains close to the mark.

The 800-Pound Gorilla

A major obstacle confronting any DCI who seeks to establish a true Intelligence Community has been what CIA officers refer to as the "800-pound gorilla" that resides in the Pentagon: the Secretary of Defense. Of the approximately $27 billion currently spent each year on intelligence, the Secretary of Defense controls about 85 percent of the total.[22] Moreover, the Nation's military intelligence agencies (including the largest, the NSA, and the most expensive, the NRO) are tied directly to both the Department of Defense and the Office of the DCI.

A result of a hasty compromise in 1947 between the founders of the CIA and entrenched military intelligence leaders anxious about threats to their domain, these blurred lines of authority created conditions ripe for bureaucratic conflict in which the DCI holds a poor hand. The Secretary of Defense enjoys much higher status in the government; he, not the DCI, is a statutory member of the National Security Council (NSC). Moreover, the Secretary of Defense (known before 1947 as the Secretary of War) has stood at the top of the cabinet's pecking order—along with the Secretaries of State and Treasury—since the beginning of the Nation's history. The DCI, in contrast, is not a member of the cabinet. President Reagan did make William Casey a member, but since then no other DCI has served in this capacity. The DCI may be the formal head of the Intelligence Community, but in terms of genuine clout in the high circles of government, he has minimal leverage over people like the Secretary of Defense.

Moreover, the defense secretary is only one of several powerful figures in the government who preside over intelligence agencies within their own departments. The Secretary of State can have considerable bureaucratic influence in the White House and on Capitol Hill and is quite capable of deflecting unwanted DCI control over the State Department's Bureau of Intelligence Research (INR).

The director of the FBI, too, is not exactly a lightweight in Washington circles. This point is obvious with respect to the legendary J. Edgar Hoover, director of the bureau between 1924 and 1972, who refused even to talk to DCI Richard Helms (1966–1973) during a CIA–FBI squabble over counterintelligence jurisdictions. More recent FBI directors—and certainly the current incumbent, Louis J. Freeh—also have had minds of their own, close ties to the Hill, and a manifest capacity to thwart DCI "interference" in bureau affairs. Despite the DCI's initial opposition, Freeh successfully expanded the presence of the FBI overseas to fight international crime, a move viewed with alarm by some senior officials in the CIA as an exercise in global empire building by the bureau at the expense of agency billets in U.S. embassies abroad. Moreover, lamented a recently retired CIA official, "The FBI is absorbing all of the agency's counterintelligence responsibilities."[23]

The less well known "program managers" who head up the other intelligence agencies (such as the director of the NSA) are also expert at shielding their operations from the DCI and at building alliances in the White House and in Congress. Furthermore, whereas the CIA is an independent, nonpolicy agency that serves the President directly (through the DCI), all the other intelligence agencies report to their policy department secretaries (whether civilian or military) as well as to the DCI.

Not surprisingly, the directors of these agencies are quick to run to their departmental secretaries for protection should a DCI become too aggressive in trying to shape their programs and budgets.

The DCI cannot depend on the President's National Security Adviser as a reliable ally in the White House. The reason is that the security adviser's views may contradict the information brought to the Oval Office by the intelligence director, and the security adviser has the considerable advantage of a suite in the West Wing and frequent access to the President.

The position of DCI, then, is not at all what it appears to be on the standard organizational diagrams: a colossus standing astride the secret agencies and driving them forward in his chosen direction, as if they were so many horses in a wagon train.

Rather, the director is primarily the titular head of the community and must depend heavily on personal bargaining skills, support in Congress, friendship ties with key departmental secretaries and program managers, and—vital to success—the President's backing. In this sense, the Office of the DCI is reminiscent of the view of the Presidency as a position of persuasion, not command,[24] although the DCI lacks the resources of funding, staff, and authority enjoyed by the President and other senior figures in the national security apparatus.

The DCI does have a few face cards in the game of political persuasion that characterizes American government. Depending on the chemistry between the two, the director sometimes has a close relationship with the President. William J. Casey was a long-time friend and confidant of President Reagan, and Robert Gates also benefited from strong ties to President Bush. In addition, the DCI has ready access to the CIA's storehouse of information gathered overseas by agents recruited by the Operations Directorate, as well as to the reports prepared by the thousands of analysts in the Intelligence Directorate (who, free of affiliation with a cabinet department, enjoy a reputation for policy neutrality).

The Secretaries of State and Defense have their wellsprings of information, too, of course, from open sources as well as from their own departmental intelligence services, but sometimes the CIA can provide the DCI with unique data and assessments, especially on global political and economic matters. In the truism, information is power and the DCI can use agency information to gain standing in the government, particularly if the President values intelligence and regularly seeks briefings from the DCI.

Military versus Civilian Intelligence

The dilemma faced by the DCI in governing the Intelligence Community can be seen in the current tug of war over "support to military operations" (SMO in the inevitable Pentagon acronym). As Operation *Desert Shield* gathered momentum in 1990, Congress heatedly debated for 4 days the wisdom of intervention to halt Iraqi aggression against its neighbor, Kuwait. Senator Sam Nunn (D–GA) agonized over the risk of high U.S. casualties that might result from the military action. Backed by former Chairman of the Joint Chiefs of Staff Admiral William J. Crowe, Jr., Nunn argued forcefully in favor of economic sanctions to punish Iraq rather than the use of an American invasion force in the heart of the Middle East.

Nunn lost the debate, but as it turned out, the ensuing fatalities on the U.S. side numbered fewer than 200. One of the main reasons for this outcome was the transparency of the battlefield for American warfighters, a result of saturating the region with intelligence surveillance platforms. The possibility in the future of ever greater battlefield transparency, allowing for still fewer body bags, has understandably whetted appetites in the Pentagon for acquiring additional intelligence resources to support the war fighters. As a consequence, "SMO" has become a popular bureaucratic battle cry inside the Pentagon among those who prepare the Secretary of Defense for annual intelligence budget negotiations with the DCI.

Naturally, DCIs also favor the reduction of U.S. casualties as far as possible during warfare; however, they have the added responsibility of reporting to the President and other policy officials on intelligence related to foreign political, economic, and societal—not just military—matters. Given the Pentagon's control already over 85 percent of the intelligence dollar, further erosion in the direction of the SMO mission would drastically reduce the budget for intelligence on these other global threats. As the staff director of the House intelligence committee has put it, "There is a need to rebuild a strategic, or what we sometimes call the national, capability to end what has been an absolute and total fixation on near-term, tactical [military] intelligence."[25]

Sometimes the bargaining over resources between the intelligence chief and the Secretary of Defense has been cordial. Indeed, Woolsey's and Deutch's ties to the defense secretary were too cozy in the opinion of some CIA officers, who feared that both men were selling out to the Pentagon's dreams of perfect battlefield transparency. Often, though, the relationship has been distant, like, in the words of a former CIA officer, "ships passing in the night."[26] In the Carter administration, Secretary of Defense Harold Brown and DCI Turner rarely saw eye to eye. In those infrequent cases when disagreements between the Secretary of Defense and the DCI are pushed into the Oval Office for arbitration, Presidents have been disinclined to oppose the military. And even if the Secretary of Defense were to lose in the White House, the Pentagon's powerful allies on the Armed Services committees in Congress are likely to enter the ring on the military's side.

The Office of the DCI is thus an incongruous leadership post, with major responsibilities for guiding national intelligence but without concomitant authority, jostled on all sides by muscular rivals and torn by deep historical and cultural divisions even within the director's own immediate home agency, the CIA. As one intelligence specialist put it, "For all the talk about community, the reality is different."[27] Indeed, it is unlikely that even James Madison (the father of institutional disaggregation in America's government) could have imagined the hyperpluralism that characterizes the Intelligence Community today. Agency autonomy is the guiding norm even within the subdivisions of the secret organizations.

The end result of this institutional fragmentation has been a steady drift away from the centrism that Harry S. Truman endorsed with his creation of a more central intelligence. Some recent steps have been taken to reverse the powerful centrifugal forces emanating from the separate departments and agencies that deal with intelligence, but they have met fierce resistance, especially from the guardians of military intelligence in the Pentagon. Even the DCI is nervous about seeking more authority. "Every time you try to give me new authority," George Tenet has remarked, "you get me in a fight with a building much bigger than mine" [that is, the Pentagon].[28]

The Elusive Quest for Intelligence Centrism

In 1996, the Aspin-Brown commission attempted to overcome some of the institutional fragmentation in the community by recommending that the DCI be given more authority.[29] When Congress addressed these and related reform proposals in the Intelligence Authorization Act of FY 1997, it gave the director some extra governing leverage, including a special Committee on Foreign Intelligence (CFI) lodged in the NSC.[30] The new CFI is chaired by the President's National Security Adviser, and its members include the DCI, the Secretary of Defense, and the Secretary of State. Although the intention of this reform was to provide more focus to intelligence issues at a high level, it achieved little more than to create still another layer in the NSC's increasingly encumbered bureaucracy.

The Aspin-Brown commission (and subsequently Congress) embraced the creation of even another new NSC committee, this one entitled the Committee on Transnational Threats. Again chaired by the National Security Adviser, its membership included the DCI, the Secretary of Defense, the Secretary of State, and the Attorney General—in short, the CFI plus one. The catchall phrase "transnational threats" is meant to include global crime, narcotics flows, and weapons proliferation, as if the NSC had somehow overlooked these menaces in the past.

Finally, Congress created in this same statute one deputy director and three assistant directors to support the DCI. The Deputy Director for Central Intelligence (DDCI, already in existence) is supposed to help manage the CIA. The new Deputy Director of Central Intelligence for Community Management (DDCI/CM) is meant to help manage the wider community. The Assistant Directors of Central Intelligence (ADCIs) are positions designed to aid the DCI and the DDCI/CM in the communitywide coordination of three core activities: administration (ADCI/A), intelligence collection (ADCI/C), and analysis and production (ADCI/A&P). With respect to the spending powers, Congress recoiled from the notion of a stronger DCI. According to the language of the 1997 Intelligence Authorization Act, the director would be allowed only to "facilitate the development of annual budget for intelligence" (as he already does, insofar as the Secretary of Defense lets him).

The DCI's most notable success in the 1997 legislation, however modest, came in the realm of selected appointment powers. That is, the Secretary of Defense must seek the "concurrence" of the DCI before appointing the program directors for the NSA, the NRO, and the National Imagery and Mapping Agency (NIMA). If the DCI did not concur, the Secretary of Defense could then take the case to the President or select another nominee. For other key appointments, including the heads of the Defense Intelligence Agency (DIA), State's INR, and the FBI, the intelligence director would only have to be "consulted" by the Secretary of Defense, the Secretary of State, and the attorney general, respectively; no concurrence would be necessary—another victory for institutional autonomy.

Toward a Protean Centrism

Should the Nation embrace the Hamiltonian impulse to strengthen the Office of the DCI, as recommended by some reformers (including the Aspin-Brown Commission)? Or in light of the political realities discussed here, would one be better off (in the British expression) to save one's breath to cool one's porridge? The presence of a strong Secretary of Defense and a large portion of the intelligence budget dedicated to military needs are facts of life unlikely to change. Nor should they, since most observers agree that America's defense requirements must remain preeminent in this Nation's hierarchy of foreign policy priorities. Nonetheless, reformers point to the unbridled centrifugal forces that dominate the Intelligence Community. They argue that America's secret agencies will continue to fall short in their duty to provide the President with cohesive civilian and military information until greater centrism is achieved (as Truman sought five decades ago) through an increase in the DCI's authority.[31]

The goal of the centrists, as one observer has astutely put it, is to achieve "the efficiencies of a 'department of intelligence' without performing major surgery."[32] Major surgery is unlikely, as the Secretary of Defense and the Pentagon's congressional allies are unwilling to allow the creation of a countervailing 800-pound DCI. Moreover, the antigovernment mood in the United States and ongoing concerns about excessive Federal spending present an unfavorable climate for the creation of a Department of Intelligence, even if that were a smart idea. The most centrists can now hope for is some modest strengthening of the DCI and a concomitant consolidation of the Intelligence Community.[33]

Former representative Lee Hamilton (D–IN), an experienced intelligence overseer, clearly stated the core objective of those reformers who seek greater centrism, namely, a more prominent role for the DCI in interagency coordination, which would also tilt the community away from the Department of Defense and toward a richer reporting of civilian intelligence:

> We don't really have a Director of Central Intelligence. There is no such thing. The DCI at CIA controls only a very small portion of the assets of the Intelligence Community, and there are so many entities you don't have any Director. There is not a Director of Intelligence in the American system, and I think we have to create one.[34]

The current chairman of the House intelligence committee agrees. "The DCI needs greater capability, since he is the chief intelligence architect," argues Porter Goss (R–FL). "We have a management problem designed for failure, and it's amazing it works as well as it does. We need more comprehensive management."[35] The chief source of the problem, in his view, is lodging the intelligence budget in the Department of Defense. The staff director for the House Permanent Select Committee on Intelligence articulated the case for a strengthened DCI:

> There is still no management of the Intelligence Community. The intelligence agencies are each managed, but there is no one in a position to make the tradeoffs within the Intelligence Community that will make a coherent, efficient organization that will function as a whole. So, we end up doing it on Capitol Hill. And I've got to tell you, if you are depending on Capitol Hill to do something as important as this, you're in trouble.[36]

A first step in remaking the DCI would be to give the office added stature, not in an unrealistic attempt to match that of the Secretary of Defense, but at least to raise the profile of the intelligence director in the national security establishment. To this end, amending the National Security Act of 1947 to make the DCI a full statutory member of the NSC (along with the President, Vice President, Secretary of State, and Secretary of Defense), and not merely an adviser to the panel, is likely to be more important than the superfluous NSC committees created by the Intelligence Authorization Act of 1997 (which place the DCI in a subordinate role to the National Security Adviser). Such a law would have to state clearly, however, that the DCI would serve on the NSC strictly in a nonpolicy capacity, only to provide information and analysis and not policy pronouncements that would contradict his role as a neutral presenter of facts and insights.

In addition, the DCI's approval of the appointment of all intelligence program directors would make the various agency chiefs more responsive to the individual supposedly in charge of the entire community. The DCI's role in preparing the annual intelligence budget could be strengthened as well, again not to have the intelligence director replace the Secretary of Defense, but to remind the Pentagon and others that the Nation's civilian intelligence needs are important, too. Except in times of war, 25 percent of the annual intelligence budget should be turned over to the DCI for civilian intelligence purposes, such as the collection of information on global political and economic matters.

In regard to consolidating the community, some important measures have been adopted since the end of the Cold War, such as the development of centers and task forces. Useful too is a new joint system set up by the CIA and the Pentagon to keep track of clandestine operations involving agents abroad, what the DCI's assistant director for administration calls "an excellent first step" and a concept "we need now to extend . . . throughout the community."[37] The melding of dispersed space reconnaissance activities under NIMA's direction is another example of consolidation. Some CIA officers worry, though, that this new organization was simply a ploy by the Defense Department to take away photo reconnaissance and imagery interpretation from the agency.

The Nation's National Photographic Interpretation Center (NPIC) was indeed once sheltered in the CIA's DS&T Directorate, and its shift into the NIMA was, in this sense, a "militarization" of this important function. Still, logic was on the side of fusing communitywide imagery and mapping components for the common task of researching global geographic details and taking note of any changes that might have strategic significance for the United States (just as signals intelligence is concentrated in another disciplinary "stovepipe," the NSA). The DCI has full access to the imagery analyses prepared by photo interpreters in the new NIMA. Nonetheless, the most important power over imagery is the ability to direct satellite and airplane cameras toward the targets of one's choice in the first place (a decision called "tasking"). This is another place where the DCI and the Secretary of Defense have often bumped heads, since NIMA is basically a combat support agency and belongs to the Department of Defense.[38]

An expansion of the program to rotate officers through different agencies as part of their career progression and a greater emphasis on common security badges, training, and the sharing of facilities would lead to better interagency cooperation.[39] Pooling recruitment data would be sensible, too. Seymour Hersh reported that U.S. Naval Intelligence recruited Jonathan Pollard, who eventually became an American spy for Israeli intelligence, without knowing that he had already flunked the CIA's recruitment tests on security grounds.[40] The CIA's recent efforts at collocation for DO and DI officers in order to increase the interaction between intelligence collectors and analysts could also be replicated among the specialties inside other agencies. The desired outcome is to build bridges that will enable people in different cultures to collaborate on assignments that cut across agency boundaries.

The organizational objective of most intelligence reformers is to build a community that is lean, flexible, and synergistic, with each agency integrated with the others and all led by a DCI with more effective management control. It is driven by a centrist vision. Reformers propose not a simple-minded model of centrism, however, headed by a potentially dangerous intelligence czar but, rather, a more fluid model that draws together different strands of the community for different tasks. This model envisions concentrating communitywide resources into the Counterterrorist Center to deal with that specific threat, or into an all-source task force for, say, an intense focus on ethnic strife in central Africa, or into a collection discipline (such as HUMINT) to blend the results of that approach to information gathering.

The model envisions a DCI with the authority to redirect community resources wherever they are necessary in future contingencies—in some instances, a rapid shifting ("surging") of capabilities from one nation or region to another. For such enduring interests as terrorism or international narcotics flows, the DCI would order a more permanent concentration of resources into new fusion centers. Increasingly, centrism would become more a matter of setting up secure electronic networks for communications among intelligence specialists throughout the community than establishing physical sites at Langley or elsewhere. These virtual fusion centers, according to a senior intelligence officer, have "made cross-cultural linkages [within the community] easier."[41] Temporary teams of visiting experts could be brought in to assist the Intelligence Community (for example, the Nation's leading academic experts on Sudan should a crisis occur there). According to this perspective, the DCI would have a continuum of coordinating strategies—a protean centrism to focus the community's efforts on the limited number of targets where the secret agencies could contribute to the already available public knowledge on foreign events and conditions.

Balancing Unity and Diversity

The main purpose of America's intelligence establishment is to provide the President and other officials with the best possible information about and insights into global events. Since the end of World War II, Presidents have generally supported the idea of a more central intelligence in place of the extreme institutional fragmentation that characterized U.S. intelligence before and during the war against the Axis powers.

Yet despite the creation of a CIA and a DCI in 1947, institutional disaggregation has remained the hallmark of American intelligence, as units within the policy departments (civilian and military) have resisted the movement toward centrism as a threat to their own authority. Unable to stop the establishment of a CIA and a DCI, the existing agencies reverted to the next line of defense: retaining as much of their original autonomy as possible within the new, more centrist framework. Although DCIs have managed to increase somewhat their control over all the intelligence agencies, the Intelligence "Community" remains essentially a confederation of disparate elements. At the other extreme, excessive intelligence aggregation would not be desirable, since each government department and agency has unique informational needs that a single organization would probably not be able to fulfill.

The problem, as always in government, is how to balance unity and diversity. The American Constitution is grounded in a theory of governance that favors institutional diversity, a disaggregation of power to ensure liberty or ambition counteracting ambition, in Madison's conception. Modern Presidents and DCIs, in contrast, worry about efficiency, having the right information at the right time, and getting things done. They seek to harness the intelligence agencies to gather and interpret worldwide information in a timely, holistic fashion, with a good balance between civilian and military reporting.

"In unity lies strategic direction and clarity," remarks an expert on America's executive branch of government. While on the one hand commending the National Security Council for exhibiting this attribute, he praises on the other hand the value of diversity displayed by the Department of State, noting that diversity encourages "sensitivity to implementation and to nuance."[42] Likewise for intelligence, greater centrism would permit the White House (through the DCI) to derive better insights from the enormous inflow of global information gathered separately by the various intelligence agencies. But if the United States were to concentrate all of its intelligence resources into a single intelligence department or perhaps a committee of the NSC, the result would be an erosion of diversity, agility, and the responsiveness that allows each intelligence element in the existing cabinet departments to respond to the needs of their individual secretaries, especially the tactical intelligence requirements of the Secretary of Defense.

Furthermore, excessive centrism would discourage competition among the secret agencies, which currently offer to the President (although not always) a range of views rather than a single, homogenized common denominator. In addition, as an intelligence expert observed, "Competition is essential for innovation."[43] Diversity of structure and a division of power in the Intelligence Community can lead to a healthy debate over the meaning of world events, a "competitive analysis" that is a valuable (if more complicated) precondition to thoughtful Presidential decisions.

Just as the homogeneity of excessive centrism would be a mistake for the Intelligence Community, so would a system that was too diverse and unwieldy and no longer served the President's needs for reliable, timely, and cohesive information—Truman's lament. Over the years, the agencies of the Intelligence Community have largely eschewed unity in favor of functional diversity, protected as they are by their department secretaries against centrism in the form of a strong DCI.

The recent growth of interagency task forces and centers suggests some movement toward greater centrism. Whether this trend will continue depends ultimately on the leadership of future Presidents. If, like Truman, they believe that greater intelligence unity is necessary, the centrist trend will continue. The adversarial, individualistic culture of the Intelligence Community may begin to approach the greater analytical integration exhibited in the British system. Even then, however, the Secretary of Defense will likely fight for the autonomy of military intelligence, the Secretary of State for intelligence (support to diplomatic operations or SDO), the FBI director for the bureau's perceived prerogatives in the war against international criminals, and on down the line.

Given what is likely, on the one hand, to be the policymaker's growing interest in quick, integrated information from the Intelligence Community on civilian and military developments around the world and, on the other hand, the enduring desire for autonomy among the intelligence agencies, we can anticipate the struggles between the values of unity and diversity to continue in the national security establishment. In light of the relatively rapid turnover of Presidents and the more permanent nature of the intelligence bureaucracy, it would probably take an intelligence failure of Pearl Harbor proportions to shock the American people and their chief executive into demanding the greater efficiencies of centrism.

Notes

[1] See especially Report of the Commission on the Roles and Capabilities of the U.S. Intelligence Community (hereafter cited as the Aspin-Brown commission), *Preparing for the 21st Century. An Appraisal of U.S. Intelligence* (Washington, DC: U.S. Government Printing Office, March 1, 1996); Task Force, Council on Foreign Relations, *Making Intelligence Smarter* (New York: Council on Foreign Relations, 1996); Allan E. Goodman, Gregory F. Treverton, and Philip Zelikow, *In from the Cold* (New York: Twentieth Century Fund, 1996); John H. Hedley, "The Intelligence Community: Is It Broken? How to Fix It," *Studies in Intelligence* 39 (1996), 11–19; National Institute for Public Policy, *Modernizing Intelligence* (Fairfax, VA: National Institute for Public Policy, 1997); and U.S. House Permanent Select Committee on Intelligence, *IC21: The Intelligence Community in the 21st Century,* 104th Cong., 1st sess. (Washington, DC: U.S. Government Printing Office, 1996), 43.

[2] On reform and abolition, respectively, see Daniel P. Moynihan, "Do We Still Need the CIA? The State Dept. Can Do the Job," *The New York Times,* May 19, 1991, E17; and Seymour M. Hersh, "Spy vs. Spy," *New Yorker,* August 8, 1994, 4. On a plea in favor of wider discretion for the intelligence agencies, see Stephen F. Knott, *Secret and Sanctioned* (New York: Oxford University Press, 1996).

[3] Stansfield Turner, *Secrecy and Democracy* (Boston: Houghton Mifflin, 1985), 185.

[4] Robert M. Gates, *From the Shadows* (New York: Simon and Schuster, 1996), 43.

[5] Bert A. Rockman, "America's Departments of State," *American Political Science Review,* December 1981, 912. Between Schlesinger and Turner came Robert M. Gates, an insider, and George H.W. Bush, another outsider—but one who avoided tampering with the CIA's staffing and operations.

[6] Gates, 140.

[7] Cohn Campbell, "Political Executives and Their Officials," in *Political Science: The State of the Discipline*, ed. Ada W. Finifter (Washington, DC: American Political Science Association, 1993), 383–406.

[8] Interviews with intelligence officials (1993–1999), Washington, DC.

[9] James Q. Wilson, *Thinking about Reorganization* (Washington, DC: Consortium for the Study of Intelligence, 1993), 1.

[10] Edward G. Shirley, "Can't Anybody Here Play This Game?" *Atlantic Monthly*, February 1998, 45–61.

[11] Quoted by Walter Pincus, "Tenet Seeks Coordination of Intelligence Gathering," *The Washington Post*, February 12, 1999, A33. The ICS is now known as the Community Management Staff (CMS).

[12] R. James Woolsey, remark to me, Oxford, England, September 24, 1999.

[13] Interviews with James J. Angleton, Washington, DC, September–December 1975.

[14] For a damaging critique of the polygraph's value, written by a scientist, see Robert L. Park, "Liars Never Break a Sweat," *The New York Times*, July 12, 1999, A19.

[15] Turner, 186.

[16] Ibid., 57.

[17] Interviews with senior intelligence officials, Washington, DC, June 8–10, 1997.

[18] Quoted in Loch K. Johnson, *Secret Agencies: U.S. Intelligence in a Hostile World* (New Haven, CT: Yale University Press, 1996), 51.

[19] Rockman, 916.

[20] Wilson, 5.

[21] Quoted in Victor L. Marchetti and John D. Marks, *The CIA and the Cult of Intelligence* (New York: Knopf, 1974), 96.

[22] Aspin-Brown Commission, 131.

[23] Remark by Frederick L. Wettering, panelist at the annual meeting of the International Studies Association, Washington, DC, February 17, 1999.

[24] Richard E. Neustadt, *Presidential Power* (New York: Wiley, 1960).

[25] John Millis, speech to Central Intelligence Retirees Association (CIRA), October 5, 1998. Not everyone at the CIA is trying to resist the SMO trend in favor of more national intelligence; some have recommended jumping on the tactical military bandwagon. As a former senior CIA officer noted, the agency "is trying hard to get in on SMO, because that's where the money is." See Wettering, remark.

[26] Charles G. Cogan, "The New American Intelligence: An Epiphany," Working Paper no. 3, Project on the Changing Security Environment and American National Interests, John M. Olin Institute for Strategic Studies (Cambridge, MA: Harvard University, January 1993), 29.

[27] Panelist's remarks at the CIA's "The Brown Commission and the Future of Intelligence," a roundtable discussion, *Studies in Intelligence* 39 (1996), 9.

[28] Comment at the National Intelligence and Technology Symposium, CIA, Langley, VA, November 6, 1998.

[29] In 1992, Senator David Boren (D–OK) and Representative Dave McCurdy (D–OK) joined forces (via S. 2198 and H.R. 4165) in an earlier attempt to strengthen the Office of the DCI. They envisioned a new Director of National Intelligence, or DNI, who would have significantly greater authority over budgets, personnel, and operations than does the current DCI. A few minor elements of their reform package made it into the Intelligence Organization Act of 1992. See Report 102–963, U.S. House of Representatives, 102[d] Cong., 2[d] sess. (Washington, DC: U.S. Government Printing Office, 1992). The more sweeping reforms of the Boren-McCurdy Act died, however, strangled by allies of the Secretary of Defense waiting in ambush inside the Hill's two Armed Services committees.

[30] See U.S. House, "Intelligence Authorization Act for Fiscal Year 1997," H.R. 3259, 104th Cong., 2[d] sess. (Washington, DC: U.S. Government Printing Office, 1996).

[31] Among others, see the report of the Aspin-Brown Commission and the U.S. House IC21 inquiry. This is not to say that other important points of view do not exist. In fact, some reformers advocate further disaggregation, especially placing the CIA's analytic staff into the various policy departments where they would have closer immediate interaction with the consumers they serve (for example, National Institute for Public Policy, *Modernizing Intelligence*).

[32] Panelist's remark at the CIA, "The Brown Commission," 6.

[33] Charles G. Cogan, formerly of the CIA, concluded, "How do you overcome the problem of a weak DCI vis-á-vis a strong secretary of defense? You can't." Comment to panel at the annual meeting of the International Studies Association, Washington, DC, February 17, 1999. For his reform suggestions within the framework of a weak DCI, see Cogan, "The New American Intelligence."

[34] Quoted in Hedley, 17.

[35] Representative Porter Goss, remarks at National Intelligence and Technology Symposium.

[36] Millis, speech to Central Intelligence Retirees Association (CIRA), October 5, 1998.

[37] Quoted by Pincus, "Tenet Seeks Coordination of Intelligence Gathering."

[38] For a view that the DCI's main concern for national (civilian) intelligence does not really require much access to SIGINT and IMINT anyway, see Ernest R. May, "Intelligence: Backing into the Future," *Foreign Affairs* 71 (Summer 1992), 63–72.

[39] The Intelligence Organization Act of 1992 recommended this rotation reform for implementation by the DCI; yet it has been honored more in the breach than in the commission, in part because many CIA officers believe they will be harmed in their internal promotion opportunities if they are away from their home offices.

[40] Seymour M. Hersh, "The Traitor," *New Yorker,* January 18, 1999, 27.

[41] Interview with the external affairs coordinator, Counterterrorist Center, Langley, VA, September 30, 1993.

[42] Rockman, 925.

[43] Bruce D. Berkowitz, "The CIA Needs to Get Smart," *Wall Street Journal,* March 1, 1999, A22.

Chapter 36

Tug of War: The CIA's Uneasy Relationship with the Military

Richard L. Russell

Public perception today is that the Central Intelligence Agency (CIA) enjoys a close working relationship with the military, but that has not always been the case. Since its inception in 1947, the CIA has traditionally had an uneasy relationship with the military. During the Cold War, the CIA's relationship with the military was strained periodically by conflicting analyses. Only since the end of the Cold War has the relationship been on more sure footing. The Gulf War underscored the need for national-level intelligence to meet the accelerating demands of the military in an increasingly technology-driven and fast-paced combat environment. Perceived shortcomings during the campaign to liberate Kuwait led to a major institutional effort to link the CIA more closely to the U.S. military by establishing the Office of Military Affairs (OMA) in 1992. The creation of the OMA, however, is unlikely to eliminate differences of analytic opinion between the agency and the military services. In fact, such conflicts will be healthy indicators of the CIA's rationale as a bureaucratic entity able to formulate independent and objective analysis precisely because it has fewer vested interests in military operations. The agency, however, must guard against being overwhelmed by the intelligence demands of the military that could spread limited analytic assets thin, further erode the quality of analysis, and derail the CIA from performing its critical mission of providing national intelligence and strategic warning to civilian policymakers.

The Bush administration's military campaign in Afghanistan against the Taliban and Osama bin Laden's terrorist network has brought attention to the CIA's role in supporting the U.S. military. The relationship, however, is poorly understood by the public and, surprisingly, even within the corridors of government. The growing body of scholarly literature on the CIA, moreover, tends to focus on human intelligence collection and covert action—the likes of which operate in the Afghan military campaign—while giving short shrift to the agency's much larger role in supporting the military with intelligence analysis.[1] This gap is startling because the impetus for the CIA's birth emerged from the 1941 military debacle at Pearl Harbor and the critical need to provide strategic warning to policymakers and the military. The CIA's ability

Source: Richard L. Russell, "Tug of War: The CIA's Uneasy Relationship with the Military," SAIS Review 22, no. 2 (Summer/Fall 2002), 1–18. Copyright © 2002 by The Johns Hopkins University Press. Reprinted with permission of The Johns Hopkins University Press.

to carry out this strategic warning function is being examined today in light of the tragic events of September 11 in New York, Washington, and Pennsylvania.

Any examination of the CIA's strategic warning capability must begin with assessing the scope of its mission and understanding how the agency's support of the military fits in its overall objectives. The CIA's primary mission is to support the needs of policymakers at the national level. As such, it allocates significant resources to support national policymakers including the President, the Vice President, the National Security Council staff, and the Secretaries of State and Defense. The demand for intelligence from these top civilian consumers increases exponentially during times of crisis, which is also when the agency is expected to commit resources to the military, including combat support intelligence.

But how far should the CIA go in serving the intelligence demands of the military services and commands? Why should the CIA be increasingly charged with supporting warfighters when the military commands are already served by intelligence staffs in each of the armed services as well as in unified and specified commands, and by the Defense Intelligence Agency (DIA)? These questions are particularly pertinent when one considers that the collective analytic resources of the military intelligence organizations dwarf those of the CIA, which tasks only a small percentage of its analytic workforce to conduct the military analysis of utmost interest to military consumers. In a post-Gulf War effort to cater to the needs of the warfighter, the CIA probably has created more of a demand for intelligence analysis than it has the means to fulfill. Moreover, serving a growing number of military intelligence demands is likely to come at the expense of supporting civilian policymakers, who rightfully have been the CIA's primary audience. The agency may be squandering its unique responsibility to act as an effective check and balance while protecting civilian policymakers from military analysis slanted by operational equities, a problem that becomes especially acute in times of war. If the CIA grows too close to the interests of the military, it will lose its objectivity and relevance to policymakers and will evolve into yet another entity of the Intelligence Community increasingly dominated by the military. Such a course of events would not be conducive to the effective civilian control of the instruments of national power that are crucial for waging war on terrorism or for defending the country against other threats.

The Second World War and Shared Institutional Roots

The CIA's roots are in the World War II organization of the Office of Strategic Services (OSS). The creator and inspiration for the OSS was its director, William Donovan. According to Michael Warner, a historian on the CIA history staff, the principal mission of the OSS was to support military operations in the field by providing research, propaganda, and commando support. Warner points out, though, that Donovan had not intended the OSS to become a "spy" agency—running espionage operations abroad—but eventually became convinced of the need for human operations that constituted one of the staple missions of the OSS's successor organization, the CIA.[2]

As part of the rapid demobilization of wartime assets after Japan's surrender that ended World War II, the OSS was disbanded in October 1945. President

Truman was suspicious of Donovan's proposal to perpetuate a combat support and intelligence agency in peacetime, fearing that such an organization might be used for domestic purposes, against U.S. citizens. As the United States emerged as a superpower, however, the need for strategic intelligence overrode Truman's concerns and required the reestablishment of an intelligence organization at the national level. Truman formed the Central Intelligence Group (CIG), which was then consolidated into the Central Intelligence Agency under the National Security Act of 1947. The CIA was to perform in peacetime many of the missions that the OSS had performed during the war. Many OSS veterans filled the leadership of the CIA, including four future Directors of Central Intelligence: Allen Dulles, Richard Helms, William Colby, and William Casey.[3]

The U.S. military also assumed some of the responsibilities previously shouldered by the OSS.[4] Special Forces personnel, like their CIA counterparts, regard Donovan and OSS as their organizational ancestors. In creating the U.S. Special Operations Command (USSOCOM) in 1987, the military consciously looked to the OSS as the model for interservice cooperation and unconventional warfare. Warner assesses USSOCOM in part as the fulfillment of Donovan's hope that combined arms special operations would become an integral part of U.S. warfighting capabilities.[5]

Military intelligence capabilities also increased dramatically after World War II. In the 1960s, the DIA was created, buttressing the military service intelligence units. The DIA was designed to meet the intelligence needs for the Joint Chiefs of Staff and the Secretary of Defense.

Cold War Discord

During the Cold War, as former Director of the National Security Agency, General William Odom, opined, the CIA's military intelligence was "almost never used by the military services."[6] The relationship was periodically exacerbated by conflicts in analytic assessments. The CIA and the military often sparred over estimates of the Soviet Union's military and strategic programs and the course of combat, first in Korea and later in Vietnam.[7]

The agency first suffered a major blow to its reputation when it failed to clearly predict the outbreak of the Korean War. As John Ranelagh, the author of a highly regarded history of the CIA, recounts, "[i]t was a situation too reminiscent of Pearl Harbor: an 'enemy' had massed its forces and launched a successful surprise attack without the United States being prepared. The CIA's overriding purpose was to prevent another Pearl Harbor, and the North Korean attack on South Korea on June 25, 1950, was too close a parallel to pass without changes being made."[8] U.S. and other forces operating under the auspices of the United Nations were subsequently surprised again when they crossed the Yalu River and were attacked by Chinese forces. Eliot Cohen observes that in a paper prepared for President Truman shortly before Chinese intervention:

> CIA analysts concluded that the Chinese could intervene effectively, but not necessarily decisively, in the Korean conflict. Believing the time for successful

intervention had passed, and that such an intervention would only occur in the context of a global war unleashed by the Soviet Union, the CIA concluded that the Chinese would continue to give only covert aid to the North Koreans.[9]

The tension and competition between the CIA and the military intelligence community became more acute during the next decade. Some of the CIA's most bitter disputes with the military centered on estimates of Soviet strategic nuclear forces, the so-called "bomber" and "missile gaps." In the early 1950s, the Air Force estimated that the Soviet Union would have a bomber force of more than a thousand aircraft within a decade, an inventory far beyond that of the United States. The CIA disagreed and argued that the Soviet industrial base was not sufficient to support such a high rate of production. In 1956, U–2 photography confirmed the CIA's hunch and showed that the Soviets did not have a large bomber fleet. By 1957, the CIA was confident that the Soviet strategic bomber force was actually much smaller, estimating it between 90 to 150 aircraft.[10] During his Presidential bid in 1960, John F. Kennedy made a political issue out of the "missile gap," which heightened public concerns that the Soviets were racing ahead of the United States technologically, a fear that was sparked by the Soviet launching of Sputnik in 1957. President Eisenhower knew from CIA analysis of U–2 photography that these fears were overblown, but he refused to jeopardize his intelligence by releasing it publicly just to calm fears. The Air Force, however, tried to use the "missile gap" as it had used the "bomber gap" to obtain larger budget appropriations.[11] This approach backfired. Indeed, part of the reason Secretary of Defense Robert McNamara created the Defense Intelligence Agency was because he distrusted what he saw as self-serving Air Force parochialism that drove its intelligence analysis during the "missile gap" controversy.[12]

The apex of the CIA and military disputes during the Cold War came during the Vietnam War. The agency took a dismal view of a host of policy issues, including the political survival of the South Vietnamese regime, prospects for the U.S.-led counterinsurgency program in South Vietnam, the bombing interdiction campaign against North Vietnamese supply routes through Laos and Cambodia, the effects of bombing against North Vietnam, and order-of-battle estimates of Vietcong irregular forces operating in South Vietnam.[13] As James Wirtz points out, a key CIA analyst responsible for order-of-battle estimates during the Vietnam War estimated that the troop strength of the Vietcong in South Vietnam was about 600,000 in 1967, twice the size of the estimate produced by the Military Assistance Command, Vietnam (MACV).[14] Although subsequent history revealed the military's conservative estimate to be closer to the mark, Wirtz astutely observes the more important lessons learned from the analytic disputes between the CIA and the military's intelligence organization during the Vietnam War:

> By the summer of 1967, CIA analysts, in contrast to officers at MACV, had established a record of skepticism about achieving American goals in Southeast Asia. Several factors probably contributed to the differences in the assessments offered by individuals working for these organizations. MACV analysts focused on battlefield events, while CIA analysts tended to integrate political, economic, and social

developments into their judgments about the conflict. Analysts working at CIA headquarters also enjoyed a degree of detachment that was not available in Saigon. CIA analysts had the luxury of focusing on the big picture, while analysts working at MACV concentrated on supporting the day-to-day conduct of military operations. In addition, it was less onerous for CIA analysts to identify weaknesses in the American war effort: the U.S. military and not the intelligence community was largely responsible for the implementation of U.S. policy in Vietnam.[15]

In short, as former CIA Director of Intelligence Ray Cline recalled, "The CIA's estimates and other analytical papers in the entire Kennedy-Johnson era were more sober and less optimistic than those of the Defense Department, particularly those of Secretary of Defense McNamara."[16]

The Vietnam War in the 1960s and 1970s was a lightning rod for controversy between CIA and military intelligence analysis in no small measure because the stakes were great for U.S. national security policy. The 1980s saw its fair share of discord between the intelligence and policy communities, though none generated as much controversy as the disputes that characterized the CIA–military relationship during the Vietnam War. The tension in the relationship was to come to the forefront again during the 1990–1991 war against Iraq, which led to the largest deployment of U.S. military forces abroad since the Vietnam War. That conflict again pitted the national-level analysis of CIA civilians against the operational and tactical-oriented military intelligence analysis. Whereas the former had few vested policy interests, the latter had significant vested interests in the course of battle.

Gulf War Turning Point

The 1990–1991 Gulf War was a watershed event in the history of the relationship between the CIA and the military. Public criticism of the CIA's analytic performance during the war by the Commander-in-Chief of Central Command (CENTCOM) forces, General Norman Schwarzkopf, was a major contributing factor to the instigation of reviews of national intelligence performance during the Gulf War. A U.S. House Armed Services committee report found that while the Intelligence Community (IC) mobilized in support of the Gulf War, some national intelligence agencies were unfamiliar with or unresponsive to the intelligence needs of the warfighter.[17] The CIA, in particular, had traditionally viewed its key intelligence consumers as civilian policymakers. In the aftermath of the successful Gulf War, lawmakers were poised to go out of their way to pay deferential treatment to the military and to funnel national-level resources toward them with little regard for the potential adverse consequences for civilian policymakers who also had critical needs for intelligence. The House committee also reported the following findings:

- There was an inability to reliably disseminate intelligence to the combat theater, which constituted one of the major intelligence failures during the war.[18]
- The IC had an excellent analytical understanding of units, locations, and equipment of Iraqi troops as well as of the enemy's military infrastructure. In addition, the community also had a good understanding of Iraq's chemical

weapons capabilities. The IC, however, had a poor understanding of Iraq's nuclear capabilities prior to the war. The Iraqis devoted enormous wealth and expertise to their nuclear weapons program and successfully shielded most of it from foreign intelligence organizations with the use of sophisticated and comprehensive denial and deception operations.[19]

- The most serious failure of U.S. intelligence during the war was the production of battlefield damage assessment (BDA). Postwar analysis showed that CENTCOM's wartime BDA of destroyed Iraqi tanks during the air campaign was inflated.[20] Although the CIA's wartime BDA was closer to the mark, the agency's analytic performance was tainted by postwar criticism, most prominently from General Schwarzkopf.[21]

The CIA was faulted for its lack of direct national intelligence support to theater commanders and for failing to integrate its capabilities into the military planning and execution processes during *Desert Shield* and *Desert Storm*. The House report found that although:

> individual CIA analysts were in regular contact with their counterparts in-theater and provided a substantial amount of useful intelligence data to Operation *Desert Storm* planners, the CIA as a whole adopted a 'hands-off' approach towards the concept of joining the organized support given combat commanders. It refused to actively participate in the Joint Intelligence Center (JIC) located in the Pentagon, and instead sent only liaison officers.[22]

In defense of the CIA's predicament, several major factors mitigated against fully participating in combat intelligence support. First, the CIA's primary mission is to support the needs of national-level policymakers. The full commitment of CIA resources toward combat support intelligence would have siphoned off limited resources needed to support national policymakers, such as the President, the National Security Council staff, and the Secretaries of State and Defense. The demand for intelligence from these top civilian consumers, moreover, increased exponentially during the Gulf War, further straining the CIA's resources. CIA officials told House investigators that they lacked the staff to join the JIC and needed to remain outside of the JIC to provide independent assessments for senior policymakers.[23]

The second mitigating circumstance to remember is that the CIA's resources and personnel—particularly for military analysis—are dwarfed by those of the DIA, the service intelligence units, and other military intelligence components. The Aspin-Brown Commission, appointed in 1996, found that the Department of Defense and its subordinate intelligence organizations spend 85 percent of the annual funds allocated for U.S. intelligence. They also employ 85 percent of all intelligence personnel.[24] The primary mission of the service intelligence components is to support field commanders, whereas they are not responsible for supporting civilian policymakers—precisely the reverse order of the CIA's priorities. Notwithstanding these constraints, the CIA answered over a thousand requests for information from CENTCOM during the Gulf War and worked on daily joint intelligence assessments with other intelligence agencies represented on the JIC.[25]

Nevertheless, the House report recommended several steps to improve intelligence agencies' understanding of the intelligence interests and demands of the theater commander in wartime. First, the report recommended frequent peacetime exercises of the theater JIC with the participation of analysts from national intelligence agencies. Second, periodic briefings should be given to senior theater commanders on the capabilities and limitations of national intelligence collection systems. Third, the committee suggested the formation of permanent CIA liaison positions on the Unified Commands (J–2 staffs) of the U.S. Commanders-in-Chiefs (CINCs). Fourth, the report supported the development by the CINCs of plans for further integration of theater intelligence capabilities. Finally, the House report recommended the creation of a single, deployable JIC that would augment a regional CINC's staff during a crisis.[26]

Institutionalizing Post-Cold War Collaboration

Notwithstanding the CIA's provision of intelligence analysis and support to the military during the Gulf War, the negative dimensions of the House report had a profound impact on the agency. Director of Central Intelligence (DCI) Robert Gates wanted to satisfy growing demands from Congress for reform while retaining control over the process. He ordered a series of reports from 14 task forces on reorganizing the Intelligence Community, including the CIA, and forwarded his recommendations to President Bush in March 1992.[27]

The Creation of the Office of Military Affairs (OMA)

One of the major changes to the CIA stemming from the task forces Gates instituted and the recommendations he presented to President Bush was increasing intelligence support to the military. To bridge the gap between the CIA and the military, Gates established the Office of Military Affairs in 1992, whose mission he described as follows:

> This Office will be responsible for coordinating military and CIA planning; strengthening the role of DCI representatives at major commands and the Pentagon; developing procedures so that the CIA is regularly informed of military needs for intelligence support; developing plans for CIA support in national, theater, and joint intelligence centers during crises; and the availability of CIA officers for participating with the military on selected exercises.[28]

> The mission of the Office of Military Affairs is to ensure that the U.S. military will have full access to a range of CIA intelligence, from raw human intelligence reports to finished multidisciplinary analysis, as well as operational support capabilities overseas. In other words, the OMA is designed to act as a "clearing house," disseminating CIA products to the military commands and complementing those intelligence materials coming from service intelligence organizations and from the DIA.[29]

The OMA had been placed under the CIA's Directorate of Operations (DO)—the agency's clandestine service, which runs global human operations—but it subsequently was moved into the DCI's office. Gates had initially created the position of

Associate Director for Operations/Military Affairs to head the OMA. His successor as DCI, John Deutch, later elevated the importance of CIA support to the military by creating the Associate DCI for Military Support (ADCI/MS) and subordinating the OMA to the Director of Central Intelligence. The move bureaucratically elevated the office out of the DO, which reflected its ability to tap the resources of the entire agency rather than rely exclusively on the clandestine service.[30]

Today, the OMA works closely with the ADCI/MS, whose office has a mandate to coordinate overall support from the Intelligence Community to the U.S. military.[31] As such, the ADCI/MS serves as the principal adviser to the DCI on military issues. The ADCI/MS also recommends, coordinates, and directs the implementation of all Intelligence Community policies in support of military force plans, exercises, and operations, while reviewing the allocation of the community's resources to ensure adequate support to the military in the fields of research and development, acquisition, plans, training, and operations. Another important task is coordinating, integrating, and "deconflicting" CIA activities with those of the military.[32]

The OMA is staffed by agency personnel from all of the CIA's four directorates—administration, intelligence, operations, and science and technology. At any given time, the OMA hosts about 100 military officers on detachment from all 4 of the armed services.[33] Military services and commanders can contact the OMA, which in turn taps the appropriate components within the CIA to answer or respond to queries from the military. The OMA is thereby able to reduce the frustration within the military that typically arises from trying to track down the appropriate CIA component for action on a given issue. The components within the CIA most frequently called upon to support the military include the DO's regional divisions, the DO's Military and Special Programs Division, the Directorate of Intelligence's Issue Managers responsible for regional and functional analytic expertise, various offices in the Directorate of Science and Technology (DS&T), and the DCI centers for counterproliferation, counterterrorism, and counternarcotics.[34] The DCI Center for Counterterrorism, for example, undoubtedly plays an important role in exploiting documents and computer files captured in Afghanistan to help CENTCOM pinpoint its elusive al Qaeda and Taliban enemies.[35]

Supporting the Military

The OMA performs a variety of tasks to link the CIA to the military. The OMA, for example, assigns DCI representatives to the staffs of the regional and functional military commands.[36] These representatives are senior agency officers, who generally serve in these assignments for 2 to 3 years. The ADCI/MS chairs the senior agency panel that selects the representatives from the candidates nominated by the CIA's deputy directors.[37] The OMA also supports peacetime exercises of the CINCs by offering scenario support and providing agency personnel as role players or controllers for war games.[38]

The OMA dispatches crisis reaction teams to bolster CIA connectivity to CINCs in time of crisis and war. It taps into the expertise of various CIA components, particularly the DO and DI, to contribute to National Intelligence Support Teams

(NISTs) assigned to joint task force commanders.[39] NISTs substantially bolster the CINC's intelligence staff with national-level intelligence. Since the Gulf War, NISTs have provided intelligence support to U.S. and multinational military operations in numerous trouble spots, including Saudi Arabia, Somalia, the Balkans, Haiti, Bosnia, Kosovo, and Albania.[40]

The OMA also sends out Crisis Operation Liaison Teams (COLTs) who perform military liaison functions to temporarily "surge" or augment stations and bases. COLTs facilitate the exchange of time-sensitive information between the CIA and the military, complement existing station support, expand station surge efforts without degrading collection against other requirements, provide around-the-clock crisis coverage, enhance the military's situational awareness and force protection posture, and provide secure communication between CIA stations and deployed military forces.[41] The OMA is also responsible for providing CIA analysts to assist Department of Defense teams conducting battle damage assessments during conflicts.[42]

In addition, the OMA supports the DCI representatives sent to military academies and war colleges (the Air, Army, Navy, and National War Colleges as well as the Marine Corps Command and Staff College). DCI representatives are fully integrated into the faculties of these schools and teach courses on intelligence to help ensure that military commanders are aware of the scope and strengths of national-level intelligence collected and produced by the CIA. They also teach courses on strategic intelligence, provide lectures on international security issues, and organize agency briefings.[43]

The OMA staff at CIA headquarters has a training and education program designed to both inform agency personnel about military intelligence needs and to explain to military audiences how the CIA can respond to their requirements. Visiting officers to the OMA include general officers and admirals, military attaches, special forces and special operations officers, war college and service school students, and intelligence officers from CIA counterparts throughout the intelligence community.[44]

The formation of the OMA has given the agency a long overdue focal point for interfacing with the military. The OMA efforts are probably paying dividends—particularly in the war effort in Afghanistan and against terrorism—by increasing the volume and relevance of CIA intelligence to the military as well as developing stronger personal ties between institutions. A former Commander-in-Chief of U.S. Army Europe, General Frederick Kroesen, attests, "[t]he cross assignment of personnel, long recognized by the services as mutually beneficial, is now producing a greater understanding between CIA operators and their Army, Navy, and Air Force counterparts."[45]

The Relationship's Path Ahead

While the OMA provides an important bureaucratic conduit for CIA and military relations, its creation has not had any significant impact on the quality of CIA intelligence. Specifically, the OMA does nothing to redress the CIA's human intelligence collection capabilities, which have been criticized in public for the failure to penetrate the conspiracy leading to the tragic September 11 events or to locate senior al Qaeda members, including Osama bin Laden, in the early stages of the Afghan campaign. Redressing these major shortcomings will require an outside and independent evaluation as well as reform of the CIA's Directorate of Operations, responsible for the global collection of human intelligence.

Nor will the creation of OMA eliminate the periodic tensions between the CIA and military intelligence organizations. The CIA lost responsibility for conducting battle damage assessments as a result of disputes with military intelligence organizations during the Gulf War. Although the muzzling of the CIA's independent voice on this score may have reduced the potential areas of analytic dispute, the move has not sharpened the military's ability to conduct objective intelligence analysis. The objectivity of the military's BDAs during the recent Kosovo war was found lacking, but its shortcomings received little public attention, in part because the CIA was not able to challenge them.[46]

The history of differing analytic assessments underscores the validity and continuing relevance of one critical rationale for the CIA's inception. The CIA is needed to provide independent and objective assessments, particularly on political-military issues, to national-level policymakers, the most important of which is the President and his or her closest advisers. The CIA's bureaucratic autonomy increases—but by no means guarantees—the prospects for the President to receive intelligence assessments that are removed from vested policy and operational interests. The military—notwithstanding the best of intentions—will likely remain more influenced by operational concerns that will taint intelligence analysis.

The rise of the OMA will pose challenges for the CIA. The military is a voracious consumer of intelligence that will put increasing pressure on the CIA to tailor its analysis to fit military needs. The CIA, with a "can-do" cultural ethic, is likely to go out of its way to meet these challenges, yet this carries associated costs. The military's demands for CIA intelligence may inundate the agency, particularly in time of war. The CIA is only one of 13 agencies in the Intelligence Community and accounts for less than one-eighth of the intelligence budget.[47] By analogy, if the CIA were a military organization the size of a modern division, brigades would represent directorates, a battalion the working-level analysts, and a company, military analysts. Quite simply, the CIA's analytic manpower is outgunned by the manpower available within the military and its CINCs. Most of the Intelligence Community already caters to the needs of the military, leaving very few of the resources to service the intelligence demands of national-level civilian policymakers.

The CIA stands at the top of the hierarchy of the multitude of intelligence organizations that constitute the U.S. Intelligence Community for several reasons. The head of the CIA, the Director of Central Intelligence, also acts as the nominal head of the entire Intelligence Community. More importantly, the CIA stands alone in the Intelligence Community as an entity that traditionally has direct access to the President. This access grants the agency a unique privilege and responsibility in the national security decisionmaking process. That unique position could be jeopardized over the long run if the agency is overwhelmed by ever-growing military intelligence requirements. As the agency services these demands, the military will increasingly look to the CIA to fill the voids left by the DIA and service intelligence components. The OMA runs the risk of marketing CIA products too successfully while agency managers fail to fill the depleted analytic ranks with the talent needed to meet growing demands for a wide variety of national security issues. The net result is likely to be a proliferation of inferior analysis tailored for military consumers, leaving civilian policymakers' needs neglected.

Indeed, the CIA's attention to military consumers may, over the longer run, degrade its ability to perform its warning mission and divert attention away from issues of interest to civilian consumers. Focusing too narrowly on the military threatens to overwhelm the handful of agency analysts who follow military affairs, leaving little time and resources for strategic analysis and warning issues that lie over the horizon. The military's operational demands—particularly in the midst of a crisis or combat—quickly overpower peacetime demands for monitoring situations in which crises have yet to occur. As one authoritative study observed, the Intelligence Community's "increasing preoccupation with military priorities since the Soviet Union's collapse has coincided with a decline in the thoroughness and quality of intelligence to civilian policymakers."[48]

Some observers may even question the wisdom of establishing a bureaucratic entity inside the CIA to support a particular consumer, noting that there are no countervailing agencies ready to service the intelligence demands of important national-level civilian consumers, notably the National Security Council, the Department of State, and, more recently, the Office of Homeland Security. Given these potential shortcomings, the challenge of balancing both tasks—fulfilling military demands channeled through the OMA while also handling other intelligence requirements for the civilian side of the national security community—will be difficult for agency managers and analysts, especially with the United States engaged in a war against terrorism.

One area of potential reform from congressional or executive action to help guard against these pitfalls would be to order the agency to trim its bloated managerial ranks that add little to fulfilling the CIA's mission and only serve to divert resources needed to hire and retain analytic experts. The agency today excels at producing bureaucrats, but fails miserably at nurturing experts needed to produce first-rate intelligence analyses.[49] As the war on terrorism rages on, the CIA—and the rest of the national security community—needs to become slimmer, smarter, and nimbler to fight adversaries determined to attack our vulnerabilities.

Notes

[1] Two noteworthy exceptions are Christopher Andrew, *For the President's Eyes Only: Secret Intelligence and the American Presidency from Washington to Bush* (New York: Harper Perennial, 1996), and Robert M. Gates, *From the Shadows: The Ultimate Insider's Story of Five Presidents and How They Won the Cold War* (New York: Touchstone, 1997). For an interesting account of CIA paramilitary operations in support of the military campaign in Afghanistan, see David S. Cloud, "Intelligence Quotient: Caught Off-Guard by Terror, the CIA Fights to Catch-up," *The Wall Street Journal*, April 15, 2002, A1.

[2] Michael Warner, *The Office of Strategic Services: America's First Intelligence Agency* (Washington, DC: Central Intelligence Agency, 2000), 22. For an account of the OSS and the origins of CIA, see John Ranelagh, *The Agency: The Rise and Decline of the CIA* (New York: Simon and Schuster, 1986), 37–142.

[3] Warner, 42–43.

[4] For a personal account of OSS "Jedburgh" operations in World War II and for a retrospective on how OSS missions in the postwar period were allocated to the CIA and the U.S. Army Special Forces, see Aaron Bank, *From OSS to Green Berets: The Birth of Special Forces* (Novato, CA: Presidio Press, 1986). For another account of OSS "Jedburgh"

operations and the formation of the CIA, see William Colby and Peter Forbath, *Honorable Men: My Life in the CIA* (New York: Simon and Schuster, 1978), 23–78.

[5] Warner, 43.

[6] Quoted in Andrew, 534.

[7] For declassified documents of CIA estimates of the Soviet Union, see Woodrow J. Kuhns, ed., *Assessing the Soviet Threat: The Early Years* (Washington, DC: Center for the Study of Intelligence, Central Intelligence Agency, 1997).

[8] Ranelagh, 186.

[9] Eliot A. Cohen, " 'Only Half the Battle': American Intelligence and the Chinese Intervention in Korea, 1950," *Intelligence and National Security* 5, no. 1 (January 1990), 138. Professor Cohen cites a CIA Memorandum, "Threat of Full Chinese Communist Intervention in Korea," October 12, 1950, in U.S. Department of State, *Foreign Relations of the United States 1950*, vol. 8 (Washington, DC: U.S. Government Printing Office, 1976), 933–934.

[10] Ranelagh, 173. For declassified National Intelligence Estimates and Special National Intelligence Estimates related to the bomber and missile gap controversies, see Donald P. Steury, ed., *Intentions and Capabilities: Estimates on Soviet Strategic Forces, 1950–1983* (Washington, DC: Center for the Study of Intelligence, Central Intelligence Agency, 1996), 5–138.

[11] Ranelagh, 322–323.

[12] Mark M. Lowenthal, *Intelligence: From Secrets to Policy* (Washington, DC: Congressional Quarterly Press, 2000), 19.

[13] For a treatment of the disputes from the CIA's perspective, see Harold P. Ford, *CIA and Vietnam Policy Makers: Three Episodes, 1962–1968* (Washington, DC: Center for the Study of Intelligence, Central Intelligence Agency, 1998).

[14] James J. Wirtz, "Intelligence to Please? The Order of Battle Controversy during the Vietnam War," *Political Science Quarterly* 106, no. 2 (Summer 1991), 247.

[15] Ibid., 246.

[16] Quoted in Ranelagh, 420.

[17] U.S. House Committee on Armed Services, Subcommittee on Oversight and Investigations, "Intelligence Successes and Failures in Operations *Desert Shield/Storm*," 103[d] Cong., 1st Sess., August 1993, 2. The term *Intelligence Community* refers to the collection of some 13 intelligence organizations that are nominally headed by the Director of Central Intelligence who simultaneous leads the CIA. For background on the Intelligence Community and its membership, see <http://www.cia.gov/ic/index.html>.

[18] Ibid., 3.

[19] Ibid., 4. For an insightful treatment of the formidable skills used to protect Baghdad's nuclear weapons program before and after the Gulf War, see David Kay, "Denial and Deception: The Lessons of Iraq," in Roy Godson, Ernest R. May, and Gary Schmitt, eds., *U.S. Intelligence at the Crossroads: Agendas for Reform* (Washington, DC: Brassey's, 1995), 109–127.

[20] "Intelligence Successes and Failures," 4. For an examination of intelligence in the Gulf War, see "What Was the Role of Intelligence?" in Thomas A. Keaney and Eliot A. Cohen, *Revolution in Warfare? Air Power in the Persian Gulf* (Annapolis, MD: Naval Institute Press, 1993), 105–123.

[21] For a fuller examination of the strengths and weaknesses of CIA's analytic performance during the Gulf War, see Richard L. Russell, "CIA's Strategic Intelligence in Iraq," *Political Science Quarterly* (Summer 2002).

[22] "Intelligence Successes and Failures," 9. For a CIA rebuttal to the charge that it failed to properly support CENTCOM during *Desert Shield* and *Desert Storm*, see "CIA Support to the U.S. Military During the Persian Gulf War," June 16, 1997; accessed at <http://www.cia.gov/cia/publications/gulfwar/061997/support.htm> (June 28, 2002).

[23] "Intelligence Successes and Failures," 9–10.

[24] Report of the Commission on the Roles and Capabilities of the United States Intelligence Community (hereafter referred to as the Aspin-Brown Commission), "Preparing for the 21st Century: An Appraisal of U.S. Intelligence," March 1, 1996, 49.

[25] "Intelligence Successes and Failures," 10.

[26] Ibid., 11.

[27] Andrew, 532.

[28] Ibid., 534.

[29] Central Intelligence Agency, Office of Military Affairs homepage; accessed at <http://www.cia.gov/oma/oma.html> (June 28, 2002). Another of the post-Gulf War reforms to the Intelligence Community was the merging of the former National Photographic Interpretation Center (NPIC) and the Defense Mapping Agency (DMA) into the National Imagery and Mapping Agency (NIMA) in October 1996. DCI Deutch and other architects of the move judged that merging the organizations would improve the quality of imagery support to the military, as well as to national-level policymakers. For background on the formation of NIMA, see A Studies Roundtable, "Creating the

National Imagery and Mapping Agency," *Studies in Intelligence* 42, no. 1 (1998). Considerable controversy surrounds the move, particularly by former CIA imagery analysts who argue that NIMA further increases the military's control of the Intelligence Community at the expense of civilian analysts and policymakers.

[30] For background, see Frederick J. Kroesen, "Intelligence: Now a Two-Way Street?" *Army* (September 1994).

[31] Office of Military Affairs homepage; accessed at < http://www.cia.gov/oma/oma.html>.

[32] Central Intelligence Agency, "Associate Director of Central Intelligence for Military Support," undated pamphlet.

[33] Office of Military Affairs homepage.

[34] Ibid.

[35] Walter Pincus and Dan Eggen, "Probe Spawns Unparalleled Intelligence-Sharing," *The Washington Post,* March 12, 2002, A9.

[36] Military commands that host DCI representatives include USJFCOM, USEUCOM, SHAPE, USSOCOM, USSPACECOM, USTRANSCOM, CENTCOM, USPACOM, USSOUTHCOM, and USSTRATCOM. DCI Representatives also are assigned to military staffs in the Pentagon such as the Office of the Secretary of Defense and the Joint Chiefs of Staff.

[37] Office of Military Affairs homepage.

[38] Central Intelligence Agency, Office of Military Affairs, Exercise Branch, "CIA Exercise Support," undated pamphlet.

[39] Office of Military Affairs homepage.

[40] James M. Lose, "Fulfilling a Crucial Role: National Intelligence Support Teams," *Studies in Intelligence* (Winter 1999/2000), 88.

[41] Central Intelligence Agency, Office of Military Affairs, "Crisis Operations Liaison Team," undated pamphlet.

[42] Office of Military Affairs homepage.

[43] Ibid.

[44] Ibid.

[45] Kroesen, 9.

[46] For background, see John Barry and Evan Thomas, "The Kosovo Cover-Up," *Newsweek*, May 15, 2000, 23–26. A suppressed U.S. Air Force report obtained by *Newsweek* found that out of the 744 "confirmed" strikes by NATO pilots during the war, Air Force investigators who spent weeks in Kosovo after the war could only find evidence of 58 successful strikes.

[47] Aspin-Brown Commission, 61.

[48] Allan E. Goodman, Gregory F. Treverton, and Philip Zelikow, eds., *In From the Cold: The Report of the Twentieth Century Fund Task Force on the Future of U.S. Intelligence* (New York: Twentieth Century Fund Press, 1996), vi. For a related discussion of the dangers posed by the military's dominance of the Intelligence Community, see Maurice R. Greenberg and Richard N. Haass, eds., *Making Intelligence Smarter: The Future of U.S. Intelligence* (New York: Council on Foreign Relations, 1996).

[49] For a provocative and informative look at the critical need for CIA and the Intelligence Community writ large to modernize and reform, see Bruce D. Berkowitz and Allan E. Goodman, *Best Truth: Intelligence in the Information Age* (New Haven, CT: Yale University Press, 2000).

Chapter 37
CIA Support to
Enduring Freedom

Anthony R. Williams

In just over 4 months, the United States organized an international coalition to pursue the al Qaeda terrorist organization on a worldwide basis, destroyed Taliban military forces in Afghanistan, drove the Taliban from power there, and turned the surviving members of al Qaeda and the Taliban into fugitives. In addition, the United States, with support from its allies, organized a temporary government in Kabul and helped it take the initial steps toward the ultimate goal of a stable government in Afghanistan.

The success to date is due to the judicious and coordinated use of the full range of American national power and the instruments provided by the American people for the application of that power. The Central Intelligence Agency (CIA) is one of those instruments, and it has played a key role in this struggle. As early as September 26, 2001, in a speech to CIA personnel, President George W. Bush cited the critical role intelligence would play in the coming struggle, noting that this would be a war that would require the best of intelligence. Since that time the President, the Secretary of Defense, and the Commander of the U.S. Central Command (USCENTCOM) have all cited intelligence as a key element in U.S. successes.

The CIA has been a key player in every American conflict since the establishment of the agency in 1947, but none has demanded a greater breadth and depth of CIA involvement than Operation *Enduring Freedom*. The CIA role has included paramilitary support on the ground in Afghanistan; intelligence collection both in Afghanistan and worldwide through agents and liaison services; coordination of the full range of U.S. national intelligence collection assets through the Assistant Director of Central Intelligence (DCI) for Collection; direct analytical support to all the military, diplomatic, law enforcement, and economic elements of the U.S. Government engaged in the war on terrorism; coordination of Intelligence Community analytical support to *Enduring Freedom* operations through the Assistant DCI for Analysis, the Chairman of the National Intelligence Council, and the Director of the Counter-Terrorist Center; and the provision of real-time automated intelligence communications capabilities to forward-based ground, air, and naval forces engaged in this struggle.

Source: Anthony R. Williams, "CIA Support to Enduring Freedom," *Military Intelligence Professional Bulletin*, October–December 2002. Reprinted by permission of the author and *Military Intelligence Professional Bulletin*.

Throughout the conflict, CIA personnel provided advice and assistance to Northern Alliance forces and target data for both U.S. aerial bombardment and Northern Alliance artillery. As recently cited in media reports, CIA teams on the ground and through the use of unmanned aerial vehicles contributed directly to the destruction of Taliban units, logistics, and losses in leadership cadres. The first American casualty in the Afghan operations was a CIA paramilitary officer, Johnny "Mike" Spann, engaged in support of Northern Alliance forces. CIA communicators provided modern communications support to CIA personnel operating throughout the Afghanistan theater and kept those elements in direct contact with U.S. military forces operating in and around Afghanistan.

CIA teams in Afghanistan also assisted in the formation of anti-Taliban units from Pashtun tribal elements in the south and elsewhere and provided coordination among and between these units as the Taliban power disintegrated and anti-Taliban forces drove deep into the country. The fact that large anti-Taliban formations of various tribal affiliations were able to converge on Kandahar in the face of intense al Qaeda and Taliban resistance with minimal friendly fire incidents speaks to the success of these coordination efforts.

As CIA personnel were operating on the ground in and around Afghanistan, the Office of Military Affairs (OMA) provided liaison support to each of the U.S. military commands, from the unified commands such as CENTCOM headquarters in Tampa to the forward-based joint forces combat commands. In some cases, such as the deployment of U.S. Special Operations Forces, CIA personnel participated directly in the predeployment and deployment operations. OMA liaison teams assigned to each of these commands have been able to reach back and task collection and analytical elements in the United States, often by means of flyaway automated communications packages provided by CIA communications. This capability has even been pushed forward to U.S. naval vessels operating in the Arabian Sea. OMA also sent additional officers to CENTCOM, Pacific Command, and Southern Command to support the permanent DCI representatives stationed there.

The CIA Counter-Terrorist Center has dramatically increased strength since the start of Operation *Enduring Freedom*. These officers are not only providing support to U.S. operations in Afghanistan, but also to U.S. military, diplomatic, and law enforcement missions worldwide in the struggle against terrorism. As part of the CIA effort to support Operation *Enduring Freedom*, scores of retired CIA officers have returned to temporary full- and part-time duty. CIA analytical, operations, and support personnel from throughout the agency have volunteered for temporary duty assignments in counterterrorist and military support activities at considerable personal inconvenience and risk.

CIA ability to provide the current level of support to America's armed forces is due in large part to efforts undertaken throughout the CIA over the past decade. The Central Intelligence Agency has been engaged for several years on the ground in Afghanistan and elsewhere in an effort to apprehend Osama bin Laden and his associates and to disrupt and destroy the al Qaeda terrorist organization. That effort has resulted in an extensive network of agents in Afghanistan and elsewhere and a cadre of

CIA officers experienced in the region ready to support Operation *Enduring Freedom* from the outset.

As a result of the after-action reviews of U.S. military operations during the 1990s, the CIA reorganized its support to the U.S. Armed Forces under the leadership of the Associate DCI for Military Support. DCI representatives are regularly assigned to all the U.S. unified commands and war colleges in order to incorporate CIA support into U.S. military doctrine. CIA liaison teams are assigned as needed to U.S. joint task forces. These representatives and additional personnel from the Office of Military Affairs have been regular participants in U.S. military exercises worldwide, thus developing the skill and experience necessary to meet the challenges imposed by Operation *Enduring Freedom.*

Chapter 38

Working with the CIA

Garrett Jones

I n 1993, I had the privilege of being a Central Intelligence Agency (CIA) student at the U.S. Army War College. During the academic year, I had some frank exchanges with my military colleagues about the Intelligence Community and how those military leaders viewed it, rightly or wrongly. The two principal conclusions I came away with were: the Intelligence Community does not know enough about the military and its operations, and the military does not know enough about the Intelligence Community and its operations.

Immediately upon graduation from the War College, I was selected as the CIA chief in Mogadishu, Somalia. Within 30 days, I was on the ground there, trying to come to grips with the quickly evolving crisis.

This [chapter] will not be about the policy disaster that took place in Somalia, however. Rather, it will seek to illuminate the working relationship between the military and the CIA, offering some of the knowledge I gained in Mogadishu and over a career. In a way, it is the incoming brief I wish I could have given to the Task Force RANGER commander and his senior staff when they arrived in Somalia.

This [chapter] is geared to the military commander and his senior staff who will be working closely with the CIA in the field, perhaps for the first time in their careers. This is not a guideline on how to do things; it is more a checklist of aspects to which you should give some thought. The [chapter]emphasizes field operations because that is my expertise; the headquarters-to-headquarters dance that occurs in Washington is a completely different animal.

Mogadishu, of course, was an extreme case. While many of the instances of close, tactical support of military operations by the CIA will in fact be in Third World countries, you can't get much more rock-bottom than Mogadishu was in 1993.

Spies Come in Different Flavors

All employees of the Central Intelligence Agency may share some commonalities, but the several types you are likely to encounter supporting you during an operational deployment will differ widely in their training, experience, and background. The type that military officers will most likely encounter during their career is an intelligence analyst. If you have attended a briefing at the Pentagon or another

---

Source: Garrett Jones, "Working with the CIA," *Parameters* 31, no. 4 (Winter 2001/2002), 28–39. Copyright © 2001 by Garrett Jones. Reprinted by permission.

senior command that was given by the Central Intelligence Agency, the briefer was probably an intelligence analyst.

An intelligence analyst is an employee of the Directorate of Intelligence. Analysts generally hold advanced degrees in academic fields that may or may not relate to your mission. They are selected for their clear analytical thinking, and they are trained and experienced in briefing senior decisionmakers and writing for publication in finished intelligence reports. They may never have met a real live "asset" (a spy), and they almost certainly have no experience in directing clandestine operations in the field.

The second type you generally encounter in direct support of your operations is a case officer. Case officers are employees of the Directorate of Operations. They are the people who recruit and run the assets. They are generally selected for their adaptability, street smarts, and ability to function independently. They are all college graduates, and if they have on-the-ground experience in your area of operations, they will be a wealth of information on how the society and culture operate and what makes the locals tick. They probably have never given a stand-up briefing to an assembled group such as your command staff, and they generally would not know a PowerPoint slide if it fell on them. Their most common written work product is the raw intelligence report.

Which type is best for you? That depends on what you want. If you're looking for research, the collation of published background material, or excellent briefing skills, you're probably better served by an intelligence analyst. On the other hand, if you're trying to find out whether a piece of information can be obtained by human assets, or what's likely going through the head of an asset who reported a piece of information, an experienced case officer is probably your best choice. There are exceptional individuals who can do it all, but it is really incumbent upon you to find out the background of the individual that you just asked to make a judgment call. Is this what he or she is good at, or did you just ask a plumber about paint selection?

Like every other organization, the CIA is not going anywhere without its talented and capable support officers. These individuals come in the form of logistics officers, communicators, specialized technicians, and people with every other arcane skill set you can imagine. Much like your support staff, these are the people who keep the wheels on the organization so that the case officers and the analysts can devote their time to their specialties. You should encourage your support personnel to meet with their CIA counterparts early and often. Not only will this promote smooth liaison between staffs, but CIA support specialists also generally have long experience in dealing with the surprises that support and logistical operations in the Third World can present. Your people may well learn something from them.

Spy Stations Come in Different Shapes

Okay, now you have your own personal nest of spies attached to your command. What does this organization look like? As is usually the case, it depends. If you are at a large command, like an area commander in chief (CINC), there probably is a CIA office that predates you. An analyst usually staffs it, and it acts as the clearinghouse through which the command receives intelligence and analysis directly from the CIA as well as a conduit for the command's requests to the CIA for information and analysis. It will also arrange the travel and housing of any CIA experts or specialists brought in to support the command. It normally has an existing place on the command's table of organization and equipment (TO&E) and usually coordinates directly with the joint intelligence officer, the J–2, or equivalent.

Moving from the least to the most ad hoc structures, the next one you might see is an intelligence support element. This is generally called a National Intelligence Support Team (NIST), though it has also been called an Incident Response Team and other terms. This is a team of CIA personnel put together to support a command when a CIA office is not already in place. It carries out the same functions as an established office, transmitting your command's requests for information and distributing incoming CIA intelligence and analysis intended for your command. The team will bring its own communications, but it will rely on your logistics support for food, housing, and office space. While the equipment and procedures are off-the-shelf items, and efforts are made to man this team with individuals who have area knowledge about your mission, it is very much a pickup team—you essentially get the luck of the draw. Staffing will depend on the size and nature of the U.S. forces involved, the location of the area of operations, the amount and type of intelligence available on potential targets, the presence or absence of a CIA field station, and other factors. In short, every NIST is different. The personnel will be very competent at what they do, but they may or may not have "on the ground" value-added for your particular mission.

The next sort of structure you might encounter is an established CIA station situated in a foreign country near the country or area that is your intended area of operations. Typically the station operates out of an in-country U.S. installation, with or without the knowledge of the host country. A good example of this would be a situation in which your command deploys or stages to a friendly country prior to conducting operations in a nearby hostile country. This is also the first time you will run into a Chief of Station (COS, pronounced like the initials C–O–S, not *coz*). The COS is the personal representative of the Director of Central Intelligence, and he is responsible for all civilian intelligence and counterintelligence activities within his area of operations. In a country where a CIA station exists, the only civilian official technically senior to the COS in the areas of intelligence or counterintelligence is the U.S. Ambassador. A good Ambassador will generally rely heavily on the COS concerning intelligence matters and will rarely overrule the COS's judgment.

This is also the first time you will run into case officers running assets in the field. These officers have real live people spying for them, and they are responsible for their assets' security and production. That said, you should remember that the CIA station was almost certainly not established to support your command or mission. The station's officers already have a full-time job going after their assigned intelligence targets; your mission is another full-time job they have just been handed.

Depending on the situation, the case officers may be able to immediately support your command with intelligence obtained from the host country's service, if they have a liaison relationship. Alternatively, some of their existing unilateral assets—assets recruited to report on another target—might just happen to have access to information that is useful to you. If you have been receiving this type of intelligence before your deployment, you are now face-to-face with the case officers who handle the assets and write the reports you have been reading. If they do not have preexisting unilateral or liaison assets who can report in support of your mission, they will have scoured the local scene to find someone who can report on the subject in an accurate and timely manner. Whatever the case, they will also transmit your requests for information to the CIA while receiving and passing along CIA reports intended for your command. Since they are already on the ground and operating, they normally will impose no drain on your logistics—in fact, they are frequently an excellent source of information for your logistics people on getting things done in the local environment.

The final configuration you're likely to see is a station that has been created especially for your mission. This station has probably existed with your force in some sort of informal limbo prior to your force's executing its mission and entering hostile territory. Its officers generally will have been running assets located in hostile territory or have a list of assets to reactivate upon the arrival of U.S. forces. The COS and case officers in this configuration generally will have a background in the geographical area in which you are operating. Initially this sort of station will be a logistics burden on your command, until you have established a viable main supply route. Once the CIA's own logistics people can move in, the station will generally be self-sustaining except for perimeter security and force protection matters. From a force commander's standpoint, this is the best sort of station to have. There will be no Ambassador or Embassy staff to divert their focus, and they will share your mission goals from the beginning.

They Are Green Tab Commanders, Too

The Chief of Station with whom you're working in the field is every bit as much of an operational commander (a green tab commander) as one of your infantry leaders or one of the commanders of your aviation elements. He has assets and case officers (Americans) on the ground and moving around in your operational area. In fact, if he's doing his job, he has assets and case officers focused in territory controlled by forces other than yours. That's why he is there. Whether it's the enemy's plans and intentions or advance warning concerning force protection, by definition the purpose of operational CIA elements is to provide you with information that you cannot obtain in any other way. The numbers and degree of intelligence operations in hostile territory will vary from situation to situation, but you should keep in mind that while the COS's operations can benefit you and your mission, your response to his intelligence—as well as actions you take as a result of other information input—can severely damage his ability to support you. The COS has the same responsibility to protect his people as you do for any of your soldiers. While both the assets and the case officers engaged in supporting your mission are aware that they must take risks, like everyone in your command they also want go home at the end of the mission.

The ever-present dynamic of protecting sources and methods versus acting on intelligence information will not go away on the battlefield. Whether you are executing an attack based on direct information obtained by assets in the field or responding to a threatening situation posed by the adversary, the conflict of protecting sources and methods and carrying out your mission will be an ongoing problem. The necessity for close liaison and communication with the COS and his officers is never more necessary than in these situations. No COS wants to lose the ability of an asset or assets to report on a target, especially when those assets have been expensive and time-consuming to put in place. That said, most COSs are mature enough to understand that sometimes that needs to be done. Where these situations arise, the COS can almost always recommend how you can go about accomplishing your mission while minimizing damage to the assets he will need to support you in the future.

Perhaps the most dangerous situation assets and case officers find themselves in, when they are operating in hostile territory in advance of U.S. forces, is when they become inadvertently involved in combat actions aimed at the enemy. By the nature of what they're trying to accomplish, they are often near or attempting to get near enemy locations—that is, your targets. The COS and his case officers have a legitimate need to preserve operational security as well as to retain sufficient flexibility in order to carry out their jobs. You, on the other hand, have a legitimate need to protect your forces and carry out your mission. There is no hard and fast rule about how to resolve these often-conflicting needs.

Perhaps a good example of this sort of conflict, and its solution, is one that occurred in Mogadishu when our case officers and assets were attempting to locate Somali warlord Mohammed Farrah Aideed. Not surprisingly, this required that our assets be located in positions frequented by Aideed's forces. The warlord's forces were hostile to both the U.S. and the United Nations (UN) presence in Mogadishu, and they regularly demonstrated their hostility by lobbing mortar shells into UN positions. The U.S. commander supporting the UN mission in Mogadishu understandably responded to these attacks with counter-battery fire. Early on, this led to some quite excited and graphic protests from assets who were operating in Aideed's territory at the direction of our case officers. Friendly fire being no more friendly to intelligence assets than anyone else, this was a problem. Fortunately, an excellent relationship existed with the U.S. military commander and his subordinates, and the organizations were quickly able to establish a simple procedure whereby case officers would be given a quiet heads-up should counter-battery fire be authorized. This permitted assets to safely depart the area, while still retaining for the commander the flexibility of responding as he saw fit to individual threats. While there were occasional glitches, and casualties did occur both to assets and case officers while operating in Mogadishu, they were never related to friendly fire.

Ops Tempo Literally Kills People

One of the primary concerns of a commander facing a hostile force is that the intelligence upon which he bases his actions, no matter from what source, must be both accurate and timely. While accuracy when dealing with human assets is often a function of the assets' training and their access to the target, timeliness often becomes a real security concern for both the case officer and the asset he is handling. Access to information is why the asset was recruited. The case officer handling the asset usually provides training in the clandestine arts. The skill of the people involved and the luck of the draw will often govern these factors. A smart asset with fair access can often through his own efforts outperform a not-so-smart asset with good access.

In normal circumstances, the timing of personal meetings with an asset or the receipt of impersonal communications from an asset is usually dictated by the level of hostility present or the threat of detection in the local operational environment. While meetings are on occasion dictated by events, as a general rule it can be stated that every personal meeting or impersonal communication holds the potential of compromising the security of an asset; thus, they occur no more often than is absolutely necessary. That being the case, the schedule of meetings or communications—that is, the need for intelligence—is carefully balanced against the threat of compromise.

You may take it as a given that the arrival of U.S. forces in a country, or in any nearby country, will generate an increased level of watchfulness on the part of both friendly and hostile counterintelligence services. This translates to a higher degree of threat for clandestine human operations. Your command's need for intelligence will always result in a dramatic increase in the frequency of meetings or communications. This increase in risk, no matter how careful the operational planning, will sooner or later result in the station or base "using up" its assets in support of your operations. While in a philosophical sense that is what intelligence operations are ultimately for, from a practical standpoint this will sooner or later affect you negatively. A source you find particularly useful may become compromised, access to information may dry up, and the difficulty in obtaining asset reports may increase. You should expect this. You should also expect that new assets will be brought on board to provide new access to targets of interest, or to replace assets who have been operationally spent. With new people doing new tasks, there are going to be screw-ups, mistakes, confusion, and missteps—one hopes they won't be fatal. Keep this in mind when dealing with information from new sources, but rest assured that both the case officers and the assets are paddling as fast as they can.

On a final note in this regard, in most countries the punishment for espionage is death or a long imprisonment for the assets, while the case officers are expelled if they are lucky. Everyone involved knows that each meeting or communication is dangerous and that the downside for mistakes is huge. Additional pressure from you or your staff is normally not constructive. Tell the case officers what you need and where your decision points are; extraneous screaming and yelling are counterproductive.

Combat Search and Rescue—We Need to Talk about it Now, Not Later

No one ever wants to court misfortune, but Combat Search and Rescue (CSAR) is a subject that must be discussed in advance. Waiting to figure out how to employ the CIA's human assets until you already have personnel on the ground threatened with capture is truly a losing proposition. Every commander being supported by a CIA element that has human assets in the field needs to address this subject before it becomes a reality. As the force commander, you can also expect to referee what will likely be the most emotional subject that will come up in the course of your relationship with your CIA counterpart.

While each situation will be different, several common threads will run through almost all settings. What do you tell the human assets, who among them do you tell, and how much do you tell them? What do you tell U.S. personnel? Do you tell the assets to actively assist the U.S. personnel to escape and evade, or tell them to just report the sighting and monitor the situation? It seems simple—you always have them actively assist, right? Not so fast. Can they really help, or will their active search for your personnel draw more attention from hostile forces than it will help? Does the asset in question have the gumption to help without falling apart from fear, or would he be more helpful providing you with accurate updates so that your own command can stage a recovery? Even if he has the nerve to hide your people, what does he do then? Try to pass them back to friendly lines, or hide them until you can get to them? How good is their security, and has the asset been upping his "profile" by reporting on hostile activity for your command? How hard are the bad guys going to look for your people—is everyone within 10 square kilometers going to be slaughtered because someone helped them? Hard decisions are better made in advance, with time for reflection, rather than on the tarmac while trying to get a rescue mission in the air.

Working out search and rescue procedures will be an emotional experience. Your staff will be talking about rescuing their friends; the COS will want to help, but also will be rightly thinking about his responsibilities to his assets—people he probably knows personally. This can turn into a nasty "us versus them" debate if you as a commander don't make it clear from the beginning that everyone has real concerns and everyone is looking for the best answer. Don't make the mistake of ignoring or taking for granted this possible resource. Cooperative planning in advance will use up some staff time, but it may save the life of one of your soldiers.

We Believe Each Other's Propaganda

Ever since the elimination of the military draft in the United States 30 years ago, the population at large has grown less and less experienced with military operations and the military life. This is true of intelligence officers as well as the general population. Few of the case officers or analysts you work with will have personal military experience as an enlisted or commissioned member of the armed services. Their experience will be what they have acquired during their careers with the CIA, and it may not have any bearing on the mission you have before you as a commander. That being the case, you need to ensure that they understand what you need and why you need it.

In many cases, the intelligence officers' pool of military knowledge is going to be what they have seen or read of the military in the media. This means they may believe that you are 10 feet tall, that you jump from airplanes equipped with only thick rubber soles, and that your mere appearance on the battlefield will suppress the enemy's fire. You should expect that you and your staff will have to educate your CIA colleagues as to what your forces can and cannot realistically be expected to do, and most important, what kind of information you need and why you need it in order to make intelligent decisions involving the safety and success of your force. What you will have going for you in this situation is that the CIA personnel you will be working with will be highly motivated to provide the information you need.

While we are speaking of misinformation, you should remember that you and your staff are in most instances going to be no better informed about the details of the intelligence profession than the general public. Few case officers ever covertly break into an enemy installation à la James Bond, and even fewer analysts ever get involved in field operations à la a Tom Clancy character. You and your people need to educate yourselves by asking lots of questions. Don't worry about asking about something sensitive—if you don't need to know, they will tell you so. While we are on the subject, what should you as the senior commander be expected to be told about an intelligence operation or asset? Almost everything. This is not transferable to your staff; you are the commander, and they aren't. The only information a case officer will be reluctant to share with you is information that will directly identify his asset. The asset's life generally rides on the disclosure of this information, and the case officer would forget it himself if he could. Other than this area, ask questions. You will be surprised by the detailed replies you will receive.

We Are Divided by a Common Language

Since you became a professional military officer, you have been befuddling and bewildering the civilians around you with the use of initials, jargon, and slang. In dealing with CIA case officers in the field, you have just met your match. CIA officers routinely use initials, slang, acronyms, and terms that have only the vaguest relationships with their standard English definitions. They do it every bit as unconsciously as you do, and like you, they slip into it quickly when they are discussing work-related matters. They are no more trying to confuse you than you are trying to confuse the civilians with whom you interact professionally. You will need to do what I am sure has been done to you on more than one occasion. Stop them and make them explain in detail what it is they are talking about. If you as an experienced commander are a bit confused, your junior staff officer—who is sitting at the table and may be involved in the execution of the matter under discussion—probably got lost somewhere after the CIA officer said "Hello." With a little good will on both sides, this can usually be sorted out fairly quickly and a shared vocabulary developed, but never hesitate to make the CIA officer explain, in English, what he is saying.

A good example of this lack of a shared common language occurred in my own experience when a senior commander was informed that a CIA station was planning a "cross-border operation" in his AO (area of operations). The commander, to whom a "cross-border operation" meant a raid by an armed force to destroy or seize a target, was justifiably upset (an understatement) at not having been consulted. He was considerably mollified when it was explained that in this case what the CIA station had meant by a cross-border operation was to give an asset bus fare to his home village with instructions to look around and report back on what he had seen. Talk to each other in plain English; it will prevent a lot of misunderstanding.

An Asset Is Not a Commando or Hero

If you are going to be the primary recipient of a human source, you need to understand a little bit about what makes them tick. Before everything else, human assets are recruited because they have access to secret information that can be obtained in no other manner. This means that not only may the asset not be a nice person, it also means he was not selected because he was brave, smart, or particularly hardworking. He needs to be frightened enough of the consequences of being caught at what he is doing to be careful, while still being enough of a risk-taker to get his information to his case officer. This requires a strong motivation on the part of the asset, especially when the case officer is not close at hand to provide constant reassurance. While money almost always plays some part in any asset's relationship with his case officer, I have always found that the best assets are at the bottom driven by revenge. Money is just a way of keeping score. Whether he is getting even with his boss, secretly showing up his classmates, or working against his government to avenge an old wrong, revenge is the flame that keeps the best assets warm at night. Thus, by definition, the best assets are pretty strange people. The case officers handling these assets normally develop a fairly complicated relationship with their assets, becoming everything from father confessor to morale booster, from disciplinarian to best buddy. Like sausages and laws, if you have a queasy stomach, you don't want to see the case officer-asset relationship up close.

What you cannot expect from an asset is that he is a junior model of one of your own troops. He is not, nor was he ever selected to be, a commando. Unless he is a very unusual asset, lying in the tall weeds and watching a target all night is not going to be his strong suit. You need to remember that his normal mode of spying is by repeating what he hears from people he meets or by stealing documents that come across his desk. If you ask him to do something new and strange, he will react like most people. He will attempt to get out of tasks he does not like, lie to his case officer if frightened, and generally not show up if pushed too far. As noted earlier, existing CIA stations were not established in order to support your mission, and existing CIA human assets were not originally recruited to support your mission. There is going to be a learning curve, and you can expect a lot of frustration on both sides before the human assets finally get the hang of what you want from them. The situation eventually gets better, but it takes a while.

Odds and Ends

What Is an Ambassador and Why Should I Care?

You have your orders from the CINC and your mission is clear. You are staging from a friendly country with an accredited and resident U.S. Ambassador, but you can ignore him or her; after all you have your orders from the National Command Authorities. Right? Wrong. The U.S. Ambassador is the personal representative of the President of the United States. Ambassadors can't exactly give you a direct order concerning your operations or force posture but they can have your orders from the CINC changed in Washington, DC, quicker than you think. The best thing for you to do as a commander operating in an Ambassador's country is to consider him as a "four-star" who lives and works in your area of operations and has the authority to look over your shoulder. It is much better if the Ambassador is a friend, not an opponent. Most of them are bright, hard-working people, and, considering the way the

United States selects its political appointees, they are generally better people than we have a right to expect.

A few tips on getting along with Ambassadors: keep them informed, treat them with respect, keep them informed, be polite with their embassy staff, keep them informed, remember that Embassy resources are limited, and, finally, keep them informed. Keeping the Ambassador informed will make or break your relationship with him or her. If the Ambassador is on your side, he can become an advocate at the echelons that are inhabited by politicians and Joint Chiefs of Staff. Conversely, an unhappy and vocal Ambassador can generate a visit from a real four-star wanting to know what the problem is. You don't have time for that sort of thing. The easiest way to handle this situation is to assign to the Ambassador a personal liaison officer. Don't slide this off to some junior officer who doesn't seem to be too busy. This is an important relationship; treat it like one. You need a smart, experienced, mid-level officer who can answer questions and handle unusual situations without becoming flustered. If you have a Defense Attache assigned to the Embassy, this can be an excellent place to put your officer, but do not rely on the Defense Attache to carry your water. He has his own agenda, his fitness report is written by the Ambassador, and he has a personal relationship with the Ambassador you may or may not want to inherit.

The presence of U.S. forces in-country always results in a dramatic rise in workload for an embassy. Having one of your officers in the Embassy that is familiar with the command structure and the individual units involved is a great resource for the embassy. Make sure your liaison officer understands that helping the Embassy deal with the presence of your command is part of his job. Whatever else the liaison officer does, make sure he gets in to see the Ambassador at least once a day, even if it is to tell him that there is nothing important going on or planned.

Use the Same Maps or at Least Know What Map the Asset Is Using

If you are fortunate enough to have human assets in the field reporting back on the location of targets or items of interest, try to use the same maps, or at least know what maps they are using to report or record the locations. It seems like a simple thing, but often it is not. The asset must preserve his own personal security, and running around in "Indian Territory" with a fistful of maps produced by the U.S. National Imagery and Mapping Agency is not the way to do it. In the Third World, Michelin Tire Company's road maps are normally widely available, innocuous, and about as accurate as the average guy on the street can safely carry. If an asset is reporting back in person or by real-time communications, attempt to arrange to keep him available for questions. Recent overhead, which you will generally be working from, and commercial Third World maps, which he will generally be working from, often take a little finessing to match up. A few short questions early in the history of a report can often clear up any confusion. The case officer handling the asset will always do his best to accurately convert his asset's report to standard grid references. However, details of great interest to you—such as avenues of approach or the height of obstacles from the ground—can often get lost in the process. Explain your needs: good case officers will take all the help they can get to turn out a better intelligence product.

Station or Base—What's in a Name?

When you get involved with a CIA operational presence overseas, you will hear the terms *station* and *base* tossed around without a lot of explanation and with no apparent distinction. There is a difference, which may or may not become important down the road. The station is the senior installation, headed by a Chief of Station (the COS). A base is a subordinate installation, headed by a Chief of Base (COB). While a base normally communicates directly with Washington, the COS, even if he is not collocated with the base, is technically responsible for all of its communications and activities. The way this normally works out in reality is that the COB runs the base's day-to-day operational activities, with the COS reserving the right to overrule him if he sees something he doesn't like. This can get sticky if a COB commits to you as a commander on some subject and then the COS has a different view. This doesn't happen often, but if you have this sort of configuration in your operational area, you need to keep the possibility in mind. Very rarely, a base will be supervised directly out of CIA headquarters in Washington. As you can imagine, putting a headquarters in the decision loop when it might be several thousand miles away is awkward, to say the least.

Not All COSs Are Created Equal

Just as it is a political fact of life that all generals are not created equal, neither are all COSs created equal. This will come into play when you or your COS are attempting to get unusual or expensive support from CIA headquarters. A more politically well-connected COS will have an easier time than a less well-connected one, no matter the merits of their respective cases. You have seen or experienced this in your own career; it is simply an inescapable fact in any large bureaucracy. Try to get an understanding of your COS's "throw-weight." When you think he is going in with a difficult request, a pointed nudge through your own channels is often helpful. Talk this over with your COS in advance; he may be able to suggest improved timing or tactics.

Experience Is Perishable

You are going to run into these folks on both sides of the operation: one of the intelligence people will have served in the military at some point, or one of your officers will have served with an intelligence organization at some point. They are going to try to anoint themselves as resident experts. Their enthusiasm is welcome, but their information and expectations are often obsolete and more than occasionally flat wrong. Make sure your communications with the COS are direct and clear, not interpreted by a resident expert on either side.

Conclusion

The purpose of this [chapter] is to give you someplace to start when working with the CIA in the field. I am sure that since my retirement, efforts have been made to institutionally address some of the problems I have raised. Unfortunately, I have found that "Murphy's Law" is a universal constant, and that Murphy always gets your forwarding address.

Chapter 39

U.S. Central Intelligence Agency Forces: Covert Warriors

Andrew Koch

Qaed Senyan al-Harthi (also known as Abu Ali) never knew what hit him. One minute the suspected al Qaeda operative and five accomplices were driving along in the Yemeni desert, the next an AGM–114 Hellfire air-to-surface missile fired from a Predator unmanned air vehicle turned their vehicle into a smoldering ruin.

The operation that caused Abu Ali's demise was part of a new U.S. strategy to strike terrorists around the world. That strategy has sought to deny terrorists safe haven and, as one senior U.S. official described it, "get them moving" in the hopes that operational security mistakes would be made.

But whether Ali's downfall was due to lax operational security or good intelligence, the strike that killed him was carefully planned and implemented by the secret warriors who form the sword-wielding arm of the U.S. Central Intelligence Agency (CIA). Called the Special Activities (SA) Division, these CIA paramilitary forces along with covert special operations force (SOF) units are fighting a clandestine "war on terrorism," details of which are rarely seen or acknowledged.

The Yemen attack is the exception that demonstrates the rule. Since the September 11, 2001, terrorist attacks on New York and Washington, the United States has conducted covert SOF and paramilitary missions against suspected terrorists around the world from Afghanistan and Colombia to Pakistan, the Philippines, Somalia, and Yemen.

They are also active in Iraq. According to U.S. military sources, CIA and SOF forces have traveled in and out of the country's northern and western areas since at least late last year. Those forces are scouting for ballistic missile launchers and suspected weapons of mass destruction sites, monitoring oil wells, looking for potential Iraqi defectors, and organizing Kurdish guerrilla forces for operations if there is an armed conflict.

Some Kurdish politicians are also being organized for their role in post-war reconstruction, mostly by the time-tested CIA tactic of buying loyalty.

But it is in Afghanistan where the SA, part of the CIA Directorate of Operations, has played its most significant role. They were the first U.S. forces sent to the country, smoothing the way for SOF and other military personnel that would follow. Working in small teams of not more than a dozen people, they organized anti-Taliban efforts, often by bribing local warlords; provided intelligence on targets the military would later strike during the air campaign; and prepared landing zones and safehouses for the follow-on SOF personnel. The CIA gave out "bags of cash" while organizing Afghan resistance to the Taliban, one official said, estimating the value of the effort at over $50 million.

The CIA personnel built on the agency's year of experience in Afghanistan and contacts with local leaders. As James Pavitt, CIA Deputy Director of Operations, explained earlier this year: "The first American team on the ground out there was CIA—for a reason. We had people with the right local languages, we had people with the right local contacts, and the right universal skills—the ability both to report conditions and, if need be, to change them for the better." The agency has received much public acclaim for this performance in Afghanistan, but the very survival of its secret SA units was in doubt less than a decade ago. By the end of the Cold War the CIA had largely scrapped its covert-action capabilities, especially its paramilitary forces.

According to an agency document, by 1993 the Special Activities Division, then called the Special Activities Staff, had declined to a staff of 190 personnel overseeing a $70 million budget. That changed, starting in July 1997, when Director of Central Intelligence George Tenet took the agency's helm and the SA and other covert-action units began to grow again. The "war on terrorism" has accelerated that trend, although the unit is still estimated to have no more than "several hundred" operators in the field—perhaps three times the 1993 total. As Pravitt notes: "You simply cannot create overnight the combination of assets—the talent, the sources, that went into the highest possible gear in defence of America after 11 September."

CIA versus Military

The growth of the CIA–SA has left some senior Department of Defense (DOD) officials wondering why they are not military missions. Moreover, they asked, why did the military, with its extensive SOF capabilities, have to rely on the CIA to prepare the ground in Afghanistan for the introduction of U.S. military forces? One senior intelligence official noted the agency's views on such a division of labor, explaining that CIA operators can deploy "in days" rather than the weeks it can take the military.

But, he added, the agency cannot sustain that presence for long periods of time due to their limited number of operational personnel. In many instances the CIA sees its role as going in first to prepare the way for SOF/military units to take over.

This, several DOD sources said, worries Defense Secretary Donald Rumsfeld because CIA operatives could start a conflict that the Pentagon would have to finish. Rather than have this happen, they said, Rumsfeld is seeking to increase the size and capabilities of SOFs capable of fighting a covert war to disrupt, interdict, capture, or kill terrorists around the world.[1]

The newly reinforced SOFs would report to Rumsfeld, not Tenet. The plans are for specialized military units to play a greater role in intelligence-gathering, special reconnaissance, and what is called "direct action," a euphemism for clandestine paramilitary operations such as that which killed Abu Ali.

A number of proposals are being floated in DOD to increase this covert military punch, although none has been approved yet. One, forwarded by the Defense Science Board (DSB), recommends creating "a new elite Counterterrorism Proactive Preemptive Operations Group."[2]

Comprising personnel with highly specialized skills including covert action, special operations, information operations, intelligence-gathering, and deception, the group would report to a specially designated coordinator on the National Security Council. At the same time, the study recommended the DOD and CIA "increase emphasis on counter-terrorism covert action to gain close target access."

Increasing DOD capabilities to conduct covert missions might be feasible in some situations, the CIA argues, but any increased SOF role in secret missions abroad would be complementary to, not competing with, the agency's activities. As the senior intelligence official noted, "there are some countries in the world where the DOD cannot easily go into."

This is due to the visibility military forces have that could carry serious political consequences for host countries with which the United States is not at war.

Small-scale civilian CIA teams can better conduct missions in such circumstances, the official argued, because they have a better ability and network to blend in. They also offer political cover due to the absence of uniforms and of public U.S. Government recognition that provides a degree of plausible deniability. Still, the official said, "when the military enters in, the agency takes on a support role."

Specialization

To conduct such missions, Rumsfeld is likely to turn to a small number of secret military units associated with the Joint Special Operations Command (JSOC) at Fort Bragg, North Carolina, which sources said is "considerably bigger in terms of operators" than the CIA–SA. These personnel already possess the requisite skills and specialization in counterterrorism (hostage rescue, close-combat operations, covert action) and counterproliferation (including materiel interdiction missions).

JSOC units include the Army's 1st Special Forces Operational Detachment–Delta, commonly known as Delta Force. Specializing in counterterrorism missions such as hostage rescues, as well as a growing counterproliferation focus, the size of the Delta Force is difficult to estimate; most military sources put it at several hundred. The Navy's Sea, Air, Land (SEAL) forces also have a covert specialized unit for similar missions called the Naval Special Warfare Development Group (DEVGRU). Formerly known as SEAL Team 6 and based at Dam Neck, Virginia, the unit is believed to comprise no more than 400 personnel. JSOC may further include a special aviation unit, possibly part of the Army's 160th Special Operations Aviation Regiment, but few details are available.

A final group, which together with Deltas and DEVGRU personnel could form the core of any increased DOD role in covert counterterrorist operations over the short term, is a highly classified Army intelligence unit once called the Intelligence Support Activity (ISA).

Now believed to be known as Grey Fox, the unit conducts covert operations, infiltration, direct action, signals intelligence, and other close-in intelligence collection that is separate from both the regular Intelligence Community and SOF, although the exact nature of its relations with the latter is unclear.

Said to be "several hundred" strong at most, members of the unit took part in SOF/CIA efforts to grab Bosnian-Serb war criminals in the Balkans during the late 1990s, several former U.S. officials said.

Despite these groups' capabilities, at least one former senior counterterrorism official questioned the wisdom of increasing the military's counterterrorism role if it came at the expense of the CIA. Units from JSOC, the official said, are very well trained for "taking down" aircraft hijackers and rescuing hostages, but asking them to conduct global interdiction missions of terrorists would be "a dramatically different role."

The official also said that despite great proficiency by JSOC forces because of their very rigorous training, before Afghanistan they had little operational experience because the U.S. military leadership had become averse to using special operations for covert missions. For example, the Clinton administration wanted to use SOF more extensively in the Balkans to go after war criminals but met resistance at DOD, with many requests for using JSOC personnel in "direct action" roles having been declined.

All CIA–SA personnel have a broad array of military and special-purpose kits available; the most publicized are Hellfire-armed Predators. Both JSOC and the CIA–SA forces, for example, were seen using Mi-8 and Mi-17 helicopters and nontraditional aircraft in Afghanistan.

Either force could use U.S. Air Force Special Operations Command's 6th Special Operations Squadron (6 SOS) aircraft, depending on the mission. The 6 SOS operates Mi-17 and Mi-8 helicopters and other foreign-built aircraft.

And while the unit primarily conducts foreign internal defense and training missions, "the squadron can also function in a direct-execution role," the command says.

Their capabilities in this regard include support for SOF missions such as exfiltration/infiltration, resupply, and airdrops from both fixed- and rotary-wing aircraft. The CIA–SA also has its own fleet of aircraft, often with civilian markings.

The CIA fleet includes foreign-built aviation assets as well as specialized Gulfstream and Boeing 757 aircraft often leased through front companies.

Equipment is not the only area these forces share resources. Many of the CIA–SA personnel come from JSOC units—either through the recruitment of retired SOFs or active troops on detail from DOD.

The CIA–SA had just over 100 personnel deployed to Afghanistan, slightly more than the number of SOFs that are understood to have been detailed to the CIA for the Afghan operations because the agency did not have enough paramilitary personnel available.

In all, U.S. SOFs totalled fewer than 500 personnel during U.S.-led Operation *Enduring Freedom* (OEF), according to Marshall Billingslea, the DOD head of the office for Special Operations and Low Intensity Conflict.

SOFs are still in Afghanistan working to track down Taliban and al Qaeda remnants, while CIA–SA personnel are conducting a similar mission in Pakistan and Afghanistan, U.S. officials say.

CIA–SA operatives worked in tandem with their SOF counterparts during *Enduring Freedom.*

Many of the small specialized SOF teams that proved crucial during OEF included a CIA–SA operative, and more SA forces were detailed to both regional planning cells as well as U.S. Central Command, to whom they reported for that conflict.

But despite these operational links, U.S. military sources complained that the two groups experienced coordination and interoperability difficulties, particularly early in the conflict.

Some senior DOD officials, for example, have complained that they were not always informed about what the CIA forces were doing nor were regular non-SOF troops well informed about their counterparts' activities.

Such complaints concerning interoperability and communications may be true at the headquarters level in Washington, one intelligence official noted, but it is not the case among the operators.

During OEF, "There [was] a total visibility between military planners at the [regional combatant commander]-level and agency planners for covert action on how to integrate their respective roles and missions," the official said. "The information goes to the most sensitive operations. There is nothing kept from [the combatant commanders]."

Still, the official said, the CIA has been looking to improve interoperability and information flow with U.S. military forces to allow more people in the field to obtain agency data quickly. In attempting one technical effort, the CIA attempted to utilize the military's communications infrastructure by using the Joint Worldwide Intelligence Communications System.

New policies and procedures are also being implemented based on the lessons of OEF. Such cooperation "is unprecedented but that is going to be growing in the future as part of the global 'war on terrorism'. . . . The relationship that [Special Operations Command] is developing with the CIA will only grow with time," the official noted.

Sources familiar with both the covert SOF and CIA units also note that overcoming interoperability challenges requires additional effort despite plans already being in place.

These challenges, the sources said, are due more to policy, doctrine, and tactics than equipment issues.

For example, military forces including specialized SOF units tend to be creatures of habit, and their doctrine, tactics, techniques, and procedures well-developed and exercised.

Others they may cooperate with, however, such as CIA and especially foreign government personnel, do not follow these procedures, forcing the SOF to improvise. "Sometimes it works out well, but other times not so great," one source said, "mostly because [of] this lack of practised co-ordination."

Legal Questions Cloud Covert Operations

As the United States embarks on covert counterterrorism operations such as that which killed Abu Ali, serious legal issues regarding the authority under which the operations are conducted have been raised.

The CIA has a detailed process in place that governs its covert action, including Presidential authorization to use lethal force. U.S. President George Bush has condoned these operations issuing a classified "finding" in September 2001 authorizing the CIA and Department of Defense to use "all necessary means" to capture if possible, but kill if necessary, al Qaeda leaders around the world. According to U.S. National Security Adviser Condoleezza Rice, Bush's authorization was "well within the balance of accepted practice and the letter of his constitutional authority."

This authorization is understood to allow the targeting of U.S. citizens working for al Qaeda overseas, although it is an implicit rather than explicit approval. Bush's new finding provides a specific list of senior al Qaeda leaders who could be targeted and the rules of engagement for doing so, such as minimizing collateral damage. This finding dwarfs the Clinton administration's orders to find and capture or kill bin Laden.

Under U.S. Government interpretation of customary international law, al Qaeda operatives are "enemy combatants" with whom Washington is at war, allowing them to be attacked anywhere, anytime without an additional legal finding. Explaining the U.S. position last December, the DOD Deputy General Counsel Charles Allen said: "Despite the fact that the terrorists present an unconventional foe, the fundamental principles of the law of armed conflict have proven themselves applicable."

Still, this premise is disturbing to some. British historian Sir Michael Howard, for example, argues that such a premise "accord(s) [al Qaeda] a status and a dignity that they seek and do not deserve."

Those who are party to an armed conflict and observe the pertinent international laws governing those activities are not liable for prosecution for attacking legitimate military targets, international customary law can be interpreted to say.

Yet neither Taliban nor al Qaeda fighters in Afghanistan were given those rights by U.S. forces. After all, U.S. officials argue, terrorist groups and their supporters do not abide by the customary rules governing armed conflict and are not given the same protections as the legitimate legal rulers of countries. This argument may extend to the question of whether killing bin Laden would violate the ban on assassinations of political leaders.

Again, U.S. officials would argue that since he and his followers do not abide by the customary rules governing armed conflict, they are not provided with the protection from the U.S. ban on political assassination either.

Moreover, Bush, in his Commander-in-Chief role, has the legal authority to order such operations under existing regulations as the leadership may be considered a legitimate target in wartime.

Even if this is the case, what about the wisdom of following such a policy? Several U.S. military officials who are skeptical of the tactic note that U.S. forces would not believe such rules are acceptable if they were applied to attacks on their own forces or personnel.

Since Bush is also Commander in Chief of the U.S. military, would he be a legitimate target for U.S. enemies during wartime, one asked.

Moreover, other military officials say, what are the standards of evidence on which lethal actions are undertaken? A fairly rigorous framework for internal and congressional oversight has been constructed in the past two decades for reviewing CIA operations, but the process for DOD-initiated lethal action is less clear.

Without a similar oversight process, a beefed-up military could be prone to the excesses that cause foreign disasters, the officials note.

Notes

[1] *Jane's Defence Weekly,* January 15, 2002.
[2] *Jane's Defence Weekly*, November 6, 2002.

The National Security Act: Excerpts

The National Security Act is the fundamental legislation of the United States in terms of intelligence. It established the National Security Council, under which serves the Director of Central Intelligence, who manages the Central Intelligence Agency. Although Congress has amended the National Security Act several times since enacting it in 1947, the Intelligence Community retains today the basic structure first envisaged by Ferdinand Eberstadt, an adviser to Secretary of the Navy James Forrestal and the act's principal architect.

The key provisions with regard to intelligence are:

SEC. 101:   The National Security Council
SEC. 102:   Office of the Director of Central Intelligence
SEC. 102A: Central Intelligence Agency
SEC. 103:   Responsibilities of the Director of Central Intelligence (including the specific role of the CIA)
SEC. 104:   Authorities of the Director of Central Intelligence
SEC. 501:   Congressional oversight of intelligence
SEC. 502:   Reporting on intelligence activities, other than covert action
SEC. 503:   Presidential approval and reporting of covert action
SEC. 504:   Funding of intelligence activities
SEC. 601:   Protection of identities of certain U.S. undercover intelligence officers, agents, informants, and sources
SEC. 701:   Exemption of certain CIA files from the Freedom of Information Act
SEC. 801:   Procedures for access to classified information.

Other sections of the National Security Act concern the structure and roles of the Defense Department and its components and are not reproduced here.

OFFICE OF THE DIRECTOR OF CENTRAL INTELLIGENCE

SEC. 102. [50 U.S.C. 4031]

(a) DIRECTOR OF CENTRAL INTELLIGENCE.—There is a Director of Central Intelligence who shall be appointed by the President, by and with the advice and consent of the Senate. The Director shall—

(1) serve as head of the United States Intelligence Community;

(2) act as the principal adviser to the President for intelligence matters related to the national security; and

(3) serve as head of the Central Intelligence Agency.

(b) DEPUTY DIRECTORS OF CENTRAL INTELLIGENCE.—

(1) There is a Deputy Director of Central Intelligence who shall be appointed by the President, by and with the advice and consent of the Senate.

(2) There is a Deputy Director of Central Intelligence for Community Management who shall be appointed by the President, by and with the advice and consent of the Senate.

(3) Each Deputy Director of Central Intelligence shall have extensive national security expertise.

(c) MILITARY STATUS OF DIRECTOR AND DEPUTY DIRECTORS.—

(1)(A) Not more than one of the individuals serving in the positions specified in subparagraph (B) may be a commissioned officer of the Armed. Forces, whether in active or retired status.

(B) The positions referred to in subparagraph (A) are the following:

(i) The Director of Central Intelligence.

(ii) The Deputy Director of Central Intelligence.

(iii) The Deputy Director of Central Intelligence for Community Management.

(2) It is the sense of Congress that, under ordinary circumstances, it is desirable that one of the individuals serving in the positions specified in paragraph (1)(B)—

(A) be a commissioned officer of the Armed Forces, whether in active or retired status; or

(B) have, by training or experience, an appreciation of military intelligence activities and requirements.

(3) A commissioned officer of the Armed Forces, while serving in a position specified in paragraph (1)(B)—

(A) shall not be subject to supervision or control by the Secretary of Defense or by any officer or employee of the Department of Defense;

(B) shall not exercise, by reason of the officer's status as a commissioned officer, any supervision or control with respect to any of the military or civilian personnel of the Department of Defense except as otherwise authorized by law; and

(C) shall not be counted against the numbers and percentages of commissioned officers of the rank and grade of such officer authorized for the military department of that officer.

(4) Except as provided in subparagraph (A) or (B) of paragraph (3), the appointment of an officer of the Armed Forces to a position specified in paragraph (1)(B) shall not affect the status, position, rank, or grade of such officer in the Armed Forces, or any emolument, perquisite, right,

privilege, or benefit incident to or arising out of any such status, position, rank, or grade.

(5) A commissioned officer of the Armed Forces on active duty who is appointed to a position specified in paragraph (1)(B), while serving in such position and while remaining on active duty, shall continue to receive military pay and allowances and shall not receive the pay prescribed for such position. Funds from which such pay and allowances are paid shall be reimbursed from funds available to the Director of Central Intelligence.

(d) DUTIES OF DEPUTY DIRECTORS.—

(1)(A) The Deputy Director of Central Intelligence shall assist the Director of Central Intelligence in carrying out the Director's responsibilities under this Act.

(B) The Deputy Director of Central Intelligence shall act for, and exercise the powers of, the Director of Central Intelligence during the Director's absence or disability or during a vacancy in the position of the Director of Central Intelligence.

(2) The Deputy Director of Central Intelligence for Community Management shall, subject to the direction of the Director of Central Intelligence, be responsible for the following:

(A) Directing the operations of the Community Management Staff.

(B) Through the Assistant Director of Central Intelligence for Collection, ensuring the efficient and effective collection of national intelligence using technical means and human sources.

(C) Through the Assistant Director of Central Intelligence for Analysis and Production, conducting oversight of the analysis and production of intelligence by elements of the Intelligence Community.

(D) Through the Assistant Director of Central Intelligence for Administration, performing community-wide management functions of the Intelligence Community, including the management of personnel and resources.

(3)(A) The Deputy Director of Central Intelligence takes precedence in the Office of the Director of Central Intelligence immediately after the Director of Central Intelligence.

(B) The Deputy Director of Central Intelligence for Community Management takes precedence in the Office of the Director of Central Intelligence immediately after the Deputy Director of Central Intelligence.

(e) OFFICE OF THE DIRECTOR OF CENTRAL INTELLIGENCE.—

(l) There is an Office of the Director of Central Intelligence. The function of the Office is to assist the Director of Central Intelligence in carrying out the duties and responsibilities of the Director under this Act and to carry out such other duties as may be prescribed by law.

(2) The Office of the Director of Central Intelligence is composed of the following:

(A) The Director of Central Intelligence.

(B) The Deputy Director of Central Intelligence.

(C) The Deputy Director of Central Intelligence for Community Management.

(D) The National Intelligence Council.

(E) The Assistant Director of Central Intelligence for Collection.

(F) The Assistant Director of Central Intelligence for Analysis and Production.

(G) The Assistant Director of Central Intelligence for Administration.

(H) Such other offices and officials as may be established by law or the Director of Central Intelligence may establish or designate in the Office.

(3) To assist the Director in fulfilling the responsibilities of the Director as head of the Intelligence Community, the Director shall employ and utilize in the Office of the Director of Central Intelligence a professional staff having an expertise in matters relating to such responsibilities and may establish permanent positions and appropriate rates of pay with respect to that staff.

(4) The Office of the Director of Central Intelligence shall, for administrative purposes, be within the Central Intelligence Agency.

(f) ASSISTANT DIRECTOR OF CENTRAL INTELLIGENCE FOR COLLECTION.—

(1) To assist the Director of Central Intelligence in carrying out the Director's responsibilities under this Act, there shall be an Assistant Director of Central Intelligence for Collection who shall be appointed by the President, by and with the advice and consent of the Senate.

(2) The Assistant Director for Collection shall assist the Director of Central Intelligence in carrying out the Director's collection responsibilities in order to ensure the efficient and effective collection of national intelligence.

(g) ASSISTANT DIRECTOR OF CENTRAL INTELLIGENCE FOR ANALYSIS AND PRODUCTION.—

(1) To assist the Director of Central Intelligence in carrying out the Director's responsibilities under this Act, there shall be an Assistant Director of Central Intelligence for Analysis and Production who shall be appointed by the President, by and with the advice and consent of the Senate.

(2) The Assistant Director for Analysis and Production shall—

(A) oversee the analysis and production of intelligence by the elements of the Intelligence Community;

(B) establish standards and priorities relating to such analysis and production;

(C) monitor the allocation of resources for the analysis and production of intelligence in order to identify unnecessary duplication in the analysis and production of intelligence;

(D) identify intelligence to be collected for purposes of the Assistant Director of Central Intelligence for Collection; and

(E) provide such additional analysis and production of intelligence as the President and the National Security Council may require.

(h) ASSISTANT DIRECTOR OF CENTRAL INTELLIGENCE FOR ADMINISTRATION.—

(1) To assist the Director of Central Intelligence in carrying out the Director's responsibilities under this Act, there shall be an Assistant Director of Central Intelligence for Administration who shall be appointed by the President, by and with the advice and consent of the Senate.

(2) The Assistant Director for Administration shall manage such activities relating to the administration of the Intelligence Community as the Director of Central Intelligence shall require.

Executive Order 12333: United States Intelligence Activities

December 4, 1981

Timely and accurate information about the activities, capabilities, plans, and intentions of foreign powers, organizations, and persons and their agents, is essential to the national security of the United States. All reasonable and lawful means must be used to ensure that the United States will receive the best intelligence available. For that purpose, by virtue of the authority vested in me by the Constitution and statutes of the United States of America, including the National Security Act of 1947, as amended, and as President of the United States of America, in order to provide for the effective conduct of United States intelligence activities and the protection of constitutional rights, it is hereby ordered as follows:

PART 1—GOALS, DIRECTION, DUTIES, AND RESPONSIBILITIES WITH RESPECT TO THE NATIONAL INTELLIGENCE EFFORT

1.1 Goals.
The United States intelligence effort shall provide the President and the National Security Council with the necessary information on which to base decisions concerning the conduct and development of foreign, defense, and economic policy, and the protection of United States national interests from foreign security threats. All departments and agencies shall cooperate fully to fulfill this goal.
(a) Maximum emphasis should be given to fostering analytical competition among appropriate elements of the Intelligence Community.
(b) All means, consistent with applicable United States law and this Order, and with full consideration of the rights of United States persons, shall be used to develop intelligence information for the President and the National Security Council. A balanced approach between technical collection efforts and other means should be maintained and encouraged.
(c) Special emphasis should be given to detecting and countering espionage and other threats and activities directed by foreign intelligence services against the United States Government, or United States corporations, establishments, or persons.

(d) To the greatest extent possible consistent with applicable United States law and this Order, and with full consideration of the rights of United States persons, all agencies and departments should seek to ensure full and free exchange of information in order to derive maximum benefit from the United States intelligence effort.

1.2 The National Security Council.

(a) Purpose. The National Security Council (NSC) was established by the National Security Act of 1947 to advise the President with respect to the integration of domestic, foreign, and military policies relating to the national security. The NSC shall act as the highest Executive Branch entity that provides review of, guidance for, and direction to the conduct of all national foreign intelligence, counterintelligence, and special activities, and attendant policies and programs.

(b) Committees. The NSC shall establish such committees as may be necessary to carry out its functions and responsibilities under this Order. The NSC, or a committee established by it, shall consider and submit to the President a policy recommendation, including all dissents, on each special activity and shall review proposals for other sensitive intelligence operations.

1.3 National Foreign Intelligence Advisory Groups.

(a) Establishment and Duties. The Director of Central Intelligence shall establish such boards, councils, or groups as required for the purpose of obtaining advice from within the Intelligence Community concerning:

(1) Production, review, and coordination of national foreign intelligence;

(2) Priorities for the National Foreign Intelligence Program budget;

(3) Interagency exchanges of foreign intelligence information;

(4) Arrangements with foreign governments on intelligence matters;

(5) Protection of intelligence sources and methods;

(6) Activities of common concern; and

(7) Such other matters as may be referred by the Director of Central Intelligence.

(b) Membership. Advisory groups established pursuant to this section shall be chaired by the Director of Central Intelligence or his designated representative and shall consist of senior representatives from organizations within the Intelligence Community and from departments or agencies containing such organizations, as designated by the Director of Central Intelligence. Groups for consideration of substantive intelligence matters will include representatives of organizations involved in the collection, processing, and analysis of intelligence. A senior representative of the Secretary of Commerce, the Attorney General, the Assistant to the President for National Security Affairs, and the Office of the Secretary of Defense shall be invited to participate in any group which deals with other than substantive intelligence matters.

1.4 The Intelligence Community.

The agencies within the Intelligence Community shall, in accordance with applicable United States law and with the other provisions of this Order, conduct intelligence activities necessary for the conduct of foreign relations and the protection of the national security of the United States, including:

(a) Collection of information needed by the President, the National Security Council, the Secretaries of State and Defense, and other Executive Branch officials for the performance of their duties and responsibilities;

(b) Production and dissemination of intelligence;

(c) Collection of information concerning, and the conduct of activities to protect against, intelligence activities directed against the United States, international terrorist and international narcotics activities, and other hostile activities directed against the United States by foreign powers, organizations, persons, and their agents;

(d) Special activities;

(e) Administrative and support activities within the United States and abroad necessary for the performance of authorized activities; and

(f) Such other intelligence activities as the President may direct from time to time.

1.5 Director of Central Intelligence.

In order to discharge the duties and responsibilities prescribed by law, the Director of Central Intelligence shall be responsible directly to the President and the NSC and shall:

(a) Act as the primary adviser to the President and the NSC on national foreign intelligence and provide the President and other officials in the Executive Branch with national foreign intelligence;

(b) Develop such objectives and guidance for the Intelligence Community as will enhance capabilities for responding to expected future needs for national foreign intelligence;

(c) Promote the development and maintenance of services of common concern by designated intelligence organizations on behalf of the Intelligence Community;

(d) Ensure implementation of special activities;

(e) Formulate policies concerning foreign intelligence and counterintelligence arrangements with foreign governments, coordinate foreign intelligence and counterintelligence relationships between agencies of the Intelligence Community and the intelligence or internal security services of foreign governments, and establish procedures governing the conduct of liaison by any department or agency with such services on narcotics activities;

(f) Participate in the development of procedures approved by the Attorney General governing criminal narcotics intelligence activities abroad to ensure that these activities are consistent with foreign intelligence programs;

(g) Ensure the establishment by the Intelligence Community of common security and access standards for managing and handling foreign intelligence systems, information, and products;

(h) Ensure that programs are developed which protect intelligence sources, methods, and analytical procedures;

(i) Establish uniform criteria for the determination of relative priorities for the transmission of critical national foreign intelligence, and advise the Secretary of Defense concerning the communications requirements of the Intelligence Community for the transmission of such intelligence;

(j) Establish appropriate staffs, committees, or other advisory groups to assist in the execution of the Director's responsibilities;

(k) Have full responsibility for production and dissemination of national foreign intelligence, and authority to levy analytic tasks on departmental intelligence production organizations, in consultation with those organizations, ensuring that appropriate mechanisms for competitive analysis are developed so that diverse points of view are considered fully and differences of judgment within the Intelligence Community are brought to the attention of national policymakers;

(l) Ensure the timely exploitation and dissemination of data gathered by national foreign intelligence collection means, and ensure that the resulting intelligence is disseminated immediately to appropriate government entities and military commands;

(m) Establish mechanisms which translate national foreign intelligence objectives and priorities approved by the NSC into specific guidance for the Intelligence Community, resolve conflicts in tasking priority, provide to departments and agencies having information collection capabilities that are not part of the National Foreign Intelligence Program advisory tasking concerning collection of national foreign intelligence, and provide for the development of plans and arrangements for transfer of required collection tasking authority to the Secretary of Defense when directed by the President;

(n) Develop, with the advice of the program managers and departments and agencies concerned, the consolidated National Foreign Intelligence Program budget, and present it to the President and the Congress;

(o) Review and approve all requests for reprogramming National Foreign Intelligence Program funds, in accordance with guidelines established by the Office of Management and Budget;

(p) Monitor National Foreign Intelligence Program implementation, and, as necessary, conduct program and performance audits and evaluations;

(q) Together with the Secretary of Defense, ensure that there is no unnecessary overlap between national foreign intelligence programs and Department of Defense intelligence programs consistent with the requirement to develop competitive analysis, and provide to and obtain from the Secretary of Defense all information necessary for this purpose;

(r) In accordance with law and relevant procedures approved by the Attorney General under this Order, give the heads of the departments and agencies access to all intelligence, developed by the CIA or the staff elements of the Director of Central Intelligence, relevant to the national intelligence needs of the departments and agencies; and

(s) Facilitate the use of national foreign intelligence products by Congress in a secure manner.

1.6 Duties and Responsibilities of the Heads of Executive Branch Departments and Agencies.

(a) The heads of all Executive Branch departments and agencies shall, in accordance with law and relevant procedures approved by the Attorney General under this Order, give the Director of Central Intelligence access to all information relevant to the national intelligence needs of the United States, and shall give due consideration to the requests from the Director of Central Intelligence for appropriate support for Intelligence Community activities.

(b) The heads of departments and agencies involved in the National Foreign Intelligence Program shall ensure timely development and submission to the Director of Central Intelligence by the program managers and heads of component activities of proposed national programs and budgets in the format designated by the Director of Central Intelligence, and shall also ensure that the Director of Central Intelligence is provided, in a timely and responsive manner, all information necessary to perform the Director's program and budget responsibilities.

(c) The heads of departments and agencies involved in the National Foreign Intelligence Program may appeal to the President decisions by the Director of Central Intelligence on budget or reprogramming matters of the National Foreign Intelligence Program.

1.7 Senior Officials of the Intelligence Community.

The heads of departments and agencies with organizations in the Intelligence Community or the heads of such organizations, as appropriate, shall:

(a) Report to the Attorney General possible violations of federal criminal laws by employees and of specified federal criminal laws by any other person as provided in procedures agreed upon by the Attorney General and the head of the department or agency concerned, in a manner consistent with the protection of intelligence sources and methods, as specified in those procedures;

(b) In any case involving serious or continuing breaches of security, recommend to the Attorney General that the case be referred to the FBI for further investigation;

(c) Furnish the Director of Central Intelligence and the NSC, in accordance with applicable law and procedures approved by the Attorney

General under this Order, the information required for the performance of their respective duties;

(d) Report to the Intelligence Oversight Board, and keep the Director of Central Intelligence appropriately informed, concerning any intelligence activities of their organizations that they have reason to believe may be unlawful or contrary to Executive order or Presidential directive;

(e) Protect intelligence and intelligence sources and methods from unauthorized disclosure consistent with guidance from the Director of Central Intelligence;

(f) Disseminate intelligence to cooperating foreign governments under arrangements established or agreed to by the Director of Central Intelligence;

(g) Participate in the development of procedures approved by the Attorney General governing production and dissemination of intelligence resulting from criminal narcotics intelligence activities abroad if their departments, agencies, or organizations have intelligence responsibilities for foreign or domestic narcotics production and trafficking;

(h) Instruct their employees to cooperate fully with the Intelligence Oversight Board; and

(i) Ensure that the Inspectors General and General Counsels for their organizations have access to any information necessary to perform their duties assigned by this Order.

1.8 The Central Intelligence Agency.

All duties and responsibilities of the CIA shall be related to the intelligence functions set out below. As authorized by this Order; the National Security Act of 1947, as amended; the CIA Act of 1949, as amended; appropriate directives or other applicable law, the CIA shall:

(a) Collect, produce, and disseminate foreign intelligence and counterintelligence, including information not otherwise obtainable. The collection of foreign intelligence or counterintelligence within the United States shall be coordinated with the FBI as required by procedures agreed upon by the Director of Central Intelligence and the Attorney General;

(b) Collect, produce, and disseminate intelligence on foreign aspects of narcotics production and trafficking;

(c) Conduct counterintelligence activities outside the United States and, without assuming or performing any internal security functions, conduct counterintelligence activities within the United States in coordination with the FBI as required by procedures agreed upon by the Director of Central Intelligence and the Attorney General;

(d) Coordinate counterintelligence activities and the collection of information not otherwise obtainable when conducted outside the United States by other departments and agencies;

(e) Conduct special activities approved by the President. No agency except the CIA (or the Armed Forces of the United States in time of war declared by Congress or during any period covered by a report from the President to the Congress under the War Powers Resolution (87 Stat. 855)) may conduct any special activity unless the President determines that another agency is more likely to achieve a particular objective;

(f) Conduct services of common concern for the Intelligence Community as directed by the NSC;

(g) Carry out or contract for research, development, and procurement of technical systems and devices relating to authorized functions;

(h) Protect the security of its installations, activities, information, property, and employees by appropriate means, including such investigations of applicants, employees, contractors, and other persons with similar associations with the CIA as are necessary; and

(i) Conduct such administrative and technical support activities within and outside the United States as are necessary to perform the functions described in sections (a) through (h) above, including procurement and essential cover and proprietary arrangements.

1.9 The Department of State.

The Secretary of State shall:

(a) Overtly collect information relevant to United States foreign policy concerns;

(b) Produce and disseminate foreign intelligence relating to United States foreign policy as required for the execution of the Secretary's responsibilities;

(c) Disseminate, as appropriate, reports received from United States diplomatic and consular posts;

(d) Transmit reporting requirements of the Intelligence Community to the Chiefs of United States Missions abroad; and

(e) Support Chiefs of Missions in discharging their statutory responsibilities for direction and coordination of mission activities.

1.10 The Department of the Treasury.

The Secretary of the Treasury shall:

(a) Overtly collect foreign financial and monetary information;

(b) Participate with the Department of State in the overt collection of general foreign economic information;

(c) Produce and disseminate foreign intelligence relating to United States economic policy as required for the execution of the Secretary's responsibilities; and

(d) Conduct, through the United States Secret Service, activities to determine the existence and capability of surveillance equipment being used against the President of the United States, the Executive Office of the President, and, as authorized by the Secretary of the Treasury or the President, other Secret Service protectees and United States officials.

No information shall be acquired intentionally through such activities except to protect against such surveillance, and those activities shall be conducted pursuant to procedures agreed upon by the Secretary of the Treasury and the Attorney General.

1.11 The Department of Defense.

The Secretary of Defense shall:

(a) Collect national foreign intelligence and be responsive to collection tasking by the Director of Central Intelligence;

(b) Collect, produce, and disseminate military and military-related foreign intelligence and counterintelligence as required for execution of the Secretary's responsibilities;

(c) Conduct programs and missions necessary to fulfill national, departmental, and tactical foreign intelligence requirements;

(d) Conduct counterintelligence activities in support of Department of Defense components outside the United States in coordination with the CIA, and within the United States in coordination with the FBI pursuant to procedures agreed upon by the Secretary of Defense and the Attorney General;

(e) Conduct, as the executive agent of the United States Government, signals intelligence and communications security activities, except as otherwise directed by the NSC;

(f) Provide for the timely transmission of critical intelligence, as defined by the Director of Central Intelligence, within the United States Government;

(g) Carry out or contract for research, development, and procurement of technical systems and devices relating to authorized intelligence functions;

(h) Protect the security of Department of Defense installations, activities, property, information, and employees by appropriate means, including such investigations of applicants, employees, contractors, and other persons with similar associations with the Department of Defense as are necessary;

(i) Establish and maintain military intelligence relationships and military intelligence exchange programs with selected cooperative foreign defense establishments and international organizations, and ensure that such relationships and programs are in accordance with policies formulated by the Director of Central Intelligence;

(j) Direct, operate, control, and provide fiscal management for the National Security Agency and for defense and military intelligence and national reconnaissance entities; and

(k) Conduct such administrative and technical support activities within and outside the United States as are necessary to perform the functions described in sections (a) through (j) above.

1.12 Intelligence Components Utilized by the Secretary of Defense.

In carrying out the responsibilities assigned in section 1.11, the Secretary of Defense is authorized to utilize the following:

(a) Defense Intelligence Agency, whose responsibilities shall include:

(1) Collection, production, or, through tasking and coordination, provision of military and military-related intelligence for the Secretary of Defense, the Joint Chiefs of Staff, other Defense components, and, as appropriate, non-Defense agencies;

(2) Collection and provision of military intelligence for national foreign intelligence and counterintelligence products;

(3) Coordination of all Department of Defense intelligence collection requirements;

(4) Management of the Defense Attache system; and

(5) Provision of foreign intelligence and counterintelligence staff support as directed by the Joint Chiefs of Staff.

(b) National Security Agency, whose responsibilities shall include:

(1) Establishment and operation of an effective unified organization for signals intelligence activities, except for the delegation of operational control over certain operations that are conducted through other elements of the Intelligence Community. No other department or agency may engage in signals intelligence activities except pursuant to a delegation by the Secretary of Defense;

(2) Control of signals intelligence collection and processing activities, including assignment of resources to an appropriate agent for such periods and tasks as required for the direct support of military commanders;

(3) Collection of signals intelligence information for national foreign intelligence purposes in accordance with guidance from the Director of Central Intelligence;

(4) Processing of signals intelligence data for national foreign intelligence purposes in accordance with guidance from the Director of Central Intelligence;

(5) Dissemination of signals intelligence information for national foreign intelligence purposes to authorized elements of the Government, including the military services, in accordance with guidance from the Director of Central Intelligence;

(6) Collection, processing, and dissemination of signals intelligence information for counterintelligence purposes;

(7) Provision of signals intelligence support for the conduct of military operations in accordance with tasking, priorities, and standards of timeliness assigned by the Secretary of Defense. If provision of such support requires use of national collection systems, these systems will be tasked within existing guidance from the Director of Central Intelligence;

(8) Executing the responsibilities of the Secretary of Defense as executive agent for the communications security of the United States Government;

(9) Conduct of research and development to meet the needs of the United States for signals intelligence and communications security;

(10) Protection of the security of its installations, activities, property, information, and employees by appropriate means, including such investigations of applicants, employees, contractors, and other persons with similar associations with the NSA as are necessary;

(11) Prescribing, within its field of authorized operations, security regulations covering operating practices, including the transmission, handling, and distribution of signals intelligence and communications security material within and among the elements under control of the Director of the NSA, and exercising the necessary supervisory control to ensure compliance with the regulations;

(12) Conduct of foreign cryptologic liaison relationships, with liaison for intelligence purposes conducted in accordance with policies formulated by the Director of Central Intelligence; and

(13) Conduct of such administrative and technical support activities within and outside the United States as are necessary to perform the functions described in sections (1) through (12) above, including procurement.

(c) Offices for the collection of specialized intelligence through reconnaissance programs, whose responsibilities shall include:

(1) Carrying out consolidated reconnaissance programs for specialized intelligence;

(2) Responding to tasking in accordance with procedures established by the Director of Central Intelligence; and

(3) Delegating authority to the various departments and agencies for research, development, procurement, and operation of designated means of collection.

(d) The foreign intelligence and counterintelligence elements of the Army, Navy, Air Force, and Marine Corps, whose responsibilities shall include:

(1) Collection, production, and dissemination of military and military-related foreign intelligence and counterintelligence, and information on the foreign aspects of narcotics production and trafficking. When collection is conducted in response to national foreign intelligence requirements, it will be conducted in accordance with guidance from the Director of Central Intelligence. Collection of national foreign intelligence, not otherwise obtainable, outside the United States shall be coordinated with the CIA, and such collection within the United States shall be coordinated with the FBI;

(2) Conduct of counterintelligence activities outside the United States in coordination with the CIA, and within the United States in coordination with the FBI; and

(3) Monitoring of the development, procurement, and management of tactical intelligence systems and equipment and conducting related research, development, and test and evaluation activities.

(e) Other offices within the Department of Defense appropriate for conduct of the intelligence missions and responsibilities assigned to the Secretary of Defense. If such other offices are used for intelligence purposes, the provisions of Part 2 of this Order shall apply to those offices when used for those purposes.

1.13 The Department of Energy.

The Secretary of Energy shall:

(a) Participate with the Department of State in overtly collecting information with respect to foreign energy matters;

(b) Produce and disseminate foreign intelligence necessary for the Secretary's responsibilities;

(c) Participate in formulating intelligence collection and analysis requirements where the special expert capability of the Department can contribute; and

(d) Provide expert technical, analytical, and research capability to other agencies within the Intelligence Community.

1.14 The Federal Bureau of Investigation.

Under the supervision of the Attorney General and pursuant to such regulations as the Attorney General may establish, the Director of the FBI shall:

(a) Within the United States conduct counterintelligence and coordinate counterintelligence activities of other agencies within the Intelligence Community. When a counterintelligence activity of the FBI involves military or civilian personnel of the Department of Defense, the FBI shall coordinate with the Department of Defense;

(b) Conduct counterintelligence activities outside the United States in coordination with the CIA as required by procedures agreed upon by the Director of Central Intelligence and the Attorney General;

(c) Conduct within the United States, when requested by officials of the Intelligence Community designated by the President, activities undertaken to collect foreign intelligence or support foreign intelligence collection requirements of other agencies within the Intelligence Community, or, when requested by the Director of the National Security Agency, to support the communications security activities of the United States Government;

(d) Produce and disseminate foreign intelligence and counterintelligence; and

(e) Carry out or contract for research, development, and procurement of technical systems and devices relating to the functions authorized above.

PART 2—CONDUCT OF INTELLIGENCE ACTIVITIES

2.1 Need.

Accurate and timely information about the capabilities, intentions, and activities of foreign powers, organizations, or persons and their agents is essential to informed decisionmaking in the areas of national defense and foreign relations. Collection of such information is a priority objective and will be pursued in a vigorous, innovative, and responsible manner that is consistent with the Constitution and applicable law and respectful of the principles upon which the United States was founded.

2.2 Purpose.

This Order is intended to enhance human and technical collection techniques, especially those undertaken abroad, and the acquisition of significant foreign intelligence, as well as the detection and countering of international terrorist activities and espionage conducted by foreign powers. Set forth below are certain general principles that, in addition to and consistent with applicable laws, are intended to achieve the proper balance between the acquisition of essential information and protection of individual interests. Nothing in this Order shall be construed to apply to or interfere with any authorized civil or criminal law enforcement responsibility of any department or agency.

2.3 Collection of Information.

Agencies within the Intelligence Community are authorized to collect, retain, or disseminate information concerning United States persons only in accordance with procedures established by the head of the agency concerned and approved by the Attorney General, consistent with the authorities provided by Part I of this Order. Those procedures shall permit collection, retention, and dissemination of the following types of information:

(a) Information that is publicly available or collected with the consent of the person concerned;

(b) Information constituting foreign intelligence or counterintelligence, including such information concerning corporations or other commercial organizations. Collection within the United States of foreign intelligence not otherwise obtainable shall be undertaken by the FBI or, when significant foreign intelligence is sought, by other authorized agencies of the Intelligence Community, provided that no foreign intelligence collection by such agencies may be undertaken for the purpose of acquiring information concerning the domestic activities of United States persons;

(c) Information obtained in the course of a lawful foreign intelligence, counterintelligence, international narcotics, or international terrorism investigation;

(d) Information needed to protect the safety of any persons or organizations, including those who are targets, victims, or hostages of international terrorist organizations;

(e) Information needed to protect foreign intelligence or counterintelligence sources or methods from unauthorized disclosure. Collection within the United States shall be undertaken by the FBI except that other agencies of the Intelligence Community may also collect such information concerning present or former employees, present or former intelligence agency contractors or their present or former employees, or applicants for any such employment or contracting;

(f) Information concerning persons who are reasonably believed to be potential sources or contacts for the purpose of determining their suitability or credibility;

(g) Information arising out of a lawful personnel, physical, or communications security investigation;

(h)Information acquired by overhead reconnaissance not directed at specific United States persons;

(i) Incidentally obtained information that may indicate involvement in activities that may violate federal, state, local, or foreign laws; and

(j) Information necessary for administrative purposes. In addition, agencies within the Intelligence Community may disseminate information, other than information derived from signals intelligence, to each appropriate agency within the Intelligence Community for purposes of allowing the recipient agency to determine whether the information is relevant to its responsibilities and can be retained by it.

2.4 Collection Techniques.

Agencies within the Intelligence Community shall use the least intrusive collection techniques feasible within the United States or directed against United States persons abroad. Agencies are not authorized to use such techniques as electronic surveillance, unconsented physical search, mail surveillance, physical surveillance, or monitoring devices unless they are in accordance with procedures established by the head of the agency concerned and approved by the Attorney General. Such procedures shall protect constitutional and other legal rights and limit use of such information to lawful governmental purposes. These procedures shall not authorize:

(a) The CIA to engage in electronic surveillance within the United States except for the purpose of training, testing, or conducting countermeasures to hostile electronic surveillance;

(b) Unconsented physical searches in the United States by agencies other than the FBI, except for:

(1) Searches by counterintelligence elements of the military services directed against military personnel within the United States or abroad for intelligence purposes, when authorized by a military commander empowered to approve physical searches for law enforcement

purposes, based upon a finding of probable cause to believe that such persons are acting as agents of foreign powers; and

(2) Searches by CIA of personal property of non-United States persons lawfully in its possession.

(c) Physical surveillance of a United States person in the United States by agencies other than the FBI, except for:

(1) Physical surveillance of present or former employees, present or former intelligence agency contractors or their present or former employees, or applicants for any such employment or contracting; and

(2) Physical surveillance of a military person employed by a nonintelligence element of a military service.

(d) Physical surveillance of a United States person abroad to collect foreign intelligence, except to obtain significant information that cannot reasonably be acquired by other means.

2.5 Attorney General Approval.

The Attorney General hereby is delegated the power to approve the use for intelligence purposes, within the United States or against a United States person abroad, of any technique for which a warrant would be required if undertaken for law enforcement purposes, provided that such techniques shall not be undertaken unless the Attorney General has determined in each case that there is probable cause to believe that the technique is directed against a foreign power or an agent of a foreign power. Electronic surveillance, as defined in the Foreign Intelligence Surveillance Act of 1978, shall be conducted in accordance with that Act, as well as this Order.

2.6 Assistance to Law Enforcement Authorities.

Agencies within the Intelligence Community are authorized to:

(a) Cooperate with appropriate law enforcement agencies for the purpose of protecting the employees, information, property, and facilities of any agency within the Intelligence Community;

(b) Unless otherwise precluded by law or this Order, participate in law enforcement activities to investigate or prevent clandestine intelligence activities by foreign powers, or international terrorist or narcotics activities;

(c) Provide specialized equipment, technical knowledge, or assistance of expert personnel for use by any department or agency, or, when lives are endangered, to support local law enforcement agencies. Provision of assistance by expert personnel shall be approved in each case by the General Counsel of the providing agency; and

(d) Render any other assistance and cooperation to law enforcement authorities not precluded by applicable law.

2.7 Contracting.

Agencies within the Intelligence Community are authorized to enter into contracts or arrangements for the provision of goods or services with private companies or institutions in the United States and need not reveal the

sponsorship of such contracts or arrangements for authorized intelligence purposes. Contracts or arrangements with academic institutions may be undertaken only with the contract of appropriate officials of the institution.
2.8 Consistency With Other Laws.
Nothing in this Order shall be construed to authorize any activity in violation of the Constitution or statutes of the United States.
2.9 Undisclosed Participation in Organizations Within the United States.
No one acting on behalf of agencies within the Intelligence Community may join or otherwise participate in any organization in the United States on behalf of any agency within the Intelligence Community without disclosing his intelligence affiliation to appropriate officials of the organization, except in accordance with procedures established by the head of the agency concerned and approved by the Attorney General. Such participation shall be authorized only if it is essential to achieving lawful purposes as determined by the agency head or designee. No such participation may be undertaken for the purpose of influencing the activity of the organization or its members except in cases where:

(a) The participation is undertaken on behalf of the FBI in the course of a lawful investigation; or
(b) The organization concerned is composed primarily of individuals who are not United States persons and is reasonably believed to be acting on behalf of a foreign power.

2.10 Human Experimentation.
No agency within the Intelligence Community shall sponsor, contract for, or conduct research on human subjects except in accordance with guidelines issued by the Department of Health and Human Services. The subject's informed consent shall be documented as required by those guidelines.
2.11 Prohibition on Assassination.
No person employed by or acting on behalf of the United States Government shall engage in, or conspire to engage in, assassination.
2.12 Indirect Participation.
No agency of the Intelligence Community shall participate in or request any person to undertake activities forbidden by this Order.

PART 3—GENERAL PROVISIONS

3.1 Congressional Oversight.
The duties and responsibilities of the Director of Central Intelligence and the heads of other departments, agencies, and entities engaged in intelligence activities to cooperate with the Congress in the conduct of its responsibilities for oversight of intelligence activities shall be as provided in Title 50, United States Code, section 413. The requirements of section 662 of the Foreign Assistance Act of 1961, as amended (22 U.S.C. 2422), and

section 501 of the National Security Act of 1947, as amended (50 U.S.C. 413), shall apply to all special activities as defined in this Order.

3.2 Implementation.

The NSC, the Secretary of Defense, the Attorney General, and the Director of Central Intelligence shall issue such appropriate directives and procedures as are necessary to implement this Order. Heads of agencies within the Intelligence Community shall issue appropriate supplementary directives and procedures consistent with this Order. The Attorney General shall provide a statement of reasons for not approving any procedures established by the head of an agency in the Intelligence Community other than the FBI. The National Security Council may establish procedures in instances where the agency head and the Attorney General are unable to reach agreement on other than constitutional or other legal grounds.

3.3 Procedures.

Until the procedures required by this Order have been established, the activities herein authorized which require procedures shall be conducted in accordance with existing procedures or requirements established under Executive Order No. 12036. Procedures required by this Order shall be established as expeditiously as possible. All procedures promulgated pursuant to this Order shall be made available to the congressional intelligence committees.

3.4 Definitions.

For the purposes of this Order, the following terms shall have these meanings:

(a) Counterintelligence means information gathered and activities conducted to protect against espionage, other intelligence activities, sabotage, or assassinations conducted for or on behalf of foreign powers, organizations, or persons, or international terrorist activities, but not including personnel, physical, document, or communications security programs.

(b) Electronic surveillance means acquisition of a nonpublic communication by electronic means without the consent of a person who is a party to an electronic communication or, in the case of a nonelectronic communication, without the consent of a person who is visibly present at the place of communication, but not including the use of radio direction-finding equipment solely to determine the location of a transmitter.

(c) Employee means a person employed by, assigned to, or acting for an agency within the Intelligence Community.

(d) Foreign intelligence means information relating to the capabilities, intentions, and activities of foreign powers, organizations, or persons, but not including counterintelligence except for information on international terrorist activities.

(e) Intelligence activities means all activities that agencies within the Intelligence Community are authorized to conduct pursuant to this Order.

(f) Intelligence Community and agencies within the Intelligence Community refer to the following agencies or organizations:

(1) The Central Intelligence Agency (CIA);

(2) The National Security Agency (NSA);

(3) The Defense Intelligence Agency (DIA);

(4) The offices within the Department of Defense for the collection of specialized national foreign intelligence through reconnaissance programs;

(5) The Bureau of Intelligence and Research of the Department of State;

(6) The intelligence elements of the Army, Navy, Air Force, and Marine Corps, the Federal Bureau of Investigation (FBI), the Department of the Treasury, and the Department of Energy; and

(7) The staff elements of the Director of Central Intelligence.

(g) The National Foreign Intelligence Program includes the programs listed below, but its composition shall be subject to review by the National Security Council and modification by the President:

(1) The programs of the CIA;

(2) The Consolidated Cryptologic Program, the General Defense Intelligence Program, and the programs of the offices within the Department of Defense for the collection of specialized national foreign intelligence through reconnaissance, except such elements as the Director of Central Intelligence and the Secretary of Defense agree should be excluded;

(3) Other programs of agencies within the Intelligence Community designated jointly by the Director of Central Intelligence and the head of the department or by the President as national foreign intelligence or counterintelligence activities;

(4) Activities of the staff elements of the Director of Central Intelligence;

(5) Activities to acquire the intelligence required for the planning and conduct of tactical operations by the United States military forces are not included in the National Foreign Intelligence Program.

(h) Special activities means activities conducted in support of national foreign policy objectives abroad which are planned and executed so that the role of the United States Government is not apparent or acknowledged publicly, and functions in support of such activities, but which are not intended to influence United States political processes, public opinion, policies, or media and do not include diplomatic activities or the collection and production of intelligence or related support functions.

(i) United States person means a United States citizen, an alien known by the intelligence agency concerned to be a permanent resident alien, an unincorporated association substantially composed of United States citizens or permanent resident aliens, or a corporation incorporated in the United States, except for a corporation directed and controlled by a foreign government or governments.

3.5 Purpose and Effect.

This Order is intended to control and provide direction and guidance to the Intelligence Community. Nothing contained herein or in any procedures promulgated hereunder is intended to confer any substantive or procedural right or privilege on any person or organization.

3.6 Revocation.

Executive Order No. 12036 of January 24, 1978, as amended, entitled "United States Intelligence Activities," is revoked.

RONALD REAGAN
THE WHITE HOUSE,
December 4, 1981

Director of Central Intelligence Directive 1/1

The Authorities and Responsibilities of the Director of Central Intelligence as Head of the U.S. Intelligence Community (Effective 19 November 1998)

This directive is promulgated pursuant to Sections 102 and 103(c) of the National Security Act of 1947, as amended (W), and Executive Order 12333.

A. Purpose

This directive establishes a system of DCI Directives (DCIDs) and subsidiary issuances, provides a summary of DCI authorities and responsibilities, assigns responsibility for the execution of certain DCI authorities and responsibilities, and provides for a process for the creation and coordination of DCI directives and subsidiary issuances. The goal of this system of directives is to enable the Director of Central Intelligence to provide timely, coordinated, and clear guidance and direction to the Intelligence Community. The process established is based on the authorities and responsibilities of the DCI as head of the U.S. Intelligence Community, as assigned by the National Security Act of 1947, as amended, Executive Orders 12333, 12951, 12958, and other statutes, Presidential directives, and National Security Council Intelligence Directives (NSCIDs).

B. The Authorities and Responsibilities of the Director of Central Intelligence Related to the U.S. Intelligence Community

The list of authorities and responsibilities of the DCI in this DCID is intended to be illustrative. Readers are directed to the citations for controlling language. In all cases, the language in the original citation is controlling. This DCID is not intended to act in derogation or arrogation of the authorities and responsibilities of the DCI or the head of any other agency, department, or organization contained in statute, Executive Order, Presidential directive, or NSCID. Furthermore this DCID is not intended to act in derogation or arrogation of any authorities and responsibilities of the DCI or the head of any other agency, department, or organization which may not be listed herein. By way of example, this DCID does not derogate or arrogate any of the authorities of the Secretary of Defense found in §105 of the National Security Act; 50 United States Code (hereafter USC) section 403-5.

1. Management
   a. General
      (1) The Director of Central Intelligence serves as head of the United States Intelligence Community; acts as the principal advisor to the President for intelligence matters related to the national security; and serves as the head of the Central Intelligence Agency. (NSA §102(a); 50 USC 403(a); see also, E.O. 12333, §1.5(a).)
      (2) To the extent recommended by the National Security Council and approved by the President, the DCI shall have access to all intelligence related to the national security which is collected by any department, agency, or other entity of the United States. (NSA §104(a); 50 USC 403-4(a).)
      (3) The heads of all Executive Branch departments and agencies shall, in accordance with law and relevant procedures approved by the Attorney General, give the DCI access to all information relevant to the national intelligence needs of the United States, and shall give due consideration to requests from the Director for appropriate support for Intelligence Community activities. (E.O. 12333, §1.6(a).)
      (4) The DCI is responsible for developing such objectives and guidance for the Intelligence Community as will enhance the capabilities for responding to expected future needs for national foreign intelligence. (E.O. 12333, §1.5(b).)
      (5) In the performance of his duties under the National Security Act, and subject to the direction of the President, the DCI may attend and participate in meetings of the National Security Council. (NSA §101(j); 50 USC 402U).)
      (6) The DCI is a member of the Committee on Foreign Intelligence of the National Security Council. (NSA §101(h)(2)(A); 50 USC 402(h)(2)(A).)
      (7) The DCI is a member of the Committee on Transnational Threats of the National Security Council. (NSA §101(i)(2)(A); 50 USC 402(i)(2)(A).)
   b. Appointment and Evaluation of Officials Responsible for Intelligence Related Activities
      (1) In the event of a vacancy in the position of the Director, National Security Agency (NSA); the Director, National Reconnaissance Office (NRO); or the Director, National Imagery and Mapping Agency (NIMA), the Secretary of Defense shall obtain the concurrence of the DCI before recommending to the President an individual for appointment to the position. If the DCI does not concur in the recommendation, the Secretary of Defense may make the recommendation to the President without the DCI's concurrence, but shall include in the recommendation a statement that the Director does not concur in the recommendation. (NSA §106(a); 50 USC 403-6(a).)

(2) In the event of a vacancy in the position of the Director, DIA; the Assistant Secretary of State for Intelligence and Research; or the Director of the Office of Nonproliferation and National Security [now, Office of Intelligence], DOE; the head of the department or agency having jurisdiction over the position shall consult with the DCI before appointing an individual to fill the vacancy or recommending to the President an individual to be nominated to fill the vacancy. (NSA §106(b); 50 USC 403-6(b).)

(3) In the event of a vacancy in the position of the Assistant Director, National Security Division of the Federal Bureau of Investigation, the Director of the Federal Bureau of Investigation shall provide timely notice to the DCI of the recommendation of the Director of the Federal Bureau of Investigation of an individual to fill the position in order that the DCI may consult with the Director, FBI, before the Attorney General appoints an individual to fill the vacancy. (NSA §106(b)(3); 50 USC 403-6(b)(3).)

(4) The DCI, in consultation with the Secretary of Defense and the Chairman of the Joint Chiefs of Staff is required to submit each year to the Committee on Foreign Intelligence of the NSC and to the appropriate congressional committees[1] an evaluation of the performance and the responsiveness of the National Security Agency, the National Reconnaissance Office, and the National Imagery and Mapping Agency in meeting their national missions. (NSA §105(d); 50 USC 403-5(d).)

c. Staffs, Committees, and Advisory Groups

The DCI is authorized to appoint advisory committees and to employ part-time advisory personnel as the Director deems necessary in the execution of the Director's functions, consistent with the terms set forth in section 303 of the National Security Act. (NSA §303; 50 USC 405; see also, E.O. 12333, §1.5(j)), "[The DCI shall] establish appropriate staffs, committees, or other advisory groups to assist in the execution of the Director's responsibilities.")

d. Congressional Reporting Requirements

(1) To the extent consistent with due regard for the protection from unauthorized disclosure of classified information relating to sensitive intelligence sources and methods or other exceptionally sensitive matters, the DCI and the heads of all departments, agencies, and other entities of the United States Government involved in intelligence activities shall keep the intelligence committees fully and currently informed of all intelligence activities, other than a covert action, which are the responsibility of, are engaged by, or are carried out for or on behalf of, any department, agency, or entity of the United States Government, including any significant anticipated intelligence

activity and any significant intelligence failure. (NSA §502(l); 50 USC 413a(l).)

(2) To the extent consistent with due regard for the protection from unauthorized disclosure of classified information relating to sensitive intelligence sources and methods or other exceptionally sensitive matters, the DCI and the heads of all departments, agencies, and other entities of the United States Government involved in intelligence activities shall furnish the intelligence committees any information or material concerning intelligence activities, other than covert actions, which is within his custody or control, and which is requested by either of the intelligence committees in order to carry out its authorized functions. (NSA §502(2); 50 USC 413a(2).)

(3) To the extent consistent with due regard for the protection from unauthorized disclosure of classified information relating to sensitive intelligence sources and methods or other exceptionally sensitive matters, the DCI and the heads of all departments, agencies, and other entities of the United States Government involved in a covert action shall keep the intelligence committees fully and currently informed of all covert actions which are the responsibility of, are engaged in by, or are carried out for or on behalf of, any department, agency, or entity of the United States Government, including significant failures; and shall furnish to the intelligence committees any information or material concerning covert actions which is in the possession, custody, or control of any department, agency, or entity of the United States Government and which is requested by either of the intelligence committees in order to carry out its authorized responsibilities. (NSA §503(b); 50 USC 413b(b).)

e. Providing and Promoting Services of Common Concern

As head of the Central Intelligence Agency, the DCI is charged with performing such additional services of common concern to elements of the Intelligence Community, which services the Director determines can be more efficiently accomplished centrally. (NSA §103(d)(4); 50 USC 403-3(d)(4); see also, E.O. 12333, §1.5(c), "[The DCI is responsible for] promot[ing] the development and maintenance of services of common concern by designated intelligence organizations on behalf of the Intelligence Community. . . .")

f. Promoting Common Administrative Practices

The DCI is charged with instituting policies and programs, in coordination with the heads of departments and agencies with elements in the Intelligence Community:

(1) to provide for the rotation of personnel among elements of the Intelligence Community, where appropriate, and to make such rotated service a factor to be considered for promotion to senior positions, and

(2) to consolidate, wherever possible, personnel, administrative, and security programs to reduce the overall costs of these activities within the Intelligence Community. (NSA §104(f); 50 USC 403-4(f).)

g. Intelligence Related Space Activities

The DCI has been assigned authorities and responsibilities under the National Space Policy, Presidential Decision Directive/NSC–49, 14 September 1996. These include, but are not limited to, the following:

(1) The DCI and the Secretary of Defense oversee those space activities necessary for national security, consistent with their respective responsibilities as set forth in the National Security Act of 1947, as amended, other applicable law and Executive Order 12333. (Presidential Decision Directive 49 (PDD–49), III (1), 14 September 1996.[2])

(2) The Secretary of Defense and the DCI are responsible for ensuring that defense and intelligence space activities are closely coordinated; that intelligence space architectures are integrated to the maximum extent feasible; and will continue to modernize and improve their respective activities to collect against, and respond to, changing threats, environments, and adversaries. (PDD–49, III (2).)

(3) The DCI is responsible for ensuring that the intelligence space sector provides timely information and data to support foreign, defense, and economic policies; military operations; diplomatic activities; indications and warning; crisis management; and treaty verification and that the sector performs research and development related to these functions. (PDD–49, III (9)(a).)

(4) The DCI is charged to work closely with the Secretary of Defense to improve the intelligence space sector's ability to support military operations worldwide. (PDD–49, III (9)(c).)

2. Analysis and Production

a. Analysis and Production of National Intelligence

(1) The DCI has full responsibility for the production and dissemination of national foreign intelligence, and authority to levy analytic tasks on departmental intelligence production organizations, in consultation with those organizations, ensuring that appropriate mechanisms for competitive analysis are developed so that diverse points of view are considered fully and differences of judgment within the Intelligence Community are brought to the attention of national policymakers. (E.O. 12333, §1.5(k).)

(2) Under the direction of the National Security Council, the DCI is responsible for providing national intelligence to the President; to the heads of the departments and agencies of the Executive Branch; to the Chairman of the Joint Chiefs of Staff and senior military commanders; and, where appropriate, to the Senate and the House of Representatives and the committees thereof. Such national intelligence should be timely, objective, independent of political considerations, and based upon

all sources available to the Intelligence Community. (NSA §103(a); 50 USC 403-3(a).)

(3) In accordance with law and relevant procedures approved by the Attorney General, the DCI is responsible for giving heads of the departments and agencies access to all intelligence, developed by the CIA or the staff elements of the Director of Central Intelligence, relevant to the national intelligence needs of the departments and agencies. (E.O. 12333, §1.5(r).)

(4) The DCI is responsible for facilitating the use of national foreign intelligence products by Congress in a secure manner. (E.O. 12333, §1.5(s).)

(5) The DCI is charged with promoting and evaluating the utility of national intelligence to consumers within the U.S. Government. (NSA §103(c)(4); 50 USC 403-3(c)(4).)

(6) The DCI is responsible for the development and implementation of such programs and policies as the DCI and the Secretary of Defense jointly determine necessary to review and correct deficiencies identified in the capabilities of the National Imagery and Mapping Agency to accomplish assigned national missions, including support to the all-source analysis and production process. The Director shall consult with the Secretary of Defense on the development and implementation of such programs and policies. (NSA §110(c); 50 USC 404e(c).)

(7) The DCI is responsible for establishing uniform criteria for the determination of relative priorities for the transmission of critical national foreign intelligence, and advising the Secretary of Defense concerning the communications requirements of the Intelligence Community for the transmission of such intelligence. (E.O.12333, §1.5(i).)

b. Reserved

3. Collection

a. Collection of National Intelligence

(1) The DCI, in his capacity as head of the Intelligence Community, establishes the requirements and priorities to govern the collection of national intelligence by elements of the Intelligence Community. (NSA §103(c)(2); 50 USC 403-3(c)(2).)

(2) The DCI, in his capacity as head of the Intelligence Community, approves collection requirements, determines collection priorities, and resolves conflicts in collection priorities levied on national collection assets, except as otherwise agreed with the Secretary of Defense pursuant to the direction of the President. (NSA §103(c)(3); 50 USC 403-3(c)(3); NSA §111; 50 USC 404f; see also, E.O. 12333 §1.5(m).)

(3) The DCI ensures the timely exploitation and dissemination of data gathered by national foreign intelligence collection means, and

ensures the resulting intelligence is disseminated immediately to appropriate government entities and military commands. (E.O. 12333, §1.5(l).)

(4) The DCI establishes mechanisms which translate national foreign intelligence objectives and priorities approved by the National Security Council into specific guidance for the Intelligence Community. (E.O. 12333, §1.5(m).)

(5) As Head of the Central Intelligence Agency, the DCI is responsible for providing overall direction for the collection of national intelligence through human sources by elements of the Intelligence Community authorized to undertake such collection and, in coordination with other agencies of the Government which are authorized to undertake such collection, ensure that the most effective use is made of resources and that the risks to the United States and those involved in such collection are minimized. (NSA §103(d)(2); 50 USC 403-3(d)(2).)

(6) The DCI is responsible for providing for the development of plans and arrangements for transfer of required collection tasking authority to the Secretary of Defense when directed by the President. (E.O. 12333, §1.5(m); see also, PDD–49, m(8)(f).)

b. Reserved

4. Program and Budget

a. Budget Preparation, Reprogramming, and Transfers, Monitoring NFIP Implementation

(1) The Director of Central Intelligence facilitates the development of an annual budget for the intelligence and intelligence-related activities of the United States by—

(A) developing, with the advice of the program managers and departments and agencies concerned, and presenting to the President, the consolidated National Foreign Intelligence Program (NFIP) budget; (NSA §103(c)(1)(A); 50 USC 403-3(c)(1)(A); see also, E.O. 12333 §1.5(n).); and,

(B) participating, in his capacity as head of the Intelligence Community, in the development by the Secretary of Defense of the annual budgets for the Joint Military Intelligence Program (JMIP) and Tactical Intelligence and Related Activities (TIARA). (NSA §103(c)(1)(B); 50 USC 403-3(c)(1)(B).)

(2) The DCI provides guidance to the elements of the Intelligence Community for the preparation of their annual budgets and approves such budgets before their incorporation in the National Foreign Intelligence Program. (NSA §104(b); 50 USC 403-4(b).)

(3) No funds made available under the National Foreign Intelligence Program may be reprogrammed by any element of the Intelligence Community without the prior approval of the DCI except

in accordance with procedures issued by the DCI (NSA §104(c); 50 USC 403-4(c). See also, E.O. 12333 §1.5(o), "[The DCI is responsible for reviewing and approving] all requests for reprogramming National Foreign Intelligence Program funds, in accordance with guidelines established by the Office of Management and Budget.")

(4) The Secretary of Defense shall consult with the DCI before reprogramming funds made available under the Joint Military Intelligence Program. (NSA §104(c); 50 USC 403-4(c).)

(5) The DCI, with the approval of the Director of the Office of Management and Budget, may transfer funds appropriated for a program within the National Foreign Intelligence Program to another such program. A transfer of funds under this authority may be made only if:

  (A) the funds are being transferred to an activity that is a higher priority intelligence activity;

  (B) the need for funds for such activity is based on unforeseen requirements;

  (C) the transfer does not involve a transfer of funds to the Reserve for Contingencies of the Central Intelligence Agency;

  (D) the transfer does not involve a transfer of funds from the Federal Bureau of Investigation; and

  (E) the Secretary or head of the department which contains the affected element or elements of the Intelligence Community does not object to such transfer. (NSA §104(d); 50 USC 403-4(d).)

(6) The DCI, in accordance with procedures developed by the DCI and the heads of affected departments and agencies, may transfer personnel authorized for an element of the Intelligence Community to another such element for periods up to one year. A transfer of personnel under this authority may be made only if:

  (A) the personnel are being transferred to an activity that is a higher priority intelligence activity;

  (B) the need for personnel for such activity is based on unforeseen requirements;

  (C) the transfer does not involve a transfer of personnel from the Federal Bureau of Investigation; and

  (D) the Secretary or head of the department which contains the affected element or elements of the Intelligence Community does not object to such transfer. (NSA §104(d); 50 USC 403-4(d).)

(7) The DCI monitors the implementation of the National Foreign Intelligence Program and, as necessary, conducts program audits and evaluations. (E.O. 12333, §1.5(p).)

b. Eliminating Waste and Unnecessary Duplication

The DCI, in his capacity as head of the Intelligence Community, is charged with eliminating waste and unnecessary duplication within the Intelligence Community. (NSA §103(c)(5); 50 USC 403-3(c)(5).)

c. Overlap Between National Foreign Intelligence Programs and Department of Defense Intelligence Programs

The DCI, together with the Secretary of Defense, is responsible for ensuring that there is no unnecessary overlap between national foreign intelligence programs and Department of Defense intelligence programs consistent with the requirement to develop competitive analysis, and for providing to and obtaining from the Secretary of Defense all information necessary for this purpose. (E.O. 12333, §1.5(q).)

d. Narcotics Intelligence Activities Abroad

The DCI participates in the development of procedures approved by the Attorney General governing criminal narcotics intelligence activities abroad to ensure that these activities are consistent with foreign intelligence programs. (E.O. 12333, §1.5(f).)

5. Relationships

a. Coordination of Foreign Intelligence Relationships

(1) Under the direction of the National Security Council, and in a manner consistent with section 207 of the Foreign Service Act of 1980 (22 USC 3927), the DCI shall coordinate the relationships between elements of the Intelligence Community and the intelligence or security services of foreign governments on all matters involving intelligence related to the national security or involving intelligence acquired through clandestine means. (NSA §104(e); 50 USC 403-4(e).)

(2) The DCI is responsible for formulating policies concerning foreign intelligence and counterintelligence arrangements with foreign governments, coordinating foreign intelligence and counterintelligence relationships between agencies of the Intelligence Community and the intelligence or internal security services of foreign governments, and establishing procedures governing the conduct of liaison by any department or agency with such services on narcotics activities. (E.O. 12333, §1.5(e).)

(3) No United States intelligence information may be provided to the United Nations or any organization affiliated with the United Nations, or to any officials or employees thereof, unless the President certifies to the appropriate committees of Congress[3] that the Director of Central Intelligence, in consultation with the Secretary of State and the Secretary of Defense, has established and implemented procedures, and has worked with the United Nations to ensure implementation of procedures, for protecting from unauthorized disclosure United States intelligence sources and methods connected to such information. (NSA §112(a)(1); 50 USC 404g(a)(1); (The statute also provides a waiver provision at NSA §404g(a)(2); 50 USC 404g(a)(2).))

b. Reserved

6. Security
   a. Protection of Intelligence Sources and Methods
      (1) The DCI shall protect intelligence sources and methods from unauthorized disclosure. (NSA §103(c)(6); 50 USC 403-3(c)(6).)
      (2) The DCI is charged with ensuring the establishment by the Intelligence Community of common security and access standards for managing and handling foreign intelligence systems, information, and products. (E.O. 12333, §1.5(g).)
      (3) The DCI is to ensure that programs are developed to protect intelligence sources, methods, and analytical procedures. (E.O. 12333, §1.5(h).)
      (4) Unless otherwise authorized by the President, only the Secretaries of State, Defense, and Energy and the Director of Central Intelligence, or the principal deputy of each, may create a special access program.[4] For special access programs pertaining to intelligence activities (including special activities, but not including military operational, strategic, and tactical programs), or intelligence sources or methods, this function will be exercised by the Director of Central Intelligence. (E.O. 12958, §4.1 and §4.4.)
   b. Classification of Imagery
      (1) The DC1 is responsible for determining whether imagery acquired by a space-based national intelligence reconnaissance system shall no longer be kept secret in the interests of national security and foreign policy. (E.O. 12951, §2.)
      (2) In consultation with the Secretaries of State and Defense, the DCI shall establish a comprehensive review of imagery from systems other than the Corona, Argon, and Lanyard missions, with the objective of making available to the public as much imagery as possible consistent with the interests of national defense and foreign policy. (E.O. 12951, §2.)
7. Other
   a. Special Activities
   The DCI is responsible for ensuring the implementation of special activities. (E.O. 12333, § 1.5(d).)
   b. Counterterrorism
   The DCI has been assigned specific responsibilities in Presidential Decision Directive/NSC–39, 21 June 1995 and Presidential Decision Directive/NSC–62, 22 May 1998.
   c. Other Authorities and Responsibilities
   The DCI, in his capacity as head of the Intelligence Community, may be directed to perform other functions by the President or the National Security Council. (NSA §103(c)(7); 50 USC 403-3(c)(7).)

C. Assignment of Responsibility for the Execution of the DCI's Responsibilities as Head of the Intelligence Community.

  1. The Deputy Director of Central Intelligence for Community Management (DDCI/CM). The DDCI/CM shall, subject to the direction of the DCI, be principally responsible for executing the responsibilities of the Director set forth in subparagraphs B.1.e., B.1.f., B.2., B.3., and B.4., above.

  2. DCI Discretionary Authority. Notwithstanding the assignment of responsibilities set forth above, the Director may assign responsibility, in whole or in part, to such other subordinate officials as he or she may choose.

  3. Implementation. The officials who are assigned responsibility pursuant to this paragraph are authorized to create such mechanisms or make use of existing mechanisms within the Intelligence Community, as may be appropriate—for the execution of their respective responsibilities.

D. System of DCI Directives (DCIDs)

  1. DCIDs. There is hereby established a system of DCI Directives and subsidiary issuances, which shall serve as the principal means by which the Director of Central Intelligence provides guidance, policy, and direction to the Intelligence Community pursuant to the authorities cited in paragraph A. All current DCIDs shall remain in force until canceled or an update is published.

  2. DDCI/CM Responsibilities. The DDCI/CM shall have overall responsibility for developing such directives and subsidiary issuances, for coordinating them with elements of the Intelligence Community, for promulgating and disseminating them, and for updating them as may be required. In carrying out these functions, the DDCI/CM may make use of such mechanisms within the Intelligence Community as may be appropriate. The DDCI/CM shall issue implementing procedures for the creation and coordination of DCI Directives and subsidiary issuances.

  3. DCI Approval. The DCI, or in his absence the Acting DCI, shall approve all DCIDs.

  4. Additional References to DCI Authorities and Responsibilities. The DDCI/CM may amend this DCID to include references to other authorities and responsibilities of the Director contained in statute, Executive Order, or Presidential directive.

George J. Tenet
Director of Central Intelligence
19 Nov 98

Notes

[1] The "appropriate congressional committees" for this purpose are defined in section 109 of the National Security Act to be: the Select Committee on Intelligence, the Committee on Appropriations, and the Committee on Armed Services of the Senate; and, the Permanent Select Committee on Intelligence, the Committee on Appropriations, and the Committee on National Security of the House of Representatives (NSA §109(c); 50 USC 404d(c)).

[2] These excerpts discuss only the unclassified provisions of PDD–49. Readers are directed to the PDD for a complete listing of authorities and responsibilities. PDD–49, III also sets out authorities and responsibilities of the Secretary of Defense, the Department of Energy, and ACDA with respect to National Security space activities.

[3] As used in this section, the term "appropriate committees of Congress" means the Committee on Foreign Relations and the Select Committee on Intelligence of the Senate and the Committee on Foreign Relations and the Permanent Select Committee on Intelligence of the House of Representatives. (NSA §112(e); 50 USC 404g(e)).

[4] A "special access program" is a program established for a specific class of classified information that imposes safeguarding and access requirements that exceed those normally required for information at the same classification level.

The USA PATRIOT Act:
A Sketch

Summary

Congress passed the USA PATRIOT Act (the Act) in response to the terrorists' attacks of September 11, 2001. The Act gives Federal officials greater authority to track and intercept communications, both for law enforcement and foreign intelligence gathering purposes. It vests the Secretary of the Treasury with regulatory powers to combat corruption of U.S. financial institutions for foreign money laundering purposes. It seeks to further close our borders to foreign terrorists and to detain and remove those within our borders. It creates new crimes, new penalties, and new procedural efficiencies for use against domestic and international terrorists. Although it is not without safeguards, critics contend some of its provisions go too far. Although it grants many of the enhancements sought by the Department of Justice, others are concerned that it does not go far enough.

The Act originated as H.R. 2975 (the PATRIOT Act) in the House and S. 1510 in the Senate (the USA Act). S. 1510 passed the Senate on October 11, 2001, 147 *Cong.Rec.* S10604 (daily ed.). The House Judiciary Committee reported out an amended version of H.R. 2975 on the same day, H.R.Rep.No. 107–236. The House passed H.R. 2975 the following day after substituting the text of H.R. 3108, 147 *Cong.Rec.* H6775–776 (daily ed. Oct. 12, 2001). The House version incorporated most of the money laundering provisions found in an earlier House bill, H.R. 3004, many of which had counterparts in S. 1510 as approved by the Senate. The House subsequently passed a clean bill, H.R. 3162 (under suspension of the rules), which resolved the differences between H.R. 2975 and S. 1510, 147 *Cong.Rec.* H7224 (daily ed. Oct. 24, 2001). The Senate agreed to the changes, 147 *Cong.Rec.* S 10969 (daily ed. Oct. 24, 2001), and H.R. 3162 was sent to the President who signed it on October 26, 2001.

This is an abbreviated versions of *The USA PATRIOT Act: A Legal Analysis*, CRS Report RL31377, stripped of its citations and footnotes.

Criminal Investigations: Tracking and Gathering Communications

Federal communications privacy law features a three-tiered system, erected for the dual purpose of protecting the confidentiality of private telephone, face-to-face, and computer communications while enabling authorities to identify and intercept criminal communications. Title III of the Omnibus Crime Control and Safe Streets Act of 1968 supplies the first level. It prohibits electronic eavesdropping on telephone conversations, face-to-face conversations, or computer and other forms of electronic communications in most instances. It does, however, give authorities a narrowly defined process for electronic surveillance to be used as a last resort in serious criminal cases. When approved by senior Justice Department officials, law enforcement officers may seek a court order authorizing them to secretly capture conversations concerning any of a statutory list of offenses (predicate offenses). Title III court orders come replete with instructions describing the permissible duration and scope of the surveillance as well as the conversations which may be seized and the efforts to be taken to minimize the seizure of innocent conversations. The court notifies the parties to any conversations seized under the order after the order expires.

Below Title III, the next tier of privacy protection covers telephone records, email held in third party storage, and the like, 18 U.S.C. 2701–2709 (Chapter 121). Here, the law permits law enforcement access, ordinarily pursuant to a warrant or court order or under a subpoena in some cases, but in connection with any criminal investigation and without the extraordinary levels of approval or constraint that mark a Title III interception.

Least demanding and perhaps least intrusive of all is the procedure that governs court orders approving the Government's use of trap and trace devices and pen registers, a kind of secret "caller ID," which identify the source and destination of calls made to and from a particular telephone, 18 U.S.C. 3121–3127 (Chapter 206). The orders are available based on the Government's certification, rather than a finding of a court, that use of the device is likely to produce information relevant to the investigation of a crime, any crime. The devices record no more than identity of the participants in a telephone conversation, but neither the orders nor the results they produce need ever be revealed to the participants.

The Act modifies the procedures at each of the three levels. It:

- permits pen register and trap and trace orders for electronic communications (for example, email)
- authorizes nationwide execution of court orders for pen registers, trap and trace devices, and access to stored email or communication records
- treats stored voice mail like stored email (rather than like telephone conversations)
- permits authorities to intercept communications to and from a trespasser within a computer system (with the permission of the system's owner)
- adds terrorist and computer crimes to Title III's predicate offense list
- reenforces protection for those who help execute Title III, ch. 121, and ch. 206 orders
- encourages cooperation between law enforcement and foreign intelligence investigators
- establishes a claim against the United States for certain communications privacy violations by Government personnel
- terminates the authority found in many of these provisions and several of the foreign intelligence amendments with a sunset provision (Dec. 31, 2005).

Foreign Intelligence Investigations

The Act eases some of the restrictions on foreign intelligence gathering within the United States, and affords the U.S. Intelligence Community greater access to information unearthed during a criminal investigation, but it also establishes and expands safeguards against official abuse. More specifically, it:

- permits "roving" surveillance (court orders omitting the identification of the particular instrument, facilities, or place where the surveillance is to occur when the court finds the target is likely to thwart identification with particularity)
- increases the number of judges on the Foreign Intelligence Surveillance Act (FISA) court from 7 to 11
- allows application for a FISA surveillance or search order when gathering foreign intelligence is *a significant* reason for the application rather than *the* reason
- authorizes pen register and trap and trace device orders for email as well as telephone conversations
- sanctions court ordered access to any tangible item rather than only business records held by lodging, car rental, and locker rental businesses
- carries a sunset provision
- establishes a claim against the United States for certain communications privacy violations by Government personnel
- expands the prohibition against FISA orders based solely on an American's exercise of his or her First Amendment rights.

Money Laundering

In Federal law, money laundering is the flow of cash or other valuables derived from, or intended to facilitate, the commission of a criminal offense. It is the movement of the fruits and instruments of crime. Federal authorities attack money laundering through regulations, criminal sanctions, and forfeiture. The Act bolsters Federal efforts in each area.

Regulation. The Act expands the authority of the Secretary of the Treasury to regulate the activities of U.S. financial institutions, particularly their relations with foreign individuals and entities. He is to promulgate regulations:

- under which securities brokers and dealers as well as commodity merchants, advisors, and pool operators must file suspicious activity reports (SARs)
- requiring businesses, which were only to report cash transactions involving more than $10,000 to the Internal Revenue Service, to file SARs as well
- imposing additional "special measures" and "due diligence" requirements to combat foreign money laundering
- prohibiting U.S. financial institutions from maintaining correspondent accounts for foreign shell banks
- preventing financial institutions from allowing their customers to conceal their financial activities by taking advantage of the institutions' concentration account practices

- establishing minimum new customer identification standards and recordkeeping and recommending an effective means to verify the identity of foreign customers
- encouraging financial institutions and law enforcement agencies to share information concerning suspected money laundering and terrorist activities
- requiring financial institutions to maintain anti–money laundering programs which must include at least a compliance officer; an employee training program; the development of internal policies, procedures, and controls; and an independent audit feature.

Crimes. The Act contains a number of new money laundering crimes, as well as amendments and increased penalties for earlier crimes. It:

- outlaws laundering (in the United States) any of the proceeds from foreign crimes of violence or political corruption
- prohibits laundering the proceeds from cybercrime or supporting a terrorist organization
- increases the penalties for counterfeiting
- seeks to overcome a Supreme Court decision finding that the confiscation of over $300,000 (for attempt to leave the country without reporting it to customs) constituted an unconstitutionally excessive fine
- provides explicit authority to prosecute overseas fraud involving American credit cards
- endeavors to permit prosecution of money laundering in the place where the predicate offense occurs.

Forfeiture. The Act creates two types of forfeitures and modifies several confiscation-related procedures. It allows confiscation of all of the property of any individual or entity that participates in or plans an act of domestic or international terrorism; it also permits confiscation of any property derived from or used to facilitate domestic or international terrorism. The Constitution's due process, double jeopardy, and ex post facto clauses may limit the anticipated breath of these provisions. Procedurally, the Act:

- establishes a mechanism to acquire long arm jurisdiction, for purposes of forfeiture proceedings, over individuals and entities
- allows confiscation of property located in this country for a wider range of crimes committed in violation of foreign law
- permits U.S. enforcement of foreign forfeiture orders
- calls for the seizure of correspondent accounts held in U.S. financial institutions for foreign banks who are in turn holding forfeitable assets overseas
- denies corporate entities the right to contest a confiscation if their principal shareholder is a fugitive.

Alien Terrorists and Victims

The Act contains a number of provisions designed to prevent alien terrorists from entering the United States, particularly from Canada; to enable authorities to detain and deport alien terrorists and those who support them; and to provide humanitarian immigration relief for foreign victims of the attacks on September 11.

Other Crimes, Penalties, and Procedures

New Crimes. The Act creates new Federal crimes for terrorist attacks on mass transportation facilities, for biological weapons offenses, for harboring terrorists, for affording terrorists material support, for misconduct associated with money laundering already mentioned, for conducting the affairs of an enterprise which affects interstate or foreign commerce through the patterned commission of terrorist offenses, and for fraudulent charitable solicitation. Although strictly speaking these are new Federal crimes, they generally supplement existing law by filling gaps and increasing penalties.

New Penalties. The Act increases the penalties for acts of terrorism and for crimes which terrorists might commit. More specifically, it establishes an alternative maximum penalty for acts of terrorism, raises the penalties for conspiracy to commit certain terrorist offenses, envisions sentencing some terrorists to life-long parole, and increases the penalties for counterfeiting, cybercrime, and charity fraud.

Other Procedural Adjustments. In other procedural adjustments designed to facilitate criminal investigations, the Act:

- increases the rewards for information in terrorism cases
- expands the Posse Comitatus Act exceptions
- authorizes "sneak and peek" search warrants
- permits nationwide and perhaps worldwide execution of warrants in terrorism cases
- eases Government access to confidential information
- allows the Attorney General to collect DNA samples from prisoners convicted of any Federal crime of violence or terrorism
- lengthens the statute of limitations applicable to crimes of terrorism
- clarifies the application of Federal criminal law on American installations and in residences of U.S. Government personnel overseas
- adjusts Federal victims' compensation and assistance programs.

A section, found in the Senate bill but ultimately dropped, would have changed the provision of Federal law which requires Justice Department prosecutors to adhere to the ethical standards of the legal profession where they conduct their activities (the McDade-Murtha Amendment), 28 U.S.C. 530B.

Charles Doyle
Senior Specialist
American Law Division
Order Code RS21203
April 18, 2002
Congressional Research Service (CRS)
    Report for Congress
Received through the CRS Web

Executive Order Strengthened Management of the Intelligence Community

By the authority vested in me as President by the Constitution and laws of the United States of America, including section 103(c)(8) of the National Security Act of 1947, as amended (Act), and in order to further strengthen the effective conduct of United States intelligence activities and protect the territory, people, and interests of the United States of America, including against terrorist attacks, it is hereby ordered as follows:

Section 1. Strengthening the Authority of the Director of Central Intelligence. The Director of Central Intelligence (Director) shall perform the functions set forth in this order to ensure an enhanced joint, unified national intelligence effort to protect the national security of the United States. Such functions shall be in addition to those assigned to the Director by law, Executive Order, or Presidential directive.

Sec. 2. Strengthened Role in National Intelligence. Executive Order 12333 of December 4, 1981, as amended, is further amended as follows:

    (a) Subsection 1.5(a) is amended to read:
        "(a)(1) Act as the principal adviser to the President for intelligence matters related to the national security;
            "(2) Act as the principal adviser to the National Security Council and Homeland Security Council for intelligence matters related to the national security; and"
    (b) Subsection 1.5(b) is amended to read:
        "(b)(1) Develop such objectives and guidance for the Intelligence Community necessary, in the Director's judgment, to ensure timely and effective collection, processing, analysis, and dissemination of intelligence, of whatever nature and from whatever source derived, concerning current and potential threats to the security of the United States and its interests,

Source: White House Website: http://www.whitehouse.gov/news/releases/2004/08/print/20040827-6.html (accessed May 20, 2005).

and to ensure that the National Foreign Intelligence Program (NFIP) is structured adequately to achieve these requirements; and

"(2) Working with the Intelligence Community, ensure that United States intelligence collection activities are integrated in:

(i) collecting against enduring and emerging national security intelligence issues;

(ii) maximizing the value to the national security; and

(iii) ensuring that all collected data is available to the maximum extent practicable for integration, analysis, and dissemination to those who can act on, add value to, or otherwise apply it to mission needs."

(c) Subsection 1.5(g) is amended to read:

"(g)(1) Establish common security and access standards for managing and handling intelligence systems, information, and products, with special emphasis on facilitating:

"(A) the fullest and most prompt sharing of information practicable, assigning the highest priority to detecting, preventing, preempting, and disrupting terrorist threats against our homeland, our people, our allies, and our interests; and

"(B) the establishment of interface standards for an interoperable information sharing enterprise that facilitates the automated sharing of intelligence information among agencies within the Intelligence Community.

"(2)(A) Establish, operate, and direct national centers with respect to matters determined by the President for purposes of this subparagraph to be of the highest national security priority, with the functions of analysis and planning (including planning for diplomatic, financial, military, intelligence, homeland security, and law enforcement activities, and integration of such activities among departments and agencies) relating to such matters.

"(B) The countering of terrorism within the United States, or against citizens of the United States, our allies, and our interests abroad, is hereby determined to be a matter of the highest national security priority for purposes of subparagraph (2)(A) of this subsection.

"(3) Ensure that appropriate agencies and departments have access to and receive all-source intelligence support needed to perform independent, alternative analysis."

(d) Subsection 1.5(m) is amended to read:

"(m)(1) Establish policies, procedures, and mechanisms that translate intelligence objectives and priorities approved by the President into specific guidance for the Intelligence Community.

"(2) In accordance with objectives and priorities approved by the President, establish collection requirements for the Intelligence Community, determine collection priorities, manage collection tasking, and resolve conflicts in the tasking of national collection assets (except when otherwise directed by the President or when the Secretary of Defense exercises collection tasking authority under plans and arrangements approved by the Secretary of Defense and the Director) of the Intelligence Community.

"(3) Provide advisory tasking concerning collection of intelligence information to elements of the United States Government that have information collection capabilities and are not organizations within the Intelligence Community.

"(4) The responsibilities in subsections 1.5(m)(2) and (3) apply, to the maximum extent consistent with applicable law, whether information is to be collected inside or outside the United States."

(e) Subsection 1.6(a) is amended to read:

"(a) The heads of all departments and agencies shall:

"(1) Unless the Director provides otherwise, give the Director access to all foreign intelligence, counter-intelligence, and national intelligence, as defined in the Act, that is relevant to transnational terrorist threats and weapons of mass destruction proliferation threats, including such relevant intelligence derived from activities of the FBI, DHS, and any other department or agency, and all other information that is related to the national security or that otherwise is required for the performance of the Director's duties, except such information that is prohibited by law, by the President, or by the Attorney General acting under this order at the direction of the President from being provided to the Director. The Attorney General shall agree to procedures with the Director pursuant to section 3(5)(B) of the Act no later than 90 days after the issuance of this order that ensure the Director receives all such information;

"(2) support the Director in developing the NFIP;

"(3) ensure that any intelligence and operational systems and architectures of their departments and agencies are consistent with national intelligence requirements set by the Director and all applicable information sharing and security guidelines, and information privacy requirements; and

"(4) provide, to the extent permitted by law, subject to the availability of appropriations, and not inconsistent with the mission of the department or agency, such further support to the Director as the Director may request, after consultation with the head of the department or agency, for the performance of the Director's functions."

Sec. 3. Strengthened Control of Intelligence Funding. Executive Order 12333 is further amended as follows:

(a) Subsections 1.5(n), (o), and (p) are amended to read as follows:

"(n)(1) Develop, determine, and present with the advice of the heads of departments or agencies that have an organization within the Intelligence Community, the annual consolidated NFIP budget. The Director shall be responsible for developing an integrated and balanced national intelligence program that is directly responsive to the national security threats facing the United States. The Director shall submit such budget (accompanied by dissenting views, if any, of the head of a department or agency that has an organization within the Intelligence Community) to the President for approval; and

"(2) Participate in the development by the Secretary of Defense of the annual budgets for the Joint Military Intelligence Program (JMIP) and the Tactical Intelligence and Related Activities (TIARA) Program.

"(o)(1) Transfer, consistent with applicable law and with the approval of the Director of the Office of Management and Budget, funds from an appropriation for the NFIP to another appropriation for the NFIP or to another NFIP component;

"(2) Review, and approve or disapprove, consistent with applicable law, any proposal to:

(i) reprogram funds within an appropriation for the NFIP;

(ii) transfer funds from an appropriation for the NFIP to an appropriation that is not for the NFIP within the Intelligence Community; or

(iii) transfer funds from an appropriation that is not for the NFIP within the Intelligence Community to an appropriation for the NFIP; and

"(3) Monitor and consult with the Secretary of Defense on reprogrammings or transfers of funds within, into, or out of, appropriations for the JMIP and the TIARA Program.

"(p)(1) Monitor implementation and execution of the NFIP budget by the heads of departments or agencies that have an organization within the Intelligence Community, including, as necessary, by conducting program and performance audits and evaluations;

"(2) Monitor implementation of the JMIP and the TIARA Program and advise the Secretary of Defense thereon; and

"(3) After consultation with the heads of relevant departments, report periodically, and not less often than semiannually, to the President on the effectiveness of implementation of the NFIP Program by organizations within the Intelligence Community, for which purpose the heads of departments and agencies shall ensure that the Director has access to programmatic, execution, and other appropriate information."

Sec. 4. Strengthened Role in Selecting Heads of Intelligence Organizations. With respect to a position that heads an organization within the Intelligence Community:

(a) if the appointment to that position is made by the head of the department or agency or a subordinate thereof, no individual shall be appointed to such position without the concurrence of the Director;

(b) if the appointment to that position is made by the President alone, any recommendation to the President to appoint an individual to that position shall be accompanied by the recommendation of the Director with respect to the proposed appointment; and

(c) if the appointment to that position is made by the President, by and with the advice and consent of the Senate, any recommendation to the President for nomination of an individual for that position shall be accompanied by the recommendation of the Director with respect to the proposed nomination.

Sec. 5. Strengthened Control of Standards and Qualifications. The Director shall issue, after coordination with the heads of departments and agencies with an organization in the Intelligence Community, and not later than 120 days after the date of this order, and thereafter as appropriate, standards and qualifications for persons engaged in the performance of United States intelligence activities, including but not limited to:

(a) standards for training, education, and career development of personnel within organizations in the Intelligence Community, and for ensuring compatible personnel policies and an integrated professional development and education system across the Intelligence Community, including standards that encourage and facilitate service in multiple organizations within the Intelligence Community and make such rotated service a factor to be considered for promotion to senior positions;

(b) standards for attracting and retaining personnel who meet the requirements for effective conduct of intelligence activities;

(c) standards for common personnel security policies among organizations within the Intelligence Community; and

(d) qualifications for assignment of personnel to centers established under section 1.5(g)(2) of Executive Order 12333, as amended by section 2 of this order.

Sec. 6. Technical Corrections. Executive Order 12333 is further amended as follows:

(a) The preamble is amended by, after "amended", inserting "(Act)".

(b) Subsection 1.3(a)(4) is amended by, after "governments", inserting "and organizations".

(c) Subsection 1.4(a) is amended by, after "needed by the President", inserting "and, in the performance of Executive functions, the Vice President,".

(d) Subsection 1.7(c) is amended by striking "the Director of Central Intelligence and" and by striking "their respective" and inserting "its".

(e) Subsection 1.8(c) is amended by, after "agreed upon", inserting "by".

(f) Subsection 1.8(i) is amended by striking "and through" and inserting in lieu thereof "through".

(g) Subsection 1.10 is amended by:

(i) striking "The Department of the Treasury. The Secretary of the Treasury shall:" and inserting in lieu thereof "The Department of the Treasury and the Department of Homeland Security. The Secretary of the Treasury, with respect to subsections (a), (b), and (c), and the Secretary of Homeland Security with respect to subsection (d), shall:";

(ii) in subparagraph (d), after "used against the President" inserting "or the Vice President"; and

(iii) in subparagraph (d), striking "the Secretary of the Treasury" both places it appears and inserting in lieu thereof in both places "the Secretary of Homeland Security".

(h) Subsection 2.4(c)(1) is amended by striking "present of former" and inserting in lieu thereof "present or former".

(i) Subsection 3.1 is amended by:

(i) striking "as provided in title 50, United States Code, section 413" and inserting in lieu thereof "implemented in accordance with applicable law, including title V of the Act"; and

(ii) striking "section 662 of the Foreign Assistance Act of 1961 as amended (22 U.S.C. 2422), and section 501 of the National Security Act of 1947, as amended (50 U.S.C. 413)," and inserting in lieu thereof "applicable law, including title V of the Act,".

(j) Subsection 3.4(b) is amended by striking "visably" and inserting in lieu thereof "visibly".

(k) Subsection 3.4(f) is amended:

(i) after "agencies within the Intelligence Community", by inserting ", or organizations within the Intelligence Community";

(ii) in paragraph (8), by striking "Those" and inserting in lieu thereof "The intelligence elements of the Coast Guard and those"; and

(iii) by striking the "and" at the end of paragraph (7), striking the period at the end of paragraph (8) and inserting in lieu thereof "; and", and adding at the end thereof "(9) National Geospatial-Intelligence Agency".

Sec. 7. General Provisions.

(a) This order and the amendments made by this order:

(i) shall be implemented in a manner consistent with applicable law and subject to the availability of appropriations;

(ii) shall be implemented in a manner consistent with the authority of the principal officers of the executive departments as heads of their respective departments, including under section 199 of the Revised Statutes (22 U.S.C. 2651), section 201 of the Department of Energy Reorganization Act (42 U.S.C. 7131), section 102(a) of the Homeland Security Act of 2002 (6 U.S.C. 112(a)), and sections 301 of title 5, 113(b) and 162(b) of title 10, 503 of title 28, and 301(b) of title 31, United States Code; and

(iii) shall not be construed to impair or otherwise affect the functions of the Director of the Office of Management and Budget relating to budget, administrative, and legislative proposals.

(b) Nothing in section 4 of this order limits or otherwise affects—

(i) the appointment of an individual to a position made before the date of this order; or

(ii) the power of the President as an appointing authority to terminate an appointment.

(c) Nothing in this order shall be construed to impair or otherwise affect any authority to provide intelligence to the President, the Vice President in the performance of Executive functions, and other officials in the executive branch.

(d) This order and amendments made by this order are intended only to improve the internal management of the Federal Government and are not intended to, and do not, create any rights or benefits, substantive or procedural, enforceable at law or in equity by a party against the United States, its departments, agencies, instrumentalities, or entities, its officers, employees, or agents, or any other person.

GEORGE W. BUSH
THE WHITE HOUSE,
August 27, 2004

Summary of Intelligence Reform and Terrorism Prevention Act of 2004

December 6, 2004

TITLE I

Director of National Intelligence

There is established a Senate-confirmed Director of National Intelligence (DNI) who shall not also serve as the Director of the Central Intelligence Agency (CIA) or as the head of any other element of the intelligence community. The DNI shall not be located in the Executive Office of the President.

National Intelligence Program

The National Foreign Intelligence Program is redesignated as the National Intelligence Program (NIP).

Authorities of the DNI

Budget Build

The DNI shall "develop and determine" an annual budget for the National Intelligence Program (NIP) budget based on budget proposals provided by the heads of agencies and organizations of the intelligence community and their respective department heads. The heads of such agencies and organizations must also provide to the DNI such other information as the DNI requests for the purpose of determining the NIP budget.

Budget Execution

The DNI shall "ensure the effective execution" of the annual budget for intelligence and intelligence-related activities. The Director of OMB must apportion NIP funds at the "exclusive direction" of the DNI for allocation to the elements of the intelligence community. The DNI is further responsible for managing NIP appropriations

Source: This document was accessed at the Senate Homeland Security and Government Affairs Website: http://hsgac .senate.gov/_files/ConferenceReportSummary.doc.

by "directing the allotment or allocation" of such appropriations through the heads of departments containing agencies or organizations of the intelligence community. Department comptrollers must allot, allocate, reprogram, or transfer NIP funds "in an expeditious manner."

The DNI "shall monitor the implementation and execution of the National Intelligence Program by the heads of elements of the intelligence community" that manage NIP programs or activities, including with audits and evaluations. The DNI shall report to the President and to Congress within 15 days of learning that a department comptroller has acted in a manner that is inconsistent with the direction of the DNI in carrying out the NIP.

Transfer and Reprogramming of Funds

NIP funds may not be transferred or reprogrammed without approval of the DNI, except in accordance with procedures prescribed by the DNI. All transfers or reprogrammings by the DNI (1) must be for a higher priority intelligence activity; (2) must support an emergent need, improve program effectiveness, or increase efficiency; and (3) may not involve funds from the CIA Reserve for Contingencies or a DNI Reserve for Contingencies. With approval from OMB and after consulting with affected department heads, the DNI may transfer or reprogram NIP funds out of any department or agency as long as the amount in a single fiscal year is less than $150 million, is less than 5% of the department's or agency's NIP funds, and does not terminate an acquisition program. These limits would not apply if the DNI obtains the concurrence of the affected department head.

Transfer of Personnel

In the fiscal year after the effective date of the Act, the DNI (1) is authorized 500 new personnel billets within the Office of the DNI, and (2) may, with the approval of the OMB director, transfer 150 personnel funded within the NIP to the Office of the DNI for not more than 2 years.

For the first 12 months after a national intelligence center is created, the DNI may transfer 100 personnel authorized for elements of the intelligence community to that center. The DNI must receive the approval of the director of OMB and notify appropriate Congressional committees of such transfers. In accordance with procedures developed between the DNI and the heads of departments and agencies concerned, and upon approval of the director of OMB, the DNI may also transfer unlimited numbers of personnel authorized for an element of the intelligence community to another such element for a period of not more than two years. The DNI may only make such transfer if the personnel are being transferred to an activity that is a higher priority intelligence activity, and the transfer supports an emergent need, improves program effectiveness, or increases efficiency. The DNI must notify appropriate Congressional committees of such transfers.

It is the Sense of the Congress that 21st Century national security threats continue to challenge the intelligence community to respond rapidly and flexibly to bring analytic resources to bear, that the Office of the DNI and any analytic centers should be fully supported with appropriate personnel levels, and the President should utilize all legal and administrative discretion to ensure that the DNI and the intelligence community have the necessary resources and procedures to meet emerging threats.

Tasking and Analysis

The DNI establishes objectives and priorities for the intelligence community and manages and directs tasking of collection, analysis, production, and dissemination of national intelligence. The DNI approves requirements for collection and analysis, including requirements responding to the needs of consumers. The DNI also provides advisory tasking to intelligence elements outside of the NIP. The DNI may establish national intelligence centers as the DNI determines necessary. To ensure accurate all-source intelligence, the DNI must implement policies and procedures to, among other things, ensure competitive analysis and that alternative views are brought to the attention of policymakers.

Personnel Management

The DNI, in consultation with the heads of other agencies or elements of the intelligence community, develops personnel policies and programs to enhance the capacity for joint operation and facilitate staffing of community management functions. An individual's service in more than one element of the intelligence community would be a condition of promotion to certain positions. The policies shall not be inconsistent with those applicable to uniformed services personnel.

In addition, the NID will prescribe regulations to provide incentives for service on the staff of the DNI, the national intelligence centers, NCTC, or other positions in support of the intelligence community management functions. It is the Sense of the Congress that policies to facilitate the rotation of personnel should seek to duplicate within the intelligence community the joint officer management policies established by the Goldwater-Nichols Department of Defense Reorganization Act of 1986 and the amendments on joint officer management made by that Act. Assignment of commissioned officers to the Office of the DNI will be considered joint-duty assignments for the purposes of the amendments on Department of Defense joint officer management made by the Goldwater-Nichols Department of Defense Reorganization Act of 1986.

The DNI has the same personnel authorities over employees of the Office of the DNI that the Director of Central Intelligence has under current law with respect to CIA employees. Employees and applicants for employment of the Office of the DNI have the same rights and protections as CIA employees under current law.

Protection of Sources and Methods/Classification

The DNI shall protect sources and methods from unauthorized disclosure and, in order to maximize the dissemination of intelligence, establish and implement guidelines for classification under applicable law, Executive orders, or Presidential directives.

Foreign Liaison

The DNI shall oversee the coordination of relationships with the intelligence or security services of foreign governments or international organizations.

Acquisition/Milestone

The DNI has the same acquisition and appropriation authorities given to the CIA Director in the CIA Act of 1949 except for that Act's section 8(b), which allows the CIA Director to expend sums made available to the CIA without regard to any of the laws or regulations relating to the expenditure of government funds. The DNI also has the same authority as the CIA Director to waive provisions of the Federal Property and Administrative Services Act of 1949. The DNI has exclusive milestone decision authority for NIP-funded major systems, except that with respect to Department of Defense programs the DNI has joint authority with the Secretary of Defense. If the DNI and the Secretary of Defense are unable to reach agreement on a milestone decision, the President resolves the conflict.

Common Services

The DNI shall, in consultation with department heads, coordinate the performance by elements of the intelligence community of services of common concern to the intelligence community that the DNI determines can be more efficiently accomplished in a consolidated manner.

Appointments

The DNI shall recommend to the President nominees for Principal Deputy DNI and for CIA Director. The DNI has the right to concur in the appointment or the recommendation for nomination of the heads of NSA, NRO, and NGA; the Assistant Secretary of State for INR; the Directors of the Offices of Intelligence and Counterintelligence at DOE; the Assistant Secretary for Intelligence and Analysis at the Department of the Treasury; the Executive Assistant Director for Intelligence of the FBI; and the Assistant Secretary of Homeland Security for Information Analysis. The DNI must be consulted for appointments or recommendations for the Director of DIA and the Deputy Assistant Commandant of the Coast Guard for Intelligence.

Office of the DNI

Staff

The DNI shall employ and utilize a professional staff in the Office of the DNI. That staff includes the Community Management Staff, which will be transferred to the Office of the DNI.

Co-Location

Commencing October 1, 2008, the Office of the DNI shall not be co-located with any other element of the intelligence community.

Deputy Directors

There shall be a Senate-confirmed Principal Deputy DNI, recommended by the DNI and appointed by the President, who shall not simultaneously serve in any other capacity in the intelligence community. The Principal Deputy DNI shall assist the DNI and serve in the absence or disability of the DNI, who may also appoint not more than four additional Deputies with such duties, responsibilities, and authorities as the DNI may assign. The DNI and the Principal Deputy may not both be commissioned officers in active status, but it is the sense of Congress that one of them should be an active duty officer, or at least have by training or experience an appreciation of military intelligence activities and requirements.

National Intelligence Council

The National Intelligence Council is established in the Office of the DNI.

General Counsel

There is established a Senate-confirmed General Counsel in the Office of the DNI, who may not simultaneously serve as the General Counsel of any other department or agency.

Civil Liberties Protection Officer

The DNI shall appoint a Civil Liberties Protection Officer.

Director of Science and Technology

There is established a Director of Science and Technology in the Office of the DNI.

National Counterintelligence Executive

The National Counterintelligence Executive is moved to the Office of the DNI.

Inspector General

The DNI is authorized to establish an Inspector General in the Office of the DNI.

Definition of National Intelligence

The bill defines national intelligence to include information gathered in the U.S. or abroad that pertains to more than one agency and involves threats to the U.S., its people, property, or interests; the development, proliferation, or use of weapons of mass destruction; or any other matter bearing on national or homeland security.

Information Sharing

The 9/11 Commission found that the biggest impediment to a greater likelihood of "connecting the dots" was the resistance to information sharing, and recommended a new, government-wide approach to information sharing. This section addresses this recommendation by requiring the President to establish an Information Sharing Environment (ISE) to facilitate the sharing of terrorism information among all appropriate Federal, State, local, tribal and private sector entities, through the use of policy guidelines and technologies.

The section provides for a staged development process, with periodic reporting. Within 180 days of enactment, a review must be conducted of current agency capabilities; in addition, a description of the technological, legal, and policy issues presented by the creation of the ISE, and how they will be addressed, must be submitted to the President and Congress. Within 270 days, the President is required to issue guidelines for acquiring, accessing, sharing, and using information, and, in consultation with the Privacy and Civil Liberties Oversight Board established elsewhere in the bill, guidelines to protect privacy and civil liberties in the development and use of the ISE. Within a year, an implementation plan for the ISE must be submitted to Congress. Finally, in two years, and annually thereafter, the President must submit a report to Congress on the state of the ISE and of information sharing across the Federal Government.

The President is also required to designate a Program Manager who [is] responsible for information sharing across the Federal Government and who is to oversee the implementation of, and manage, the ISE. The Program Manager is to serve for two years, during the planning and initial implementation of the ISE; after that, recommendations are to be made for the future management structure of the ISE. During the initial two-year start up period, this section also establishes an interagency panel, based on the Information Sharing Council created by Executive Order 13356, to advise the President and Program Manager and to facilitate interagency coordination in the development and implementation of the ISE.

Privacy and Civil Liberties

Privacy and Civil Liberties Oversight Board

This section creates a Privacy and Civil Liberties Oversight Board within the Executive Office of the President that would ensure that privacy and civil liberties concerns are appropriately considered in the implementation of laws, regulations, and executive branch policies related to efforts to protect the Nation against terrorism. The Board's responsibilities encompass both advice and counsel and oversight and would include reviewing regulations and policies, including information sharing guidelines, and providing advice to the President and departments and agencies in the Executive branch. The Board would be required to report at least annually to Congress on its major activities.

The Board would be composed of a chairman, vice chairman, and three other members appointed by the President. The chairman and vice chairman would be Senate-confirmed and the chairman may serve on a full-time basis. All members would serve at the pleasure of the President.

In order to carry out its responsibilities, the Board is authorized to have access to information from departments and agencies. If the requested information is necessary to withhold to protect national security interests, as determined by the National Intelligence Director, in consultation with the Attorney General, or sensitive law enforcement, counterterrorism or ongoing operations, as determined by the Attorney General, the information may be withheld. The Board is also authorized to make written requests to persons outside of government to produce information, documents and other evidence. If the person to whom such a request does not comply within 45 days, the Board is authorized to notify the Attorney General and the Attorney General, in his discretion, could take such steps as are appropriate to ensure compliance with the request.

Sense of the Congress on the Designation of Privacy and Civil Liberties Officers

This section is a Sense of the Congress that each Executive department or agency with law enforcement or anti-terrorism functions should designate a privacy and civil liberties officer.

Analysis

Alternative Analysis

Not later than 180 days after the effective date of the Act, the DNI shall establish a process and assign an individual or entity the responsibility of ensuring that elements of the intelligence community conduct alternative analysis as appropriate. Not later than 270 days after the effective date of the Act, the DNI must submit a report to the Congressional intelligence committees concerning implementation.

Safeguarding Objectivity in Intelligence Analysis

Not later than 180 days after the effective date of this Act, the DNI shall identify an individual within the Office of the DNI who shall be available to analysts within the Office of the Director of National Intelligence to counsel, conduct arbitration, offer recommendations, and, as appropriate, initiate inquiries into real or perceived problems of analytic tradecraft or politicization, biased reporting, or lack of objectivity in intelligence analysis. Not later than 270 days after the effective date of this Act, the DNI shall provide a report to the Congressional intelligence committees on implementation.

Analytic Integrity

Not later than 180 days after the date of the enactment of this Act, the DNI shall assign an individual or entity to be responsible for ensuring that finished intelligence products produced by any element or elements of the intelligence community are timely, objective, independent of political considerations, based upon all sources of available intelligence, and employ the standards of proper analytic tradecraft.

The individual or entity assigned responsibility shall perform, on a regular basis, detailed reviews of finished intelligence product or other analytic products by an element or elements of the intelligence community covering a particular topic or subject matter; and shall be responsible for identifying on an annual basis functional or topical areas of analysis for specific reviews. Each review should include, among other things, whether the product or products concerned were based on all sources of available intelligence, properly describe the quality and reliability of underlying sources, properly caveat and express uncertainties or confidence in analytic judgments, and properly distinguish between underlying intelligence and the assumptions and judgments of analysts. Not later than December 1 each year, the DNI shall submit to the Congressional intelligence committees and other entities a report containing a description and the associated findings of each review.

Preservation of Authorities

The bill provides that the President shall issue guidelines to ensure effective implementation of the authorities provided to the DNI in a manner that respects and does not abrogate the statutory responsibilities of the Director of OMB and the heads of Executive branch departments.

National Counterterrorism Center

The National Counterterrorism Center (NCTC) is established in the Office of the DNI. The Director of the NCTC is Senate-confirmed and may not simultaneously serve in any other capacity in the executive branch. The Director of the NCTC reports to the DNI on budget and intelligence matters, but to the President on the planning and progress of joint counterterrorism operations (other than intelligence operations). The NCTC will conduct "strategic operational planning," which is defined to include the mission, the objectives to be achieved, the tasks to be performed, interagency coordination of operational activities, and the assignment of roles and responsibilities. The NCTC Director shall monitor the implementation of strategic operational plans and shall obtain relevant information from departments and agencies on the progress of such entities in implementing the plans.

National Counterproliferation Center

The President shall establish a National Counterproliferation Center (NCPC) not later than 18 months after the date of enactment. The President may waive this requirement if the President determines that it does not materially improve the government's ability to halt the proliferation of weapons of mass destruction. Such a waiver shall be made in writing and it must be submitted to Congress.

National Intelligence Centers

The DNI is authorized to establish national intelligence centers to address intelligence priorities, such as regional issues. These centers shall have primary responsibility, in their areas of intelligence responsibility, for providing all-source analysis and for identifying and proposing to the DNI intelligence collection and production requirements. The DNI shall ensure that the centers have sufficient personnel and that the intelligence community shares information in order to facilitate their mission. Each center shall have a separate budget account.

Joint Intelligence Community Council

There is established a Joint Intelligence Community Council (JICC), chaired by the DNI, which is composed of the Secretaries of State, Treasury, Defense, Energy, and Homeland Security, as well as the Attorney General and such other officers as the President may designate. The JICC shall assist the DNI by advising on budget and other matters and by ensuring the timely execution of the programs, policies, and directives of the DNI.

Education and Training

The DNI develops a comprehensive education, recruitment, and training plan to meet the linguistic requirements for the intelligence community. The DNI is further responsible for establishing an integrated framework that brings together the educational components of the intelligence community to promote joint education and training. Finally, the DNI establishes an Intelligence Community Scholarship Program, to provide college scholarships for students in exchange for service within the intelligence community.

Open Source Intelligence

The DNI shall ensure that the intelligence community makes efficient and effective use of open source information and analysis. It is the Sense of Congress that the

DNI should establish an intelligence center for the purpose of coordinating the collection, analysis, production, and dissemination of open source intelligence, and the DNI must report to Congress on this matter.

Effective Date/Implementation Plan

Title I shall take effect not later than six months after enactment. The President shall submit to Congress an implementation plan not later than 180 days after the effective date. Not later than 60 days after the appointment of the initial DNI, the DNI shall appoint individuals to positions within the Office of the DNI.

"Lookback" Provision

Not later than one year after the effective date of the Act, the DNI shall submit to the Congressional intelligence committees a report on the progress being made to implement this title and such recommendations for additional legislative or administrative action as the DNI considers appropriate.

TITLE II

Federal Bureau of Investigation

Improvement of FBI Intelligence Capabilities

The FBI will improve its intelligence capabilities through the development of a national intelligence workforce. The FBI Office of Intelligence shall be redesignated the Directorate of Intelligence.

Personnel Authorities

The FBI Director is given greater flexibility in establishing analyst positions and corresponding rates of pay. The FBI is given additional authority to raise the mandatory retirement age to 65 years of age for up to 50 FBI employees per fiscal year through September 30, 2007.

Federal Bureau of Investigation Reserve Service

The FBI has discretionary authority to establish and train a reserve service for the temporary reemployment of up to 500 former employees of the Bureau during periods of emergency. Reserve members are not subject to a reduction in annuity.

Use of Translators

The Attorney General will submit annual reports to the Judiciary Committees of the House and Senate regarding the Department of Justice's translator program.

TITLE III

Security Clearances

The President designates a single entity to oversee the security clearance process and develop uniform standards and policies for access to classified information. The President also designates a single entity to conduct clearance investigations. Additional investigative agencies could be designated if appropriate for national security and efficiency purposes. Reciprocity among clearances at the same level is required.

A national database is established to track clearances. The head of the entity selected to oversee the security clearance process evaluates and reports to Congress on the use of available technology in clearance investigations and adjudications. The head of the entity is further responsible for consulting with Congress and adjudicative agencies to develop a plan to reduce the length of the security clearance process within five years.

TITLE IV—TRANSPORTATION SECURITY

Subtitle A—National Strategy for Transportation Security

This section implements key 9/11 Commission recommendations with respect to transportation security by requiring that the Secretary of Homeland Security develop and implement a national strategy for transportation security.

Subtitle B—Aviation Security

These sections implement 9/11 Commission recommendations to improve passenger prescreening (including improved use of the "no fly" and "automatic selectee" lists), and to ensure that these watchlists do not violate privacy or civil liberties. It also implements a recommendation to give priority attention to screening passengers and their bags for explosives.

This subtitle also directs the Transportation Security Administration to develop a plan for implementing improved explosives detection equipment. Other provisions help protect air marshals, improve performance of airport screeners, and enhance in-line baggage screening. Additional provisions improve pilot licenses, general aviation security, biometric technology, and technology to protect against shoulder fired missiles.

Subtitle C—Air Cargo Security

Pursuant to a general 9/11 Commission recommendation to improve air cargo security, this subtitle requires the Transportation Security Administration to develop better technologies for air cargo security, authorizes funding for equipment and research and development, requires the Department finalize its air cargo regulations within 8 months, and requires a pilot program to evaluate the use of currently available and next generation blast-resistant containers.

Subtitle D—Maritime Security

This subtitle directs the Transportation Security Administration to begin screening passengers and crew of cruise ships against comprehensive consolidated terrorist databases within 180 days. It also requires certain maritime-security plans, reports, and assessments to be completed in a timely manner.

Title V—BORDER PROTECTION, IMMIGRATION, AND VISA MATTERS

Subtitle A—Advanced Technology Northern Border Security Pilot Program

This subtitle permits the Secretary of Homeland Security to carry out a pilot program to test advanced technologies that will improve border security between ports of entry along the northern border of the U.S., requires a report to Congress, and authorizes appropriation of such sums as may be necessary to carry out the pilot program. Among the program's features would be the use of advanced technology for border surveillance, and operation in remote stretches along the border with long distances between 24-hour ports of entry and a relatively small presence of border patrol agents.

Subtitle B—Border and Immigration Enforcement

Border Surveillance

This section requires the Secretary of Homeland Security to submit to the President and Congress a plan for the systematic surveillance of the southwest border of the U.S. by remotely piloted aircraft, and to implement such plan as a pilot program. Among the missions of this program would be the interdiction of the illegal movement of people, weapons, and other contraband across the border, and assisting in the dismantling of smuggling and criminal networks along the border. This section also authorizes the appropriation of such sums as may be necessary to carry out this provision.

Increase in Full-Time Border Patrol Agents

This section requires the Secretary of Homeland Security, in each of fiscal years 2006 through 2010, to increase the numbers of border patrol agents by not less than 2,000, subject to available appropriations. In addition, this provision would require a number of agents equaling at least 20% of each year's increase in agents to be assigned to the northern border.

Increase in Full-Time Immigration and Customs Enforcement Investigators

This section requires the Secretary of Homeland Security, in each of the fiscal years 2006 through 2010, to increase the numbers of Immigration and Customs Enforcement investigators by not less than 800, subject to available appropriations.

Increase in Detention Bed Space

This section requires the Department of Homeland Security, in each of the fiscal years 2006 through 2010, to increase the number of beds available for immigration detention and removal operations by not less than 8,000, subject to available appropriations. It would also require the Secretary to give priority for the use of these additional beds to the detention of those charged with removability under section 237(a)(4) or inadmissibility under section 212(a)(3) of the Immigration and Nationality Act.

Subtitle C—Visa Requirements

In-Person Interviews of Visa Applicants

This section requires an in-person consular interview of most applicants for nonimmigrant visas between the ages of 14 and 79. It includes certain waivers that may be granted by consular officials or the Secretary of State.

Visa Application Requirements

This section requires an alien applying for a nonimmigrant visa to completely and accurately respond to any request for information contained in the application.

Revocation of Visas and Other Travel Documentation

This section makes the revocation of a nonimmigrant visa by the State Department grounds for removal. The visa revocation would be reviewable in a removal proceeding where the revocation provided the sole ground for removal.

Subtitle D—Immigration Reform

Bringing in and Harboring Certain Aliens

This section increases criminal penalties for alien smuggling and requires the Secretary of DHS to develop an outreach program in the U.S. and abroad to educate the public about the penalties for illegally bringing in and harboring aliens.

Deportation of Aliens Who Have Received Military-Type Training from Terrorist Organizations

This section renders deportable any alien who has received military training from or on behalf of an organization that, at the time of training, was a designated terrorist organization.

Study and Report on Terrorists in the Asylum System

This section requires the General Accounting Office to conduct a study evaluating the extent to which weaknesses in U.S. asylum system could be exploited by terrorists.

Subtitle E—Treatment of Aliens Who Commit Acts of Torture, Extrajudicial Killings, or Other Atrocities Abroad

Inadmissibility and Deportability of Aliens Who Have Committed Acts of Torture or Extrajudicial Killings Abroad

This section renders inadmissible and deportable any alien who has ordered, incited, assisted, or participated in conduct that would be considered genocide under U.S. law, and any alien who committed or participated in an act of torture or extrajudicial killing.

Inadmissibility and Deportability of Foreign Government Officials Who Have Committed Particularly Severe Violations of Religious Freedom

This section renders inadmissible and deportable any alien who, while serving as a foreign official, was responsible for or directly carried out, at any time, particularly severe violations of religious freedom.

Waiver of Inadmissibility

This section amends the waivers of inadmissibility for aliens who have participated in Nazi persecution, genocide, or the commission of any act of torture or extrajudicial killing.

Bar to Good Moral Character for Aliens Who Have Committed Acts of Torture, Extrajudicial Killings, or Severe Violations of Religious Freedom

This section prevents a finding of good moral character with respect to any alien who is inadmissible for having participated in genocide, torture, extrajudicial killing, or particularly severe violations of religious freedom.

Establishment of the Office of Special Investigations

This section creates within the Criminal Division of the Department of Justice an Office of Special Investigations to detect, investigate, and take legal action to denaturalize any alien who is inadmissible for having participated in genocide, torture, or extrajudicial killing.

Report on Implementation

This section requires the Attorney General, in consultation with the Secretary of Homeland Security, to submit to the House and Senate Judiciary Committees a report on the implementation of this subtitle.

TITLE VI—TERRORISM PREVENTION

Subtitle A—Individual Terrorists as Agents of Foreign Powers ("Lone Wolf" Provision)

Sec. 6001 authorizes the issuance of warrants under the Foreign Intelligence Surveillance Act of 1978 (FISA) for individuals involved in international terrorism, but not affiliated with a known terrorist group. The authority is subject to a sunset at the end of 2005.

Sec. 6002 requires semiannual reports by the Attorney General to the House and Senate Committees on Intelligence and Judiciary regarding the number of persons targeted for FISA orders allowing electronic surveillance, searches, and access to records; the frequency of use of information in criminal proceedings; and summaries of significant legal interpretations of the Act and copies of decisions of FISA courts. Such reports are to be submitted in a manner consistent with the protection of the national security.

Subtitle B—Money Laundering and Terrorist Financing

This section authorizes funding for a series of technology enhancements to improve the data maintained by the Department of Treasury's Financial Crimes Enforcement Network (FinCEN), while reducing compliance burdens on financial institutions. It also reauthorizes the National Money Laundering Strategy and the Financial Crime-Free Communities Support Program.

Subtitle C—Money Laundering Abatement and Financial Antiterrorism Technical Corrections

This subtitle makes a number of technical corrections to the USA PATRIOT Act. It also makes permanent the provisions of title III of the USA PATRIOT Act, which include only provisions related to money laundering and financial transactions, by repealing section 303 of the Act, which provides that the provisions of title III will terminate after September 30, 2004, if both Houses of Congress enact a joint resolution to that effect.

Subtitle D—Additional Enforcement Tools

This subtitle contains miscellaneous additional financial tools to combat terrorism. For instance, it authorizes the Secretary of the Treasury to produce currency and other security documents at the request of foreign governments. It directs the

Secretary of Treasury to prescribe regulations requiring the reporting to FinCEN of certain cross-border transmittals of funds relevant to the Department of Treasury's anti-money laundering and anti-terrorist financing efforts. It requires a report from the Secretary of Treasury regarding U.S. efforts to combat terrorism financing. It contains a provision that restricts federal examiners of financial institutions, for one-year upon leaving the Federal Government, from accepting compensation for employment from a financial institution for which the examiner had responsibility for examining.

Subtitle E—Criminal History Background Checks

PROTECT Act

Sec. 6401 extends for 12 months a pilot program for criminal history background checks on volunteers at mentoring groups.

Criminal History Background Checks

Sec. 6402 establishes a mechanism by which authorized employers of security guards can request criminal history background checks of employees using existing State identification bureaus.

Sec. 6403 requires the Attorney General to report to the Committees on Judiciary of the House and Senate regarding criminal history record checks that are statutorily required to be conducted by the Department of Justice. The AG is to make recommendations for improving, standardizing, and consolidating existing background check programs for non-criminal justice purposes.

Subtitle F—Grand Jury Information Sharing

Sec. 6501 allows the sharing of grand jury information about terrorist threats with state, local, tribal, and foreign government officials. This provision, originally enacted as part of the Homeland Security Act, did not take effect due to the failure to take account of changes made to the grand jury rules by the Supreme Court. It also allows the disclosure of grand jury information to a foreign court or prosecutor for use in an official criminal investigation.

Subtitle G—Providing Material Support to Terrorism

The first section in this subtitle makes it illegal to knowingly receive military-type training from a designated foreign terrorist organization. In order to be prosecuted for this offense, a person must have knowledge that the terrorist group is so designated or that it engages in terrorist activity or terrorism, as defined by statute.

The second section in this subtitle makes a number of changes to the statutes prohibiting the provision of material support to terrorists and designated foreign terrorist organizations. Key changes include:

- The changes made to current law by this section are subject to a sunset date of December 31, 2006.
- It clarifies the definitions of several types of material support—training, personnel, and expert advice or assistance—in order to respond to rulings by the U.S. Court of Appeals for the Ninth Circuit. Also in response to the Ninth Circuit's concerns that "training" and "expert advice or assistance" could in-

clude constitutionally-protected speech, this provides that nothing in the section can be construed to abridge rights protected under the Constitution.

- This provision also clarifies current law's requirement that the defendant knowingly provide material support to a designated foreign terrorist organization. This provision makes it clear that under this section, the defendant must know that the organization has been designated as an foreign terrorist organization by the Secretary of State, or that it engages in the type of terrorist activity that can cause an organization to be designated.
- This provision also includes a provision allowing a person to apply to the Secretary of State, acting in concurrence with the Attorney General, for a waiver in order to provide personnel, training, or expert advice or assistance to a designated foreign terrorist organization. The Secretary of State cannot grant the waiver if any of the material support may be used to carry out terrorist activities.

The third section in this subtitle makes two changes to the statute prohibiting terrorist financing. First, it ensures that the concealment of the proceeds of funds can be prosecuted, in addition to the concealment of the funds themselves. Second, it modifies the statute so that it is criminal to conceal funds when they are to be used to support terrorism, in addition to when they have been used to support terrorism.

Subtitle H—Terrorist and Military Hoaxes

The first section of this subtitle establishes criminal penalties for hoaxes relating to terrorism, or the death or disappearance of a member of the Armed Services during a war. A violation of either offense is punishable up to 5 years in prison. If serious injury results from the hoax, the defendant may be imprisoned up to 20 years, and if death results, the defendant may be imprisoned up to life in prison.

The second section of this subtitle increases the maximum penalties for obstruction of justice and false statements in terrorism cases from 5 years to 8 years in prison.

The third section of this subtitle makes a technical amendment affecting the statute prohibiting acts of terrrorism transcending national boundaries. Federal jurisdiction over such crimes exists, among other cases, when any facility of interstate or foreign commerce is used in the offense. However, the definition of "facility of interstate or foreign commerce" is unclear as to whether facilities of foreign commerce are truly covered. This provision would make it clear that they are covered.

Subtitle I—Weapons of Mass Destruction Prohibition Improvement Act

Sec. 6802 expands Federal jurisdiction over crimes involving weapons of mass destruction and re-establishes chemical weapons as weapons of mass destruction.

Sec. 6803 provides that a person who participates in or provides material support to a nuclear weapons or weapons of mass destruction program of a foreign terrorist organization is subject to imprisonment for up to 20 years. Makes possession, attempt to possess, or conspiracy to posses a radiological weapon subject to imprisonment for a period of a term of years, up to life.

Subtitle J—Prevention of Terrorist Access to Destructive Weapons Act of 2004

Sec. 6903 strengthens penalties for the production, possession, and use of missile system designed to destroy aircraft. It establishes a fine of up to $2 million, mandatory minimum penalties of not less than 25 years for; and life imprisonment if death of another results from violation of the prohibitions.

Sec. 6904 strengthens penalties for the production, possession, and use of atomic weapons. It establishes a fine of up to $2 million; a mandatory minimum penalty of 25 years; and life imprisonment if death of another results from a violation of the prohibitions.

Sec. 6905 strengthens penalties for the production, possession, and use of radiological dispersal devices. It establishes a fine of up to $2 million; a mandatory minimum penalty of 25 years; and life imprisonment if death of another results from a violation of the section's prohibitions.

Sec. 6906 strengthens penalties for the production, possession, and use of the variola virus. It establishes a fine of up to $2 million; a mandatory minimum penalty of 25 years; and life imprisonment if death of another results from a violation of the sections's prohibitions.

Sec. 6907 adds the offenses described in Sec. 6903–6906 to the offenses for which wire taps can be authorized.

Sec. 6908 adds the offenses contained in Sec. 6903–6909 to the crimes listed in the definition of "Federal crime of terrorism" contained in 18 U.S.C. 2332b(g)(5)(B).

Sec. 6909 adds to the crimes identified in Sec. 6903–6906 to the list of predicate crimes for the crimes of money laundering and providing material support or resources to designated foreign terrorist organizations

Sec. 6910 amends the Arms Export Control Act by adding the crimes listed in Sec. 6903–6906 to the crimes for which individuals who are convicted or indicted can be denied export licenses.

Subtitle K—Pretrial Detention of Terrorists

This provision adds federal crimes of terrorism punishable by more than 10 years in prison to the list of offenses that are subject to a rebuttable presumption of pretrial detention. The defendant would be able to obtain bail if he could show the judge that he was not a flight risk or a danger to the community. A similar presumption exists for federal drug crimes punishable by more than 10 years in prison, and certain other crimes.

TITLE VII—9/11 COMMISSION IMPLEMENTATION ACT OF 2004

Subtitle A—The Role of Diplomacy, Foreign Aid, and the Military in the War on Terrorism

This subtitle reflects and implements 9/11 Commission recommendations regarding the importance of using all elements of national power, including diplomacy, military action, intelligence, covert action, law enforcement, economic policy, foreign aid, public diplomacy, and homeland defense to win the war on terrorism. It includes findings and a Sense of Congress on the role of terrorist sanctuaries in providing support for terrorist operations and the need to identify terrorist sanctuaries and develop and implement a strategy to eliminate such sanctuaries. It includes a provision that would amend the Export Administration Act to include a government's actions to prevent and eliminate terrorist sanctuaries as a criterion for the licensing for export of sensitive dual-use technology to that country. It also amends current law to ensure that the State Department Patterns of Global Terrorism reports include assessments of the actions countries have taken to prevent their territories from being used as terrorist sanctuaries.

This subtitle includes findings regarding Pakistan's role in countering the growth of terrorism, and a Sense of Congress that the United States should make a long-term commitment to ensuring a stable and secure future in Pakistan, as long as its leaders remain committed to combating extremists, with a range of assistance to Pakistan. It includes language extending the ability of the President to waive foreign assistance restrictions on Pakistan for fiscal years 2005 and 2006.

This subtitle includes a series of provisions entitled the "Afghanistan Freedom Support Act Amendments of 2004" designed to provide flexibility to United States assistance to Afghanistan. Among other things, these provisions amend the Afghanistan Freedom Support Act of 2002 to make permanent a Coordinator for Assistance for Afghanistan, authorize the Coordinator to support and develop education, the rule of law, democratic and cultural institutions in Afghanistan, and repeal the current law prohibiting assistance to Afghanistan. It authorizes such sums as may be necessary to the President for each fiscal year from FY2005–FY2009 to provide assistance to Afghanistan.

The subtitle includes findings regarding the need to strengthen the relationship and dialogue between the United States and Saudi Arabia. It includes findings regarding the need to combat the stereotypes of the U.S. in the Muslim world and a Sense of Congress that the Government of the United States should offer an example of moral leadership in the world that includes a commitment to treat all people humanely and encourage reform, freedom, democracy, and moderation in the Islamic world.

The subtitle recognizes the importance of integrating public diplomacy into the planning and execution of foreign policy. It requires an annual strategic plan be prepared and implemented for public diplomacy policies. The conference report calls for the Foreign Service to recruit individuals with expertise and professional experience in public diplomacy, and to emphasize the importance of public diplomacy skills and techniques in Foreign Service training. It also requires Foreign Service promotion boards to consider whether a Foreign Service Officer has demonstrated public diplomacy skills.

The subtitle includes provisions encouraging the President and the Secretary of State to support and expand the work of the United Nations democracy caucus, and to undertake reform of membership in United Nations bodies and other multilateral institutions. It directs the State Department to require multilateral diplomacy training for Foreign Service Officers and civil service employees.

The subtitle authorizes the President to expand international exchange programs and calls for a long-term and sustainable investment in promoting engagement with countries with predominately Muslim populations. It also establishes a pilot program to provide grants to students from countries with predominantly Muslim populations to study in American-sponsored school in their countries. The subtitle includes findings regarding the need to improve education in the Middle East and authorizes the President to establish an International Youth Opportunity Fund to provide financial assistance for the improvement of public education in the Middle East.

The subtitle includes findings regarding the importance of economic development in combating the breeding grounds for terrorism and declares it is a Sense of Congress that a comprehensive United States strategy to counter terrorism should include economic development policies. It authorizes to be appropriated such sums as may be necessary for each of fiscal years 2005 and 2006 for the Middle East Partnership Initiative, a program that is currently authorized in law, and expresses the Sense of Congress that a significant portion of those fund should be made available to promote the rule of law in the Middle East.

The subtitle recognizes the need to cut off funding for terrorists and emphasizes the importance of targeting terrorist financial facilitators It includes a provision that eliminates the current requirement that designations of Foreign Terrorist Organizations (FTOs) lapse after two years unless renewed by the Secretary of State and replaces this requirement with procedures allowing entities designated as FTOs to petition the Secretary every two years to have their designations revoked, and a mandatory review of designations after five years if they have not previously been reviewed as a result of a petition.

The subtitle includes a provision requiring that the President submit to Congress not later than 180 days after the date of enactment a report on the activities of the United States government to carry out this title. The subtitle also includes amendments to the Case-Zablocki Act to require the Administration to submit all international agreements to Congress.

Subtitle B—Terrorist Travel and Effective Screening

This subtitle requires the Director of the NCTC to submit to Congress a strategy for combining terrorist travel intelligence, operations and law enforcement into a cohesive effort to intercept terrorists, find terrorist travel facilitators, and constrain terrorist mobility domestically and internationally. This section also requires improvements in technology and training that will assist border, consular, and immigration officers in detecting and combating terrorist travel. The subtitle establishes in law the Human Smuggling and Trafficking Center, which includes an interagency program devoted to countering terrorist travel. Additionally, the subtitle requires the Secretary of Homeland Security, in consultation with the Director of the NCTC, to establish a program to oversee DHS's responsibilities with respect to terrorist travel and establishes a Visa and Passport Security Program within the Bureau of Diplomatic Security at the Department of State to strengthen efforts to prevent theft and misuse of U.S.-issued passports and visas.

This subtitle also provides authorization for an increase in the number of consular officers by 150 per year from fiscal year 2006 through 2009 and ensures that there will be at least one full-time anti-fraud specialist at all high-fraud diplomatic and consular posts where visas are issued unless there is a full-time employee of the Department of Homeland Security assigned to such post pursuant to section 428 of the Homeland Security Act. Other provisions in this subtitle include a section encouraging international agreements to track and curtail terrorist travel through the use of fraudulent documents and a section encouraging international agreements to establish international standards for transliteration of names into the Roman alphabet for international travel documents and name-based watchlist systems.

This subtitle also includes provisions that strengthen control over access at U.S. ports-of-entry. The subtitle calls for the accelerated deployment [of] a biometric entry and exit system that would help verify the identities of individuals entering and leaving the U.S. based not just on the identity documents they carry, but on their physical features. The subtitle also calls for individuals entering into the U.S., including U.S. citizens and visitors from Canada and other Western Hemisphere countries, to bear a passport or other document sufficient to denote citizenship and identity. Additionally, the bill requires DHS to promulgate minimum standards for identification documents required of passengers seeking to board domestic flights subject to Congressional approval.

The subtitle also includes programs that "push out our borders" by increases the screening of threatening individuals before they reach the U.S. These measures include expanding the program that places U.S. immigration experts at foreign airports both to provide expert advice to airlines and foreign immigration officials concerning individuals bordering flights bound for the U.S., and increasing the number of foreign airports where visitors will be "pre-inspected" before reaching the U.S.

Finally, the subtitle requires the establishment of new standards to ensure the integrity of the three basic documents Americans use to establish their identity—birth certificates, state-issued driver's licenses and identification cards, and social security cards. The provisions in the subtitle establish new requirements to ensure that the applicant for the identity document is actually the person whom the applicant is claiming to be and the physical security of the document. States would receive grants to assist them in implementing new birth certificate and driver's license requirements.

Subtitle C—National Preparedness

The Incident Command System

This section expresses the Sense of Congress that the United States needs to implement a 9/11 Commission recommendation by adopting a unified incident command system and significantly enhancing communications connectivity between and among all levels of government and emergency response providers.

The National Capital Region Mutual Aid

This section authorizes mutual aid for first responders in the National Capital Region. A recommendation of the 9/11 Commission, this provision removes obstacles to mutual aid by addressing liability and other issues that arise when first responders in jurisdictions neighboring and including the nation's capital provide assistance to other jurisdictions in the region.

Enhancement of Public Safety Communications Capabilities

This section establishes programs for the enhancement of public safety communications interoperability, and urban and other high-risk area communications capabilities. It authorizes the establishment of an office within the Directorate of

Science and Technology to carry out programs related to SAFECOM and other related programs. It authorizes the use of multi-year commitments by the Secretary of Homeland Security when funding public safety interoperable communications projects at the state and local level, and mandates reports to Congress on the development of national voluntary consensus standards for public safety interoperable communications.

Regional Model Strategic Plan Pilot Projects

This section establishes pilot projects in no fewer than two high threat urban areas to develop a regional strategic plan to foster interagency communications.

Private Sector Preparedness

This section expresses the Sense of Congress that the Department of Homeland Security should promote adoption of voluntary national preparedness standards for the private sector.

Critical Infrastructure and Readiness Assessments

This section requires the Department of Homeland Security to report to Congress on its assessment of critical infrastructure protection needs and the readiness of the Government to respond to threats against the U.S.

Report on the Northern Command and Defense of the United States Homeland

This section expresses the Sense of Congress that the Secretary of Defense should regularly assess the adequacy of the Northern Command's plans and strategies.

Subtitle D—Homeland Security Grants

Homeland Security Grants

This section expresses the Sense of Congress that Congress must act to pass legislation in the first session of the 109th Congress to reform the system for distributing grants to enhance state and local government prevention of, preparedness for, and response to acts of terrorism.

Emergency Preparedness Compacts

This section requires FEMA to establish a program supporting the development of emergency preparedness compacts.

Office of Counternarcotics Enforcement

This section elevates and expands the duties of the Counternarcotics officer in the Department of Homeland Security. The Director of this office is tasked with coordinating policy with respect to counternarcotic activities.

Subtitle E—Public Safety Spectrum

Public Safety Spectrum

This section requires studies of the need for allocation of additional spectrum for first responder needs and to assess strategies that may be used to meet public safety telecommunications needs. A separate provision expresses the Sense of Congress that Congress must act in the first session of the 109th Congress to establish a comprehensive approach to the timely return of analog broadcast spectrum as early as December 31, 2006.

Pilot Study Regarding Warning Systems

This section provides for a pilot project similar to the AMBER alert network to notify the public in the event of a terrorist attack.

Subtitle F—Presidential Transition

This section requires the outgoing administrations to provide the president-elect with a classified, compartmented summary of specific threats to national security. Each major party presidential candidate would have discretionary authority to submit the names of transition team members shortly after their nomination to expedite the issuance of security clearances. The President-elect is directed to submit the names of candidates for national security positions as soon as possible after the date of the general election to expedite the issuance of security clearances. The language expresses the sense of the Senate that nominees for national security positions should be processed in an expeditious manner.

Subtitle G—Improving International Standards and Cooperation to Fight Terrorist Financing

This subsection works to better combat terrorist financing by requiring better coordination and building on international coalitions. It states the Sense of Congress that the Secretary of the Treasury should continue to promote the dissemination of international anti-money laundering and combating the financing of terrorism standards. It expands reporting requirements for the Secretary of Treasury to include assessments of progress made in these areas. It also requires the Secretary of Treasury to convene an inter-agency council to develop policies to be pursued by the United States regarding the development of common international anti-money laundering and combating the financing of terrorism standards.

Subtitle H—Emergency Financial Preparedness

This subtitle would provide a number of measures to enhance emergency financial preparedness for fiscal authorities and markets.

Chapter One provides for enhanced delegation authority for the Secretary of the Treasury to appoint a Fiscal Assistant Secretary in the absence or inability to serve of the current Fiscal Assistant Secretary. Under current law, the Secretary may only appoint "an officer" of the Treasury Department. The new provision would make any Treasury employee eligible for such appointment. The Fiscal Assistant Secretary is the head of the Fiscal Service, an entity in the Treasury Department comprised of the Bureau of Government Financial Operations and the Bureau of the Public Debt.

Chapter Two empowers the SEC to take action in an "emergency" to maintain or restore fair and orderly securities markets, ensure "prompt, accurate and safe" transaction settlement, and prevent disruptions of markets or market activities. Such action shall last for 10 business days, but may extend up to 30 calendar days should the public interest require. The action can only pertain to markets and actors normally within the SEC's jurisdiction. The Secretary of the Treasury is given comparable authority over markets for government securities. In addition, the subtitle contains a

"Sense of Congress" that insurance and credit rating firms should consider a firm's "compliance with standards for private sector disaster and emergency preparedness" when assessing the firm's insurability and creditworthiness. This is consistent with the 9/11 Commission Report, which made the identical recommendation.

TITLE VIII—GENERAL PROVISIONS

Subtitle A—Intelligence Matters

Intelligence Community Use of National Infrastructure Simulation and Analysis Center

This section provides that the National Intelligence Director shall establish a formal relationship, including information sharing, between elements of the intelligence community and the National Infrastructure Simulation Center.

Subtitle B—Department of Homeland Security Matters

Homeland Security Geographic Information

This section creates an Office of Geospatial Management under the Chief Information Officer in the Department of Homeland Security to coordinate the geospatial information needs of the Department. Geospatial information, which includes maps, charts, remote sensing data and images, and aerial photographic images, is an integral tool used by most government agencies.

Subtitle C—Homeland Security Civil Rights and Civil Liberties Protection

Homeland Security Civil Rights and Civil Liberties Protection

This subtitle includes the provisions of the Homeland Security Civil Rights and Civil Liberties Protection Act of 2004. These provisions would codify existing responsibilities of the Officer for Civil Rights and Civil Liberties at the Department of Homeland Security, which include assisting the Secretary of Homeland Security in developing, implementing, and reviewing Department policies and procedures to ensure civil rights and civil liberties are appropriately considered; overseeing compliance with constitutional, statutory, and policy requirements relating to civil rights and civil liberties; and investigating complaints.

This subtitle also provides that the Officer for Civil Rights and Civil Liberties and the Privacy Officer of the Department of Homeland Security coordinate on programs, policies, and procedures that involve civil rights, civil liberties, and privacy considerations.

This subtitle also provides for the Inspector General of the Department of Homeland Security to designate a senior official within the Office of the Inspector General who would be responsible for coordinating the activities of the Office with respect to civil rights and civil liberties and consulting with the Officer for Civil Rights and Civil Liberties.

Protections for Human Research Subjects of the Department of Homeland Security

This section requires the Department of Homeland Security to ensure that the Department complies with the protections for human research subjects in Title 45, part 46 of the CFR, widely known as the "Common Rule." The Common Rule specifies how research involving human subjects is to be conducted and reviewed, including requirements for obtaining informed consent. While these protections have been adopted by 17 federal departments and agencies to date, the Department of Homeland Security has not yet become a signatory to the Common Rule.

Subtitle D—Other Matters

Amendments to Clinger-Cohen Act Provisions to Enhance Agency Planning for Information Security Needs

This provision amends the Clinger-Cohen Act to explicitly require federal agencies to emphasize information security from the earliest possible stages of a new system's IT capital planning and investment decision-making process.

Enterprise Architecture

This section requires the Federal Bureau of Investigation (FBI) to continually maintain and update an enterprise architecture; and maintain a state of the art and up to date information technology infrastructure that is in compliance with the enterprise architecture of the FBI. Specifically the FBI is required to develop a detailed outline or blueprint of its information technology that will satisfy the ongoing mission and goals of the FBI and that sets forth specific and identifiable benchmarks. The Director of the FBI shall report to the House and Senate Judiciary Committees on whether the major information technology investments of the FBI are in compliance with its enterprise architecture and identify any inability or expectation of inability to meet the terms set forth in the enterprise architecture.

Financial Disclosure and Records

This section would require the Office of Government Ethics to submit a report to Congress evaluating the financial disclosure process for executive branch employees within 90 days of the date of enactment; require the Office of Personnel Management to electronically submit a list of Presidentially appointed positions to each major party candidate after his or her nomination; and require the Office of Government Ethics, in consultation with the Attorney General, to report to Congress on the conflict of interest laws relating to federal employment. The provision would also require each agency to submit a plan to the President and Congress that includes recommendations on reducing the number of positions requiring Senate confirmation.

Extension of Requirement for Air Carriers to Honor Tickets for Suspended Air Passenger Service

This provision would extend an existing provision of law requiring airlines to honor, under certain conditions, tickets issued by bankrupt carriers that have suspended passenger service.

Selected Readings

Benjamin, Daniel, and Steven Simon. *The Age of Sacred Terror: Radical Islam's War Against America.* New York: Random House, 2002.

Berkowitz, Bruce D., and Allan E. Goodman. *Best Truth: Intelligence in the Information Age.* New Haven: Yale University Press, 2000.

Bohn, Michael K. *Nerve Center: Inside the White House Situation Room.* Washington, DC: Brassey's, Inc., 2002.

Coll, Steve. *Ghost Wars: The Secret History of the CIA, Afghanistan, and bin Laden, from the Soviet Invasion to September 10, 2001.* New York: Penguin Press, 2004.

Godson, Roy, Ernest R. May, and Gary James Schmitt, eds. *U.S. Intelligence at the Crossroads: Agendas for Reform.* Washington, DC: Brassey's, Inc., 1995.

Grabo, Cynthia M. *Anticipating Surprise: Analysis for Strategic Warning.* Lanham, MD: University Press of America, 2004.

Heuer, Jr., Richards J. *Psychology of Intelligence Analysis.* Washington, DC: Center for the Study of Intelligence, 1999.

Hulnick, Arthur S. *Fixing the Spy Machine: Preparing American Intelligence for the Twenty-First Century.* Westport, CT: Greenwood Publishing Group, 1999.

Keegan, John. *Intelligence in War: Knowledge of the Enemy from Napoleon to al-Qaeda.* New York: Alfred A. Knopf, 2003.

Jeffreys-Jones, Rhodri. *Cloak and Dollar: A History of American Secret Intelligence.* New Haven: Yale University Press, 2002.

Johnson, Loch K. *Bombs, Bugs, Drugs, and Thugs: Intelligence and America's Quest for Security.* New York: NYU Press, 2002.

————. *Secret Agencies: U.S. Intelligence in a Hostile World*. New Haven: Yale University Press, 1998.

Lowenthal, Mark M. *Intelligence: From Secrets to Policy*. 3ᵈ ed. Washington, DC: CQ Press, 2006.

The 9/11 Commission Report: Final Report of the National Commission on Terrorist Attacks upon the United States. New York: W.W. Norton, 2004.

Pillar, Paul R. *Terrorism and U.S. Foreign Policy*. Washington, DC: The Brookings Institution Press, 2001.

Shulsky, Abram N. *Silent Warfare: Understanding the World of Intelligence*. Rev. 3ᵈ ed. Washington, DC: Brassey's, Inc., 2002.

Sims, Jennifer E., and Burton Gerber, eds. *Transforming U.S. Intelligence*. Washington, DC: Georgetown University Press, 2005.

Treverton, Gregory F. *Reshaping National Intelligence for an Age of Information*. Cambridge: Cambridge University Press, 2001.

About the Contributors

Roger Z. George has recently joined the Sherman Kent Center, part of the CIA University's Sherman Kent School for Intelligence Analysis. He completed a 3-year teaching assignment at the National War College, where he served as the DCI's faculty representative from 2001–2004. Dr. George has been a career intelligence analyst at CIA for 25 years and is a member of the Senior Analytic Service (SAS). He has also served as a Policy Planning Staff member in the Department of State from 1989–1991, was the National Intelligence Officer for Europe from 1991–1995, and was the director of the Policy and Analysis Group for the Assistant Secretary of Defense for International Security Affairs, from 1995–1997. He has taught international politics at Brandeis University, Occidental College, and UC–Santa Cruz and was a postdoctoral research fellow at Stanford University prior to government service.

Robert D. Kline is currently working as an independent consultant after recently retiring from the U.S. Department of Defense, where he served for more than 25 years as a senior executive. He was on the faculty of the National Defense University from 2000–2003 and taught in the Department of National Security Strategy at the National War College. Prior to serving at the Department of Defense, Kline was a senior analyst at the U.S. General Accounting Office, the investigative arm of Congress, where he also served on the staff of a Member of Congress.

Matthew M. Aid is an associate managing director of the Washington office of Kroll Associates and a former Russian linguist and intelligence analyst with the Department of Defense.

Christopher M. Andrew is professor of modern and contemporary history at Cambridge University and the author of *For The President's Eyes Only: Secret Intelligence and the American Presidency from Washington to Bush, Eternal Vigilance? Fifty Years of the CIA*, and *The Sword and the Shield: The Mitrokhin Archive and the Secret History of the KGB*.

Michael R. Bromwich is a litigation partner in the law offices of Fried Frank and has served as inspector general of the Department of Justice. He has written on law enforcement, criminal justice, and oversight issues for *The New York Times*, *The Washington Post*, and *The Boston Globe*.

James B. Bruce is vice chairman of the Director of Central Intelligence Foreign Denial and Deception Committee and has taught at the National War College.

Charles G. Cogan is a senior research associate in the Kennedy School at Harvard University and a former senior operations officer at the Central Intelligence Agency. He is the author of *The Third Option: The Emancipation of European Defense, 1989–2000,* and *French Negotiating Behavior: Dealing with La Grande Nation.*

Jack Davis is a former national intelligence officer and analyst at the Central Intelligence Agency and consultant to the Intelligence Community.

Yahya A. Dehqanzada is a research associate at the Carnegie Endowment for International Peace.

Michael B. Donley is vice president of Hicks and Associates, Inc., and has held senior positions with the Senate Armed Services Committee, on the National Security Council staff, and at the Department of Defense.

Ann M. Florini directs the Projects on Transparency and on Transnational Civil Society at the Carnegie Endowment for International Peace, and has held positions at the Rockefeller Brothers Fund, Georgetown University, University of California at Los Angeles, the United Nations Association, and the Brookings Institution.

Randall M. Fort served as Deputy Assistant Secretary of State for intelligence and research and also as special assistant for national security affairs to the Secretary of the Treasury.

Richard S. Friedman is a retired Army officer who has worked as a senior analyst, assistant national intelligence officer, and staff operations officer at the Central Intelligence Agency.

John C. Gannon is staff director for the House Select Committee on Homeland Security and has served as deputy director of intelligence and chairman of the National Intelligence Council.

Glenn W. Goodman, Jr., is editor of *The ISR Journal: Intelligence, Surveillance and Reconnaissance.*

Michael I. Handel was professor of strategy at the Naval War College and taught at the U.S. Army War College, and is the author of *Intelligence and Military Operations* and *Masters of War: Classical Strategic Thought.*

James W. Harris is senior analyst at Centra Technology and formerly was chief of the strategic assessments group in the Directorate of Intelligence at the Central Intelligence Agency.

Norman B. Imler is a retired operations officer at the Central Intelligence Agency and served as director of the Sherman Kent Center for Intelligence Studies at the National War College.

Loch K. Johnson is the Regents Professor in the School of Public Policy at the University of Georgia and formerly was a staff member on the Senate Select Committee on Intelligence.

Garrett Jones served as a case officer at the Central Intelligence Agency in Africa, Europe, and the Middle East.

Larry C. Kindsvater is a career analyst at the Central Intelligence Agency and has served as the executive director for Intelligence Community affairs within the Director of Central Intelligence Community Management Staff.

Andrew Koch is Washington bureau chief of *Jane's Defence Weekly*.

Mark M. Lowenthal is the assistant director of Central Intelligence for analysis and production and previously was staff director of the House Permanent Select Committee on Intelligence.

John D. Macartney is a retired Air Force officer who served as commandant of the Defense Intelligence College and also taught at the National War College.

Carmen A. Medina is a career analyst at the Central Intelligence Agency.

John Montgomery is a former analyst on the National Security Council staff.

Cornelius O'Leary is a former director of the White House situation room.

James M. Olson teaches in the George Bush School of Government and Public Service at Texas A&M University and previously served in the Directorate of Operations at the Central Intelligence Agency.

Marvin C. Ott is professor of national security policy at the National War College and a faculty fellow in the Institute for National Strategic Studies. Previously he was a professional staff member and deputy staff director of the Senate Select Committee on Intelligence.

Martin Petersen is a career officer at the Central Intelligence Agency and currently serves as Deputy Executive Director of the agency.

Reed R. Probst has served at the U.S. Army War College and was a career analyst at the Central Intelligence Agency.

Harvey Rishikof is visiting law professor at the National War College. Formerly he served as legal counsel to the deputy director of the Federal Bureau of Investigation, administrative assistant to the Chief Justice of the United States, and dean of Roger Williams University School of Law.

Victor M. Rosello is a lieutenant colonel in the Army who has served as an intelligence adviser to the Salvadoran armed forces and participated in Operations *Just Cause* and *Desert Storm*.

Richard L. Russell taught in the Near East–South Asia Center for Strategic Studies at the National Defense University and previously was a military analyst at the Central Intelligence Agency.

Thomas W. Shreeve is director of the Intelligence Community case study program and was an analyst at the Central Intelligence Agency.

L. Brit Snider has been a professional staff member of the Senate Select Committee on Intelligence and served as inspector general of the Central Intelligence Agency.

Michael Warner is a career officer at the Central Intelligence Agency and served as deputy chief of history at the Center for the Study of Intelligence.

Anthony R. Williams is the Director of Central Intelligence faculty representative at the U.S. Army War College and a career military intelligence analyst at the Central Intelligence Agency.

James J. Wirtz is professor of nuclear strategy, international relations theory, and intelligence at the Naval Postgraduate School and the author of *The Tet Offensive: Intelligence Failure in War*.

Amy B. Zegart is assistant professor of policy studies in the School of Public Policy and Social Research at the University of California, Los Angeles, and previously served on the National Security Council staff and worked at McKinsey and Company.